MUSICAL
EVENTS

MUSICAL EVENTS

A Chronicle: 1980–1983

Andrew Porter

GRAFTON BOOKS

A Division of the Collins Publishing Group

LONDON GLASGOW
TORONTO SYDNEY AUCKLAND

Grafton Books
A Division of the Collins Publishing Group
8 Grafton Street, London WIX 3LA

First published in the USA by Summit Books,
A Division of Simon & Schuster, Inc., 1987
Published in Great Britain by Grafton Books 1988

These essays first appeared in *The New Yorker*

British Library Cataloguing in Publication Data
Porter, Andrew
Musical events: a chronicle, 1980–1983.
1. Western music, 1750–1983 – Critical
studies
I. Title
780'.9

ISBN 0-246-13311-2

Printed in Great Britain by
Robert Hartnoll (1985) Ltd, Bodmin, Cornwall

Set in Baskerville

FOR
WILLIAM SHAWN,
IN
GRATITUDE

CONTENTS

INTRODUCTION

9

PART I

1980–1981

15

PART II

1981–1982

123

PART III

1982–1983

299

INDEX

489

INTRODUCTION

This book continues the chronicle of *Music of Three Seasons: 1974–1977* and *Music of Three More Seasons: 1977–1980*; it is another record of three years' musical events compiled, initially in the columns of *The New Yorker*, by a music critic who, while living most of the time in New York, likes to use travel, tapes, recordings, and radio to give some touches of national and international perspective to the New York musical scene. In a preface to *Music of Three Seasons* I wrote of a feeling for "place" made sharper by my move, after twenty years of working in London, to New York. A feeling for "place" in all its aspects: the place on the map of a work's composition and the place, the building, of its first performance; the historical, social, political, and, for that matter, acoustic considerations that may have influenced the form it took; its place within a composer's oeuvre; the place—suitable or not in acoustics, "atmosphere," associations—of the particular performance under review; and, perhaps most important, the place that the work can or should hold today in our society and culture.

Every critic has his special interests. Three of mine are contemporary music, operas of the past in contemporary performances, and contemporary music theatre. I was tempted to reorder these weekly reviews into categories, with long sections on those three topics and others on, say, remarkable performers of our day, established or emergent; music of the sixteenth, fifteenth, and earlier centuries given a new hearing in the changed circumstances of the modern world; the revival of music from the past on authentic instruments, in historical performing styles. But any attempts at categorization broke down. For example, the last piece in this book, based on the Carnegie Hall recitals at which Alfred Brendel played all Beethoven's piano sonatas, would plainly belong to an "eminent performers" section, but it touches on several other topics: the history of the Beethoven-sonata *intégrale*; recordings of the sonatas made over the last half-century; my personal memories of past performances; the way memory may play tricks and adjust itself over the years; speculation on whether contemporary timbre preferences have been colored by the sound of high-fidelity records; and consideration of the fact that—as Brendel himself puts it—"whenever we hear Beethoven on a present-day instrument, we are listening to a sort of transcription."

These and related themes run through or beneath several pages of this book. The one about contemporary timbre preference, for example, surfaces in an account of the five concert halls—in New Orleans, Baltimore, Peoria, Eugene, and Toronto—that opened within a fortnight in 1982. The one about the matching of music and the instruments of its performance is treated in various accounts of Handel's, Haydn's, Beethoven's music played on instruments that its composers would—or would not—have recognized. I hope these are not mere repetitions but, rather, presentations in different contexts of some of the ideas about music and its execution which came to the fore during the years under review: considerations of general practice as exemplified—or contradicted—by a particular performance.

A recurrent concern is the importance of recordings. They have been with us all this century. They have become increasingly important, in many different ways. Commercially, for one: the recording industry (in that phrase must be included audio-visual recordings on tape and on disc) now plays a part in determining the repertory and the casting of operas in the world's principal opera houses, and the repertory and the choice of soloists for the world's great orchestras, especially on their international tours. On another level, recording—achieved with a simplicity and, since tape cassettes came into use, economy not possible before—provides contemporary criticism with a new tool. The critic faced with an attractive but initially baffling composition, and not faced with an overnight deadline, often has the chance of listening to that work twice—or twenty times—again before having to shape and order his thoughts about it. (Publishers and performers are generally coöperative; I'm not suggesting that critics attend concerts with illegal tape recorders concealed in their coats.) Recordings also provide points of comparison that can help a critic to decide whether a work previously acclaimed (or decried) that now proves disappointing (or exhilarating) may do so because of an inadequate (or superior) performance.

There are performers who declare proudly that they never listen to the recordings made by their their predecessors lest they be "influenced." That seems to me like a declaration that they feel they have nothing to learn—that Casals has nothing to say to a modern cellist, or Gemma Bellincioni, whom Verdi admired as Violetta, to a contemporary interpreter of La traviata—or, even, that a composer himself, an Elgar, Copland, Bernstein, Berio, should be allowed no say in the way his music sounds. Rejecting that view, I do not hestitate to urge, for example, a modern Werther to listen attentively to recordings made by the great Werthers of the past—from Ernest Van Dyck, who created the role, onward—as a stylistic guide, an inspiration, a revelation of possibilities that he may choose to emulate, to refashion to accord with his own perceptions of the role and his own technique, or to scorn, but that he should at least know and consider. Familiarity with the achievements of great interpreters from the late nineteenth century onward has been made easier—for performers and listeners alike—by two developments of our day: abundant reissues of recordings from the past, and modern technology's ability to recover from the old, scratchy grooves far more musical "information" than was once thought to have been inscribed there.

Recordings play another part when they give a critic's readers the chance to hear for themselves what the critic is writing about. Performance criticism from centuries before ours must be taken on trust. No one living knows what Wilhelmine Schröder-Devrient, Giuditta Pasta, Maria Malibran, Liszt, Paganini really sounded like; but performances by Rosa Ponselle, Renata Tebaldi, Maria Callas, Arthur Schnabel, Jascha Heifetz are amply "documented." When some *laudator temporis acti* reminisces, makes comparisons, complains that things are going to the dogs, his younger readers can readily hear for themselves whether he is right, or merely *difficilis, querulus, castigator censorque minorum.* (Since Horace is no longer read in every schoolroom, let me translate those famous lines from the *Ars Poetica*: "testy, picky, a praiser of bygone days when he was a boy, reproving and finding fault with the new generation.") I'm a critic who looks to, listens to, and tries to learn from the past, and who tends to throw a fair amount of "history" into his reviews. But that past is valued chiefly for what it has to offer the present.

When some new work discovered, discussed, and enjoyed is available on record, I like to tell readers about it. (I have, of course, removed from the reviews details of broadcasts once forthcoming, now long past, but have added some references to subsequent recordings.) When a work that pleases has been played at a concert, all a critic can do is to describe it and to urge further performances; but when it has appeared on a record, readers have a chance of hearing and enjoying it for themselves. That sentence is repeated from a 1979 review based on the publication of the LaSalle Quartet's record of Alexander Zemlinsky's Second String Quartet. The review began: "Musicians delight in sharing their discoveries and enthusiasms. Performers champion works they love. And one of the rewards of a music critic's life is being able to share delight with more than an immediate circle of acquaintances." I hope this book reads as, above all, an enthusiastic chronicle. There are passages of crossness in it, but usually of censure for performances that, it seemed to me, distorted or obscured the delights of a work that I love. I have been reproached for being over-generous toward, promiscuously adulatory about, new music—for a Dodo-like attitude ("At last the Dodo said, '*Everybody* has won, and, *all* must have prizes'")—and should explain here that less than half the new music I hear actually gets written about. The big works that appeared during these years are dwelled upon. The progress of our major composers is traced. But, by and large, from the large amount of new music heard only those pieces that made some favorable—or, at least, memorable —impression are mentioned. This is a personal and a partial chronicle. There is a long gap in the dating for 1981, when for a while I deserted criticism for academe and lived in Berkeley, California. (On my return to New York, I found I was able to catch up with much of what had been happening there.) The steady stream of standard orchestral fare from the New York Philharmonic and of standard operas revived, night in, night out, by the Metropolitan Opera and the New York City Opera goes largely unrecorded, and must be understood as a ground-bass to musical events more exciting; the new productions and the appearances of striking new artists are reviewed. I have struck out some sentences that merely filled in the details of what a particular bill contained. I have retained references to early works by composers and early performances by artists who later become well known, and have added [in brackets and italics, thus] a few postscripts noting subsequent developments.

The collection is dedicated, fondly, to William Shawn, the inspiring editor of The New Yorker, who in 1972 invited me to join the New Yorker team. Let me repeat what I said in the preface to Music of Three Seasons. A pianist who, after years of struggling with instruments where some notes are out of tune and some notes stick, is offered a well-tuned, well-regulated instrument, precise and responsive, may feel as I did when I came to write for The New Yorker. The simile can be extended: it is as if that pianist, before presenting any piece to the public, is invited to play it before a small, critical audience of experts attentive to each aspect of what he does. I am deeply grateful to Mr. Shawn; to my particular editor, Susan Moritz (who shares my love for Mozart but is sadly uncomprehending of Wagner's genius); to Eleanor Gould Packard, whose nice reading gives a writer the feeling of having a personal Fowler focussed upon his work; to Sara Lippincott, then Martin Baron, and their team of checkers—in these years Dwight Allen, Peter Canby, David Green, Nancy Franklin, Patti Hagan, and Richard Sacks —who saved me from misnaming, misquoting, miscounting; and to the many other members of the New Yorker family who play an active part in the preparation of columns that appear over my name.

At Summit Books, Ileene Smith encouraged me at each stage of this compilation; Andrée Pages read it with an alert eye; and Gerold Ordansky and Sydney Wolfe Cohen compiled the index that enables Handelians, Verdians, Wagnerians, admirers of Elliott Carter or of Milton Babbitt to turn at once to what most concerns them.

A final, pedant's note on dating (from one who wrestles often with the discordant information about singers' birthdays and about world premières which appear in various sources). Issues of The New Yorker bear a Monday date but appear during the previous week. The convention followed in these pages is that "this week" refers to the week (starting on a Sunday) in which the issue appears, not to the week of the Monday by which it is dated. Month references, however, are determined by date issue. So, for example, in a review dated "November 2, 1981," "last month" would mean October but "Tuesday last week" would mean October 20, not October 27.

Andrew Porter
New York
January 1987

PART
I

1980–1981

SUPPLE SONG

September 15, 1980

NED ROREM'S NEW CYCLE, *The Santa Fe Songs,* composed for the Santa Fe Chamber Music Festival, is a lyrical and beautiful work. The twelve poems that form its text are by Witter Bynner, who lived in Santa Fe. I make little of them, but Rorem has made much: music of eloquence, unselfconscious charm, and fine, inventive workmanship. The settings are for baritone, piano, and string trio, and the medium is deftly and diversely handled. Much of the time, the four instrumentalists are as much "singers" as is the baritone. In the sixth song, their lines weave three limpid, tender spans (in slow mazurka rhythm), divided by brief, unaccompanied statements from the singer. The ninth song begins with an extended, rapturous monody for the cello. The eleventh is a mysterious *scorrevole* movement for the three strings, into which, on just two notes, the singer whispers the strophes of the Bynner poem. The cycle is true chamber music for five alert performers, not songs with accompaniment, yet at the same time it is a true song cycle, dominated by the singer. The climaxes are outbursts of soaring, full-throated vocal melody.

Some of Rorem's recent works—*Book of Hours,* for flute and harp; *Romeo and Juliet,* for flute and guitar; *A Quaker Reader,* for organ (all available on CRI)—have left me unsatisfied: the ideas have been elegant, often beautiful, but the working has seemed thin. *The Santa Fe Songs,* on the other hand, is refined but not thin, delicate but not slight. One criticism made of the piece was that since piano quartet is traditionally a weighty medium the writing for it should have been broader, bigger. That seems to me unfair. Brahms's three piano quartets may be big pieces both in structure and in sonorities, but there are other ways of composing for these forces. Rorem's movements are short—the cycle of twelve songs lasts about half an hour—and only in the first song, at the close of the fourth, and at the climax of the last is there a large, full sound. An instrumental stretch in the seventh song is marked *fff,* and its coda *ffff,* but the texture there is linear and open, not massive. The predominantly clear, uncluttered working of the cycle constitutes one of its charms. In the tenth song, Rorem writes a catchy melody that for most of its length uses just three notes—A, the B-flat above, and the G below, in the key of F (slipped a third higher in

17

the central section)—and the very occasional excursions beyond that narrow range tell strongly. The second song is threaded through by a piano ostinato on just two notes, C and D, arranged to form a four-beat passacaglia theme in triple meter which sets up gentle rhythmic tensions. There are many other examples of an economy that is pleasing and not at all schematic, for the composer's imagination is rich. His familiar virtues—unforced rhythmic variety of declamation, naturalness of pace, quick response to verbal colors, and command of a decisive cadence—are everywhere apparent. So is the sovereign virtue: expressive melody. The poems he has chosen include a summer, a winter, a fall, and finally an ecstatic spring scene. The underlying theme of the cycle seems to be an exploration of various memories that gather at last into an affirmation of returning joy.

Rorem was composer-in-residence at this year's Santa Fe festival (the eighth). *The Santa Fe Songs* had its first performance there; his *Day Music* and *Night Music,* for violin and piano, and his powerful, moving song cycle *War Scenes* were also done. (All three works are recorded by Desto.) From Santa Fe, the festival ensemble went to Seattle for a week of music-making, and then came to New York, where it gave six concerts, each of them preceded by a brief recital, on consecutive days, in Alice Tully Hall. All were broadcast live by WNYC, and I am reviewing *The Santa Fe Songs* as it was heard over the air. The baritone was William Parker; Ani Kavafian, Heiichiro Ohyama, and Timothy Eddy were the violinist, the violist, and the cellist; the piano part was played by the composer. Mr. Parker has a beautiful voice, a refined style, and a winning manner. In lyricism, smooth phrasing, and timbre, he recalls Gérard Souzay; like Souzay, he can also seem at times to lack energy, vigor, verve. (Souzay was a cultivated Don Giovanni, but the animal spirits of the character eluded him.) The first of Rorem's *Santa Fe Songs* begins with swift, driving utterances, sweeping and leaping through the range from low B-flat to the tenth above as they evoke the march of modernity through the West. The instruments in the Tully Hall performance pounded, pulsed, and glittered, but Mr. Parker's delivery of the bold phrases had a by-the-skin-of-his-teeth quality. The second subject, a calm arpeggio poised over the "mountain-town... with something left... of the ancient faith and wisdom of St. Francis," displayed his ability to spin romance through eloquence of timbre. He rose to all the romantic moments, and gave an admirable performance of the cycle. He will sing it better still, I think, when he phrases more freely and gives more color and variety to individual words.

Two days later, the evening concert was preceded by a Debussy recital. It began with the third sonata, for violin and piano, delicately—perhaps rather too delicately—played by Franco Gulli and Enrica Cavallo. Then Mr. Parker and Mr. Rorem joined in two song cycles, *Le Promenoir des deux amants* and the *Trois Ballades de François Villon.* When composers play the piano well—as Poulenc and Britten did, as Rorem and William Bolcom do—they prove to be inspiring "accompanists," and not only in their own compositions. When Poulenc played Fauré or Debussy, and when Britten played Purcell or Schubert, the sense of the music and the significance of particular details were revealed with rare vividness. Mr. Rorem's playing of the Debussy cycles had the same sort of character. He might have composed the music himself, one felt, so subtly and so vividly did he communicate its nuances. And most of Mr. Parker's singing was exquisite.

The concert proper began with a neat but understated—and essentially characterless—account of Verdi's string quartet, led by Mr. Gulli. It lacked portamento, it lacked passion, and in the final movement it lacked violence of dynamic contrasts. (There are just a few entries marked *f*, and for the rest Verdi indicates either *pp* and *ppp* or *ff* and *fff*.) The Santa Fe artists are a group of expert chamber-music players who have been together often enough and long enough to know one another's work well. Their performances are drawn from a roster of five violinists, two violists, two cellists, a horn player, and (besides Mr. Rorem) four pianists—a shifting personnel that precludes any constant "corporate personality" such as a permanent quartet or trio achieves but, given the excellence of the players, can bring other rewards. The Verdi quartet was followed by Ravel's trio for violin, cello, and piano, which leapt into life because the violinist, Ani Kavafian, and the cellist, Ralph Kirshbaum (who had plunged back into chamber music just two days after his triumph, in London, as cello soloist of Tippett's new Triple Concerto), are players of arresting temperament who hold listeners intent on every phrase. The pianist, Edward Auer, was correct but less remarkable. In Brahms's horn trio, which closed the concert, Mr. Auer was the pianist, James Buswell was the violinist, and Dale Clevenger, first horn of the Chicago Symphony, gave the performance its character by his potently personal inflections.

When I last wrote about *The Pirates of Penzance*, after its City Opera revival three years ago, I suggested that a good cast for the piece would be Joan Sutherland, Marilyn Horne, Placido Domingo, and Sherrill Milnes. Or, if the work were to be done in Italian translation, with sung recitatives, Montserrat Caballé, Fiorenza Cossotto, José Carreras, and Piero Cappuccilli. The New York Shakespeare Festival production of *The Pirates*, which played this summer in the Delacorte Theatre, in Central Park, used vocal resources more modest and—inevitably in the large open-air, open-sided theatre—relied on amplification to get the voices across. Moreover, Sullivan's music had been rescored—resourcefully—for a stringless combo (dominated by two noisy trumpets), and that, too, was amplified. The music reached its listeners from loudspeakers high above the stage. Nevertheless, admirers of Gilbert and Sullivan, once their ears had adjusted themselves to the sound, could enjoy an attractive, animated, and even in its way stylish account of the opera. Its romance, its charm, and its high spirits were all done justice to.

Linda Ronstadt, the leading lady, had accurate and pretty coloratura for Mabel's waltz song. Lower down, she sounded short-breathed, and the "insert aria" borrowed from *H.M.S. Pinafore,* Josephine's "Sorry her lot," did not suit her. Rex Smith was a bonny Frederic and a better actor than one usually sees in the role. Though he did not have the voice for the music—there was little between a husky, sexy murmur and a raw blare when he sang out—his phrasing was accomplished and his words were clear. Clarity and musical alertness distinguished all the performance, prepared and conducted by William Elliott; one seldom hears Sullivan's music delivered with so excellent a sense of when to pause, when to press on. The show had its bizarre aspects, to be sure. Tony Azito turned the police sergeant into an India-rubber Latin, and Graciela Daniele's choreography tended to confuse the stolid constabulary with light-footed traffic cops. But everything was lively and cunningly paced. "The theme of *The Pirates of Penzance,*" Shaw once wrote, "is essentially the same as that of Ibsen's *Wild Duck.*" Wilford Leach had directed Gilbert's play attentively and subtly. Although George Rose's Major-General Stanley was disfigured by touches of the primping, mincing, all-purpose camp that players of *Don Pasquale* and *Falstaff* sometimes affect, his enunciation and timing of the patter song were virtuosic. Patricia Routledge's Ruth was no trombone-voiced virago but a spry, entertaining veteran. Kevin Kline played the pirate king as Douglas Fairbanks might have done. The chorus was dapper.

In an age that is serious about *Lucia di Lammermoor* and *Il trovatore, The Pirates of Penzance* acquires renewed freshness. The music is good enough to reward vocal prowess of the highest level—and good enough, too, to prove intoxicating even with moderate voices when it is as skillfully and spiritedly performed as it was here.

[*The production later enjoyed runs on Broadway and in London's West End, and was recorded on Elektra.*]

OPERETTA

September 22, 1980

ERIC BLOM, writing in Grove about Sir Arthur Sullivan, remarks that although Offenbach may be saucier and Johann Strauss may display more "peppery verve," Sullivan is their superior technically and "also in the matter of inventive variety and emotional range." Blom concedes that even at his best Sullivan "fell short of Mozart's greatness"; but, he concludes, of operetta "he has so far remained the outstanding master, and after him the later Viennese operetta showed a steep descent and the twentieth-century musical comedy a disastrous downfall." True? Largely true, I'd say; the operettas of Lehár, Heuberger, Kálmán, Oscar Straus, Leo Fall, and Robert Stolz don't come within striking distance of *Die Fledermaus* or of Sullivan. (Nor does any other of Strauss's operettas which I know—but that's another matter.) How should one define "operetta"? In Grove, Blom proposes "comic opera, not necessarily on a small scale as to size, but light in character both in its subject and its music." That admits opera buffa, which is rather different. (Confusingly, Offenbach favored the term "opéra-bouffe" for his operettas.) Can one draw a line that will not run through parts of *The Magic Flute*? Are Smetana's *Bartered Bride* and his *Two Widows* not operettas in their first versions? Does *Fidelio* not start as an operetta? Is Puccini's *La rondine* an operetta? The questions can perhaps be left to dictionary-makers. Enough to say that the stage pieces of Johann Strauss (except *Ritter Pázmán*), of Offenbach (except *Les Contes d'Hoffmann*), and of Sullivan (except *Ivanhoe*) *are* operettas, and are sparkling triple peaks at the center of a terrain with boundaries indefinite and disputed. ("Operetta," Saint-Saëns remarked at the opening of the American Conservatory in Fontainebleau, in 1921, "is a daughter of opéra comique who went astray; but·daughters who go astray are not always without charm.") Musical comedy has no independent entry in the current Grove, but Blom glanced at it wryly in his account of operetta:

> New York caught up with [operetta] just in time to produce some engaging examples (Gershwin, Jerome Kern), but by their time—the early 20th century—it had begun to degenerate into "musical comedy" (Amer. "musicals"), in which plots had become stereotyped and often sentimental, both humour and music were sadly enfeebled, and artistic pretensions were upheld only by increasingly lavish and not often correspondingly tasteful productions which failed to sustain the vitality of operetta as a musical species of art.

Just in time, indeed! *Die Fledermaus* and works by Offenbach and Sullivan reached New York within months of their European premières; *The Pirates of Penzance* opened here. The New Grove, due soon, will, I trust, deal more generously with musicals. Gershwin has received Schoenberg's imprimatur. (Thrice in Schoenberg's *Style and Idea*, Gershwin appears in a sentence with Offenbach and Johann Strauss.) Kurt Weill was a great composer who wrote musicals. And the serious opera critic is happy to give his attention to operas of entertainment from all ages—Bach to Bernstein; Cherubini to Kern, Reginald De Koven, and Cole Porter; Haydn to Victor Herbert; Sullivan to Stanley Silverman.

Blom's words about the steep descent of later Viennese operetta recurred to me when, the day after visiting Sullivan's *Pirates* in the Park, I saw Sigmund Romberg's *The Student Prince* at the State Theater. The City Opera began the season with a new production of that piece and played it for a run of thirteen performances. (There was alternate casting in the leading roles.) Odd choice. This is Offenbach year; the centenary of his death falls next month. All over Europe, there are commemorative revivals of more than just *The Tales of Hoffmann*. (The

BBC, for example, is putting on a series of the lesser-known one-act operettas.) Beverly Sills and her company missed a chance. They could have done *Bluebeard* or *The Brigands*. They could have made a splash with the spectacular *Geneviève de Brabant*. If they wanted a familiar title, they could have mounted *Robinson Crusoe*. There was no adventure in dragging out Romberg's *Student Prince* for another airing. And it was not even particularly well performed.

Strictly, *The Student Prince* is not, of course, a *Viennese* operetta. Romberg, who came to this country in 1909, was the Shuberts' house composer, and the piece—after tryouts in Atlantic City and Philadelphia—appeared at the Jolson Theatre, in 1924. (It was Romberg's seventh theatre score that year.) Richard Traubner, writing in the City Opera program book, says he has traced no production in Vienna itself. But in style and in substance *The Student Prince* is a thorough Viennese operetta, written by an Austro-Hungarian composer who had been a pupil of Heuberger and was for a while an assistant manager of the Theater an der Wien, where not only *Fidelio* but also *Die Fledermaus* and *The Merry Widow* saw the light. The plot, drawn from the play *Old Heidelberg*, is a variation on *Giselle*, with the difference that the plebeian heroine does not go mad but realistically accepts the fact that a royal match is not for her; Prince Charming marries a princess, and Cinderella is left with a memory to cherish "deep in her heart." Although the working is slight, the dramatic predicament, the conflict between dreams and duty, between romance and regal obligation, is real enough—recurrent in history and often effectively treated on the stage. In Handel's *Semele*, the heroine's plight is lifted to a divine level, and her ambition causes her destruction. In *La traviata*, it is given a demi-monde setting and a different ending. Aeneas was semidivine, and his beloved was royal, but essentially Karl Franz of Karlsberg, the Student Prince, must choose whether to act as Aeneas or as Edward VIII did. It doesn't matter that Romberg handled the theme lightly and decoratively; with more serious music, *The Student Prince* would be an opera, and it was not intended to be that. It does matter that much of his music is poor. The central section of the well-known serenade ("Overhead the moon is beaming") is a miserable run of rosalias. Romberg put out some attractive ideas—the start of Kathie's waltz aria ("I'm coming at your call, For orders large or small"), the fizzy "Come boys, let's all be gay, boys," which follows it—but, like Meyerbeer, he had small ability to sustain an initial melodic felicity through a whole number. And his command of harmonic movement keeps faltering. The score is for the most part an alternation of sentimental waltzes and jolly student ensembles. Echoes of Strauss and of Lehár are plentiful. Stretches of the music slip down agreeably; then dreary sequences or clumsy harmonic shifts prove distressing.

The City Opera production was curiously cast. Jacque Trussel can be a powerful, direct, and even passionate tenor, but neither in timbre nor in manner does he display the easy romantic charm or the brio that an operetta hero needs. James Agate found Allan Prior, London's first Student Prince, in 1926, a "chubby, confident personage in whom there was no possible wistfulness," but on records Prior's bright, excitable singing proves irresistible. Leigh Munro's Kathie was accurately sung but had little character. The main vocal pleasure was provided by Kathryn Bouleyn, in Princess Margaret's few phrases. Jack Hofsiss, the director, had not found any apt or consistent style for the piece. Various veterans of the company were allowed to don their standard, all-purpose comic manners. The basic contrast between the oppressive splendors of the court and carefree student life was muted by the décor: the court settings—the gloomy palace room of the prologue and the magnificent state room of Act III, with Karl Franz as King—were replaced by a romantic garden. Dorothy Donnelly's dialogue had been reworked by Hugh Wheeler, and cheapened.

On the first night, the pacing was far from sure, and the contrast with the expert timing and sure execution of *The Pirates of Penzance* was great. But then I had heard *The Pirates* toward the end of a five-week run, which had been preceded by two weeks of previews, whereas *The Student Prince* opened "cold." I went back to sample the seventh performance, to hear the other cast and to see if the show had been played in. It did run a little less awkwardly, but no significant reworking had been done; the stretches of dead dialogue and the crude "cameo" performances remained. The alternate Karl Franz, Henry Price, sang weakly and was unaristocratic, registering boyish charm with a nonstop grin. But the alternate Kathie, Elizabeth Hynes, was delightful—bright and full in timbre, lively in manner. And most of her words were intelligible. On the whole, the show would have benefitted from miking. I am no champion of amplification in the opera house, but when the choice is between that and not hearing the words, it is the lesser evil. (In London's main concert hall, electronics —not audible as such, but delicately applied—improve the acoustics, and listeners are grateful.) Andrew Meltzer conducted, without subtlety. The strings sounded thin. The original orchestration was not by Romberg himself but by Emil Gerstenberger. There is another, bright orchestration by Hershy Kay, used in the recording with Roberta Peters and Jan Peerce. For the Mario Lanza movie, the score was syruped. The City Opera uses an orchestration by Dale Kugel.

The City Opera's *Student Prince* played to full houses. From that point of view, it was a success. But from the company that performed Weill's *Street Scene* so precisely, so sensitively, it was an unworthy offering.

Buxton, in the North of England, a spa from Roman to Edwardian times and still a popular resort, is the site of Britain's newest summer festival. It is a pleasant town with some good architecture. Chatsworth, the great house of the Dukes of Devonshire, is not far away. The fifth duke engaged John Carr, a Palladian architect, to build the Crescent, the Square, and the Stables that make Buxton a minor Bath. For the sixth duke, Wyatville and later Paxton laid out parks and gardens. Soon after the railway arrived, in 1867, the pretty Victorian Pavilion was built. To it were added a circular concert hall and, in 1903, an opera house—an elegant Edwardian-rococo theatre by the prolific Frank Matcham. The festival planning is thematic. Last year, Walter Scott was the inspiration, and *Lucia di Lammermoor* the opera performed. This summer, the central figure was Shakespeare. Ambroise Thomas's *Hamlet* and Berlioz's *Béatrice et Bénédict* were produced, each for six performances. The Symphonie Fantastique and its sequel, *Lélio*, were given in a manner intended to evoke the first performance, in 1832, at which the actress Harriet Smithson, hearing Lélio's cry "Oh, if only I could find her, the Juliet, the Ophelia whom my heart calls out for," realized that the composer was calling to her. (The next year, they were married.) In the Buxton Museum and Art Gallery, there were images of Miss Smithson in her Shakespeare roles and another show of Shakespeare heroines in the nineteenth century, dominated by Mrs. Siddons and Ellen Terry. The Shakespeare-Fletcher *Two Noble Kinsmen* and Tom Stoppard's *Rosencrantz and Guildenstern Are Dead* were revived. The Symphonie Fantastique was also played in Liszt's piano transcription; Berlioz's *Nuits d'Été* was done in both its orchestral and its piano dress. Peter Maxwell Davies's new children's opera, *Cinderella*, had its English première, with children from local schools.

I thought less well of the *Hamlet* than most of my colleagues did. Thomas Allen, England's leading young baritone, has the voice for the role, but his playing the night I saw him was stolid. Christine Barbaux (Yniold and Barbarina in Karajan recordings of *Pelléas* and *Figaro*), the Ophelia, was efficient but unimaginative. Thomas' *Hamlet*, like Gounod's *Faust* (which had the same librettists, Michel Carré and Jules Barbier), simplifies the motivations and emotions of its original. At the heart of the opera lie Hamlet's ardent love for Ophelia, her all-consuming love for him, and their despair when circumstances drive them apart. Unless the love scenes are played more tenderly, poignantly, and passionately than they were at Buxton, the opera loses its main point. The rest is largely decoration on a vast, colorful Opéra scale, calling for a larger stage, chorus, and orchestra than Buxton could provide. For no good reason, the action was transferred to a nineteenth-century court, which does not suit the drama. But the presentation, even though not full-scale, or "faithful," was intelligent, careful, and handsome to look at. The Buxton Festival's young directors, Anthony Hose and Malcolm Fraser, were conductor and director. Josephine Veasey was a powerful Gertrude. Thomas' score is an effective and excellent composition, uniting charm and invention with thorough craftsmanship. It would not be surprising if this operatic *Hamlet* returned to the international stage.

[*The San Diego Opera mounted* Hamlet *in 1978, with Sherrill Milnes as Hamlet and Ashley Putnam as Ophelia, and four years later the production was revived by the New York City Opera. I wrote no reviews, for the piece was done in my English translation. Let me pay tribute now to Mr. Milnes's powerful, passionate Hamlet and Miss Putnam's limpid, accurate, and touching Ophelia.]*

A HALF-AND-HALF AFFAIR

September 29, 1980

WHEN EDWARD DENT, in an essay on Donizetti that he contributed to *Fanfare for Ernest Newman* (1955), declared that "the grandeur and genuine passion of *Anna Bolena* and other operas of that type lies not in the arias, but in the force and rapidity of the dialogue," he was stating —perhaps overstating—something that Donizetti's early-twentieth-century detractors and champions both tended to overlook. Actors are required to animate that dialogue. Fine vocalism is not enough in itself to make a Donizetti opera dramatic. If it were, *Lucia di Lammermoor* would hardly have been laughed off the stage after a single performance when Toti Dal Monte and Dino Borgioli sang it at Covent Garden in 1925. And the New York City Opera revival of *Anna Bolena*, which has a cast of uncommon vocal accomplishment, would be a more gripping affair. In some ways, Donizetti's dramatic music is more difficult to perform than Wagner's. If a soprano has the notes and the tone for Isolde, the music can do the rest: the phrases are expressive in themselves. But some of Donizetti's most celebrated phrases are "nothing"—of no musical interest—until an actress makes them expressive in the theatre.

When nineteenth-century critics wrote of great nineteenth-century singers, they devoted as much attention to acting, gestures, stances, turns of the body, and flashes of the eye as to purely vocal prowess. Giuditta Pasta, for whom Anna Bolena and Bellini's Norma were composed, in 1830–31, sang her last London season in 1837, when her voice, Henry Chorley tells us, was steadily out of tune and painful to the ear. But since the grandeur of her style and her wonderful musical perceptions were unimpaired, she remained "none the less the 'Queen and wonder of the enchanted world of sound.'" Chorley recalls her as Romeo "raising tenderly a long lock of hair from the brow of the deceased" as she sang "Ah, mia Giulietta." His recollection of Pasta as Medea—a role "musically and dramatically composed by herself out of the faded book and correct music of Simone Mayr's opera"—is even more vivid:

I *see*, too, her magical and fearsome Medea.... The air of quiet, concentrated vengeance seeming to fill every fibre of her frame—as if deadly poison was flowing through her veins—with which she stood alone, wrapped in her scarlet mantle, as the bridal procession of Jason and Creusa swept by, is never to be forgotten. It must have been hard for those on the stage with her to pass that draped statue, with folded arms, that countenance lit up with awful fire, but as still as death, and as inexorable as doom. Where, again, has ever been seen any exhibition of art grander than her Medea's struggle with herself ere she consents to murder her children?—than her hiding the dagger, with its fell purpose, upon her bosom, under the strings of her distracted hair?—than her steps to and fro, as of one drunken with frenzy, torn with the agonies of natural pity, yet still resolved on her awful triumph?

Visual memories. And others, of a final concert, in 1850, when Pasta returned to London with a voice "broken, hoarse, and destroyed," a voice whose "state of utter ruin...passes description," and essayed some scenes from *Anna Bolena*. In the duet with Jane Seymour, her utterance of the single word "Sorgi!" and "the gesture with which she signed to her penitent rival to rise" revealed the old greatness. In the finale, "when, on Ann Boleyn's hearing the coronation music for her rival, the heroine searches for her own crown on her brow, Madame Pasta wildly turned in the direction of the festive sounds, the old irresistible charm broke out."

The point need not be pressed on anyone who saw and heard that imperfect yet matchless vocalist Maria Callas as Anne Boleyn, Medea, Norma, Violetta; or, for that matter, on anyone who saw and heard Beverley Sills as Anne Boleyn, Elizabeth (in Rossini's and Donizetti's operas), Mary Stuart, Violetta. Great operatic singers are great actresses, and the eye responds to and remembers them as keenly as the ear. There could be a long discursion here about ways in which the ear can persuade the eye and transform a staid elderly tenor into an ardent young poet (Björling's Rodolfo in later years) or a mountainous soprano into Wagner's agile warrior-maid. But it is not needed: operagoers understand, instinctively at least, the mysteries of operatic acting, and it is only some modern directors who confuse the values of the "straight"—or spoken—theatre with the more complicated workings of the lyric stage.

After the run of the operetta *The Student Prince*, the City Opera turned to *Anna Bolena*. There was a cast able to meet the technical demands of Donizetti's music; indeed, some exceptionally florid passages, omitted in most modern revivals—notably the G-major section of the Act II trio, with its taxing arpeggios and runs for the bass, and the testing double aria for the tenor in Act II—had been reinstated and were accurately voiced. Yet the performance lacked the "grandeur and genuine passion" Dent wrote of. Most *Anna Bolena*s I have seen, even those less capably sung, displayed those qualities. What was wrong with this one? Three things, I think: staging, conducting, and declamation.

Anna Bolena had its first twentieth-century revival in Donizetti's native Bergamo, in 1956. The Scala production the following year, with Callas as its heroine and Luchino Visconti as its director, brought the opera to prominence and reëstablished Donizetti as the composer of more than *L'elisir* and *Don Pasquale, Lucia* and *La Favorite*. Other productions soon followed, and *Anna Bolena* reached the City Opera in 1973. Sills was the heroine, Tito Capobianco the director, Ming Cho Lee the scenic designer, and José Varona the costume designer. For the revival, the show has been newly staged by Jay Lesenger in the existing décor. Mr. Lee's unit set, variously decked to suggest the different localities, is acoustically admirable. Two slanting solid walls seem to throw the sound forward, out into the house, and the singers are excellently audible. This is good. But the scenes are visually monotonous and lack romance. Moreover, a large square platform at center stage, mounted by three steps, cripples the direction and cripples the action of the singers. Up and down they go, up and down, pausing at times to stand or sit on the steps. Any naturalness of dramatic movement is precluded. As a first step, a director with any feeling for the visual manners of nineteenth-century opera would surely throw out the platform. A historically precise reconstruction of Tudor court behavior may be neither possible nor theatrically effective today, but one can fairly ask for a style in which historical possibility, nineteenth-century operatic convention, and the susceptibilities of a modern American audience are more plausibly reconciled. The ladies of the court should not sit on the ground while their queen is standing—or at any other time. Percy should not grab the king's arm while addressing him in public. This was a staging of movements imposed (when the king told Percy not to kiss the royal hand in submission, Percy "reacted" by reeling right across the platform), not of—what the opera needs—movements, glances, and gestures apparently spontaneous and natural, yet tremendous, revelatory, which make vivid what the characters are saying, feeling, and thinking: the kind of acting that Chorley described and that Callas and Sills provided. Instead of that, there were "clever director's touches": much play with the added figure of the young Princess Elizabeth (looking more than two years old); the intrusive presence on stage of the executioner brought over from Calais to strike off the queen's head. The lighting, "designed" by Gilbert V. Hemsley, Jr., would have shamed a provincial circus; it depended largely on spotlights pointed with variable accuracy in the direction of the principals. Charles Wendelken-Wilson's conducting was insensitive, unshaped. Textually, things were better. The overture was omitted, but several of the little mid-movement cuts that disfigured most earlier presentations of the opera had been healed. (At Glyndebourne in 1965, six movements were omitted and five drastically abridged.) This City Opera *Anna* is probably the fullest, except on records, that has been played in our century.

The old opera critics looked carefully at the work of the hairdresser, the wigmaker, and the costumer, and assessed their contributions to an interpretation—while holding the individual singer responsible for the result. They did not name those minor functionaries or go on about stage direction and lighting. Rarely did they mention a designer or a conductor. They and their readers could take for granted, as we cannot, that a prima donna's eyes would be visible, that there would be a series of scenes representing the stage pictures, at different depths, which the composer held in his mind's eye while he composed; and that the musical director would faithfully support and second the refinements of the singers' art. Things have changed. Chorley would no doubt chide me for talking about stage direction, scenery, and conductor before naming any of the cast. I would protest that singers of our day, even when performing in the operas of his day, have resigned their primacy and have allowed directors, designers, and conductors to take the lead and put their stamp on a presentation.

When Donizetti composed *Anna Bolena,* in 1830, he was on his mettle. He had just extricated himself from a burdensome Neapolitan contract that required him to turn out four new pieces a year. He had now to prove himself before the Milanese public; his earlier Milan piece, *Chiara e Serafina* (1822), had been a failure. His librettist was again the fine poet Felice Romani, more experienced than he had been when he wrote *Chiara.* The greatest soprano and tenor of the day, Pasta and Giovanni Battista Rubini, had been engaged for him—more accurately, he for them—and the great bass Filippo Galli was in the company. When such a cast is assembled, then, in Romani's words, "the poet can throw away the pale melodramatic rubbish known as 'librettos' and soar to the heights of lyric tragedy; the composer can leave in his desk his worn-out stock of routine phrases and eternal cabalettas, and rise to dramatic truth and the music of passion." Donizetti's response—with forceful, eloquent dialogue, set pieces that break out of the Rossinian mold, high melodic density, and thoughtful, expressive instrumental passages—is a matter of musical history. Formally, the opera is satisfying—especially the second act, where linked elegiac choruses cradle a duet, a trio, and two arias, neither of them for the heroine, and then introduce her tremendous finale of three successive arias. Act I is an exposition leading by swift steps to a crisis; Act II a long, beautiful resolution. Dramatically, the opera is well planned: the royal vices that Anne excited to become queen work on to compass her downfall. Anne appears in six of the seven scenes. Proud, spirited, ambitious, once ruthless but now remorseful that she sacrificed love to gain dominion and is thus authoress of her own tragedy, she is one of Donizetti's most fully drawn heroines. Jane Seymour, impetuous, feminine, caught in a web not of her weaving, is also a living character. So is Henry: even at his most villainous moments, there is bigness, majesty in his music. Percy, Anne's first love, and the minstrel Mark Smeaton are more conventional, but their roles are rewarding.

Performers should probably start, as Donizetti did, with the text. In the City Opera performance, a scream of torment from Smeaton, unwritten by the composer, breaks into the second chorus of Act II. This touch from *Tosca* (reinforced in the finale by a Smeaton with his eyes put out) embellishes the historians' speculation that the youth's confession was elicited by the threat of torture, but sounds inappropriately from a council chamber where a formal trial is being held. Worse, it flatly contradicts a clear statement in Romani's text: that Smeaton was tricked, not tortured, into his confession. It's no good approaching Donizetti with the cynical thought that the words don't matter. Anne is brought to life by recitative phrases like:

Ambitious, I wished for a crown,
And a crown I have—of thorns!

The words and the music look trite on the page. Properly timed, inflected, "acted," they can be overwhelming. But I wonder how many people in the State Theater followed them.

Which raises the question of language. *Anna* was essayed in Italian. A Romani text needs to be followed; and it is surely absurd for an all-American cast to play a drama to an American audience in a foreign tongue. There are several English translations of *Anna Bolena*. Joseph Reese Fry's was heard in Philadelphia and New York in 1844. Charles Jefferys's was heard in London in 1847. Modern versions have been made by Royce Isham and by Chester Kallman (used at Santa Fe in 1959). I don't know them. But I do feel sure that—despite the inevitable losses in pure sound—an English translation would have helped the singers, the audience, and the work. Most of the singers could pronounce Italian. But they weren't communicating with their listeners.

Olivia Stapp, who some years ago sang such roles as Carmen, Santuzza, Menotti's Magda Sorel—and Jane Seymour—with the company and has since then been making some name for herself abroad in a wide-ranging soprano repertory, returned to New York in the title role. She was thoroughly efficient but did nothing affecting, delicate, or exciting enough to call forth warmer epithets. No phrases etched themselves on the memory except the famous "Giudici! ad Anna!"—and that stood out only because it was crudely overdone. The voice is agile and, except below the staff, powerful. Jane Seymour, like Adalgisa in *Norma,* is a role for a young soprano which mezzo-sopranos have long appropriated. Susanne Marsee was fluent, lustrous, but a little monotonous; her words did not have much inflection or color. Rockwell Blake, the Percy, showed the surest command of the style: the ability to mold the phrases, to play with timing and timbres, to "present" the music. He attacked and sustained confident high D's. Samuel Ramey's bass coloratura was brilliant. He can sing his role. Now he must learn to enact it—find a stance, a gait, a look for Henry VIII. He had no presence or majesty. Mimi Lerner's Smeaton was loud and full. The comprimarios, Ralph Bassett as Lord Rochford and James Clark as Hervey, were both good.

TANTANTARA!

October 6, 1980

FROM A musical point of view, the celebrations that attend the opening of a new concert hall are perhaps best avoided. When Minneapolis opened its fine new Orchestra Hall, in 1974, I waited awhile, until both the brouhaha and the Minnesota Orchestra itself had settled, before going to report on it. If I was tempted to attend the first concerts in San Francisco's new concert hall, the Louise M. Davies Symphony Hall, and fell, let me plead in extenuation that there were musical lures: *Happy Voices*, the latest adventure in David Del Tredici's long "Aliceaed"; Mahler's Eighth Symphony, which tests a hall to its limits; and (a bonus for a New Yorker whose local grand-opera season has been delayed by the strike of the Met orchestra and chorus) a chance of catching at the same time the opening productions of the San Francisco Opera—*Samson et Dalila, Simon Boccanegra,* and *Die Frau ohne Schatten.* But physically the hall was not quite finished: here and there carpets were unlaid, walls were unpainted, and entrances that will one day admit the public were still blocked. And acoustically the hall was quite unfinished: not merely the "fine tuning" but even the basic "rough tuning" remained to be done. The inaugural gala—thousand-dollar tickets, champagne flowing as if from public fountains, and a final shower of balloons over the stage and of confetti in the form of musical notes over the audience—was more a social than a musical event. Later in the season, when the fine tuning has been done and the San Francisco Symphony has found its ears in the new surroundings, will be the time to report on the hall as a home for music. Meanwhile, some first impressions.

The architects of the Louise M. Davies Symphony Hall—named for the patron who donated five of the twenty-eight million dollars it cost —are the San Francisco office of Skidmore, Owings & Merrill, in association with Pietro Belluschi. The building stands across the street from the War Memorial Opera House, in San Francisco's Civic Center, and among those City Beautiful neoclassical and neo-Renaissance monuments—elegant echoes of St. Peter's, the Invalides, the Bibliothèque Sainte-Geneviève—it seems at first sight something of an underbred interloper. The main façade is a quadrant of glass and concrete, buttressed at ground level with semicircular concrete planters. A bulbous "string course" rings the building, looping out at each end of the quadrant to embrace two excrescent semicircular balconies. Through the glass, cylindrical columns—too widely spaced— are visible. The glass of the third floor is decked with thick pendant half-mullions, "teeth," whose purpose is obscure. There is no grand entrance, only a marquee off to one side. The place could be a classy bus station or air terminal. I looked and looked at it, trying to like it better—and liked it less. Getting into it for the first concerts recalled subway approaches at rush hour; anyone with a seat in the orchestra must first climb to the second floor and then descend through narrow passages, slowed by steps, to reach the doors leading into the auditorium. Things will doubtless improve when other entrances from the street are opened, but the plan shows unaccountably poky public spaces for so many people: the hall seats three thousand. There is no grand foyer. But there is space at street level, it seems, to tuck in, later, the restaurants, cafés, and bookshop that an audience should find in a city's principal concert hall.

Once inside, the spectator has a striking first impression. Sight lines are excellent, and the place doesn't feel as enormous as it is. In plan, the auditorium is shaped like a plump pear—a circle with an extrusion for the orchestral platform. The main floor is raked, the platform level. There are two balconies, stepped into open boxes as they dip toward the platform, and the lower balcony continues right around the hall, forming a chorus gallery (or providing "backstage" seating) where it runs above and behind the orchestral platform. The seats are upholstered in dusty rose (on mine, the pile of the plush ran the wrong way, impelling me ever forward), and the rest at the moment is white or cream. The floor beneath the audience's feet is bare concrete; the orchestra plays on wood. The rows run unbroken by aisles, but there is ample space between them for people to pass by those already seated. (In the old concert halls—Vienna's, Boston's—the audience is packed in more tightly, and good acoustics take precedence over convenience.) The ceiling is studded with projecting pyramids, and the balcony fronts and the side walls are studded with built-in "Frisbees," to scatter the sounds coming from the platform. These replace the coffering, cornices, corbels, niches, pilasters, and statues of the old concert halls, but they look rather silly and do not have the dramatic effect of the "cube explosion" Hugh Hardy designed for a similar purpose in Minneapolis. In general, the architectural detail seemed coarse, particularly where the curved balcony front embraces the platform like a fat white bolster, but it should all look different when all the painting is done. There are many slots in the ceiling. Some of them admit air. Through others, banners descend, and these banners are intended to control the reverberation time of the hall, between mid-frequency extremes of 2.1 and 1.5 seconds. Over the players are suspended about two dozen large reflecting discs—flying saucers—of clear acrylic plastic.

The acousticians are the Cambridge firm of Bolt Beranek & Newman, remembered by the general public as the first to be employed on New York's Philharmonic Hall. In other BBN buildings—among them Harvard's Loeb Drama Center, Ottawa's National Arts Center, the opera house in Bloomington (possibly America's best), and the remodelled Orpheum in Vancouver—I have listened to music with pleasure.

Philharmonic—now Avery Fisher—Hall in its latest edition is acoustically the work of Cyril Harris, as is Minnesota's Orchestra Hall. In lay paraphrase, Harris's aim would seem to be a warm, vibrant, resonant space that lives and "breathes" with the music. (In Fisher Hall, the floor under one's feet throbs at climaxes.) And BBN's aim would seem to be a rigidly unsympathetic concrete enclosure concerned with directing the "energy" produced by players as precisely, efficiently, and agreeably as possible. On the whole, I find BBN acoustics accurate but unhelpful, unflattering; bad orchestras don't sound better. Harris believes in what might be called "inherent" acoustics, in which the shape and the construction of the hall determine the sound. BBN incorporates "tuning devices" and other variables—San Francisco's banners and saucers. But the hoists and winches to adjust them are not yet in full working order. I hope I can report later on sound warmer, rounder, more glowingly beautiful than we heard at the opening concerts.

As a schoolboy in Marin County, David Del Tredici played the White Rabbit in a musical version of *Alice*. Twenty years later, in 1968, he began composing the long series of *Alice* pieces that has engaged him for the last twelve years: *Pop-Pourri*, the four-movement *Alice Symphony*, *Adventures Underground*, *Vintage Alice*, *Final Alice*, and—still in progress —a full-evening piece, *Child Alice*, of which *Happy Voices* is the second installment to appear. Part I of *Child Alice*, *In Memory of a Summer Day*, an hour-long setting, for soprano and large orchestra, of the prefatory verses to *Through the Looking-Glass*, was heard in St. Louis earlier this year. Part III, *All in the Golden Afternoon*, a half-hour setting, for the same forces, of the prefatory verses to *Alice's Adventures in Wonderland*, is due in Philadelphia next spring. Part II is to consist of two instrumental interludes: the first, *Quaint Events*, is in preparation, and *Happy Voices* is the second. It is an orchestral fugue, lasting about seventeen minutes, using, eventually, five themes, which are cast for the most part in an easy popular idiom. The large orchestra includes special bells rentable from—appropriately—the Carroll Musical Instrument Service Corporation. The first three fugue subjects are not single-voice but two-part themes, harmonized in thirds or tritones, and so the texture quickly becomes thick. The opening stretches of the piece are ingenious and agreeable, and the whole is a remarkable tour de force. The rhythms are playful, beguiling. But when everything gets going the accumulation proves self-defeating. At the climax, in the composer's words, "when one theme has struggled to the fore, the other motives, like a gang of howling furies, are not far behind, below or above, seeking to wrest it from its sovereign place," and "every possible contrapuntal device is now given full exuberant play." One saw everyone bowing or blowing away like crazy—and heard nothing but a dense din whose only followable feature was a rag melody blared out by the brass. Then there was a quiet coda. At the end, a wind machine sighs and an off-stage soprano voice sings, "All in the golden afternoon." In the score, this is marked "Concert-Ending." Presumably, in a full performance of *Child Alice* it is also the start of Part III.

The composer regards the instrumental interludes of his *Child Alice,* he says, as some of the improvised stories Lewis Carroll told to Alice Liddell and her sisters while they were rowing on the Thames but did not write down afterward. What kind of story could this one have been? Del Tredici says he has one in mind but will not reveal it. I enjoy the romantic and poetic aspects of his *Alice* music but lose him when he becomes strident, vociferous, dense, thunderous. Then I recall the Tenniel illustration to the close of the Lion and the Unicorn chapter in *Through the Looking-Glass,* when in distress Alice "put her hands over her ears, vainly trying to shut out the dreadful uproar." *Alice's Adventures in Wonderland* and *Tristan und Isolde* appeared in the same year, 1865. Alice, W. H. Auden once suggested, is "an adequate symbol for what every human being should try to be like." At times, Del Tredici seems to confuse that sweetly reasonable, intelligent, tidy-minded, and well-behaved heroine with the hysterical, passionate, undisciplined Isolde who cried out to wave and wrack to destroy the ship and all on it. Or—to put things on a purely musical level—he becomes overexuberant, raises the volume too high, writes too many notes, lets rip. All the *Alice* pieces with voice specify an *amplified* soprano; I find it hard to believe that Alice, even at her most emphatic, would ever resort to a public-address system. Del Tredici has something to say, about childhood, tenderness, memory, innocence, and the nature of love. Also about nightmares, and possible dark currents beneath these tales told on a sunny river. He is a generous and romantic composer. But he gets carried away. I'd remind him of an earlier river refrain: "Sweete Themmes! runne softly, till I end my Song."

The inaugural concert, conducted by Edo de Waart, now in his fourth season as music director of the San Francisco Symphony, began with Berlioz's *Roman Carnival,* which the orchestra has played under all but two of its conductors—from Henry Hadley, in 1912, onward. It had a bright performance, with crisp detail and an eloquent English horn, Robert Royse. After *Happy Voices,* there was Mendelssohn's G-minor Piano Concerto—a work the twenty-year-old Del Tredici played with the Symphony in 1957. The soloist was now the seventy-seven-year-old Rudolf Serkin, who gave a wise, courteous performance, a little graver than those we usually hear but beautifully fashioned. The second half was Beethoven's Fifth Symphony. When Mendelssohn played the first part of it to Goethe, in 1830, the old man said, "This arouses no emotion but astonishment. It is grandiose." After a long pause, he added, "It is very great, quite wild; it makes one fear the house may fall down." When the symphony was first played in San Francisco, in 1856, a critic reported that the later movements "caused many to yawn." De Waart's performance aroused no emotion in me at all. There it was, the celebrated composition, accurately executed, without eccentricity. And nothing especial happened. But, as I suggested, the concert was not primarily a musical occasion. The conductor was interviewed by television during the intermission, and he was under the cameras while he conducted. When Fate knocked at the door, many of the audience, still outside with the champagne, missed the summons.

If the climax of *Happy Voices* was loud, Mahler's Eighth Symphony the next night was louder still. Theodore Schultz, BBN's technical director of architectural acoustics, told me that at a rehearsal of it his meter rose to read a hundred and one decibels—five more than it had ever registered before in a concert hall. Performances of the "Symphony of a Thousand"—Mahler dubbed the première, in 1910, a "Barnum and Bailey show"—used to be rare and tremendous events. Now they are common. (This month, Solti conducts it in Chicago and WNCN broadcasts the concert in New York the next day, and Ozawa and the Boston Symphony bring it to Carnegie Hall for two performances.) The San Francisco performance was perhaps premature. An organ has been planned for Davies Hall, but it is not yet there: with an electronic roar of E-flat, the symphony got off to a bad start. But on the whole the first part, the "Veni, creator," went well, impetuous and urgent, with strong choral singing. In the second part, picturesqueness, sentiment, and "saturated" tonal beauty were missing. Some of the soloists were poor. The string playing was plain, without emotional portamento. One remained on earth.

A final word for the admirable program booklets, edited and largely written by Michael Steinberg, the Symphony's artistic adviser and publications director. They have all the merits of the program booklets he produced for the Boston Symphony when he held a similar post there. Content, thoroughness, printing, and paper all put New York programs to shame. Mr. Steinberg sets compositions in musical and in San Franciscan history, and he recalls links between them: Berlioz's jest about and Del Tredici's playing of the Mendelssohn concerto; Mendelssohn's and Berlioz's encounters with the Beethoven symphony. These are essays coherently devised for a particular program, not notes pulled from stock. They deserve careful reading, not rapid scanning, and they prepare the way for receptiveness to the music. Of course, there should also be a shop in the hall where the books and records that Mr. Steinberg recommends, and the scores of the pieces to be played, can be bought in advance.

[*The acoustics of Davies Hall have been somewhat improved, but it is still not a "warm" place. An organ was installed in 1984.*

Del Tredici's 137-minute Child Alice *had its première in 1986, in Carnegie Hall; it seemed to me an indisciplined, self-indulgent work. An account of* All in the Golden Afternoon *appears on p. 468.*]

GRAND OPERA

October 13, 1980

UNTIL THIS season, the San Francisco Symphony and the San Francisco Opera shared the splendors of the War Memorial Opera House, built in 1932. Splendors for the audience, that is. In an essay in the inaugural program book of the Louise M. Davies Symphony Hall, which opened last month, Robert Commanday, the critic of the *San Francisco Chronicle,* recalled that in 1965 there appeared "vivid descriptions of the Opera House with the 'Queen Anne front and Mary Ann back,' leaking 'like a sieve from roof to basement,' jammed with debris and dirt, imposing trying, costly, often dangerous work conditions on the Opera, Symphony, Ballet, and guest artists." And the Symphony, which played under a shell built into the stage house on concert nights, was not happy with the sound. Things became better for the Opera when in 1976 the pit was enlarged, so that Karl Böhm could conduct *Die Frau ohne Schatten* with Strauss's full orchestra; and better still last year, when a large extension was added to the back of the house. Now that the Symphony has moved across the street to its new home in Davies Hall, both it and the Opera are giving longer, overlapping seasons, and the latter has recruited its own, independent orchestra.

Eight years ago, I declared in *The New Yorker* that "internationally, the San Francisco Opera has the reputation of being America's first: the big company that most successfully combines excellent casts, enterprise in the choice of repertory, and a serious approach to dramatic presentation." That impression had been formed before I came to America, by reading *Spielpläne,* cast lists, and reviews. It was confirmed on my first, opera-hopping tour of this country, in 1964. Subsequent visits to San Francisco have not shaken it. Let me stress—before St. Louisans and others write indignant letters—that I am talking about international grand opera. The San Francisco season is short—only three months this year—and so Kurt Herbert Adler, the intendant, does not have James Levine's annual task of trying to keep a long season going while many of the good singers and conductors are busy elsewhere. In San Francisco, I have heard things less than first-rate but have never—even at the worst performances—been bored by an underrehearsed or routine performance, slung on because the schedule required it. There is a festival feel to the productions, yet it is not pure *stagione*—a term that implies pickup casts assembled for a few specific shows. The big houses today strive for a balance between *stagione* and "repertory"—a term that implies the continuity of a resident, developing company and many different productions in active use. Covent Garden has moved toward *stagione;* it offers high-level casting but limited fare. (For the second half of October, only *Lucia* and a single

Figaro are on the Royal Opera bills; in November, only *Figaro*, *Otello*, and *Tosca*. December is devoted to four *Hoffmanns*.) Maestro Adler has found a way to combine advantages of both systems. The productions of his junior troupes—Western Spring Opera, Western Opera Theater, Brown Bag Opera, the Merola Opera Program, and the American Opera Project (which puts on new American works)—provide year-round continuity, enrich the repertory, and open to young singers a path that has led some of them, by way of secondary roles in the grand fall season, to international stardom.

The War Memorial Opera House is very large. It seats 3,052 people —about a thousand more than La Scala or Covent Garden. There are some bad seats in it. I once had one, way back in the orchestra under the overhang of the balcony. After an act, I managed to sneak forward —and then a performance that had sounded dull and distant came to life. Otherwise, I have been fortunate and have regularly enjoyed big-house acoustics that put the place in the Teatro Colón and Scala class: rich, full, and warm, not daunting to young voices, and easily set ringing.

The 1980 season began with Saint-Saëns' *Samson et Dalila,* an opera that refuses to die, despite sniping at its oratorial rig and academic manners: Mendelssohn, Gounod, and neoclassicism went into its making; the bacchanale brings to mind Sir Despard's remark, in *Ruddigore,* "We only cut respectable capers." I have seen *Samson* in Paris, Britain, and Italy but most often in America. When the Met revived it in 1971, the *Times* asked, "Is there any justification for giving Saint-Saëns' *Samson et Dalila* today?" and, despite an admirable performance, answered no. The authors of *The Record Guide* opine that "as a drama it hardly exists, but a number of charming airs and ensembles ensures its survival." The charming airs are Delilah's "Printemps qui commence," "Amour! viens aider ma faiblesse," and "Mon coeur s'ouvre à ta voix" (to which Samson adds some important phrases). To hear Germaine Cernay sing the first and last, on old Columbia records, is to be captivated. Mezzo-sopranos, whose only other repertory chance as prima donna of a serious opera has been in *Carmen* (well, until *Werther* recently became fashionable), welcome the opera. But only one Delilah I have heard—Rita Gorr in her Paris début season (1952) and at the Met twelve years later—has fully commanded the range, the style, timbre both voluptuous and delicate, and perfect French. When Shirley Verrett sang Delilah at La Scala in 1970, she looked stunning and acted electrically but lacked the deep notes of the role. Ten years later, in San Francisco, she still looks stunning and acts with intensity, but the voice —which in the interim has been screwed up at times for Norma, Tosca, and Amelia in *Ballo,* then dropped again for Orpheus and Azucena—has taken a beating. Delilah's low notes were now forced out in exaggerated chest, the middle was often unsupported, and only an occasional high note shone with something like the old luster.

Martinelli recorded Samson's "Arretez, ô mes frères," and Caruso recorded "Vois ma misère," but they are not tunes one remembers; *Samson et Dalila* belongs to the mezzo. Nevertheless, big tenors have not disdained the other title role—Mario Del Monaco, Jon Vickers, and now in San Francisco Placido Domingo. Domingo was in admirable voice, big and free, but on the night I heard him (it was the fourth performance) he sang full out *all* the time, as he sometimes does, and was therefore unmoving—all voice and no character. Wolfgang Brendel, as the High Priest, had the sharpest declamation—and the worst French. In minor roles, the grave, beautiful bass of Kevin Langan (a graduate of the Merola Opera Program), as the Old Hebrew, was outstanding. Scenically, things were flimsy. Douglas Schmidt's sets and Carrie Robbins's costumes, which took their inspiration from Alma-Tadema, were decorative. Nicolas Jöel's stage direction was light and mannered rather than fervent. The temple collapse was a feeble affair. In general, a more respectful attention to the stage directions and to the Bible was called for. Julius Rudel usually conducts French opera—*Pelléas, Werther*—sensitively, but his account of *Samson* was hardly more than neat, efficient, and perhaps a trifle flashy.

San Francisco gave the American première of *Die Frau ohne Schatten* in 1959. Four years ago, it mounted a second production—a version of the staging directed by Nikolaus Lehnhoff and designed by Jörg Zimmermann that has been seen in several European houses. For two acts, it is a delicate, picturesque production in what—despite the quashing of some symbolic actions—is perhaps the finest *Frau* décor since Emil Preetorius's. The traditional stage plans are pretty well retained; the magic scenes are airy and fantastic, the earthy scenes substantial. Things go wrong in Act III, where a back-to-front presentation of the temple—the petrified Emperor squats near the prompter's box—upsets the dynamics of the action.

This year, there was a seasoned cast in the principal roles. For more than a quarter century, Leonie Rysanek has been the reigning Empress. She is still radiant. In her performance, the sensuous beauty, the sentiment, and the spiritual content of this complicated and ambitious opera find their embodiment. (But her delivery of the crucial "Ich—will—nicht," shouted out in a histrionic manner, was new to me and not pleasing.) The Dyer's Wife is a fairly new role in Birgit Nilsson's repertory. (She did it first in Stockholm five years ago, in the Lehnhoff-Zimmermann production.) She sang it strongly; her interpretation was vulgar and obvious. Ruth Hesse's Nurse was as ill-voiced and approximate as ever, and James King's Emperor as stolidly reliable. Gerd Feldhoff's Barak was firmly voiced; the role needs greater warmth and breadth of tone and of character. Berislav Klobučar conducted with a good sense of colors and of general pacing; there was too little fine, bewitching detail. The sound picture was often marred by having offstage voices—and some that should be onstage—piped in over loudspeakers. Among the young singers, Rebecca Cook, a bright Falcon; Mr. Langan and Thomas Woodman (the baritone who impressed me so much in Central City last year), as two of the Watch-men; and James Hoback, as an astonishing Apparition of rippled golden nudity materializing to tempt Miss Nilsson, deserve mention.

Simon Boccanegra was revived in the décor by Pier Luigi Pizzi first seen in Chicago in 1974—décor not unhandsome in itself but inept for, destructive of, Verdi's musical drama. That Chicago *Boccanegra* gave impetus to the founding of the American Institute for Verdi Studies, one of whose aims is to offer performers a clearer idea of what Verdi's operas are about. Sonja Frisell, who directed the San Francisco revival, cannot be blamed for everything that was wrong about the staging; the décor imposes its limitations. But surely it would not have been hard to refashion Act III into some semblance of a private room (it seemed mere chance that Simone was the first to drink from a pub-lic pitcher; he fell asleep not at his desk but, awkwardly, perched on a public bench), and in Act III to follow the stage direction, tied in detail to the music, for Simone's death. Authorized production books were published for Verdi's operas from *Les Vêpres siciliennes* to *Otello*. The most elaborate of them are those for *Simon Boccanegra* and *Otello*, and while there are various reasons that can justify a director's depar-ture from or adjustment of their prescriptions, there is no excuse for changes that render the result dramatically or musically less effective. If, for example, the offstage chorus of the Act II finale—which "must begin very far off" and then at the reprise on "Le guelfe spade cin-gano" surge forward, four or six choristers abreast, until the last eight measures are cried loudly from the left wings—is sung from a station, as it was in San Francisco, an effect Verdi intended is lost.

The production book is not a straitjacket, any more than the score is. Its authors (Giulio Ricordi compiled it, but Verdi's and Boito's hands can be discerned in what it says) remark that the stage plans for the Act II finale, worked out for Scala acoustics, may need modification in other theatres. After a very close account of the Council scene, they continue, "But it is not the dry description of a gesture, of a step back-ward or forward, that can make this dramatic development, this suc-cession of episodes and terrible passions, effective on the stage. The production merely indicates in a material fashion and in its chief points the various positions that for musical or dramatic reasons the soloists and the chorus must adopt." When those have been mastered, interpretation can begin. Then it is up to *"supremely intelligent actors"*—with (shall we add today?) a director to inspire them—"to dig to the depths of the musical conception and the dramatic conception, both at once, and thus achieve the aim of gripping and stirring the audience." Miss Frisell chose to end the tremendous scene not in Verdi's way but with Demon King contortions from the Doge, fancy lighting effects, and a flat contradiction of the specific statement that no one suspects Paolo to be the object of the Doge's curse.

Renato Bruson took the title role. He has a very beautiful voice, beautifully deployed, but is just a shade dull in the part. Margaret

Price was Amelia. She is perhaps the only big-league soprano around able to sound all the music amply, accurately, and securely. She may not be a particularly compelling or vivid actress, but, unlike Mr. Bruson, she does inflect phrases in a way that creates character. (Did she, I wonder, try the direction to start Amelia's aria looking out to sea and to turn to the public only at "Ma gli astri e la marina," but then find it ineffective in the San Francisco theatre?) Cesare Siepi was still a noble, moving Fiesco. Giorgio Lamberti's Gabriele was bright in sound but unpolished in style. In the smaller roles, it was not, for once, the Paolo, Frederick Burchinal, who caught the ear (he seemed concerned more with sound than with sense) but the Pietro—once again Mr. Langan. Lamberto Gardelli's conducting was masterly, though there were passages where more give, a greater readiness to stretch the phrases, would have been welcome.

HALL

October 20, 1980

NEW YORK CITY has a new large concert hall, part of the Lehman College Center for the Performing Arts, in the Bronx. It seats 2,318. It has good acoustics and is an attractive place, on the marge of a spacious campus with lawns, trees, and a diverse architectural landscape of 1930s academic Gothic and 1960 Marcel Breuer. The Lexington Avenue No. 4 train stops one block away, and the D train two blocks away, so the hall is easily reached from Manhattan. There is a restaurant. The concert hall, a theatre, an experimental theatre, and a recital hall in the college's music building make up the performing spaces of the Center, whose "complex" also includes a library and an art gallery. In some ways, it is like a second Lincoln Center in a peaceful setting, without the concrete expanses, busy traffic, and encircling skyscrapers. The concert hall opened at the end of last month with a concert by the New York Philharmonic. The second event—the hall can also be used as a theatre—was *La traviata*, the inaugural performance of the National Opera Touring Company, the New York City Opera's new touring division.

The architects are David Todd (the designer of Manhattan Plaza) and Jan Pokorny; the acoustic consultant is Ranger Farrell. Building was begun in 1973 but was interrupted after two years by the city's financial crisis. (Lehman College is part of the City University.) The *AIA Guide* (1978) called the unfinished buildings "eye-catching but... more prima donnas than anything else." That's harsh. Finished, they make up a romantic place that predisposes one toward enjoyment of a performance. The concert hall is asymmetrical, an assemblage of trapezoidal forms suggesting zoo architecture (Toronto's pavilions, Casson's elephant house in London). It is unpretentious—elaborately

39

designed but simply, even barely, executed in concrete, limestone, and glass. Within the irregular auditorium, the orchestra seats fan out in five unequal vanes; the rightmost of them climbs sharply to become one with the balcony, which is treated as a lively cluster of interlocking steep terraces. The side walls are elegantly ribbed with narrow concrete blocks. The ceiling is a mosaic of large white panels with darkness visible through the spaces between them. Similar white panels surround and roof the platform, which is framed by a red curtain. The floor, raked to give good sight lines (and hearing lines?), is carpeted. At the opening concert, I thought I had never heard the Philharmonic so clearly, so intimately. At a first assessment, I would rate the acoustics of Lehman Hall—may we henceforth call it that?—above those of Avery Fisher Hall, as being more immediate and intimate, but a little below those of Carnegie Hall, as being less warm and responsive. The other public spaces, the foyers and lobbies, are plainly decorated, interestingly shaped on varied, linked levels, and meager; American architects often seem to forget that an audience takes up more room in intermissions, walking, talking, eating, drinking, than when it is packed into orderly rows. In fair weather, it doesn't matter at Lehman Hall: outside, a broad, tree-lined terrace and its open, ample undercroft (part of the walkway system that links all the college buildings) give onto a wide lawn, and there is also a stepped forecourt that looks ideal as a site for informal summer concerts.

The Philharmonic program began with two works by composers on the Lehman College faculty: Ulysses Kay's symphonic essay *Markings* and John Corigliano's Clarinet Concerto—pièces d'occasion on this occasion but, as Zubin Mehta, who conducted, pointed out, pieces that on their own merits had already been taken into the Philharmonic's repertory. The orchestra played Corigliano's concerto on its European tour this summer. The Bronx performance confirmed what the critic of the Malmö *Arbeten* wrote of the soloist, Stanley Drucker: "Here is a clarinettist with an almost improbably superb technique, a sound that is divine, and a radiance very few musicians possess." Then Brahms's Second Symphony. The Philharmonic is making a better sound than it has made for years: string tone fuller, woodwinds more nearly in tune (but still some brass glare at climaxes). If Mr. Mehta had not adopted the eccentric modern seating plan—top strings all clumped to his left, double-basses lopsidedly off on the right—one might even have heard rich, balanced, Brahmsian sonority. Mr. Mehta's account of the work was unimpressive.

For the Touring Company's *Traviata*, Frank Corsaro restaged his celebrated City Opera production—a thoughtful, detailed, and delicate realization in which the nuances of timing, phrasing, glance, and gesture are determined by keen psychological observation of the characters and their plights. "What is she thinking?," "Why does she say *that*?," "What would she *do*?" are good questions for a Violetta to start with; they must be followed—and evidently they were—with "What should *I* do to make the audience believe in her?" Elizabeth Pruett, singing her first Violetta, gave a performance both moving and precise. And well sung: other important questions—"*Why* this high note, slur, corona, change of harmony?"—had, it was clear, also been considered. Sometimes the careful thought that had gone into the answers was too patent; later in the run—the company has embarked on a five-week, twenty-five-city tour—Miss Pruett will surely play and sing more freely. "Non sapete—quale affetto" needs more agitated, less strictly *a tempo* phrasing. The dropping seventh of "unico raggio di bene" calls for portamento. For the three solo outpourings of the second finale ("Ah perchè venni," etc.), the tempo should broaden. Already Miss Pruett's performance is distinguished in conception and in many fine points of musical execution. She sings "Addio del passato" so affectingly that she could profitably omit some "business" (with Germont's letter, a prie-dieu, a crucifix, a rosary) that adds nothing to—dispels, rather—the emotional force of what Verdi and she are saying.

The personal dramas are vividly enacted, but Mr. Corsaro's reading of Alfredo's character is not mine—or, I think, Verdi's. (Would the shy, modest youth who for a year has worshipped Violetta at a distance go into a public clinch with her at their first meeting, during the brindisi? Is the extreme complacency that Mr. Corsaro makes him so unsubtly express in Act II—he ended "De' miei bollenti spiriti" relaxed on a sofa, with his feet up—not belied by the ardor and intensity of the music?) William Livingston was an eager, impassioned little Alfredo, singing his heart out in bright, forward tones. He reminded me of Luigi Infantino. What I missed in the production was Verdi's "subtext" of social protest and freethinking assertion. Perhaps that was inevitable in a small-scale presentation. The chorus numbered a dozen: the *deserto che appellano Parigi* was hardly *popoloso,* and the Act II dance divertissement was omitted. Miss Pruett caught the heroic note, but her adversaries were immature. Vernon Hartman, the Germont, forced up his volume to a point where steadiness and pitch became uncontrolled. And in this hall there was no need for anyone to push. Although it seats more than Covent Garden—and exactly the same as Kennedy Center's opera house—everything the young cast sang and everything the small orchestra played (a much reduced scoring was used) was excellently audible. "If only people could hear half so well in the State Theater," I heard a member of the City Opera say. The words were consistently clear, and so there was less excuse than usual for performing the drama in a foreign tongue. How many people really *followed* Violetta's and Alfredo's exchanges in the brindisi?

Among the comprimarios, Rose Benedetto, the Annina, caught the ear with her easy, unforced singing. The scenery was dowdy. The lighting was crude: follow-spots for two acts, and a demonstration in Act III of how much better a realistic action looks without them. Yet it was a *Traviata* that held the attention securely. In an unstylish modern way, Victor DeRenzi's conducting had life and love in it; now he must study the way that singers of Verdi's day phrased this music.

Bizet's *Pêcheurs de perles* has come to the City Opera, and it is welcome, for it is a work good to sing and good to hear. When the opera first appeared, at the Théâtre-Lyrique in 1863, alternating with *Figaro*, Berlioz alone proclaimed its merit; after eighteen performances, it was dropped. Ten years after Bizet's death, in a new version, with the weak ending recomposed, it began to turn up on the world's stages, and in 1889 Emma Calvé and the publisher Sonzogno, who had the Italian rights, brought it to prominence. That year, Calvé sang the opera all over Italy (in Naples, with Fernando De Lucia) and reintroduced it to Paris, in Italian, at the Gaîté. In 1893, in yet another revised version, she relaunched it in French at the Opéra-Comique. (And there it stayed; I used to see it in the fifties in what looked like—but, the annals assure me, were not—the sets Calvé sang in.) In 1896, Calvé introduced it to the Metropolitan, in an abridged version. But in New York the opera did not take. It was twenty years before it returned to the Met, for three performances with Frieda Hempel, Caruso, and Giuseppe De Luca. And that, it seems, was the last professional staging it had here before the City Opera's. *Pêcheurs* has taken now. All five performances were sold out; it returns in the spring [*and has returned several times since then*].

The Théâtre-Lyrique première was probably a swagger affair: the theatre went in for spectacle, and *Pêcheurs* is Bizet's most massive score (except for *Ivan IV*). The 1863 critics found it noisy; one dubbed it a "fortissimo in three acts." The City Opera staging, directed by Cynthia Auerbach, is simple, sensible, and not unpicturesque. Robert O'Hearn's spare set, first seen in Miami, has plenty of usable flat space, flanked by platforms and beehivey Brahmin objects that can be variously grouped. Palm trunks frame the scene, and on the backcloth a Klimtian painted moon rides above a romantic ocean. (But in this Ceylon the light, the only out-of-style feature of the show, comes from elsewhere—largely from spotlights none too accurately pointed at the actors.) The exotic atmosphere is not neglected, but the emphasis is thrown on the soloists and their music—not on the Meyerbeerian choruses, dances, and large scenic effects. That matches a work whose main enchantments are supple, subtle melodies, delicately accompanied.

There were two casts, both accomplished. In the first, Diana Soviero was a sweetly flexible Léïla. Marianna Christos, a few days later, was even better; she had devised a character for the priestess, and it gave character to her singing. *Pêcheurs* may not be much of a drama. In his Bizet biography, Winton Dean observes that "Léïla remains the typical suffering soprano, Nadir the aspiring tenor who is all emotion, no brain, and little brawn...while Zurga, like other stage baritones, is required to veer between ferocity and magnanimity as the situation demands." Yet something more than lovely music can be found in the roles. Miss Christos showed how, in her portrayal of a girl at once devout yet sensual, gentle yet resolute; in Léïla there is something of Micaëla, something of Carmen. Miss Christos's timbre can recall that of Maria Callas at its most limpid and steady—still carrying a touch of fascinating resin. Where most of the soloists could pronounce French, she commanded it, and brought the phrases to life. The Carmen quality came forward strongly in the Act III duet with Zurga, where, indeed, some of Carmen's most striking phrases are foreshadowed. This duet is not one of the famous numbers in *Pêcheurs,* but as done by Miss Christos and David Arnold it brought the house down. Its opening exchanges may recall Meyerbeer, but the singers continue now like Carmen and Don José, then like Aida and Amonasro. Almost with disbelief one discovers that Verdi could not have heard *Pêcheurs* before composing *Aida*—unless he was invited to an early rehearsal—for he left Paris two months before the première. The number was fortified by the restoration of two passages cut in the 1893 revision. And there was a splendid Zurga. Mr. Arnold, too, created a character. He, too, commanded the language and made every phrase arresting. And he voiced the music in a cultivated baritone of precise focus, of the kind one longs to hear in French opera and so seldom does hear. He also acted well. Dominic Cossa, the first-night Zurga, sang with feeling but more roughly.

The first-night Nadir, Barry McCauley, displayed a tenor similarly apt for this music: ductile, flexible, and unforced. Although he can, I know, float the high B's of "Je crois entendre encore" (the traditional high C has, alas, been expunged from the City Opera score) in a radiant falsetto of poignant sweetness, as the old tenors used to do, on the first night he chose to sing them fully. He stuck to the notes and essayed no gracing of either the melodic lines or the meter. With profit he could study De Lucia's recordings of the romance, the chanson, and the tenor's first duet with Léïla (readily available now in the Rubini album of De Lucia's earlier recordings)—if not to copy that most individual of stylists, then to be inspired by the possibilities De Lucia suggests, and to adopt those of them that he finds good. Mr. McCauley is no actor, but he sang so extraordinarily well that one feels justified in asking still more of him. Joseph Evans, the other Nadir, was more ordinary—conscientious and acceptable. In the pit, Calvin Simmons made a promising but puzzling City Opera début. The promise lay in the lilt and animation of his conducting and in his poetic response to Bizet's exquisite instrumental inventions. The puzzles were two: his inability to keep the chorus in time and his persistence in a strict, metronomic beat through passages—notably the climaxes of the tenor-baritone duet and the second soprano-tenor duet—that cry out for rubato. He, too, could learn from De Lucia.

In 1954, a Sadler's Wells production of *Pêcheurs* took a half step toward restoring Bizet's 1863 score. In 1973, the Welsh National Opera production went all the way, and passages that survive only in the first vocal score were orchestrated by Arthur Hammond. (The autograph and the 1863 performing materials have disappeared; without them, we can only guess at Bizet's *first* version, before "theatre cuts" and rehearsal revisions were made. Early manuscript librettos, the first printed libretto, and the 1863 vocal score all yield different readings.) In 1975, Bizet's publishers, Choudens, issued a fourth edition, the "Welsh version." It has been recorded on Angel, and it is used by the City Opera (although the libretto sold in the theatre corresponds to the second, 1880s score). The main text of the "Welsh score" retains the tenor-baritone duet in its familiar, posthumous version, where a reprise of the big tune replaces the stirring stretta that Bizet composed, and banishes the stretta to an appendix. This stretta can be heard on the Angel recording; I hope it will be heard in the State Theater at the spring revival. The other big difference is the excision of the final trio, "Ô lumière sainte," which may have been composed by Benjamin Godard, and the reinstatement earlier in the scene of the soprano-tenor duet to almost the same words, which Bizet composed. It's not great music, but it will sound better than it does when the singers and conductor don't treat it as a military quickstep. Bizet's own surviving finale is weak—one understands why successive editors have tinkered with it—but it is the best we have. Maybe his *ur*-finale—with a reprise for the lovers of "Ô lumière sainte" rather than the tune that belongs to Nadir and Zurga—will turn up one day. Miss Auerbach has tinkered, too. To the 1863 music she has added a stage direction from the unauthentic 1893 score; the offstage lovers reappear on a distant rock. Here it looks like a *Flying Dutchman* apotheosis-in-the-sky. That can very easily be put right.

More Bizet, please. For a start, *The Fair Maid of Perth* and the one-acter *Djamileh*. Then, *Ivan IV*.

The City Opera has revived its *Don Giovanni*, new last spring. Only Carol Vaness, the Anna, remains from the earlier cast. Samuel Ramey, its Don, now plays Leporello. John Cox is still listed as the director, Jay Lesenger is named as the stage director, and there have been changes in the production. Not having seen the original, I cannot apportion blame for the poor staging of the revival, which is sometimes slackly traditional, at other times feebly innovatory. There was a rather distinguished cast, but, as Shaw wrote after a Covent Garden presentation in 1889, "I cannot say that the performance was an adequate one. A musical critic does not write that often in a lifetime about *Don Giovanni*—unless, indeed, he is given to writing the thing that is not." Mahler is often said to have said, in his role as an opera director, "Tradition ist Schlamperei," or "Tradition is slovenliness." What he really said was something like "What you people call tradition is mere slovenliness." He was damning easy, thoughtless repetition of old routines; he was far too intelligent not to value the "tradition" that represents the accumulated wisdom of generations of operatic interpreters: a treasure house of possibilities from which sensitive performers—singers, conductors, and directors—take what they find to be good, true, and suited to their own abilities, and to which they add their own discoveries and perceptions.

More than tradition is scorned when a composer's instructions are flouted. Goethe, that experienced theatre and opera director, once declared that opera has "a fundamental advantage that the spoken drama lacks: the full score, the expressed will of the composer, insuring that tone, expression, movement and bodily position cannot be mistaken." Even if Mozart had not signalled with his triple "si cava la maschera" the exact moments in the Act I finale at which Ottavio, Elvira, and Anna unmask, a Mozart director should hear those moments in the music and not get them wrong. If he chooses to play fast and loose with a masterpiece, he should perhaps rewrite Da Ponte's words and recompose Mozart's score to suit his ideas. On a simple, literal level, the "gigantic mouthfuls" of a "tasty dish" which Leporello refers to suggest something more than spoonfuls of soup; Giovanni should not cry "eccellente marzimino" while raising a glass of *white* wine to his lips. On a more serious level, it is absurd for the Commendatore's statue to say "Leave the dead ones in peace" (when, according to the stage directions, Giovanni has whacked several monuments) if the setting has been shifted from a cemetery to "a stonemason's yard." And the tremendous scene plays at half strength when the awe and eeriness of a nocturnal cemetery and the sense of near-blasphemy have been tossed aside in a silly bid for novelty. The City Opera ending is equally false to Mozart's drama: Giovanni is bound and carried off by his servants. One could write an opera with that dénouement: rebellion in the servants' hall, master frightened by a hoax and then borne off, his villa fired. But Mozart didn't.

Crippled by the direction and cribbed by a poky set, the singers could hardly shine. Miss Vaness, muting the temperament that made her Vitellia in last season's *Titus* so lustrous, sought pathos and tenderness in Anna's music. She found it in an account of "Non mi dir" which was beautiful, moving, and exciting. "Or sai chi l'onore" needed more spirit and broader phrasing; some endings were clipped. (Has any previous Anna ever chosen to *sit* before launching into that passionate, fiery declaration?) Heather Thomson's Elvira showed more spunk. At the start, there was harshness at the top of her voice, but it flowed evenly and truly through an admirable "Mi tradì." Gwenlynn Little's Zerlina was ordinary. The sense of Alan Kays's Ottavio escaped me. He had painted his face to resemble an owl; when during Leporello's aria Anna swooned, he turned his back on her. But then he handled "Il mio tesoro" with great tenderness. Samuel Ramey's Leporello was well sung. Justino Diaz has the looks, the figure, the physical presence, and the voice to be a splendid Giovanni. Thirteen years ago, both Sarah Caldwell, in Boston, and Giancarlo Menotti, in Spoleto, directed him in

45

the role. Yet he was, and he remains, no more than promising. The ingredients are right, but nothing happens.

John Mauceri conducted. He used the regular conflation of Prague and Vienna versions, and also included Elvira's recitative after the catalogue aria. First steps had been taken toward restoring the necessary appoggiaturas, but Miss Vaness left a hole in the middle of "Non mi dir," before the reprise; in fact, all Mozart's invitations to extempore cadenzas and bridge passages were gracelessly declined. That Mr. Mauceri loves the score was evident. A slowish allegro assai at the start of the first finale meant that Zerlina did not have to peck at the eighth-note arpeggios; a slowish andante to follow allowed the romantic instrumental parts to be savored. But somehow the result was also a bit sleepy. And neither the first nor the second finale had the weight of accents or the extremes of dynamic contrast to make them tremendous. The staging seemed to have got into the sound. The whole thing lacked passion and conviction. *Don Giovanni* did not, in the words of City Opera's current slogan, "come alive." A cynic might remark that it hardly matters when many in the audience are probably not following the text in detail (the drama was played in Italian) and many of them care nothing for Mozart's music: again and again, applause crashed out before a movement had reached its tonic close.

BUZZ, BUZZ!

October 27, 1980

WHILE THE Philharmonia Orchestra, from London, was playing three Viennese symphonies and one Russian symphony at its Carnegie Hall concerts last week, American musicians were giving the American premières of some British works. Philip West's Alice Tully Hall recital, on Sunday, entitled "An Evening of English Music for the Oboe," began with Britten's early Phantasy Quartet, Opus 2, for oboe and string trio, and his *Six Metamorphoses after Ovid,* for solo oboe, and it included the American premières of his *Two Insect Pieces* (1935) and his *Temporal Variations* (1936), both for oboe and piano, and both but recently published. The *Insect Pieces*—the Grasshopper and the Wasp—are slight, brief scherzi, one hoppity-skippity, the other a thing of darting zigzag flights from the oboe and angry buzzing, now loud, now soft, from the piano, with a sting in the coda. Mr. West and his pianist, David Burge, treated them solemnly, steadily, and missed the fun. The graphic vividness of the final episode—on the page the lines seem to track an increasingly infuriated wasp, homing in at last on its target—was given no correspondingly picturesque sound image. And that was surprising, for Mr. West and Mr. Burge are both known to be witty men. As I have had occasion to observe before, Puritan hangups persist in American "classical" music-making. Even the merriest men can turn sobersides when they put on the old soup-and-fish and step out in front of an audience. Oboists, I'm told, daren't smile; embouchure must determine the set of their lips. But surely their eyes can twinkle and their music can smile? I'd never before heard the Bacchus movement of the *Metamorphoses*—which represents "the noise of gaggling women's tattling tongues and shouting out of boys"—played in so careful and unintoxicate a manner. Would it be wrong to suggest that British music and therefore British executants—or is it vice versa?—are the most relaxed of any, the least formal, the readiest to reach out to audiences and share enjoyment with them? Handel was British by choice and by adoption; most of his music was written for London. Mr. West and Mr. Burge played his G-minor Sonata, Opus 1, No. 6, and played its sparkling movements too earnestly.

Temporal Variations is a substantial, often entertaining composition—theme, seven variations, and "resolution"—lasting about fifteen minutes. Subtleties of motivic, harmonic, rhythmic, and textural transformation show Britten's innate command of musical science, and the piece also has charm and wit—more than were revealed by a prim, inhibited performance. Britten's almost Expressionist range of dynamics and accents was narrowed. The variation called "Oration" was not declamatory; "Commination" didn't sound like a string of colorful curses. The stress of the germinal motif seemed to fall on the second, not on the accented first, note. The recital ended with Arthur Bliss's Oboe Quintet (1927), written, as the Phantasy Quartet was, for Leon Goossens. Mr. West was joined by four of his colleagues on the Eastman faculty. (Since one celebrated review of the composition began "Five oboes is an unusual combination," perhaps I should specify that they were four distinguished string players, versed in chamber music, making up an ad-hoc string quartet.) Bliss's "absolute" music has its champions, but I, though I liked the man very much, am not among them. The *Pastoral: "Lie strewn the white flocks"* is beautiful; the film music (notably *Things to Come*) and the three ballets are strong and effective. But the Oboe Quintet and its stronger successor the Clarinet Quintet now seem to say little, to do little, even in performances more freely romantic than that of Mr. West and his colleagues. It was a disappointing recital from a player who is a master of his instrument, a scrupulous and dedicated musician, and an explorer of new repertory. No sparks flew; no fire was kindled.

The next day, William Walton's *Façade* 2 had its American première, at a concert in the Symphony Space given by the Caecilian Chamber Ensemble. *Façade*, Walton's most famous composition, has an intricate history. In brief, there were eighteen "numbers"—Edith Sitwell poems recited in tempo to musical accompaniment from wind quartet, cello, and percussion—at the first public performance, in 1923. Eleven of them were retained at the next performances, in 1926, and seventeen new settings were added. Only five of the originals survived at the ISCM performance, in 1928. The following year, Miss Sitwell, with

Constant Lambert as her partner, made the first of her three *Façade* recordings—eleven numbers, all of which were taken into the "definitive" suite. This was published only in 1951. Like *Pierrot Lunaire*, it consists of thrice seven settings. It has become the familiar *Façade*. Then in 1977, Walton's seventy-fifth-birthday year, eight of the earlier *Façade* pieces were revived, by the English Bach Festival, and were prepared for publication. While reading the proofs, the composer decided to reject three of them and replace them with three other numbers, and "radically to rework and reorder the music." The quotation is from the recently published score of *Façade 2*, which comes from the Oxford University Press. (*Façade 2* has also been recorded, as a prelude to *Façade*, on an O.U.P. disc distributed here by Peters International. Cathy Berberian and Robert Tear are the speakers.) This summary history could be complicated by consideration of the *Façade* orchestral suites; the different scores, with different contents, used for the Ballet Rambert's and the Royal Ballet's *Façade*; and the three (at least) *Façade* poems that Walton has also set as songs.

Study of *Façade* would not be ado about nothing. The piece has a touch of magic in it and more than a touch of genius. On several counts, it is an important work in musical history. Nicholas Kenyon suggested one of them in his *High Fidelity* review of the O.U.P. recording: "The effect of its success on Walton's composing career seems in retrospect to have been disastrous.... It is ironic that while Michael Tippett, for example, has become ever more searching in the works of his later years, Walton had to celebrate his seventy-fifth birthday by returning to a youthful triumph of forty years before." Anyone concerned with Mascagni, who never repeated the success of *Cavalleria*, Leoncavallo (ditto with *Pagliacci*), or Rossini, who conquered the musical world while he was young and after *William Tell* retired into almost forty years of near-silence, must speculate on this phenomenon. (Tippett, Schütz, and Verdi, writing ever greater music into an advanced age, are the opposite types.) Then, there is the matter of bringing "popular" idioms into "serious" music, with its bearing on Debussy, Ravel, Stravinsky, Krenek. Walton's tango, foxtrot, and popular song, with its smoochy saxophone, precede those of Kurt Weill. *Façade* also throws its own light on the mysterious marriage of the sounds and rhythms of words to those of instruments. When I was a schoolboy, Edith Sitwell's writing—her essays and her poetry—opened my ears to the *sounds* of English, to niceties of weight, length, speed, vowel colors, and the percussion of consonants. (As antidote to this heady stuff, there was the daily sound of the Prayer Book and the Authorized Version, and plenty of Gibbons and Purcell to be sung.) Today, I make students slowly read aloud

> *Jane, Jane,*
> *Tall as a crane,*
> *The morning light creaks down again*

and listen to the sustained vowels. And hear the muted music of

> *Jumbo asleep!*
> *Grey leaves thick-furred*
> *As his ears, keep*
> *Conversations blurred.*

And learn to join distinct consonants to vowels short and long with

> *Madam Mouse trots,*
> *Grey in the black night!*

Years ago, I wrote in a *Façade* review of the incantatory effect on me of Sitwell's verses, chanted from nursery days onward, and of the imagery with which she had filled my life. From Sunset Boulevard, Dame Edith sent a generous letter, explaining what she had tried to achieve with her *Façade* poems. The work's long genesis, the refinements and rejections spread over nearly a decade, are enough to indicate that *Façade* was more than a jeu d'esprit on Sitwell's and Walton's part. *Pierrot Lunaire* had appeared in 1912, *The Soldier's Tale* in 1918; they lay behind this further experiment with sounds and sense. The score of *Façade* 2 gives no hint of how radical Sir William's latest reworking of its contents has been, but several of the "new" pieces—at least two of them go back to the 1923 score—show sparer textures and less exuberantly detailed working than those of the familiar *Façade*. The mood is often close to that of *Pierrot*.

The Caecilian performance, conducted by Gerardo Levy, was instrumentally brilliant. The reciter was rhythmically exact but otherwise had little to recommend her. She adopted fancy voices, added camp or coy "expression," shimmied, swung her hips, waved her arms, "sang" in lines of *Sprechstimme*, and did almost everything except pronounce the words clearly and beautifully. Although she used a microphone, the rapid numbers became an incomprehensible gabble. (The audience had been given broad-sheets with the texts of all the poems, clearly reproduced but useless: the lights in the hall were turned out.) In three recordings, Dame Edith herself set a standard for *Façade* recitation. That exquisite patrician art may well be inimitable; at least, it should be studied by any prospective *Façade* interpreter. After a while, I tried to shut out the voice and attend only to the virtuosity of the instrumentalists and Walton's "compositional art." It's one way of listening to *Façade*, but not the way its creators intended.

"An American Trilogy," at the New York State Theater, is a bill of three new one-act operas. The best of them is Stanley Silverman's *Madame Adare*, with a libretto by Richard Foreman. The plot turns on some loose and surely inaccurate equation of mental instability with interpretative genius. "If you were well, Madame," says the Psychiatrist, "if I had cured you, Madame, nothing would have remained seething inside, forcing those glorious notes from your beautiful throat, Madame." Madame Adare, it's true, replies, "That's garbage, doctor," and so both sides of the argument are presented. She then shoots the Psychiatrist and "becomes a sexy movie star on the basis of such notoriety." Hindemith's *Neues vom Tage* treated the second limb of the plot more wittily and precisely. The libretto is a loose, unpolished, undergraduate piece of work. Silverman's score—Weillish but without the bite and the depth of human feeling that give Weill's music its greatness—is dapper and inventive. A pity, though, that Silverman didn't take the chance when writing for the City Opera (which commissioned the piece) of advancing beyond the idiom of *Dr. Selavy* and *Hotel for Criminals,* small-house successes, to produce something more ambitious, more potent—something that really uses and needs opera-house resources.

Thomas Pasatieri's *Before Breakfast* is a monodrama that was written three years ago for Beverly Sills to do on television. The libretto is an expansion and prolongation, by Frank Corsaro, of O'Neill's brief dramatic monologue with the same title. Cocteau's one-woman play *La Voix humaine,* a not dissimilar work, is possibly more effective theatre "straight" than in Poulenc's operatic version, but Poulenc's score added a "dimension" of thoughts, emotions, and reminiscences, and some of it is elegant, distinguished music. Pasatieri's score strikes me as worthless, sub-Menotti stuff. There is an elaborate production, by Mr. Corsaro, in a richly detailed period set, by Lloyd Evans. (The refrigerator light that goes on when the door opens is surely an anachronism.) Marilyn Zschau does what she can to give life to this stagy confection. Her talents would be better employed in Schoenberg's *Erwartung*.

Jan Bach's *The Student from Salamanca* is a farce with a libretto by the composer based on Cervantes' interlude *The Cave of Salamanca,* with touches from *The Jealous Old Man.* The first few minutes, of bright neoclassical chatter, are sprightly. With increasing dismay, one sits on through more than an hour of less amusing, less inventive larkiness. For some reason, the lusty, witty Student is played, by Allan Glassman, in a lugubrious hangdog manner; the rest is produced, efficiently, in the primping, Mickey Mousing caricature style thought appropriate to operatic comedy. The words are clear—even those of the old husband, John Lankston, who is required to sing his patter music with a lisp. Bach has technical skill. Beverly Evans, as Cristina, the maid, is brilliant. Was this score, winner of a nationwide competition for new one-act operas, really the best that turned up? Better, in that case, to have awarded no prize and strengthened the "Trilogy" with some existing opera that deserves a New York production.

The City Opera production of *Silverlake,* an entertainment derived from *Der Silbersee,* a play by Georg Kaiser with music by Weill, has been recorded by Nonesuch and revived at the State Theater. In an essay accompanying the records, Kim Kowalke, the author of *Kurt Weill in Europe,* remarks that "*Silverlake* is not *Der Silbersee.*" Indeed no. *Der*

Silbersee was the last strong great statement of the Weimar Republic's lyric stage; an earnest, emphatic, brave, and beautiful fable illumined by some of Weill's keenest and deepest music—his *Fidelio*, one might say. It appeared in February 1933; Hitler was already Chancellor. Nine days after the première, the Reichstag was burned; in March, Weill's scores and Kaiser's plays were proscribed. To make *Silverlake*, Kaiser's drama (called by its first director "ten times tougher than any Brecht play") has been rewritten by Hugh Wheeler, who is cited in Mr. Kowalke's essay as saying, "The original play is so difficult and highfalutin I could barely make out what it was all about." And Weill's score has been diluted with his incidental music for Strindberg's *Gustav III*. Played as background music through the dialogue, it blunts the force of the *Silbersee* movements when they arrive. One of them, the "Hungerlied," is omitted.

Der Silbersee, at once a heavy play and a musically demanding opera, is hard to perform. The complete score was first heard only in 1971, at the Holland Festival, in a concert version for which David Drew had devised a context true to Kaiser. (Tapes and a pirate recording circulate; an authorized recording in good sound would be welcome, for Gary Bertini's conducting was sensitive and committed.) For repertory use in a New York theatre, some adaptation was doubtless inevitable. But the City Opera version lacks force, feeling, and faithfulness; it misrepresents the tone, the spirit, and the content of the work. Like *The Magic Flute*, *Der Silbersee* balances sacred, operatic, and popular elements in a topical play-with-music whose concerns are timeless. Some opera company with a social conscience—Boston? Minnesota?—should revive it. At the State Theater, Harold Prince's smart, superficial staging was not even slickly executed. Julius Rudel's conducting was glib, unimpassioned. Among the newcomers to the cast, Mr. Lankston, as Olim, made sense of his role and was altogether admirable. On the first night of the revival, the voices were amplified; miking is preferable to inaudibility, but the sound here was tinny.

In the Good Shepherd-Faith Church—on West 66th Street, a few doors from the blood bank—Heinrich Marschner's *The Vampire* (1828) was produced by the Encompass troupe. The opera has a place in Romantic history; the young Wagner was influenced by it. But the orchestral playing was so loud, the staging so silly, and the singing so strenuous that I left Lord Ruthven to his wicked devices and fled a block north, to the Abraham Goodman House, where Steven Kimbrough, having begun a recital with songs by Alexander Zemlinsky and Mahler, was continuing it with songs by Franz Schreker. Schreker's early songs, written in student days, are fairly conventional, but the Five Songs of 1909—Mr. Kimbrough sang three of them—are arresting studies in Schreker's "deliquescent" style, where "fused" harmonies and rhythms glow around the words. An aria from the opera *Der ferne Klang* and a fairly late song, "Das feurige Männlein," proved even more striking. Mr. Kimbrough is a remarkable singer, with a cultivated, easily flowing baritone of fine quality and a rare command of words and rhythms.

EMOTION

November 3, 1980

IN MY younger days, I heard Mahler's Eighth Symphony at decent intervals: in 1948, conducted by Adrian Boult; in 1959, by Jascha Horenstein; in 1964, by Charles Groves. Deryck Cooke's program note for the second of these—the fourth-ever performance of the work in London—began, "To hear Mahler's Eighth Symphony in the flesh is an experience as rare as it is tremendous." Those early performances made a great impression on me. I have lost count of later ones. Within the space of a month, I have just heard three different performances of the symphony: in San Francisco, where Edo de Waart conducted it with the San Francisco Symphony in the new Louise M. Davies Symphony Hall; from Orchestra Hall in Chicago, whence the inaugural concert of the Chicago Symphony's ninetieth-anniversary season, conducted by Georg Solti, was widely broadcast; and in Carnegie Hall, where it was conducted by Seiji Ozawa at the Boston Symphony's first New York visit in its hundredth-anniversary season. The eighty-minute progress, with immense forces, from the urgent, ardent summoning of a Creator Spirit to a heaven where "the ineffable is enacted" and—in the Jungian parlance of the new Boston translation—"Eternal-*anima* compels us on" used to be no everyday event but a huge, exciting adventure earnestly embarked on by both executants and audience. Now that the adventure is no longer rare—now that conductors and listeners are ready to take it in their stride—has it also become less tremendous? I asked the question four years ago, when the Philharmonic's "Mahler-month"—a series of concerts at which Pierre Boulez conducted Symphonies Nos. 3, 7, and 9, Erich Leinsdorf No. 5, and James Levine the rest—had left me not unadmiring but something less than overwhelmed, exalted, shattered. And I decided that the answer is yes—and yes to a similar question about any of the symphonies— except when it is conducted by someone who seems less to "command" the work than to be commanded by it, by a conductor in (disciplined) surrender to the flow and surge and swell of the music and to its emotional dictates. Mahler's forms are easily apprehended; in performance, they must be charged by feeling. Boulez's lucid, "analytical" performances proved cold; at best, they were correctives to emotionally messy, unconsidered, callow, or stalely routine interpretations. Since then, I have heard three Mahler performances in which form and feeling, technical delicacy and sensuous beauty of execution, mastery and mystery conspired to transport listeners: Solti's of the Fifth, with the Chicago Symphony, and Abbado's of the Fourth, with the Philadelphia Orchestra, both in Carnegie Hall in 1977; and now Solti's of the Eighth.

This Eighth as far surpassed Solti's 1972 recording of the work as his 1977 Carnegie performance of the Fifth surpassed his 1970 recording. I heard it, as I said, over the air. The performance was carried "live" from Chicago to Europe by way of a broadcasting satellite. The relay was a co-production of that admirable Chicago station WFMT and the European Broadcasting Union. Leo Black, of the BBC, came over to direct it. The national stations of Britain, Ireland, France, Belgium, Italy, West Germany, Sweden, and Canada and about a hundred and fifty local American stations broadcast the concert. (But in Europe at least, I'm told, the Eighth did not make it all the way through. Fifty-five minutes in, some wires got crossed: a diaper commercial began to mingle with the Mahler's elevated strains, and then, understandably, a fuse blew. The BBC, which was feeding the relay to the other countries, switched to its "cover," the 1972 recording.) In New York, however, a tape (undiapered) of the concert was broadcast the next day, by WNCN. The sound was not up to BBC standards. In the second movement, between the harp arpeggios and the "Mater Gloriosa" entry that they herald, there was an audible change of tape, accompanied by a drop in volume. But it was good enough to leave a listener rapt, awed, exhilarated, trembling at the grandeur and beauty of Mahler's visionary work.

The simplest point of excellence to describe is the superlative instrumental playing of the Chicago Symphony; the San Francisco and Boston orchestras were not in the same class. When the march theme of the first movement was passed from horn chorus to oboe chorus, to flute-and-bassoon chorus, and back to the horns and was then scattered through the orchestra, one felt one had never heard wind playing so rhythmically precise, perfectly balanced, and purely tuned. To embark on direct comparisons of orchestral and choral timbre would be unfair: the San Franciscans were playing in a hall with unfinished acoustics; the Bostonians were packed onto the Carnegie stage in a curiously lopsided way, with double-basses banished to the right outfield, where they could provide no deep, firm foundation to the sound. But the Chicago string tone, at any rate as heard from loudspeakers, was fuller, warmer, richer, more beautiful than the "live" tone at the other performances. The Chicago Symphony Chorus (which used a properly German, not an Italianized, pronunciation of the Latin) was livelier, more accurate in attack, than the others. The children who take the part of Blessed Boys carolled more liltingly. But the Chicago Eighth was memorable above all for the breadth, warmth, and profundity of Solti's reading. He has always been an energetic and exciting conductor. He has regularly secured technically first-rate playing. But sometimes it seemed that his concern was with execution, with orchestral virtuosity, with excitement for excitement's sake. This

Eighth, as exciting, as "vital" as anything he has done, was breathed in long spans. All the tempi and all transitions between them seemed natural, inevitable. The first movement was a heartfelt invocation, the second a "drama" of vision upon vision, mystic and beautiful. The preparation for and then the "placing" of each great moment—such as the massed cry of "Accende lumen sensibus"—was exactly right. The solo singers were fervent. By comparison, de Waart's performance was a well-meaning sketch, Ozawa's was shallow, lightweight, and shrill.

Violent physical reactions to Mahler's music—bouts of weeping, for example—are too well-documented to be dismissed as merely personal critical indicators of a performance's merit. (A rehearsal for the first performance of the Sixth Symphony left its composer, his wife recalled, "sobbing, wringing his hands, unable to control himself.") More than just emotion—which Boulez considered a "somewhat primitive reaction" to Mahler's music—is brought into play. A great performance of the Eighth Symphony touches on all that its listeners may have thought about religion, philosophy, and art; about individual striving and collective achievement. The Second Symphony, its composer said, asks, and tries to answer, "the great question: 'Why did you live? Why did you suffer? Is it all nothing but a huge, cruel jest?'" The Third Symphony was intended to be "a work of such magnitude that it actually mirrors the whole world." It leads its listeners from awe, chaos, brutality, and terror, through emerging order, a delight in nature's beauty, and a yearning for something still higher, to a passionate, glowing "musical enactment" of bliss. That's what it should do. Zubin Mehta's performance, at the Philharmonic early last month, left me unmoved. I began to fear that—unless Mahler's music has been overrated—I'd lost my ability to respond to it. Solti's performance of the Eighth reassured me that I hadn't.

BEVERLY!

November 10, 1980

On Monday last week, at a gala celebration within the frame of the *Fledermaus* party scene, Beverly Sills gave her farewell operatic performance. Gianna Rolandi was the Adele, Kitty Carlisle the Orlofsky, Alan Titus the Eisenstein, and Richard Fredricks the Falke. Julius Rudel conducted. The place was the State Theater; the company was the New York City Opera, of which Miss Sills is now general director. She was Rosalinda—the role in which she had made her City Opera début, twenty-five years before. Among those who came to Prince Orlofsky's party to sing or play to the guest of honor were Mary Martin, Carol Burnett, Donald Gramm, Placido Domingo, Eileen Farrell, Leontyne Price, James Galway, Sherrill Milnes, Ethel Merman, Dinah Shore, and

54

Renata Scotto. Trumpets rang out across Lincoln Plaza to summon the public to the show.

I first heard Beverly Sills at her Scala début, in 1969, as Pamira in *The Siege of Corinth,* and marvelled at her prodigious facility in rapid singing. Rossini's score had been decorated up to the hilt, and the prima donna's divisions, graces, runs, and leaps were astonishing in their ease, accuracy, and brilliance. But equally impressive and still more moving was her feeling for Rossini's long, slow melodies. Pamira's prayer in Act II, "Du séjour de la lumière," is an air of essentially simple outline touched with sudden delicate fioriture; tracing them, gently pressing on the chromatic syncopations of the second verse, Sills was poignant. I recall her appearance—the tall, romantic figure on the prow of Mahomet's ship (the set was changed when *The Siege* came to the Met), a lovely physical image of the character and her plight. In a review, I praised all this with enthusiasm but added some reservations concerned with the want of solidity, of firm core, in the tone. Over the years, as I heard and saw more of Sills—a Lucia at Covent Garden in 1971, then many roles at the State Theater; in Boston, the Daughter of the Regiment, Bellini's Juliet, and Gilda; Violetta at the Met—the reservations remained but my admiration and affection for her grew. Sills is a "second-generation" Marchesi pupil by way of her teacher, Estelle Liebling, and to Miss Liebling she attributes what in her memoirs she describes, not quite accurately, as "a solid technique." Liebling

stressed breath control, and my whole technique of singing is based on it. As a result, I know how to sing. Even when I have laryngitis and cannot speak, I am almost always able to sing.

And she has never been unarresting. What she has not commanded is the tonal security and evenness for which Marchesi pupils—Melba, Emma Eames—were famous. It is often said that one has to have seen Sills on the stage—have seen her Manon, her Lucia, her Cleopatra, her Elizabeth in *Roberto Devereux*—to understand the esteem in which she is held. Not necessarily so. There are good pages about her in John Steane's *The Grand Tradition* (1974), which is a survey of singing on records. His account begins:

Beverly Sills . . . achieves profundity perhaps more genuinely than any other singer discussed in this section [among them, Joan Sutherland, Teresa Berganza, Marilyn Horne], but it is in spite of her timbre rather than because of it. The voice is light, and, in itself, shallow; it is beautiful only on high, the middle register being thin and the upper notes on the stave becoming slightly tremulous under pressure. Her technique is often superb, and her high florid singing is delightful to the ear. But the interesting thing, finally, is that she is so satisfying, not as a sweet-sounding, highly-trained nightingale, but as a singer of remarkable intellectual and emotional strength.

55

Then comes a page on details in Lucia's first aria and the "specific insight" that makes Sills's performance of it in some ways more gripping than those of Tetrazzini, Sutherland, and "even Callas." Sills played some sixty roles—with a pang one writes that past tense—and recorded nineteen complete operas (the tally excludes what is available only on pirate or private disc or tape), ranging from *The Ballad of Baby Doe* in 1959 to a *Rigoletto* published last year. But most of her records were made in the seventies, when her voice was unsteadier, more fragile, less pretty than on the earlier discs. She had used it unstintingly: eight Toscas in seven days (in Cleveland in 1957) are among the annals of the busy twenty years before Cleopatra in *Giulio Cesare*, at the State Theater in 1966, brought her to international prominence. The four roles Sills thinks she has done best, she says in her memoirs, are Baby Doe, Manon, Cleopatra, and Elizabeth. All are recorded. The first is moving, delicate, exquisite—but already the long notes at the end are unsteady, not firm and pure. Cleopatra's last aria displays, in Mr. Steane's words, "the most beautiful scale-work, brilliant semiquaver runs, the most accurate and compact of trills, and an absolutely dazzling display in the *da capo* section." *Manon* was recorded too late—after the *Devereux*—but it is a captivating impersonation. *Roberto Devereux*—the recording appeared early in 1970, and later that year the opera inaugurated the Donizetti "royal trilogy" at the State Theater—was a landmark in Sills's career. The passionate energy of her declamation, the use of virtuosity for dramatic ends, the force and vividness of her characterization, and the ability to charge a few simple notes of recitative with potent emotion are all remarkable. Yet it may be that historians will also trace the decline of her voice from her unsparing use of it in the heavy, dramatic role. The interpretative qualities brought to that Elizabeth were those I admired most during the decade I heard Sills regularly: as Lucia, the other Donizetti queens, Bellini's Elvira, Lucrezia Borgia. Her artistry grew. Her Met Violetta, in 1976, was memorable. Her last New York performance in a whole opera, a year ago, as Joan the Mad in *La Loca,* the opera Menotti wrote for her, was electrifying. There was also the bubbly side: the sense of mischief, sparkle, and infectious fun that she brought to the Daughter of the Regiment, Rosina, the Merry Widow, Fiorilla in *The Turk in Italy*. Sometimes it went too far—when she became not those specific heroines of these operas but just the Beverly we all love, cutely inviting us to join in the fun.

A full study of Sills must be written by someone who heard her from early days. Her career belongs to the history of music in America. There were very famous American prima donnas before her. But Lillian Nordica and Emma Eames became famous abroad before they returned to their homeland; Rosa Ponselle made her operatic début directly at the Metropolitan, beside Caruso and De Luca, as the heroine of *Forza*. Sills is homegrown, and a diva of the people. She toured in operetta for the Shuberts in the 1940s. She made her operatic début as Frasquita in a Philadelphia *Carmen,* in 1947. Throughout her career, she has remained in the best sense of the word a trouper, known to, heard by, audiences across the country. Television appearances have also made her a household pet. Since P. T. Barnum imported Jenny Lind, ballyhoo has been part of the operatic scene. Sills's biographer must weigh the role played by the modern "media," able to inflate the popular reputation of, say, a Pavarotti out of all proportion to his artistry. I don't think the publicity—the *Newsweek* and *Time* covers, and all the rest—harmed Sills's artistry. She is too scrupulous a musician. But it may have affected her repertory, thrown too much emphasis on the bright, merry heroines, sent too many Merry Widows, Regimental Daughters, and Rosinas scampering across the country at the expense of the tragic heroines. And it possibly accounted for a carping note found in many of her reviews: a corrective to unthinking, "unhearing" popular adulation.

Last week's show, billed as "Beverly!," was her farewell performance on the stage. It was a moving occasion. Memories of all I have heard her do came flooding back. But it was not her farewell to opera. Now that the last bubbly heroine has been sung (for the record, Sills's final appearance in a full role was as Adele in a San Diego *Fledermaus* last month; Joan Sutherland was the Rosalinda), she can give all her attention to the company as director. She is equipped for the role on many counts. She knows the American operatic scene, across the country, from within. She has the trust and loyalty of her colleagues and of the public. During her first year of office—she was precipitated into the post while she still had singing engagements to fulfill—she assembled a company in which many of the country's most gifted young singers shine. Some of them she has brought back home from European houses. Casting is stabler. The repertory is adventurous. Two further tasks are urgent. The first is to do something about the acoustics of the State Theater. As for the second: armed with her wisdom and her experience, she must guide City Opera productions from their first, planning stages—meddling where necessary, editing, urging, explaining, gently and firmly correcting whatever is false, unhelpful, perverse, or silly. [*The acoustics of the State Theater were spectacularly improved, by the prescriptions of Cyril Harris, in 1982. Firm artistic guidance of the City Opera productions has been less evident.*]

Otto Nicolai's *The Merry Wives of Windsor* (1849) is a delightful opera, one in which "wit, merry humors, the wildest jesting, craft, and daring"—as evoked by Mistress Ford at the start of her aria—conspire with charm, in music well enough composed to beguile the nicest ear. Mozart, Weber, Donizetti, and Mendelssohn were Nicolai's musical godparents, and what they bestowed on him he used well. He hesitated before tackling a *Falstaff* opera—only a Mozart, he declared, was fit companion for a Shakespeare—but when he did so he produced a work that even Verdi's masterpiece on the same subject (1893) has not extinguished. The New York City Opera staged *The Merry Wives* in 1955, with Phyllis Curtin as Mistress Ford and William Wildermann as Falstaff. Twenty-five years later, it has come up with a new production, which is enjoyable but does not do full justice to the piece. Mr. Wildermann returns, and around him a potentially good cast, including several of those gifted young singers, has been assembled. But neither the staging nor the musical direction is stylish. On the first night, there was no sign that anyone had striven to introduce these singers to the musical style of the mid-nineteenth century. It was hard to believe, for example, that Carol Vaness—a soprano of boundless possibilities who was about half as good as she should have been—had been coached in Mistress Ford's aria by Margarethe Siems, Erika Wedekind, Lotte Schöne, and Lotte Lehmann (with all of whom, thanks to the phonograph, she could easily have studied); or that Stephen Dickson, the fine young baritone who made his City Opera début as Ford, had listened attentively to the Leopold Demuth and Wilhelm Hesch recording of the famous duet in Act II.

The stage director is Lou Galterio, the designer John Conklin. Can they have conned the score closely? The opera, as its title suggests, is set in Windsor, not in a German provincial town. The epoch Nicolai adopted was the start of the seventeenth century, not the mid-nineteenth century. The first scene should play in a yard between the Ford and the Page houses, not in a thronged, bustling *Marktplatz*. The second scene is a room in Ford's house—but surely not the laundry room, hung with washing, which is hardly where Mistress Ford would receive her titled visitor. In fact, the washing hangs on a platform in the middle of the market square, whose buildings, painted on panels, enclose six of the seven scenes, while the platform is differently decked. (For the seventh scene, the panels are reversed, to show painted trees.) The set is pretty but monotonous. The central platform, that once fashionable scenic device, inhibits easy, natural movement across the stage, and an action that turns at times on closed rooms, locked doors, privacy, and peeking loses its sharpness out in the open. The staging was in other ways insensitive. In Act II, Scene 2, Nicolai writes six measures of excited entrance music for Anne Page, as she runs in after Fenton's aubade; Mr. Galterio brought Anne in during the aubade, and the entrance music meant nothing. The aubade tells of the lark singing and soaring in the sky above; Mr. Galterio pinned it to earth with stock business around a caged dove. The final scene begins with moonrise in Windsor Forest, pictured in some of Nicolai's most celebrated pages. In the State Theater, the moon was already high when the curtain rose; the light remained constant, and the magical lunar crescendo accompanied a rustic muster.

Julius Rudel conducted. The overture went well; it was delicately shaped, prettily nuanced. But much of the rest was dispatched in a brisk, efficient, no-nonsense manner, with the dance rhythms metronomic, uninflected. Singers were allowed to deliver recitative in rigid

4/4. There was little rubato; there were none of the surprising added cadenzas, holds, hurryings, piquant pointing of individual notes and words by which generations of earlier Nicolai singers brought his music to life. The show had energy but not grace. The characters were unrealized sketches. Mr. Wildermann's Falstaff was excellently clear, and firm and forward in tone, but it was a stock comic portrayal, not a rounded individual portrait. (Incidentally, he is surely the leanest Falstaff that has ever trod the stage.) Miss Vaness's singing was simply beautiful: an accurate flow of lustrous if too studiously "covered" tone. She lacked merriment, high spirits, audacity. Mistress Ford needs sharper words, brighter colors, more animated phrasing. One seldom has cause to chide a singer for being too smooth, too even; but this portrayal suggested a Donna Elvira ill at ease in a comedy role, re-membering at times—usually too late—that she should smile, and then wanly simpering. RoseMarie Freni, as Mistress Page, had more dash, but not enough voice for the Act III ballade. (Schumann-Heink did the role at the Met in 1900.) The young lovers, Janice Hall and Vinson Cole, sang truly but too forcefully, preferring volume to sweet-ness and gentleness of tone. Mr. Dickson sounded good, but his man-ner was callow, his timing uncertain. In general, the spoken dialogue suggested amateur Shakespeare, and on the singing Mr. Galterio had imposed not in-character actions but irrelevant business. Mistress Ford fooled with a dime-store hand mirror during her aria. When the music began to dance, as Nicolai's often does, the singers shuffled into D'Oyly Carte routines. (That they did so without conviction was tribute to their musical instincts.) This was disappointing from a director usually ready to trust a work and guide his cast into creating charac-ters.

The English translation helped neither the singing nor the acting. There are at least nine English versions of *The Merry Wives*. The huck-ster in the lobby of the State Theater, crying "Libretto of the opera!," sells the abridged Krehbiel text, of 1886; what's sung is the Josef Blatt version. (Since I'm in the translation business myself, I should declare that Miss Sills invited me to undertake a new *Merry Wives* for this pro-duction; but I recommended Leonard Hancock's version, used at Wex-ford in 1976.) [*More about this* Merry Wives *production on page 65.*]

The Juilliard Symphony's first concert of the season, in Alice Tully Hall, brought together a rare work and a once common but now fairly rare one: Liszt's Symphony to Dante's *Divine Comedy* and César Franck's Symphony. James Conlon conducted. The Dante symphony is a rum piece, assembled from largely conventional material (as Edward Sack-ville-West once remarked, the terrors of Hell are depicted in music that might "usher in the Demon King in a pantomime"), yet often quirky in its details, and sometimes beautiful. Mr. Conlon held it to-gether but achieved cohesiveness at the cost of drama and rhetoric; the declamatory nature of the work is emphasized by the lines of Dante set under some of the themes. The Franck, at first, was too tightly shaped. The second subject didn't swoon; there was no emotional portamento from the strings. The dry acoustics of Tully Hall need an extra charge of fervid Romanticism. When Mr. Conlon reached the second trio of the middle movement, he was readier to surrender to the flow of the music; the clarinets were freely expressive. The finale went well. The student orchestra played with its customary verve and gleam, but the woodwind chorus needs finer tuning.

CHARACTER

November 17, 1980

SINCE I last wrote about Mahler, two weeks ago, the Cleveland Orchestra and Loren Maazel have played the Sixth Symphony in Carnegie Hall; a tremendous performance of the Sixth by the Chicago Symphony and Claudio Abbado has appeared on record (Deutsche Grammophon); and, also in Carnegie, first the San Francisco Symphony and Edo de Waart and then the London Symphony and Abbado have played the Fifth. All Mahler's symphonies are disturbing when properly played, and the Fifth, if not one of the most "shattering," can unsettle a listener as thoroughly as any. For two movements, it is despairing, insecure, even hysterical. The second movement (marked "tempestuous in its motion, with the greatest vehemence") at last reaches firm ground, apparent confidence, in the bravely affirmative D-major chorale. The collapse of that confidence into terror, isolated cries of despair, and a final mutter is one of the cruellest episodes in music. What follows? A D-major waltz kaleidoscope; the passionate bliss of the Adagietto; a D-major finale telling of a composer's joy in creation as he combines sonata, rondo, and fugue forms in one exuberant movement. The chorale reappears, and this time its foundation is not undermined. But, recalling what happened before, can one now trust those shining towers of sound to stand? Are they a baseless vision?

With unfaltering mastery, Abbado traced the faltering, uncertain progress of the symphony. The music flowed through him. He is very nearly a complete Mahler conductor: emotional, excitable, and instinctive; disciplined, precise, and attentive to both passing details and the large form. Where some interpreters go too far and others not nearly far enough, his judgment of accent, emphasis, rubato, tempo change seemed exactly right, and to be felt rather than calculated. A merit of Abbado's Mahler performances is that each one of them becomes a new, fresh adventure, and that each symphony is given its distinct character. The Fifth is a thing of paradox. The emotional content of the first two movements is irreconcilable with that of the rest; the contrast should tear the symphony apart. And yet it holds. At times, echoes of the bright, lyrical *Wunderhorn* world can be heard, but they are thrown back in the hard, spare sound of the middle-period scoring and are no longer consolatory. There are intimations of what is to come in later and perhaps deeper works. When Mahler told the conductor Willem Mengelberg that the Fifth was "very, very *difficult,*" he must have been thinking as much of its matter as of technical difficulties. In each Mahler symphony, as Deryck Cooke once remarked, "we are taken into a different world," and in the Fifth this sense of a new world—and a difficult one—is especially strong. Literary programs, sung texts, picturesqueness are left behind. It is a new, strenuous beginning. In the Fifth, Bruno Walter said, Mahler "is now aiming to write music as a musician."

That "complete" above is qualified only because Abbado, like many modern conductors, seems to fear the full, expressive string portamento that is an essential part of Mahler's music. The composer who notated his intentions so carefully distinguished between ordinary, taken-for-granted portamento, marked by no more than a common slur, and emphatic, emotional portamento, indicated by a straight line drawn between the notes in question and often accompanied by a marking like "seelenvoll." When he wants to insure that a slide reaches the pitch of the new note just before the new beat, he makes that clear (as in the Adagio of the Ninth). His notation also suggests whether big upward-swooping attacks—of an octave, a tenth, then a twelfth in the central bars of the Adagietto of the Fifth—should come before or on the beat. In successive recordings of the Adagietto one can trace the gradual drying out of portamento in our century. Mengelberg, who was long associated with Mahler, recorded it in 1926, gluing the slurred notes together with very full portamento. Walter, also long associated with the composer, recorded it in 1938 with the Vienna Philharmonic, using slightly less portamento but still a great deal. When Walter recorded the complete symphony, in 1947, it was with the New York Philharmonic and with still less portamento—yet the rising fourths of the Adagietto melody *are* carried right through by the violins, then by the cellos, as they are not in, say, James Levine's 1978 recording and were not in the Abbado performance. This is not a minor point or just a matter of taste and fashion. When Mahler marked the cello solo over the drumroll in the second movement "klagend" and drew a portamento line up the rising seventh, he meant something specific, and the meaning is lost if the music is not played as written. Solti's later Mahler performances have become more eloquent since he has begun to use portamento stylishly and freely.

The London Symphony at this showing was not an orchestra to set beside Chicago's, Vienna's, or Philadelphia's. It sounded good but— even though one saw names like Jack Brymer and Martin Gatt in the personnel list—slightly anonymous: there was not that sense of individual voices which marks the greatest Mahler performances. The string tone was strong, but hard and bright rather than rich. One can find excuses. The players were nearing the end of a long transcontinental tour. But a visiting orchestra should be in top form at a Carnegie appearance. The concert began with Mozart's A-major Symphony, K. 201, in a performance lithe, elegant, and unsatisfying. The orchestra was reduced but top-heavy: the effect was firsts-with-accompaniment, winds somewhere in the background, and no crunch in the counterpoint. The finale was too fast to let the sixteenth-notes be heard. In both works, Abbado favored the modern, lopsided platform arrangement.

Rossini's *La Cenerentola* is a romantic and lovely opera. The City Opera has a staging of it, new this year, by Lou Galterio, which blunts the delicate points and is mounted in garish scenery and costumes, by Rouben Ter-Arutunian, inherited from the 1953 production. Nevertheless, the work comes across: it is well sung, and Brian Salesky conducts it with love, poise, polish, and understanding. His strings have lightness, energy, and grace, his woodwinds the right combination of wit and lyrical beauty. His tempi were consistently well set. The music was now exhilarating, now melting, and ever bewitching. Just about Mr. Salesky's only failing was not to have persuaded his singers to sing recitative in lively speech rhythms.

Catalogues of staging faults grow tedious. In brief, then: The buffo characters were reduced to farcical stock. Cinderella's sisters, real people as Rossini and his librettist, Jacopo Ferretti, limned them, became frumps and freaks. Clorinda was required to sing her trickiest coloratura standing on one leg or bourréeing across the stage. Dandini was heavy, charmless—a painted caricature, not a witty servant. D'Oyly Carte routines turned some ensembles into "production numbers." *La Cenerentola* is a *Cinderella* without the supernatural, a comedy of human character. No pumpkin, no mice, and no fairy godmother, but in her stead a philosopher, Alidoro, who has taught his pupil prince to do as his heart directs and to rate human worth above rank and riches. That Ramiro falls in love with Cinders is just a first step; his test comes when he discovers that she is, apparently, of mean station, and it is passed when he chooses her as his bride all the same. Alidoro's important role, in fact, was cruelly cut in this production: he lost his aria (either "Vasto teatro è il mondo," by Luca Agolini, not Rossini, yet part of the original conception, or "Là del ciel," which Rossini added later) and two significant recitatives. The other big cut was of Don Magnifico's third aria. Appetites are small these days: when Marietta Alboni sang Cenerentola at Her Majesty's in 1849, the opera was followed by a selection from the ballet *Fiorita,* the last act of *Norma,* and "A New Ballet, in Five Tableaux, Entitled *Electra,*" with Carlotta Grisi and the younger Taglioni. The City Opera *Cenerentola* lasted about three hours, and some twenty minutes of that was devoted to an extra intermission, which broke Act I into two. Remove it and the missing music could be restored within a three-hour span. Nevertheless, I shouldn't really be complaining; I heard more of Rossini's score than I have ever heard before in the theatre. The great Act II sextet was done in extenso; Clorinda's aria (by Agolini) was included; and there were few of those little snicks—four bars here, eight bars there—by which Rossini's balanced forms are habitually disfigured.

Susanne Marsee was a charming heroine, touching in lyric cantabile, fluent in divisions. All she missed was Cinderella's sense of humor. June Anderson sang Clorinda's aria brilliantly. Rockwell Blake, a wooden actor but a virtuoso Rossini tenor, was fleet, graceful, and astonishing in his account of Ramiro's music. The others—Alan Titus (Dandini), James Billings (Don Magnifico), Ralph Bassett (Alidoro), and Dana Krueger (Thisbe)—were clear. The ensembles were well balanced and rhythmically polished. The choral singing (male voices only) was abominable. Sometimes it faltered; sometimes individual voices could be heard bawling.

The opera was done in English; the translation, by Gimi Beni, is passable, if less witty than Arthur Jacobs's. The latter appears in the English National Opera guide to *La Cenerentola*, published by the Riverrun Press. I recommend it; it also contains several good essays on the work. Shouldn't the City Opera be publishing some guides of its own?

The company's revival of *Giulio Cesare* can be recommended to historians of Handel performance curious to see and hear the way his operas were done in the dark days, not long ago, before people took him seriously and realized that he was a great dramatic composer who meant what he wrote. Handelians can also take pleasure in the forthright, well-shaped singing of Delia Wallis, in the role of Sextus. The iniquities of the City Opera edition, prepared by Julius Rudel in 1966, have often been rehearsed (at the American Musicological Society meeting in New York last year, the Handel scholar Winton Dean cited it as the locus classicus of a great masterpiece reduced to dramatic nonsense), but perhaps the gravest charges should be briefly restated, since—surprisingly, regrettably—the show has been brought back with all its crimes broad blown.

Giulio Cesare is an opera Handel composed with unusual care. It has a good plot, a cast of fully drawn characters, and a heroine of infinite variety—one who in the course of eight airs, two great accompanied recitatives, and a duet develops, as Dean puts it, "from a frivolous flirt into a woman capable of profound tragic feeling," and is "comparable with Shakespeare's heroine." Handel refashioned or replaced seven of those eight airs before he was satisfied with the result. In Act III, Cleopatra, captured by her brother Ptolemy and fearing that Caesar is dead, sings the poignant "Piangerò." But at the City Opera she sings it when, disguised as her maidservant Lydia, she first meets Caesar. Words and music become meaningless. In Act II, Caesar is captivated by the voluptuous vision—the nine Muses in consort accompanying

"V'adoro pupille"—that Cleopatra has contrived. Then (in Handel's scheme) the vision is closed from view; alone in the "delicious grove," Caesar carols with birdcalls from the solo violin as he sings of his desire. In the City Opera revival, a shard of the air is allowed him; then Cleopatra—still as Lydia—comes forward, and prematurely the two embark on the duet with which Handel celebrated the happy end of all the action. Cleopatra's first air is a tripping number in which she taunts and teases her brother. Here she seems to address it to her eunuch Nirenus; Ptolemy is not present.

Cesare is one of Handel's longest operas—an uncut Birmingham production in 1977 ran four hours and ten minutes—but not impossibly long. Still, *some* abridgment for repertory use can be forgiven. At the City Opera, rather more than half of the original (1724) score gets done. Although twenty-one of Handel's thirty-one airs are represented (plus that shard for Caesar, an addition since 1966), only three are complete. In several of them, a peculiarly unhappy form of cutting—internal snips within the main divisions—plays merry hell with Handel's balanced forms. Let me pass with a rapid shudder over the sound of the clangorously amplified harpsichords and the inappropriate use of an organ as Cornelia's continuo instrument. The production—directed by Tito Capobianco, choreographed by Gigi Denda—requires the singers to glide about gracefully, attitudinize, wave their arms, and dance through instrumental introductions and ritornellos. Mr. Capobianco's failure to understand the piece, to hear the drama in the music, is underlined by a program note in which he declares that Handel's "heroes, his villains, his shepherdesses and his queens are not real characters." His attempt to "parade these courtiers...with the subtle threads of their olden elegance" is unconvincingly, sometimes risibly executed. Ming Cho Lee's unit set obscures the sharp design of Handel's scenes.

In 1966, Beverly Sills, the Cleopatra, carried the show, and it, in turn, carried her to international fame. The new incumbent is Gianna Rolandi; her rapid singing was deft, but she lacked purity and steadiness of tone and accuracy of pitch. To the grand tragic role of Cornelia, Diane Curry brought a twinkle that could not be subdued; with a little encouragement, she could be hilarious. Dominic Cossa was a passable Achillas. Caesar and Ptolemy are alto roles; at the City Opera they are sung an octave too low, in the bass register, with the customary unhappy results. Marks to Robert Hale and Donnie Ray Albert for trying. The imported conductor, Ralf Weikert, from Frankfurt, showed no particular Handelian virtues.

There are at least two English translations of *Giulio Cesare* that have been proved in performance: Brian Trowell's, used in Birmingham and also in London, where Janet Baker sings Caesar; and Richard Bradshaw's, used in San Francisco last year, when Carol Vaness sang Cleopatra. The City Opera does the work in Italian; there might be something to be said for that if the language were more tellingly sung (many lines proved incomprehensible) and if the house lights were left up, eighteenth-century fashion, so that the audience could glance at its librettos.

Last week, I had some hard things to say about the City Opera's production of Nicolai's *The Merry Wives of Windsor* but remarked that it was enjoyable. So I went back to enjoy it again, at the fourth performance, when there was a largely new—and, as it happened, a largely superior—cast. Glenys Fowles, the Mistress Ford, was a *merry* wife, sparkling and resourceful. She and Muriel Costa-Greenspon, the Mistress Page, reminded us—as their predecessors had not—that the opera is, among other things, Fiordiligi's and Dorabella's revenge upon menfolk. They played to and sang with one another as a well-matched pair. The new lovers, Carol Gutknecht and Bruce Reed, were lyrical, sweet, and true. Page was now cast at strength in the person of Ralph Bassett, whose strong, pure bass is bravely projected. Stephen Dickson has grown swiftly into the role of Ford, which he voiced and acted with the keenness and force missing before. Norman Large and Harlan Foss had polished their deft portrayals of Slender and Caius. The new Falstaff, Herbert Beattie, was even leaner than his predecessor—lean of voice, too, and generally lacking in the knight's abundance, although his sound and his words were clear.

An enchanting opera! If Nicolai had not died young—in 1849, aged thirty-eight, and soon after the première of *The Merry Wives*—the history of German music might have been different. Who else so skillfully and so beguilingly combined and built upon felicities of Mozart, Beethoven, Weber, Mendelssohn, Rossini, and Donizetti?

Two more things for Miss Sills to do before the City Opera returns in the spring: persuade her box-office staff and her ticket-takers to welcome, or at least be cheerful and pleasant to, her guests; and check what librettos the theatre sells. The *Merry Wives* muddle I mentioned last week. The *Cenerentola* is in Italian and English—but not the English the company sings. For *Giulio Cesare*, the Program Publishing Company, which produces all these, has issued two different librettos. A few days before the show, when I wanted to bone up on the text, the box office sold me an English-only version (English of a sort: the first scene is set in "a spacious plane"); it translates the original text and is unrelated to the Rudel version. The edition that does represent it, in Italian and English, was being sold on the night of the performance—too late to be useful.

TEMPERAMENTS

November 24, 1980

AT A fortepiano recital in Merkin Hall last month, Malcolm Bilson played Haydn, C. P. E. Bach, Mozart, and Beethoven, and, for encores, accompanied Susan Robinson in Schubert and Mozart songs. His instrument, built by Philip Belt, was modelled on the Anton Walter fortepiano now in the Mozart House in Salzburg. A piano of beautiful tone, it can also be admired on Mr. Bilson's latest record, a coupling of Mozart's sonatas K. 332 and K. 333 (Nonesuch). Two days after the recital, Mr. Bilson spoke, played, answered questions, and invited his listeners to try the Belt-Walter for themselves at a lecture-demonstration in the musical-instruments gallery of the Metropolitan Museum. There are—as I have often remarked before—many pages of Mozart, Haydn, Beethoven, and Schubert which on a modern Steinway, Baldwin, or Bösendorfer simply cannot be played as the composer wrote them. Though fingers may sound the notes, the intended dynamics, phrasing, detailed articulation, and balance of textures are beyond the capacity of a concert grand. Let me draw attention again to Mr. Bilson's article in the April 1980 issue of *Early Music,* in which four such passages—by Mozart, Beethoven, and Haydn—are discussed. At the Met demonstration, the pianist began with a simple example—the start of the "Pathétique," that thick low chord marked *fp.* Hit it really *f* on a modern piano and it will not die to *p* before the time for the continuation arrives.

Timbre, lightness and directness of action, swiftness and precision of damping—the light wooden frame, the thin strings, the small, leather-covered hammers—conspire to produce a sound that is clear, singing, and compact. The modern concert grand is not an insensitive instrument. It has its uses. But it was not designed to match the sensibilities of Mozart's, Beethoven's, or Schubert's music. Iron-framed, massive, it aims at resonance, "full" tone, power, and sostenuto; as Grove puts it, thirty-ton inner tensions result in "a sostenuto unknown to Beethoven or Schumann or Chopin," let alone Haydn or Mozart. I needn't go on. To hear Classical music played on a piano of the Classical age—and, for that matter, early-Romantic music played on an early-Romantic piano—is to be convinced. Unless, of course, the player or the instrument is poor.

Mr. Bilson, a superior player on a superior instrument, was able to be bolder, wittier, braver in his contrasts, more delicate and various in his phrasing, and truer to the text than colleagues who must "edit" and adjust the music before feeding it to their modern monsters. There was a new, further interest in the recital, and there is on the latest Nonesuch record: Mr. Bilson no longer uses equal-temperament tuning but has adopted "well-tempered" tuning, in which all keys are available but the common keys are more consonant than remote ones. Therefore, some tonalities are comfortable, smooth, consolatory, and others are keen, edgy, tense. Key colors, key characteristics—the subject of much debate and speculation—are sharply distinguished. I won't pretend that at the recital I was conscious of unusual tuning, except perhaps on a subliminal level. I merely thought the effect of modulations and sudden key shifts—the D-major statement in the first movement of Beethoven's F-major Sonata, Opus 10, No. 2; the chromatic adventures in the Andante of Mozart's K. 333—was even more noticeable and more telling than usual. One responded to harmony as well as to timbre and touch with added alertness. But at the Met lecture the tuning differences were made clearly audible: the start of the "Pathétique" slow movement took on different emotional shadings when played in transpositions. On the Nonesuch record, the B-flat-minor excursions of the K. 332 Adagio sound more affecting than ever. I don't know what people with absolute pitch, their mental A finely tuned to 440, make of it. For the recording, Mr. Bilson used A = 423, and, at the recital, A = 430. Key character is usually attributed to a combination of familiar associations (Mozart's G-minor vein, for example), the resonances of the violins' open strings, and the "natural" keys for woodwinds and for brasses. It has also been suggested that the very words "sharp" and "flat" may color one's reactions, making A major (three sharps) seem bright and E-flat major (three flats) solemn; that the very same chord may sound bright when it is thought of as C-sharp and tender when it is thought of as D-flat. When we add the factor of unequal temperament, giving different degrees of consonance to the tonic triads, there is good reason why Mozart's A major should continue to sound "bright" even to an absolute-pitcher who hears it as closer to A-flat.

At Mr. Bilson's recital, two things pinned one to the twentieth century: the unhappy lighting scheme currently favored in America—bright on the platform and dim in the hall, setting the performer apart from his listeners—and, more serious, an electrical buzz in the ceiling loud enough to fill the music's silent moments with sound. (When listening to a fortepiano, one listens very intently, and a hall free of any adventitious noise is more than usually necessary.) In fact, the two things were related, I learned: the dimming of the lights caused the buzz.

The buzz was back at Mary Sadovnikoff's fortepiano recital there some days later. She played Mozart, Haydn, and Beethoven on a Belt copy of a J. L. Dulcken instrument. (It once belonged to Mr. Bilson, and on an earlier Nonesuch record of his it can be heard in the Beethoven Opus 27 sonatas.) This was a less remarkable event. Either the pianist or her piano was in less than top form. The instrument sounded neither "well-tempered" nor purely in tune by any system, and the octave below middle C seemed to dominate all: whether above or below the ostinato triplets, the second theme of the "Tempest" Sonata hardly made its way through them. In the finale, and in that of Haydn's A-flat Sonata, Hob. 46, Miss Sadovnikoff tended to rush her fences.

For the first concert of its season in Alice Tully Hall, Clarion Concerts and its music director, Newell Jenkins, joined by the Canterbury Choral Society, revived Carl Loewe's oratorio *Die sieben Schläfer von Ephesus* (1833). Loewe is remembered as a prolific songwright (his collected songs fill seventeen volumes; Fischer-Dieskau has not yet tackled a complete recording, though he has made some fine Loewe records) and probably best known as the composer of "Tom der Reimer," one of the prettiest of all songs. The Seven Sleepers—whose tale appears in the Koran and was told by Gibbon—provide matter for a romantic libretto. Loewe responds to the moment when after nearly two centuries of slumber the seven brothers wake in their cave, and voice after voice—from bass to soprano—strikes up steadfastly to praise the Lord. But his response is hardly inspired. The work is bland, with picturesque touches—violas and cellos making an evening murmur at the start of Part III. The composer at his most melodiously inventive and attractive appears in a duet between the boy Malchus, a soprano, and his great-grandnephew Antipater, Proconsul of Ephesus, a tenor. The work, no revelation of neglected glory, was unfailingly agreeable. The oratorios of Spohr and Sigismund Neukomm, once popular, are heard no more: *The Seven Sleepers* showed us something of what was happening between Beethoven's *Christus am Ölberge* (1803) and Mendelssohn's *Elijah* (1846). A duet for Antipater and his wife catches echoes from Beethoven; a final solo and chorus flowing smoothly over long pedals anticipate Mendelssohn at his most serenely mellifluous. In a decent cast, the basses Richard Crist and Robert Briggs were outstanding. Susan von Reichenbach sang Malchus clearly and resolutely. The large chorus made a surprisingly small sound even when in full cry, but the dry hall, no friend to voices, may have been partly to blame. There are churches in which the oratorio would have flowered more richly. It was done in German, but English text sheets were provided.

It was sixteen years ago that Elisabeth Söderström last sang at the Metropolitan, where she took such roles as Susanna, Sophie, Marguerite, Adina, Rosalinda. Since then, to hear the great soprano in the theatre New Yorkers have had to travel. Her repertory ranges from Monteverdi, through Gluck, Mozart, and Beethoven, to Debussy, Britten, Henze, and contemporary Swedish operas; she is preëminent now as the heroines of Richard Strauss and of Janáček. For London Records, she has recorded Janáček's *Kát'a Kabanová* and *The Makropulos Affair*. In San Francisco, where she first appeared three years ago, as Kát'a, her Jenůfa this season has been a revelation of operatic art at its highest. *Jenůfa*—does it still need saying?—is one of the great operas of our century. Suffering and despair have not been more keenly shared. Attending it is a searing experience. Poor little Butterfly draws easy, enjoyable tears; *Jenůfa* is drama and music on another level. It would be unbearable but for the composer's tenderness and compassion. Out of the tragedy and the horror, understanding and love are born.

Söderström first played Jenůfa in a Stockholm production, eight years ago, directed by Götz Friedrich. (When it came to Edinburgh in 1974, the editor of *Opera* called it "one of the most emotionally shattering evenings I have ever experienced" and Söderström's Jenůfa "one of the great experiences of our day.") In a brief autobiographical volume, *In My Own Key*, just published (Hamish Hamilton), the soprano recalls Friedrich's dictatorial methods with a touch of sharpness:

> "I can't carry out definite movements until I know what sort of person I'm supposed to be, can I?" I said. "I don't even know her yet."
>
> "But I do," said Götz. "Do it like this." Not until I saw the finished production...did I give way. I realised then that I was nothing but a small piece of a gigantic puzzle, and I was so impressed that I swallowed my objections to his interpretations of some of the scenes in the third act. Against my inner conviction, I played them as the producer wished me to. But it seemed cowardly and false.

In the San Francisco *Jenůfa,* there was not a false or uncommitted instant. When the curtain rose, Jenůfa stood with her back to the audience; a few bars later, she ran upstage to watch for her lover's return. In Söderström's stance and her gait, the girl was already revealed—eager, apprehensive, willful yet vulnerable. Her every move through the developing drama was eloquent; not a glance or a gesture was stagy or calculated in effect. (*In My Own Key* has some good pages on "physical" interpretation.) She wore Jenůfa's clothes, not theatrical costumes. Her body, its placing, its weights, seemed to be that of a different woman from the elegant, youthful interpreter of the Countess in *Capriccio* and from the elegant, ageless, haunted interpreter of Elina Makropulos. The voice was quite different, too: Jenůfa brought out a fresh, full, girlish timbre, as young as that of Söderström's Tatyana but quite different in character. Söderström is not young, but she sounded and seemed it, and she was singing better than ever, with a richer range of colors. Even in the huge San Francisco house, and over the big orchestra, her voice soared easily. Only in the final duet, where Jenůfa's sustained B-flats lift the throbbing music to its long dominant pedal, did she tire a little. The sound was still radiant.

There are two great women's roles in *Jenůfa.* Sena Jurinac, Vienna's memorable Jenůfa in 1964, moved in 1978 to the role of Jenůfa's foster-mother, the Kostelnička, and she sang it again in San Francisco. Another marvellous performance: every gesture and every phrase truthful, eloquent. The climactic B at the close of Act II rang out pure, unfrayed, with dramatic-soprano force. Elsewhere, her voice did sometimes sound worn, but there was still beauty in the singing, of sound as of expression. I have loved the two sopranos for years: Jurinac was Glyndebourne's prima donna from 1949 to 1956; Söderström, who came to Glyndebourne in 1957, has been her successor there. Together, they now scaled new heights of achievement, bringing long experience and sure technique to roles whose directness, honesty, and subtlety peculiarly matched their special art, temperaments, and understanding.

The large cast seemed to be inspired by them and was without weakness. William Lewis (the Met's Števa in 1974) was poetic. Allen Cathcart (the Laca of the Welsh National Opera and the Scottish Opera productions) was unobtrusively subtle. The principals hardly needed any further "direction"; Michael Rennison, the director, and Leni Bauer-Ecsy, the designer, provided a workable framework within which they could appear to advantage. (But the flared perspective of Act II made the Kostelnička's house seem needlessly immense.) The conducting of Albert Rosen (who gave the Dublin première of *Jenůfa*, in 1973) had character and strength. The opera was done in Moravian, learned parrot-fashion by most of the cast but sung with conviction. Although I've forgotten what little Czech I once knew, I didn't mind; I was glad to hear the original sounds, and have heard the piece often enough in English or German for mental "subtitles" to run. But *Jenůfa* is unlikely to become the repertory opera it deserves to be (and is now in much of Europe; since 1977 four of Britain's full-time companies have been playing it) except in the language of the audience.

EXOTICS

December 1, 1980

BORODIN's *Prince Igor* is a beautiful, strangely neglected, and often maligned opera. The New Grove calls it "tableauesque and disjointed" and talks of "loose design." A case against it is easily made. The libretto is episodic, and the action can be summarized in a sentence: Igor leads his forces against Khan Konchak and the Polovtsy, is captured and lavishly entertained, escapes, and returns home. Two touches of subplot add variety without affecting the action: Igor's brother-in-law Galitsky proves a dissolute regent; Igor's son Vladimir and the Khan's daughter Konchakovna fall in love. Borodin, a part-time composer, wrote the opera piecemeal, across eighteen years, changing the scenario from time to time. After his death, it was assembled and in large part orchestrated by Rimsky-Korsakov and Glazunov. Yet on the rare occasions that I have seen *Prince Igor* in the theatre—a Zagreb production in London, a Bolshoy production in Paris, and now one in Bloomington, given by the Indiana University Opera Theater—it has seemed not episodic, not a patchwork, and not undramatic but a noble and successful epic opera of an unconventional kind.

When Borodin had sketched about half of it, he set down some account of his aims:

> My whole manner of dealing with operatic material is quite different [from that of the other Russian nationalists]. As I see it, superfluous detail has no place in opera. Everything should be drawn in bold strokes, as clearly and vividly as is practically possible for voice and orchestra.

His starting point had been a detailed scenario by V. V. Stassov, which rounded off the action with the wedding feast of Vladimir and Konchakovna—the Polovtsy defeated, Galitsky in jail. In 1869, the year Mussorgsky completed the first version of *Boris Godunov,* Borodin began *Igor.* Then for five years—disheartened, perhaps, by the Maryinsky's rejection of *Boris*—he put it aside. I have not seen it suggested, but it strikes me as likely, that the production of the revised *Boris,* in 1874, encouraged Borodin to return to his opera. He simplified Stassov's scenario and brought it closer to the old *Lay of Igor's Campaign* (there is an English translation by Nabokov), which makes no mention of a Polovtsian defeat. He introduced Igor at the start (Stassov had reserved him for Act II), crying "Forth, to fight Russia's foes," and gave him much the same words for his final utterance. This is the opera's heroic theme; it sounds through Igor's music in the Polovtsian acts, and its strength is not really compromised by the intoxicating, glamorous music lavished on the Polovtsians and their magnificent, Tamburlaine-like Khan. Between the "bold strokes" are no explanatory transitions; *Prince Igor* has something in common with Tippett's *King Priam* in its lapidary technique. The audience is presumed to know the plot in advance (a brief program note can achieve this), while the composer makes vivid and universal its high moments and high emotions. Yaroslavna, Igor's wife, voices the grief and fears of all women whose men are at war. Galitsky stands for irresponsibility in high places; Yeroshka and Skula, genial rogues, show it in common men. Vladimir and Konchakovna suffer the conflict of lust and duty. Konchak is a conqueror who can afford careless magnanimity. To complain that they are not fully rounded individuals is to miss the point. Deliberately (or so it seems to me), not through incompetence, the composer presented his characters only in epic moments. And his *Prince Igor* became an "epic" opera in both the Brechtian and the ordinary senses of the word. Borodin's musical genius has never been in question. The Mighty Handful seem to have deemed him the most inspired of their band, and their regret that academic administration, chemical research, his campaign to let women study medicine, and the exigences of his sickly, neurotic wife kept him so much from composition is easily shared. Yet the music of *Igor,* I believe, seems greater still when its colors, its networks of subtle motivic allusions, and the contrasts between elevated or emotional Russian strains and the glittering, exotic Polovtsian rhythms and melodies are heard as part of a carefully patterned musical drama.

The case for *Igor* is most convincingly argued by a performance, and the Bloomington production made out a good case. The scale was large: a chorus of a hundred and thirty, a ballet of thirty-six. The orchestra, conducted by Bryan Balkwill, was bright. The show had spirit. Max Röthlisberger's sets were big and handsome. (If the Met wishes to mount an *Igor* in borrowed décor, it could well use them.) Bodo Igesz's staging was straightforward and sensible. The Polovtsian Dances were re-created on Fokin lines by Nicolas Beriozoff. I was gripped and stirred by the piece. Nevertheless, it did not seem to have received quite the long, loving, and detailed preparation one expects a campus presentation to have had. There was abundant vocal talent in the cast I heard but not much evidence that the young singers had steeped themselves in the particular sounds and style of Imperial Russia—that Nova Thomas (Yaroslavna) had been listening for months to, say, Nina Koshetz, Laura Rice (Konchakovna) to Eugenia Zbruyeva, Larry Paxton (Vladimir) to Leonid Sobinov, Tim Noble (Igor) to Vladimir Kastorsky, Mark Lundberg and Kevin Maynor (Galitsky and Konchak) to Lev Sibiriakov. From those artists and their like they could have learned more of the distinctive Russian manner, in which notes are held through for their full value and are pressed close, one to the next, in a seamless legato; in which syllables are caressed, each of them pronounced as if it were something precious. The plangent lyricism, the cultivation of timbres exceptionally limpid, voluptuous, or grandiose, the tricks and flicks of Russian coloratura, the swells and the meltings—of these there was too little. In several numbers, the singers seemed to be hurrying, moving on rather than savoring. But Miss Thomas was touching, and Mr. Noble was—well, noble. Two clear, forward tenors in small roles, Neil Jones (Ovlur) and Daniel Brewer (Yeroshka), had the right approach.

Cutting was heavy, as it usually is. I have yet to hear the full sequence of numbers which opens Act III, after the Polovtsian March, played in a theatre. But there at least a large clean cut was made; more disfiguring was the reduction of the Konchakovna-Vladimir duet to a few phrases. Nevertheless, the effect of the whole was exhilarating. This *Prince Igor* joins Boston's *Russlan* and Bloomington's *Christmas Eve*, done in 1977, to remind our regular companies that there is more to Russian nineteenth-century opera than *Boris* and the two familiar Tchaikovskys.

Meanwhile, the French revival continues. The Dallas Civic Opera has just done Delibes' *Lakmé*, and has done it well. In my young days, *Lakmé* was an Opéra-Comique staple; only *Carmen, Manon,* and *Werther* notched up more performances there. From 1932 to 1946, it was also a Met staple, with Lily Pons. Today, it's rarish; productions with Joan Sutherland (Seattle in 1967, Sydney in 1976) and with Christiane Eda-Pierre (Wexford in 1970) stand out in the annals. *Lakmé*, we are told, needn't be taken too seriously. I thoroughly enjoyed it in Dallas because the executants *had* taken it seriously, not in any unstylish modern way (it was not, for example, presented as a tract on the iniquities of British colonial rule) but as a refined and exquisitely fashioned essay in late-nineteenth-century exoticism. The production originated in Trieste. The sets, by Pasquale Grossi, were beautiful and looked like Gérômes brought to life. The staging, by Alberto Fassini, was precise. (The lighting, alas, was crude.) Nicola Rescigno's conducting was sensitive. Best of all, the piece was uncommonly well sung.

Ruth Welting, who in recent years has sometimes sounded rather hard and pert, had found again the sweet, gentle, limpid tones and manner that made her early Lucias so touching. All the notes of the Bell Song were clearly and sweetly struck, and the number was not just a showpiece. Lakmé's anxiety—she knows her father is using the song as a trap to catch her lover—was also sounded; the coloratura was urgent and poignant as well as accurate and pretty. Alfredo Kraus, the Gerald, was his usual polished self. The voice has lasted well, and he phrased with distinction. But, as often, he seemed self-centered, an artist intent on his own elegant performance rather than a hero deeply in love with the particular soprano of the evening. Paul Plishka was a grave, powerful Nilakantha.

I've not seen many Dallas productions—four in sixteen years—and shouldn't generalize about the standards and style of the company. But all four have been of high merit and have represented an approach to opera that becomes increasingly rare: eminent singers; rich, handsome spectacle; thoughtful presentation; staging without willfulness or eccentricity. This *Lakmé* was a model of how to revive French opera in a large American house. The sung-recitative version, Delibes' own, was used, yet a feeling of opéra-comique delicacy and charm was preserved. Although the décor was picturesque and impressive, the main focus was not on designer or director but on the singers—and on *all* of them, not just on a prima donna or a primo tenore. The smaller parts —led by David Holloway's Frederick and Carolyne James's Mistress Benson—were well taken. The opera seemed to have been revived not "for" anyone, not even for the admirable Miss Welting, but because everyone concerned liked and believed in the piece. *Lakmé* is not a great opera. *Prince Igor* is. But that's another matter. I'm not one to despise elegant, cultivated entertainment on the foothills—provided that the heights are not neglected. And in Dallas they're not; the annals of the company make impressive reading.

BEACON

December 8, 1980

A MUSICAL event of high importance has been the publication, by Macmillan, of the New Grove Dictionary of Music and Musicians, edited by Stanley Sadie. Grove (or Grove's, as Americans tend to call it) first appeared, in fascicules and then in four volumes, between 1877 and 1890. The preface by Sir George Grove—that remarkable man whose first job, appropriately, had been building lighthouses—is reprinted in the New Grove and remains apt. "It is designed for the use of Professional musicians and Amateurs alike," and directs its attention to "all the points, in short, immediate and remote, on which those interested in the Art, and alive to its many and far-reaching associations, can desire to be informed." Once again, "the articles are based as far as possible on independent sources, and on the actual research of the writers." "Fresh subjects have been treated, new and interesting information given, and some ancient mistakes corrected."

The New Grove—the sixth edition—appears in twenty handsome, clearly printed volumes, each of them close on nine hundred pages. It is a "new" Grove, not just a revision, in many ways. Folk music, popular music, and non-Western "serious" music are considered more fully than ever before. It remains a British publication, but the British contributors—according to the editor's estimate in his preface—now make up only about a fifth of the total number. And about a third of the contributors are American. Detailed catalogues and substantial bibliographies are among the features that reflect the Germano-American academic approach to music, and valuable they are. But, the editor says, "we have tried to ensure that something of the fine humane traditions of the earlier editions of Grove are to be seen in our pages," for "intelligent critical and evaluative writing still have a place in musical lexicography." Indeed they have. First impressions of the New Grove are altogether favorable. It is at once useful and readable. Any volume I take up I find hard to put down again.

To mark the Expressionist show at the Guggenheim, two performances of Schoenberg's *Pierrot Lunaire* were given in the museum's subterranean auditorium. Schoenberg was himself an Expressionist painter, and his *Pierrot* is conventionally rated a masterpiece of Expressionist music. In the New Grove's Schoenberg entry, by O. W. Neighbour, it is discussed along with *Das Buch der hängenden Gärten, Erwartung,* and *Die glückliche Hand* under the rubric "Expressionist works." But to my ears and eyes a gap between *Pierrot,* with its refined, detailed texture and exquisite facture, and the characteristic colors, forms, and imagery of Expressionist painting grows ever wider. (The concertgoers were not invited to seek analogues; unaccountably, the exhibition was closed to them.) Mr. Neighbour remarks:

> As a painter Schoenberg's amateur status severely limited the scope and quality of his achievement, but allowed him to feel that his hand was guided without his conscious intervention, whereas in music he had to pay for the benefits of mastery by reckoning with its censorship.

The Guggenheim *Pierrot* was the coolest, most laid-back, least Expressionist account of the piece I've ever heard. Schoenberg's instruction to the reciter of the poems—hair-sharp rhythms, indicated notes just touched and then let go, declamation neither singsong nor naturalistic—has led to a variety of interpretations, from glissando stylized moaning, freakish and extraordinary, to something close to song along the melodic lines he indicated so precisely. The composer's own 1940 recording has Erika Stiedry-Wagner pattering out the poems almost as accompaniment to the music of the instrumental quintet. Nine years later, he deplored that balance as an overreaction to performances where all attention had gone to the reciter, "while the themes (and everything else of musical importance) happen in the instruments"; perhaps, he said, he "forgot that one must, after all, be able to hear the speaker." Back in 1922, he had protested that if people "were musical, not a single one of them would give a damn for the words." In later life, he declared that for English-speaking audiences *Pierrot* should be done in English. The Guggenheim performance was done in German, and so another element entered the *Wort-oder-Ton* amalgam.

At the very first performance of *Pierrot Lunaire*, in 1912, the players were behind screens, and Albertine Zehme, dressed as Colombine, was in front of them. At the Guggenheim, the players were to one side of the stage, and Maureen McNalley—an elegant Schiele-like figure with red hair, a red boa, and a black dress, topped later by a cloak and a Pierrot hat—declaimed each "song" (the word seems inescapable) from a different place, under different lighting. The presentation, directed by Robert Engstrom, may sound fidgety but was in fact effective, and the balance was admirable: as Schoenberg remarked, separating reciter and players "contributes a great deal to the distinctness of the speaking part, and also gives the instruments their due, so that the music can really come into its own." Miss McNalley declaimed lightly and clearly, without rhetoric, and was perfectly audible, never drowned. Brilliantly she caught "that light, ironical, satirical tone in which the piece was originally conceived" (Schoenberg in 1940). She sustained her pitches. She suggested a singer "marking" rather than an actress reciting; if Yvette Guilbert had tackled *Pierrot*, it might have sounded like this. The playing of the instrumentalists, conducted by Joel Thome, was admirable, apart from an unsteady, too heavily throbbing flute in "Der kranke Mond."

Stravinsky once called *Pierrot* the "solar plexus as well as the mind of early twentieth-century music." Its spectrum of pain, strangeness, romance, poignancy, and wit has proved greater than any single performance can compass—from the silent screams of the protagonist in Glen Tetley's *Pierrot* ballet (which *is* an Expressionist interpretation) to Miss McNalley's understated virtuoso version. All sensitive performers reveal some new facet of the work. [*The Guggenheim performers later made a recording of* Pierrot, *on MMG.*]

Soon after his death, in 1521, Josquin Desprez was praised by Castiglione, Rabelais, and Martin Luther. In 1567, the humanist scholar Cosimo Bartoli wrote that if Ockeghem had been music's Donatello, Josquin was her great Michelangelo. In the eighteenth century, Burney pronounced Josquin "the Giant of his time" and laid specimens of his music before the common reader. And today, as Jeremy Noble remarks in the New Grove's Josquin entry (a masterly essay, marshalling the facts and gently yet firmly assessing the speculations of recent scholarship), "that Josquin was the greatest composer of the high Renaissance, the most varied in invention and the most profound in expression, has become almost a commonplace of musical history." Last Sunday's concert in the Music Before 1800 series in Corpus Christi Church was devoted to Josquin. The Pomerium Musices, ten strong, directed by Alexander Blachly, sang his *Malheur me bat* Mass, interspersed with a frottola, motets, and chansons. Some of the juxtapositions were surprising: before the Easter motet "Victimae paschali," three young men voiced a girl's amorous regret for the loss of her boyfriend, and after it another trio (soprano, tenor, and bass) announced in concert that each had set her mind to acquiring a new one. The modern convention that women may sing masculine songs but not vice versa—sopranos appropriate "Der Musensohn," but tenors don't tackle "Die junge Nonne"—evidently didn't hold in the Renaissance. A varied, vivid picture was given of Luther's "joyous, spontaneous, and abundant" composer.

The *Malheur me bat* Mass, Mr. Noble remarks, shows "the Janus-faced quality of Josquin's genius (and the difficulties this poses for historians)." The details of Josquin's life and the chronology of his works are a puzzle with some important pieces missing and others not yet in place. The big Josquin volume that resulted from the big Josquin festival-conference held in New York in 1971 is (among other things) a gripping detective story of clues discovered, ciphers cracked, and alibis examined. ("Where Was Josquin from 1479 to 1486?" is a subheading in Edward Lowinsky's chapter; "'Ut Phoebi Radiis': The Riddle of the Text Resolved" is the title of Virginia Woods Callahan's contribution.) On the ground of style, Mr. Noble would place the *Malheur me bat* Mass rather later than Mr. Lowinsky and (in his program note) Mr. Blachly do—on the ground that in 1480 *malheur* had indeed struck the prelate who may have been Josquin's patron at the time. In any event, the "calculated fantasy" (Noble), the "flowing melody and felicitous expressivity" (Lowinsky), the "exalted climaxes" of the Gloria and the Credo and the "diabolical intricacies" of the Agnus (Blachly) were bravely and movingly turned into living music by Mr. Blachly and his choir, a virtuoso group of gifted individuals who together make a wonderful sound. Sometimes the timbre of the lower voices struck me as perhaps a shade too relaxed, soft-grained, "refined"; the tension that should be drawn through long melodic spans was slackened. The altos (countertenors) were keen and bright, the sopranos shining and excellently steady.

Pierrot Lunaire is made of carefully fashioned lines that must be placed one against another with rhythmic exactitude although the precise pitch distance between them is not always crucial. In Schoenberg's recording, Stiedry-Wagner indicates the melodic shapes, more or less, but does not adhere to the written pitch levels. Charles Rosen, in his acute little Schoenberg monograph, carries the idea into the instrumental parts with his arresting suggestion that the clarinet line in "Der Dandy," for example, could be played a semitone too high or too low "and (although some effect would be lost) the music would still make sense," since "the harmonic consistency is concentrated within the individual lines." Josquin's no less expressive counterpoint, on the other hand, requires pure tuning of line against line as well as accurate rhythmic placing. At the Corpus Christi concert, the intonation, except for an errant moment in "Victimae paschali," was admirably true. But occasionally in the rhythmic aspect one had the impression of singers with eyes on the beat rather than ears on one another—as if Mr. Blachly were ruling audible barlines across the flow of the music. (His singers find and rap out dance-rhythm episodes—in the Agnus, for example—with a piquant effect, almost, of little drums beating.) It scarcely needs saying that in the best Josquin performances a listener responds both to lines and to the resultant "harmony"; but a perfect, natural-seeming balance between expressive linear flow and accurate, not overemphasized, vertical coincidence—and also between colorful incident and the large "architectural" spans—is hard to achieve. In this respect, Mr. Noble's recording of the *L'Homme armé* (sexti toni) Mass, with the Josquin Choir (Vanguard), is a model. The Pomerium Musices accounts of the elaborate "Virgo salutiferi" and the exuberantly inventive "Victimae paschali" were models, too. All in all, this was a concert of rare merit: great music performed with care, devotion, and uncommon accomplishment, in an agreeable and acoustically apt building, to an attentive audience. Among the Pomerium Musices virtues is its utterance of texts sacred or secular as if they meant something. Text sheets with translation were provided, but the clue to deciphering the nonsense Latin in "Ut Phoebi radiis"—read the solmization syllables backward—was teasingly withheld.

OF DAMES, OF KNIGHTS, OF LOVE'S DELIGHT

December 15, 1980

VIVALDI CLAIMED, late in life, that he had written ninety-four operas. The figure has been doubted—only fifty-five or so operas by him have been identified—but its preciseness suggests that the composer drew up a list, and modern scholarship suggests that the claim should be taken seriously. In that case, among the prolific giants of the Baroque only Alessandro Scarlatti, Reinhard Keiser, and perhaps Antonio Caldara were more prolific than he. His tercentenary fell in 1978. That year, London heard *Griselda*, Paris heard *La fida ninfa*, and New York heard *Farnace* in concert performances. *L'incoronazione di Dario* was staged in Siena, and *Orlando furioso* in Verona. Recordings appeared of *Tito Manlio*, *Orlando furioso*, and *L'Olimpiade*. *Orlando furioso* has now been produced by the Dallas Civic Opera, with great success. It seems to have been the first Vivaldi opera staged in this country. May others follow soon. The combination of beautiful melodies, fine singing, and spectacular décor made it a hit with the public. Who could ask for more?

Well, in Dallas those who knew Vivaldi's opera, and even those who knew only its libretto, which is by Grazio Braccioli, could and did ask for more. Around the first performances of its *Orlando* the Civic Opera, in conjunction with the Meadows School of the Arts at Southern Methodist University, had convened a four-day international symposium on the theme "Opera and Vivaldi: Reflections of a Changing World." Bold undertaking: unless the dramaturge of a troupe has done his work with unusual thoroughness, or unless the conductor and the director of a show are themselves keen scholars, such symposia invite critical scrutiny of a performance from people who know far more about the piece concerned than its performers do. Each scholar may have studied in detail only one aspect: how the composer intended his work to be staged, sung, accompanied, acted; how the vocal lines should be decorated; how continuo chords and cadences should be played, and by what instruments; and so on. By the time all have exchanged information and commentary, and have descried the special characteristics of the work both within the composer's oeuvre and in relation to opera of his day, they share a formidable body of knowledge and understanding—assembled and made public too late for the performers to take advantage of it. The Dallas symposium was particularly useful in that it included several scholar-performers who have themselves conducted, directed, sung in, played in, and edited Baroque operas—who have formed and tested ideas in the theatre and discovered that they work. Perhaps it should have been held a year ago. At any rate, whoever next puts on Vivaldi's *Orlando* and whoever next puts on, takes part in, or, for that matter, attends a Baroque opera should be able to do so with mind, ears, and eyes sharpened by what was revealed at the Dallas symposium. [*The proceedings of the conference have now been published:* Opera & Vivaldi, *edited by Michael Collins and Elise K. Kirk (University of Texas Press).*]

Braccioli's libretto was written in 1713 for the composer Giovanni Alberto Ristori and the Teatro Sant'Angelo, in Venice. The following year, Vivaldi produced a different *Orlando* opera, *Orlando finto pazzo,* for the same theatre and again to a Braccioli libretto, and then followed it with a new version—the music partly his, partly Ristori's—of the 1713 show. Thirteen years later, now a very experienced opera composer, Vivaldi returned to *Orlando furioso,* recomposing much of the music but retaining some of his 1714 numbers and also a little of Ristori's work. This 1727 *Orlando furioso* was also performed at the Sant'Angelo. Modern revivals have used a text derived from it.

The 1954 Grove stated flatly that "Vivaldi's vocal music has been entirely forgotten." Although that's no longer true, the old textbook view of his operas reappears in the New Grove: "Viewed dramatically, the operas merely supply what was expected of a composer working within narrow and at the same time universal conventions." The sharp satire contained in the prescriptions of Benedetto Marcello's *Teatro alla moda* still tends to be taken as truth: the poet "will write the whole opera without formulating any plot"; the composer "will take care never to read the whole opera." And the evening will consist of a long, loose string of arias devised solely to display the varied vocal abilities of the performers, divided by screeds of recitative. After hearing *Tito Manlio, L'Olimpiade, Farnace,* and *Orlando,* we know better. Each creates and inhabits a world of its own. *Orlando* is a skillful and attractive essay at capturing and transforming episodes of Ariosto's poem for the lyric stage. Although the numerous exploits of the epic, Braccioli says in his 1713 preface, roam half the world, he has limited his scene to Alcina's enchanted island and taken as his main action the love, the madness, and the recovery of Orlando. But "the love of Bradamante and Ruggiero, the love of Angelica and Medoro, the various inclinations of Alcina, and the diverse passions of Astolfo serve to accompany this action and lead it to its end." Ariosto's military theme—the conflict of Christendom with the infidel invader (which was being waged again when he wrote, seven centuries after the Carolingian battles he told of)—is unsounded in the opera, but seven of the leading characters are here. The women are Angelica, proud Princess of Cathay, a Helen who has turned the heads of half Europe's heroes and driven the mightiest of them mad, who spurns them all only to lose her heart to the humble Saracen soldier lad Medoro, with his black eyes and golden curls; Alcina, King Arthur's sister, an old woman still greedy for sensual pleasures, her irresistible beauty preserved by artifice; and Bradamante, an early Leonore, the shining type of heroic, loving woman—clear-eyed and ever true to her errant, unfaithful Ruggiero.

The men are Medoro, passive and beautiful; the impetuous Ruggiero; the adventurous English prince Astolfo, who journeys into space to find the cure for his cousin Orlando's madness; and Orlando himself, his noble mind o'erthrown when he learns that the haughty Angelica has bestowed herself on another—the observed of all observers quite, quite down. By allusions, elisions, brief narratives (as of Astolfo's space trip), and ingenious transformations and inventions to tease and please the connoisseur of Ariosto, Braccioli covers a surprising amount of the poem, and does so with Ariostan bravura. He wrote for listeners who knew the epic; and with Barbara Reynolds's fluent, readable translation available in Penguin there is no reason that anyone who goes to Vivaldi's opera today should not know it. The libretto is a subtle and colorful achievement. In the opening scenes, the characters are brought to the island and identified, and their relations to one another are defined. Then, as in *Figaro* but against a background of bright chivalry and romantic marvels, love and the effects of love in all their variety—idyllic tenderness, steady devotion, deceit, infatuation, lust, frivolity, jealousy, obsession—are explored in a carefully balanced drama.

In composing this unusual opera, Vivaldi, as John Walter Hill noted in one of the symposium's most valuable papers, broke an oft-cited opera-seria "rule"—that each aria should be in a different genre from that of its predecessor—by grouping within each of the opera's nine stage settings arias of a similar type: bravura, parlante, cantabile, etc. And thus he achieved a diversity subtler, less mechanical, than that of the automatic contrasts mocked by Marcello: one hears a similar emotion—resolve, tenderness, whatever—catching different people differently. And in other ways Vivaldi, like the best of his colleagues, bent and broke the conventions with dramatic surprises: by embarking on an aria without recitative; by cutting a number short; by keeping a singer onstage after an apparent "exit aria." Such effects lose their singularity if, in a modern performance, the conventions are everywhere disregarded. For Orlando, he composed remarkable mad scenes, violent, pathetic, and vivid.

In Dallas, the literary, narrative, formal, and dramaturgical aspects of *Orlando* had been treated with disdain. The first four scenes and most of the fifth were omitted. After an overture, Orlando—unintroduced, unmotivated—stepped forth and launched into the fifth aria of the score. The edition used was an abbreviated and partly disordered version of the opera prepared by Claudio Scimone for the 1978 recording and the Verona production. Further cuts were made in it. Something over two and a half hours of music—between two-thirds and a half of the original score—was done. Snail's-pace recitative, with cadences protracted, extended the playing time. Sometimes it was organ-accompanied. In not looking beyond the Scimone text for his source, Nicola Rescigno, the conductor and the artistic director of the Dallas Opera, could be likened to a theatrical director who, introducing *Hamlet* to America, was content to do so from the prompt script made for an earlier production which contained about half the original and shuffled some of the scenes about. There were practical reasons for the decision. The Scimone score and parts existed, ready to play and sing from. Décor and staging keyed to the edition, both by Pier-Luigi Pizzi, had been borrowed from Verona. The protagonist was that of the Verona production and of the recording, and she may have been reluctant to restudy her role. One can appreciate such reasons and still regret that Dallas took over as a package deal a presentation evidently conceived in accordance with what Daniel Heartz, in the New Grove, describes as "received opinions, still regrettably widespread," about opera seria: that it "had been static and entirely predictable, both dramatically and musically; that its only interest had lain in music, not in drama." Such views lend license to editors and directors who decide, quite wrongly, that opere serie need jollying and refurbishing before a contemporary audience can enjoy them. Of course, in our enormous modern theatres, and before audiences unwilling to devote five or six hours to a show, there must be compromise. But, as Winton Dean says in his *Handel and the Opera Seria*, it should be no more than an adjustment between the ideal and the practicable: "A compromise between what a great composer desired (provided it is practicable) and what we happen to be accustomed to is not a valid artistic operation. It is a piece of intellectual slovenliness."

I wish the work of Braccioli and Vivaldi had been treated more seriously and sensitively. Nevertheless, Dallas's *Orlando* package was filled with good things, and I enjoyed them thoroughly. The title role was written for a woman. Marilyn Horne sang it with astounding and resistless virtuousity, bravura, brilliance, and power. She looked unfortunate, clomping about in buskins, costumed in a voluminous black dress, a huge cloak in some filmy, feminine fabric floating out behind her. But I'll go part of the way with the Covent Garden chairman who remarked after Tetrazzini's first London Violetta, "Let her sing the role in a top hat if she chooses, provided she sings it so well." Ellen Shade was a lovely Angelica, particularly in the expressively molded lines of her second-act aria, "Chiara al pari di lucida stella." Gwendolyn Killebrew produced rich, lustrous sound as Alcina, but a cleaner, more accurate focus on the notes was needed. Rose Taylor was a brave, pleasing Bradamante. (The role was written for Maria Caterina Negri, who eight years later created the same character in Handel's *Alcina*.) The high notes of James Bowman, the Ruggiero, were more powerful than those of most countertenors but were not always pleasant to hear. Astolfo, sung in Dallas by the bass Nicola Zaccaria, was the only low voice in 1727, but here, as in Verona, the role of Medoro had been dropped an octave. Dano Raffanti revealed a tenor of exceptionally beautiful quality, one to send a thrill of pleasure through the listeners by the freshness, purity, and firmness of its timbre.

The music was treated with care. Under Mr. Rescigno's baton, it moved well. Decorations of the vocal lines were interesting. Cadenzas were surprising both in the right and, sometimes, in a wrong, out-of-period way. A viola obbligato to Medoro's only remaining aria was exquisitely played; the flute obbligato to Ruggiero's "Sol per te, mio dolce amore" was wobbly. (The instrumentalists joined the singers onstage.) Vivaldi's score is, among other things, a treasure house of affecting and exciting melodies, and musically there was a great deal to admire. There was also matter for the eye. In conjunction with *Orlando*, the Opera and the Meadows School had mounted a splendid Vivaldi exhibition, and here one could see the way operas were staged in his day. It is not Mr. Pizzi's way. The floor of the Dallas stage was a perilous alpine slope, of some shiny black substance, which dropped sheer into the orchestra pit except where two bridges came out toward the audience. The side and back walls were of dusky mirror—a striking if modish device. (It worked even better in the Bologna Comunale, reflecting Bibiena architecture as background to the Gluck *Orfeo* Mr. Pizzi designed for Luca Ronconi.) The magical machinery specified in the score was handled simply: the flying horse on which Ruggiero arrived a mere statue pulled on from the wings; two plastic tubes doing duty for the fountains of oblivion and desire from which he drank; two gilt rocks flopping forward to represent the avalanche that should precipitate an imprisoning cavern around Orlando. But there were some big scenic strokes elsewhere: a wall of painted mirror, spanning the stage, that pivoted up to make a reflecting sky. Scene changes were swift and ingenious, but, like Mr. Pizzi's direction, they obscured the dramatic design of the work. Whoever mounts an opera seria does well to preserve the prescribed scene changes, entrances, and exits. They are part of the musical and dramatic scheme. The rich costumes—Orlando's excepted—happily recalled Tiepolo's Orlando frescoes in the Villa Valmarana.

LANDMARKS

December 22, 1980

THE BIG "landmarks" of contemporary music—the headline-hitting long compositions for large forces—are usually slow to reach New York. Those met with in recent years can be counted on the fingers of one hand: Philip Glass's *Einstein on the Beach*, done in 1976; Pierre Boulez's *Pli selon pli*, in 1978, sixteen years after its completion; Peter Maxwell Davies's Symphony, in 1978, and an exception in that the Philharmonic played it within eight months of its première; and, most recently, Luciano Berio's *Coro*, brought to Carnegie Hall this season by the Cleveland Orchestra. Meanwhile, *Coro* has also turned up on record, from Deutsche Grammophon—one of a clutch of contemporary-music releases which also includes Karlheinz Stockhausen's *Stern-*

klang. (That open-air "park" music for five separate groups is something that might well have been mounted in Central Park before now.) *Coro,* commissioned by West-German Radio, had its first performance in Donaueschingen, in 1976. It was then sung and played at the Venice Biennale and at the Holland Festival, and in 1977 a revised version had its first performance in London, at the Proms, in the Albert Hall. Since then, it has been heard in Paris, Rome, Jerusalem, and Tel Aviv. In all these performances the Cologne Radio Chorus took part, and it came to America to join the Cleveland Orchestra in introducing *Coro* to Cleveland, Boston, New York, and Washington.

Coro continues the line of Berio's "archetypal" compositions: the symphony called *Sinfonia,* the opera called *Opera,* the recital called *Recital,* and the concerto (for two pianos and orchestra) called *Concerto.* No more than them is it in forces or form a conventional specimen of its titular genre. The "chorus" consists of forty soloists, each with her or his separate line. Each singer sits or stands beside an instrument of roughly equivalent range, to constitute a symbiotic duo. The instruments, plus two percussion batteries, an electronic organ, and a piano, make up the orchestra. Seating plans prescribed in the score cover three dimensions: platform risers are "essential...because all singers and players must be seen by the audience." (On the Carnegie platform, this requirement was not completely met.) *Coro,* like the other Berio works mentioned, is among other things a composer's musical answer to such questions as "What has symphony/opera/recital/concerto/chorus meant to people through the ages?" and "What can it mean to listeners today?" In a talk that Berio gave before the London performance, he declared that whereas a composer of the past could confidently set forth his vision of a Utopia where "all men become brothers," a composer of today can honestly do no more than "recapture certain simple aspects of that vision." The full choral cries that punctuate *Coro* are based on two stark lines from poems by Pablo Neruda. One, from his nihilistic years, is "The pale day dawns." The other, written after his conversion to Communism, is "Come and see the blood in the streets." In the last section of *Coro,* it is cried as answer to a question:

> *You will ask me why this poem*
> *doesn't speak of dreams, of leaves,*
> *of the great volcanoes of my native land?*
> *Come and see the blood in the streets.*

But in *Coro* the dreams and the leaves also play a part.

The massed voices and instruments give out in stern, powerful chords these bleak words of the individual poet. They break through a tapestry of songs—solos, duets, trios, and part-songs—that are settings, usually with chamber-music accompaniment, of lines from folk and traditional love songs and work songs taken from all over the world: from North and South America, Polynesia, Africa, Persia, Yugoslavia, Italy, and ancient Palestine (the Song of Songs). The languages used are English, German, French, Italian, and Hebrew. Love and work, Berio said in that London talk, have been the foundations of his life. The melodies, with one exception, are of his own invention; the techniques by which they are treated are sometimes his own adaptation of folk techniques—for example, a hocketing procedure used by the wooden-trumpet bands of the Central African Republic. ("Hocket," or hiccup, is a medieval term for the dovetailing of sounds and silences.) After the lyrical Sioux love song and the lilting Peruvian choral dance that make up the opening section comes the first harsh, forceful summons, "Venid a ver." What are we to come to see? No answer is vouchsafed yet. An alto breaks into a Polynesian love song. "Venid a ver" sounds again, brief, peremptory. Male voices take up the Polynesian song—same words but a different tune. Then the Neruda line is extended: "Venid a ver la sangre." And it continues to sound as a tragic refrain through an expanding vision of men and women loving and working, in simple communities and in cities, throughout the world. In a note on the record cover, Berio suggests different ways of approaching *Coro*. On the simplest level, it is "an anthology of diverse ways of 'setting to music.'" Then, it is

> like the plan for an imaginary city realized on different levels, which produces, assembles, and unifies different things and persons, presenting their collective and their individual characters, their distances one from another, their relationships and their conflicts within borders at once real and ideal.

The work has a solidly harmonic foundation. The ever-changing—sometimes related, sometimes independent—episodes of its linked songs Berio likens both to events taking place in the large landscape and to "musical images inscribed like graffiti on the harmonic wall of the city."

To perceive the composer's intention is not difficult. To hear and feel and respond to it in more than a generalized way—that of noting obvious contrasts of attractive lyricism or dance rhythms with loud, massy statement—I found hard, both in London three years ago and in Carnegie. It was only after repeated playings of the record that things started to fall into place. *Coro,* which lasts nearly an hour, is a vastly ambitious score, simple in its ground plan, simple in its textual juxtapositions, but far from simple in its musical procedures. In ages hence, it may perhaps come to be regarded as a twentieth-century masterpiece—by a visionary, a creator, and a poetic, all-embracing yet intensely personal musician with a wonderful ear.

I am not competent to assess the Carnegie performance, which was conducted by Lorin Maazel, for I was still finding my way into the music, but it seemed to me that he had mastered the score and that his orchestra of forty-four soloists played confidently. The virtuoso Cologne chorus is expert at pitching and expert at rhythm. Some of the voices are beautiful, and some of them are no more than serviceable.

I'd like to hear an English-speaking choir tackle *Coro* someday, for English is the language most used in Berio's libretto, and the Germans' singing of the language was unidiomatic. It was a matter not just of pronunciation ("Today iss mine ... Vake up voman") but of inflecting the composer's melodies with more than their notated or "instrumental" values, of making vivid the words as well as the musical shapes; on the record, it is striking that a new eloquence and freedom inform the singing when the text goes into German. From where I sat, the Carnegie platform tended to compress the sound, to close the distances between what should be far-flung details, to draw the walls of the imaginary city to a smaller circumference than they had compassed in the Albert Hall. On the other hand, the sheer physical impact of the terrifying refrains was greater in New York.

Berio, Stockhausen, Luigi Nono, and Michael Tippett could be deemed "visionary" composers of our day in the sense of being creators who look at the world and its history, and in their public, social works address that world as poets, prophets, and judges. Tippett is engaged on a large public work commissioned for the Boston Symphony's centenary—an evening-long oratorio, *The Mask of Time*, the first part of which, it is reported, will be "a kind of creation myth for our own time," and the second "a consideration of man and time more within history." Tippett's latest completed score is a stretch of pure music, a Triple Concerto, lasting just over half an hour, for violin, viola, and cello soloists and an orchestra of moderate size and unusual constitution (single flute/piccolo/alto flute, oboe, and English horn/bass oboe, but four clarinets). It had its première at the London Proms in August, and its North American première in Toronto the following month. The concerto is a work of abundant lyricism and invention, and very beautiful. The soloists are regarded as three distinct individuals, not a string trio. At the start, each in turn establishes a separate character in an exuberant, rapturous, cadenza-like outpouring. Then the three join in a stretch of tranquil music derived from the coda of Tippett's Fourth String Quartet. Although the three lines are quite independent, they conspire to create a single mood, serene and radiant. Unconventional counterpoint of this kind—a simultaneous flow of apparently improvised, unrelated, yet marvellously complementary melodies—marks much of the new score. There is a synthesis of Tippett's early exuberant polyphony and the leaner, motivic style of his middle period. There are links with both earlier and recent pieces: in the first movement, bold juxtapositions, rather than developments, and virtuoso brass writing continue the vein of the Fourth Symphony.

The concerto has three movements, linked by interludes. The first movement is a vigorous presentation of idea upon idea; a "second subject" marked by repeated falling ninths, glissando (anticipated in the cello's opening cadenza), is particularly striking. Then the first interlude, a magical passage, catches an echo from the woodland-dawn music of Tippett's first opera, *The Midsummer Marriage*: melodies steal out from alto flute and from bass oboe, and horns call softly, through a shimmer of nine solo violins and an enchanted sparkle of gentle tuned percussion. The slow movement is the heart of the concerto. It is based on a long, lovely, consolatory tune with decorative arabesques, spun from the notes A, B-flat, C, D, and E-flat—F major with a flattened seventh, and sung out over an F pedal, yet somehow Eastern in effect. (The sounds and structures of Balinese music played upon Tippett shortly before he began composing the concerto, and he has owned their influence. His battery includes five tuned gongs.) The three soloists play the tune in octaves, but the viola has the lowest line; the cello is two octaves above it, the violin an octave above that. The timbre is extraordinary, and so is the change of timbre when viola and cello switch positions for the cadential phrases. The movement continues with long duets for solo cello with bass oboe, and violin with alto flute. Between them, there are strange passages where· progress is arrested but movement is not stilled: aspen music, one might call it. Then the main tune sings out once more. The movement ends with a quiet, elegiac glissando sigh reminiscent of the "breath of the forest" motif in Britten's *Midsummer Night's Dream*. It appears several times; and toward the end of the work there seems to be another, possibly unconscious tribute to Britten: an ostinato from the three soloists which recalls the fugue subject of his *Young Person's Guide to the Orchestra*. With an effect that continues to shock me each time I hear the concerto, the second interlude breaks out in sophisticated big-city sounds—untuned percussion, suggesting a jazz kit, streaked with brief brass-ensemble riffs. The first part of the finale, built of statements and varied restatements of an energetic sequential theme, is perhaps the only passage in the rich work where Tippett's invention falls below his most inspired. The heights are regained when the opening cadenzas and the serene "trio" are recapitulated with a new, wonderful intensity. And suddenly the piece is over.

The Toronto soloists were Steven Staryk, Rivka Golani-Erdesz, and Daniel Domb; the orchestra was the Toronto Symphony, conducted by Andrew Davis. In London, the soloists were György Pauk, Nobuko Imai, and Ralph Kirshbaum; the orchestra was the London Symphony, which had commissioned the piece, and the conductor was Colin Davis. The concerto is not easy to play, to balance, or to shape. The Toronto players did well by it, but although I heard two performances, I still wondered whether I was hearing an imperfectly realized account of a more beautiful and more cogently constructed work than appeared or whether my London colleagues had been immoderately ecstatic in their reviews. Now a tape of the Prom performance has reached me, and all is explained. That first performance was far more coherent; both the soloists and the orchestra were braver, more precise in placing and balancing detail against detail, more impassioned in tone and spirit. Colin Davis's almost instinctive understanding of Tippett's music is well known, and to instinct he and his players have added long experience—as their recordings of the first three symphonies and the Concerto for Orchestra bear witness. [*In 1983, a Philips recording of the Triple Concerto appeared, made by its first interpreters.*] More than one Tippett score that seemed at first overelaborated in its textures or awkward in its construction remained "unrevealed" until Davis took it up. Then what had been found labored became luminous, what had been considered clumsy was clarified, and the composer was acclaimed as a master whose unconventional technical procedures were not merely novel but precise and eloquent.

LIGHT

December 29, 1980

THE METROPOLITAN OPERA has reopened, and, as the first opera of its season, gave the New York première of the completed, three-act *Lulu.* James Levine conducted. John Dexter directed. Teresa Stratas was the heroine. It was a performance on a high level, and one that came far closer than the others I have seen—the première, at the Paris Opera, and the American première, in Santa Fe—to stilling any doubts about the work while making much of what has never been in question: its beauty, richness, and theatrical vitality. Before writing any more about this detailed, careful, and impassioned execution of a detailed and impassioned score, I want to hear and see it again.

The Met's official "opening night," two days earlier, was devoted to Mahler's Second Symphony, for orchestra and chorus—as if in graceful acknowledgement that the Met orchestra and the Met chorus, whose requests for better treatment had kept the house dark for so long, are indeed the backbone of the company. The symphony's sobriquet, the "Resurrection," also made it an appropriate choice. But the performance was nothing much. Mr. Levine, who conducted, has never struck me as the "outstanding Mahler interpreter" that the New Grove calls him. His reading lacked flow, emotional phrasing, eloquence. There were some carefully considered details, isolated points that pleased. If the Met is to continue to give concerts—and I trust it will, for an opera-house orchestra needs to come up and take the limelight from time to time—thought must be given to their staging. At this concert, the pit floor was raised to stage level and most of the players were out on it, packed tight in a long, narrow line. First and second violins were divided left and right, and that was good, but the double-basses were clumped at third base, which spoiled the balance. Without risers, the woodwinds hardly breached the wall of strings. The salvos of the heavy percussion, a battery stationed out in front of the proscenium arch, proved hard to bear. Behind the orchestra, the stage was set shallow, and the chorus, a hundred strong, was banked up in front of the *Don Carlos* towers. It sounded unaccountably scrawny—particularly in the tenor division. Marilyn Horne, the alto soloist, sounded hollow and had little legato. Judith Blegen, the soprano soloist, soared sweetly.

The Met's Wagner-Strauss concert last season, rich-toned and exciting, had led one to hope for more—for fuller string sound, clearer woodwinds, more accurately tuned brass, and tidier ensemble. Excuses are easily found. An orchestra that has not played Mahler's music before—and has not played under Mahler for seventy years—can hardly be blamed for not getting it right first time. And *Lulu*, which *was* played (and conducted) with great eloquence and intensity, had no doubt hogged the rehearsal time.

Pierre Boulez's latest composition, his first for orchestra in five years (since *Rituel*), is *Notations*, a work of uncommon brilliance and attractiveness. Daniel Barenboim and the Orchestre de Paris gave the first performance, last June. Zubin Mehta and the Philharmonic introduced it to New York the day before *Lulu*. *Notations* lasted about twelve minutes in Paris and about fourteen minutes here, but it may grow longer. It has already grown from four short piano pieces—four from a set of twelve—that Boulez composed in 1945 when he was a student in Messiaen's harmony class at the Conservatoire. He plans to make orchestral versions of the eight others, too, and in June the Orchestre de Paris is due to play as many as are ready. The composer's program note is brief:

> Originally very short pieces for piano, reëxamined after more than thirty years and "developed" for orchestra—less a matter of orchestration than, as Berio would say, of "transcription." What more need be said but that the character of each piece is defined, isolated, fixed in a single expressive mode, and that the relationship between the pieces is essentially one of contrast?

The pieces that make up the piano *Notations* last, I'm told, perhaps a minute or so each, and each delineates a single idea. In the orchestral *Notations* the idea has, as it were, been passed through a many-faceted bright prism and broken into a thousand linked, lapped, sparkling fragments—a twinkling spectrum that falls across a very large orchestra whose individual players are stirred into sound when the light touches them. As now arranged, the four movements make up a small symphony. The first of them is a thing of sudden attacks, swells, and decays. The second is a scherzo. The third is a lyrical slow movement of almost Messiaenic lushness, with yearning melodies that wind their way across a richly scored background. The finale is a terse modern *Rite*—a percussion-dominated dance of bright colors which sets the pulses racing. There is no sense of miniatures inflated, bagatelles become bombast: all is delicate, precise, limpid, even when there are some ninety staves on the page and the volume is high. In his busy conducting years, Boulez set his baton—well, his hands, for he didn't use a baton—to many a modern composition in which instrumental lines proliferate until nothing is heard clearly. *Notations* is among other things a demonstration of lucid orchestration for such forces. And more than that. As soon as the piece begins, one knows one is—in a phrase from Isaiah Berlin's latest collection of essays—sailing in first-class waters. That mind has always been dazzling. The twenty-year-old student had genius. The fifty-five-year-old composer, conductor, and, at IRCAM, commissar of vanguard music is again our model of clear thinking, musical intelligence, and exhilarating aural adventure. His *Notations* cuts like a bright sword through many contemporary thickets.

The Group for Contemporary Music and Parnassus joined forces last month for the first concert of their seasons and drew a good house to the Symphony Space. George Perle's Concertino, for piano, fourteen winds, and (in just the closing pages) timpani, had its New York première, with Robert Miller as the pianist. It is a captivating piece: nine minutes of witty, elegant, distinguished music. Perle's renown as an analyst and scholar may have diverted some of the attention that should be given to his merits as a composer. Last week, WQXR broadcast his Short Symphony, recorded at its Tanglewood première this summer. The performance, by the Boston Symphony under Seiji Ozawa, was rather vague, smudged in some of its details, but good enough to reveal the arresting quality of the score. Perle's aim—put bluntly, to find ways of reconciling our traditional (tonal) ways of hearing and understanding with the richness of serial procedures—is an important one, but what matters to listeners is his achievement: the vividness of the melodic gestures, the lively rhythmic sense, the clarity and shapeliness of his discourse, and, quite simply, the charm and grace of his utterance. A vein of romance often runs through both the harmonies and the timbres.

The other new work in the Group-Parnassus concert was Anthony Korf's *A Farewell*, a longish, ambitious piece for twenty winds and percussion. The winds are treated as five separate and coherent choirs (four flutes, two oboes with two bassoons, and so on). *A Farewell* is an intelligent composition that presents some grave, beautiful sounds and thoughts. Korf has a good ear. But after a time one lost sense of direction. The program began with Varèse's noble, mysterious *Intégrales* and ended with Charles Wuorinen's Tuba Concerto (1970), scored for the uninviting ensemble of solo tuba with twelve winds and twelve drums. It includes an exciting percussion cadenza.

The Light Opera of Manhattan's Christmas production is of Victor Herbert's *Babes in Toyland*, billed as possibly the first full-scale New York revival of the piece in half a century. It is not an Urtext version. For the sake of young audiences, the book has been rewritten by William Mount-Burke, the director of LOOM, and Alice Hammerstein Mathias, daughter of a famous librettist. The wicked uncle is gone, the toys don't turn lethal, and the nursery-character extravaganzas yield to a straighter-line narrative. Some numbers have been brought in from other Herbert scores. Yet the result is delightful. Herbert was a skillful, scrupulous, and inventive composer. "Full-scale" may be rather a grand epithet for a show accompanied—albeit skillfully and sensitively—by piano and electric organ, but the piece has been put on with style and spirit, in colorful sets (Michael Sharp) and costumes (James Nadeaux). In the large cast (twelve soloists, toy corps of eighteen), Claudia O'Neill and Jeff Severson are the charming babes, and Karen Hartman is a nimble toy mouse. Moreover, it was a rare pleasure to hear opera in a theatre—the Eastside Playhouse—where without any forcing every word could be caught, and even the lightest voices told.

TRUE REFLECTION

January 5, 1981

THE PRODUCTION of the three-act *Lulu* is one of the Metropolitan Opera's high achievements. By all concerned it is executed with rare intensity, accuracy, and passion, and it is the most faithful presentation of Berg's opera I have seen. James Levine conducts it with a long, broad line, a vivid feeling for passing dramatic incident, and the ability to find and express the sense of each particular sound—rhythm, chord, or instrumental color. To this staggering great score Berg brought a mastery of just about all devices known to opera. (Well, not massed choruses, though in the ensembles of Act III his refined variant of the device is used.) He reconciled rigorous formal structures with music that moves flexibly in response to the pressures of the plot, and freely expressive lyrical melody—character or emotion manifest in the curve of a vocal line—with consistent serialism. Mr. Levine's conducting, authentically Bergian, combines the instinctive theatrical eloquence of such a *Lulu* interpreter as Karl Böhm and the intellectual precision of such a one as Pierre Boulez. Erich Kleiber used to conduct *Wozzeck* in this way, but I never heard him do so with as secure and responsive an orchestra as Mr. Levine commands. The solo violin should have had his name in the cast list; he has an important role in the drama, and Raymond Gniewek played it luminously. The contributions of the solo viola (Michael Ouzounian) and of, unidentified in the program, the saxophone (Vincent Abato) and the piano (Warren Jones) were also outstanding. On the first night, the horns pushed too hard at climaxes; by the third their melodies were warm and urgent without glare.

If *Lulu* had somehow no words, no libretto, it could still be acclaimed as a musical masterpiece—and as a musical drama with a "plot" apprehensible through the forms alone. Berg's pupil Philipp Herşcovici suggested, in a contribution to the Berg Society's seventh newsletter, that in *Lulu* the *Formgestalt* of Wagner's music-dramas (as descried by Alfred Lorenz) came to full fruition; if Schoenberg's D-minor Quartet and Chamber Symphony had already pointed a way to juxtaposition and "interpenetration" of forms, Berg's new achievement was to give such intercutting a specific function, as "the organic bearer of the dramatic events." Berg's own introductory lecture to his *Wozzeck* was concerned mainly with matters of formal organization, but at the end of it he said, in effect, "Forget all I've told you when you attend the performance." Listening now to *Wozzeck* and to the even more elaborately constructed *Lulu,* we don't forget such things, however. The form is part of the drama. When the first subject of a heroic symphony returns, or when Wagner ends *Tristan* by recapitulating a stretch of Act II, more than another hearing of a good tune is involved: a fuller sense, extending now over both passages, is revealed; a structure is completed. And as the third act of *Lulu,* withheld from the world until last year, becomes familiar, and Berg's intended restatements and new conjunctions are heard, the fuller sense of music long admired in the truncated version —the tense Sonata for Lulu and Dr. Schön, Lulu's self-revelatory Lied, Alwa's intoxicated Hymn to Lulu's beauty—is revealed at last. Some strange things have been written about the third act; for example, "Nothing particularly new is offered, nor is any new light thrown on the characters" (a critic in *Opera* after the Frankfurt production). One could as sensibly—and more accurately—observe that the Liebestod adds nothing particularly new to the rest of *Tristan.* Yet I must own that it was only after the Met production—the first, with the partial exception of Santa Fe's, in which Berg's opera has not been "recomposed" by a stage director—that I *felt* as true what George Perle's writings and my own perusal of the score had made me want to believe.

A distinction made between "musical" and stage drama recalls remarks in Tovey's essay on the overtures Beethoven wrote for *Fidelio*: "The trouble with *Leonora No. 3* is that...it is about ten times as dramatic as anything that could possibly be put on the stage"; and, more generally, "We shall never understand the aesthetics of opera (nor even of instrumental music) until we realize that dramatic expression on the stage is merely more immediately effective [than dramatic expression in instrumental music]." Herşcovici also mentions *Fidelio,* as a work that "exists entirely independent of its libretto." Both men simplify and overstate the case, in reaction to what used to be said of the *Fidelio* libretto: that it is dramaturgically clumsy, and that the subject matter —the rescue of a prisoner from a provincial jail—is too small for Beethoven's sublime music. Similar charges have been brought against *Lulu:* that the abrupt, cartoon-strip style of the Wedekind plays on which it is based, their deliberately violent mingling of farce with tragedy, jars with Berg's lovingly romantic music, and that in any case the subject matter is revolting. I confess that after the Paris and Santa Fe productions I voiced some doubts along those lines. Ernst Krenek, in the course of his careful, sensitive "Marginal Remarks re *Lulu*," in the latest Berg Society newsletter, says:

> It is astonishing that Alban Berg could live for years in intimate mental contact with this repulsive crew of shady derelicts and desperate clowns and crooks and care with unflagging dedication for their musical well-being.

But he concludes:

> In *Lulu* we are transported by the magic charm of its nostalgic beauty, full of admiration for a work so passionately conceived and lovingly completed by its maker, notwithstanding the flaws it has inevitably inherited from the unwieldy model to which it was inextricably wedded from its inception.

Krenek's observations were prompted by the Santa Fe production. Twenty-six years ago, Donald Mitchell published in *The Music Review* a perceptive appreciation of the opera "as it stands" (the score of Act III had been seen by very few people), in which he concluded reluctantly that "what goes on in the orchestra pit and on the stage fail to match," since Berg had altered the character of Wedekind's heroine without sufficiently altering Wedekind's text. Ten years later, in the same magazine, Perle came to Berg's and to the operatic Lulu's defense, partly by citing what happens in Act III, partly by claiming that Berg had by his music both more effectively conveyed the mythic aspect of Lulu (suggested in Wedekind's titles, *Earth Spirit* and *Pandora's Box*) and "realized, far more consistently and convincingly than does the spoken drama, the character of Lulu in her human incarnation." For "Berg's humanization of Lulu makes far more dramatic sense than Wedekind's ambiguous and inconsistent characterization."

Another line of defense can be added. In all the *Lulu* productions, two-act or three-act, that I've seen except the Met's (by Günther Rennert, Wieland Wagner, Patrice Chéreau) and in those I've read about (by Sarah Caldwell, Frank Corsaro, and, recently, Götz Friedrich and Joachim Herz), it *has* been true that "what goes on in the orchestra pit and on the stage fail to match." (Even in Santa Fe, in Colin Graham's generally scrupulous staging, Lulu died onstage; for Harry Kupfer, in Frankfurt, she dies in Schigolch's arms.) That's not Berg's fault. What goes on in the orchestra pit dictates in detail what should happen on the stage. Actions are "notated" almost like a musical line; arrows indicate exactly where they should occur. (Schön is required to pen a letter word by word in tempo.) Displacing the moves or inventing different actions has an effect comparable to displacing Berg's instrumental entries by a few bars or writing in new musical lines. Not all composers were also stage directors who composed the stage action as a part of their scores, but Wagner was, and Verdi was, and perhaps most of all Berg was—not all the time (Berg's production notes for *Wozzeck* indicate "scenes in which the fantasy of the producer is given much greater leeway") but often enough to make the stage directors who miss these points seem crude and unmusical.

The critic's plea for theatrical as well as musical accuracy is often misunderstood. Following a composer's wishes doesn't mean that productions all over the world will be stereotypes, any more than all performances of, say, *Otello* are musically identical because musicians try to sing and play the notes Verdi wrote. (The *Otello* production book says, in effect, "Learn the right notes and the right moves—and then the real business of interpretation can begin.") Mr. Chéreau's staging of *Lulu*, in Paris, was a striking, imaginative, effective, and very personal interpretation of the Wedekind plays; it had little to do with Berg's opera. At the Met, John Dexter's production of *Lulu*, subtle, sensitive, and unassuming, is concerned with "what's there" and with making that as vivid as possible. When it does go wrong and strike a false or feeble note, the reason is infidelity to Berg. In Lulu's Lied, Teresa Stratas, instead of "lowering the revolver," kept it pointed at Schön and sang at him menacingly; a key passage was wrongly characterized. A little earlier, Schön's Othello-like attempt to strangle Lulu was gratuitous. Miss Stratas's calm, cool demeanor in the Arietta at the end of the scene contradicted Berg's "appassionato" and "eindringlich," and the music took the wrong expression. (Julia Migenes-Johnson, who sang the second and third performances, when Miss Stratas was ill, got it right.) In the final scene, Lulu and Jack were late on their exit, still moving during the quiet bars that introduce the Nocturne, when all that should happen (but at the Met didn't) is a change from lamplight to glaring moonlight. Jack's casual murder of Geschwitz took too long. (Other, small points: Lulu's remark about liking best to walk barefoot on her rich carpets makes less sense if she is barefoot already; odd of the Schoolboy to keep his cap on in Lulu's drawing room.) One noticed these things because they were exceptions. The Lied—as one discovered from a rehearsal sequence shown in an intermission of the televised *Lulu*—was in fact directed by Miss Stratas herself, along the lines of the Paris production.

Working for once with, not against, the music, the performers became vivid. No more than any other soprano around could Miss Stratas compass the full vocal demands of the title role. (Has there been a singer since Margarethe Siems—Strauss's first Chrysothemis, Marschallin, and Zerbinetta, a Queen of the Night, Aida, and even Isolde—who commanded the necessary registers, coloratura, power, steadiness, and vocal charm?) On the first night, Miss Stratas was strident and squealy at the top, but as an actress and an artist she is electric. One believed in the fifteen-year-old girl who made men lose all self-control. As the draggled whore of Act III she seemed still beautiful: makeup and wig were realistic, but by some illusion one beheld her through Alwa's and Geschwitz's and Berg's adoring, infatuated eyes. (The elegiac Portrait Quartet of Act III, in which Alwa's Hymn to Lulu's beauty is recapitulated, was somewhat too strenuously sung.) The opera is less "about" Lulu than about the behavior and the emotions of the men—and the woman—who degrade and ruin themselves for her. By men she is, in turn, ruined and destroyed. Lulu's character, Krenek suggests, "is not so much mysterious as it seems vague." Miss Stratas was not too specific but direct, unaffected, honest—true as a bright steel mirror remains true while reflecting a diversity of images. At the second performance, Miss Migenes-Johnson stepped in as understudy, without a full rehearsal, and gave a remarkable performance. She was secure, even more accurate than Miss Stratas, and happier in the high reaches. In the middle ranges, her voice proved a little small for the monster house. Some touches of American-girl sexiness were inappropriate, but by her second performance (which I saw on television) they were already fewer.

Franz Mazura was a strong, credible Dr. Schön, a rounded and complete character. Kenneth Riegel sang Alwa's music beautifully. He acted clumsily; eyes that should have been on Lulu were ever slewing round to catch Mr. Levine's beat. Evelyn Lear, once a famous Lulu, played a dignified and moving Geschwitz, but the long high notes at the end were not pure, tender, or beautiful. Andrew Foldi's Schigolch is a virtuoso performance. Lenus Carlson (Animal Tamer and Acrobat), Hilda Harris (Schoolboy—but with a touch of tomboy sparkiness she must subdue), Frank Little (the Painter) were admirable. Nico Castel's Marquis was neither well nor tellingly sung, and so the big duet with Lulu lost the importance it should have. Otherwise, the large cast was without weakness.

The Met chooses to shield its audience—those members of it not fluent in German—from the full impact of *Lulu* by performing it in a foreign tongue. It is being needlessly protective. The subject matter is sordid; in this Pandora's box, no Hope is left behind. Berg's music, his widow said, has a beauty and a truthfulness that efface everything hateful and repulsive in the text, leaving only an unquestionably great masterpiece. It's not quite true about the effacing. But this Met production—free of gratuitous sensationalism; adopting no more of Wedekind's shock effects than Berg himself chose to adopt, but not shirking the crude or the comic episodes; drawing its drama as much from the score as from the stage; and holding all in careful balance—proves that from passion, morbid obsessions, healing and wholesome sympathy, and musical genius Berg did indeed distill a masterpiece.

HOOKING LEVIATHAN

July 27, 1981

"THE LEAR of Shakespeare cannot be acted," Charles Lamb said. "The contemptible machinery by which they mimic the storm which he goes out in, is not more inadequate to represent the horrors of the real elements, than any actor can be to represent Lear; they might more easily propose to personate the Satan of Milton upon a stage, or one of

Michael Angelo's terrible figures." A. C. Bradley, calling the play Shakespeare's greatest achievement and grouping it with *Prometheus Bound, The Divine Comedy,* and "even with the greatest symphonies of Beethoven and the statues in the Medici Chapel," also deemed it a "defective drama" and "too huge for the stage." What *could* be acted was Nahum Tate's Lear. In 1681, in Lamb's vivid phrase, Tate "put his hook in the nostrils of this Leviathan, for Garrick and his followers, the show-men of the scene, to draw the mighty beast about more easily." He banished the Fool, devised a romance between Cordelia and Edgar, and provided a happy ending; and for a century and a half Tate's Lear trod the stage. Betterton, Garrick, Kemble played him. So did Kean, although in 1823 he restored a tragic close. Then, in 1838, Macready returned to Shakespeare. On June 18, 1847, as he noted in his diary, he "acted King Lear with much care and power, and was received by a most kind and sympathetic and enthusiastic audience." Verdi, who was in London, may well have been one of that audience. Jenny Lind, the prima donna of his forthcoming *I masnadieri,* certainly was, for Macready recorded the excitement her presence aroused. Four days earlier, Verdi had probably seen Macready act Macbeth "in very ablest manner"; he said later he had seen *Macbeth* in London, and the dates fit. He had just composed his own *Macbeth* and in 1845 had planned a *Lear* opera for London. Macready had hesitated to restore the Fool, despairing of an actor to impersonate "the sort of fragile, hectic, beautiful-faced, half-idiot-looking boy that he should be," but had then found his performer in Priscilla Horton (better known to music history as Mrs. German Reed). Verdi, who considered making a *Lear* opera on and off from 1843 to 1865—and very much on between 1850 and 1857—after his London visit cast the Fool as a woman.

What cannot meetly be said may sometimes effectively be sung. Operatic versions of *Lear,* written and unwritten, add a chapter to the long stage history of the play. Many composers have dreamed of a *Lear* opera: notably Verdi and Benjamin Britten, who hoped to use Peter Pears as the Fool and Dietrich Fischer-Dieskau in the title role. Only lesser men have got their hooks in firmly enough to land a finished score, and only one of their scores, Aribert Reimann's, which had its première in Munich three years ago and its American première in San Francisco last month, has made any mark. A glance at other, forgotten operatic *Lears*—there are at least five—reveals an interesting variety of grappling techniques.

The *Re Lear* of Antonio Cagnoni, who was fifteen years younger than Verdi, remained unperformed but was published. Echoes of Tate sound on. Act II includes a love duet for Cordelia and Edgar. Edgar's chief aria begins "O celeste Cordelia," to a stepwise ascent, and includes other echoes of an aria that the same librettist, Antonio Ghislanzoni, had written for Verdi's Radamès. Regan launches a brindisi and has a mad scene in which she sees spectres of Gloster and her father. The Fool is a soprano. Alberto Ghislanzoni's *Lear,* to his own text, appeared in Rome in 1937. I have seen only the libretto, a skillful piece of condensation but conventionally "operatic." Over the sleeping Lear, Cordelia sings, to her own harp accompaniment, "un'antica e dolce canzone de la terra celtica." The Fool is a tenor. Two years later, an odder *Re Lear*, Vito Frazzi's, appeared in Florence. The librettist, Giovanni Papini, declares in a preface that he must have been mad to lend his name to that "indispensable, indefensible" operatic adjunct called a libretto, madder to lay hands on Shakespeare, and maddest to mutilate the play by suppressing Cordelia. Only friendship for Frazzi, he says, led him to commit such a crime. All that remains of Cordelia is a voice from on high joining Lear's at the close. The division-of-the-kingdom scene has gone: Kent tells Edgar about it in an opening conversation. The Fool is a soprano.

Alberto Ghislanzoni's and Frazzi's operas were made in the knowledge of Verdi's struggles with *Lear*, after several of his many letters on the subject had been published. These letters amount to a correspondence course in opera-making. In his adventurous, unconventional *Macbeth* Verdi wrote, if not the first opera with a plot drawn from Shakespeare, the first that can in any significant sense be called Shakespearean. In 1850, he announced his intention of treating all Shakespeare's principal plays, and that year he drew up a very workable four-act synopsis of a *King Lear* opera. Sending it to Salvatore Cammarano, he said that although *Lear* might seem at first sight too vast and complicated for operatic treatment, the difficulties were not insuperable provided that old formulas were abandoned and it was "treated in a new, vast way, without respecting the conventions." Cammarano, a master librettist, died before much work had been done. Verdi turned next to the inexperienced Antonio Somma, and by 1856 a libretto was complete. I have been reading it (there is a microfilm in the American Institute for Verdi Studies, in New York), and now it seems plain that one reason Verdi did not compose his *Lear* is that he had saddled himself with a dreadful libretto, one he could not believe in. Reasons that he gave at various times, to various people, were that the available casts were inadequate, that Meyerbeerian spectacle was lacking (that was to the director of the Paris Opera), that the storm terrified him, and that the Fool eluded him.

Verdi's thinking about Shakespeare was formed first by his energetic response to the poet "whom I have had in my hands since earliest youth, and whom I read and reread constantly." It was colored by A. W. Schlegel's influential *Lectures on Dramatic Art and Literature*, many pages of which are appended to the translation of Shakespeare, Carlo Rusconi's, that Verdi used. (It still stands by his bed in Sant'Agata.) Schlegel's *Lear* commentary dwells on the five characters—Lear, Cordelia, Edmund, Edgar, the Fool—whom Verdi designated to both Cammarano and Somma as his five principals. Schlegel also claims that the combination and interweaving of two parallel but contrasting plots "constitutes the sublime beauty of the work." That must have given

Verdi pause when he reflected on Somma's treatment. For Somma, exhorted by the composer to be more concise, hit at last on the desperate expedient of removing the subplot: his final version has no Edgar, no Gloster. Verdi approved at first, calling the excision "a hundred-per-cent gain," but wondered how the end could be effected without Edgar's challenge and duel. To retain a quartet on the heath, an Old Herdsman was introduced, and "Blow, winds" became a quartet for Lear, Kent, the Fool, and this Herdsman. A multiple chorus of courtiers, ladies, knights, and pages, singing the praises of "ricca Albion" and its new rulers, opens the next scene; a love duet for Regan and Edmund closes it. More chorus work appears at the "tribunal" (an episode that Verdi deemed "very original, very moving"); it takes place with the participation of "una moltitudine di pastori, giovani, vecchi e fanciulli colle lore donne." The composer was curiously polite to Somma about his work, but his final letter on the subject, in 1856, expresses a certain (well-justified) dissatisfaction. Nine years later, when *Lear* was mooted for Paris, he said that Shakespeare would have to be followed closely; any tampering destroyed the originality and character that made his work so powerful.

The libretto of Reimann's *Lear*, as of his previous opera, *Melusine*, is by Claus H. Henneberg. It is based on the German translation of Johann Joachim Eschenburg (1777), which Henneberg describes as "harder, clearer, more theatrical"—than what, he does not say; presumably the Schlegel verse translation. (Beethoven—according to Anton Schindler—also preferred Eschenburg's Shakespeare to Schlegel's, finding the latter "stiff, forced, and at times too far from the original.") Henneberg's libretto is largely a straight and not unskillful abridgment, but there are odd additions. One is crucial: the first presentation of the protagonist. Verdi, concerned lest Lear's motive for disinheriting Cordelia seem "childish, perhaps even absurd in our day," sketched a version of Shakespeare's opening scene in which Gloster refers to the aging King's whims and quick petulance, but Somma persuaded him out of it. Others, too, have sought to diminish Lear's initial magnificence and "rationalize" his conduct. In 1955, John Gielgud played him as a dodderer from the start. Henneberg's first stage direction says, "At times it seems that Lear is almost overcome by sleep, and the procession falters"; and the King's first speech acquires the invented aside "Ah, ah, this longing for sleep." From this line—according to an essay by Reimann that accompanies a Deutsche Grammophon recording of his *Lear*—"the path trod by [Lear's] psyche begins." We see a senile, crumbling wreck, not Shakespeare's great image of authority. The opera, it seems, has missed the point of the play.

There are two acts, the first about eighty-six minutes long, the second about an hour, with the division falling after Shakespeare's Act III, Scene 6, as Lear is led to Dover. At that point, not only the Fool but also the loyal Kent disappears. (Presumably, Shakespeare used one actor to double Cordelia and the Fool. His play seems to be constructed that way. The Fool keeps reminding us of Cordelia during her long absence, from I.1 to IV.4. The concinnate wordplay of Lear's "And my poor fool is hang'd"—referring to Cordelia—resists translation into either German or Italian.) To provide chorus work, Gloster is accompanied by a search party and, earlier, Henneberg adopts Goneril's (and Peter Brook's) view of Lear's knights, giving them a rowdy drinking song. They are not "men of choice and rarest parts, That all particulars of duty know." As if Shakespeare's horrors were insufficient, he requires Regan herself to pluck out Gloster's second eye. Much, much is cut, but, surprisingly, six lines of the Fool's "Merlin's prophecy" speech, commonly regarded as an interpolation, are retained.

It became plain that Britten, like Verdi before him, would not compose a *Lear* opera; Fischer-Dieskau, in 1968, asked Reimann to write one for him instead. The two had given recitals together, and in 1960 Reimann had composed two works for Fischer-Dieskau, *Fünf Gedichte von Paul Celan* and *Ein Totentanz. Zyklus* followed in 1971, and *Wolkenloses Christfest* in 1973. Meanwhile, as Reimann's essay reveals, he hesitated about *Lear* for four years, planned and pondered for four more, and composed most of the opera in 1976–77. It appeared at the 1978 Munich Festival with the triple peals of publicity insured by a Fischer-Dieskau "creation," a new production by Jean-Pierre Ponnelle, and a big opera published by the house of Schott. I read the reviews and was not tempted to go. I heard the recording and found disappointingly little music in the piece. Having now seen and heard it, in San Francisco, I think no better of it. When *Lear* was announced as the new production of the San Francisco Opera's summer season, the critic of the San Francisco *Chronicle,* Robert Commanday, deplored the choice, and he was right. *Lear* has achieved a certain modish réclame, but there are many contemporary operas with a stronger claim to be heard.

Reimann is, at least, an efficient composer. Everything is carefully thought out. The three sisters are three contrasted sopranos: Cordelia lyric, Goneril dramatic, Regan dramatic-coloratura. Lear is a heroic baritone. Edmund is a robust tenor, Edgar a lyric tenor with a coloratura extension up to high F to use in his Poor Tom impersonation. Kent is a tenor, Gloster a bass-baritone. The Fool, designated a speaking role, is asked occasionally to pitch rather than speak his songs. The good characters, Cordelia and Edgar, share a lyrical note-row moving by small steps. The bad characters, Goneril, Regan, and Edmund, sing various kinds of vigorous, jagged music. Much of the time, Lear himself merely recites in unmeasured, largely monotone chant. A big orchestra makes a great deal of noise, often in long-sustained, impenetrably dense cluster chords. By way of contrast, there are quiet, gentle episodes: as Edgar assumes the guise of Poor Tom, motifs drawn from his row steal out on solo flutes (bass rising through alto to the regular instrument, then down again) against a soft string blur; Edgar continues the strain with florid wordless melisma high above the staff (suggested, Reimann says, by his hearing a muezzin in Jerusalem); Cordelia's return is signalled by a sweet, slow triple canon on her row, from muted violins; a parallel passage—two solo violins in high, melodious canon—accompanies her principal aria. All this is intelligently planned and deftly executed. One can read Reimann's composition diary—his account, say, of a vision of the storm music which came to him one night in 1977—and then follow the working out of his notions in the score, and admire his intelligence, seriousness, industry, and dexterity. But those are not virtues enough to insure a powerful music drama. For all the elaborate artifice, the music itself is commonplace—unworthy of a *King Lear*.

The opera might make a slightly more favorable impression in another production. Mr. Ponnelle is not a man to give first place to a composer, and this show, a reworking of the Munich première for the San Francisco stage, is more "Ponnelle's *Lear*" than Reimann's—or Shakespeare's. (The season also included a vulgar travesty of Verdi's *Rigoletto* devised by Mr. Ponnelle—a demonstration that even *that* opera is not director-proof but can be unmoving when every effect intended by the composer is countermanded.) Mr. Ponnelle's *Lear* staging is striking but drab, on a single set—a realistic heath of reeds and rocks laid out on a platform within a stage house stripped bare to its outer walls. Court and palaces are throneless. Courtiers pick their way through bushes and boulders. There is much to be said for playing Shakespeare's *Lear* on a bare stage and letting the poetry create the pictures, less for mounting an operatic *Lear* planned in distinct scenes (one of them multiple), with curtain rises and curtain falls indicated, in a set that makes a specific locative statement modified only by the floor's ability to move up and down in various patterns. The storm, however, was effectively brought on by clusters of bare horizontal rods lowered from the flies: economical but not contemptible machinery. Reimann wrote instrumental interludes between his scenes; Ponnelle in his unit set fills them with pantomime, some of it gross. The lyrical music of Cordelia's return here accompanies Edmund's tupping of Goneril against the proscenium arch. The bad characters are rendered as caricatures: Goneril and Regan drop into the comedy routines of the Ugly Sisters in a crude *Cinderella* pantomime; Edmund gesticulates and grimaces as if parodying a Kabuki actor. The Fool is a wizened, croaking mini-Lear draggling on in his royal crown and mantle after Lear has been divested of his. It amounts to a comic-strip account of the play enacted against sound effects.

In San Francisco, the opera was done in English—a "back-translation" into pidgin Shakespeare by Desmond Clayton. As a translator of four Shakespeare operas, I sympathize with anyone who must choose between misquoting very famous lines and mismatching the music. But where Reimann writes unmeasured monotone declamation, without rhythmic or melodic significance, Mr. Clayton's attempts to match the syllable count of the German seem perverse. The storm monologue went thus: "Blow, winds, blow!" Orchestral racket. "Crack your cheeks, winds!" Orchestral racket. "Rage and blow!" Orchestral racket. And so on. There was perhaps some idea of avoiding archaisms. Gloster's "But have I fall'n or no?" became "Did I then really fall, or not?" Yet "Off, off, you lendings!" remained. "Regan, don't do that!" was blunt for Lear's reproachful "O Regan! will you take her by the hand?"

In a Ponnelle production, individual singers are apt to count for little, but two of those in the San Francisco *Lear* made their mark. Helga Dernesch, as Goneril, was trenchant—arresting in every gesture, powerful and precise in all she sang. And David Knutson's Edgar —his Poor Tom a blend of Peter Quint, the Hindu Merchant in *Sadko*, and the Simpleton in *Boris*—spun limpid, tender vocalises in touching tones where tenor flowed into countertenor without audible break. The voice was small for Edgar's challenge. Edgar is a protean role. In the straight theatre, it is hard enough to find a virtuoso to compass the credulous youth, the feigned madman, and the hero who at the end of the play agrees to rule the realm; on the lyric stage, harder still. Thomas Stewart, an artist of force and feeling, took the title role. Reimann's score and Mr. Ponnelle's production do not help a Lear, as Verdi's scores do a Macbeth or an Othello, toward an arresting interpretation; rather, they create awkwardnesses of diction, timing, and characterization. Mr. Stewart strove to overcome them. The other principals were Emily Rawlins (Cordelia), Rita Shane (Regan), Jacque Trussel (Edmund), William Lewis (Kent), Robert Lloyd (the Fool), and Chester Ludgin (Gloster). All had worked hard. Gerd Albrecht conducted.

PACIFIC SONG

August 3, 1981

WHEN THE San Francisco Symphony moved to its new home, Davies Hall, across the street from the Opera House, and the San Francisco Opera, which had hitherto drawn on Symphony players, engaged its own stable orchestra, both companies were able to give longer and overlapping seasons. This summer, while the Symphony held a Beethoven Festival in Davies Hall, the Opera embarked on a summer season, its first ever. Twenty-eight performances were given, of five operas: *Lear, Don Giovanni, Die Meistersinger, Rigoletto*, and *L'incoronazione di Poppea*. Earlier, Spring Opera Theater, or SPOT, a cadet division of the company, played a season of five operas, in English, and in the smaller Curran Theater: *Figaro, The Grand-Duchess of Gerolstein*, Gounod's *Romeo and Juliet*, and, in a double bill, Monteverdi's *Il ballo delle ingrate* and John Eaton's *The Cry of Clytaemnestra*.

San Francisco lies in an area well stocked with Baroque performers. Trained continuo players abound. The numerous campuses sound with early music. An informed public exists. But *Poppea* and *Il ballo* were entrusted to house conductors, David Agler and Willie Anthony Waters, who are not Monteverdi stylists but beat time through what should be freely declaimed. Instead of harnessing special scholarly skills to opera-house routine—to the benefit of both—the company relied on the latter, with results that did small service to Monteverdi. Mr. Agler and his cast were saddled with Raymond Leppard's elaboration of *Poppea*, a period piece (made in 1962, for Glyndebourne) that sounds expressive when Mr. Leppard himself is in charge but in other hands inhibits spontaneity. Tatiana Troyanos sang the heroine's music in a voice afflicted by a slow, heavy vibrato. The Nero, Eric Tappy, perhaps confused by differences from the Harnoncourt edition he has lately been singing, resorted often to unpitched shouting. Wolfgang Brendel, the Otho, had the best voice in the cast, but he is a baritone; Otho's music, composed at mezzo pitch, suffers most grievously of all from Mr. Leppard's transpositions. Julien Robbins delivered the Captain's few lines admirably. For *Il ballo*, Denis Stevens's straightforward and sensible edition was employed. The players were onstage, but only the harpsichordist-conductor took advantage of the fact to watch and follow the singers they accompanied. The phrasing was absurdly square. The whole was close to parody.

Don Giovanni was played in an open set, by Toni Businger, of tall golden lattices against a black ground. Costumes were also black and gold, Ottavio's gray duds excepted. It looked pretty but suggested ballet décor and allowed the tensions of Mozart's drama to leak out through the wings. Giovanni and Leporello were two veterans, Cesare Siepi and Giuseppe Taddei. The New Grove writes of their careers in the past tense, but there they both were, giving their familiar, accomplished performances and still far from voiceless. The women were young. Carol Vaness is a promising Anna; her words and her tone both need bringing forward for the promise to be realized. Lella Cuberli was an accomplished Elvira, accurate and steady. Pamela South's Zerlina was brightly American. Gösta Winbergh's Ottavio was stylishly sung; he is among the best Mozart tenors around now. August Everding, the director, had not formed these diverse elements into any dramatic whole. I've never known a *Don Giovanni* so little gripping. The new young Hungarian conductor Ádám Fischer left an odd impression—as if he had some ideas about the opera deep inside him but were unwilling to communicate them to cast or orchestra. The production of *Figaro*, by Virginia Davis Irwin, exemplified modish practices noted by Desmond Shawe-Taylor in a review of Covent Garden's new *Don Giovanni*: "to overdo everything, to invent a vast amount of unnecessary and frequently harmful stage activity, and to override the intentions and scorn the dramatic skills of librettist and composer." A Laurel and Hardy pair of comic servants, bringing on a bed, held the limelight during Susanna and Figaro's first duet and again, up on a ladder and adjusting chandeliers, during the Count's scena at the start of Act III. Mr. Agler conducted with a cool elegance so unfeeling, so unresponsive to the moves of Mozart's score that one began to wonder how musical he was.

Rigoletto, the revival of a Jean-Pierre Ponnelle production, of 1973, was worse. It became "Rigoletto's Dream"—perhaps the whole opera, for during the prelude the jester stared out into space; perhaps just what happened after the quartet. Rigoletto was onstage for Gilda's murder. During the tender final duet, he resumed his initial pose, not looking at or touching his daughter. (She had to open her own sack.) Instead of hearing the live Duke's voice ring out—a chilling moment in every other production—he saw the Duke and Gilda waltzing together. Earlier, the courtiers were a grimacing, putty-nosed, lipsticked crew of caricatures, who bounced up and down on their toes in time to "Questa o quella." Sparafucile was a second hunchback—"Pari siamo" indeed! Act II was dominated by a large curtained bed, with Gilda and the Duke on it while Rigoletto sang "Cortigiani." At his "Miei signori, perdono, pietate...tutto al mondo ell'è per me," the courtiers shook with laughter. Garbis Boyagian was a lightweight Rigoletto, Patricia Wise a pallid Gilda, and Peter Dvorský a crude Duke. But they were permitted no chance to be moving. From the director who also gave us the *Dutchman* as "The Steersman's Dream," what next? *Tosca* as the Sacristan's dream? *Norma* as Clotilde's?

The Grand-Duchess was plebeian rather than elegant, broad rather than witty in its humors, and not very pretty to look at, but Randall Behr conducted with spirit and David Eisler was a clean, lively Fritz. In the title role, Sheila Smith lacked presence; she was no Hortense Schneider—or Régine Crespin. I never hear *Romeo* without thinking what an excellent piece it is—tender melodies, exquisite scoring, refined craftsmanship in all its workings. Soon, all but general impressions (and some numbers already familiar from famous recordings) fade; detailed admiration wakes anew at the next encounter. SPOT's version of the five-act *grand opéra* was scaled down: no magnificent décors, sumptuous ballet, or massed choruses. The Romeo, William Pell, was handsome but dull. The Juliet, Deborah Longwith, phrased attractively. Mark Flint conducted ably. Something came through. It did, too, in the even smaller presentation (which I saw in a far larger theatre, Sacramento's Community Theater) toured by Western Opera Theater, or WOT. This is another cadet branch of Kurt Herbert Adler's operatic family, and this year it made an extensive tour, taking *Romeo* and *L'elisir d'amore* through sixteen Western and Midwestern states. Roughly speaking, WOT's young principals sing subaltern roles for SPOT, and SPOT principals take subaltern roles in the international seasons. Yet another cadet branch, Brown Bag Opera, in May gave eight performances of Henry Mollicone's latest "portable" opera, *Emperor Norton*, for four singers and three players.

There is concern because Mr. Adler's successor, Terry McEwen (he takes over next year), has wiped out SPOT, at least for a year. It has been going for twenty years. In 1961, six operas were each given a single performance in the big house (Marilyn Horne and James King sang in *Carmen*). Over the years, the pattern shifted to a repertory season of several operas in a smaller theatre. One of them was usually contemporary *(Death in Venice*, Thea Musgrave's *Mary, Queen of Scots*, operas by Carlisle Floyd, Douglas Moore, Robert Ward, Conrad Susa), one an eighteenth-century revival *(Clemenza di Tito, Giulio Cesare)*, one a rarish later work *(La rondine, Les Pêcheurs de perles)*. It is a good formula, which enlarges the Bay repertory, gives Americans a chance to enjoy opera as Europeans enjoy it, in a house of less than monster size, and brings forward new singers: Norman Treigle, Frederica von Stade, Brent Ellis, Maria Ewing, Carol Vaness are names in the SPOT annals. Summer opera for 1982 is, however, assured: *Giulio Cesare*, in English, and *The Rake's Progress* are among the works announced. There is talk for the future—nothing definite so far—of collaboration with the Symphony in a Mozart summer festival (making San Francisco a "Salzburg West") and of a new *Ring* ("Seattle South"?). [*The San Francisco* Ring *did come about:* Das Rheingold *and* Die Walküre *in 1983* (see page 458), Siegfried *in 1984, and three full cycles in 1985.*]

Die Meistersinger was the hit of the summer season. Mr. Adler conducted it himself, with a breadth, a warmth, a rightness to show that Reginald Goodall is not the only conductor left who remembers how moving Wagner can be when he is handled with love and lyricism. Sachs was Karl Ridderbusch, expert in the role. In personality, he may not seem as noble, lovable, and poetic as Hans Hotter or Paul Schöffler was, but he sings the notes so steadily and so surely that Wagner does most of the rest. Eva was Hannelore Bode, a peaky, glassy vocalist but a captivating interpreter and actress. Walther was William Johns; his looks and acting were awful, but he sang the role amply and lyrically. A first-rate Beckmesser, Gottfried Hornik, rightly strove to sing his serenade and prize song as beautifully as Beckmesser could, and left it to Wagner to make the jokes. His characterization was complete; the Act III exchanges with Sachs were oddly affecting. Roberto Oswald's décor is a shade flimsy and fancy but not perverse. Peter Brenner's staging encouraged overreaction (the apprentices needed a stiff dose of bromide) but was not eccentric. Much was wrong. But then much is wrong with most *Meistersinger*s. There was enough right in this one to make it deeply moving—indeed, overwhelming. There were cuts, including some of David's recital of modes and verses of Beckmesser's serenade, of the cobbler's song, and of the prize-song composition. But the final scene was complete, for once. And it was joy to be rapt again in the kind of *Meistersinger*, wonderful even though imperfect, that I knew in Bayreuth, Munich, and London. Neither New York house in the last decade has come so close to the heart of the great opera.

And so to modern times. I wrote about *Lear* last week and about

Clytaemnestra after its Bloomington première, last year. Four of the Bloomington principals—notably Nelda Nelson in the title role and Timothy Noble as Agamemnon—came to San Francisco, but the performance, brilliantly conducted by Richard Bradshaw, was quite different: warmer, freer, more lyrical, more passionate. The merits of Eaton's opera seem to increase on every hearing. Whereas *Lear* sounded contrived, uninspired, noisy, hollow, *Clytaemnestra* is filled with richly expressive, eloquent music.

I spent the first half of this year in Berkeley. All around, there was much music worth hearing, and next week I hope to write about some of what happened in concert halls. Here is a brief report on some of the operatic activity outside San Francisco itself. On the Berkeley campus, Alan Curtis led the American première of Stefano Landi's *Sant'Alessio,* with Judith Nelson in the title role. Semistaged, on the platform of Hertz Hall, it served as a tryout for the full production that Mr. Curtis has now conducted in Rome. This 1631 opera, with a libretto by the future Clement IX, taxes a modern listener's sympathies, for the saint's virtue consists in concealing his identity from wife, mother, father, and friends. On his wedding night, he fled the family palace; now he lives, unrecognized, as a beggar beneath its staircase. The music is often moving, especially in keen plaints that one humane word from Alexius could have ended.

On the Davis campus, it was interesting to see a *Freischütz* staged in décor based on nineteenth-century designs and techniques: painted flats, mechanical special effects, no follow spots. Very romantic it looked. The costumes resembled those of the 1821 première, corrected in accord with Weber's own objections to some aspects of them. Singing, acting, and orchestral playing were poor, but the enterprise pointed a way toward making the opera seem less silly than on the modern stage it often does. A Wolf's Glen true to the libretto—complete with toy owl, eyes agleam and wings flapping—was oddly exciting.

On the Mills campus, Robert Ashley's *Perfect Lives (Private Parts),* put on in the Pompidou Center, in Paris, last year, was given. Subtitled "An Opera in Seven Episodes," it apparently deals with the drabness of life in the Midwest. Mr. Ashley himself stood centerstage, declaiming interminable monologues into a microphone; his words were inaudible. On his left, "Blue" Gene Tyranny, in a spangled blue outfit, bashed out nonstop—well, something a bit harder than cocktail-lounge music, but along those lines. On the right, a young woman and man sometimes added commentary. A rhythm accompaniment thundered from loudspeakers, while a few small television screens showed Midwest landscapes and closeups of Mr. Tyranny's be-ringed and bleeding hands. The sound was amplified to a level that I feared might prove permanently deafening, and after three long, long episodes I fled.

The Berkeley Symphony gave a concert performance of Janáček's

Mr. Brouček's Adventures, in a Berkeley church—another American première. It was a bit rough and unready, and Kent Nagano, a conductor too cool and unromantic for my taste, had his work cut out keeping things more or less together. Quade Winter sang agreeably in the title role. There was a deft new English translation, by Ross Helper.

An excursion northward led to the Seattle Opera's new *Tristan* and another evening of rapt enjoyment. As with the San Francisco *Meistersinger,* although much was wrong, enough was right to inspire surrender to the work. Above all, Johanna Meier (who is now singing Isolde in Bayreuth) was in radiant, soaring, unforced, and beautiful voice. Edward Sooter, the Tristan, was reliable but unromantic. Richard Clark, the Kurwenal, is someone to note; his baritone is exciting in timbre. Siegwulf Turek's décor, achieved largely by light, produced beautiful effects of sea and sky. Lincoln Clark's staging had its awkward moments—Isolde sat on the deck; Tristan, after declaring that it would be unsafe for him to leave the helm, put the vessel on autopilot; in Act II, lovemaking on bare boards looked more uncomfortable than rapturous—but basically things were more or less all right. Henry Holt's conducting was both urgent and supple, and after six years of *Ring*s the Seattle players had become fine Wagnerians.

In the south, San Diego's Verdi Festival offered Verdi's second and third operas: *Un giorno di regno,* the composer's first and worst failure, withdrawn from the Scala stage after a single performance; and *Nabucco,* his first and in some ways greatest triumph, performed at La Scala more often in a single season than any other work in its two-century history. *Un giorno* was done in my English translation, and so I'll say no more about it. And I'll say little about *Nabucco,* since the production, differently cast, comes to the City Opera next month. Cristina Deutekom can flash out exciting notes in cabalettas, but in cantabile her tones were unsteady, and her impersonation of the spirited, spitfire heroine was tame. Kari Nurmela's baritone was sonorous, monochrome, strongly projected, and admirably steady—so steady that some out-of-tune singing became painful. Maurizio Arena's conducting did not encourage the free, abundant rubato and portamento by which singers of or close to Verdi's own day once made his music expressive.

BAY LAURELS

August 10, 1981

AROUND San Francisco Bay, composers are clustered, it seems, more densely than anywhere else in the country but New York. And their works are played. During six months I spent in Berkeley, I could probably have heard new music every night—given nothing else to do, 'satiable curtiosity, and readiness to motor often to Mills, Stanford, and points between or to cross the bridge to the city. Or so it seemed, and an occasional check on a week's programs confirmed it. There were two festivals: a weekend entitled New Sounds San Jose, at which three of four concerts were devoted to "the Bay Area scene," and a wider-ranging week in San Francisco, New Music America 81, with up to eight events a day. Those were special. What impressed me still more was the large part contemporary music plays in what might be called everyday musical life. The San Francisco Opera mounted John Eaton's *Cry of Clytaemnestra* and Aribert Reimann's *Lear*. The San Francisco Symphony gave the American premières of Tōru Takemitsu's *Far Calls. Coming, Far!* and Bruno Maderna's Oboe Concerto No. 3; the local première of Witold Lutoslawski's Variations on a Theme of Paganini; and the first performance of John Adams's *Harmonium*. (Edo de Waart, the Symphony's conductor, describes his commitment to contemporary music as "gigantic"; I arrived in California too late for the Symphony's all-modern concert series, in the Galleria, and its Davies Hall performances of Richard Felciano's *Orchestra* and Otto Ketting's First Symphony.) The Oakland Symphony season included Lou Harrison's Concerto for Violin and Percussion, Adams's *Common Tones in Simple Time,* and (a commission) Olly Wilson's *Trilogy.* The Berkeley Symphony played Oliver Messiaen's *Transfiguration;* Messiaen came over to give his blessing, and Yvonne Loriod to play the piano part. The Boston Symphony, on a visit, played Peter Maxwell Davies's Second Symphony.

Berkeley-based, I did not even have to leave the campus to hear some of these: the San Francisco and Oakland orchestras brought them to the big university auditorium. To a smaller university auditorium, Hertz Hall, the Audubon Quartet, the pianist Robert Miller, the duo pianists Karl and Margaret Kohn, the baritone William Parker, and the Berkeley Contemporary Chamber Players brought other new music. The University Chorus sang David Ellis's *Sequentia IV*; the University Symphony played Seymour Shifrin's Three Pieces for Orchestra. There was plentiful new music from student ensembles. Mills and Stanford were also busy. At Mills, for example, the soprano Jane Manning, muse of many British composers, gave her first American recital, introducing, amid Warlock, Boulez, and Berio, works written for her by Richard Rodney Bennett, Anthony Payne, and Judith Weir (*King Harald's Saga*, a three-act opera, lasting less than ten minutes, in which, unaccompanied, she plays eight characters and the chorus). Other ensembles—the San Francisco Contemporary Music Players, the Arch Ensemble, the New Music Ensemble—have regular series. Many of the concerts are broadcast.

A long string of one-sentence, two-epithet reviews would make dull reading, and not everything I heard was worth writing about. Let me record the general impression of vitality and of new music's looming larger, relatively, than it does in New York. We probably have no less of it here, but round the Bay they do not submerge it in quite so full a flood of standard repertory and standard big-name performers. There must be various, mutually supporting reasons for the happy state. The composer Charles Boone, introducing the San Jose festival, suggested as one that the heritage of two great teachers, Sessions at Berkeley and Milhaud at Mills, was still bearing fruit. The concentration of universities certainly plays its part, packing the area with composers, performers, and educated listeners. (At the San Jose festival, composers from six Bay campuses and from the San Francisco Conservatory were heard.) Further, there is, Boone said, no "established hierarchy" into which new works must fit; indeed, old-style-Princetonian orthodoxy from Berkeley, disciplined electronics from Stanford's Center for Computer Research in Music and Acoustics, undisciplined and messy neo-expressionism ground out in the Mills of today, and romantic minimalism from the Conservatory were on display cheek-by-jowl. One expects to hear a composer's music played on the campus where he teaches; here off-campus performances were also common. To mention only composers on the Berkeley faculty: I heard music by Andrew Imbrie in San Francisco, and by Felciano, Wilson, and Robert Stine in San Jose. Works by Edwin Dugger and Walter Winslow were brought back to Berkeley by visiting artists. The daily papers and the weeklies kept this activity before the public, for every newspaper—there are many of them around the Bay—seems to employ a team of busy critics, and editors must believe that modern music matters. Alfred Frankenstein, the music critic of the *San Francisco Chronicle* from 1934 to 1965, helped to plant the belief; his last piece of writing before he died, in June, was a letter to his old paper exhorting the Symphony to make fuller use of local performers and composers.

What stood out? Or, rather, what stands out in memory now? I was in California to talk and teach, not to review, and kept no mental or pencilled notes to enlarge on soon after the event. In an odd way, the impressions that remain with me are not always of what seemed most important or enjoyable at the time. Here is a short list: the elegant workmanship of two trios, Frank Larocca's for violin, viola, and cello and Wilson's for violin, cello, and piano; the refined strength of Imbrie's new cycle, *Roethke Songs,* sung by Nina Hanson (as I listened, I thought the vocal line angular, but I reread the poems now and find that it etched poetic images); the sound of Heinz Holliger's oboe winding and winging through Maderna's rhapsodic, loose-knit concerto; the puzzling but arresting inventions in two precursors—one a dramatic scene and one a piano suite—of the opera after Marcel Duchamp's *La Mariée mise à nu par ses célibataires, même* that Charles Shere has been working on for years; the romance of Michael McNabb's electronic *Dreamsong,* already admired at its New York performance two years ago; the swift, delicate traceries of Felciano's *from and to, with,* for violin and piano (the rich, beautiful ideas of his choral piece *The Captives,* which I heard on tape, moved me still more); and three compositions by Adams, who teaches at the San Francisco Conservatory, directs its New Music Ensemble, and is contemporary-music adviser to the Symphony.

One of the Adams pieces, *Phrygian Gates*, for piano, was already familiar. (It was played in New York in 1979, and is now recorded, along with his *Shaker Loops*, by 1750 Arch Records, a Berkeley label.) *Common Tones in Simple Time* (1979), taken up by the Oakland Symphony, is a fresh, very pretty, shimmering piece, aptly described by its composer as "a pastoral with a pulse." With his latest and largest work, *Harmonium*, the San Francisco Symphony commission, Adams takes a big step forward. He has said, "Minimalism really can be a bore—you get those Great Prairies of non-event—but that highly polished, perfectly resonant sound is wonderful." In the earlier, attractive, and strongly fashioned pieces, he could be said to be working out and acquiring mastery of a musical language frankly, avowedly, derived from the sounds and moto-perpetuo patterns of Steve Reich but more copious in thematic incident, swifter in color shifts, and more varied in moods. A program note tells of his citing Charles Rosen's observation that Schoenberg created a "universe coherent and rich enough to offer possibilities beyond the development of an individual manner" and of his suggesting that he stands to Reich rather as the other members of the Second Viennese School did to their founder. In *Harmonium* (the title refers to a concord of sounds, not a cottage organ), Adams uses his flexible new language to compose large-scale settings of Donne's "Negative Love" and Emily Dickinson's "Because I could not stop for Death" and "Wild Nights." His "highly polished, perfectly resonant sound" *is* wonderful. So is the large, long control of harmonic tension and resolution. *Harmonium*, for large choir and orchestra, lasts thirty-four minutes. The orchestra should record it. [*The orchestra did record it, on ECM/Warner.*]

Not all the Bay music I heard was modern. At midnight on Holy Saturday, in the little St. Joseph of Arimathea Chapel of Berkeley, where ancient rites are revived, I attended the Paschal Vigil Mass, one of the great dramatic services of Christendom—a symbolic enactment of death conquered by the Resurrection, a literal enactment of darkness yielding to light, and fast to feast. The opera critic within me murmured that the production and the lighting effects needed more rehearsal and that some of the words (the intercession of saints seldom called upon by Anglicans—Agatha, Anastasia—is invoked) should have been more fervently uttered. But the chant, chanted here in English translation by a small (mixed) choir directed by Richard Crocker, was sensitively shaped. Plainchant, the foundation of all Western music, should be heard in a liturgical setting.

St. Joseph's has a good German organ, built by Jürgen Ahrend and tuned to Werckmeister III, a temperament that makes all keys available but gives to each a distinct character. (Not all the pipes were perfectly in tune, however.) On Fridays at noon, Larry Archbold, an accomplished player and cogent interpreter, gave a long, ambitious series of recitals entitled Organ Music of J. S. Bach and his Predecessors—German, Dutch, Italian, French, Spanish, or English groups with a big Bach work as finale. Too often at organ recitals one tends to listen to the instrument; here one quickly discovered what the little two-manual, twelve-stop instrument could do, and began to listen only to the music.

Eighteenth-century sounds I now miss in New York are those of domestic keyboards. The house that I rented in Berkeley held five instruments, the oldest in date—but most modern in timbre—being a Walter fortepiano of the kind that Mozart favored, the others reproductions of more ancient instruments. Only that abundance—not, in Berkeley, the presence—of old instruments was exceptional. Almost every day there, my conviction that the modern Steinway is an unsuitable medium for Mozart, Beethoven, and Schubert grew deeper as I listened to sounds the composers themselves would have recognized. The nineteenth-century highlight was two impassioned performances of Verdi's Requiem, in Hertz Hall, conducted by Richard Bradshaw, with the University Chorus and Orchestra and professional soloists. Here, again, an accurate feeling for style brought music of the past to new life. Mr. Bradshaw showed an instinctive command—it is rare today—of the natural movement, the dynamic surge and ebb and flow, the unwritten but essential rubato of Verdi lines. (It was in high contrast to a polished, driven performance, on television, conducted by Riccardo Muti, which eschewed rubato, portamento, expressive molding of the phrases.) David Rosen, who is editing the Requiem for the new Verdi edition, had made significant, audible corrections to the usual printed text. The soloists phrased freely and emotionally. Rebecca Cook, a young soprano with the San Francisco Opera, floated warm, full lines and rose to a thrilling high C. Timothy Noble, the bass, was urgent and vivid.

The acoustics of Davies Hall, the home of the San Francisco Symphony, have been improved by the provision of new reflecting "saucers" above the orchestra—the old ones were warped—but the sound can still not be called warm or "living." In standard repertory, Mr. de Waart seemed a decent but dull conductor—which is at least preferable to a musically indecorous, flamboyant conductor. The Oakland Symphony plays in a 1931 *art moderne* palace lovingly restored, the Paramount, of such splendor that the setting almost steals the show. Calvin Simmons, its conductor, puzzles me. He is gifted and musical, but in performances of Mozart, Schubert, Richard Strauss, Prokofiev, Vaughan Williams he put precision before phrasing, energy before expression, to an extent that made one want to lock him in a library of Mengelberg, Furtwängler, and Beecham records, where he might learn that making music means more than playing the right notes, crisply, elegantly, in strict tempo. Then he led an account of Britten's *Spring Symphony* so fresh and *felt* that one's heart went out to him.

Back in New York, the plazas of Lincoln Center come to life with open-air summer music. The first strains I heard on return were those of the newly discovered Mozart symphony, K. 19a, in F major, composed in London when Mozart was nine; the Mostly Mozart Festival gave a run-through of its opening concert out in the open, playing to a happy throng under the trees of the north plaza, beside the pool. The symphony is a delightful piece, fashioned in the manner of John Christian Bach, with inspired Mozartian touches in its first movement. Most evenings, the Guggenheim Concert Band has been playing in Damrosch Park, at the southwest corner of the Center. J. C. Bach composed for Vauxhall Gardens; Mozart played in Ranelagh Gardens. Damrosch Park and the summer café and kiosks on the main plaza provide between them a rough modern suggestion of those musical pleasure places. The bandshell, a soaring concrete mihrab, seems to carry an echo of Vauxhall's "Moorish-Gothick" bandstand. An evening of Leonard Bernstein's show music, given by the National Chorale, reminded us of his wit, metrical vivacity, and melodiousness. The band concerts reached their climax in a "festival" devoted to John Philip Sousa and Victor Herbert. Both men, near-contemporaries, were bandmasters. Herbert conducted the famous Twenty-second Regiment Band of the New York National Guard before he went to the Pittsburgh Symphony. He is remembered mainly for his operettas, and Sousa for his marches, but both composers were prolific in both veins. The "festival" designation was earned by the planning: successive programs explored influences (Offenbach, Wagner, Johann Strauss); pièces d'occasion (for Pittsburgh, Atlanta, Buffalo expositions, President Garfield's Inauguration); "connections and legacies" (outstanding was *A Chant from the Great Plains,* a symphonic episode, of 1919, treating an Omaha Indian theme in amplest *Rheingold* manner, by Carl Busch, conductor of the Kansas City Symphony and a composer unknown to Grove), exotica (*The Kaffir of Karoo,* from Sousa's *Tales of a Traveler*); theatre music. In Lincoln Center Library, there were related morning "seminars." The performances, however, did not always attain festival standard. Several pieces sounded underrehearsed. Ainslee Cox, the Guggenheim Concert Band's music director and conductor, was an unobservant accompanist to his soloists. I preferred the dapper, traditional style of the guest conductor, Leonard B. Smith, music director of the Detroit Concert Band.

Brass bands and military bands (the latter term not necessarily implying anything more bellicose than the addition of woodwinds to the brasses) have their part to play in serious music. In American opera houses, I have only twice heard *banda* music excitingly performed: in San Antonio's production of *Rienzi,* and, by West Point players, in the Sacred Music Society's performance of Meyerbeer's *Il crociato.* (Records of that stirring performance, by the way, have just been released on the Voce label.) I hope Beverly Sills has engaged a crack marching band for the City Opera's *Nabucco* next season. At the first *Nabucco,* according to Verdi's memoir, the audience burst into applause when the *banda* came marching in.

GOSPEL OF PEACE

August 17, 1981

PHILIP GLASS's opera *Satyagraha,* commissioned by the city of Rotterdam, had its first performances there and in Amsterdam last September, and its first American performances, last month and this, in Artpark, Lewiston, in upstate New York. The subtitle of the piece is "M. K. Gandhi in South Africa 1893–1914," and the title means something like "the firmness of truth." In Gandhi's words, "truth *(satya)* implies love, and firmness *(agraha)* engenders and therefore serves as a synonym for force." The term was coined to describe the principles of the movement by which Gandhi, first in South Africa and then in India, sought to better the lot of his countrymen. Satyagraha is linked to ideas of passive resistance and civil disobedience. Gandhi distinguished it from the former: "While in passive resistance there is a scope for the use of arms when a suitable occasion arrives, in Satyagraha physical force is forbidden even in the most favourable circumstances.... In passive resistance there is always present an idea of harassing the other party...while in Satyagraha there is not the remotest idea of injuring the opponent."

This subject matter was chosen by Glass; the libretto is by Constance DeJong; and their opera has an interesting and important plot. There are three acts, each lasting about fifty minutes. The first scene—like that of a Venetian *dramma per musica* in the days when opera was young—is allegorical: the confrontation at the start of the Bhagavad-Gita. The army of Prince Arjuna is ranged against that of his adversary Duryodhana. Arjuna, seeing friends and kinsmen in both camps, hesitates to embark on carnage. The Lord Krishna reassures him: "Recognize this war as prescribed by duty.... Give up this vile faintheartedness. Stand up, chastiser of your foes!" The princes on their high chariots are resplendent in the colorful costumes of Indian traditional drama. As light gathers, the opposed armies are revealed as Indian and European, and between them Gandhi is present, in pure, shining white. The scene is related to Gandhi's own decision on a night in 1893 when, a young barrister on his way to Pretoria, thrown off a train for not travelling as a nonwhite should, he shivered at Maritzburg station and decided not to flee to India but to stay and work for his people. All the text of the opera is taken from the Bhagavad-Gita, which Gandhi described as "an infallible guide of conduct" and "my dictionary of daily reference," and it is sung in the original Sanskrit. Scene 2, a tranquil interlude, is set on an ashram, a coöperative farm that he founded. In Scene 3, the Indians take a vow before God to resist the Black Act, which requires them to carry at all times finger-printed certificates of registration. Act II, also in three scenes, has a similar pattern, with heightened action. In the first scene, Gandhi, landing in Durban after six months abroad, is attacked by a white mob and rescued by the wife of the superintendent of police, who literally takes him under her umbrella. In Scene 2, the coöperatively owned press that prints *Indian Opinion,* the newspaper Gandhi founded, turns out the first issues. In Scene 3, satyagraha has its baptism of fire when the Indians, tricked into voluntary registration by an unfulfilled prom-ise, cast their cards into a caldron of flame. Act III is a single, slow, ritualistic representation of the satyagrahis' Newcastle March, in 1913, which led at length to the passing of the Indian Relief Bill. Gandhi returned to India, to pursue there his vision of a free, united, peaceful nation. In South Africa, "firmness of truth" had achieved its end—for a while. The last words of the opera are "Whenever the law of right-eousness withers away and lawlessness arises, then do I generate my-self on earth...thrusting the evil back and setting virtue on her seat again." Above the stage at the back, the three acts are presided over by, in turn, figures of Tolstoy, Tagore, and Martin Luther King, Jr.—three advocates of nonviolence. The final image is of Gandhi looking to King.

Satyagraha, then, is a political opera as *Fidelio,* David Blake's *Toussaint,* and John Eaton's *Danton and Robespierre* are political—*faits historiques* reënacted in song, interesting and stirring in themselves and inviting thought about their significance for audiences of today. They do not preach, but they present: this is what happened; trace the moral for yourselves. *Satyagraha* is a grave, formal, lyrical, and beautiful work. The events of the twenty-one years are presented as if they formed a day in history: the opera opens in an antelucan glimmer and moves through midday brightness and afternoon splendor on to dusk and, at last, a starry night, in which, one by one, the satyagrahis are arrested and dragged off while Gandhi's gentle, insistent song of firmness sings on. The settings, designed by Robert Israel and lit by Richard Riddell, are not rich agglomerations, like Robert Wilson's for his *Deafman Glance,* or stark and geometrical, like Wilson's for his and Glass's opera, *Einstein on the Beach,* but spare, distinguished, exquisitely composed tableaux of light, form, and color. The nearest sights to them I have seen were "magic pictures" by Wieland Wagner: the second act of his 1956 Bayreuth *Meistersinger,* where in a dense blue dusk the white elder flowers glowed and the outlines of Nuremberg housefronts were lightly traced; the Elysian Fields—white-robed figures in slow proces-sion—in his Munich production of Gluck's *Orfeo.* Did Appia influence Mr. Israel's strong, simple structures, early Corot his delicate tonal ef-fects of distance, and kathakali the points of jewelled Oriental bril-liance? I am not sure whence he took his inspiration, but his stage pictures are among the most distinguished the lyric theatre has produced in recent years. One specific influence is recorded. In an essay on the opera, Miss DeJong declares that the big skies and broad meadows of Cape Breton, in Nova Scotia—where composer, librettist, and designer met in the summer of 1978 to discuss their ideas—played a part in giving shape to their spectacle.

Satyagraha is based on a historical narrative. It is hardly at all an exploration of individual characters: the roles of Gandhi's wife, his secretary, and three fellow-workers are as one-dimensional—though vivid within that dimension—as those in an old morality play. Above all, the opera is a ritual celebration of a way of thinking and a way of acting. Last week, I suggested that John Adams, another composer sometimes called a "minimalist," had in his *Harmonium* moved on from constructing music that "expresses nothing but itself" to music that is linked to real life outside the concert hall. In *Satyagraha*, Glass has done so, too. His *Einstein* was a collaboration with Wilson, and his *Dance* a collaboration with Lucinda Childs, but the scores for those pieces can lead independent and hermetic existences. Heard without the "visuals," they create self-sufficient worlds of their own. But no one could listen to the *Satyagraha* score without realizing that the music is about more than its sounds, structures, figurations, and procedures. Glass has not simply embraced conventional opera. By leaving the text in Sanskrit, a language followed by few, he has renounced a chief part of opera's expressive means. (Many opera companies achieve the same effect, of course, by performing in tongues that most of the audience, and on occasion some of the singers, do not command.) Following a drama in an unknown language without a line-for-line crib is always interesting. One discovers just how communicative pure timbre and inflection, declamation united to glance and gesture but devoid of verbal sense, can be. I have been deeply moved by and, in a limited way, have "followed" Noh drama on a temple stage, kathakali round a blazing fire, and ta'azieh in a village street packed with a sobbing or shouting throng. I count them among my most exciting dramatic adventures. (Authentic surroundings played a part; in a formal Western theatre, under electric lights, much of the magic is lost.) But there is a difference. Most of the audiences *were* following the words; the texts of those dramas were not meant not to be understood. Glass's use of Sanskrit in *Satyagraha* is perhaps closer to Peter Brook's use of orghast, a language the poet Ted Hughes invented, in *Orghast,* a drama (or opera, or ceremony, or rite) Brook created in Persepolis ten years ago. No one understood orghast at first, or was meant to. Gradually, some of the vocabulary, at least, revealed itself, for the language had Romance and Nordic roots: *palom* was "dove," *lugh* "light," and *glittalugh* "star." But learning the language in that way was not the point—precisely not the point. Brook's intention was that the audience should respond directly, spontaneously, to the sounds uttered—sounds that would carry an emotional and dramatic charge even though listeners did not grasp their precise sense. He strove for a new "openness," an intuitive, direct kind of communication, in some ways closer to that of music than to that of speech. Similarly, Glass eschewed intelligible words and deliberately sought eloquence on another level. I understood far less of the Sanskrit than I did of orghast—well, none of it, in fact. But the libretto is published in English translation, and I read that before the performance.

Other elements are more conventionally operatic. In earlier scores, Glass used voices as lines in the general texture, as instruments of his ensemble, but in *Satyagraha* (as Schoenberg once remarked when explaining his system of distinguishing main from subsidiary voices) "the human voice is always *Hauptstimme.*" In the pit is not a typical Glass ensemble—such as the *Einstein* quintet of two electric organs and three wind players doubling on flutes, saxophones, and clarinets, all heavily amplified—but an orchestra of conventional strings and woodwinds, with electric-organ continuo. No brasses or percussion. No amplification. The Artpark players came from the Buffalo Philharmonic. The Artpark Opera Chorus, of thirty-one, sang precisely and fervently. *Satyagraha* is an unusual opera readily performable by usual opera companies. The Stuttgart Opera stages it in October. The Artpark production comes to the Brooklyn Academy of Music in November.

And the music? In timbres and in timing, it departs from Glass's earlier scores, but it is constructed in his familiar manner. For those unfamiliar with that manner, let me attempt a description: moto-perpetuo figuration; slow-moving diatonic harmony; chord progressions many times iterated; brief repeated figures, fragments of melody often scalic, rather than any long "tunes." For a start, imagine the first prelude of Bach's *Forty-eight* played in strict tempo with each measure repeated and a further repeat sign at every fourth bar; add in some extra sixteenth-notes here and there, to vary the meter but not the pace of the sixteenths. The opera begins with fourteen statements of the chord sequence F minor, E-flat, D-flat, C, traced in arpeggio figuration in even eighth-notes. But the number of eighths in each measure varies from five to six to seven to nine. There follow sixteen measures built over F-minor scales, rising and falling, the leading note alternately E-flat and E-natural, with sustained notes above to limn the initial chord sequence. That sequence then returns nine times in measures of eight, of nine, then of eight even eighth-notes, with the chords after the first no longer in root position (the bass rises four steps instead of falling four), and with two-voice mirror arpeggiation. Then the initial, simpler version is heard seventeen times. The next four statements of the progression have rising scales—F minor, E-flat, D-flat, C—in the bass and sustained harmonies above. The next twelve statements have three-voice arpeggiation. And so on. Enough has been said, perhaps, to suggest why the style is dubbed "minimal": the whole of the long scene is built on a hundred and forty-three repetitions of that four-chord progression. But the working is far from simplistic. One would have to say a great deal more to describe the variety, the interest, the fascination of what happens within the sequence—the changes of meter (placed on an unwavering pulse of eighth-notes), texture, and timbre, the carefully spaced and carefully placed vocal entries. Each of the two-hundred-odd bars of the second scene consists of the chords D minor, G major with an F-natural, A minor. The third scene is built on an eight-bar ground bass whose first four bars are C, B-flat; C, B-flat; C, B-flat; C, B-flat. There is a coda made from fifty alternations of F and E-flat chords. But the varied figuration, the timing, the scoring, the meter of the coda are brilliantly controlled. The sense of a mass vow solemnly sworn and reaffirmed is vividly conveyed.

The counts above are taken, of course, from the score. A listener stirred by an opera does not consciously count to 143 (or even to 12). There were passages in *Satyagraha,* however, when I did find myself, I confess, "counting"—working out how the music was made rather than simply responding to it. Glass sometimes uses a wheels-within-wheels simile to describe his methods and their relation to Indian music: "Cycles of repeating rhythms going on at the same time, like little wheels turning inside big wheels and all the revolutions are different and at a certain time they come out together." There were episodes in *Satyagraha* where one became conscious of the wheels going round, of a mechanical *Fortspinnung* ill-matched to the humane subject matter. Another objection—it applies to much minimal music—might be: a surfeit of consonance, not enough opposition. The grinding seconds of the white mob at the start of Act II—their chorus recalls the peasants' mocking chorus at the start of *Der Freischütz*—provide just about the only crunchy moments of the evening. Musically and dramatically, this is the only presentation of the violence satyagraha encountered; the final scene is presented in dreamlike slow motion.

The longest melody is that of Gandhi's aria-finale: a white-note scalic rise, in even quarters, from E to E, with the last note sustained. It was sung thirty times over. (Counting here was easy, since the aria falls into five strophes vocally identical, although differently accompanied and harmonized—once with bothering parallel octaves.) It reflects, as I said above, Gandhi's gently insistent, unalterable resolve; but by the fourth strophe I felt the point had been made. Generally, however, I trust Glass's sense of timing. And in *Satyagraha* the dramatic narrative and the practicalities of the opera house have trimmed and tempered the long, long expositions and developments deployed in such a score as his *Music with Changing Parts.* The opera has been likened to *Parsifal* in its slow, ritual tone. Musically, in its exploration of varied movement over ground basses it is perhaps closer to the more formal episodes in Monteverdi.

The performance—staging by Hans Nieuwenhuis, based on David Pountney's at the Holland première—seemed to me as good as can be. Douglas Perry's singing, as Gandhi, was clear, powerful, lyrical, sweetly in tune, moving; he sounded like Lohengrin. Claudia Cummings, as

Miss Schlesen, Gandhi's secretary, was radiant and pure. Everyone sounded good. Glass's smooth, diatonic vocal writing plainly brings out the best in voices. Christopher Keene's conducting was secure and committed. The performance moved unfalteringly.

This was my first visit to Artpark. The name may be trendy, but the place is exhilarating: a state park beside the gorge of the Niagara River (the Falls once fell there, before their gradual move seven miles upstream), laid out, by Hardy, Holzman & Pfeiffer Associates, in a way that disposes the visitor toward enjoyment and makes his spirits rise. The theatre, designed by Vollmer Associates, is a fine building—a modern and larger Bayreuth, seating twenty-three hundred, with acoustics that, like Bayreuth's, seem to amplify and enhance singers' voices against an orchestra sound clear and full yet always in balance. Why has Artpark not become the home of an annual East Coast *Ring*?

[*An Artpark* Ring, *conducted by Christopher Keene, began in 1985, with* Das Rheingold, *and continued in 1986 with* Die Walküre.

The New York City Opera has recorded Satyagraha, *on CBS, with Douglas Perry as Gandhi, Claudia Cummings as Miss Schlesen, and Mr. Keene as conductor. The company has not staged the opera, but in 1984 it staged Glass's next opera,* Akhnaten. *My own responsiveness to minimalism in opera—to minimalism of all kinds—soon diminished. But* Satyagraha *and* Akhnaten, *both in New York and in Europe, have drawn eager audiences.*]

MELODIOUS FALLS

August 24, 1981

GLENS FALLS, on the Hudson, makes little of its chief claim to fame: what should be the best-known of all American literary sites, the cave under the falls where since 1826 the imagination of America and Europe has taken shelter with Cora, Uncas, and their companions. Even before *The Last of the Mohicans,* the place was celebrated. There Edward Stanley (later Lord Derby, the translator of Homer) remarked to James Fenimore Cooper, "Here is the very scene for a romance," and planted the seed of the novel. The dying Schubert took solace in the *Mohicans* and, in his last letter, asked his friend Schober to send him more Cooper. What musician could read unstirred the account of the Glens Falls cave filled with song?

> The air was solemn and slow. At times it rose to the fullest compass of the rich voices of the sweet maidens, who hung over their little book in holy excitement, and again it sunk so low, that the rushing of the waters ran through their melody like a hollow accompaniment. The natural taste and true ear of David, governed and modified the sounds to suit their confined cavern, every crevice and cranny of which was filled with the thrilling notes of their flexible voices.... The singers were dwelling on one of those low, dying chords, which

116

the ear devours with such greedy rapture, as if conscious that it is about to lose them, when a cry, that seemed neither human nor earthly, rose in the outward air, penetrating not only the recesses of the cavern, but to the inmost hearts of all who heard it.

Since schoolboy days, I have wanted to visit the romantic site. But today there is no trace of the spiral stairway from the bridge over the Hudson which, my WPA guide to New York State (1962 printing) assures me, leads down to the cave. Attempts to scramble across from the east bank were thwarted by fences and thick undergrowth. Baffled, I returned to the town library and learned there that in 1962, when the state assumed responsibility for the bridge, it destroyed the stairway. But a few miles to the north the lake Cooper loved best, Lake George, is still beautiful and, despite all the sport on its surface, would still be peaceful were its shores not polluted with canned music. An occasional musket or cannon shot from the bastions of Fort William Henry reminds a romantic of history. (Lake George was far from peaceful in *Mohicans* time.) Brief, cheery recitals from a blowzy calliope aboard a pleasure steamer have a certain popular charm. But nonstop Baroque Muzak piped out from loudspeakers in the trees is hard to bear. (Blessed by all musicians be those isolating musical earmuffs that have succeeded roller skates as the latest craze.)

Between Lake George and Glens Falls, in the auditorium of Queensbury High School (which seats less than nine hundred), the Lake George Opera Festival is held. It began twenty years ago, in a lakeshore hall; this year the President himself wrote to congratulate the festival on two decades of "excellence in artistry." It has a fine record of playing American operas, but at the 1981 festival that side of things is left to two matinée shows, piano-accompanied, given by the American Lyric Theater, a group of young singers who gather for summer studies; and the main festival productions are of a musical, *Man of La Mancha,* and of *Carmen* and *The Abduction from the Seraglio.* I saw the last. It was not the sort of Mozart production I like best. The synopsis in the program book was ominous. It began: "Overture: On a beautiful early morning inside the guarded, locked gates of the Seraglio, the harem girls dance and bathe in the palace garden." A choreographer, Judith Haskell, as well as a director, Nancy Rhodes, was named, and there was choreography in plenty: four people took part in the first duet, and six in Osmin's solo "Ha! wie will ich triumphiren"; the Rondo alla Turca, scored, was inserted to provide a full-company chase sequence after the abduction. The order of the later numbers was altered, and Belmonte's "Wenn der Freude Thränen fliessen" was omitted. The designer, Michael Anania, had ignored what seems to me an *Abduction* designer's first task: if the drama is to work, there must be a clear definition of inside and outside, and who can get where.

Mozart's opera does pose problems. Some of the arias are long. Konstanze is expected to sing two of the longest, "Traurigkeit" and

"Martern aller Arten," in succession, and the second has a sixty-measure instrumental introduction, with concertante flute, oboe, violin, and cello solos, dividing her last spoken and her first sung words of defiance. My feeling is that director and singers should meet such challenges, try to rise to Mozart's intentions, not revise his work to make things easier for themselves. A good Konstanze, with her eyes, her bearing, perhaps a well-judged move or two, can make eloquent what she thinks and feels; a good Pasha seconds her by the way he looks and listens; and meanwhile the concertante instrumentalists "speak." But in the Lake George performance Konstanze and the Pasha *talked* through the introduction—a couple bickering to background music. During the aria proper, Konstanze moved from base to base, pursued by the Pasha, who grabbed at her. She finished vocal paragraphs and then shook him off.

The overture is marked "Presto." In the 1920s, Richard Strauss drew up Ten Golden Rules for a young conductor, and the ninth of them was "When you think you have achieved the fastest *prestissimo* possible, then double the tempo." But in 1948 he added an amendment addressed to Mozart conductors: "Halve the tempo." Mark Flint, conducting, took the overture rather too fast, and its rapid figures were not properly sounded. (An early rehearsal with slackened strings, slackened bows, and those nineteenth-century devices chin rests and endpins removed from the instruments can help players—and their conductor—to take a first step toward a truer Mozart style. A tiny first step only—eighteenth-century techniques are not easily acquired or modern instruments quite so easily modified—but, as such experiments have shown, a helpful one.) Still, since Mozart's overture had been demoted to accompany dance, pantomime, and merry jest, it did not matter too much. When the singers' voices came into play, Mr. Flint's tempi settled, and he showed a nice response to the marvels of the score. The singers—Charlotte Ellsaesser and Alan Kays as the noble pair, Lauran Fulton and James Longacre as their servants, Richard Crist as Osmin—were all fairly able. But when they were not thinking about their movements they seemed to be concentrating more on tone than on sense. Giuseppe Taddei, San Francisco's latest Leporello, made some wise remarks on this subject which were reported in that company's *Don Giovanni* program book:

When you're singing, you should express the meaning of the words as much as possible with the voice. Then the voice comes with exactly the right color. That's the logical and simple secret. Instead, many artists only want to make big and beautiful sounds and think only about the voice. If they thought of the words instead, the voice would come by itself, if, of course, it's there in the first place.

The English words of this particular *Abduction* were by Wesley Balk, and although they were not always happy (in his first aria Belmonte sang something like "I pray that I might find her and all her suffering end," which lay on the music in a way to suggest that he hoped to find all, not just a part of, Konstanze's suffering end), most of the time they ran well. The singers could have made more of them. When Konstanze sees her lost Belmonte, she should breathe his name, as she launches the Act II finale, with rapture and wonder; Miss Ellsaesser sang it loudly, fiercely, almost angrily. Mr. Kays had lost the naturalness, the straightforwardness, that made his Sam in the City Opera's *Street Scene* so winning. In the little auditorium, both of them could have dared to be lighter, more direct, more charming. In general, the execution suggested careful study rather than spontaneity and truth.

Nevertheless, I enjoyed the evening. The study *had* been careful. The performance was not uncaring. And Mozart poured all his youthful genius into this comedy as, shortly before, he had poured it into a serious opera. Everything he knew, had learned, was capable of—elaborate arias, amusing songs, poignant ensembles, expressive instrumental writing—is on display. The faults of *Die Entführung* are those of abundance.

A NOBLE MIND O'ERTHROWN

August 31, 1981

JAKOB LENZ'S play *Die Soldaten* (1776) influenced Georg Büchner's play *Woyzeck* (1837). Alban Berg's opera *Wozzeck* (1923), based on Büchner's play, in turn influenced Bernd Alois Zimmermann's opera *Die Soldaten* (1964), based on Lenz's play. [*A review of Zimmermann's opera appears on page 202.*] In 1778, Lenz lived for a while near Strasbourg with the pastor Johann Friedrich Oberlin. Oberlin's funeral oration was spoken by the father of Büchner's fiancée, and his papers passed to a family Büchner knew well. Drawing heavily, sometimes word for word, on Oberlin's diary, Büchner wrote his novella *Lenz* (1835). It seemed inevitable that sooner or later some composer would write a *Lenz* opera drawing together strands from Lenz, Büchner, Berg, and Zimmermann. In 1979, the young German composer Wolfgang Rihm (born in 1952) did so. His chamber opera *Jakob Lenz* had its première in Hamburg that year, and has now been taken up by several German and Austrian houses. With welcome speed, it has also crossed the Atlantic. To make the chain of cross-references complete, it should really have been staged here by Oberlin College, which is named for the pastor, but in fact it was done by the Indiana University Opera Theatre, in Bloomington, last month, as the 199th production of that enterprising company.

Whether by design or not, Büchner's *Lenz* is a fragment, and it owes much of its disturbing quality to that fact. It opens without preamble or explanation: "On the twentieth Lenz went through the mountains.

The peaks and high slopes covered with snow, gray rock down into the valleys, green fields, boulders, and pine trees." (I cite the translation in Henry J. Schmidt's thorough and helpful edition of Büchner's works.) With Büchner's Kafkaesque seventh sentence, it has been claimed, modern European prose was born: "He felt no fatigue, but at times he was irritated that he could not walk on his head." Lenz reaches Oberlin's manse. The narrative tells of his fits of suicidal madness alternating with sweet calmness. Suddenly it breaks off. From Oberlin's diary one can fill the gap: the pastor, after a suicide attempt by Lenz which alarmed all the household, decided to send him back to Strasbourg under escort. Büchner resumes with a final paragraph about the journey, describing a magnificent Rhine sunset and a moonlit night that seems to flood the earth with gold. "Lenz stared out quietly.... Again he made several attempts on his life but he was too closely watched." He arrives in Strasbourg and appears to act rationally. "So he lived on." He is a Werther without self-dramatization, and Büchner is a narrator who eschews Goethe's rich romanticizing vein. The prose slips between lyricism and dryness, from a plain account of things as they happened to an evocation of sights as they seemed to Lenz, whose reactions to nature were extreme. The style is jerky, the tone is oddly elusive, and the novella presents an unforgettable picture of schizophrenia.

To turn this prose into a text for music—for lyric drama—cannot have been easy. Michael Fröhling's libretto treats incidents of the book but handles it freely, reshaping it in a series of thirteen distinct but continuous episodes. Several of them are monologues—as it were, new, freely composed Lenz poems. Rihm's opera, which lasts about eighty minutes, is almost a monodrama, a modern song cycle, for the protagonist (a baritone). Pastor Oberlin (a bass) is a small role, and Christoph Kaufmann, a friend of Lenz (a tenor), one smaller still. (Fröhling converts Kaufmann into a kind of dark adversary, rather like Griswold in Dominick Argento's Poe opera.) There is a group of six solo voices, who represent, usually, inner voices conversing within Lenz himself but sometimes Nature become articulate and sometimes real village personages in the narrative. The orchestra is an unconventionally constituted chamber ensemble of eleven: two oboes, clarinet, bassoon; trumpet and trombone; three cellos; harpsichord; percussion.

"Putting a person like Jakob Lenz on the stage," Rihm wrote in the Hamburg Opera magazine before the première, "is complicated only because he himself conceals many stages within him. These everpresent stages must be revealed by the music." "Pluralism" may be a catchword today, but it seems the right word to describe the unaffected, all-embracing, frankly eclectic—and, given the subject, dramaturgically apt—quality of Rihm's score, which ranges from naïveté to neo-Expressionism, from melodiousness to extremes of tortured, unnatural modern vocalism. From the various kinds of musical monism championed in postwar years, the composer has appropriated whatever might be expressive. There is a directness in his work which makes it very striking and a shapeliness that saves it from being a magpie nest of diverse manners. It is easy to hear why *Lenz* has, deservedly, been a success. Rihm and Fröhling presumably counted on an audience that could bring to bear on their piece some knowledge of Lenz and some of Büchner. In Bloomington, the ties with historical *Sturm und Drang* were deliberately cut. No attempt was made to suggest Lenz as Goethe described him:

> Small, but of pleasant appearance, a dear little head whose delicate form perfectly matched his dainty, somewhat blunt features; blue eyes, blond hair...a gentle, almost cautious gait, a pleasant, hesitant manner of speech, and behavior alternating between reserve and shyness.

In the words of the director, Ross Allen, the Bloomington production sought "a more timeless interpretation of conditions and problems of which we are now increasingly aware." Something was lost, I think— the resonances sounding from the past into the present which so often constitute not merely the charm but also the essential point of a serious work of art. In general, I am against modern-dress presentations of historical or mythological dramas; an attempt to underline points of "relevance" or contemporaneity merely blunts them. But, given the premise, the Bloomington execution was brilliant. Mr. Allen's direction was crisp and compelling. Max Röthlisberger's décor, blending interior with realistic landscapes, was strong, subtle, and distinguished. Thomas Baldner, who had also made the English translation, conducted a secure and cogent performance. Michael Smartt played the title role with boundless assurance. If he had soaked himself longer and deeper in Lenz, in Büchner, and in Rihm's score, he might, I think, have played it with more variety. He seemed to view the opera as one long, vivid mad scene. He was vivid indeed but monochrome. There are passages in Büchner's *Lenz* and corresponding passages in Rihm's opera of eloquent, rational, and beautiful discourse, and if these are extravagantly supercharged the tragedy of the noble mind o'erthrown is obscured. The schizophrene becomes a monomane.

The Bloomington opera house, which seats 1,460, is one of the best in this country, but it was a little too large for the chamber opera. The writing for the small orchestra did not tell as strongly as it should. Hamburg's opera house is slightly bigger (it seats 1,650), but in Hamburg *Lenz* was given in the Opera's intimate studio theatre. *Lenz* was a highlight of Bloomington's summer festival of contemporary music, Music of Our Time, which also included new, commissioned orchestral pieces from Lukas Foss (*Dissertation*) and Milton Babbitt (*Ars Combinatoria*).

PART
II

1981–1982

APOLLO'S SON

September 21, 1981

THE ENGLISH National Opera's 1981–82 season opened with a new production of *Tristan and Isolde* distressing to look at but musically overwhelming: it had been prepared (during rehearsals of a year and more) and was conducted by Reginald Goodall. Since it was sung in my English translation, I'll say no more about the performance, beyond a word for Alberto Remedios's ardent, poetic Tristan. The merits of Mr. Goodall and of his Isolde, the young Scottish soprano Linda Esther Gray, and of his Marke, Gwynne Howell, can also be admired in the London Records album of the Welsh National Opera's original-language *Tristan*.

Like the New York City Opera, the English National offers some summer operetta—this year *The Merry Widow*, which in August alternated with the *Tristan* and with a remarkable new production of Monteverdi's *Orfeo*. Fifteen years ago, the company used to play Monteverdi's opera in a rich realization by Raymond Leppard; now it uses a more stylish edition, by John Eliot Gardiner, who also conducted. The English Baroque Soloists, along with some English National strings and brass, provided the accompaniment. The production had opened on tour, in Nottingham's little Theatre Royal; any fears that the old instruments might sound too small in the Coliseum, the English National's London home, which holds over two thousand, were swiftly allayed. The floor of the orchestra pit was set high. Cornetti, clarini, and sackbutts rang out bravely. Continuo harpsichords and chitarroni gave ample support to the singers. In ritornellos, the handful of strings seemed even too loud at times. Musically, this was an attempt at an authentic performance, led by a specialist in the style. Scenically, it was something quite different, directed by a young Australian, David Freeman, who cites Martha Graham, Peter Brook, and Jerzy Grotowski as influences on his work. (Mr. Freeman has founded small operatic ensembles, which he calls Opera Factory, in Sydney, in Zurich, and now, under English National auspices, in London.) The 1607 music drama, sung by highly trained singers and accompanied by expert instrumentalists, was here acted as if by present-day descendants of the Thracians among whom Orpheus once sang. The production, one read in the program book, "is set in a contemporary peasant village on the Eastern shores of the Mediterranean." The costumes were a modern motley with ethnic touches. The décor was chiefly pretty cloths or carpets suspended, and some portable rocks on which the company could sit or stand. Divine intervention by Apollo was signalled by the waving of a golden cape. The lighting was simple, strong, and effective. No attempt was made to resolve the evident contradictions: between a High Renaissance court entertainment and an open-air rustic mystery play; between adherence to a verbal and musical text written by two highly cultivated, scholarly artists and the adoption of a simple, improvisatory acting style. (The piece was still recognizably Monteverdi's opera—unlike, say, Grotowski's thorough reworking of *The Constant Prince,* which was no longer recognizably Calderón's play.) Mr. Freeman had been, in fact, not so much a "director," imposing his ideas on a cast, as the "coördinator" of an action in which the twenty individual singers had devised for themselves "natural" ways of expressing emotions and had invented for themselves antique, pastoral wedding rites and a representation of souls in Stygian or Hellish torment. By Graham, Brook, or Grotowski standards, much of the movement was naïve (a criticism that invites the retort "Why should peasant acting—or an enactment of peasant acting—be polished?"). The "natural" reaction to grief—throwing oneself to the ground—was indulged in often enough to lose its expressive force. At such times, the firm hand of an old-fashioned director was missed; also when a chorister's obtrusive mime was allowed to steal attention from the hero's principal song.

Orfeo, the first great opera, is itself a masterpiece in which tensions of many kinds are balanced: between word and note, acting and singing, monody and madrigal, free declamation and strict, formal musical designs, instruments as accompaniment and (in Orpheus' "Possente spirto") as "actors," scenery decorative and scenery dramatic. In fact, the various operatic reforms through nearly four centuries can be defined as returns to or adjustments of these balances that Monteverdi established so long ago. There are many possible ways of presenting the piece. The company's earlier production was done in colorful abstract décor, and in Italian. Kent Opera's version, directed by Jonathan Miller, reflected the harmonious proportions of Poussin in its stage pictures. The Juilliard's, three years ago, mimicked to fine effect a luxurious Baroque spectacle. Mr. Freeman evidently took his cue from the undimmed directness of Monteverdi's musical expression— the immediacy, now as in 1607, of vocal gesture and harmonic pang. The scenic metaphor chosen was, of course, no less artificial and exotic to a modern audience than any attempt to simulate the original performance by Duke Vincenzo's company would be, and it looked a little old-fashioned—"Zagreb sixties" in manner and aspect, a carrying over into the opera house of once popular staging ideas that the straight theatre has explored pretty fully. But it worked. And the questions it raised led to the central mysteries of opera's power over men's minds and hearts. This was no Simple-Simon or Monteverdi-for-the-masses redaction. Although on one page of the program book Mr. Freeman remarked that "perhaps today a rock singer such as Roger Daltrey or Mick Jagger...is the nearest contemporary equivalent" to Orpheus, on other pages writings by Plato, Dante, Gaffurius, Pico della Mirandola, Lorenzo de' Medici, and Edgar Wind were brought to our attention.

The singing was accomplished, especially that of Anthony Rolfe Johnson, one of the English National's leading Mozart tenors, in the title role; of Jennifer Smith as the incarnation of Music, who introduces the opera; and of John Tomlinson, as Charon. Three countertenor shepherds were excellently and agreeably audible. All were fluent in division and decoration. The ensembles were well balanced and precisely timed. Yet something was lacking, and its absence lessened the eloquence and dimmed the delights of the evening: the singers made little of the words. Nonverbal theatre—or, at any rate, theatre in which words are not treated as the prime medium of communication—was in vogue some years ago: Grotowski's *Constant Prince* and Brook's production of *A Midsummer Night's Dream* are instances. (Nonverbal theatre of another kind is common in opera houses where performances are given in tongues uncomprehended by either cast or audience.) For Monteverdi it won't do; like Giuseppe Verdi, he was a composer who accorded primacy to the text. "Aim to serve the poet rather than the composer" was the burden of Verdi's instructions to his *Macbeth* interpreters, and Monteverdi's expressed intention was to make his music the handmaiden of the text. Those formulations are, of course, too simple: Alessandro Striggio's libretto for *Orfeo* and the Verdi-Piave-Maffei libretto for *Macbeth* are *drammi per musica*—plays written for a composer to set. They need to be *sung*, not spoken. But the way to sing them expressively, to bring the music to life, is to start by expressing the words—whether those words be the original Italian or, as in this production, a translation. Anne Ridler's English version, sensitive to the shapes of Monteverdi's lines, was used. Although the *Orfeo* cast did not commit the common fault of subordinating sense to vocal tone, it did seem concerned more with "enacting" the text than with uttering it distinctly and affectingly. Many of Anne Ridler's words were quite simply unintelligible. Verbal values—the natural speech rhythms of the translation—were often subordinated to metrical observance of the printed note values. Both conductor and director must be chided for not having urged the artists to "speak" with the passion and vividness they brought to their acting. It might have helped to raise the pit floor higher still and station the continuo players where they could see and follow the singers they accompanied. Recitative relayed through a conductor must always be recitative to some extent dulled.

Yet for both the audiences and, evidently, the cast, this unorthodox *Orfeo* was an exciting, valuable, and stirring enterprise. In an age when, on the one hand, critics and, increasingly, the public are calling for a return to traditional presentations—for operas done in a manner their creators would recognize as reasonable accounts of their work—while, on the other hand, several celebrated directors move farther and farther the other way, this simple, careful, adventurous, and uncostly production afforded new evidence that there can be nonhistorical stagings of old works which do them no violence; that imagination and intensity count for more than mere expenditure on machinery and décor; that limitations of stage or of budget—such as in postwar years Günther Rennert knew in Hamburg and Wieland Wagner in Bayreuth—can still be turned to virtue. Scenically, those morals could be drawn. The musical moral was equally plain: that works sound most eloquent and most beautiful when executed as closely as possible in accord with the sounds and style their composers knew. There is a paradox here, but then opera has ever been a matter of paradoxes, inconsistencies, and compromises. (To touch on just one: although operas are best heard in the original language, the words of many operas need to be understood not just in general but in detail; so compromise is inevitable when borders are crossed.) Like *Orfeo* itself, this production of it sought a new synthesis. Challenging some tenets of contemporary execution and confirming others, it set both traditionalists and modernists thinking. To several current debates—about style, language, old instruments, small-scale operas in large houses—it made a practical contribution. Best of all, it presented *Orfeo* as what Monteverdi meant his opera to be: at once a narrative, an allegory, and a living demonstration of music's power.

HURRAH! HURRAH!

September 28, 1981

THE PHILHARMONIC began its season with Karlheinz Stockhausen's *Jubiläum,* or *Jubilee,* Opus 45, an occasional piece commissioned to celebrate the hundred-and-twenty-fifth anniversary of the Hanover Opera House, in 1977. Occasional but substantial: *Jubilee,* which lasts fifteen minutes, is composed for large orchestra with quadruple winds, and it is rich in music. The work is a passacaglia whose emphatic, shapely fifteen-note theme—a twelve-note theme extended at the close in a cadence pattern—is played through ten times, eight of those times by basses, bassoons, and plate bells. They form one of the four groups—the "ground bass" group—into which the orchestra is divided both texturally and spatially on the platform. By other instruments, these statements of the theme, which opens on C and closes on a dominant-sounding G, are variously doubled, harmonized, colored with overtones. Against and around its powerful, measured stride (broken by pauses rather in the manner of a chorale fantasy), bright, busy lines—

transformations of the theme at various tempos, often accelerating or slowing down; exuberant, decorative glissandos—are spun. "Jeder für sich"—"Each man for himself"—is a recurrent instruction: the players thus directed achieve independence both of the conductor and of one another, so that, in the words of the preface to the score, "new melodies constantly result from the interaction of the lines." The basic structure is simple and audibly apparent. The detailed working is intricate, and the areas of freedom—the playgrounds mapped out for individual instrumentalists—are carefully plotted. *Jubilee* was revised last year, and when the revised score had its première, in London (from the Philharmonia Orchestra, conducted by Andrew Davis), the composer provided a long and largely mathematical program note. (In New York, the note was dropped in favor of a lucid introduction by Benjamin Folkman.)

The eager, luminous counterpoint and the glittering instrumentation could be enough in themselves to sustain interest in the progress of the piece, but other arresting things happen. Twice "the entire orchestra STOPS—no one moves!" That instruction precedes two dramatic episodes designated "sound windows"—opening onto extensions of the traditional concert space. In the first of them, a brass quintet— four trombones and tuba—swells into the stillness, uttering the theme as a solemn chorale; the players are stationed in an isolated box or else (as at the Philharmonic performance) behind the audience. In the second, an invisible oboe quartet, backstage, intones the theme in a subdominant transposition. Then, there are important, virtuoso roles for six soloists—horn, trombone, violin, flute, oboe, piano—each of whom except the last signals his entrance by standing up to play. The trombone is asked either to deliver his solo from a box "with characteristic gestures" or else (as happened here) to advance slowly from the back of the hall, through the audience, playing the while. Demeanor and deportment make a contribution to many Stockhausen works; in this one, the "sound window" brasses are directed to join the main body on the platform, for the final massed statement, "with posture and pace ceremoniously stylized."

Jubilee, then, brings together and concentrates in assured, personal fashion many ideas and devices of contemporary writing for large orchestra. It was Stockhausen's last orchestra piece—*In Freundschaft*, Opus 46, also of 1977, was his last chamber piece—before he turned to the composition of the seven-day opera *Licht* (of which, so far, *Thursday* and a part of *Tuesday* have been brought to performance). *Jubilee*, which Stockhausen intended to be "festive, spectacular, full of confidence," has a consummate quality. It is not one of his largest or most ambitious undertakings and was evidently composed to be accessible both to conventional symphony-orchestra audiences and to conventional symphony orchestras. (An authorized "chamber" version, achieved simply by omitting the third and fourth wind parts, further stresses the practicality of the work.) On the simplest level, *Jubilee* reassures those reluctant to follow Stockhausen's more meditative and mystical flights that he is still a master of notes. It does nothing to disturb the "only one conclusion about Stockhausen's style" reached in the New Grove: that "he has gathered together in a great synthesis all the means available to the composer of the twentieth century, not excluding his heritage from the past, and that he has drawn from serial thought the techniques—indeed, the new language—which can present them in a fashion at once ordered and elemental." The Philharmonic players, conducted by Zubin Mehta, sounded confident but not always convinced; some of the contributions seemed more dutiful than joyful in their phrasing. The balance—each of the soloists is amplified—was not always happy: from my seat I could hardly hear the piano. Nevertheless, *Jubilee* provided an exciting start for what promises to be an uncommonly interesting season.

At the London Proms—fifty-six concerts that pack into eight weeks a matchless feast of music—I heard last month a slighter specimen of "modern music without tears": Witold Lutoslawski's Double Concerto, for oboe, harp, and chamber orchestra (1980), composed, like Hans Werner Henze's *Doppio Concerto* and Ernst Krenek's *Kitharaulos,* for Heinz and Ursula Holliger. The piece was something of an instant hit at its London première last year, and the finale was encored. So it was at the Prom. It's a deft, slim, agreeable composition, with a perky, neo-Prokofiev finale. Another double concerto, Priaulx Rainier's Concertante for Two Winds (oboe, clarinet, and chamber orchestra), had its première at an earlier Prom. Like all her work, it is delicate, distinguished, strong and sure, yet unassertive. In an age of modes and movements, Rainier's voice remains distinctive, unique. I found the Concertante elusive—more so than, say, her Cello Concerto or *Aequora lunae*—but enjoyed each musical statement even while missing a sustained argument.

London critics sometimes take the Proms for granted. They seem to me at once a model and a miracle. Where else can one attend a Birgit Nilsson concert for eighty pence (about $1.50) or hear whole operas with star casts for that price? I got to London too late for the British première of Maxwell Davies's Second Symphony and left it too soon for the British première of Boulez's *Notations,* the world première of John Buller's *The Theatre of Memory,* a B-minor Mass with original instruments, and eight hours (from 11 P.M. to 7 A.M.) of Indian music. But my three-week stay did bring Mahler's Third Symphony conducted by Haitink; his Fifth conducted by Abbado; Henze's First; a *Gurrelieder,* whose impact was somewhat diminished by its being heard two days after the English National Opera's *Tristan*; a Rossini Stabat Mater, dully conducted by Giulini; and three Prom operas: *La forza del destino,* in the original St. Petersburg version (Martina Arroyo back in full, free voice), the Glyndebourne *Ariadne auf Naxos* (Helena Döse its radiant heroine), and Mozart's *Lucio Silla* (with a fine cast led by Felicity Palmer and Arleen Augér). That left no time for a rival attraction, the eighteen concerts of London's South Bank Summer Music, a festival now under the direction of Simon Rattle, with choice performers (Elisabeth Söderström, Alicia de Larrocha, Támás Vásáry) in choice programs (Weill, Fauré, Gershwin, Bartók).

One big Prom event was the second performance of John Tavener's *Akhmatova: Requiem*. (The first performance was given a week earlier, at the Edinburgh Festival.) It is a setting, in Russian, for soprano and an orchestra of strings, brasses, and percussion, of the poem cycle *Requiem*, Akhmatova's memorial to the sufferings of those whose relatives, friends, and loved ones were arrested in the Stalin years:

> In the terrible years of the Ezhov terror I spent seventeen months in the queues outside Leningrad prisons. One day...a woman with frozen blue lips who stood behind me...breathed in my ear (we all spoke in whispers there), "Would you be able to describe this?"
> And I answered, "I would."

Akhmatova's first husband was shot; her third husband and her son were sent to labor camps. *Requiem,* a powerful and beautiful sequence assembled over many years (the earliest poem is dated 1935, the latest 1961), reaches a climax in a Stabat Mater in which she cites phrases of the Russian Good Friday liturgy. Tavener amplifies these, and elsewhere he has added other lines (a recurrent "Give repose to the souls of thy servants") of the Orthodox liturgy. These are sung by a bass, accompanied only by a tolling of deep bells and a shimmer of small ones. The work, which lasts about forty-five minutes, has a ritual framework within which are enclosed the poet's outbursts of personal grief and passion and her compassion for all who suffered similarly ("I have worked a generous protecting veil for them").

Tavener's music is grave, uncomplicated, direct, created on a large scale and set down with a sure ear for affecting sonority. In those earlier big pieces of his—the huge Crucifixion meditation *Ultimos Ritos* and the opera *Thérèse*, about St. Theresa of Lisieux—there were passages where I felt that surefire formulas of magniloquence, ecstasy, and mystic passion were being perhaps too easily employed. Not so in *Akhmatova: Requiem*. Everything is felt, urgent, disciplined, worthy of the subject. Phyllis Bryn-Julson sang the long, taxing role most movingly. John Shirley-Quirk, in the bass solos, was light of voice for music that seemed to call for a resonant Russian bass. Gennadi Rozhdestvensky conducted, and with this concert nobly ended a three-year tenure as chief conductor of the BBC Symphony.

LEADING LADIES

October 5, 1981

IT WAS unwise of the Metropolitan Opera to open the season with Bellini's *Norma* without having engaged a soprano equipped to meet the challenges of the leading part. Renata Scotto essayed it, and she came to grief. During the last decade, she has undertaken the tremendous role several times—in Turin, Palermo, Cincinnati, Houston, Philadelphia, Florence, and Vienna—but she had not sung it before in New York. Nature endowed Miss Scotto with a delightful lyric soprano. She made her London début in 1956, singing as promising and pretty a Mimì, Violetta, Adina, Lucia, and Donna Elvira as one could hope to hear. With careful nurture, voices grow. Nine years later, Miss Scotto reached the Met as a bewitching Butterfly. But soon thereafter she began to move into a still heavier repertory and to gain force at the cost of freshness, purity of timbre, and evenness of dynamic flow. In 1972, I praised the dramatic force she brought to a Carnegie Hall *Lombardi,* but feared lest "artistic ambition lead her to punish that beautiful voice."

Various paths lead to the Norma summit. The opera's seconda donna, Adalgisa, was evidently conceived by Bellini for what we might call a soprano d'agilità (although in his day there was less categorizing: Amina, in *La sonnambula,* and Norma were composed for the same singer, Giuditta Pasta). His first Adalgisa, Giulia Grisi, soon became a famous Norma. Giuseppina Strepponi, later Verdi's wife, sang Adalgisa in 1835 and Norma the following year. The great Lilli Lehmann, the Met's first Norma, sang the comprimaria role of Clotilde, Norma's handmaid, in her early Prague seasons (1866–68) and then Adalgisa before—having mastered Donna Anna, Beethoven's Leonore, and Isolde—she felt herself ready to tackle Norma, a role she deemed "ten times as exacting as Leonore." In our day, Joan Sutherland has sung both Clotilde and Norma, bypassing Adalgisa; mezzo-sopranos have long since appropriated that role (which in the early years of the phonograph we find recorded by Lakmés, Gildas), and at least two of them—Shirley Verrett and, notably, Grace Bumbry—have made the ascent to Norma. But Normas are not easily found. An essay in the opening-night program recalls that the first eight decades of Met history produced only five—Lehmann, Rosa Ponselle, Gina Cigna, Zinka Milanov, and Maria Callas. Thirty-five years elapsed between Lehmann's Norma and Ponselle's, and it was only in her tenth Met season that Ponselle undertook the part. After Ponselle, Kirsten Flagstad learned it but decided against singing it; Dusolina Giannini took it as far as a dress rehearsal and then withdrew. In the past Met decade, however, there have been six different Normas, and each of them has

had something to offer. We should not conclude that heroines qualified to don the druidess's mantle have suddenly become abundant.
Richard Bonynge, introducing Miss Sutherland's recording of the
opera, summarized the role's requirements as "the greatest dramatic
ability, superhuman emotional resources, the greatest bel-canto technique, a voice of quality and size, and I dare say many more attributes
as well." And Ester Mazzoleni, a celebrated Norma of the 1910s and
'20s, remarked in a 1977 *Opera News* interview:

> I simply cannot understand what is happening nowadays. They all sing
> Norma—the coloraturas like Deutekom, Sutherland, and Sills, the lyrics like
> Scotto and Cioni, the spintos like Caballé, whom I admire in certain roles very
> much. But how can they do justice to this terrifying score? It is a travesty of
> what Bellini wrote, and the audience takes a lot of punishment.

The Met audience did. Miss Scotto is a serious and determined artist.
If will alone could have driven her voice through the music, it would
evidently have done so. But "Casta Diva" was a disaster. Sustained
notes were often unsteady. The repeated A's at the climax lurched
over, both times, into a sharp and strident B-flat, a curdled scream.
The descending scales of the cabaletta were slithers. At coloratura passages she grabbed—and missed. By intention, the performance was
powerful, earnest, and never perfunctory; Miss Scotto plainly does not
share Beverly Sills's opinion, set out in her autobiography, *Bubbles*, that
"Norma is not a very difficult role" and that "there are some lines . . .
that always make me want to giggle." Miss Scotto was strongest in
fierce declamatory recitative, as in the exchanges with Adalgisa before
"Mira, o Norma." In passages of sustained melodic forcefulness, she
pushed her voice to its limits. There was nothing in reserve to compass
changes of color; everything was delivered in one hard, clear, high-
pressure tone. Elsewhere, there were soft, gentle, floating notes, and
some of them were beautiful. But, through either miscalculation or
technical trouble, the "thread of voice"—a necessary weapon in any
Norma's armory—was not evenly spun, and important statements
faded in and out of audibility. Estimates of Miss Scotto's acting differ.
The dear, bright little bundle of earlier days has acquired a grand
manner that sits oddly on her small frame. I tend to admire it; she
does everything so confidently. But I see why some people think it slips
into the absurd.

Adalgisa was Tatiana Troyanos—a new Met assumption, although
she sang the part with Caballé at La Scala four years ago. It lies high
for her; the peak notes were reached, but they were pretty raw. She is a
gauche actress. There is a rich sound to her voice. I wish she would
essay the sustained A-flat of the phrase "Io l'obbliai" with the "messa di
voce assai lunga" that Bellini asks for, instead of just belting it out.
Placido Domingo recorded the part of Pollio in 1973, with Caballé, but
he has waited eight years to bring it to the stage. He began badly,
blaring out the conversational remarks to his friend Flavius as if he

were an Othello embarking on "Esultate!" The subsequent aria was rough and loud, though his tone was fine. In the duet with Adalgisa, he seemed to have overlooked the instruction "con tutta la tenerezza." In a plain, blunt way, however, he offered a passable performance. Bonaldo Giaiotti's Oroveso was passable, too, provided one didn't look for the nobility and grandeur with which the role can be invested.

No one seemed very much interested in anyone else, and the drama dragged. If Miss Scotto's technical execution was faulty, the others lacked delicacy, refinement—the individual touches, vocal and dramatic, by which imaginative singers bring Bellini's opera to life. The approach of the conductor, James Levine, did not encourage them to finesse. He laid out foursquare metronomic rhythms. He was energetic and assured, and less crude than in his 1973 recording (with Sills as its heroine), but he showed almost no feeling for sensitive, flexible shaping of Bellini's melodies. The staging, by Fabrizio Melano, was plain and for the most part inoffensive. But without batting an eyelid the chorus heard the news that its priestess had broken her vows and betrayed her country. A spread-eagled sacrificial victim dominating the first scene struck a false note. Desmond Heeley had revised his scenery, but not sufficiently in accordance with the requirements of the plot. There was no sacred oak for Norma to cull mistletoe from. (They brought her a pre-cut bunch.) There was no bronze shield for her to strike. (She gestured toward a gong in the sky.) Two of the prescribed settings—the "luogo solitario" and the "tempio d'Irminsul"—are dispensed with; both scenes were played back in the "foresta sacra" of the opening.

Abigail, the heroine of Verdi's third opera (and first great success), *Nabucco,* is a shorter role than Norma, but while it lasts it makes vocal demands on its singer scarcely less extreme. Indeed, it asks for even more in the way of vigorous leaps (up to two octaves in extent), violent declamation, and extravagant dynamic contrasts. Abigail's scena ed aria "Anch'io dischiuso un giorno" is a "Casta Diva" recomposed in the *canto d'azione* that Verdi's contemporaries recognized as something new; in her duet with Nabucco, she takes up and extends a fiendish roulade cadence of Norma's in her duet with Pollio; and her death scene quotes the "Casta Diva" climax of repeated notes, syncopated, swelling to the semitone above. The City Opera, for the production of *Nabucco* that opened its season (after summer operettas), had wisely engaged as Abigail a prima donna who can sing Norma, Grace Bumbry. Not all the coloratura was securely in place. In tender passages, the tone was not always limpidly beautiful. But she was fiery, regal, and exciting. The stage and the music came to life whenever she appeared.

There was not much else to enjoy, apart from the firmly voiced phrases of John Broecheler, in the title role. (As an actor, he was almost clownish.) Zechariah needs a deeper bass than Justino Díaz's, and his low notes were pale. The second soprano sang awkwardly, and the tenor bawled. Nicola Benois' set is a clumsy affair of two giant staircases, unsuited to an opera where crowds must rush on and off. The stage direction, by Ghita Hager, was village-hall. "Va, pensiero" from a chorus seated around as if at a picnic loses its emotional force. Worst of all, Imre Pallo's conducting was small, short-breathed, unshaped. Who would have thought that a performance of this rousing opera could have so little blood in it?

Mr. Pallo also drained much life from the revival of Donizetti's *Maria Stuarda*, two days later. The show, directed by Tito Capobianco in 1972 (for Sills), has now been restaged by Mr. Melano, and its worst stylistic solecisms are removed. Maralin Niska, the Elizabeth, was ugly of voice but arresting in her use of it, and she is a cogent actress. She made much of the text. ("It is the convoluted, ornate Italian of the libretto that is hard to master in this opera," she said in an interview.) More than Miss Scotto, more, even, than Miss Bumbry, she made one sit up, attend, feel, and understand. The Leicester, Henry Price, was also a vivid performer, albeit with a frayed tone; he, too, gave dramatic life to the score. Alan Titus was Talbot. His voice held a new weight, warmth, and fullness. He seems to be growing naturally, happily, without forcing the pace, into a fine romantic baritone.

As for the heroine, Ashley Putnam, she puzzled me. She was in good voice. She looked attractive. And yet she made less of an effect than one would have expected from such virtues as hers. Mary's long final sequence of *confessione, preghiera,* and *aria del supplizio,* broken only by the carefully written choral *inno di morte,* proves overwhelming in almost any performance of *Maria Stuarda,* but here it was not. Three things, perhaps, conspired to dim it: Mr. Pallo's wan, feeble conducting; Miss Putnam's failure to pronounce the Italian words vividly; and —harder to describe but related to the preceding—a want of ardor and intensity in the phrasing. Miss Putnam lacked majesty. She was too young, too consciously girlish a queen. She came to the confrontation with Elizabeth with hair tumbling like a coltish schoolgirl's. Yet much was right, much was moving. Given more sensitive direction, musical and dramatic, Miss Putnam could surely become a memorable Mary.

In *A Hundred Years of Music* (1938), Gerald Abraham wrote that "at best one can hope to hear nothing more than occasional concert excerpts from Donizetti...or a sporadic half-dead 'revival' for the benefit of some star singer." The fifth edition of Grove (1954) allotted just three and a half pages to Donizetti, and concluded:

> With the passing of the great virtuosi, the music written for them, the music which fed that fashion, was bound to suffer. Facile, sentimental melodies can no longer sustain the interest or be supposed to represent adequately dramatic action, and Donizetti seldom rises above that standard.... *Lucia* continues to hold the stage in Italy.

But in the New Grove Donizetti rates seventeen (larger) pages, and in our day Donizetti performances are common. It was Maria Callas, above all, who brought his serious works besides *Lucia* back into esteem and showed the world how much virtue *Anna Bolena* and *Poliuto* contain. Joan Sutherland, Beverly Sills, and Montserrat Caballé set other serious operas of his before wide publics. And they fed those publics' appetite for novelty without newness. I doubt whether Donizetti will ever again—well, for a long time, at any rate—be as lightly dismissed as he was in the first half of our century. Enough work has been done to demonstrate that there is more than prima-donna fodder in his scores. Nevertheless, those scores call imperatively for prima donnas; approximate and unstylish performances won't do. Unless some new stars of magnitude arrive—singers who refine natural endowment by careful study—it cannot be long before his works figure less prominently in the international repertory.

ODYSSEY

October 12, 1981

HANS WERNER HENZE'S *Barcarola* for large orchestra, given its American première by the Philharmonic last month, is a romantic twenty-minute "tone voyage" that laps the listener in beautiful sounds and lulling rhythms; cajoles him with a melancholy viola solo; calls him to attention, several times, with brazen signals; and leaves him at last in contemplation of a serene, shimmering vision. The piece has a program, which starts out, "This boating song was sung by ferryman Charon on a crossing of the river Styx." Before the barcarolle begins, there is a long embarkation scene: a low, tugging swell; a summons from a trumpeter who remembers the hollow fifths of *The Flying Dutchman;* some impassioned cantilena; strains of the Eton Boating Song, which was used in Henze's opera *We Come to the River* to symbolize moneyed military coarseness of fibre; much other incident. "Charon's boat crosses the river at night." From time to time, he blows his horn in the darkness, and these calls are "like poles planted in the quicksand, resisting the current." The musical development, we are told, may be likened to the mingling in the mind of memories and new insights at the approach of death, "and the fragments of memory appear to the traveller as colorful visions flashing on the horizon, on the unknown shore." The bark beaches on the chord that opens the third act of *Tristan,* but here it does not resolve into F minor and anguished yearning. Instead, the percussion flickers. Muted strings glister. "On the horizon, the traveller perceives a small island shining in the morning light, rubs his eyes, blinks, and knows: this is Ithaca." The references in program and score touch on themes in other recent Henze works: his ballet *Orpheus*; his *Tristan,* for piano, orchestra, and tape (which also cites the start of Wagner's Act III); his new version of Monteverdi's *Il ritorno d'Ulisse*. Even if the program were suppressed, one would still have the impression of calm, steady progress accompanied by intense and varied emotions, and of new ways of thinking about old, familiar things.

Henze is a bewilderingly prolific composer. Music of many kinds pours from him; in recent years I have not been able to keep up with the stream. But it was delightful to encounter so soon the *Barcarola*. It was commissioned for the Zurich Tonhalle Orchestra and played by it in April 1980, and has since been played by at least seven other European orchestras. In its romantic richness, the work recalls Henze's 1953 cello concerto *Ode to the Westwind,* but although the orchestra is indeed large—triple winds, two saxophones, six horns—the textures are less luxuriantly dense than those of the earlier piece. Most of the sounds are bewitching, and several players have eloquent solo episodes. The Philharmonic's first viola, Sol Greitzer, was outstanding. Zubin Mehta conducted.

Edward Barnes's Concerto for Piano, Percussion, and Strings, which was given its first performance last month, also has a program. Its subtitle is "Fifteen Verses After Passages by Sam Shepard," and the passages are the "eagle" narrative that opens and the "eagle" dialogue that closes Act III of Shepard's play *Curse of the Starving Class.* Both are strong and vivid; the final image—eagle and cat in midair, cat clawing the eagle to death and refusing to be dropped, until both come crashing down—is painful. The passages were printed in the program book, "to make it possible to listen and follow along," but I doubt whether anyone could follow along very closely. In the score, however, the verses are tagged with phrases—"Doin' some suicidal antics," "All of a sudden he comes. Just like a thunder clap"—that make the correspondences clearer. This is a rum piece by an evidently fluent, talented young composer. (Born in 1957, he came to attention last year when the Juilliard staged his opera *Feathertop.*) Torrents of notes for the piano (played here with panache by the composer himself). Almost "single-line" music, driving ever onward, sometimes at a relaxed pace, Coplandish, but more often furiously. Little counterpoint but lots of busy accompaniment in the form of ostinatos, flurries, lush added-note harmonies. Hard to describe: imagine Granados become the pianist of a modern pop group.

The concerto was given at the first of a Music Today series conducted by Gerard Schwarz at the Merkin Concert Hall. Each program in the series includes a "classic" (Schoenberg, Stravinsky), one piece by an older and one by a younger American master, and a new work. The first concert, string-based, opened with Wallingford Riegger's *Study in Sonority,* for ten violins. Then, after the Barnes, Milton Babbitt's *Correspondences,* for string orchestra and tape (1967). It's a difficult piece for both listeners and players, and too difficult for me, whose ear cannot order the profusion of very short motifs—a sparkling barrage of brief exclamations—into connected musical discourse. In a platform discussion, Babbitt declared that Mr. Schwarz and his players had done brilliantly. Finally, the orchestral version of Schoenberg's Second String Quartet. Possibly an East Coast première, Mr. Schwarz said, though that seems unlikely, since the score was published in 1929. [*Astrid Varnay, the NBC Symphony, and Dimitri Mitropoulos, I later learned, had performed it on December 23, 1945, in NBC's Studio 8-H.*] In the new medium, the first movement becomes more evidently a waltz, and the last two movements turn into richly accompanied arias. The soprano, Margaret Chalker, voiced the lines beautifully, with clear, fresh, steady tone, but did not bring Stefan George's poems to life. Mr. Schwarz had assembled an ensemble of first-rate young players. It was a concert on a high level.

Merkin Hall is the concert hall of Abraham Goodman House, the Hebrew Arts School, newly named. Since it opened, three years ago, we have all been singing its praises. Just north of Lincoln Center, on 67th Street, it offers what the Center has long lacked—an attractive, intimate concert hall with good sound and good sight lines, well scaled for solo recitals, chamber music, and small orchestras. It seats 457. It is booked for a busy season of near-nightly concerts, and the bills promise a feast of old music (this month, English pieces of the early fifteenth century, from Pomerium Musices), classical music (Haydn on original instruments), and abundant modern music.

The Met had engaged respectable casts for its half-*Ring*—*Rheingold* and *Siegfried*—but the first two performances were poor. The scenes are murky derivatives of the luminous, enchanted pictures that Günther Schneider-Siemssen created for Karajan in Salzburg a decade ago. (Brünnhilde hailed sun and light under a gray, lowering sky.) Erich Leinsdorf's conducting was brisk, professional, prosaic. Except in the second act of *Siegfried*, where from the prelude on there was color, incident, and drama, nothing much happened musically—nothing seriously wrong, nothing memorable, nothing to engage mind or emotions in the great work. Is a workaday *Ring*—even a workaday half-*Ring*—better than no *Ring* at all? I'm not sure. The Met can plead practicalities—inability to devote the first month of its season, as Covent Garden did last year, to nothing but two fully rehearsed *Ring* cycles. But even by repertory standards these were two pretty shabby performances.

No discernible stage direction may be preferable to an egocentric director's antics. In the old days, I thrilled to many a performance where little time had been spent on the staging. But then there was an accepted standard of appropriate—and eloquent—Wagnerian behavior. Kirsten Flagstad, Astrid Varnay, the Konetzni sisters, Hans Hotter, Ludwig Weber knew what to do, how to act the music. The Met shows, however, were a medley of singers doing their own things—an anthology of "touches" picked up in other, eccentric productions—and singers doing nothing but standing around and singing. What possessed the Wanderer, played by Donald McIntyre, to rise while answering the third question of the riddle scene, cross the stage, rub Mime's nose in the runes of the spear, brandish the spear on high, and then strike the ground as if summoning Loge at the end of *Die Walküre*? A bright lightning flash followed. The stage directions are unambiguous: Wotan, still seated, "as if involuntarily touches his spear to the ground; a slight thunder is heard." What possessed Siegfried, played by Manfred Jung, to clamber up and perch "boyishly" on the high anvil? He looked absurd.

Das Rheingold brought the New York début of Heinz Zednick, that alert, arresting Mime; by *Siegfried* he had become altogether too fussy and fidgety. Ragnar Ulfung dried the lyrical beauty from Loge's aria, as Gerd Brenneis did from Froh's arietta. Franz Ferdinand Nentwig was a passable but small-scale Wotan. The giants—John Macurdy and Aage Haugland, as Fasolt and Fafner—were the real thing. They, at least, lent a touch of distinction to the evening. I enjoyed some unforced, gentle, lyrical singing from Mr. Jung in the second act of *Siegfried*. Elisabeth Payer, the new Brünnhilde, has a voice that from G to B above the staff is amazingly loud. If the Statue of Liberty were to give tongue, she might let out an A like Miss Payer's in "Kein *Gott* nahte mir je!" Her high C's were unpleasant, and on the staff her voice lost quality and character. Her singing was unrhythmical.

Until *I puritani* returned to the State Theater, opera this season failed to "dazzle the imagination" (the Met's claim in its advertisements) or more than intermittently "come alive" (the City Opera's). But the *Puritani* held its listeners from start to finish, and this was no small feat, for it is a difficult piece to bring off. When Donizetti recomposed it (just about) as *Lucia di Lammermoor,* he and his librettist, Salvatore Cammarano, arranged the traditional numbers—soprano's entrance aria, love duet, largo concertato, bass's narrative aria, mad scene, etc.—in a traditional sequence of proved efficacy, and provided a rational plot. Whereas *I puritani*, as the editor of *Opera* once wrote, "probably takes the first prize for the most ridiculous plot of any opera now in the repertory." At the City Opera, however, it was not ridiculous at all. The music, as Bellini intended, portrayed convincing plights, and one did not stop to ask why Elvira, minutes before her marriage, should be the only person in a fortress bustling with preparations who was unaware that it was about to take place. A single prima donna with supporting cast cannot bring *I puritani* to life; composed for a quartet of great singers, it is an ensemble opera. There are only two unequivocally solo numbers—the baritone's cavatina and the bass's romanza—although several of the ensembles are dominated by a single voice. Bellini called the mad scene a "trio."

Gianna Rolandi's first Elvira was a success—carefully prepared, accurately and touchingly sung, stylish and delicate in its phrasing. She was at her best in fleet decorated music. A troublesome vibrato in sustained cantilena spoiled the start of the mad scene. Her face was unbecomingly painted, and her wig was untidy; she is a more attractive woman than she was allowed to appear. The vibrato is a danger signal to heed; the looks can easily be put right. With his first Arturo, John Aler takes a big step forward. I didn't know there were still tenors at once versed in niceties of bel-canto style (had Mr. Aler been listening to Bonci records?) and able to carry in a large theatre—not with volume but with clean, clearly projected tone. Mr. Aler sailed up to the C-sharp of "A te, o cara" and the D of "Vieni fra queste braccia" so easily that I almost expected him to essay the high F's of "Credeasi, misera." (He didn't, however.) He was handsomely and flatteringly costumed. Pablo Elvira, a good Riccardo, took a while to get into his stride; his best singing came after the aria. In "Suoni la tromba," it was his bad luck to be pitted against the much bigger bass of Paul Plishka, a splendid Giorgio.

The conductor, Theo Alcantara, missed the sunrise romance of the opening pages. There were wrinkles in Carl Toms's backcloth. Jack Eddleman's staging began unpromisingly: soldiers marked time as they sang, and Mouldy, Shadow, Wart, Feeble, and Bullcalf had evidently been recruited in the Puritan cause. There was far too much sitting on the ground. Riccardo sat to sing "Ah! per sempre." Elvira sat to sing "Vieni al tempio." She began "Vien, diletto" sitting and then lay flat on her back. This jarred with the keen sense of style brought to the music but did not spoil the evening. More important on the balance sheet were Mr. Alcantara's feeling for the shape and progress of the movements, his sure handling of pace, climax, and large form; the handsomeness of Mr. Toms's settings; and Mr. Eddleman's presentation of real people who suffered and rejoiced. No *Puritani* I've seen, however starry—at Covent Garden, the Met, the San Carlo, Glyndebourne—gave a more favorable account of Bellini's fresh, adventurous opera than this one does.

A FINE RESOURCE

October 26, 1981

AN ENTHUSIASM for old music played on old instruments runs, rather surprisingly, through the pages of Bernard Shaw's collected music criticism. In 1894, between reviews of the Handel Festival (with Melba, Albani, Santley among the soloists) and Covent Garden's latest new opera, Shaw hailed the birth of Arnold Dolmetsch's first clavichord "as, on a moderate computation, about forty thousand times as important" as either. The year before, he had remarked that "if we went back to the old viols...and the old harpsichords, I suppose we should have to begin to make them again" and was concerned lest they be designed for ears dulled by the daily racket of "passing trains, factory hooters, fog signals, and wheel traffic." He had heard "a new harpsichord manufactured by a very eminent Parisian firm of pianoforte makers," and "not only did it prove itself a snarling abomination, with vices of tone that even a harmonium would have been ashamed of, but it had evidently been deliberately made so in order to meet the ordinary customer's notion of a powerful and brilliant instrument." Low volume, allied to fineness of detail, was something Shaw valued. He complained keenly of the sonic trespass committed by neighbors owning an iron-framed modern piano, or even a modern fiddle, "a terribly powerful instrument in neighborhoods where only millionaires can afford to live in detached houses." ("How much pleasanter it would be to live next to Mr. Arnold Dolmetsch, with his lutes, love viols, and leg viols.") Low volume, however, was but one advantage of the new-old instruments. Low cost was another; Shaw reckoned that a clavichord, "an individual work of art," could be made and sold for the price of a fourth-rate mass-produced piano. But the principal merit was musical. "Above all, you can play Bach's two famous sets of fugues and preludes, not to mention the rest of a great mass of beautiful old music, on your clavichord, which you cannot do without great alteration of character and loss of charm on the piano."

That was nearly a hundred years ago. Today, many things are better, and some worse. Brutal harpsichords of the kind Shaw deplored continued to be made but are now generally discredited. (Some linger on in concert halls and opera pits, and are still needed for a few contemporary concertos composed with their qualities in mind.) Skillful, loving reconstructions of musical instruments of the past are common, and original old instruments are sensitively restored. Techniques for sounding the instruments are mastered, and "authenticity" need no longer suggest faltering, scratchy tone and rocky intonation. The phonograph has, on the one hand, caused domestic intrusion far worse than any Shaw suffered—the sledgehammer thump of amplified rock bass—but, on the other hand, it has made the sounds of earlier centuries widely available. The musician who prefers to hear Bach's cantatas, Mozart's symphonies, Beethoven's piano sonatas played on instruments their composers would have recognized can now readily do so. And corresponding live concerts, particularly in university towns, become commoner.

Attempts to recapture the sounds composers had in mind loom large in the music-making of our day. The early-music movement Shaw welcomed has moved on into the Classical period. Performances of Haydn's, Mozart's, Beethoven's, Schubert's keyboard music on light, clear Viennese keyboard instruments are no longer rare, and their music can be played as it was written—not adapted in various ways to the sonorities of a modern grand. At the other end of the century, in the late-Romantic orchestral repertory, portamento is beginning to return. Perhaps gut E strings on the violins will follow—or will protest-

141

ing animal lovers prevent it? Adrian Boult thinks that orchestral string tone was ruined when steel E strings became standard. But more than a hundred seven- or eight-month-old lambs, Grove says, must be slaughtered to provide a single double-bass string, and "September is the month for fiddle-string making." A return to the old, balanced orchestral seating plan, which Boult is one of the last conductors to uphold, would help to re-create authentic late-Romantic sound with less bloodshed. With the Oakland Symphony, Calvin Simmons has made a start; his first violins sit left, his seconds right. But for music of the mid-nineteenth century—the Romantic age, which provides pianists with a great part of their repertory—less has been done. There are a few recordings; on a Oiseau-Lyre disc, for example, Malcolm Binns plays Chopin's Barcarolle on an 1847 Broadwood such as Chopin himself played at his last recital, in London. And earlier this month Kenyon College, in Gambier, Ohio, organized a two-day symposium entitled Erard vs. Steinway, whose participants were able to test the aptness of Romantic pianos to Romantic piano music with their own ears and fingers. It was an event to set people listening and thinking. The choice of instrument for Schumann's keyboard music, Malcolm Bilson once remarked, is even more crucial than for Beethoven's, "because as pianos developed, and as pianistic style developed, they became ever more interrelated." *The Book of the Piano*, a handsomely illustrated anthology edited by Dominic Gill and just published by the Cornell University Press, contains an acute and stimulating essay by Charles Rosen on "The Romantic Pedal," and there he analyzes specific Schumann passages showing how "the sonority of the piano has now become a primary element of musical composition, as important as pitch or duration. Not since Couperin and Domenico Scarlatti had the actual sound of a keyboard instrument provided the basic material of music."

There is, of course, no single "right" Romantic piano. Liszt enthusiastically and promiscuously endorsed many different brands in the course of his long career but seems to have been most faithful to his Erards. Other composers had their favorites. A few miles from Gambier, there is a farmhouse jam-packed with a wide variety of pianos— the collection of Edmund Michael Frederick. Among the instruments is a mid-century Pleyel such as Chopin favored, preferring its tone and touch to the more sophisticated action of an Erard. (Clara Schumann agreed with him, to judge by a letter she wrote to Robert in 1839: "If only I knew how to begin playing on a Pleyel without offending Erard, who has shown me every possible kindness.") There is a Streicher grand of the late sixties, twin to the instrument Brahms owned; essentially it is a Viennese fortepiano built large, with a wooden frame, though iron-braced, and with Viennese action. (Schumann and Brahms, Grove tells us, "never wavered in their allegiance to the Viennese piano.") There is a series of London Erards, dated 1850, 1856, and about 1873, and an 1893 Paris Erard such as Ravel owned and composed for. Visiting, hearing, and playing upon this collection formed the centerpiece of the Kenyon symposium. It opened with a demonstration and discussion in the college's concert hall at which three pianists—Raymond Dudley, Charles Fisk, and Paul Posnak— moved between the 1856 Erard and a modern Steinway grand, playing extended passages now on one, now on the other. Mr. Frederick and Benjamin Wiant, a piano restorer and piano connoisseur, were on hand to answer technical questions. Then, on the second day, Mr. Dudley played a full recital on the Erard, of Schumann, Chopin, and Liszt.

Perhaps *un peu d'histoire* may be helpful here. In 1859, in New York, the firm of Steinway more or less invented the modern grand piano, with its solid cast-iron frame and its "over-stringing." (The bass strings cross the frame diagonally, lapping the tenor strings.) Steinway's strings were thicker and under very much heavier tension than those of earlier instruments; the hammers that struck them were much larger and heavier. The result—for technical reasons that need not concern us here—was a great increase both in volume and in sustaining power. The strings could be more energetically activated, and their disposition on the soundboard allowed the energy to be discharged gradually—whereas in earlier pianos an initial, sharp impact sound is followed by a swift "decay" and a softer, subtler afterglow. The loud, "singing" Steinway triumphed at the Paris 1867 Exposition, and many European manufacturers enthusiastically adopted the "American system." Not all, and not some of the most famous. All the pianos in Mr. Frederick's collection are "straight-strung" (the strings run parallel down the cases), and all have composite frames of wood or of wood braced with iron.

Liszt invented the modern piano recital. Liszt, Chopin, and Schumann can be said to have invented modern piano writing. And their music is bound up with the instruments it was written for. But which instruments suit it best? Roughly speaking, there are two views. According to the Liszt scholar Alan Walker, "only when the great firms of Steinway and Bechstein produced their powerfully reinforced instruments in the 1860s did the Romantic repertory of the 1840s come into its own." Wagner took things further when in an 1879 testimonial to Steinway he declared:

> Our great tone masters, when writing the grandest of their creations for the pianoforte, seem to have had a presentiment of the Ideal Grand Piano, as now attained by yourselves. A Beethoven Sonata, a Bach Chromatic Fantasy, can only be fully appreciated when rendered upon one of your pianofortes.

But who thinks that way about Bach now? Who will think that way about Chopin once he has heard Chopin's music rendered in the gentler tints and finer, thinner lines drawn by a mid-century Pleyel such as Chopin played? In the Erard vs. Steinway demonstration-discussion at Kenyon, the earlier instrument won every round but one:

Charles Fisk suggested—and demonstrated—that on the powerful Steinway it is easier to begin Schumann's F-sharp-minor Sonata in a broad, grand way suggestive of the large events to follow. But Mr. Fisk, who had initially been invited to Kenyon as a Steinway champion, had discovered, he said, that the more he played on the Erard the more his arguments fell away and his loyalties altered. So it became a somewhat lopsided "match"—a clear win on points for the earlier instrument. The burden of the three pianists' comments and demonstrations seemed to be: it is usually possible on the modern Steinway to simulate the effects the composer intended, but in order to achieve them adjustments—to directions for pedalling, dynamics, indications of touch, even suggested tempos—have to be made. On the Erard, with its cleaner sounds, its more complicated timbres, its sharp attack and swift decay, the composers' original piano writing is idiomatic, natural. Pedal marks such as the one in Chopin's A-major Prelude which Robert Collet (in *The Chopin Companion*, edited by Alan Walker) deems "very risky" reveal their sense. Melodies stand clear of their accompaniment. Everything falls into place. Passage after passage—the second of Schumann's *Davidsbündlertänze*, with its sighing motif, the start of *Faschingsschwank*, Chopin's C-minor Nocturne—made the point, and Mr. Dudley clinched it by playing the huge climax of Liszt's *Funérailles* on the Erard with tremendous effect. Conclusion: pre-Steinway piano music is best played on a pre-Steinway piano.

A tidy and satisfying conclusion! I wish I could leave it at that. But the final recital disturbed it, bringing reservations and riders. Not Mr. Dudley's fault: his playing was large, sensitive, romantic, now rapt, now fiery. He knows Erards, for he owns one himself, and in a program that spanned forty years of Romantic literature—Schumann's Arabesque and Fantasy, a group of Chopin mazurkas and the Barcarolle, Liszt's *Funérailles* and *Mephisto Waltz*—he showed all its abilities. The mazurkas—Chopin's most intimate music—were perhaps most beautiful of all. At the start of the Schumann Fantasy, the passionate left-hand figure could surge unsubdued and sustain the big melody without swamping it. The Barcarolle's cantabile thirds floated lightly on the lapping left-hand figure. *Mephisto* took on a new snap and sparkle. Erard tone is less homogenized than Steinway tone; Steinway deliberately sought, achieved, and was lauded for evenness. Evenness is often a virtue—but not necessarily so in music that presumes distinct shadings in the different registers of a keyboard.

Why, then, the reservations? They were caused by physical factors: the size of the hall—a lofty six-hundred-seater, with a seating plan not intimate—in relation to the Erard's volume, and the state of the instrument itself. Erards carry well. Liszt played them in the Drury Lane Theatre and the Paris Opera. H. R. Haweis heard one at the 1851 Crystal Palace Exhibition (where Chickering displayed a straight-strung grand with a solid cast-iron frame):

I remember perfectly well falling into a kind of dream as I leant over the painted iron balcony and looked down on this splendid vista. The silver-bell-like tones of an Erard—it was the thousand-guinea piano—pierced through the human hum, and noise of splashing waters, but it was a long way off.

Yes, Erards carry. But, it seems, they do not fill an even fairly large hall with big, big sound as Steinways can. At the Kenyon demonstration, in an audience vote of preference after Mr. Dudley had played the start of the Fantasy on both instruments, the one hand lifted in favor of the Steinway appeared in the gallery at the back of the hall. I sat there for part of the recital and missed, in the middle movement of the Fantasy, that sense of extra power in hand which can make the triumph march so exciting. The *Funérailles* climax heard in the body of the hall also proved less overwhelming than at the demonstration where I was close to the piano. As for condition: the Erard, 125 years old, had been lovingly tended, but I doubt whether even its owner would claim it as the smoothly efficient, utterly reliable piece of machinery that a modern Steinway in peak form can be. Perhaps there will be a move to build new Romantic pianos, as now we do new fortepianos. They would be very expensive: the detailed craftsmanship inside the Erard, Mr. Frederick said, makes the insides of a modern Steinway look like dime-store work.

One further, rather technical point: not the least of Steinway's achievements was to "tune" his strings—a complicated matter, depending on where they are placed and where they are struck—so that the sound of unwanted natural harmonics is minimized. At the 1867 Exposition, Berlioz admired not only the Steinway's "splendid and noble sonority" but also the near-elimination of the "terrible resonance of the minor seventh" that afflicted the low notes of other pianos. This resonance occasionally sounded from the 1856 Erard: a curious seventh-ghost, for example, hung over the E-flat chord that ends the middle movement of the Fantasy.

No open-and-shut matter, then. Things to be said on both sides. And practicalities to consider. For a centuries-spanning program, a good Steinway is surely the best all-purpose single instrument. For large Romantic music in a large hall, it may well be more satisfactory. And perhaps even for large Romantic music in a fairly small hall—at least, to ears still habituated to modern sound levels. But something that would be most welcome, valuable, revelatory—the Kenyon symposium proved it—would be abundant recordings of Chopin played on a Pleyel, Liszt and Ravel on an Erard, Brahms on a Streicher. Pianists, whatever their own instruments may be, would learn much. (Not all have Horowitz's apparently instinctive genius for making his Steinway sound like just about any kind of piano he wants it to be.) So would all listeners. I doubt whether anyone left the symposium without a feeling that some long-familiar pieces had been met at last on their "home ground," had been seen at last in their true colors, and had revealed new aspects of their characters in the encounter; or without thoughts that will color the way he next plays or listens. Records are revealing, live experiences even more so.

HARP OF THE NORTH!

November 2, 1981

READING Walter Scott's *Lady of the Lake*—in preparation for the Houston Grand Opera production of Rossini's *Donna del lago*—was an unexpected pleasure. Earlier attempts to get through it had faltered on such lines as

> *Onward, amid the copse 'gan peep*
> *A narrow inlet, still and deep,*
> *Affording scarce such breadth of brim*
> *As served the wild duck's brood to swim.*

But this time I managed to push on with James Fitz-James to that airy point he won

> *Where, gleaming with the setting sun,*
> *One burnish'd sheet of living gold,*
> *Loch Katrine lay beneath him roll'd,*

and then, once Ellen had appeared, guiding her swift skiff across its waters, I was caught. The poetry of *The Lady of the Lake* lies not in its words but in its keenly imagined—if conventionally described—landscapes. The narrative is arresting. The pace of its telling is cunningly varied. And what Verdi called *situazioni*—striking encounters, confrontations made for ardent theatrical music—abound. Moreover, the poem is shot through with songs. (The last of them reaches the heroine's ears from a tower where her lover, like Leonora's Manrico in *Il trovatore*, is imprisoned.) Small wonder, then, that in the year of the poem's publication, 1810, it reached the stage as a play with musical numbers; that in 1811 it appeared at Covent Garden as a musical drama, *The Knight of Snowdoun*, the first of Henry Bishop's numerous Scott "musicals"; that Schubert found music for seven of its songs; and that Rossini, so we are told, was fired by his reading of the poem to instruct Leone Tottola to fashion a libretto from it. Bishop's piece is not an opera; the principal characters—Ellen, James, Roderick, Douglas—do not sing. *La donna del lago*, launched in Naples in 1819, is the first Scott opera and an early example of the Romanticism that was to fill Europe's theatres with Northern landscapes evoked in sounds, words, and paint and beneath the lamps of increasingly inventive designers. Meanwhile, landscapes evoked in Romantic instrumental sound filled concert halls: beside Bellini's *I puritani di Scozia* and Donizetti's *Lucia di Lammermoor* there appeared Berlioz's *Waverley* and *Rob Roy*, Mendelssohn's *Hebrides* and "Scotch" Symphony.

In Weber's *Freischütz*, the only opera of its day to challenge the popularity of Rossini's operas, romantic nature was harnessed by a composer determined to create, he said, "a work of art in which all the parts form themselves into a beautiful whole"—as opposed to Italian operas that consist of "a few brilliant gems, regardless of their setting." The ease with which Rossini's gems could be made to shine in disparate settings seems to support Weber's view. ("Tanti affetti," the rondo-finale of *La donna del lago*, reappeared in Rossini's next opera, *Bianca e Falliero*, while in *La donna*, from a Paris production of 1824 to a Florence production of 1958, a quartet from *Bianca* commonly replaced "Tanti affetti.") In our age of loving restoration, however, we begin to discover that operas as their composers first conceived and created them may have more integrity than was once supposed. Well-founded claims have been made for Handel, and persuasive claims for Vivaldi, those two princes of self-plagiarism. In Houston, *La donna del lago* was done in a new, pure critical edition by Colin Slim, and, apart from some recitative cuts, it was done pretty well complete. (The first act lasted about a hundred minutes, the second about an hour.) If anyone was left unconvinced that the piece has what Verdi called a *tinta* or *colorito*—a distinct, individual color and character—the fault lay probably in the staging, not in Rossini.

Many an eighteenth-century simile aria drew parallels between natural phenomena and emotional disorder—tempest without and turbulence in the soul:

> As the helmsman on the ocean
> Fears the stroke of wave and wind,
> So my heart with keen emotion
> Feels the blows of love unkind.

It was a conventional conceit, one that allowed a composer to write wind-and-wave figuration. Then, at the start of *Iphigénie en Tauride*, Gluck brought the storm itself onto the stage even as it raged in Iphigenia's heart. But his is a formal neoclassical storm. Rossini was more picturesque, more romantic, in the final scene of his early opera *Tancredi*. The stage directions prescribe "a mountain chain, precipitous gorges, torrents tumbling down to form the Arethusa; forests partly covering mountain and plain; Etna in the distance; the sun in the west, glowing upon the sea," and so on. Rossini painted it all in rich music that recurs to punctuate Tancred's observations that "the streams' fearful clamor, the winds' grim raging 'mid the crags" increase his unhappy brooding on Amenais' apparent infidelity.

In *La donna del lago*, the correspondences are less specific, not spelled out so precisely, but—as in Scott—they are implicit. In Houston, Ming Cho Lee's scenery was too drab. He saw a Scotland under misty gray skies, not Scott's and Rossini's colorful, sun-drenched scenes:

> The western waves of ebbing day
> Roll'd o'er the glen their level way;
> Each purple peak, each flinty spire,
> Was bathed in floods of living fire.

Jane Greenwood had designed picturesque costumes for the clansmen but was less happy with the principals and least happy with the star of the show, Marilyn Horne, who took the transvestite role of Malcolm Graeme:

> Of stature tall, and slender frame,
> But firmly knit, was Malcolm Graeme.
> The belted plaid and tartan hose
> Did ne'er more graceful limbs disclose;
> His flaxen hair of sunny hue
> Curl'd closely round his bonnet blue.

Three men—James, Roderick, and Malcolm—love Ellen, but she loves only Malcolm. In the poem, he is something of a cipher. Scott admitted it in an 1811 letter:

You must know this Malcolm Graeme was a great plague to me from the beginning.... I gave him that dip in the lake by way of making him do something; but wet or dry I could make nothing of him. His insignificance is the greatest defect among many others in the poem; but the canvas was not broad enough to include him, considering I had to group the King [James], Roderick, and Douglas.

Bishop's librettist, Thomas Morton, simplified Scott's grouping by omitting Malcolm; at the end, Ellen marries Roderick. But in Naples in 1818–19 the great contralto Rosmunda Pisaroni had joined the company, and so Rossini had to provide roles for her, which he did in *Ricciardo e Zoraide, Ermione,* and *La donna del lago.* Isabella Colbran remained the prima donna, the *protagonista*—Zoraide, Hermione, the Lady of the Lake—but Rossini's Malcolm is far from insignificant. He alone is allotted two full arias. (Ellen, James, Roderick, and Douglas have one apiece.) Miss Horne sang them in spectacular fashion: her cantabile was dulcet and finely wrought; her coloratura glittered. Although not of stature tall, and slender frame, she could have been more becomingly costumed. In high-heeled boots, a short, saucy tartan skirt, and a nipped-in black velvet jacket, she must have envied the choristers their full kilts and plaids.

Ellen, a soprano role (Kiri Te Kanawa took it in a 1969 London production), was the mezzo-soprano Frederica von Stade. Her timbre was beautiful in the mezzo range but edgy on the heights. An attractive and accomplished artist, she would be more captivating still if she were readier to link her lovely notes into flowing, shapely lines. The wigmaker had missed Scott's account of Ellen's "wild luxuriant ringlets...

Whose glossy black to shame might bring The plumage of the raven's wing." That famous first sight of the heroine alone in her boat was smudged by the provision of a boatman. These particularities matter. *La donna del lago* is not just any old Italian opera of lovers' tiffs and trials but a work that—as Philip Gossett points out in an *Opera News* article—was inspired in spirit and often in detail by Scott. Much in Houston was conventionalized.

Claudio Scimone was a routine conductor, making little of the marvellous atmospheric effects in the score. Dano Raffanti was no Black Sir Roderick, nor was Rockwell Blake the chivalrous James V. They were two arm-waving tenors. (Mr. Blake's fleet, accurate divisions were astounding, but his voice often sounded ugly.) Frank Corsaro directed as if he had no confidence in the piece. Usually, his work contains characters and has character. Here there were singing dummies and irrelevant diversions, in the form of a menagerie, an antlered Highland Falstaff capering about, a masked ball. Rossini's carefully planned scene structure was broken by two unwanted scene changes introduced into the first musical number.

I should add that this is an account of the opening night. Friends I trust tell me that at later performances everything went better and that the singing carried all before it, as in Rossini it can. A first-night verdict must be that the beautiful opera had been ambitiously cast but not enough thought and time had been spent on presenting the cast, and the work, to fullest advantage.

When Rossini settled in Paris, he worked out more fully and consistently reforms that in his earlier pieces had been compromised by the hurly-burly of Italian operatic life. In the sublime closing pages of *Guillaume Tell*—forerunner to the perorations of *Das Rheingold* and *Götterdämmerung*—his employment of scenery as dramatic symbol, as drama in itself, reached new heights. (The huge Alpine landscape is painted as much by the music as in the scene shop.) Before *Tell*, he reworked two of his Neapolitan operas, *Maometto II* and *Mosè in Egitto*, in a large, serious manner; the second became *Moïse et Pharaon*, a grand, moving, and powerful music drama. *Moïse* has not lacked praise but in this country, at least, has lacked performances. The Opera Company of Philadelphia's recent production (in Italian translation, as *Mosè*) was apparently the first staged here since 1860. It was a more consistent and convinced kind of performance than Houston's *Donna del lago*. There was a distinguished international cast, but the opera took precedence of the singers. Franco Colavecchia had designed simple, striking, handsome sets. James Assad's stage direction was aptly severe yet not unpicturesque. Alessandro Siciliani is a Rossini conductor with a fine command of pace and shape. All things worked together. Lella Cuberli, a true soprano (the Ellen of a *Donna del lago* in Pesaro in September), was an affecting, accurate, and stylish Anaï; the more I hear this young American artist, the more she impresses me.

Julia Hamari was an accomplished Sinaïde. The two tenors, Antonio Savastano and Krunoslav Cigoj, were decent except when they sang too loud. To the title role Jerome Hines brought dignity, presence, and some noble utterances, but his voice is not what it was.

Other opera in brief: Birgit Nilsson's first Metropolitan Dyer's Wife, in *Die Frau ohne Schatten,* was very loud and impressive except at the close of Act II, when she parted from the pitch and was merely loud. Eva Marton's Empress was loud, firm, and true, but hardly radiant or delicate. Mignon Dunn was a strong Nurse, who really sang the music, Franz Ferdinand Nentwig a lightweight Barak, and Gerd Brenneis an unlyrical Emperor. The production—décor by Robert O'Hearn, direction by Nathaniel Merrill—holds up well. Erich Leinsdorf was a clear, competent conductor, solving all "problems" deftly, but was utterly prosaic.

The revival of Janáček's *Cunning Little Vixen,* at the City Opera, was a delight, even if the children's-book sets and cuddly animals, from Maurice Sendak designs, sentimentalize Mr. Corsaro's keen, intelligent (and not uncontroversial) production. Gianna Rolandi took the title role precisely. Michael Tilson Thomas's conducting was at once fine-grained and stirring.

With Miss Rolandi become fox, the City Opera fielded an alternative *Puritani* cast. June Anderson, the new Elvira, lacked something of Miss Rolandi's charm and pathos, but she sang like a young Sutherland; she was strong, brilliant, and confident. Chris Merritt played Lord Arthur as a great booby and sang bravely, if not gracefully. Richard Fredricks was a forthright Sir Richard, and Justino Díaz a grandly generous Sir George except when the role sank beneath his effective compass.

CELEBRATION

November 9, 1981

AMONG THE works the Boston Symphony Orchestra commissioned to mark its fiftieth anniversary, in 1931, were Stravinsky's Psalm Symphony and Prokofiev's Fourth Symphony. Among those it commissioned to mark its seventy-fifth, in 1956, was Roger Sessions's Third Symphony. This year's centennial commissions range widely, and the celebrations continue into 1985. Peter Maxwell Davies's Second Symphony appeared earlier this year. Michael Tippett's full-evening oratorio *The Mask of Time* is billed for 1984. Roger Sessions's Concerto for Orchestra had its first performance on October 23.

Sessions will be eighty-five next month. His concerto is the work of a great composer at the peak of his powers. It lasts about fifteen minutes, is for large orchestra, and is in three linked sections: Allegro, Largo, and Allegro maestoso. The composer's own program note on it is brief. After a paragraph recalling his debt to the Boston orchestra, from the age of fourteen ("I have often said that the orchestral *sound* of the Boston Symphony as I first heard it impressed itself on my musical memory and strongly affected my own style of orchestral writing"), it continues:

> In the first section, alternately playful and lyrical, the woodwinds play a very prominent role; this is followed by a slow section...In this part, a solemn Largo, the brass instruments play the main role...A contrasting middle section extends the register by introducing the high woodwinds and more movement. After a climax the music of the previous Largo returns...A trumpet call...introduces the final section, which is festive in character. A short concluding statement, three phrases long, brings the piece to a quiet end.

Anyone deciding from that that the strings must play less than their usual dominant role would be right. There are no specifically string episodes, although when the strings do carry the burden of the argument for a few measures the effect is beautiful. They join in tuttis but otherwise seldom play all together. Divisions of the family contribute individual lines to the texture and at times support the winds with doubling or by shaping a new melody culled from the notes of various wind parts. Sessions's Concerto for Orchestra is not at all like Bartók's Concerto for Orchestra (which was also composed for the Boston Symphony, in 1943). Instead of sharp-cut, distinct, contrasting movements and the effect of spotlights playing upon now one part of the platform, now another, there is a single, intricate, poetic span. One ascends it with animated tread, moves with slow wonder across the central reach, speeds pace again toward its close, and at the end pauses for a moment, quietly rapt, to consider both the journey made and the realms to which it may lead. The concerto is exuberantly contrapuntal, like most of Sessions's music, but the sound is not thick. Back in 1959, when Tossy Spivakovsky and the New York Philharmonic, under Leonard Bernstein, played Sessions's Violin Concerto, Elliott Carter observed that to divide Sessions's work into three periods—Impressionist beginnings around 1923, Neoclassic from about 1926 to 1937, and thereafter Expressionist—could shed some illumination even while doing violence to the facts. Two decades later—a heroic-romantic opera, the great Whitman cantata, and five symphonies later—divisions are even harder to make. I recall Carter's remark because "Impressionist" is a word I reach for in trying to describe the scoring of the new concerto—the Impressionism of *La Mer*, which is richly and rigorously constructed, and filled with picturesque detail at once motivically controlled and set down so surely that the "picture" moves and dances. The solo wind melodies (toward the close of the central section, there is a wonderfully serene, lyrical period for solo trombone while flute, oboe, then flute again trace soft, ecstatic larksong high above) and a recurrent ticktock of the xylophone, a deft touch swiftly restabilizing the pulse after passages rhythmically ambiguous, suggest links with Sessions's previous work, the Ninth Symphony, which appeared in 1980.

In a 1950 essay, "How a 'Difficult' Composer Gets That Way" (reprinted in *Roger Sessions on Music,* the collected essays published by Princeton), Sessions said, "I would prefer by far to write music which has something fresh to reveal at each new hearing than music which is completely self-evident the first time, and though it may remain pleasing makes no essential contribution thereafter." New hearings—except of the works that are recorded—are hard to come by. Boston played the First Symphony in 1927, the Third in 1957, and has played neither since. The New York Philharmonic commissioned the Eighth Symphony for its 125th-anniversary celebrations, in 1968, played it then, and has not played it since. The Philharmonic's record of Sessions performances is poor indeed: the Second Symphony in 1950, the Violin Concerto in 1959, the Eighth Symphony in 1968, the Third in 1976. (The BBC Symphony has probably done more of Sessions's music than any American orchestra.) Some major works await a New York performance—among them the opera *Montezuma* and the cantata *When Lilacs Last in the Dooryard Bloom'd* (a piece that many would put into Columbia's hand if she could hold but a single score representing this country's highest musical achievement). *Montezuma,* however, is due at the Juilliard in February (see page 205). In an article on Sessions written for the December issue of *Keynote,* WNCN's lively, valuable music magazine, David Hamilton suggests that not only listeners but also performers are missing much they might enjoy, and he essays some matchmaking:

> The Violin Concerto is a natural for Itzhak Perlman, who would relish both its technical challenges and its expressive potential. The *Idyll of Theocritus* I commend to Jessye Norman and Colin Davis; it's just the kind of high-protein music for which they command the emotional range and intensity. And there are symphonies enough to go around: for Claudio Abbado, Michael Gielen, Bernard Haitink, James Levine, Leonard Slatkin, Edo de Waart—all of whom should find significant aspects of Sessions's musical language congenial and stimulating.

Seiji Ozawa conducted the Boston performances (and New World recording) of *Lilacs* in 1977, and now the Concerto for Orchestra, and so may be counted something of a Sessions champion (even though he and the orchestra have now set out on a world tour to play only Beethoven, Schubert, Stravinsky, Bartók, and Webern to audiences in Japan, France, Germany, Austria, and London). The performance of the concerto was, I thought, conscientious rather than idiomatic. The details hadn't yet fallen into place. Not all the melodies *sang.* (But the first trombone, Ronald Barron, was poetic.) The tempo of the outer sections was surely a shade slow. The score proposes more variety of dynamics than we heard. But then performers and listeners alike need to find their way into Sessions's music. Later Boston performances—if ever the orchestra does play the concerto again—will surely reveal a work still more eloquent and exciting. And other conductors, other orchestras will surely take up with enthusiasm a piece so vigorous, so beautiful, and—for listeners, at least—so little "difficult."

[In 1982, Sessions's Concerto for Orchestra was awarded the Pulitzer Prize for Musical Composition. The Boston Symphony and Mr. Ozawa recorded the work, on Hyperion.]

Sir Michael Tippett is seventy-six. His first three string quartets are early works, composed between 1934 and 1945, before his huge lyrical flowering in the opera The Midsummer Marriage. Beethoven—and specifically, Tippett recalls, annual Beethoven cycles played in London by the Busch and the Léner quartets during his student days—was the large influence on them. By the time he composed the Third, he also knew Bartók's quartets. The three are rewarding pieces (the Lindsay Quartet has recorded them on a Oiseau-Lyre disc), all marked by formal adventure—each contains at least one fugue—by a love of Tudor polyphony as found in viol fancies, and by an exuberant, dancing quality all Tippett's own. Beethoven has never been far from Tippett's music and is very near the surface in the Piano Concerto, the Third Symphony, and the Third Piano Sonata. When Tippett composed a Fourth String Quartet, in 1977–78, he wrote a Beethoven-steeped finale, with imagery derived explicitly from the Grosse Fuge. Before it, a long, lyrical Andante carries the main charge of the work. The first movement is a mysterious "coming-to-birth" introduction—ponticello chords trembling into life and line—which leads without break into a vigorous linear Allegro. Tippett's late style is not less lyrical or exuberant than his early style (though less abrupt than the middle style of King Priam and the Second Piano Sonata), but it represents utterance pared to essentials—almost in the manner of Beethoven's late Bagatelles. A surprising amount of the string writing is in only two real parts.

The Lindsay, which introduced the new quartet at the 1979 Bath Festival, played it at Carnegie Recital Hall last month, and it was good to hear. Before it, Haydn's Opus 74, No. 3; after, Beethoven's second "Razumovsky." Those performances had the intensity, the freedom, the sharp musical insights for which the Lindsay is in Britain so much praised. The quartet, a colleague there once wrote, "is remarkable not only for the strength and panache of all its members, but for the collective concentration with which it pursues its sharply defined musical purposes. There is a strong sense that each player is given his head, and yet that all the heads seem to think the music the same way." And so, indeed, it did seem. But I was unprepared for quite so much faulty intonation; perhaps string quartets, like pianos, can be shaken out of tune by travel.

FINDING THE RIGHT PATH

November 16, 1981

ON ALL Hallows Eve, both New York houses played *Rigoletto,* the Metropolitan in the afternoon and the City Opera in the evening. Anyone attending both productions could assemble—except in point of staging—an outstanding performance of Verdi's opera. The Met's seat prices ranged from sixty dollars to eleven, the City Opera's from twenty-five dollars to three-fifty. The apter voices for Gilda and the Duke of Mantua were to be heard at the latter house. Carol Vaness, tackling her first Gilda, gave a performance at once beautifully studied, delicate, and passionate. She has a young, full lirico spinto, for which voice the role is written. (The first Gilda, Teresa Brambilla, was an Abigail in *Nabucco,* an Elvira in *Ernani*; the first Elvira, Sofia Loewe, was Verdi's first choice for Lady Macbeth.) Miss Vaness is a brave, spirited singer ready to dare, well able to ride the storm trio, to crown the climax of the quartet, to ring out in "Sì, vendetta" if the conductor ignores Verdi's repeated pianissimo markings. She can float limpid, affecting high notes and turn accurate, shapely coloratura. Her trills were neat. Vinson Cole displayed a tenor at once firm and beautiful, supple and shining. Both artists were clear, sure, effortless, and unroutined. At the Met, Judith Blegen, on a smaller scale, sang an exquisite "Caro nome" and was exquisite in all four duets. By purity of projection, she carried in passages that really need an ampler voice than hers. She is a singer who lends distinction to all she does, and her Gilda was very pleasing. Juan Lloveras phrased even more seductively than Mr. Cole, especially in "È il sol dell'anima," and he has more assurance on the stage, but his voice is a less even instrument, and at times the timbre clouded over.

In the title role, the Met's Matteo Manuguerra was outstanding. Although he lacks the reserves of power Sherrill Milnes can draw on for "Cortigiani!" his performance was rounded, consistent, securely voiced, and unflagging. Moreover, he knows the one or two rules that all family fools must observe: that a jester, paid to be funny, must jibe, joke, and jollify. In the first scene, Mr. Manuguerra was properly quaint and amusing, whereas the City Opera's Richard Fredricks, a dour fellow, would soon have had half-a-crown stopped out of his wages. Nevertheless, Rigoletto is one of Mr. Fredricks's best roles. He sings it strongly, even formidably. But the performance suffers from his acquiescence in Frank Corsaro's direction of the opera.

Mr. Corsaro's Rigoletto treats Monterone's curse (the opera's original title was "La Maledizione," and the curse motif begins and ends it) as a joke, and laughs it off with each arm around a willing wench. We may deduce if we like that inwardly he is disturbed, but Mr. Fredricks does

154

nothing to demonstrate it. On the way to the house where Gilda has been installed (it is miscalled Rigoletto's dwelling by both Met and City Opera programs; plainly he doesn't live there himself), the jester has recourse to strong drink and is required to play the start of Scene 2—the duet with Sparafucile and "Pari siamo"—as a drunk scene, sip-sip-sipping away. It is psychologically possible, but it is not what Verdi had in mind. If Verdi had wanted a tipsy Rigoletto, he would have said so, and written music to that effect. If in the following scene Verdi had intended Rigoletto during "Solo per me l'infamia" to spurn his daughter, throw her to the ground, strike her, he would have said so. But, again, it is possible behavior. In the final scene, for Rigoletto to leave Gilda lying, just before "Lassù in cielo," and run for a second time to batter on the tavern door as if to ask for his twenty scudi back—services inadequately rendered!—seems to me an impossible reading of Rigoletto's character, the words, the music, and the scene.

Throughout the show, the staging parts company from the stage directions. Gilda addresses the scena of "Caro nome" to a still present Duke. Ten attendants play various roles in the scena of the Duke's "Parmi veder le lagrime"—in the score, a soliloquy. The courtiers' narrative chorus becomes unheeded accompaniment to a dog show. Six women besides Gilda figure prominently in this act and destroy Verdi's strong, deliberate device of a stag affair that throws the single victim into relief. The program's "Cast (in order of appearance)" begins ominously: first, Rigoletto (for whom Verdi devised a sudden, striking, later entrance); second and third, "Daughter of Count Monterone" and "Clown," two Corsaro additions to the composer's dramatis personae and both given protuberant invented roles. (Two jesters compete for attention at the City Opera court.) After years, now, of watching Corsaro productions, I am less ready than once I was to dismiss them as merely perverse, obtuse, and vulgar. I admire his evident insistence that actors should act and react not merely "after the book" but in accord with sound, perceived psychological reasons, and admire the effect he has—vivifying at best and at the least purgative—on modern singers who are content to let directors (and conductors) do much of their thinking for them. (Mr. Manuguerra is exceptional: when invited into the San Francisco *Rigoletto* earlier this year to fill in for an absent protagonist, he sensibly refused to enact some of the rubbish with which Jean-Pierre Ponnelle had weakened the final scene.) I think I can see, as a rule, what Mr. Corsaro is after. But his execution often leaves the impression of a director determined above all to do something different—one incapable of following orders, who thinks he's a better dramatist than Verdi, Monteverdi, Rossini, Debussy, Janáček. Mr. Corsaro is not a poor dramatist, even if some of his devices—eye-catching animals, much onstage donning and doffing of clothes—become Corsaro cliché. His work is arresting, not boring. But his revisionist hand weakens much of what it touches—when he fights his authors instead of finding and using their strengths. The Houston

Donna del lago I wrote about two weeks ago was Corsaro versus Rossini, not a triumphant collaboration. Prising out new, keen details of behavior, stitching in any loose ends of timing or action, finding diversion for passages he deems boring, he is apt to miss composers' simpler, straightforward, large effects. *Rigoletto* (like *La traviata*) would not have held the stage solidly for a hundred and thirty years had it been in need of drastic dramaturgical overhaul. To question tradition is admirable. To reject too readily a century and more's accumulation of others' insights and discoveries is foolish. (At the Vienna Opera, it was not tradition but "what you people call tradition"—unthinking acceptance of established practices—that Mahler denounced as slovenliness.) Moreover, I sometimes think Mr. Corsaro's operatic understanding incomplete and his musical horizons limited—when he focusses too intently on the librettos and strives to improve them. Many librettos are on the printed page poor plays indeed, inviting revision. But, as Lee Strasberg says in a foreword to Mr. Corsaro's book *Maverick*, "Opera is drama in music, not drama with music." In the chapters of *Maverick* that follow, there is little to suggest any appreciation of theatrical power inherent in musical forms, and in his practice Mr. Corsaro often denies himself or diminishes that power.

The City Opera's *Rigoletto*, I should add, was a revival of a 1969 Corsaro production, not fresh from his hand but carefully re-created by a talented staff director, Jay Lesenger. However, the master—he told me so in an intermission—approves it. If I go on at length about Mr. Corsaro, it is because he is a major force in American opera, a force largely for good—but not wholly—and a man I like, respect, admire, and enjoy arguing with. The staging of the Met's *Rigoletto*, a revival of John Dexter's 1977 production, is less provocative. In an earlier volume, I detailed its obvious mistakes. Some of them have now been righted; others are ineradicably linked to Tanya Moiseiwitsch's misconceived revolving-tower unit set. Both *Rigoletto*s look handsome, but the City Opera's, designed by Lloyd Evans, houses Verdi's action more aptly. Within the Met staging, the principals can give delicate and intelligent performances, and they did.

At the City Opera, Henry Lewis was a conductor of no particular merits other than simple vitality; some passages were rushed. At the Met, Giuseppe Patané was a conductor versed in *Rigoletto* lore—supple, sensitive, and exciting. The Met's limpid, steady first flute, Michael Parloff, made much of the important role Verdi assigned him; the City Opera's flute was more ordinary. [*John Wion, the City Opera's regular first flute, later wrote to tell me that he was not playing that evening.*] As I said, one had to hear both performances to discover the opera. At the Met, two-thirds of the duet "Ah! veglia, o donna" was cut (something I thought now happened only in small-town Italian houses). At the City Opera, Rigoletto was allowed his solo strophe, but Gilda's reply was rudely interrupted after twelve measures. (Why spoil a balanced musical design to save twenty seconds?) In both houses, Gilda's and the

Duke's farewells were abridged, and the latter's "Possente amor" was reduced to a single strophe. Both Dukes piously endorsed the nineteenth-century Venetian censor's alteration of the order to Sparafucile, in Act III, for "tua sorella" to a meaningless order for "una stanza." Miss Vaness, however, did sing the coda of "Caro nome" as Verdi wrote it, staying on B during "Gualtier Maldè" (and very beautiful it was); Miss Blegen rose to the E's of the printed score. Miss Vaness elected to sing the long, smooth rising scale in "Caro nome" staccato. Both sopranos overlooked the portamento slurs on "tempio" and "Iddio" in "Tutte le feste."

Both houses have also been playing *La traviata*. The opera turns on its heroine, and the Met's Catherine Malfitano has what Verdi himself described as "the best qualities for a Traviata—a beautiful face, spirit, and theatrical presence." And she has youth. She has learned, it seems, from great Violettas past and present, yet taken from them only what will fit her own vivid portrayal. Not an inflection, gesture, or glance seemed untrue. The effect was spontaneous, and thrilling. She sings the music honestly and beautifully: this was one of the most *audible* performances I have ever heard in the huge house. "Con voce debolissima," Verdi wrote over Violetta's entry in the Act II finale, "con voce bassa senza suono" for her reading of the letter in Act III, and "un fil di voce" on the A's that end each strophe of the aria. Miss Malfitano obeyed those instructions memorably. The Alfredo, Giuliano Ciannella, was a less cultivated singer but bright, ardent, and credible. The pair played well together. Brent Ellis was a decent if not exceptional Germont. Nicola Rescigno conducted in a fleet, light way, with little rubato, and, for once, instead of disliking that I thought it matched the youthful urgency of his cast. He is a cunning and expert accompanist. Balance was perfect. Colin Graham's production, new last spring, is admirable: fresh, honest, lively (Flora's party is particularly successful); filled with well-observed, truthful, and—except for a tiresome drunk in the first scene—unstagy details; not cranky, and supple enough to contain and enhance the individual contributions that changing casts may bring to it. Miss Moiseiwitsch's scenery is handsome, unspectacular, and realistic—large enough for the scale of the house, intimate enough for the drama. (I wonder if Mr. Corsaro saw the show, and, if so, what he made of it. It seemed to me to fulfill most of what he requires of an operatic presentation.)

The City Opera has at last retired Mr. Corsaro's celebrated 1966 production of *La traviata* (it had Patricia Brooks, Placido Domingo, and Dominic Cossa as its first cast), and replaced it with an undistinguished version directed by Lou Galterio in cheap-looking scenery designed by Zack Brown, with costumes—largely hideous—designed by Patton Campbell. (Mr. Corsaro's version has its memorial in two stimulating chapters of *Maverick* and its progeny in good ideas that have found their way into various other performances.) The lighting—like that of all City Opera shows I've seen this season except *The Cunning Little*

Vixen is often provincial primitive. An intermission breaks the flow of Act II, whose first scene is moved out-of-doors, into a sort of yard. Diana Soviero was an able, well-schooled, capable heroine, but somewhat monotonous of timbre and unmoving. Barry McCauley's Alfredo was blunt and plebeian. William Stone's Germont was ordinary. Mario Bernardi conducted. Luchino Visconti once set out—in Spoleto in 1963—to produce "una *Traviata* poverissima," after the splendors of his Scala version with Callas. The results were peculiar but not unarresting. The City Opera *Traviata* looks and sounds merely dowdy.

The City Opera's revival, from the spring, of *Attila*, Verdi's ninth opera, was—unlike its new production of *Nabucco*, Verdi's third opera —bold, confident, handsome, and splendid. More: it revealed—as productions in Florence, London, Newark, Washington did not—the irresistible power of the once-popular piece. After the Washington production, in 1976, I concurred in the generally unfavorable verdict on the work but added, "I still hope to encounter, one day, a performance that will make me change my mind." I have done so. Everyone set about the piece in the right way—with vividness, gusto, a sense of its picturesqueness, and a feeling for what Julian Budden rightly calls "moments of tenderness and beauty." The title role lies ideally for Justino Díaz's ringing basso cantante. He has the vocal powers and physical presence for the part. Marilyn Zschau, the Odabella (another Loewe role), entered as if fresh from a Brooklyn beauty parlor rather than the smoky battlefield (does no one edit the City Opera divas' makeup?), but there was both vigor and luster in her accurate, energetic singing. Enrico DiGiuseppe, the Foresto, and Richard Fredricks, the Aetius, were strong. Even the comprimario, James Clark, as Uldino, was gleaming. And in Sergiu Comissiona the company fielded one of the two superior conductors it has so far brought forward this season. (The other was Michael Tilson Thomas in the *Vixen*.) He led, shaped, surged, drew urgent playing from the orchestra, supported the singers firmly. Ming Cho Lee's scenery is plain, but Hal George's costumes are resplendent. Lotfi Mansouri, directing, handled the masses well: the moment when Attila's advance upon Rome was checked by a chorus of children and virgins proved as thrilling as Verdi hoped it would be. Ralph Bassett had the voice but not the grand bearing for Pope Leo the Great (a role billed as "Leone, an ancient Roman"—another City Opera submission to nineteenth-century Venetian censorship).

Verdi's sixth opera, *I due Foscari,* was last month given a concert performance by Eve Queler's Opera Orchestra of New York. Carlo Bergonzi played Jacopo Foscari. He can be a wonderful stylist, "the last of the Verdi tenors," master of supple lines and melting effects such as Caruso, Bonci, Gigli commanded, and he can be an undisciplined performer indulging in late-Gigli vices—the grunt preliminary, good notes clung to for as long as they can be held. In this *Foscari,* he was both. Francesco Foscari is the part in which I have most often heard

Renato Bruson. In Naples in 1968, he was monotonously loud; in the Teatro Colón in 1979 he gave a noble, poetic performance; for Miss Queler he reverted to loudness and seemed more intent on displaying a voice than on creating a character. Neither tenor nor baritone was always nice about pitch. The Lucrezia (as at the Colón) was Margarita Castro-Alberty, a shining ex-Juilliard soprano in the Caniglia mold, with a large, beautiful voice; broad, high cheekbones; big, bright eyes; and a strong frame. It was an evening of full, uninhibited singing rather than a careful artistic account of the sombre, unconventional opera.

One of the sharper sentences in the New Grove ends Michael Steinberg's entry on Vladimir Horowitz: "Horowitz illustrates that an astounding instrumental gift carries no guarantee about musical understanding." Well, maybe he thinks with ears and fingers, but it would be hard to say that the account of six Scarlatti sonatas—shapely, captivating, irresistible—which opened Horowitz's recital in the Metropolitan Opera House this month lacked musical understanding. It would have been hard not to surrender to everything he did. Chopin's fourth and first Ballades, Liszt's B-minor Ballade, and three Rachmaninoff Preludes completed the program; a Chopin waltz, a Rachmaninoff polka, and a Scriabin study formed the encores. Horowitz has always been mannered, willful, quirky. Accents fall in unexpected places. Rhythms and phrasing can be very odd. But his command of articulations, textures, dynamic balances, and pedaling is supreme. He has wit. Every detail of these performances had been polished for our delight. What can one do but marvel and be glad?

Clarion Concerts began its twenty-fifth season, in Alice Tully Hall, with the overture to Salieri's *Europa riconosciuta,* the opera commissioned to inaugurate La Scala, in 1778. It's a dramatic storm piece. The concert continued with three movements of Salieri's symphony—the only symphony in the Grove list of his surprisingly few orchestral compositions. The Larghetto is exquisite, a dialogue between muted, murmuring strings and woodwinds. The Scherzo and Trio is conventional but includes a piquant use of the violins' open G string. The finale is an extended Rondo with a catchy main theme and an entertaining close. Then came one of Salieri's two piano concertos, the C major. His orchestral concerns, to judge by these pieces (all of them billed as American premières), were less with large structure and dramatic discourse than with passing attractive inventions, melodic or instrumental. And the music certainly was attractive.

But Clarion, eighteenth-century champions and introducers to New York of much worthwhile music, will have to come to terms with 1980s ideas of how eighteenth-century music should be played—and on what instruments. Newell Jenkins, conducting, used a top-heavy string body (6–5–4–3–1) in a lopsided modern disposition. Kenneth Cooper played the Salieri on a (rather bleak) fortepiano, a copy of a Walter, which balanced ill with the modern instruments of the orchestra. For a Mozart concerto in the second half (K. 488, in A), he moved to the hall's Steinway, and that raised new problems, since he played the instrument as if it were uncongenial to him. In this Mozart second half, Mr. Jenkins gave the American première of twenty-eight newly discovered measures for *Die Entführung*. In Act I of the opera, the Pasha Selim and Konstanze enter on a pleasure craft "preceded by another boat with a janissary band on board." This new janissary march is presumably what the band played—some of the "bezaubernde Musik" with which Selim had been hoping in vain to soften Konstanze's heart.

The Group for Contemporary Music opened its twentieth-anniversary season, at the 92nd Street Y, with a program of four "classics"—two solos, two chamber concertos—that drew a large audience. Harvey Sollberger gave a refined, lyrical account of Varèse's *Density 21.5*, and Raymond DesRoches a taut, arresting account of "Saëta" and "Canaries" from Elliott Carter's Pieces for Four Timpani. Charles Wuorinen's Chamber Concerto for cello and ten players, one of his most brilliant and shapely pieces, should perhaps be termed specifically a Group classic. The Group gave the first performance, in 1964, and in 1971 recorded it (for Nonesuch) with the same splendid soloist, Fred Sherry, as at this concert. The classic status of Berg's Chamber Concerto, for piano, violin, and thirteen winds, is not in doubt, but it is an awkward piece to bring off. It often sounds dense, clogged, airless—and overextended in its finale. Despite two eloquent soloists—Robert Black, piano, and Benjamin Hudson, violin—it seemed that way here, I thought: like a masterwork manqué, but one well worth hearing. The Boulez recording on Columbia is the only performance I know that is spacious and clear.

A LOFTIER STRAIN

November 23, 1981

THE UNIVERSITY of Maryland at College Park, outside Washington, has an admirable chorus, conducted by Paul Traver. In its library, it has the collection of the Handelian scholar J. M. Coopersmith. And recently it has established a Center for Renaissance and Baroque Studies. In 1979, the university chorus and the Smithsonian Chamber Players joined to give the first Washington-area performances of Handel's first English oratorio, *Esther,* in an edition prepared by Howard Serwer, of the Music Department, with his Baroque-music seminar; and this Maryland *Esther* was taken to the Handel Festival in Halle, Handel's birthplace. From these foundations, there rose this month the Maryland Handel Festival—a three-day event, with three concerts in the Memorial Chapel of the university and, in the Library of Congress, a two-session international symposium in which eminent Handelian scholars—Winton Dean, J. Merrill Knapp, Paul Henry Lang, Jens Peter Larsen, Alfred Mann, Walther Siegmund-Schultze—took part. The choice of the main work to be performed, *Messiah*, was conservative, but its execution was not uncontroversial. Handelian passions run deep and, like torrents in summer, can suddenly rise to o'erflowing. Moreover, *Messiah* in particular holds so special a place in most musicians' hearts that reaction to any performance of it may well be as susceptible of Jungian as of musicological analysis. I know it in myself, as I strive for accurate listening, clear of the personal associations that cluster thickly around several of its numbers, and I sensed it at the Maryland performance, as the air became charged and the distress of one of the distinguished visitors grew so keen that after the first part he had to flee the chapel.

The edition Mr. Traver used was that of Watkins Shaw, published by Novello. Shaw's full score, careful and unexceptionable, presents the notes Handel wrote and little else except some suggestions for rhythmic alteration and some added trills—clearly indicated as editorial. But his complementary vocal score is more freely embellished. Handel set the words "He was despised, despised and rejected" to a melody thirteen notes long—a note to a syllable except for two sixteenths on the last syllable of the second "despised." Shaw adds seven notes more, in the form of slides, passing notes, and twiddles. His preface to the vocal score points out that the embellishments are editorial, but since they appear on the main staff, a singer is tempted to sing them unquestioningly—with the result that Handel's original clear, beautiful outline is then never heard. Adornments of this kind are by some modern Handelians eagerly welcomed, by others despised and rejected, and both camps adduce historical evidence to support their preferences. Handel himself wrote a somewhat elaborate and fanciful cadenza for the air "He was despised." But about adding cadenzas—provided they are kept within eighteenth-century bounds, and do not go rocketing into Rossinian, Bellinian, or Verdian territory—and about moderately decorating da capos there is little dispute. It is mucking around with a melody before ever it has been heard as written and varying it out of all recognition that rouse passions. The castrato Guarducci, who sang in English oratorios in the late 1760s, after Handel's day, once said to Burney:

> The English are such friends to the composer, and to simplicity, that they like to hear a melody in its primitive state, undisguised by change or embellishment. Or if, when repeated, *riffioramenti* are necessary, the notes must be few and well selected, to be honoured with approbation.

But then Guarducci, as Dean observes in his great book on the Handel oratorios, was singing before an audience "already affected by the movement to sanctify the oratorios." And so the argument goes back and forth. Peter Wishart's published album of ornamented *Messiah* arias and Dame Joan Sutherland's renditions of what a famous conductor once called her "Mad Scenes from *Messiah*" represent two aspects of the modern taste for adornment. In a 1972 essay reprinted in the Maryland program book, Larsen compares two recorded performances, a quarter century apart, of the opening recitative and air "Comfort ye...Ev'ry valley." Aksel Schiøtz's, which appeared in 1940, "at its time...seemed sensationally new because the performance of aria accompaniments...in Handel's scoring for string orchestra only —without added wind parts—was still highly unusual." Robert Tear's, which appeared in 1967 (in a *Messiah* conducted by Charles Mackerras), "is anything but unadorned. The solo performance is totally dominated by a modern tendency towards richly embellished vocal interpretation. One can in no way escape the impression that the soloist wants to show his audience how well he masters the art of ornamentation. His singlemindedness in this respect is completely naïve—though taken seriously in wide circles." And so historicism in one case

> leads to the omission of added nineteenth-century orchestration, restoring the freedom with which a gifted singer can present the glorious melodic flow of Handel's music. In the second case it leads to the false conclusion that Handel's oratorio solos are to be treated like the bravura arias of operas, with constant elaboration of the musical text—a wealth of vocal virtuosity in which the original music is nearly lost.

Larsen's words are loaded. In Handel's day, there were already complaints about overadornment. Early in the nineteenth century, Mrs. Billington, mistress of bold inventions and rapid divisions, was admired for not "gambolling" when she sang Handel's sacred music. (But that "sacred" is a question-begging word.) A Schirmer 1912 vocal score of *Messiah* boldly cites Hugo Goldschmidt's 1907 study of Baroque vocal adornment: "The interpreter's work is no mere execution.... His task is rather to seize the vital conception of the art-work, to blend it with his own ego and the views of his period, and thus to imbue it with life and effectiveness." The views of any period are varied: from the same evidence different conclusions are reached. Opposed contemporary views clash resoundingly in the issues of *Opera* from June to September, where Dean and Mackerras—both of them *Giulio Cesare* editors—and their supporters disagree on many Handelian matters. And when it comes to *Messiah*, then, as I suggested, more than musical passions seem to be fired. (Larsen charges that noble singer Janet Baker with committing "appalling examples of exaggerated ornamentation" in a recording of "O thou that tellest.") One soprano sings the "liveth" of "I know that my redeemer liveth" to two G-sharps; another alters the notes to A and G-sharp. Either way, a shudder of disapproval runs through part of the audience.

I agree with Larsen. A confluence of tendencies each good in itself —the wish to make familiar music sound fresh, and to free Handel's oratorios from Victorian heaviness; a fuller recognition of how dramatic, even "operatic," they often are; a delight in virtuoso "star" singing—has led to overexuberant and frequently tasteless ornamentation. Moreover, when new discoveries about authentic performance practice are made there is a natural desire to test them to the hilt. A *Musical Times* exchange over another of our modern "historical fashions" is relevant. In the May issue, a reviewer of Bach's orchestral suites recorded by the English Concert complained that "every long note is like an overdriven love affair, with hectic advance and retreat." In July, Robert Donington suggested that the current craze for such "lozenge dynamics" (sustained notes soft-loud-soft, or the "Harnoncourt lurch") is a "particular bit of authenticity which has gone wrong, or should I say got out of hand." In October, Trevor Pinnock, the director of the English Concert, pointed out that he had made the record three years ago, in a putting-it-to-the-test period, and that since then "the orchestra has developed a style which is less dependent on this feature than that of almost any other Baroque ensemble that I know."

Fashions in performance change fast. Today's orthodoxy becomes tomorrow an old misunderstanding. But the good and the true remain: the baby born during the fad for "terraced dynamics," for example, waxes bonny while the bilge that once surrounded him is gone. Mr. Traver, to judge by the Maryland *Messiah,* is still in an overenthusiastic stage, discovering the delights of decoration, for to the Shaw edition he had added still more adornment, written into choral and instrumental lines; and much of this was hard to accept. When a Handel melody takes the step of a third, the small leap was often filled in with a passing note. In "I know that my redeemer liveth," the violin seemed to be playing precomposed variations without regard to what the singer, Phyllis Bryn-Julson, did; the result sounded more like a musicological dispute than a serenely declarative duet. In one respect, however, Mr. Traver clung to yesterday's practice: at the close of recitatives he held back dominant and tonic chords until the voice had finished, instead of striking in with the cadences where Handel wrote them. (Propulsive, foreshortened cadences, today's new thing, prove vivid and convincing in performance.) And he left awkward gaps between the numbers that should follow swiftly one upon another.

So there were things to question and argue about. The performance as a whole was spirited, shapely, thoroughly rewarding. The chorus, consisting of about a hundred light, clear voices, was firm, lithe, rhythmical, and well balanced. (The full complement was used only in the bigger numbers.) Mr. Traver has a fine command of the dance rhythms that underlie so much eighteenth-century music. Nothing was heavy or labored. There was much joy in the performance, and where majesty was called for, it was not missing. The solo quartet contained one Baroque specialist, the countertenor René Jacobs, whose steady tone, beautiful melodic and rhythmic articulation, and chaste, discerning adornments tended to show up the more ordinary manners of the three "modern" singers—Miss Bryn-Julson, John Aler, and Donnie Ray Albert. The first was not in good voice: has much leaping around in the service of contemporary music taken a toll of the evenness, pure timbre, and accurate intonation that we expect of her? Mr. Aler displayed his newfound strength and fullness of timbre, and he sang with fervor. Sometimes he and Mr. Albert were louder than necessary. The orchestra was modern, and of moderate size. Practicalities enjoin the former: no point in making a fuss. No doubt the Maryland festival will one day command a Baroque band (I noted a face or two familiar from Aston Magna on the platform), and no doubt even before that the Baroque movement will start to temper the players' vibrato, their bright, modern attack, and their modern approach to phrasing.

The festival began with Handel's four Coronation anthems, in splendidly brave performances. Most of the Maryland campus buildings are vaguely neo-Wren in style, in Wren's plainest, Chelsea Hospital manner. The chapel is like a City church, with pews and galleries, but totally unadorned. (No hint whether Mithras, Mars, Moses, the Messiah, Muhammad, or Mammon is revered there.) It proved a shade unresonant for *Messiah* and distinctly too dry for the Coronation anthems, whose carefully planned figuration and slow, sure harmonic gait flower in the long-sounding spaces of Westminster Abbey. The anthems were divided by three of the Opus 4 Organ Concertos, played by Catharine Crozier on a rather cramped-sounding little chamber organ.

At the second concert, Miss Bryn-Julson, the soprano Linda Mabbs, and Mr. Jacobs paired variously to sing Handel duets, including, interestingly, those that share material with five numbers of *Messiah*. (It has been suggested that they are "sketches" for the great work—Handel's "Wesendonk-Lieder.") They sounded somewhat underrehearsed. They were framed between four of the Opus 6 Grand Concertos, conducted by Mr. Traver in a manner to make one exclaim afresh at Handel's greatness. The Concerti Grossi—does it need saying?—are marvels of invention in melody, in harmony, in texture, in form. They provide the sort of delight that inspired Haydn does. Perhaps it does need saying: they figure too seldom in chamber-orchestra programs.

The Maryland Handel Festival is intended as an annual event. For next year, the first version of *Esther* is billed, to inaugurate a series of all Handel's English oratorios in order of composition. Exciting prospect.

[*For an account of the second festival, and* Esther, *see page 369.*]

MUSIC IN THE SILENCE OF THE NIGHT

November 30, 1981

ELLIOTT CARTER'S *Night Fantasies,* for piano solo, was composed in 1979–80, at the request of four American pianists who have all been notable performers of his music: Ursula Oppens, Charles Rosen, Paul Jacobs, and Gilbert Kalish. Miss Oppens played it first, at the Bath Festival, in June 1980, and returned to England that October to play it in ten other British cities: London, Brighton, Bedford, Manchester, York, Liverpool, Huddersfield, Nottingham, Leicester, and Birmingham. The Arts Council of Great Britain maintains a Contemporary Music Network to insure that at least some major performances will be more than one-time, one-audience affairs, and the BBC saw to it that everyone in Britain had a chance of hearing Carter's latest composition. (In America, it should have been, but wasn't, broadcast prominently, coast to coast.) Miss Oppens then gave the American première, in Chicago, last February, and has since played it in Tokyo and Venice. Mr. Jacobs played it in Detroit last March, and both pianists played it at the Monadnock Festival last summer. Mr. Rosen played it in Toronto in June. It reached New York at last when Mr. Jacobs played it in his recital at the 92nd Street Y on November 11. Mr. Kalish will play the piece in Germany next November. Miss Oppens is billed to give the New York deuxième at her Metropolitan Museum recital on February 11.

Night fantasies! There are famous accounts, each of them purporting to be related in the composer's own words, of the way nocturnal inspiration visited Mozart and Beethoven. The Mozart passage was published by J. F. Rochlitz in 1815:

> About my way of composing, and what method I follow in writing works of some extent, I can really say no more than the following.... When I am, as it were, completely myself, entirely alone, and of good cheer—say, travelling in a carriage, or walking after a good meal, or during the night when I cannot sleep—it is on such occasions that my ideas flow best and most abundantly. *Whence* and *how* they come, I know not; nor can I force them.... All this inventing, this producing, takes place in a pleasing lively dream.

The Beethoven passage appeared in 1880 in Louis Schlösser's "Memories of Beethoven":

> You will ask me whence I take my ideas? That I cannot say with any degree of certainty: they come to me uninvited, directly or indirectly. I could almost grasp them in my hands, out in nature's open, in the woods during my walks, in the silence of the night, at earliest dawn.... They are roused by moods, which... are transmuted into tones that sound, roar, and storm until at last they take shape for me as notes.

165

Both passages have long appealed to romantic commentators. Both, alas, have been declared to be inventions. Back in 1858, Mozart's biographer Otto Jahn decided that the remarks Rochlitz published "cannot be by Mozart" but thought that a genuine Mozart letter underlay them. William James, in 1907, still adduced them as evidence that "great thinkers have vast premonitory glimpses of schemes of relation between terms, which hardly even as verbal images enter the mind, so rapid is the whole process." The Schlösser passage is called into question by Maynard Solomon in the latest number of *Music & Letters*, and his demonstration that it is essentially a rewriting of Rochlitz's invented Mozart letter seems to me incontrovertible. The "alas" must stand. What Rochlitz and Schlösser wrote is reluctantly rejected. It ought to be true. Every insomniac knows those moments "during the night when I cannot sleep," "in the silence of the night, at earliest dawn," when "ideas flow best and most abundantly," and responds to the notion that a genius—a Mozart, a Beethoven, an Elliott Carter—can recapture those ideas ("take out the bag of my memory" is the phrase Rochlitz attributed to Mozart), formulate them, phrase and frame them, find notes for them, and set them down for mankind's instruction and delight.

In his song cycle *A Mirror on Which to Dwell* (1976), Carter made music for Elizabeth Bishop's poem "Insomnia." One thought obsessed the sleepless poet there—that of a reversed, mirror world in which "you love me"—but her poem contains the line that gives Carter's cycle its title; and *Night Fantasies*, it seems to me, may have a starting point in the song and the poem. The composer has described his new work as a nocturne "suggesting the fleeting thoughts that pass through the mind during a period of wakefulness at night."

Music historians like making distinctions. There is a sense in which Verdi can be categorized as a *Tagkomponist* and Wagner as a *Nachtkomponist*—despite the "transfigured night" scene in *Falstaff,* when Windsor Forest glows with a mysterious, Keatsian enchantment, and the scenes in *The Ring* that should (but in modern productions seldom do) shine in the sun's full ray. Thoughts of *Tristan* color thoughts of Wagner (and, thanks to Cosima's diary, we can now share more of Wagner's dreams than those he found music for). Haydn, surely, is a "day composer," while Mozart eludes categorization, unless we project the symbolic conflicts in *The Magic Flute*—of dark forces with those of day, unruliness with limpid order—into many of his compositions. Elliott Carter is too close to us to be pigeonholed, but the light of day shines on his string quartets, on his Duo for violin and piano, on *Syringa:* skies are clear above and around them; Arizonan or Attic suns illumine their details. The dreams in his Symphony of Three Orchestras are daydreams. *Night Fantasies* is luminous, too, but with gleams, flickers, sudden patches of iridescence, or the clear, thin shine of moonlight, which can create a new world of visual values even as night thoughts can strangely distort the values of day and make unexpected things seem important. As an analogy to *Night Fantasies,* the composer has suggested Schumann's *Kreisleriana.* Indeed, he has called the piece "a sort of a contemporary *Kriesleriana*," and a revealing approach to it can be made through Alfred Brendel's excitable yet cohesive new recording (on Philips) of those eight wayward, elusive Schumann fantasies. Carter's *Night Fantasies,* like *Kreisleriana,* contains episodes of contrasting character, but in his work the episodes run into one another, overlap, recur in fragments, reappear with altered emphases. As another analogue, Carter has cited poems of Mallarmé where (as David Schiff put it in a program note) "phrases and thoughts and images are ambiguously dovetailed, so that multiple readings are not only possible but inevitable."

Carter's other piece for solo piano, the Sonata, appeared in 1946—thirty-five years ago—but he has since then written extensively for the instrument: in the Double Concerto for harpsichord and piano, the Piano Concerto, and the Duo, and also in the Concerto for Orchestra and the Symphony of Three Orchestras (the piano parts of which were first played by Mr. Jacobs). He has always sought specific inspiration in the physical, acoustical properties of the instruments he writes for. The players in his Brass Quintet play kinds of music only brass instruments can make, and trumpets, horn, and trombones further show their distinct musical characters. The Duo is—among other, more important things—a treatise on the differing natures of violin and piano. All composers, of course, endeavor to write music apt to the instruments that are to play it. Carter is special, I think, in the way his explorations of a new, personal musical language extend to incorporate facts of instrumental tone production until they become a part of that new language, both enriching and advancing it. A remark of Charles Rosen's about Schumann's piano writing which I quoted last month applies also to Carter's piano writing: "The sonority of the piano has now become a primary element of musical composition, as important as pitch or duration." Carter has a practical ear. He hears what he writes, he writes for performers, and although he makes huge demands of them, he writes music for them that is rewarding to play. And that, perhaps, does need saying, for one still hears him charged with composing paper music, dense with mathematical intricacies and unnecessarily difficult for both performers and listeners. The charge should not survive a single hearing of *Night Fantasies* as it is played by Miss Oppens or by Mr. Jacobs.

For the work is beautiful. One uses the simple epithet as one might use it of a Chopin nocturne. At the start, a series of soft, far-flung chords, tranquillo, touched in a note or sometimes two notes at a time, "sets the stage." An F on the bass staff and a C-sharp on the treble staff are recurrent—two bright fixed points in a soft-shining, mysterious firmament. Suddenly, fantastico, those two notes dance away into a brilliant, agitated dazzle, like—in Peter Grimes's simile for a sky become bewildering—"the flashing turmoil of a shoal of herring." Fantasy follows upon fantasy. Ideas are pursued, relinquished, half captured; new ideas steal in or dance in. At the center of the piece, a scherzo, "capriccioso," subsides into a "recitativo collerico" that sounds like an attempt to formulate a grave summation. But night thoughts can't be pinned down: the scherzo returns to blow the recitative away, and the fantasy procession continues.

In the Piano Sonata, Carter used the piano's resonances, overtones, and pedalled sonorities as part of the material to be composed with. In *Night Fantasies,* the range of pianoforte effects is immensely expanded. The whole gamuts of pitch, touches, textures, dynamics, and pedal effects are drawn on with a master's hand. Outré devices are not employed: the pianist's fingers remain on the keyboard and don't go poking or scratching at the strings; fists or forearms are not crashed down on clusters. Carter's instrumental writing always respects the inherent nature of the instruments he composes for and employs the sounds they were devised best to make. He hears and uses the piano as Liszt, Chopin, Schumann heard and used it—and also Ravel, for there is a sense in which *Night Fantasies* could also be dubbed "sort of a contemporary *Gaspard de la nuit,*" as a virtuoso piece that tests a player's technique and taste to the utmost. But he writes music of a kind that has not been heard before. The Carter chords—part consonant, part dissonant, and wholly satisfying—the Carter harmonic sequences, the Carter scorrevole passages of outlines rapidly traced, the Carter sonorities, and the bewitching Carter metrics here find memorable pianistic expression. And there are melodies. Melody, it has been rightly said, is essentially vocal gesture, but the piano's "voice" has a more than human span, and so Carter's melodies range freely through the octaves.

While *Night Fantasies* was being written, the composer suggested that each of the four pianists for whom it was intended would find in it passages particularly suited to his or her personality. It would be a brave critic who dared distribute the four main expressive indications —tranquillo, fantastico, appassionato, and capriccioso—among the four executants. Puccini was once accused of tailoring his arias to fit comfortably on ten-inch or twelve-inch record sides. If Carter had made *Night Fantasies* last fifteen minutes or less, we might have had the Oppens, Kalish, Jacobs, and Rosen interpretations of it gathered on a single long-playing disc, and that would have been an enthralling document. But *Night Fantasies* lasts twenty minutes. I've heard Miss Oppens's BBC performance (on tape) many times now. She gives a thoughtful, lyrical, flowing account, at once beautiful, brilliant, and coherent. I've heard Mr. Jacobs play the piece only twice—at a "preview" and at the Y recital. He gave an incisive, cogent, brilliant, very arresting performance. Now I long to hear Mr. Rosen and Mr. Kalish play it, too. And then Alfred Brendel and Maurizio Pollini. For *Night Fantasies,* which no single performance can exhaust, may well be our century's next pianistic landmark after Pierre Boulez's Second Sonata.

That work, which appeared in 1948, when Boulez was twenty-three, was iconoclastic—a young genius's new, defiant advance. Carter will be seventy-three next month. His *Night Fantasies* is a mature genius's advance, embracing previous piano music, explaining much of it, and saying new, beautiful things.

[*The score of* Night Fantasies *is published by G. Schirmer. The work has been recorded by Charles Rosen on Etcetera, by Paul Jacobs on Nonesuch, and by Aleck Karis on Bridge.*]

MUSICA BRITANNICA

December 7, 1981

PITTSBURGH HELD a British Festival in November—concerts, operas, plays, lectures, films, and exhibitions devoted to British art. The core around which it grew was three concerts of British orchestral music played by the Pittsburgh Symphony under André Previn. The plan for those was born when the British Council, short of money, had to abandon a scheme for a series of such concerts to be given in New York by one of the London orchestras but agreed to help underwrite some Pittsburgh programs instead. Mr. Previn, during a decade as principal conductor of the London Symphony Orchestra, became a champion of "conservative" British music (more accurately, of British music that, however advanced it might once have seemed, in the seventies appealed chiefly to conservative musical taste). With the LSO, he recorded Vaughan Williams's nine symphonies and a deal of Walton and Britten. But his enthusiasm for the repertory, he says, dates back to student days and the impressions Walton's Viola Concerto and Britten's *Peter Grimes* made on him then. The bulk of the Pittsburgh programs consisted of Vaughan Williams (the Tallis Fantasy, of 1910, and the Fifth Symphony, of 1943), late Elgar (the Cello Concerto, of 1919), Walton (the Violin Concerto, of 1939, and the Second Symphony, of 1960), and early Britten (*Les Illuminations*, of 1940). But each of the first two programs included a contemporary work—Tippett's Triple Concerto (1980) and Oliver Knussen's Third Symphony (1979)—and the third included a seventeen-year-old piece, Variations on a Theme of Karl Amadeus Hartmann, by John McCabe. The three programs were then brought to New York—two of them were played in Carnegie Hall, the third in Avery Fisher Hall.

First, a word about the orchestra. The *Times* critic of the first concert, while loftily dismissive of the music played, noted "the improved quality of the Pittsburgh orchestra both in its solo players and in ensemble cohesion" and the "full, pure, and velvety" sound of its strings. The *Times* critic of the third concert said that the "Pittsburgh Symphony seems an honorable but not distinguished orchestra." I'd put it rather more warmly than that, and rate the orchestra above, say, the

New York Philharmonic, if somewhere below the Chicago Symphony and the Philadelphia. The Pittsburgh string tone was certainly fuller, warmer, more "singing" than New Yorkers hear except at the Met and from the best visitors. The woodwinds did not draw attention away from the music onto individual virtuoso prowess, but the episodes of important solo work—the alto flute's duetting with the solo violin in the Tippett concerto, the English horn in the romanza of Vaughan Williams's Fifth—lacked neither accomplishment nor eloquence. The brasses never blared out, as Chicago brasses can, to stun us and swamp their colleagues on the platform. Most important—and hardest to describe—was the "feel" of an orchestra that loves and believes in the music it plays, that seeks to communicate its enjoyment, that listens and makes the audience listen, too. In short, Mr. Previn has, to judge by these concerts, led the Pittsburgh Symphony into America's top orchestra league. It was well tuned. It was well balanced, and when it sounded less than ideally balanced the reasons seemed to be, first, the lopsided seating plan Mr. Previn favors (high strings clumped on the left, low strings clumped on the right) and, second, the conductor's tendency to stress the top line even in such passages as the allegro in the first movement of Vaughan Williams's Fifth, which should be a fugato dialogue between equals, not a first-violin theme with accompaniment.

I wrote about Tippett's new concerto after its performance in Toronto last year (page 85). The Pittsburgh performance was keener—more sensitive, masterly, and beautiful. There were three fine soloists, leaders of their sections: Fritz Siegal, violin; Randolph Kelly, viola; and Anne Martindale Williams, cello.

A British critic has called Knussen "the most formidably equipped composer of his British generation." (He is twenty-nine.) Another finds that his sound has "a vitality and physicality unequalled by any of his contemporaries." I've been away from England too long to assess the comparatives, but his Third Symphony is certainly a rich and wonderful stretch of orchestral sound—a brief piece (lasting about fifteen minutes) packed with arresting and beautiful ideas. It was a long time in the making. In January 1973 Knussen began work on a symphonic poem about Ophelia planned to consist of, he wrote in a program note, "a turbulent preparatory movement, the crucible out of which Ophelia's madness is born," followed by "a set of dances (a sort of wordless setting of Ophelia's mad songs), and a slow cortège-finale suggested by the famous Pre-Raphaelite pictures." Michael Tilson Thomas requested the work for the Boston Symphony, but a year later only the first section, "Introduction and Masque," was ready; Mr. Thomas conducted it in Boston in 1974. Five years—and several smaller, related compositions—later, the Third Symphony had its first performance, at a London Prom, also conducted by Mr. Thomas. It was now a diptych; there had meanwhile appeared *Ophelia Dances*, No. 1, for chamber ensemble (which was played in Pittsburgh by the

Pittsburgh New Music Ensemble during the festival). The "masque" reaches its climax in a huge, sustained twelve-note chord. It leads directly into the "cortège," a set of variations on a slow chorale theme treated as a ground across which the ideas of the first part, altered but still recognizable, pass in review.

Knussen was thrown into the limelight when at the age of fifteen he conducted his Opus 1, a First Symphony, with the LSO. Several commissions followed that confident start; so did a period of uncertainty, when ideas flowed as freely as ever but getting them into shape, finding the definitive form for each piece, proved difficult. Knussen's Second Symphony, settings of Georg Trakl and Sylvia Plath, was commissioned for the 1970 Windsor Festival, but only a preliminary version, without the finale, was ready in time. The whole symphony was performed at Tanglewood in 1971, conducted by Gunther Schuller, and then a corrected version was heard in Boston in 1972. Knussen's list of works shows compositions unfinished and several others revised years after their first performances. There are separate pieces (Opp. 14, 16, and 15: *Autumnal*, for violin and piano; *Sonya's Lullaby*, for piano; *Cantata*, for oboe and string trio) that he likes to have performed as a sequence. Between other works there are cross-references. And, in general, there is a sense of work in progress and of ideas so rich, profuse, and ambitious that getting more than a part of them down on paper tends to elude the composer. But in the finished works that do appear there is no lack of confidence, no fumbling. The Third Symphony is lucidly and strongly constructed. One may feel some disproportion between the scale of the music—the sheer quantity of striking inventions it contains, the ampleness of the layout for large orchestra—and its duration. That feeling may result simply from foreknowledge of the symphony's genesis. The conjunction of bigness with brevity is certainly very bold. And, as I said, the sound of it all is wonderful. The piece made an indelible impression.

Variations on a Theme of Karl Amadeus Hartmann is a student piece. McCabe composed it in 1964, when, aged twenty-five, he went to study at the Munich Hochschule. The Hallé Orchestra played it in 1965, and since then it has been quite often heard and admired, rightly, as a composition in which impeccable workmanship and a quiet, pleasing imagination, disciplined but not unemotional, are combined. McCabe is an all-round and thorough musician—a fine pianist, a critic and author (monographs on Rachmaninoff and on Bartók's orchestral works), and a prolific, accomplished composer. He goes his own way, as Hartmann did—not raising waves, yet not failing to give satisfaction to mind and ear in all that he writes and plays.

To attempt any conclusions about the state of contemporary British music from those three works would be foolish; it would be like pronouncing on the state of contemporary American music after hearing, say, Elliott Carter's and David Del Tredici's latest compositions and a student work by John Harbison. Nor could late Elgar, early and middle Vaughan Williams, early Britten, and middle Walton present any coherent picture of British music from 1910 to 1960. Impressions only: Yo-Yo Ma was a marvellously commanding soloist in the Elgar Cello Concerto, voluptuous and noble of tone, passionate in his phrasing, Amfortas-like in the tragic episode of the finale. But he overdid the "expression," I thought, in the long pastoral theme of the first movement. It sounded rhetorical—not one of those melodies the composer wanted to hear played "like something you hear down by the river." But there is distinguished precedent for Mr. Ma's approach: he follows the Casals and Jacqueline Du Pré line, not that of W. H. Squire, Paul Tortelier, and Anthony Pini. In Walton's Violin Concerto, Kyung-Wha Chung played with gleaming bravura and unbounded efficiency. But it's not a work I have ever warmed to; I wish Pittsburgh had chosen the poetical Viola Concerto instead. In *Les Illuminations,* Susan Davenny Wyner sacrificed purity of pitch and timbre to volume; the singer of Carter's *A Mirror on Which to Dwell* could surely have given a more delicate, less declamatory performance.

Mr. Previn is a most "musical" interpreter as well as a conductor who inspires admirable playing. He felt the pieces. And *I* feel insular if I suggest that there is, let's say, more to Vaughan Williams's Fifth Symphony than Mr. Previn found in it. (If asked to define just what, I'd put the Boult and the Previn recordings into the questioner's hand and invite him to hear the differences.) It is tempting but too easy to claim a quality of "essential Britishness" that eludes foreign conductors (and well nigh impossible to define it). Many years ago, I praised in print a Sargent performance of Delius. Sir Malcolm wrote to me to say how pleased he was that someone other than Sir Thomas Beecham had been allowed to be a good Delius conductor: proclaiming Delius a one-conductor preserve limited and diminished the merits of his music. By extension, it would limit and diminish the merits of British music to assert that only Britons can conduct it properly. (In any case, there is Toscanini's glorious recording of the "Enigma" as proof to the contrary.) All the same...

Mr. Previn's most brilliant performance was of Walton's Second Symphony. I heard its première, twenty-one years ago, and had not heard it since. Even then, it traversed no new symphonic ground, opened no new horizons. But—I've turned up my original review—"there can be great pleasure in traversing known country by a new route, with a new and lively companion as guide." The symphony conveys a sense of enjoyment and is marked by unaffected vigor. It bubbles into being like a spring before one's feet: over a light play of strings and celesta, woodwinds and then strings throw up an arched motif that is the inspiration and driving force of the first movement, a phrase whose intervals and harmonic implications are dynamic. The middle movement is a luxurious lento, a romantic dream troubled by some harsher passages included more for form's sake, it seems, than through any emotional necessity. The finale is slightly pat—a set of

variations on a twelve-note (not serially treated) passacaglia theme—
but brilliantly worked.

There is a hint of defensiveness in that 1960 review—as if I needed
to apologize for admiring something so old-fashioned as the Walton
Symphony. In Britain, the Glock years—soon to be the Glock and
Boulez years—had begun, when accounts of what Peter Maxwell
Davies, Harrison Birtwistle, Alexander Goehr, and their contemporaries were doing filled the columns of the musical press, while Britten,
Tippett, and Elisabeth Lutyens were the older composers who held
our attention. Elgar's symphonies and Violin Concerto, Vaughan Williams's and Walton's music meant less to us. We weren't unjust to it, I
like to think, but our enthusiasms, our championship, went elsewhere.
(We also put in our individual claims for "unjustly neglected" composers. Alan Rawsthorne was one of mine.) The period falls between
the fifth edition of Grove (1954), in which Elgar, Vaughan Williams,
Walton receive more loving attention than we gave them, and the sixth
edition (1980), where once again—judiciously, and without immoder-
ate claims—they are held in high esteem. There is a study to be written about the way Britain's musical and political advances were being
made, it seems, hand in hand. And the latest reports from London—
of poor attendance at contemporary-music concerts, and of a play-it-
safe, less adventurous orchestral repertory resulting from, it has been
argued, the new "fund raising" from commercial and industrial
sources, rather than reliance on enlightened state support—suggest
that the new conservatism has infected the artistic life of the country.
The British Festival program brochure began with a dull "message of
goodwill" from Margaret Thatcher. In the programs, only the Tippett
and the Knussen could be called unconservative choices of repertory.
But that does not mean that there was not much good music to be
heard. The festival was in itself an adventure. Pittsburgh and all who
contributed to it earn our gratitude.

EXCURSIONS

December 14, 1981

THE STANDARD work on Leoš Janáček, Jaroslav Vogel's careful, loving,
and thorough study, is available now in a full English translation (published by Norton), and that is good news. The book, which is subtitled
"A Biography" but contains much musical commentary, was first published not in Czech but in German translation, in 1958. Four years
later, an English version appeared, inaccurate and abridged; musicians
unable to read the Czech original (which was published in 1963) had to
stick with the German volume. The new English edition, edited and
revised by Karel Janovický, includes a catalogue of works and a bibliography, and takes account of Janáček research done in the decade

since Vogel—a friend of the composer and a fine Janáček conductor —died.

In his introduction, Vogel remarks that Janáček had "two teachers to whom he remained faithful throughout his life: nature and the simple human being who was, for him, what the mythical man was to Wagner," and that "thanks to these two teachers, he made his greatest contribution: truthfulness, even to the point of ruthlessness, if necessary." It is this quality of truthfulness, more and more fully appreciated, that brings Janáček's operas to the world's stages with increasing frequency. In America this year alone, the City Opera has done *The Makropulos Affair* and *The Cunning Little Vixen*; Baltimore has done *Jenůfa*; Houston has done *Káťa Kabanová*; and the Indiana University Opera Theater, in Bloomington, has just given, as its two-hundred-and-second production, the American stage première of *Mr. Brouček's Excursions*. (Earlier this year, the Berkeley Symphony put on an underprepared concert performance.)

Mr. Brouček is the Janáček piece companies tend to be shy of. (It was the last of his mature operas to reach the London stage, in 1978.) But whenever it is done, it captivates. Mr. Brouček is a comfortable Prague burgher—a landlord—and fond of beer. One night, outside the Vikárka Inn, he looks up at the moon wistfully—no taxes there, no leaky roofs to repair. His head nods. He wakes up on the moon, where his Prague acquaintances are metamorphosed into lunar beings. The hero's dream projections of everyday life refashioned by subconscious evaluations and wishes give the work some psychological interest, but a good part of the moon excursion is taken up with satire. The artists who frequent the Vikárka are transformed into a self-adulatory lunatic circle, reciting silly, pretentious poems and spending hours in ecstatic contemplation of ridiculous pictures. Aesthetes and art unrelated to life are made fun of, but the philistine Mr. Brouček also comes in for some censure. The moon-dwellers feed only on the scent of flowers; he takes a piece of a sausage from his pocket and starts to munch. Because they are so absurd, he (in Vogel's words), "far from disgusting us with his down-to-earth materialism, gradually gains the better part of our sympathies"—which may not be what Janáček originally intended. Mist covers the scene. Mr. Brouček flies off on Pegasus. The lunar hymn turns into the farewells of artists leaving the Prague inn, and, as the first act ends, a very drunk Mr. Brouček is carried home.

There are at least three Pragues present in the artistic experience of the Western reader and music lover, and discoverable still by the visitor to that great city. One is Kafka's, sinister and secret, with the tyrannical Castle brooding over the life of the town. Another is the warm, romantic, joyful, and very beautiful place made for love, friendship, merry company, and music—and this Prague finds magical expression in *Mr. Brouček*. The principal singers in the first act are a pair of young lovers—Málinka and Mazal, a new Nannetta and Fenton—and the orchestra. Their romantic, moonlit pages before and after Mr. Brouček's lunar trip breathe the distilled enchantment of being in love in and with this most lovable of cities. The third Prague is heroic, drenched in stirring patriotic history—the city founded by Libuše, celebrated by Smetana, and lit, unto our own day, by martyrs burning for Czech freedom. This is the setting for the second act of Janáček's opera, Mr. Brouček's excursion to the fifteenth century. Janáček took nine years over the excursion to the moon, but the second excursion was completed in a matter of months, in 1917. "The great day is approaching," he wrote. "Will the star of hope shine out?... The more dreadful the time, the swifter the rush of musical ideas." The opera was dedicated to Tomáš Masaryk, a founder and the first President of the independent Czechoslovakian state.

This time, the talk at the Vikárka has been of secret passages leading from the Castle to the Old Town. Mr. Brouček stumbles out of the inn and in a dream goes stumbling on through a secret passage that leads him to fifteenth-century Prague and into the heart of a Hussite rising. Again, his cronies appear in new guises. There is some fun with anachronisms—Mr. Brouček's curious dress, his knowledge of the forthcoming battle's outcome—but basically the tone is heroic, and there is a stirring use of Hussite hymns. Mr. Brouček is recruited. A pike is put into his hands. But, alas, he proves a coward and grovels before the first German soldier he meets. The Hussites condemn him to be burned in a barrel—and in a barrel he wakes up next morning outside the inn.

Janáček declared that he wished his countrymen to be disgusted by Mr. Brouček's behavior and to stamp on such people wherever they met them—especially within themselves. But his innate humanity tempered the theme so that one cannot feel very indignant at Mr. Brouček's reluctance to become a hero. The composer's generosity and warmth of personality were incompatible with the one-sided presentation that keen, tidy satire requires. The patriotic pageantry is rousing; an elegy for the fallen is poignant; but we can't lose sympathy for the amiable little burgher caught up in it all. Similarly, in the moon act Janáček's natural lyricism invested his intended parody of a tenor's high-flown lament with a tone that rings passionate and true. How can anyone not love him?

An unusual opera, then, and a difficult one to bring into focus, but rich, filled with beautiful, brilliant, strange, and moving music. Some episodes are lunatic and glittering, some poetic and tender, some patriotic and noble, some funny; and through it all Janáček's genius for thematic metamorphosis is evident. The interlude transporting Mr. Brouček from fifteenth-century back to nineteenth-century Prague is one example among many of the composer's musical mastery transcending the libretto's ambivalent tone and, in several places, shaky construction. Fragments from both dreams swirl about the hero, hold steady for a moment, then drift elusively away as he returns to waking life. To verbalize what is expressed would be very hard; to mistake the experience it tells of is impossible.

The Bloomington décor, by Max Röthlisberger, was distinguished. At the start, a projected view of the city led to one of the Charles Bridge, seeming vividly present, stretching before us, inviting us to step out of the auditorium and cross into the quarter where the Vikárka (which was then realistically represented) still stands. Bryan Balkwill conducted the score with an ideal combination of sharp-edged accuracy and tenderness. The orchestral playing was very good. Carlos Alexander's direction was less sure; there were passages of clumsy, unconvinced acting and occasional uncertainties of tone. Joseph Levitt portrayed a Mr. Brouček without the customary good humor and geniality; the hero won less of our amused affection than he usually does. It was an adept portrayal, justified by the composer's pronouncements but not, I feel, by his music. The best voice in the lively young cast was that of Philip Skinner, as Würfl, the innkeeper, and his later transformations. The Málinka became edgy when her line rose. The Mazal was patchy but had some good moments. The work was sung in Norman Tucker's English translation, and the English was not particularly well handled. "Weak hands" was given the stresses of "weakens," "fancy dress" those of "fanciful." But the opera triumphed. It always does.

TRIPTYCH

December 21, 1981

THE METROPOLITAN OPERA marks the centenary of Stravinsky's birth, which falls on June 17 next year, with a triple bill entitled "Stravinsky" and comprising *The Rite of Spring, The Nightingale*, and *Oedipus Rex*. The show is conducted by James Levine and is staged by the team responsible for "Parade," last season's Satie-Poulenc-Ravel triple bill: John Dexter as director, David Hockney as designer, and Gil Wechsler as lighter. They have devised a long, strenuous evening, carefully prepared, uncompromisingly severe, and filled with interest for musician and theatregoer alike. It is largely a dance event (the *Rite* has been choreographed by Jean-Pierre Bonnefous, and *The Nightingale* by Frederick Ashton), but the foreground is occupied by Mr. Levine and his orchestra—which is to say, by Stravinsky's scores. The orchestra pit has been raised high; it is now less a "pit" than a shallow depression between the spectators and the stage. The wooden wall that usually divides the orchestra from the "orchestra" (thus the confusing American terminology; would that the British "stalls" or the French "parterre" had been naturalized) is replaced by a clear plastic screen. In some earlier productions, Mr. Levine and Mr. Dexter sought to bridge the "mystic chasm" that Wagner opened between stage and auditorium—the orchestra pit that toward the end of the nineteenth century became a regular feature of opera-house design. The sets for their *Entführung* and *Mahagonny* jutted through the proscenium frame. "Stravinsky" is their boldest endeavor to place audience, orchestra, and actors together in one room, and to create a vividness and an immediacy, theatrical as well as acoustical, that are otherwise easily lost in the enormous Met, a late-nineteenth-century opera house writ huge. The soprano and tenor of *The Nightingale* stand in the pit and are clearly visible to the audience; when not singing, they lean over the edge of the stage and watch the action along with the other spectators. The narrator of *Oedipus*, enthroned in the pit, in front of the prompter's box, is also visible. So, more prominently than usual, is the conductor. But the sight lines are cleverly planned so that the stage pictures are not masked.

An austere front curtain used before and after each of the three works, and also during scene changes, is black and is decorated simply with Stravinsky's name and the date 1882, beneath a lyre schematically represented as a circle crossed by five vertical lines. All three pieces are staged within a black cyclorama studded with graffiti of faces chalked up as if by a child—ovals containing two dots for eyes, two dashes for nose and mouth. For the *Rite*, there is also a large roundel at the back depicting three tree trunks, a sheet of water behind them, and, across the water, a group of triangular hills whose form suggests a view of the Sydney Opera House. The roundel's basic colors are red trunks, intense blue water, and acrid green hills, but the colors change and glow as various lights are played upon them. For the second scene, a tangle of brightly colored branches descends to cap the trunks. The stage floor bears a circle. In Mr. Hockney's costumes, there are echoes of Nicholas Roerich's costumes for the first *Rite*, and throughout the evening there seem to be deliberate allusions to earlier Stravinsky productions—as if not just the composer but seventy years of his works in the theatre were being celebrated. Mr. Bonnefous' choreography includes images derived from what we know of Nijinsky's choreography for the first *Rite*, but it misses the power, the weight, the heavy surge of the score. In general, it is too light, long-limbed, and decorative—not charged, mysterious, frightening. One can watch it without feeling anything stir in one's own body. It's the music that sets the pulses beating faster, the blood racing.

The Nightingale opens with a circle of blue ripple on the floor, and on it the Fisherman. Then a tall white-and-blue banner descends as a central backdrop for the shore scenes, rippling and fluttering like the Noguchi curtain for Stravinsky's *Orpheus*. Cook, Chamberlain, and Bonze are stylized commedia-dell'-arte chinoiserie figures. The face motif on the backcloth, already echoed in the *Rite* by faces set up on poles, here proliferates into faces on poles carried by the courtiers; their own faces are masked. Against the sombre black surroundings, almost everything is blue until the Japanese envoys in lacquer red and their glittering, jewelled mechanical nightingale arrive. Cyril Beaumont, in his book about the Diaghilev ballet, recalls of the 1914 *Nightingale* little more than a ring of blue lanterns; glowing blue-and-white lanterns, shaped like pineapples, add a pretty touch to Mr. Hockney's décor.

The Nightingale is a magical score, and even today the composer's treatment of timbres, rhythm, and time proves astonishingly modern. (Stravinsky began the opera in 1908, before *The Firebird,* and completed it after the *Rite,* in 1914.) If ideas from Mussorgsky and Debussy flowed into it, some delicate passages in Boulez's *Pli selon pli* seem to have flown from it. But it is a tricky work to stage. Stravinsky attributed its later neglect to the difficulty of finding an apt companion piece. (At La Scala in 1926, it was a curtain-raiser to *Hansel and Gretel.* In Rome in 1928, it followed *La sonnambula.* The Met première, in 1926, paired it with Falla's *La vida breve.* At the City Opera in 1963, it preceded Honegger's *Joan of Arc at the Stake.*) The original Benois décor was spectacular, but the most beautiful and most touching production I have seen was also the simplest—designed and directed by Colin Graham, at Sadler's Wells in 1960. (It was done with *Oedipus.*) In the new Met version, some of the charm, some of the poetry, and most of the wit are lost. Partly, it is a simple question of scale. Despite the collaborators' efforts to make the huge house more intimate, much of the fragile, exquisite instrumental detail escapes. Partly, the decision to sing the piece in Russian is to blame. *The Nightingale* is, among other things, an allegory of the power of music and of the nature of musical inspiration, and needs to be followed in words as well as sounds.

Nightingale and Fisherman are sung by Gwendolyn Bradley and Philip Creech. She has a sweet and flexible soprano, not quite limpid enough for the role; he has a supple but not quite sharp-focussed tenor. The roles were elegantly danced by Natalia Makarova and Anthony Dowell. Ashton's choreography is a graceful anthology of attractive, familiar ideas, not quite specific, it seemed to me, either to the opera or to this staging of it. Claudia Catania was a delightful Cook. Mr. Levine conducted the music with a light, subtle, and affectionate hand.

Of *Oedipus,* Stravinsky wrote, "I had begun to visualize the staging as soon as I started to compose the music. I saw the chorus first, seating in a single row across the stage and reaching from end to end of the proscenium rainbow." In the Met's new *Oedipus,* the choristers, some sixty men, are seated in a double row spanning the proscenium arch. They wear dinner jackets and black ties. On a high platform behind them, the principals, similarly clad (Jocasta in a long black dress), and wearing black gloves, sit on modern chairs. Behind each, there stands a handsome waiter holding on high a tall white half mask. These attendants place the masks on the soloists when they rise and move centerstage to sing, and otherwise stand like waxworks, distractingly still. Centerstage, a high, gold-striped screen rises above a red semicircle— echoing the formalized lyre of the curtain. The stripes are projected by light, and similar stripes are projected on the sides of the proscenium arch and the approaches to it. The colors, red and gold, are those of the auditorium itself. The all-in-one-room idea becomes dominant. At one end of the room, a formal, solemn drama is enacted. It is almost like a court scene: conductor and orchestra in the foreground; then the narrator on his throne; then the chorus; then, one might say, defendant, prosecutors, and witnesses. (Oedipus is his own judge; he passes and executes sentence upon himself.)

Oedipus and Tiresias were Richard Cassilly and John Macurdy, the Oedipus and Messenger of the City Opera *Oedipus* twenty-two years ago, conducted by Stokowski. Both were strong, incisive, commanding, but Mr. Cassilly's sustained notes became unsteady. Franz Mazura's Creon was less precise. Tatiana Troyanos's Jocasta was uneven, often very imposing. The narrator, Mr. Dowell, was in ringing voice. "I detest the speaker device, that disturbing series of interruptions," Stravinsky wrote (in *Dialogues and a Diary*), "and I do not much like the speeches themselves." But there they are, and "alas, the music was composed with the speeches, and is paced by them." Mr. Dowell dealt with them admirably. But the rather classy British accent he adopted accorded ill with his mispronunciation of "deities" and a slip or two over classical names ("Crayon," "Lie-oose"). "The music?" Stravinsky continued. "I love it, all of it, even the Messenger's fanfares, which remind me of the now badly tarnished trumpets of early 20th-Century-Fox." Mr. Levine conducted as if he loved all of it, too.

Conclusions? Hard to reach. The evening—I've now seen it twice— proves exhausting. It would be more successful, I think, if the *Rite* were omitted. There is evidence everywhere of hard thought and good, strong ideas, but the attempt to impose some "unity" by the recurrent use of masks and circles is neither here nor there; the three works are very different, and all that matters is how the masks and circles work in each of them. *Oedipus* seemed a less exciting *drama* than usual—maybe because one was tiring by then, maybe because, as Ingmar Bergman once told Stravinsky, "a mask may be beautiful, and it can be a useful façade for all sorts of things, but the price, which is loss of contact, is too great." (He said he would stage the opera without masks.) One goes away with a dominant impression of that huge stage hung in black; despite the glowing roundel in the *Rite* and pretty moments in *The Nightingale*, the austerity of the spectacle mutes the colors of Stravinsky's music. But it is a big, serious achievement; something new for the Met; and a landmark in New York's operatic history.

AWAY, ABOVE THE CHIMNEY TOPS

December 28, 1981

PUCCINI REMAINS popular. Of the sixty-nine performances billed in the Metropolitan Opera's winter brochure, twenty-six—more than one in three—are of works by Puccini. In London next year, the Royal Opera plays nothing but *La Bohème* for two weeks. The Met has just mounted a large, elaborate new production of *La Bohème*, designed and directed by Franco Zeffirelli. At first sight, it is a revised version of Zeffirelli's celebrated *Bohème* production for La Scala nineteen years ago—revived there often, taken up by other houses, and (not adequately) filmed. But there has been rethinking and reworking. The attic set is new, and the dramatic emphasis has changed, in ways that may be disconcerting and disappointing to a simple Puccini-lover and are interesting to anyone concerned with the reasons for Puccini's lasting success. The show has been reviewed as if it were no more than a conventional, traditional production writ large. In this country, Zeffirelli has seldom had his due as an operatic thinker. His scenic effects do, of course, draw a Met audience's easy, mindless acclaim. (On the first night, the music of Act II was *four* times drowned by applause for the spectacle.) There certainly is a showman side to his work; as the New Grove puts it, "no *coup de théâtre* has proved too extreme for him in the interests of bold Romantic spectacle." Six hundred people filled the stage in his Scala *Aida*, and nearly three hundred appear in Act II of the Met *Bohème*. He aims to give spectacular pleasure, and would be a lesser director if he didn't. But the showman is also an operatic interpreter of genius. Like it or not (and I'm not sure how much I do like it), this splashy new *Bohème* is as much a serious-minded "statement" as was the Met's sombre Stravinsky evening a few days before.

Is elaboration necessary? *La Bohème* is an undemanding opera to stage. Its scenic requirements are simple. Covent Garden's 1899 sets, inaugurated by Melba and Fernando de Lucia, did good, hard service for seventy years. (Through 1938, there were only four years when the opera was dropped from the bills; in 1948 Peter Brook redirected it in the old sets, which then put in two more decades of annual service—missing only two seasons—until in 1969 they were at last retired.) Being built to the composer's requirements, after designs supplied by his publisher, this décor worked well, and unobtrusively framed the merits of generation after generation of bohemians: among those of my time, Victoria de Los Angeles (1950) and Teresa Stratas (1961), who both chose Mimì as a Covent Garden début role; Renata Scotto (1962) and Mirella Freni (1964); Jussi Björling (1960) and a new young tenor called Luciano Pavarotti (1963). Those performances were "created" by the singers and took no added color from staging or scenery. I remember individual excellences. I forgot—until I flicked through some old reviews—how often I cited as still valid the composer's own complaint about Covent Garden: that it felt the engagement of a "star" or two was enough, and paid little attention to ensemble or mise en scène.

Puccini could not make that complaint of the new Met version. But he, who identified so strongly with his characters, who wanted listeners to throb and sob along with them, might object to something else—the oddly distanced effect of the drama as it is presented here, and the unexpected and hardly Puccinian "theme" that seems to emerge: How unimportant these young people and their ephemeral loves, their dreams and pictures and poems are! They live and die as mayflies on the great stream of life. The distancing is achieved in several mutually confirming ways. The attic of the first and last acts is small and far away, set well back behind two realistically built rows of rooftops. "For the first time," Zeffirelli said in an interview, "audiences will have a sense of the immensity of Paris, and the smallness of this little group's place—the actual space of a garret." In many *Bohème* productions, the studio is rather larger than life, too spacious for strict realism; but symbolically that is not inappropriate. The audience is invited to enter a room where what goes on looms larger than anything in the great world without. The emotions are contained, and they fill the stage from side to side. But the Met audience observes some people moving in a distant loft, which might be on the far side of Amsterdam Avenue and is only one among many in the huge, crowded city. In Act II, our principals are then lost in the busy throng; sometimes when we hear them singing it is hard to spot where they are. In the prescribed décor, their supper table is set well forward, stage left, always dominant; in Zeffirelli's, it is central, set back by a lane's width, and sometimes masked by the crowd. In Act III, there is much coming and going beyond the prescribed diversions of the score, and again the effect is to remind us that the bohemians are not the only people in the world who have troubles. One's expectation of a new set for Act IV—a closeup on the principals—was not fulfilled. The rooftops returned.

Another, linked intention seems to have been to reduce the set-piece effect of solo numbers that usually stand out in relief: "Che gelida manina," "Mi chiamano Mimì," Mimì's farewell, Colline's coat song. They have been directed with applause-inhibiting closes, in a way to flow continuously into what follows. But—at any rate, on the first night—the bold idea was not carried through: instead of proceeding, conductor and singers waited for the usual applause, which then arrived, late, as an awkward intrusion. It would be moving to hear an unbroken sequence of "Che gelida manina . . . Mi chiamano Mimì . . . O soave fanciulla" (as one can on records), to hear Rodolfo lap the D-flat of Mimì's "Addio, senza rancor" with the D-flat of his "Dunque: è proprio finita," to hear Colline pass straight into recitative at the end of the coat song. (I seldom attend a *Bohème* without thinking that "Vecchia zimarra" might effectively be omitted; and then remind myself that Puccini, who cut so much while the opera was being made—an act in the courtyard of the house where Musetta lives, Schaunard's misogynist solo—knew what he was about. All the same, it might be worth trying.) If the singers prefer applause, the direction should be altered to take account of it.

The librettists of *La Bohème*, Giuseppe Giacosa and Luigi Illica, declare in a preface to their text that they aimed to preserve the essential spirit, the characters, the atmosphere, and the episodic quality of their source, Henry Murger's *Scènes de la vie de Bohème*. When the opera first appeared, critics were disconcerted by the "impressionistic" nature of both the plot and the music. But now, as Mosco Carner remarks in his Puccini biography, "countless performances year in year out have blunted our ears to the fact that Puccini's is one of the most original creations for the lyrical stage and the first opera in history to achieve an almost perfect fusion of romantic and realistic elements with impressionist features." Zeffirelli's production removes veils of familiarity, sharpens our ears, and invites us to think again about the work. There is more of Murger in it than usual, though Zeffirelli is too sensible, and too much of a musician, to fall into the modern trap of "directing" a source rather than what a composer has made of it. His Rodolfo is not Murger's Rodolphe: "A young man whose face could hardly be seen for a huge, bushy, many-colored beard. To set off this prognathic hirsutism, a premature baldness had stripped his temples as bare as a knee. A cluster of hairs, so few as to be almost countable, vainly endeavored to conceal this nakedness." But his Rodolfo is scruffy and unshaven. In forming his Mimì, Zeffirelli may have recalled a sentence that the librettists significantly omitted from the Murger quotation introducing their first act: "At certain moments of boredom or bad temper, her features assumed an appearance of almost savage brutality, so that a physiognomist might perhaps have recognized the signs of either a profound egotism or a complete lack of sensibility." For Rodolfo to blow out his own candle when Mimì's has been extinguished by the draft is a common, unpleasing, rather cheap bit of added business. Zeffirelli not only used it but made it seem as if Mimì had deliberately blown out her candle, too. Many a provincial Rodolfo scores a cheap laugh by tidying his hair when he hears a woman's voice outside the door; Zeffirelli not only retained that business but then had Rodolfo further check his appearance in a glass before answering Mimì's knock. In Puccini, all is drenched in romance. Fate furthers the affair: chance blows out both their candles in turn; as if by accident, Rodolfo's hand touches Mimì's in the dark. Rodolfo, as he says in the final duet, merely assists destiny by pocketing the key. In Zeffirelli's version, it's a knowing, calculated pickup from the start, on both sides. Mimì gives a triumphant smirk when she sees Rodolfo find the key; she deliberately advances her hand to be grasped by Rodolfo's. The effect is not unrealistic (except in the lighting plot, when two spotlights track the lovers through the darkened room). Mimì and Rodolfo were, after all, both experienced seducers. But it destroys the tenderness and the delicacy of Puccini's scene, in which they behave like two young, shy people increasingly attracted to one another—a scene in which tension should mount gradually toward the full-throated release of the octaves at "Ah! tu sol comandi, amor!"

Teresa Stratas is a piquant, fascinating, attractive Mimì. She plays the role with more resource than she did at Covent Garden twenty years ago, still looks young, gives vividness and meaning to every phrase, and shapes the musical lines fully. Renata Scotto's Musetta is a serious and carefully studied portrayal, but she went too far at the close of Act II. "Saucily revealing her foot," says Puccini; Miss Scotto kicked her skirts up over her head. Her waltz song veered disconcertingly between shrillness and inaudibility; the prayer in Act IV was under better vocal control. José Carreras, as Rodolfo, was disappointing. He seems to have passed from City Opera promise to international routine; the voice was dark, ordinary, not fresh and bright. For Richard Stilwell, distinguished as Pelléas, as Ulysses, as a Mozart baritone, to be essaying Marcello seemed precious like slumming, but, in his restrained, patrician way, he gave a plausible performance. Allan Monk and James Morris were a decent Schaunard and Colline. The lack of any remarkable solo singing—of phrases that stir one in the theatre and live on in memory's ear—matched the resolutely unsentimental approach. The acting was intimate and detailed, as if for the cinema. It will probably work wonderfully on television. The Met's closeup photographs look like film stills. In the enormous theatre, the effect of remoteness is further increased; everything stays in long shot.

The Scala *Bohème* was possibly the most beautiful operatic show of our day. (In Balzac's *Les Paysans*, a young man coming upon a magnificent natural landscape remarks, "Ma foi, c'est presque aussi beau qu'à l'Opéra.") Courbet, I suppose, was Zeffirelli's inspiration, and the result was Courbet brought to life. One remembers not still, painted pictures but magical effects of changing light in the large studio, and, in Act III, a snowscape that reached not to a canvas backcloth but to a point where the eye could penetrate no farther through diminishing gradations of light, within which moving figures were glimpsed. The special merits of that 1963 staging gradually seeped away. The enchantments of the first cast—Mirella Freni and Gianni Raimondi, Eugenia Ratti and Rolando Panerai, all more sharply, if more traditionally, characterized than their Met counterparts—faded as they grew older or as others took their places. Scenically, Zeffirelli's Met *Bohème* stands to his Scala *Bohème* much as his Met *Falstaff* and *Cav and Pag* do to those he created for Covent Garden. They are not straight reproductions. There are a few improvements, but much of the detail is coarser. Some of the freshness of first discovery is gone. Reworking has brought overworking. The Met's attic set, as I said, is new. In Act II, the trees that formerly lined the boulevard above the quayside café have been felled, and the buildings look more like painted scenery, less real. In Act III, the wide central emptiness—bleak, marvellous image of a life without love—has now been filled by a snowbank and by trees. These central acts both look shallower than they did at La Scala, and are less magically lit. On the other hand, the Met's stage machinery allows Acts I and II to be played without an intermission, and that is a gain.

The Scala *Bohème* was memorably conducted by Herbert von Karajan, who is both a great conductor and a delicate accompanist—especially admirable in Donizetti and Puccini. At the Met, James Levine had not engaged a Puccini conductor but undertook the assignment himself. His enthusiasm for the inventions of the score was evident; so was his inability to find the natural, idiomatic flow of the music. For all I know, he may be able to recite cantos of the *Divine Comedy* by heart, but he conducts Italian opera as if he didn't speak the language fluently, didn't feel the weights and colors and meanings of words that should inflect the music. Nor is he nice enough about stage-pit balance.

Violetta and Mimì were contemporaries, despite misleading indications of epoch in the scores. (The score of *La Bohème* says "about 1830"; that of *La traviata* sets the action "about 1700.") The *Scènes* were running in *Le Corsaire* in 1848, the year Dumas' novel *La Dame aux camélias* appeared. *La traviata* can well bear—may, indeed, benefit from—some passing presentation of social injustices that have made Violetta a fallen woman. But, while the Goncourts described Murger's *Scènes* as "a triumph of Socialism," Puccini's opera can hardly be forced into a political mold. (Mimì makes her piecework as seamstress seem a romantic and charming occupation.) The English National Opera's *Bohème* hints at darker things—but more explicitly in the program notes than in the staging. The Met's is an essay in desentimentalization, achieved by sinking Puccini's foreground figures deep into a large frame. It's an interesting production.

New York's third *Traviata* production of the season was put on by the Juilliard American Opera Center, in an amateurish-looking and bloody staging directed by Andrei Serban. At Flora's party, Paquillo mimed killing five bulls, and that can pass, for the chorus sings of it. But Paquillo's Andalusian inamorata dabbled her fingers in their blood, smeared it over her face and bosom, licked it, and that is not acceptable party behavior. In the last scene, Violetta brought up blood by the cupful and wiped it from her hands on Germont's letter—that letter which in Verdi's opera she cherishes so dearly. The drama was apparently set in an almost bare loft. It held a few screens in the first scene for Violetta's guests to play peekaboo among. "Tanto lusso" in the second scene was represented by some cushions scattered about on the floor (this Violetta was a parterre letter writer) and a suspended piece of cloth, which Germont tore down at the end, to signify to the simple-minded his irritation that Alfredo should go off in quest of his beloved. Flora decked the loft with hanging rugs and some gilt chairs, which won a round of applause. In the last scene, it was furnished with a truckle bed, a washstand, a chair, and a closet.

The staging was a mixture of modern clichés (the corpse of Violetta lying front stage to start and end the opera; the return of Alfredo in person at the close of Act I; pantomimes during the preludes) and rude, false invention. There was double casting. In my cast, Roseann Del George suggested that in a less foolish production—one that allowed the singers natural expressiveness and worked with the grain of the score—she might be a moving heroine. Her "Addio del pasato" was affectingly and subtly sung, and technically accomplished. Michael Austin, the Alfredo, had several good notes and no character. Christian Badea, conducting, sometimes pushed ahead of singers he should have been accompanying, and showed little sense of Verdi style.

Erich Leinsdorf, in his wise, detailed, and valuable book *The Composer's Advocate: A Radical Orthodoxy for Musicians* (Yale), remarks, "Today special courage may be required to sweep away the detritus of misinterpretation and reveal a composer's work as he first constructed it. Ironically, faithful interpretation of a great master's wishes often seems not conservative but radical." It was sad to see the Juilliard School lending countenance to modern misconceptions, and sad to see and hear promising young American artists thus led astray—*traviati*.

BLAZING, RADIANT

January 4, 1982

WHEN BERLIOZ reached Rome, he hastened to St. Peter's. "Sublime, overpowering! Michelangelo, Raphael, Canova on this side and that.... And the intense stillness, the solemnity.... As I thought of the glorious role that my own art must play there, my heart began to beat with excitement." Architecture, sculpture, and painting, he said, may form the body of a building, but "music is its soul, the supreme manifestation of its existence." He looked for the organ and for the St. Peter's choir that should be numbered in thousands. He discovered a little instrument on wheels, concealed behind a pillar, and learned that there was a choir of eighteen, augmented to thirty-two on major feast days. But the "aural vision" of a vast building brought to life by large, solemn music never left him. In the Requiem, first performed in Les Invalides in 1837, and the Te Deum, first performed in Saint-Eustache in 1855, he composed music worthy of St. Peter's—music to set huge resonant spaces sounding, with timbres and resonances undreamed of before, harmonies that move slowly but purposively, solo melodies that seem to steal out and rise like incense smoke, fanfares that ring through every vault. (When the Philharmonic performs those works, it might well play its concerts in St. John the Divine. Fisher Hall cannot do justice to them.) In his memoirs, Berlioz described four of his works as "architectural": those two sacred pieces and two that are secular—the Funeral and Triumphal Symphony (which he conducted with a drawn sword *en cortège* through the streets of Paris while the ashes of the 1830 heroes were transported from a Requiem Mass in Saint-Germain to interment in the Bastille column) and the cantata *L'Impériale*. The Requiem, the Te Deum, and the Symphony are familiar; recordings are easily come by. *L'Impériale* is a rarity. So far as I know, it is unrecorded. What was billed as the American première, and in a program note more cautiously described as "probably the American première," was given last month by the Brooklyn College Chorus and Orchestra, in the Whitman Hall of Brooklyn College.

"Secular" is perhaps not the just word for the Funeral and Triumphal Symphony. For the fanfare that introduces its Apotheosis, Berlioz "imagined a trumpet-call of archangels, simple but sublime, boundless, glittering, an immense radiance swelling and resounding, proclaiming to earth and to Heaven the opening of the Empyrean gates." But *L'Impériale*—unless one believes in the divine right of kings—is wholly secular. It glorifies Napoleon III. It was composed to celebrate the prize-giving by the Emperor at the 1855 Exhibition in the Palace of Industrial Products. The first performance was interrupted when the music overran into time set aside for a speech by the Emperor's cousin. The author of the text, a Captain Lafont, may have believed in divine right. His high-flown lines suggest it:

> *Bearing the oriflamme*
> *In his brazen talons,*
> *The eagle with wings of flame,*
> *Sovereign arbiter,*
> *Opens his deep eyelid*
> *To the billows of the star of light,*
> *And reappears in the skies,*
> *Blazing and radiant.*

Lafont continues, "For, as once the Messiah did, the imperial dynasty that God Himself revived and that glory brought to birth has emerged from the tomb." Repeated cries of "Vive l'Empereur!" form the refrain.

Berlioz learned in youth to play the flageolet, the flute, and the guitar. "Can anyone fail to recognize in this judicious choice the hand of Nature urging me toward the grandest orchestral effects and the Michelangelesque in music?" He is both the most delicate and the grandest of scorers. He enjoyed large orchestral forces. At a concert after the 1844 Exhibition of Industrial Products, he played Beethoven's C-minor Symphony with thirty-six double-basses, the *Freischütz* overture with twenty-four horns, the *Moïse* prayer with twenty-five harps. And "my thousand and twenty-two performers moved with the unanimity

186

of the members of a first-rate quartet." For *L'Impériale* at the 1855 Exhibition, he had twelve hundred performers. In the score of the cantata, the apt number of instrumentalists on each line is specified, amounting to two hundred players in all. There is a first chorus of forty voices, and a second chorus "far more numerous." Then the last ten pages, the final paean in praise of Napoleon III, bear the instruction "Entry of a military band (ad lib.) doubling all the wind instruments." Berlioz held the baton in his right hand, and with his left activated an "electric metronome" that relayed the beat to five sub-conductors "in the huge area that the performers occupied." The ensemble, he says, was marvellous.

America, which has both a tradition of accomplished, spirited campus bands and an abundance of enclosed performing spaces too large to be adequately filled by symphonic forces of conventional size, should now be the country where Berlioz's big works receive their due. One needs both the bands and the spaces. When Colin Davis conducted the Funeral and Triumphal Symphony in Regent's Park twenty years ago with the Massed Bands of Her Majesty's Brigade of Guards, the performers were plentiful but the open-air acoustics diminished the grandeur of the score—as they did, Berlioz says, when the work was played through the Paris streets. (It was an indoor performance, in the Salle Vivienne, that moved Wagner to write of the Symphony, "It is noble and great from the first note to the last. Free from sickly excitement, it sustains a noble patriotic emotion which rises from lament to the topmost heights of apotheosis.... I must, along with my joy and conviction, state that this symphony will endure and will inspire courage so long as there is a nation known as France.") I've been stirred by the strains of the famous University of California Marching Band. It should play Berlioz's large scores regularly. Brooklyn College also has a fine band—certainly fine when I last heard it, under Dorothy Klotzman, playing at the Ives centenary celebrations. But it didn't play in *L'Impériale*. Berlioz makes provision for performances by "an ordinary orchestra"; and in a small hall, he says, four solo voices may replace the first chorus. In Whitman Hall, which is not exactly small, there was a solo quartet, an orchestra of fifty-three, and a chorus of a hundred; to the final paean sixty children's voices—those of the Brooklyn College Preparatory Center Chorus—were added. A certain spectacular effect was achieved: the tots were dressed in red, white, and blue, and at the climax they waved tiny tricolors. But there wasn't really enough *noise*; and the festivity was diminished by the half-darkness into which the hall had been plunged. It was difficult to read the carefully prepared texts and translations. At concerts, one should be able to take in printed words at a glance, without peering, and then concentrate on the performers. But the bad old habit of dimming lights dies hard.

L'Impériale is, of course, an occasional piece. It might be amusing to devise a new text, hymning, let's say, a victorious football team, a popular college president, or an Olympic hero, but it is probably better to keep the cantata as a stupendous Second Empire monument. Berlioz wrote music to match such lines as:

Never was brow crowned
With such an immortal aureole;
As if in a living symbol,
The people are incarnate in you.
You guide them by your genius,
They sustain you by their valor.

By rewriting as a triplet the four sixteenths that start "Vive l'Empereur!" the refrain could be sung to the words "Hail to the Chief," but it is hard to think of any present-day figure for whom the splendors of the music would not seem excessive. The references to Napoleon III in Berlioz's memoirs are few and hardly enthusiastic, but the composer had been fired early by the Napoleonic legend. He contemplated a symphony on "The Return of the Army from Italy." He composed a *Cinq mai* cantata. He was present at the funeral, in Florence, of the future Emperor's brother: "It was a sight to conjure with, yet not so awe-inspiring as the thought of who it was that lay there: the very name set great echoes ringing in my mind. A Bonaparte! *His* nephew, almost *his* grandson." There is no hollowness in the score of *L'Impériale*. Whatever the composer's opinion of the hyperbolic text may have been, the triumph in his music is wholehearted. Simplicity and majesty combine. The work celebrates, one might say, the amazing power of music to celebrate.

In Brooklyn, *L'Impériale* crowned a choice and well-planned program of music for chorus and orchestra. Before it, there were Brahms's *Schicksalslied* and his *Nänie*, and then three wonderful Berlioz pieces: *La Mort d'Ophélie*, the *Funeral March for the Last Scene of "Hamlet,"* and the setting for triple choir of Victor Hugo's "Sara la Baigneuse." Harry Saltzman—best known as the director of a smaller choir, the Sine Nomine Singers, in an earlier repertory—conducted. He was most successful with the plaintive purling of the Ophelia ballad and with the seductive lilt to which Sarah swings in her hammock above the pool. The *Hamlet* march needed heavier accents. (The chorus's contribution, although it is only offstage cries of "Ah!," adds much to the effect of the piece.) *L'Impériale* needed heavier, crisper accents, more bandmasterly snap and showmanly flamboyance. Brahms was done in German, Berlioz in French, and the slight pallidness that normally attends singing in foreign tongues—the result of the words not being vividly expressed—was not altogether avoided. Nevertheless, it was a concert to delight lovers of Berlioz and confirm them in their admiration for his genius.

Not all Berlioz's thoughts in St. Peter's were of solemn, elevated music:

I liked spending the day there when the summer's heat became unbearable. I would take a volume of Byron and, settling myself comfortably in a confessional...would sit there absorbed in that burning verse. I followed the Corsair's bold journeys over the waves; I adored that character, at once inexorable and tender, pitiless and generous, strangely composed of two apparently contradictory sentiments—hatred of the human race and love of a woman.

Something of that Byronic character informs the overture Berlioz finally called *Le Corsaire*, although he first called it *La Tour de Nice* and then *Le Corsaire rouge*—the French title of Fenimore Cooper's *The Red Rover*. He composed the first version in 1844. The previous year, Verdi had suggested Byron's *Corsair* as an operatic subject for Venice. In 1846, he decided to compose it for London; Piave prepared a libretto, and Verdi "sketched a few of the things I found most congenial." *Macbeth, I masnadieri,* and *Jérusalem* intervened, and then Verdi completed *Il corsaro* in 1848. It was first performed in Trieste, and got a bad press. Until recently, it has continued to fare ill in the Verdi literature: "With the exception of *Alzira,* this is the worst opera ever written by the composer" (Francis Toye); "Another piece of hack-work" (Frank Walker in the fifth Grove). Verdi dispatched the score from Paris and did not (as was his wont) supervise the première himself; he composed it to discharge an irksome contract with a publisher he disliked ("I shall never write an opera of much importance for that detestable and uncouth Signor Lucca"). Those facts may have encouraged commentators to underrate the piece. The first twentieth-century production of *Il corsaro*—in London in 1966, with Pauline Tinsley as its heroine—showed that, so far from being hack-work, it is one of Verdi's most audacious early operas, filled with arresting formal and instrumental inventions whose effect can hardly be guessed at from the piano-vocal score. What that London production revealed a 1976 Philips recording (with Montserrat Caballé, Jessye Norman, and José Carreras) then confirmed. An even more exciting performance—the opera's American première—was given, in concert form, in the Fine Arts Center at Stony Brook on December 12. It came to Town Hall four days later. The Stony Brook performance was more spacious.

Verdi scholarship had meanwhile turned up a letter in which the composer gives instructions to Marianna Barbieri-Nini, the opera's first heroine, as detailed and subtle as those he sent her while she was preparing to create Lady Macbeth for him. (It was printed in English for the first time in the Stony Brook program.) It chimes with other things he wrote about the piece. "I couldn't hope to find a finer, more passionate, and more musicable subject," he said. In Act I, Conrad the corsair leaves his beloved Medora and sets off to attack the Muslims. In Act II, he loses his chance of conquest by leading his men away to rescue the women of Pasha Seyd's harem, which has caught fire. Returning with the Pasha's favorite, Gulnare, in his arms, he is captured; so are most of his gallant men, similarly encumbered with odalisques. In the first scene of Act III, Gulnare, who has fallen in love with Conrad, stabs the sleeping Pasha and escapes with Conrad. Meanwhile, back home, Medora, believing Conrad dead, has taken poison. Conrad and Gulnare arrive just in time to sing a trio with her. She dies in his arms, and Conrad flings himself off a cliff. Plenty of action, but, as Julian Budden remarks, narrative rather than drama. It's the music that makes *Il corsaro* exciting—wildly exciting in places. The combination of an old-style libretto and an "advanced" score on which both the adventure of composing *Macbeth* and firsthand experience of French opera have left their mark makes it at once strange and adventurous.

The Stony Brook performance—presented by the Long Island Opera Society in conjunction with the American Institute for Verdi Studies and the State University of New York at Stony Brook—had a fine cast. Gulnare was Sarah Reese, a new soprano of high promise, with a gleaming voice and the power, the flexibility, the dramatic energy, and the variety of accent that all Verdi heroines need. Medora's exquisite strains were delicately sung by Carolyn Val-Schmidt. Conrad was Carlo Bergonzi, than whom there is no more winning Verdi tenor. He makes others seem plain and plebeian, even when some of his more melting effects strike one as perhaps a bit much. Seyd was strongly sung by James Dietsch. Three comprimario roles were featly taken by Robert Guarino. The Stony Brook Chamber Symphony played with fire and finesse (good solo viola and solo cello, Susan-Lee Pounders and Frederick Chao; good solo oboe, Jeffrey Spaulding). The Stony Brook University Chorus was a shade feeble. David Lawton conducted, and he is a Verdian of such outstanding merits that I trust Mr. Levine and Miss Sills are vying to tempt him out of academe and into Lincoln Center. No Verdi conducting of such style and spirit has been heard in either of their houses this season. [*More about* Il corsaro *on page* 274.]

GRACEFUL, PASSIONATE, POETIC

January 18, 1982

SAMUEL BARBER'S last composition, completed in short score in 1978, soon after the Third Essay for Orchestra, was an eight-minute piece for oboe and string orchestra, intended to be the middle movement of an oboe concerto—one of the Philharmonic's series of concerto commissions for its own members to play. But the outer movements were not written. The piece, put into full score after Barber's death, last year, by his pupil and friend Charles Turner, now stands on its own, with the title *Canzonetta*. The Philharmonic, under Zubin Mehta, gave the first performance last month, with Harold Gomberg, the orchestra's first oboe from 1943 to 1977, as the soloist. It is a graceful and endearing work, based on a charming and shapely lyrical melody, deftly treated. It needs, I think, a simpler and more modest kind of interpretation than Mr. Gomberg's. His phrasing was emphatic, and he did some odd things to the score: appropriated a first-violin line, and turned some measured strains into a free-tempo cadenza. Barber was a fastidious and sure artist. *Canzonetta* is slight but elegantly written. A week or two before, while I was in England, I listened to his early String Quartet (1936) played by the Lindsay String Quartet in a concert broadcast from Birmingham. Its Adagio, rescored for full strings, has become famous; the movement sounds even better with the lean, careful original textures. The outer movements show buoyant invention. The concert began with Haydn's Opus 71, No. 2. The alert, invigorating performance confirmed the Lindsay's high reputation, and confirmed that at its rather disappointing New York recital earlier this season it was indeed below top form.

The International String Quartet, a Bloomington-born group, last month played Richard Felciano's *Crystal*, a delicate and poetic study in sonorities and spacings, at the first of two Carnegie Recital Hall concerts. *Crystal* was commissioned for the International by Brown University, where it is quartet-in-residence. There followed a strong, polished performance of Bartók's First Quartet. The second half was Beethoven's C-sharp minor. This performance, too, was polished, but it lacked character. The International has well-nigh flawless intonation and excellent ensemble. Its tone is sweet and true. But there was no energy of thought in the discourse—only a series of "problems" smoothly and efficiently solved. I felt so unsatisfied that after the concert I listened to—of course—the Busch recording. Few live chamber-music concerts provide so keen and exquisite a delight as does hearing a fine Haydn quartet at home, on radio or phonograph—light and temperature adjusted to one's needs. Few live Beethoven-quartet performances are given in halls silent enough and before audiences still enough to allow undisturbed, unfaltering concentration on the music.

I was in London to hear some French opera. Last year was a French-opera year there: *L'Africaine*, *Samson et Dalila*, Gluck's *Alceste*, and (presented by the English Bach Festival) *Castor et Pollux* at Covent Garden; *Roméo et Juliette*, *Louise*, and *Pelléas* at the English National Opera. In the last five days of November, one could choose, in London alone, between the new productions of *Alceste, Louise,* and *Pelléas*, and *Tosca* (with Domingo), *The Seven Deadly Sins* and *Les Mamelles de Tirésias*, Pauline Viardot's *Cendrillon*, Alessandro Scarlatti's *Il trionfo dell'onore*, Malcolm Williamson's *English Eccentrics*, Lars Johan Werle's *Dreaming about Thérèse*, *Falstaff*, and the National Theatre's new *Oresteia*, with a score by Harrison Birtwistle. That's a lot of music-drama in just four days. (On the Sunday there were no theatrical performances, but Covent Garden put on a gala concert with Joan Sutherland.) I went to *Alceste*, *Louise*, and *Pelléas*, and otherwise spent much time in front of the radio, catching up on what had been happening in the wide world of music.

Alceste is Gluck's noblest and most ambitious opera. In Paris earlier this century, the big dramatic sopranos—Félia Litvinne, Germaine

Lubin—sang it. Marjorie Lawrence sang it at the Met in 1941, and in 1952 it was as Alcestis that Kirsten Flagstad made her Met farewell, singing the part in English. Janet Baker chose Alcestis for her Covent Garden farewell. (She has announced her retirement from the stage— but not from the concert platform—with this Alcestis, Donizetti's Mary Stuart at the English National in the spring, and then Gluck's Orpheus at Glyndebourne this summer.) Alcestis' solos were transposed down a tone for her (all but "Divinités du Styx," which remained in B-flat)— not as far down as they were for Pauline Viardot in 1861, but enough to alter their heroic-soprano character. No matter: Dame Janet is our "classical" opera heroine—or hero—par excellence, the most vivid Dido (both Purcell's and Berlioz's), Diana (Cavalli's), Orpheus, Penelope (Monteverdi's; would she had also undertaken Fauré's), Idamantes, and Vitellia of our day. She commands the qualities of directness, force, and intensity. She gives passionate expression to the words and to the musical lines. She combines wholehearted generosity with dignity, control, and an eschewal of anything sentimental, showy, or false. She is the most honest of singers. I wish I had heard and seen her as Beethoven's Leonore—a part she has not tackled—even had it meant transpositions of the kind Malibran practiced in *Fidelio*. She should have done it with Jon Vickers as Florestan. He is in some ways her male match—in force, expressiveness, ardor, honesty, and passion. (There is a difference. Mr. Vickers sometimes pushes too far and cracks the mold of the role he appears in.) I have followed Miss Baker's career from her début, in 1956, in the Oxford University Opera Club's production of Smetana's *The Secret*. I missed some things: the Dorabella in Scotland, Walton's Cressida at Covent Garden, the Charlotte at the English National (but not the wonderful early Handel performances in London and Birmingham). And I've not always been a no-reservations admirer; some "but"s have appeared in my reviews. She is in the company of Flagstad, Astrid Varnay, Callas, Hans Hotter, Vickers—indelible singers I'm glad I'm old enough to have heard and seen on the stage. For various reasons, Dame Janet has shunned the American opera houses. It was well worth crossing the Atlantic to hear her Alcestis.

Let me get three "but"s out of the way. First, for good but sometimes also for ill, Dame Janet is a potently dramatic but not a conventionally "theatrical" performer, and in operas that need a touch or two of flashy showmanship—*Maria Stuarda* among them—she lacks flamboyance. Second, she is at her very best singing in English (as she sang Octavian, Berlioz's Dido, his Margaret). She has learned languages and certainly knows how to use them, but it is by mother-tongue communication that she touches audiences most deeply. The Covent Garden *Alceste* was sung in French. Third, she sometimes seems rapt in her roles, with a single-mindedness, a self-absorption, that sets her aside from the circumstances of the actual performance on the boards around her. It enhanced her Penelope, that isolate heroine whose thoughts are ever on the absent Ulysses. It worked wonderfully for the single-minded, self-absorbed Vitellia. But as Alcestis, while in her solos she made her devotion to the idea of Admetus shiningly apparent, she conveyed little such love toward the actual, physical Admetus of the evening, Robert Tear. Perhaps I am being unfair. On the first night, Mr. Tear was ill; in the third act he stopped singing altogether and mimed his role while another tenor, David Hillman, sang the lines in from the pit. Could any Alcestis in such circumstances be wholly convincing? Yet when Regina Resnik sang Amneris, and Varnay sang Ortrud, and Callas sang Violetta, while they were onstage one seemed to see and even hear the others through *their* eyes and ears; everyone else, whether able or not, took life and light from them. Dame Janet is certainly a "transfigured" performer; onstage, she appears to be made of some finer, rarer substance than mere mortal clay. But she does not have that strange, compelling power that can transfigure everything around her. She herself was incandescent. Her recitatives were aflame. The lines of the arias were thrillingly molded. The voice is mature now, and not quite as fresh in timbre or as free as before, but it is still filled with beautiful, ample sounds that seem to touch the very nerve of feeling. At her soft phrases, the house held its breath. Her singing was fearless, generous, and marvellously detailed.

The production was vaguely, not confidently, neoclassical. Washes of romantic amber light sentimentalized Roger Butlin's scenes. Walls rising in mid-act like garage doors to allow entrances, and a chorus partly masked, partly not, suggested a timid compromise between tradition and "modernity." (I preferred the precise geometry of Hugh Casson's décor for the 1953 Glyndebourne *Alceste*.) John Copley's staging was sensitive but rather soft. The chorus fell too often into compassionate clinches. There was a moment in Act II when courtiers who should have been onstage called in their comment from the wings and irresistibly suggested eavesdroppers at the royal keyhole. The important dances and the final divine descent *in machina* were muffed to a point where they aroused the audience's mirth. But Charles Mackerras is a marvellous Gluck conductor. That was apparent from the start of the overture. Pace, accent, and utterance were precise and very exciting. He phrased with an eloquence to match the heroine's. From his modern orchestra he drew timbres skillfully adjusted to the music. He combined a scholar's understanding of the style with practical flair and great dramatic instinct.

The Paris revision of *Alceste* (1776), not the original Vienna score (1767), was used, and for a large house it is probably the right choice. Few commentators have risked expressing a clear preference for either version; each of the two has its particular virtues—and drawbacks. Noble and elevated and great as *Alceste* is, it is also monotonous. As Ernest Newman wrote, the opera "is preëminently a drama of one idea; the burden of the play is sorrow and lamentation, which simply shifts from Admetus at the beginning of the drama to Alcestis in the subsequent acts." When Gluck revised the piece for Paris, he added some great things, and added, too, Hercules' swashbuckling entry, which does afford some contrast in Act III but disturbs the tone more awkwardly than effectively. At Covent Garden, when Alcestis herself was not onstage a tinge of boredom was sometimes mingled with admiration for Gluck's long stretches of "noble simplicity."

The English National Opera's *Louise*, a co-production with the Opéra Royal of Liège, had clumsy, lumpish scenery, with side walls of mirror, designed by René Allio, and an unromantic Julien, John Treleaven. But it was superlatively well conducted, by Sylvain Cambreling —Charpentier's score became a long, captivating tone poem—and it had a bewitching heroine in Valerie Masterson. The dozens of bit parts brought forward one good piece of singing after another. The company is in fine shape.

Pelléas was directed by Harry Kupfer, of the Berlin Comic Opera, in décor by Reinhard Heinrich "based on designs by Peter Sykora," who designed Mr. Kupfer's *Pelléas* in Dresden three years ago. It's hard to describe it without making it sound awful, and yet this was one of the strongest, sharpest, and most moving accounts of *Pelléas* I have ever heard—because it was so well sung, so well acted, and so well played.

A huge moth-eaten moth or moldering bird of prey rose from the stage after the first scene and hung there, eye-catchingly, sometimes flapping its wings a bit, until at the end it descended to envelop all the principals—all except little Yniold, who stepped clear, up to the footlights, and was left literally holding the baby. This "obliteration" of Golaud and Arkel along with Pelléas and Mélisande is an unhappy directorial gloss. Mélisande entered the castle as a ray of truth, honesty of feeling (even though she tells lies), and naturalness. She is destructive but is eventually destroyed. Debussy's tragedy requires us to see the castle life persisting after that ray's extinction. The House of Usher fell; Allemonde continues. Otherwise, the décor was chiefly two mobile, self-propelled greenhouses, illuminated within but never entered, with flat, practicable roofs reached by staircases. They weren't *too* bad. They arranged themselves into spaces that provided good areas to act and move in. Only the *fontaine des aveugles*—it looked like a plastic wall fountain, such as one might see in a motel lobby, clipped to one of the greenhouses—was woefully inadequate to carry the symbolic charges attached to it.

The opera was sung in a new English translation, by Hugh Macdonald. *Pelléas* is often declared to be "untranslatable," but it is not. Perhaps the operas whose music is most closely tied to particular speech rhythms and inflections—Monteverdi's, Mussorgsky's, Janáček's, Debussy's—gain most from translation even while in another way they must lose most. (The paradox arises from the fact that the more nearly a musical line is linked to its words, the more imperative it is that the words be used and understood.) In a BBC talk on the eve of the première, Mr. Macdonald suggested that "many opera translations are too reverential to the music." His translation is not reverential. He has rewritten Debussy's vocal lines freely to fit his own idiomatic and accurate English—too freely, I thought, in some phrases where the composer's rhythms and intervals are even more important and eloquent than the words, where musical motifs are the chief carrier of the "sense." Not only because this was a *Pelléas* (unlike those of Covent Garden, the Met, and the City Opera) in which the actors sang in their own tongue to an audience whose tongue it is, too, did it seem as if a veil had been removed; but the translation played its part.

So did the naturalness of the actors. Mr. Kupfer restricted his heavy symbolic underlining to the décor, and presented a drama played by "real people." Eilene Hannan was a near-ideal Mélisande: neither the fey, frail wraith of some productions nor the knowing, willful little bitch sometimes produced in reaction but a straightforward, credible, touching, understandable young creature. Her singing was true and beautiful. Robert Dean, the Pelléas, had the same directness. Neil Howlett (Golaud), John Tomlinson (Arkel), and Sarah Walker (Geneviève) were all distinguished. Rosanne Brackenridge, the Yniold, sang well but, buttoned tightly into a blue suit, looked like a plump bellhop. A real boy, when one with a voice can be found, is in every way preferable. The musical direction—Lionel Friend's on the night I attended, Mark Elder's at a performance four days earlier, which was broadcast —was at once lucid and poetic.

A word in praise of the English National's program books, edited by Nicholas John. Each is a small work of art, carefully designed, carefully printed on good paper. That for *Louise* contained, among much of interest, some new material gathered from the composer's nephew. That for *Pelléas* brought together related essays, aperçus, poems, and images from Debussy, Maeterlinck, Poe, Munch, Rossetti, Carlyle, Pascal, Botticelli, and Yeats into a true "*Pelléas* Book." And advertisements are grouped at the ends, on pages easily disposed of.

Joshua Rifkin and his Bach Ensemble brought their "chamber" performance of Bach's B-minor Mass to the 92nd Street Y this month. The arguments for a "one voice to a part" interpretation which Mr. Rifkin advanced in a program note seem to me questionable on both historical and musical grounds. I can't believe that the great Sanctus was composed for a vocal sextet (and not only because when I played continuo for performances of the Mass conducted by Albert Coates he would urge me to draw the thirty-two-foot pedal reed at those striding bass octaves). But the performance itself, which drew a full house, was rewarding to hear. The clarity of the textures, the gentle timbres of the old instruments (lovely flute playing from Christopher Krueger), and the light, clear, neatly phrased solo singing conspired to please. Mr. Rifkin sometimes plodded, but he led the "Dona nobis pacem"—eight voices now, two to a part—to a sure, fine climax.

LOVE'S MAZES

February 22, 1982

IN 1954, Edward J. Dent wrote:

> The only way to understand Handel's operas is the logical one: to begin with the librettos and read them word for word from beginning to end, and to do the same with the full scores, never allowing oneself to skip a note of the recitative, however "dry" it may appear to be. It is fatal to regard a Handel opera (or indeed any opera) as no more than a string of famous arias; it is a drama, inseparable from its action and stage setting.

A year later, the Handel Opera Society, formed under Dent's inspiration, staged its first production, of Handel's *Deidamia*. *Hercules* followed in 1956, and *Alcina*, with Joan Sutherland as its heroine, in 1957. For the last twenty-three years, the Society has generally put on two Handels a year at Sadler's Wells. (Last year's pair was *Partenope* and *Belshazzar*.) In 1959, two other Handel opera series began: in the little Unicorn Theatre, in Abingdon, and at the Barber Institute, in Birmingham. (There it was that Janet Baker sang Irene in *Tamerlano*, *Ariodante*, and *Orlando*.) Most of Handel's forty-odd operas have now been revived—some of them in several productions—in the country where he lived and worked. Most of the mistakes that can be made in their performance have long since been made. By trial and error, by blunder and bold adventure, answers were found to the "problems"— of dramaturgy, of voice type, of staging, of instrumentation—that they pose to modern performers and to modern audiences. But the lessons provided by two decades of steady performance remained largely unlearned by the big companies. I've not seen the English National's recent *Giulio Cesare* (which is to be re-created in San Francisco this year), but Covent Garden's *Alcina* and the English National's *Semele* were sorry examples of a refusal to take Handel's dramas seriously, and the New York City Opera's *Cesare* was a travesty.

The American Repertory Theatre, at the Loeb Drama Center, in Cambridge, is now presenting an *Orlando* conceived closely in accord with Dent's counsel. Except for repeats in the overture, this *Orlando* is done complete—all the arias, all the recitative. It is playing (to full houses) for a run of forty performances, which means that the singers, drawn on any night from a double-cast pool, can try new refinements, inflections, and musical variations; that the performance grows; and that Cambridge and Boston enthusiasts can visit it again and again, discovering both differences and new beauties in a score performed with detailed, dedicated commitment.

Dent declared roundly and rightly that *Orlando* has "a very good libretto" and that "the moral aspect of this opera is interesting." The titular hero is Christendom's doughty champion distracted from his mission and driven to madness by his unrequited love for Angelica, Queen of Cathay. She, who spurned the hands of half Europe's princes, has fallen in love with the African soldier boy Medoro. That much is familiar from Ariosto. Handel adds two more characters: the shepherdess Dorinda, deserted by Medoro when the highborn Angelica crossed his path and dazzled him; and the mage Zoroaster, part counsellor and part conjurer, who cares for Orlando and finally cures him of his infatuation. Like *Figaro* and *Così fan tutte*, the piece explores the intricacies and responsibilities of love in music that makes manifest and vivid its pangs, its joys, and its ambiguities. Act I ends with a trio in which Angelica and Medoro, happy with one another, try to console Dorinda, and each strand of feeling is surely spun. Act II is a breathtaking sequence of beautiful, emotional arias culminating in Orlando's famous mad scene. Four years after *Orlando*, Handel himself had a breakdown. His first biographer, John Mainwaring, remarked on the "violence of his passions" and continued:

> How greatly his senses were disordered at intervals, for a long time, appeared from an hundred instances, which are better forgotten than recorded. The most violent deviations from reason, are usually seen when the strongest faculties happen to be thrown out of course.

The mad scene of Handel's *Orlando* when violently and passionately enacted—as it was in Cambridge—is an incident to arouse pity and terror. And Orlando's sudden return to reason, effected in the opera by a philter brought from starry regions by an eagle, adumbrates Handel's own restoration at Aix-la-Chapelle: "His cure, from . . . the quickness, with which it was wrought, passed with the Nuns for a miracle." In short, *Orlando* when properly performed seems real. The magic apparatus of its plot becomes a metaphor for human experience.

The Cambridge performance is given in modern dress and with contemporary imagery. The first stage direction in the original libretto is:

> Night. A Country with a Mountain in Prospect; *Atlas*, on the Summit of the Mountain, sustaining the Heavens on his Shoulders; Several Genij at the Foot of the Mountain; ZOROASTER leaning on a Stone, and contemplating the Motions of the Stars.

The Cambridge synopsis reads:

> The scene opens at Mission Control, Kennedy Space Center, Cape Canaveral. Zoroaster—scientist, magician, and Project Supervisor—is studying distant galaxies of the solar system.

He studies them, of course, on a screen, with winking lights below. Where Handel's scene changes to a glade with Dorinda's pastoral cot, Cambridge's shifts to a clearing in the Everglades where Dorinda has parked her Airstream camper. When Zoroaster, to shield Medoro from the jealous Orlando, causes "a large Fountain to rise out of the

Earth and conceal him," a steel drinking fountain appears for Medoro to duck behind. At the close of Act II, Handel's Zoroaster dispatches Orlando in an aerial chariot; in Cambridge, a rocket lifts off. Act III's Temple of Mars becomes a Martian landscape.

In the telling, this may sound like adolescent ingenuity. In practice, the Cambridge collaborators have devised apt and effective imagery to replace the marvellous stage machines of the Baroque theatre. The sets are designed by the painter Elaine Spatz-Rabinowitz; the costumes are by Rita Ryack; the lighting is by James F. Ingalls; Peter Sellars is the director. Their stage pictures are beautiful. Image after image remains graved in the mind: Dorinda, in cutoff jeans, apostrophizing the nightingale as she stands in the warm glow from her camper door; Angelica, a Main Line heiress kitted in impeccable riding clothes, pinned to a silver panel by a shaft of cold blue light; Orlando, a romantic figure in his orange space suit, flexing his muscles as he recalls the feats of Alcides and of Peleus' son. The opera is not altered. The characters and their plights remain those Handel portrayed so keenly. Clumsily executed, or conceived in a spirit of prankishness, such a production would be intolerable. But this *Orlando* is brilliantly, gracefully, and precisely handled. (Entertainingly, too: the element of visual extravaganza is a necessary component of Handel's drama.) Mr. Sellars is twenty-four. His work seems to me the newest and most exciting I have encountered on the operatic stage since—well, since Giorgio Strehler's. His *Orlando* is more accurately inventive and more musical than were, say, Peter Brook's and Peter Hall's earliest essays in opera. His cast must sometimes be as active as those in Brook's *Midsummer Night's Dream*, but whereas in that exhilarating show Shakespeare's poetry, ill spoken, took second place, in this one Handel's music, very well sung, is paramount. In the trio, the three singers move through intricate, mazy patterns that seem not a gloss on the music but a marvellous, living enactment of it. Mr. Sellars's control of the long phrase, of stillness, of sudden shifts of direction, of musical and emotional counterpoints struck me as near-miraculous. And his control of the stage-audience relationship (houselights were left on, as they were in Handel's day) was rare and wonderful.

A cast of expert young singers sang lightly, fluently, and truly. Jeffrey Gall, a countertenor, was a poignant and powerful Orlando. So was his alternate, Sanford Sylvan—a baritone, but one with a clear timbre that made the octave transposition less distressing than usual. Jane Bryden was a fine-drawn, patrician Angelica; her alternate, Janet Brown, was more vulnerable, and very sweet of voice. Mary Kendrick Sego and Pamela Gore were both admirable in portraying a good-natured, burly, winning Medoro. At both performances I saw, Sharon Baker was a quicksilver, captivating Dorinda, and James Maddalena a suave, spry Zoroaster. Handel—I cite Dent again—"made no concessions to the vanity of conductors; in that golden age of opera they did not exist." Craig Smith was such a conductor as singers and directors dream of working with. He set apt tempi, phrased eloquently, was responsive to each turn of the drama, and evidently welcomed each surprising, unrehearsed flight of fancy with which the singers embellished their lines.

Budget restrictions precluded the touches of recorders and horns that should occasionally color Handel's basic orchestra of oboes, bassoon, strings, and continuo. The opera is sung in Italian, but a bilingual libretto is available for a dollar. *Orlando* continues through March. The performance discovers all Handel's richness, variety, wit, humanity, and genius.

[*For an account of a very different—and also very satisfying—production of Handel's* Orlando, *see page 403.*]

Lorenzo Da Ponte in his memoirs cites Ariosto as one of his "first masters," and ideas from *Orlando Furioso* lie not far beneath his libretto for *Così fan tutte*. The plot is a sophisticated development of the tale told in Ariosto's Canto 43, where woman's fidelity is put to the test. The prima donna borrows her name from Ariosto's heroic Fiordiligi, who followed her beloved to the wars. In an aria for Guglielmo (which Mozart later replaced with a shorter one), the baritone declares himself more helplessly infatuate than Orlando, more deeply smitten than Medoro. The libretto, written to be heard by and please educated people, is as rich in classical allusions as any that Handel set. Venus, Mars, and Vulcan—a triangle familiar to Mozart's Figaro—reappear. Penelope, Pallas, Jove, Mercury, Artemis, Charon, the Eumenides, the Phoenix, and the Hydra pass in procession. Fiordiligi when roused to highest indignation rounds on the importunate suitors with a line of Virgil, converting "Velut . . . rupes immota resistit" into "Come scoglio immoto resta."

Così fan tutte is an opera, like *Orlando*, every word of whose libretto deserves attention. It would be sensible of the Met, which has just mounted a new production of the piece, to leave the houselights up so that listeners could follow it. The show is sung in Italian. (The old Victorian translation, by the Reverend Marmaduke E. Browne, alters names but captures the tone in such lines as "Then, for strength, could Samson beat us? Or, for learning, Epictetus, Saint Augustine, or Servetus?") Literary skill is but one of the opera's varied merits. The White Queen trained herself to believe six impossible things before breakfast. To enjoy *Così* fully, the listener should learn to hear it in at least six possible, if incompatible, ways simultaneously. *Così* is an artificial, mannered comedy, with a plot providing what Alfred Einstein described as "the aesthetic satisfaction that we get from a chess problem well solved"; and it is a work proclaiming profound truths about human character and human behavior. The four lovers, Dent said, are "more like marionettes than human beings"; and they are also four recognizable, distinct, living, breathing people. The score is Mozart's loveliest and most extended divertimento—a radiant sequence of movements scored for six voices and orchestra, each movement employing different forces—and it is a developing music drama. It is precisely and delicately constructed and balanced; yet Act II contains a sequence of five arias that Hermann Abert could describe as "without peer in its monotony among Mozart's mature works." It is an improbable tale of fidelity and devotion destroyed in an instant by flightiness and frivolity; and it is a believable account of events that might really happen—reflecting, indeed, Mozart's real-life transference of his affections from one Weber sister to another. There is a parody element in the music—"Come scoglio" is a highly extravagant protestation— but Fiordiligi in that aria is patently sincere and means every word she sings. And what of Ferrando's mock wooing in the duet "Fra gli amplessi," and of Fiordiligi's heartfelt surrender? Do they speak in accents other than those of true love? One of the marvels of Così is that we need not answer that question but can welcome both the truth and force of the sentiments and the contrivance of the situation.

The Così performances I have enjoyed most have been those that took their starting point in individual characters and personalities carefully observed and fully portrayed; that left the ambiguities (and particularly Fiordiligi's feelings for the "absent" Guglielmo and the disguised Ferrando, and theirs for her) unresolved, as in real life such ambiguities often are; and that ended with the original couples reunited—shaken by their emotional adventures, wiser, a little more mature. Romantics have long argued that the mispairing in the central scenes reveals the true matches—that the emotional Fiordiligi and Ferrando are meant for one another, as are those realists Dorabella and Guglielmo. By this reckoning, Don Alfonso is either a perceptive character-reader whose wager is a brilliant stroke of psychological counsel or a cynic whose jest inadvertently does much good. The logical consequence is that the betrothal ceremony begun in spoof should go ahead in earnest. Alfonso's last words to the women are "I deceived you, but the deception undeceived your lovers, who will henceforth be wiser.... Join hands, take partners, kiss, and keep silent. All four of you now laugh, as I laughed and will laugh." And all four follow his advice, praising a life where laughter and reason can weather every storm. After Figaro and Don Giovanni, Così proclaims sentiments that Jane Austen and George Eliot would recognize. But who joins hands with whom? The historical answer, the libretto's answer, the only possible answer, is plain. At the same time, it is a measure of Mozart's insight into the human heart that the question can even have been asked.

The new Met production, which is directed by Colin Graham, answers the question wrongly. During the closing pages, Ferrando and Guglielmo, reconciled to their original loves, then catch one another's eyes, shrug, and coolly switch partners for the final exchanges. The women react hardly at all. The effect is casual and cynical, and it is unprepared for. The message seems to be "What does it matter who mates with whom?" Mozart's music has been telling us that such things matter very much. The coarse, frivolous comment would have done more harm had not the performance by that time ceased to claim much serious attention. The drama was enacted (at any rate, on the second night) by five melodious puppets and only one real character. She was Dorabella, in the person of Maria Ewing. And Miss Ewing was wonderful. No need to repeat the encomiums that her Dorabella at Glyndebourne, in 1978 (in Peter Hall's wonderfully fresh, truthful production), won. She was the same impulsive, spontaneous, ever-arresting young woman, quick to respond to every turn of events. So long as she was on the stage, then—provided one attended only to her—Mozart's drama was alive. Kiri Te Kanawa moved blandly through the role of Fiordiligi, making lovely sounds undisturbed by any emotion or any sharp consonants. ("Come scoglio immoro resa conra i veni" was what one heard.) Kathleen Battle's Despina was a sketch that needs filling out with more vivacious Italian. David Rendall's singing as Ferrando was fluent and well shaped; his characterization was stock. James Morris, oddly cast as Guglielmo, was often raucous and roaring. And even Donald Gramm, usually so polished, witty, and resourceful a performer, made next to nothing of Don Alfonso.

The opera was given uncut, as it rarely is. In itself, that is a virtue, but not if it was the reason that James Levine, conducting, rushed through so many numbers at breakneck speed. Recitatives were gabble-gabble and gobble-gobble, not witty discourse. The first three trios and the aria "Ah lo veggio" (which Mozart marked allegretto but Mr. Levine took at an allegro assai) were the most disconcertingly rapid. Mr. Levine's Mozart is often graceless, despite his evident affection for the music. With a stick, he beat out every beat of the score, emphatically, insistently. The effect was breathless, unlinear, not shaped to the words and their sense, and not taking life from—but, rather, inhibiting any eloquence in—the singers. Harmonic events that should be placed and dwelt on passed by unheeded. He used what sounded like too large, heavy, and bright an orchestra, sunk deep in a pit. He is an energetic and excited conductor, but in Così his gait was not that of a limber, Mozartian athlete—a Beecham, a Walter—ready to relax, responsive to each bewitching surprise along the way.

Hayden Griffin's scenery is an arrangement of moving screens and panels against a clear sky, with cutouts at the back—somewhat in the manner of Luciano Damiani's wonderful décor for Strehler's great Entführung at Salzburg, but less distinguished and beautiful in execution. The lighting, by Gil Wechsler, is admirably bright and clear. The stage direction—until the final blunder—is neat and could be called inoffensive were it not an offense to treat a Mozart opera as if it were not the most important thing in the world.

SOLDIERS

March 1, 1982

J. M. R. LENZ'S *Die Soldaten,* written in 1775 (the year of Mozart's *La finta giardiniera*) and published in 1776, is a remarkable play. With its short scenes, ellipses, "jump cuts," and ta'azieh-like techniques for bridging space and time, it seems more advanced than Büchner's *Woyzeck* and Wedekind's *Lulu* plays—on which it plainly left a mark—and than most of Brecht's dramas. (In ta'azieh—Persian religious dramas —one may hear a letter being indited in one city and, simultaneously, being read by its recipient in another.) The terse, vivid tragedy traces the degradation of a middle-class girl into a soldiers' whore. The main characters are officers in Armentières; Marie; her family; and her bourgeois betrothed, who enlists, becomes a batman, and poisons the soup of the officer chiefly responsible for Marie's fall. In the penultimate scene, Marie, now a drab, solicits, unrecognized, her own father. (The confrontation recalls Henryson's *Testament of Cresseid* and adumbrates one in Schreker's *Der ferne Klang.*) In the final scene, a colonel and a countess coolly debate the advisability of establishing official military brothels.

Die Soldaten remained unstaged, it seems, until Max Reinhardt produced it during the First World War. In 1930, Manfred Gurlitt, who four years earlier had set *Woyzeck,* made an opera of it, which played in Dusseldorf, Prague, and Berlin. Then in 1965, in Cologne, Bernd Alois Zimmermann's *Die Soldaten* appeared—an opera, the New Grove rightly declares, "widely acknowledged as the most important in German since those of Berg." Other productions followed—in Cassel, Munich, Dusseldorf, Nuremberg, Hamburg, most recently Frankfurt —and German troupes took the piece on tour, to Britain, Italy, Holland, Sweden. The Cologne production was recorded, by Wergo. Opera companies less firmly grounded and solidly subsidized than those of Germany looked eagerly at *Die Soldaten* but fought shy of it, for it is a hard piece to perform: the Munich production is said to have had 377 vocal and 33 orchestral rehearsals. Last month, the American première of *Die Soldaten* was presented by the Opera Company of Boston.

Sarah Caldwell both directed and conducted. The show demonstrated at once her ambition and adventuresomeness, the vitality that informs all she does, and the unsatisfactory nature of American operatic life, which makes a first-rate performance of such a work as *Die Soldaten* all but impossible. European productions are usually long rehearsed, with a stable cast and orchestra, and are then played for season after season. The Boston *Soldaten* was put together in a matter of weeks, with singers and players assembled for the occasion, and only a preview and three performances were scheduled. (In the event, as a result of an orchestral dispute a week's rehearsal and one performance were lost.) So, on the one hand, it was underprepared; on the other hand, weeks of intensive hard work, difficult roles newly learned, and an elaborate set were put to but brief use. The Met or the City Opera should have undertaken *Die Soldaten* years ago, should have revived it regularly, and should have played it the length and breadth of the country. It is a work that both performers and audiences need to grow into.

Zimmermann was drawn to Lenz's play, he said, less by its social content than by its treatment of time and "timelessness." In a written introduction to the opera, he cited sentences of Joyce ("Put all space in a nutshell"), Pound ("All ages are present. The future stirs in the souls of few"), and Lenz himself ("I will give you one hundred instances which still remain one"). The epoch of the opera's action is "yesterday, today, and tomorrow," and visual and musical imagery of all ages is drawn upon. The play expands and is charged with the large, despairing tragic vision that filled Zimmermann's later works. The opera ends with a world destroyed: the dust from an atomic explosion settles, and a chant of "But deliver us from evil" fades into darkness and silence. The piece is "total theatre." In the composer's words, "architecture, sculpture, painting, musical theatre, spoken theatre, ballet, film, microphone, television, tape, and sound techniques, electronic music, concrete music, circus, the musical, and all forms of motion theatre combine to form the phenomenon of pluralistic opera," and the composer's task is "'merely' ... to concentrate and intellectually coördinate the new discoveries of recent years." *Die Soldaten* was initially conceived for performance in a theatre where twelve stages, each with its attendant musicians, surrounded the audience. Cologne, which had commissioned the piece, declared it unperformable, and Zimmermann made the current "performing version," which still calls for an orchestra of over a hundred (fifty-four independent string parts), for seventeen soloists, for actors and dancers, for films projected on three screens. One café scene is accompanied by a percussion toccata provided by soloists and chorus as, in strictly notated rhythms, they tinkle cups, clink glasses, slam down cards, chatter. Three cadets tap out or stamp out a dance glorifying military life in contrapuntal rhythmic patterns notated in 7/8 broken by bars of 1/8, 5/8, and other meters. The vocal lines are hard to pitch and hard to time. All forms of utterance from full-throated song to naturalistic speech are employed, and the singers must be able to pass from one to another not only within a phrase but even between syllables of a word. "In some scenes of this opera," Zimmermann wrote, "I have employed speech, singing, screaming, whispering, jazz, Gregorian chant." In an extended lyrical trio for three women, almost every note carries its own dynamic indication. Most productions have simplified the composer's more elaborate scenic requirements. Those for the start of Act IV—a phantasmagoria of multiple, simultaneous scenes, in which all the principals appear and some of them are doubled by actors, and again by dancers, and again on three simultaneous films—are particularly intricate; I doubt whether any theatre could compass them fully, or whether any audience, except after studying the libretto and the original play, could follow what happens in more than a general way.

Zimmermann's musical complexities do not seem unnecessary. As Lord Harewood writes in Kobbé, "what impresses the listener at the end of a performance is the clarity of organization, the audibility of the text, the subtlety of the sounds he has heard." The vocal lines, for all their angularity and awkward leaps, prove eloquent—at any rate, in the original German. The sounds and inflections of the words apparently determine the melodic contours. The Boston *Soldaten*, however, was sung in an English translation that was excellently audible but often seemed forced and unnatural in declamation. Miss Caldwell had engaged a cast of able singers. (Outstanding were Phyllis Hunter as Marie, Beverly Morgan as her sister, Joseph Evans as her betrothed, Richard Crist as her father, and Timothy Noble, John Moulson, and John Brandstetter among the officers.) Everyone—down to three perky tap-dancing cadets—seemed perfectly confident. How accurate the performance was I cannot say; to judge of that one would have to listen to a tape while following the score. But the effect—unlike that of the deft Dusseldorf production I heard in 1971, which was conducted by Günther Wich, or that of the Cologne recording, which is conducted by Michael Gielen—often suggested an enthusiastic approximation. Several episodes were impressive, moving, beautiful. Others seemed imprecise. I heard the preview and the first performance. I wish one could have returned to, say, a tenth performance, in which the ensembles had settled, the balances had been adjusted, and what was sketchy had become sure. Miss Caldwell evidently has a vision of what *Die Soldaten* might be, and she earns our gratitude for a remarkable achievement—even if it was a bold, vivid stab at, not a finished rendering of, Zimmermann's lucid and overwhelming masterpiece.

In New York, the Met has come up with a leaden new production of Rossini's *Il barbiere*, redeemed in part by the performance of its heroine, Marilyn Horne. True, she looked matronly and in Act II suggested the Zia Principessa in Puccini's *Suor Angelica*. Her acting was broad, but it was irresistibly naughty, mischievous, and alive. And her vocalism was prodigious. In true Rossinian style, she kept us guessing what the next notes might be. Would she leap an octave, plunge an octave, add a trill, fly into inventive divisions, or even sing a passage familiar from the score? The twinkling of this star was filled with delightful surprises.

Around her, the Met had assembled a cast of what sounded like comprimarios—men whose singing might pass muster in some dim provincial house. John Cox's stage direction was busy but humorless.

Andrew Davis's conducting was lyrical in intention but heavy. Robin Wagner's revolving décor added two more sets to the three Rossini calls for: the prettiest of them was seen only in transitions, and the most elaborate was used only to accompany the final passage of the Alma-viva-Figaro duet. Has the *Barber* ever seemed so long and, except when Miss Horne was singing, so shapeless and dull?

A MAGNIFICENT EPIC

March 8, 1982

THE GREAT American opera, Roger Sessions's *Montezuma*, comes closer to receiving the production it deserves; perhaps a full-scale presentation by the Metropolitan Opera will mark the composer's hundredth birthday, which falls on December 28, 1996. *Montezuma*, composed between 1941 and 1963, was first performed in Berlin in 1964. Sarah Caldwell gave the American première in Boston twelve years later. And now *Montezuma* has reached New York: the Juilliard American Opera Center mounted three sold-out performances of it last month.

Let me repeat some of what I said after the Boston première. The Matter of Mexico, recounted most memorably in W. H. Prescott's *History of the Conquest of Mexico*, is the great American epic—as stirring as the Matter of Arthur or the Matter of Troy, as romantic and adventurous as *Orlando Furioso* or *The Faerie Queene*. It has the added charm and interest of being true, and the importance of treating moral and political themes still raised by the news in our daily papers—for it deals with invasion; with the imposition of foreign rule; with the clash of religions; with commercial exploitation; with patriotic resistance, coups, and palace revolutions; with the disruption of a stable agricultural society by conquerors whose motives are mixed. Further, it is a tale of marvels—the Spaniards' first sight of Montezuma's glittering capital, riding on the vast lake in the clear, high air, is a vision that still stirs imaginative hearts—and of high heroic adventure, including a New World anabasis; and it is a tale of strong, sharp, complicated characters in conflict. One of Cortes's lieutenants, Bernal Díaz, set down his firsthand account of the expedition in simple, vivid words. Prescott, drawing on the accumulated resources of Charles V's archives, amplified them in his great history. Even the Conquest of Peru, the conflict of Pizarro and the Inca, which Prescott also chronicled, and which Peter Shaffer turned into a successful play, *The Royal Hunt of the Sun*, and Iain Hamilton into a lyric drama done by the English National Opera—even that matter, as the historian remarked, "notwithstanding the opportunities it presents for the display of character, strange, romantic incident, and picturesque scenery, does not afford so obvious advantages...as the Conquest of Mexico. Indeed, few subjects can present a parallel with that, for the purposes either of the historian or the poet. The natural development of the story, there, is precisely what would be prescribed by the severest rules of art.... It is a magnificent epic, in which the unity of interest is complete." It is also a tragedy. Díaz, after describing Mexico City and its surroundings, "like an enchanted vision from the tale of Amadis... things never heard of, seen, or dreamed of before," reflects that "today all that I then saw is overthrown and destroyed; nothing is left standing." Small wonder, then, that the Matter of Mexico inspired operas. One of the earliest was Graun's *Montezuma*, of 1755, with a libretto by Frederick the Great. (It was done in Boston in 1973.) The most celebrated before Sessions's was Spontini's *Fernand Cortez*, of 1809. (It was done by the Met in 1888 with forces that, according to the critic H. E. Krehbiel, "rivalled in numbers those who constituted the veritable Cortez's army, while the horses came within three of the number that the Spaniards took into Mexico.")

Sessions's *Montezuma* captures the scale, the seriousness, and the romance of the subject in music that is powerful, splendid, colorful, and generous. But it is not an opera made for easy public success. The case of Berlioz's *Les Troyens* is perhaps not irrelevant. That epic, too, had its champions from the start but was by many not unintelligent people long deemed a clumsily made, noisily ill-scored, impracticably long, and even amateurish opera—at best, a masterpiece by intention maimed by inexpert execution. It needed performances by enthusiasts convinced that the "awkwardness" and the greatness were inseparable to gain unstinted public acceptance; and a century passed before it had its first complete—well, all but complete—production (at Covent Garden in 1957). Any fool, as Brahms might have said, can hear what is "wrong" with *Montezuma*: it is too densely and busily composed and too heavily scored (the orchestra is that of *Turandot* plus a fourth clarinet and a fourth trumpet—slightly smaller than Verdi's in *Don Carlos*); and G. Antonio Borgese's libretto is "impossible," mainly but not only because of the syntactical torment it inflicts on natural English word order. "Bread and wine needs a man to fight and die" and "Black is beyond the moon, the sky" are characteristic lines, and there are some that even on the printed page, let alone when they are sung out in the theatre, resist parsing—such as these remarks of Malinche, Cortes's Indian mistress, to her lord:

> *Art thou the restituted king, the arisen one?*
> *Some doubt, blame thee a demon, dread*
> *as blackened flame of volcanoes, this beard,*
> *through which thou breath'st me,*
> *human as a god.*

I missed the Berlin première. The productions in Boston and New York were certainly put on by committed champions. Boston's was directed and conducted by Miss Caldwell. New York's was directed by Ian Strasfogel and was conducted by Frederik Prausnitz, who has long been a distinguished exponent of Sessions's music. (He has recorded the Eighth Symphony, and the Ninth is dedicated to him.) The Boston theatre, the Orpheum, had no pit; despite the ardent spirit that informed the enterprise, its impressiveness, and some fine performances, the result was unbalanced, and it was often hard to hear exactly what was supposed to be happening in the score. The Juilliard Theatre has a pit. The instrumental perspectives were more clearly limned, and under Mr. Prausnitz the Juilliard Orchestra played very well. In many ways, it was a clearly focussed musical presentation. But the problems posed by Sessions's textures were not solved. The pit is not deep, and it was not even depressed to its full depth; the house is fairly small. Student instrumentalists find it hard to play difficult music softly, and Mr. Prausnitz, probably wisely, made no evident moves to keep the orchestra down. The score was vibrantly and radiantly alive, and that was thrilling. But the instruments often took precedence of the voices and covered what they should have accompanied, and that is precisely what Sessions did not want. In a prefatory note to the score, he wrote, "The vocal parts of this work constitute always its principal melody." Moreover, most of the words were inaudible.

That had the somewhat dubious advantage, of course, of making objection to Borgese's stilted diction largely irrelevant. A few passages did come through that revealed bold rewriting of the text by the director. Where Borgese's phrases suggest crossword-puzzle clues, Mr. Strasfogel's revised wording solved them and supplied the answers. Borgese's Montezuma refers to "the tame high deer, feather-maned, rampant skyward to span with cotton hair'd harvest the ranges"; Mr. Strasfogel changed the first words to "the horses we need." Borgese's Malinche sings, "All rosy, stalking on important stilts, troop-shuttling from pond to bank"; Mr. Strasfogel wrote in "flamingos." I am not sure that he was right thus to clarify. During the last decade, I have modified my first dislike of the libretto's diction. (A National Public Radio broadcast of the Boston production, in a recording that favored the voices more than the theatre did, brought a chance for reassessment.) It seems to me now an awkwardness that, since Sessions accepted it, we, too, must accept—as an integral part of his opera. He chose this stylized language for his work, and it makes its effect. Changing it changes not only the "tone" of the drama but also its music, for the vocal lines—the "principal melody"—are largely determined by Borgese's verses. And it is not enough to sing them with the correct pitches, the written durations, and clear pronunciation. In that prefatory note, the composer spelled out his intention:

Rhythmic detail in the vocal delivery should be performed according to the natural inflection of the English language, rather than to a rigid and literal adherence to the note values as indicated in the score. These note values represent an approximation, on the composer's part, to the rhythm of English pronunciation and, of course, an indication of the desired expressive stress as embodied in the vocal line. His musical intention will be most completely realized if the above principle is applied without any constraint except that demanded by a firm metrical background.

The principle applies to most vocal music, and it is one insufficiently observed by many American singers. Strict adherence to written note values, unmodified by the inherent shape of the words, sacrificing text to tone, and "sounding the bar lines" dull many recitals and opera performances. (The Chamber Opera Theatre's recent production of Thea Musgrave's *The Voice of Ariadne*, in the Marymount Manhattan Theater, contained sentences of stilted, unnaturally inflected English declamation that reduced the expressiveness of that imaginative, beautiful score.) Let me, not for the first time, commend Harry Plunket Greene's *Interpretation in Song* (Da Capo Press), and especially his pages on prosody and meter. The singers of *Montezuma* must, I believe, learn to love Borgese's text and to respond to it as Sessions did, and sing it with all the eloquence at their command. Then, even if some of the words still prove inaudible, the vocal lines will in themselves be expressive.

There are people inattentive to words who happily attend operas performed in tongues that not they or, on occasion, the singers understand. Even for them, *Montezuma* is a special case: because much of its "action" is close-argued dialogue on subjects political and religious which must be followed in detail; because exceptional care is needed to place the vocal lines in the foreground; and because both score and drama are constructed on a framework of narratives. The narrator is Bernal Díaz in old age, inditing his history; the scenes he remembers then take shape on the main stage. Incomprehensible narratives are of but limited interest, and the Juilliard's Díaz, Robert Keefe, had a voice of loose focus in the high register, and fuzzy articulation. Would it have helped, I wonder, to move him in front of the proscenium, or even to amplify him electrically? (I suppose those things were tried and found not to work well.)

Before long, *Montezuma* should be performed in a theatre with a deep, Bayreuth-like pit, and after rehearsals numerous enough to allow fine adjustment of the balances. And audiences should be able to buy the libretto when they buy their tickets. A vocal score is available, but not, so far, a libretto. When it is published, it should probably be annotated. Mr. Strasfogel, so far as I could hear, wrote out Díaz's references to "expert Circe," "yearning Ariadne," and "haughty Medea," not especially recondite personages, but left in other allusions—to the Duke Valentino Borgia and his procurator Don Ramiro de Orco—that surely do need explanation. I enjoyed the Juilliard *Montezuma* more than many people did, I suspect, because I had done some homework —had read Díaz, Prescott, and Borgese and knew what the characters were meant to be saying. But even those who heard only sounds, not an interesting discourse, in, say, the long dialogue for Malinche and Cortes that ends Act I must have recognized that the Juilliard production was a stunning achievement, and one carefully matched to the resources available. Ming Cho Lee's décor, if not the romantic, colorful scenery described in the score, created a series of evocative, dramatically charged pictures, completed by Beverly Emmons's fine lighting and Mr. Strasfogel's strong, imaginative staging. Designer and director worked economically, precisely, and to potent effect. It was a distinguished production. The large tableaux of Act II—the famous first meeting of Cortes and Montezuma on the causeway leading to the capital, and an Aztec sacrifice on the great pyramid of the city—were both brilliantly handled. Not all the singers fulfilled Sessions's requirement that "the vocal parts...except in a very few passages where a declamatory mode of delivery is expressly indicated...are to be sung in an expressive *bel canto* style throughout," but most of them did. The performances became increasingly confident; the third of them was excellently lyrical. In true Sessions fashion, Mr. Prausnitz's conducting combined freedom and firm underlying pulses.

Hei-Kyung Hong's Malinche was beautiful to hear and to watch, sensitively sung and sensitively acted. James Dietsch, a vigorous Cortes just a little thick and backward of voice, Robert Grayson as Montezuma, and Cornelius Sullivan as the fiery Alvarado were the other principals. (In his long cast list, the composer distinguishes between principal, secondary, and "episodic" roles.) Keith Olsen sang the young Bernal bravely. Charles Damsel's matching of text to musical phrase, in the part of Cuauhtemoc, was outstanding; and two characters designated as episodic—the interpreter Aguilar and a veteran—were raised to well-nigh principal status by the clear, well-focussed baritone, sharply defined words, and alert stage presence of Nicholas Karousatos. The work of the Collegiate Chorale was somewhat disappointing. The long final chorus of nepheliads—clouds—which provides the unconventional, beautiful close of the opera suffered from another balance problem unsolved: their voices, instead of welling out like a "sonic veil" to cover the stage where Malinche mourns the dead Montezuma, emerged thin and insubstantial from the upper reaches of the theatre. One cut was made: of bars 625–688 in Act II, Montezuma's plea for religious tolerance.

At last week's free one-o'clock Wednesday concert in Alice Tully Hall, given by the Juilliard Conductors Orchestra, I enjoyed as gripping an account of the first movement of César Franck's Symphony as I have heard in years. The conductor was Andrew Litton, a Juilliard student, twenty-two years old, who in January won the BBC's Young Conductors Contest. His handling was broad, long-breathed, very exciting, with phrases lovingly molded. The interpretation was positively Furtwänglerian both in its romantic freedoms and in its sense of steady, purposeful impetus. The second and third movements were ably conducted by another Juilliard student, David Alan Miller, twenty-one.

Double standards, maybe—but one often finds more musical vitality, energy, freshness, and keenness in accomplished student perfor-

mances than in those of seasoned professionals. I'd gladly exchange
some of the conducting we've heard in the Lincoln Center houses
lately for Mr. Litton's.

[*Both young conductors have made good. Mr. Litton became the Associate
Conductor of the National Symphony, and now has a flourishing international
career. Mr. Miller is the conductor of the New York Youth Symphony, with
which he has introduced several striking new orchestral compositions.*]

BABBITT ON BROADWAY

March 15, 1982

A FEW years ago, the name of HK Gruber began turning up on the
international scene. In Gruber's native Vienna, it was already well
known. In 1961, Gruber, aged eighteen (a former Vienna Choirboy
and a descendant of the F. X. Gruber who composed "Silent Night"),
became the double-bass of the ensemble Die Reihe—roughly, Vienna's
Speculum Musicae. His Opus 3, Concerto for Orchestra, was prominently performed in 1966. The ensemble MOB art & tone ART, which
he founded in 1968 with the composers Kurt Schwertsik and Otto M.
Zykan, toured the festivals. His *Frankenstein!!*, a "pan-demonium for
baritone chansonnier and orchestra," had its première in Liverpool in
1978, conducted by Simon Rattle, and its American première at Tanglewood in 1980, conducted by Gunther Schuller. A chamber version
appeared at the 1979 Berlin Festival, and last month it reached New
York, at a Speculum Musicae concert in Tully Hall. It was given along
with compositions by Milton Babbitt, Hugo Wolf, and Alvaro Cordero-
Saldivia. The audience seemed unsure what to make of it. And so, I
thought, did the players. New York concerts still tend to be formal
affairs. (What has happened to those Group for Contemporary Music
events in the students' café of the Manhattan School—candles burning, wine flowing—of a few years ago?) New York players still tend to
be straitlaced, straight-faced, earnestly correct. HK himself was the
chansonnier, burly, beaming, engaging, and in sharp contrast to those
around him (except the percussionist Gordon Gottlieb, who is a true
"performer" as well as a fine player). *Frankenstein!!*, as the program
note told us, has roots in cabaret, but it was presented in a format that
Gruber has described as "an inherited ritual that has lost any flexibility" and as "unfriendly to new music." Symphony Space would have
been an apter locale, and the Bottom Line or the Village Gate a locale
apter still. The only bodily cheer Tully Hall offered its guests was cold
water—a minor matter, but indicative of a deeper gulf between American and European concertgoing. The lunar Palace of Art that Janáček
made fun of in *Mr. Brouček's Adventures* is not far from New York reality.

Those who bought tickets for the Speculum concert should have been advised at the box office to read in advance the September 1978 issue of *Tempo,* which provides a context for *Frankenstein!!* in the form of essays on the Wiener Gruppe (whose central figure, the poet H. C. Artmann, wrote the texts Gruber uses), the MOB ensemble, and Gruber himself, and by Gruber on music and politics. In the current debate on the reasons for contemporary composers' alienation from the wide public, Gruber's voice is worth hearing. Until the mid-sixties, as David Drew, the editor of *Tempo,* remarks, vanguard composing had its strict orthodoxies; then "the secession of composers brought up in the Darmstadt-Cologne milieu... gave rise to new constellations in several countries," and "whether the composers proceeded in a neoromantic direction (as for instance in West Germany) or a Marxist one (e.g. West Germany also, and Italy) and/or a minimalist or systemic one (in most countries) they have been much criticized for turning their backs upon a vast range of new possibilities for the future of music— at the very least, the range from, say, IRCAM to Princeton." In the country where the neoromantic George Rochberg's first opera, *The Confidence Man,* is due in Santa Fe, where Frederic Rzewski's variations for piano on the Chilean song "The people united will never be defeated!" is a critical hit, where the minimalist Philip Glass is the only living composer who can pack the Met, where Glass and Steve Reich are just about the only living composers who draw full houses at Carnegie Hall—but where "Princeton" still dominates orthodox vanguard activity—these things need thinking about. And the Speculum concert set one thinking.

Frankenstein!! is a pop piece. The verbal imagery includes James Bond, John Wayne, Superman caught with his pants down, and Batman and Robin in bed together. The musical imagery ranges from Bach and Mozart, through Weill and (above all) Stravinsky, to sleazy nightclub wailings. The orchestration includes Swanee whistles, kazoo-type toy saxophones, lengths of plastic hose pipe that whee and whoo when the players whirl them above their heads, and paper bags to be blown up and busted. I'm not sure that *I* know what to make of it all. But I am sure that Gruber is a composer through and through, a synthesist and a creator, a careful craftsman and a thinker—zestful, serious, and unboring. Now we must hear his Violin Concerto,... *of shadow fragrance woven* (1978), which is said to be lyrical, personal, and intense and to open a new path between Berg and Stravinsky that modern audiences can joyfully tread.

Babbitt, who has taught at Princeton for more than forty years, writes program notes about his works so repellent as to prompt suspicion that he fears lest anyone do something as simple as merely enjoy his music. A note on his *Arie da Capo* (1974), for five players, which began the Speculum concert, tells of "models of similar, interval-preserving, registrally uninterpreted pitch-class and metrically-durationally uninterpreted time-point aggregate arrays." The piece itself falls gratefully, if not simply, on the ear. The Wolf songs were "Herr, was trägt" and "Wunden trägst du," with their piano parts gravely and exquisitely scored by Stravinsky for three clarinets, two horns, and string quintet. The sonorities are beautiful. In the Stravinsky album assembled by the composer's widow and Robert Craft, a color plate of two autograph pages provides a fascinating glimpse of small adjustments made by that precise ear. Cordero-Saldivia's *Ausencias* (1981), composed for Speculum, seemed a piece of careful construction to formula, though one of the "two musics that... coexist, interfere, complement and eventually absorb each other" (the composer's note) was quite pleasantly lush.

Three days earlier, in Symphony Space, the Group for Contemporary Music presented a program both elegant and nourishing: three works by Babbitt and three by Stefan Wolpe, the composers alternating. Babbitt's *Dual* (1980), for cello and piano, eluded me, for I heard no song in it, only sounds. But I am eager for a second hearing. His *Paraphrases* (1979), for nine winds and piano, is hardly less "pointillistic"—bitty, exclamatory, hiccupping—in texture but is also colorful and approachable. *Paraphrases* was written for Anthony Korf's Parnassus ensemble, which introduced it in 1980, played it again here, and has recorded it for CRI. Babbitt's *Elizabethan Sextette* (1979), six Elizabethan poems set for six female voices, unaccompanied, was positively charming, for all the composer's talk of "closely related, but relatively, quantitatively uninterpreted underlying ordered pitch-class lines, combinatorial pairs of lines, and six-part aggregates." Rum fellow, Babbitt—and delightful, engaging fellow! The New Grove talks well of his "highly ordered, multiplex sound universe" and reminds us that he's also a sports fan. What's his 1946 Broadway musical, *Fabulous Voyage*, like? Perhaps selections from it could appear on a double bill with *Frankenstein!!* Of Wolpe, we heard the lyrical *Songs from the Hebrew* (1938), the fine, taut String Quartet (1969), and his last composition, the Piece for Trumpet and Seven Instruments (1971), which is a stunning example of his refined, precise writing, at once passionate and economical, and of his laconic wit.

Thirty-two of New York's finest performers took part in the rewarding, well-attended concert. Seven of them appeared again at the Speculum concert, where *Frankenstein!!*, written for audiences less special than New York's vanguard faithful, suddenly cut through the rarefied post-tonal atmosphere with bothering effect. Like Schwertsik, whose set of linked aphorisms on these matters appeared in the *Oesterreichische Musik-Zeitschrift* in 1975 (and in English in *Tempo* for March 1979), I "am happy to live at a time when so many different musical concepts of the past and the present are accessible. This multiplicity teaches us to be careful and unassuming when we come across the new, and the unknown. Moreover, it invites us to hear right through the surface of the sounds and musical gestures, and to reach the heart of all music." But how many accept the invitation? Not only in this country, but perhaps more emphatically here than elsewhere, "serious" music means increasingly the sort of thing purveyed by a Pavarotti or by WNET's "Gala of Stars." Commerce and its publicity machines channel public attention toward profitable performers in popular repertory. (And not only in this country: the London *Times* list of "Classical Best Sellers" includes in all seriousness Placido Domingo's "Perhaps Love" and his "Tangos.") Standards sink. Discernment grows dimmer. Living composers accept that by only a choice few will their music be heard with eagerness, sympathy, and understanding. Composing for those few, they move still farther from anything that a wide public wants to listen to and the most celebrated performers want to play or sing.

There are exceptions: Gruber, Bernstein, David Del Tredici, and William Bolcom among the bridge-building composers, Maurizio Pollini among the world-famous executants. And it's not a new bother, as every music historian knows. But it has grown worse. A century and a half ago, people complained if instead of brand-new symphonies, sonatas, and operas they were offered old, familiar pieces; Philharmonic and Metropolitan subscribers don't complain. Giuditta Pasta delighted in creating new roles that living composers had written for her; Renata Scotto and Montserrat Caballé plainly don't. At the same time, with each passing century the body of "essential listening" grows larger, and, moreover, in our day the span of the repertory has reached backward as well as forward. (In Pasta's day, neither *Pelléas* and *Wozzeck* nor Monteverdi's *Orfeo* and *Poppea* existed as works that self-respecting companies should do; Handel's operas had not been rediscovered, and Henze's hadn't been written.) Listeners faced with the new multiplicity are tempted to adopt Boulez's view: that great works of the past still worthy of attention rise above a "waterline" everything below which, whether good or bad, should be ignored. It's a view I find hard to accept. Ascending foothills helps one to understand views from the summits; and there is too much to be learned from—and enjoyed in—the lesser, aspirant works. Who would restrict Verdi to, say, his six greatest operas, and ban performances of Mozart's *Lucio Silla* and *Re Pastore*, Wagner's *Die Feen* and *Rienzi*? The last two have been heard in New York recently: more of that later (see page 215).

The City Opera began its spring season with a concert performance of *Die Feen*. The repertory includes one fairly new opera, Carlisle Floyd's twenty-seven-year-old *Susannah;* one early Verdi, *I lombardi;* and a new production of *Medea* by Cherubini, a composer Beethoven much admired. Early in the season, the company did a *Figaro* as distinguished as one could hope to see anywhere—admirably sung, delightful to look at (in décor by Carl Toms), executed with dedication and in detail, natural and unaffected in its flow. Samuel Ramey in the title role is unrivalled. It was as Figaro that I first heard him, aged thirty-three, at the City Opera seven years ago. On the stages of the world (he went on to sing Figaro at Glyndebourne and, for Strehler, at La Scala; also in

Aix-en-Provence, Hamburg, Holland, and Vienna), the performance then admired has been tempered and polished. Now he "plays with the music" as great singers can, throws vocal and verbal wit into recitatives, draws on his large range of timbres and dynamics with stylishness and spontaneity. He was cheerful, ardent, vulnerable (in Act IV), and various. He looked as striking as he sounded—lean, alert, often literally on his toes: a Toledo-blade adversary for the Count. Perhaps he was even on the edge of peacocking through the part. But a hairline between being Mozart's Figaro to the fullest and exhibitionism remained uncrossed, and the result was thrilling.

Elizabeth Hynes was a captivating Susanna, warm, sweet, and pure in tone, gentle but lively, delicate but never meagre. Carol Vaness, the Countess, was in glowing voice. She produced a kind of young-Rethberg sound—full, supple, and sure in its moves from note to note. Her recitatives were vivid. William Stone's Count was sharply drawn, trenchant, attractive. This Countess and Count were City Opera "firsts"; so were Nadia Pelle's keen Cherubino, Judith Christin's lovable, funny Marcellina, Dan Sullivan's substantial Bartolo, and Martha Toney's Barbarina. John Copley's production, new in 1977 and fresh again in his revival of it for this cast, was carefully, expertly, and lovingly worked. All the characters rang true. Irrelevant jokes were few. And the sense of time—of a real day during which events and emotions from a real past come together in crisis—was strong. Imre Pallo conducted; his overture was a scamper, but thereafter the score was sensitively handled. Hans Sondheimer's lighting worked well, except when a crude spotlight tracked the Countess down the staircase of Act III. The production has been switched from the Martins' translation into the original. While in general it makes small sense for American singers to sing to Americans in Italian, for my part I own that when I have translated an opera (as I have *Figaro*) and therefore know the text thoroughly, then I prefer to hear it in the original—provided, of course, that the singers command the language as well as most of this cast did. Appoggiaturas were in short supply, and reprise variations nonexistent.

Some ninety years ago, Bernard Shaw chided Covent Garden for "rattling the drying bones" of *Un ballo in maschera* while Hermann Goetz's *The Taming of the Shrew* was not performed there. A few years earlier— as we find in one of the previously uncollected reviews now collected in the three volumes of *Shaw's Music* (Dodd, Mead)—he had called Goetz's piece "the greatest comic opera of the century, except Die Meistersinger." References to it recur. It is "really great work" (1889). And Goetz

has the charm of Schubert without his brainlessness, the refinement and inspiration of Mendelssohn without his limitation and timid gentility, Schumann's sense of harmonic expression without his laboriousness ... while as to unembarrassed mastery of the material of music, shewing itself in the Mozartian grace and responsiveness of his polyphony, he leaves all three of them simply nowhere. Brahms, who alone touches him in mere brute musical faculty, is a dolt in comparison to him. You have to go to Mozart's finest quartets and quintets on the one hand, and to Die Meistersinger on the other, for work of the quality we find, not here and there, but continuously, in the symphony in F and in The Taming of the Shrew. [1893]

As late as 1947, Shaw was urging the opera, "Mozartian in its melody," on the BBC. Goetz (1840–76) is now best known as the composer Shaw admired. What did he admire in him? Decent craftsmanship, well-knit and jolly ensembles, and a copious flow of amiable but uninspired melody are all I've ever been able to hear in *Der Widerspenstigen Zähmung*, and the Manhattan School of Music's able production last month revealed no more. It's pleasant, time-passing music set to an unpleasing play. ("An atrocious play," Shaw called it in 1892.) Kate's aria of sentiment in Act III, "Die Kraft versagt," endorses the underlying moral: that women secretly enjoy being violated, and fall in love with men who tame their independence. The opera was sung in English, but the name Petruccio, whose pronunciation Shakespeare took the trouble to indicate by his "-chio" spelling, was given a "k" sound.

YOUTHFUL SPLENDOR

March 22, 1982

LATER, BETTER Wagner has long been the enemy of good early Wagner. *Die Feen, Das Liebesverbot,* and *Rienzi* are operas that have more good music in them, and more music-drama, than several pieces by lesser men which get trotted out on the stages of the world. Even too much music: all three are long, and by very heavy cutting they are spoiled. Each has had probably only one complete performance ever—prepared by the BBC and broadcast early in 1976. The BBC's uncut *Die Feen* contained three hours and twenty minutes of music, *Das Liebesverbot* three hours, and *Rienzi* four hours and forty-five minutes. The stage productions I have seen—three *Rienzi*s, two *Liebesverbot*s, and (in Bayreuth, but not in the Festspielhaus) a single *Feen*—have all been abridged, a Munich *Rienzi* almost to "highlights." But *some* careful cutting can be accepted. At least two of those shows—a *Liebesverbot* at Nottingham University and a *Rienzi* in San Antonio—were carefully and not too severely cut, and in each case the opera proved wonderfully exhilarating.

When Shaw heard the overture to *Die Feen,* in 1889, he enjoyed it. Declaring that the twenty-year-old chorus master who had composed it was no crude amateur, even if he was "a crude Wagner," he wrote of "a charm in this Vorspiel that is wanting in the empty and violently splendid overture to Rienzi," and continued with sentences that foreshadow modern commentary on the whole opera: "It is more Wagnerian, for one thing. For another, it has youthful grace and fancy as well as earnestness." With *Die Feen* (1833), textbook opinion runs, Wagner started out on the right path, one that ran from *Der Freischütz*, *Fidelio*, and Heinrich Marschner's *Der Vampyr*. (The list of influences is the composer's own.) Then he strayed for a while. He succumbed to the heady delights of Italian opera—particularly of Rossini's *Otello* and Bellini's *I Capuleti*—and composed the Italianate *Das Liebesverbot* (1835), declaring that "the keynote of my conception...boldly tended to exalt unrestrained sensuality." *Rienzi* (1838–40) was something else—an attempt at an extra-grand grand opera that would rescue its composer from the grind of provincial operatic life. With *The Flying Dutchman* and *Tannhäuser*, Wagner then found his path again. Meanwhile, *Rienzi* served its purpose. It appeared in Dresden in 1842, and all Europe flocked to see it. It made Wagner's name as surely as *Nabucco*, another opera produced in 1842, made Verdi's.

The account is true as far as it goes but leaves out a lot: how far the three operas differ from their models; what they have in common; and, not least, how interesting and enjoyable they are. Each carries a strand of autobiography. That Arindal, the hero of *Die Feen*, should achieve immortality through the power of music was Wagner's own addition to his source, Gozzi's *La donna serpente*. When refashioning *Measure for Measure* into *Das Liebesverbot*, Wagner changed Shakespeare's Angelo into Friedrich, an earnest German governor who in his soliloquy voices a recurrent Northern dilemma: simultaneous intoxication with and reprobation of captivating Mediterranean frivolity. The manner of the music and the theme of the opera are one, and the soliloquy, shot through with reminiscence motifs, marked by *Tristan*-adumbrating harmonies, is a scena of self-realization unmatched until much later in the century. Every Anglo-Saxon whose surrender to Rossini's *Otello* is accompanied by a twinge of Protestant guilt, who delights in Donizetti but reflects that there are Bach cantatas he has not heard, understands and responds to it. *Rienzi* is an opera about a grandiose visionary whose lofty dreams outsoar the comprehension of the masses. It needs no hindsight from *Tristan*, *Die Meistersinger*, *The Ring*, and *Parsifal* to find in the young Wagner the genius who gave dramatic and musical form to important concerns: love, sex, religion, and politics. None of the three early operas is a mere mindless entertainment. They share copiousness of melodic invention. They have energy, vivacity, and brilliance.

Die Feen has a plot somewhere between *The Magic Flute* and *Die Frau ohne Schatten*. Although the name Gozzi does not appear in the Strauss-Hofmannsthal correspondence, Strauss knew *Die Feen* well. He prepared its first performance, which was given in Munich in 1888. Plot synopses of *Die Feen* and *Die Frau* can start identically: "The hero, out hunting one day, pursued a white hind, which turned into a beautiful woman; and she became his wife. The time has now come when she must decide whether to acquire mortality and stay with the husband she loves or return to her supernatural kingdom." Things diverge thereafter and then draw close again in the final scenes of test and trial, but in Wagner's opera it is the woman who is turned to stone and the man who must rescue her. Wagner's motif for "Verwandelung in Stein," starting on E, with G-sharp flattened to natural on the word "Stein," perhaps sounded on in Strauss's memory when he wrote his similar "Er wird zu Stein" motif for *Die Frau. Die Feen* is an adventurous and imaginative piece. Its merits, however, were but faintly apparent in the feeble, unconvinced concert performance that began the City Opera season. After two acts, I could bear no more, and left to enjoy Act III in a recording of the BBC presentation.

The concert performance of *Rienzi* that Eve Queler and her Opera Orchestra of New York mounted in Avery Fisher Hall a week later was something quite different: splendid, spirited, filled with zest and excitement. There was a strong basic chorus, the Choral Guild of Atlanta. Rienzi's Messengers of Peace were the boys of the St. Thomas Choir, who entered in procession through the hall. Rienzi's army was the United States Coast Guard Academy Singing Idlers, who marched off to battle, down the aisles, with drawn swords. At the hall's corners, trumpets blew. No stage director was named, but the concert performance was put on with theatrical flair. Anyone not stirred by it would have had to be a cold fish indeed. Wagner handled crowd scenes more nobly than Meyerbeer; Acts III and IV of *Le Prophète* are cold, dry imitations of Acts III and IV of *Rienzi. Rienzi*, like *Le Prophète*, calls for only three principals—tenor, mezzo, and soprano. William Johns, robust, ringing, sometimes a little rough, was the Rienzi. Julia Hamari, a cultivated singer but a shade underpowered for her role, was the Adriano. April Evans, deputizing for Elisabeth Payer, sang boldly as Irene. Just over three hours of music was included.

Next year, Miss Queler, please give us *Das Liebesverbot*.

The City Opera's first new production of the spring season was of Italo Montemezzi's *L'amore dei tre re* (1913), an opera that older critics who remember Mary Garden or Rosa Ponselle as its heroine and Ezio Pinza as the old, blind king, Archibald, who strangles her, recall with affection. Donald Grout, in his *Short History of Opera*, calls it "one of the best Italian tragic operas since Verdi's *Otello*" and writes of "enduring beauty," "refinement of style," and "memorable moments of classic breadth." The City Opera production, designed by Beni Montresor and directed by Frank Corsaro, looked quite handsome but was badly lit. The singing was decent (Samuel Ramey's, as Archibald, more than that), not voluptuous. Maternity had claimed the soprano originally billed, and illness the intended tenor. John Mauceri's conducting was ardent, but the orchestral tone was meager. I thought it a boring, faded opera, less striking than Zandonai's *Francesca da Rimini* (1914), which Miss Queler revived in 1973. Both pieces are products of an Italian movement away from verismo toward high-minded D'Annunzian lyric drama; *Tristan*, both directly and filtered through Puccini, and *Pelléas* bear upon the music. For *Francesca*, Tito Ricordi drew from D'Annunzio's play a libretto that moves in varied meters. The libretto of *L'amore dei tre re*, drawn from Sem Benelli's play, is in un-rhymed hendecasyllables throughout (except in a funeral chorus), and that may have something to do with the way the music seems to ramble on and on. One or two moments bring Prokofiev to mind. Perhaps Prokofiev heard Montemezzi's opera in Chicago in the 1921–22 season, when *The Love of the Three Oranges* and *The Love of the Three Kings* were both on the bill.

The Met has put on a new production of Offenbach's opéra comique *Les Contes d'Hoffmann*, which may be the most often performed of his works but is the least entertaining of the dozen or so of them I have heard. The most corrupt of the many *Hoffmann* editions available, the one furthest from its composer's intentions, was used (Covent Garden also chose it for its big production in 1980), but textual discussion can wait until the City Opera brings out its alternative version, next year. The Met show is a hit. Its chief stars are the set designer and the director, Günther Schneider-Siemssen and Otto Schenk. The house machinery—providing stages that rise, stages that sink, stages that roll forward from the distance—is used to spectacular effect. Gaby Frey's costumes and Gil Wechsler's lighting enhance the scene. The coloring is somber—browns and grays predominate; Hoffmann's four loves are dressed in pure white—and the detail is lavish. It's all very good to look at. There has been no attempt to make a serious or consistent drama of the piece—the patchwork Choudens edition precludes that —but the tone is right, and so is the undertone: beneath the fun there is a hint of grotesquerie, even diablerie, which is aptly Hoffmann-esque.

The Olympia act is the high point, and its Doll Song is a tour de force on the part of Mr. Schenk, of Ruth Welting—the springiest, wittiest, and most charming doll one could hope to see, and strong, sweet, and accurate in her singing—and of Michel Sénéchal, the Cochenille. The whole act is filled with elegant, stylish invention. The chorus's work is brilliant. Andrea Velis is a vivid Spalanzani, and Michael Devlin, who plays all four villains with polished bravura, is a virtuoso Coppélius. Placido Domingo is Hoffmann. He's had much experience in the role: he recorded it ten years ago with Joan Sutherland; he was the Hoffmann of the 1980 productions in Salzburg and Covent Garden. He plays and sings with confidence, generously, wholeheartedly, but the style is not quite right. The manner is too beefy for the music. He lacks grace, delicacy, Gallic lightness of touch. Perhaps M. Sénéchal, who has those qualities in abundance, should coach him in the part. (And why does this Hoffmann make his first entrance as an unshaven, lurching sot, not a romantic poet?) Giulietta, an unrewarding role in this edition, was Tatiana Troyanos. Antonia was Christiane Eda-Pierre, who did not suggest a fresh-voiced ingénue. Riccardo Chailly conducted a dapper, alert performance, not quite lilting enough in the barcarolle or the sextet.

CANTATE DOMINO

March 29, 1982

RICHARD TARUSKIN and his Cappella Nova provide some of New York's most valuable concerts. They light the pages of music history into life with, at once, ardent belief and polished technique. Their latest program, sung first in Corpus Christi Church and a week later in St. Joseph's (where I heard it), was a composite Easter Mass of fifteenth-century music from northern Europe. Like everything else I have heard the Cappella do, it was beautiful. The choir can make a listener happy, with many a winding bout of linked sweetness long drawn out with giddy cunning, the melting voice through mazes running; and it can make him thoughtful in anthems clear that dissolve him into ecstasies and perhaps even bring all Heaven before his eyes. At the least, it takes him into a world where the dry pages of Gustave Reese's *Music in the Renaissance* turn into eloquent sound, and the footnotes break into flower. The Cappella's programs are adventures of discovery: presentations of what the singers and their director have found by, as it were, following with their voices along paths pointed out by historians—paths that often lead through unpublished music. The concerts are communicative. They glow with a sense that the performers are eager to show and share wonders they have come upon.

The Cappella's Johannes Ockeghem explorations are "documented" —made available for repeated, enthralled listening—on two fine Musical Heritage records. Two years ago, I wrote about its revelation of Heinrich Isaac's grandeur in sacred music, and there was further championing of Isaac in the Easter Mass: the Gloria was taken from his Missa Paschale. Like much Isaac, it calls to mind Fiordiligi's simile in *Così fan tutte:* as a rock resists the onslaught of winds and tempest, so the cantus firmus is unshaken by the florid writing that beats against it. This Gloria is a stunning example of Isaac's inventiveness, his craftsmanship, and his affecting power. The word "suscipe" is suddenly set to simple chords that make the listener catch his breath. From Isaac there came, too, the Introit, the Gradual, Alleluia, and Prose, and the Communion: Cappella Nova programs have continuity. But the "featured" composer of the evening was Ockeghem's great contemporary Antoine Busnois, Charles the Bold's musician, "who today is far too little known," said the program note. Every music student knows *about* him, and his song "Fortuna desperata," a hit in its own time, to judge by the many arrangements that were made of it, has now become a hit of the Renaissance revival. But modern performers give most of their attention to Busnois' secular music. Cappella Nova included the Sanctus of his "O crux lignum" Mass, the Easter Sequence "Victimae paschali," and two motets, both settings of "Regina coeli." All of them revealed his strangely elegant deployment of very long and metrically elaborate lines, florid and unpredictable, quirky as Janáček's. The motets were breathtaking. This is all that Grove has to say about them: "Busnois composed two four-part settings of 'Regina coeli.' One, in which the cantus firmus is in the bass, shows evidence of being modelled on a 'Salve regina' by Ockeghem. The second incorporates the cantus firmus in canon." Not a word to suggest that the second, in particular, is one of the loveliest stretches of music ever written. I suppose it must be heard to reveal its more than structural merits. The program was rich and was assembled from a wide knowledge of this repertory. Nine settings of "Christ ist erstanden," drawn from various sources, formed verses of the Hymn. Three Easter chants wove through the music as leitmotifs. Jacques Barbireau provided the Kyrie, Johannes Tinctoris the "Ite missa est," and Anon.—in a Vatican codex, the Trent codices, and the Glogauer Liederbuch—the rest.

In the past, I sometimes felt that Mr. Taruskin could be too insistent a champion. It was a fault on the right side, and better than blandness, but a fault all the same when he squeezed expressiveness out of the music too hard and screwed tension up in an almost unseemly manner. No longer. Although his gestures still seemed often to be saying "Give me more, more," his singers did not overdo things. The music flowed securely and convincingly. There was excitement—Alleluias that broke forth like dazzles of radiant light—and there were soft phrases that caressed the ear like Gigli at his most dulcet, but nothing was exaggerated. Everything was finely judged. The singing of the twenty-one-voice choir was well balanced, well tuned, firm, and excellently supple. There are women on the upper lines, but their timbre was not unmeetly feminine. St. Joseph's, a Greek Revival temple in the Village, is a friend to voices.

A day after the Cappella Nova concert, Steve Reich's latest composition, *Tehillim*, had its New York première, in the twentieth-century galleries of the Metropolitan Museum. On ears still tuned to the refined, delicate workmanship, the subtleties, and the sophistication of Renaissance church music, *Tehillim* fell brashly at first. A sudden change from candlelight to neon glare or from Burgundian illuminated manuscripts to large modern canvases painted with bold, bright acrylics would be no less startling. Still, the world is full of a number of things, and *Tehillim*, which aims at instant appeal and accessibility to listeners of all kinds, is a substantial, carefully made, and colorful work. "Tehillim" is the Hebrew word for "Psalms," and the piece is a setting for four female voices—high soprano, two lyric sopranos, alto—and instruments of texts from Psalm 19 ("The heavens declare the glory of God; and the firmament sheweth his handywork"), Psalm 34 ("What man is he that desireth life, and loveth many days, that he may see good? Keep thy tongue from evil, and thy lips from speaking guile.... Seek peace, and pursue it"), Psalm 18 ("With the merciful thou wilt show thyself merciful"), and Psalm 150 ("Praise him with the timbrel and dance: praise him with stringed instruments and organs"). The accompaniment includes four "timbrels" (tuned tambourines without jingles), a quintet of stringed instruments, and two electric organs; also flute, piccolo, two clarinets, oboe, English horn, maracas, marimbas, vibraphone, and crotales. The voices, winds, and strings are amplified. *Tehillim*, which lasts half an hour, was commissioned jointly by the radio stations in Stuttgart and Cologne and the Rothko Chapel, in Houston. Two movements were played in Stuttgart in June last year, and all four in Cologne in September. Several European performances followed, and in November the piece was done in the Rothko Chapel. An orchestral version—with full strings, unamplified—opens the Philharmonic's 1982–1983 season.

The work begins with a soprano singing a lilting, tricky, catchy tune, accompanied by tambourine taps and clapping hands. The rhythm is elusive, with anything from four to eight eighth-notes to a measure. The melody is "modal" (Locrian, I suppose: B to B on the white notes, but here up a fourth, with a B-flat in the key signature). The effect is exotic: people to whom I play the start (on tape) guess it to be something recorded in the Middle East. The tapping and clapping patterns grow denser. A second voice strikes in, in canon. Strings add slow-moving drone harmonies. (The amplified strings, played non-vibrato, sound oddly reedy and, again, exotic, suggesting the kamancha, or Persian spiked fiddle.) All four voices take up the melody in four-part canon. Then just one voice sings it again. The movement dances along in a pretty moto perpetuo of flexible meters. Tempo does not change for the second movement, but tunes and textures do. It is homophonic; voices in parallel sixths add a lush touch, and voices in parallel fifths a medieval one. So far, there has not been, except in key signatures, a sharp or flat in sight. The melodies are all "modal," and the harmonies are diatonic added-note chords. But the third movement becomes chromatic, and it moves, more slowly than its predecessors, over a seductive, Caribbean-sounding beat from marimbas and vibraphones. The text is delivered stichomythically, with voices paired in parallel thirds, fourths, fifths, or sixths for each statement and response. The final Laudate resumes the initial tempo, recapitulates the techniques employed in the preceding movements, and mounts to a climax of hallelujahs.

In a program note, the composer gives instances of his word painting: a "crystal-clear A-flat-major triad" on the word "good"; an unexpected G-natural in C-sharp minor, creating a tritone *diabolus in musica,* at the word "perverse"; a subtle conversion of that G-natural to a leading note into G-sharp at the word "subtle." But since *Tehillim* is sung in Hebrew, the weddings of word to tone can hardly be apparent to most listeners. What they hear is a syllabic patter—"Im-chah-síd, tit-chahsáhd, Im-ga-vár ta-mim, ti-ta-máhm"—until "Ha-le-lu-yáh" rings out at the close. The score bears few dynamic indications, and those mostly *mf* and *f*. There is, perhaps, something slightly "machine-made" about the sonic effect—the result of the even dynamics, the rubatoless, unvarying tempos, and the amplification, and also of the near-constant doubling of the vocal lines by winds or electric organs. Still, it is plain that *Tehillim* is the work of a composer and not just a constructor, and it is far less schematic than Reich's earlier pieces. At the Metropolitan Museum performance, it was preceded by part of his *Drumming* (1971) and by his *Music for Mallet Instruments, Voices, and Organ* (1973). To their sparkle and vivacity it adds a new flexibility of meter and a new feeling for expressiveness. George Manahan conducted the composer's regular ensemble, Steve Reich and Musicians. The balance was somewhat awry; the voices—Jane Bryden, Rebecca Armstrong, Jay Clayton, and Pamela Wood—did not dominate, as plainly they should, and the piccolo screamed with painful shrillness. But it was a spirited performance, and everyone except the *Times* critic seemed to enjoy it.

Choral music of the twentieth century was both sung and enacted at the third of the Brooklyn Philharmonia's Meet the Moderns concerts, given earlier this month in the Lepercq Space of the Brooklyn Academy of Music. Five choirs—one from the city, three from the state, and one from Connecticut—came to take part, each contributing a number to the bill. Its coördinator, Frank Ledlie Moore, declared in a program note that "choral drama provides the best possible context for hearing the subtlety and the beauty of great music," and invoked Greek drama and "the great celebrations in medieval and renaissance cathedrals." The idea is interesting, but the execution faltered. The performances were varied in approach—and in accomplishment—but only small steps were taken toward justifying Mr. Moore's large claim. By professional standards, this was on the dramatic side not a competent show. The performers probably learned more from it than the audience did. It seemed woefully underrehearsed, and, in particular, the special problems presented by the Lepercq Space—a long, lofty, narrow, rectangular room—were scarcely addressed. The spectators were banked up at either end, while the choirs sang and acted in the space between them. David Buttolph's staging of Jacob Avshalomov's *Tom O'Bedlam,* which opened the bill, used the room most successfully; there was a sense that a band of wandering beggars—played by the SUNY Binghamton Chorus—had made its way into a market square and was addressing the crowd around it. Schoenberg's *Friede auf Erden,* sung and enacted by the Ithaca College Choir, conducted by Lawrence Doebler, was the most ambitious and elaborate piece of staging. John Stevenson, president of the Dalcroze Society of America, had patterned the motet in space after the structure of the music and the sense of the text. (The choreography would have been more communicative had the piece been sung in English, not German.) But when half the chorus faced one way and half the other, to share the music between the east audience and the west audience, balance and ensemble suffered. And when the singers united at the climax, they addressed their passionate appeal to a blank brick wall.

Moore's own *Wagadougou* had its first performance. The title refers not to the modern city of that name but to the legendary African city that Herodotus wrote of and that the ethnologist Leo Frobenius still heard being sung about early in this century. In a preface to the score, the composer affirms that his work "will come across memorably if it is performed with precision and with what actors call projection of emotion." And I think it might, for it seems to be a deft and imaginative composition. But the performance by the Hartwick College Choral Theater Ensemble was thin. Hans Werner Henze's *Moralities* had what was billed as its first staged performance. (Can it have been? These "three scenic plays by W. H. Auden from fables by Aesop" have been around for a long time—since their first performance at the 1968 Cincinnati May Festival—and an English-German score with two-piano accompaniment, "for school performance," was published in 1969.) It is a slight work, but not as feeble a work as the Craven Singers, conducted and directed by Dorothy Craven, made it seem.

Thea Musgrave's *The Last Twilight,* a theatre piece for large chorus, semichorus, and supers, accompanied by twelve brasses and percussion, had its New York première. A setting of D. H. Lawrence's "Men in New Mexico," it was written for the New Mexico D. H. Lawrence Festival, in 1980. The first performance was given in the open-air spaces of the Paolo Soleri Theatre, in Santa Fe, with campfires, torches, and processions. The Brooklyn performance, by members of the Schola Cantorum and other choruses, conducted by Hugh Ross and directed by Maroun Azouri, was constricted; no use was made of the varied levels and distances that the Lepercq Space can provide, and again that brick wall was much addressed. This was no more than a sketch of what *The Last Twilight* might be—just enough to let one guess at Musgrave's large, romantic, picturesque evocation of New Mexico's landscape and history, seen in a terrible and beautiful Lawrentian vision. Musgrave's writing for voices and brasses, drums, and bells is inspired.

DOWN IN THE VALLEY

April 5, 1982

IN THE 1961 supplement to the fifth edition of Grove, Carlisle Floyd, his reputation made by the success of *Susannah,* rated an entry of more than a column. But the New Grove dispatches him—twenty years and five operas later—in a brief paragraph from whose grudging sentences no reader could guess at his importance on the American operatic scene. If there is a national repertory to be discerned here, it is—at any rate, on the far shores of the Hudson—founded largely on Floyd's work. His latest opera, *Willie Stark,* had its première in Houston a year ago. I missed it then but caught up with it on television last September and thought it a dexterous and accomplished piece. Those epithets, while more favorable than most of those I read at the time of the première, are hardly enthusiastic. There is something about Floyd's operas that pleases the public but often inhibits simple, unreserved praise from critics. Defining what it is is not easy. Perhaps a starting point can be found in some thoughts about lyric drama he included in an autobiographical note written in 1956, soon after *Susannah;* they still seem to represent his views fairly.

First of all, librettos (Floyd writes his own) should be qualified "to meet all the stipulations of competent playwriting—for instance, careful, logical structure, thorough motivation both in plot and in character development, a reasonable balance between characters and situations...as well as a sustained emotional atmosphere and a well-defined conflict and at least partial resolution." Next, "the presence of a 'theme' which is never tiresomely didactic" is desirable, for it is "time that opera took it upon itself to make some comment on contemporary life and timeless human problems." About music he then says little except that music and drama, "if necessary, should be capable of existing autonomously," and that "the fusion of the two should enhance and make each more significant." Finally, he states his commitment to American subject matter:

> When composers of operas in this country have managed to create works as unequivocally American in spirit and locale but as universal in theme and application as we find, say, in *The Scarlet Letter,* I believe we can feel that we have developed a type of lyric theatre that may stand without apology yet in graceful acknowledgment of its predecessors in Europe.

Of Floyd's nine operas, all but two—*Wuthering Heights* and the one-act *Markheim,* after the Robert Louis Stevenson story—have American settings. (The count is eleven if one includes *Fugitives,* which he has withdrawn, and the monodrama *The Flower and the Hawk.*) The four full-length operas of his I have heard—*Susannah, Of Mice and Men, Bilby's Doll* (after Esther Forbes's *A Mirror for Witches*), and *Willie Stark* (after Robert Penn Warren's *All the King's Men*)—fulfill his requirements for dramatic structure, balance of character and situation, an inner "theme" that comments on contemporary affairs, and American subject matter. With a commitment that rivals Smetana's in Bohemia or Britten's in Britain, he has striven to create a national repertory. He has studied the best international models and learned the international language of successful opera in order to speak it in his own accents and to enrich it with the musical and vernacular idioms of his own country. *Willie Stark* is a political opera that picks up some threads from Marc Blitzstein's political operas, some of its dramaturgy (I suspect) from *Evita,* and some of its musical manners from Broadway ballads. It is a bold and adventurous work. Over the air, on the screen, the Houston production, which was directed by Hal Prince and was conducted by John DeMain, seemed to me brilliant. Eugene Lee's classical set combined the architecture of government and a sense of Greek tragedy. (Simply to stand in the portico of Cass Gilbert's courthouse on Foley Square is a dramatic adventure.) Timothy Nolen in the Huey Long title role presented a living man who could be larger than life. Jan Curtis's Sadie was incisive. In the theatre, Julia Conwell's poor diction as Anne may have dimmed the role, but a television listener could glance at a libretto in his lap. Alan Kays's Jack was a shade pallid, but perhaps the fault is Floyd's: Jack is the narrator of the novel, and turning an ever-present "I" into another member of a cast is never easy. The opera probably benefitted— as the Met's *Bohème* did—from the closeups that television favors. Big-theatre (or "real") opera and television opera are different things. (Someone who knows Maria Callas in action only from filmed performances can have little idea of the way her acting carried in a large house.) But *Willie Stark* on television was a success.

Last month in New York, there were two performances of Floyd's most successful opera, *Susannah,* to be heard within three days—the first a WNYC broadcast and the second a revival at the City Opera. The success of *Susannah* can be measured by the fact that in this country alone it has had at least two hundred different productions since its première, in Tallahassee, Florida, in 1955. The City Opera has staged four of them, while over the years eight directors have mounted the piece there. The latest of them is Lou Galterio, who has revived it in the sets that Ming Cho Lee designed in 1971 for Robert Lewis's staging. Bruce Ferden conducted. The broadcast was a recording of the Cincinnati Opera's 1979 production, conducted by Christopher Keene.

When I first saw *Susannah*—it was done by the Kentish Opera Group in 1961, and in London seven years later—it seemed to me to have an ethos as exotic and a plot as improbable as anything in *Ernani* or *La forza del destino.* The time was "the present," and the scene a Tennessee valley. Was it possible that "in this day and age," even in Tennessee, four grown, married men could be morally shocked by the sight of a pretty girl taking a dip in a secluded spot on her own property, and seek to hound her out of the valley? I have since learned that it is possible. I looked forward to an American production in which the atmosphere of bigotry and hypocrisy would be authentically and powerfully re-created, for the motivations of *Susannah* need careful handling. A community's rounding on a member who does not conform is a good operatic subject, but the reasons for the malice must be made clear. *Susannah* (which was composed against the background of McCarthy witch-hunting) crosses a theme of *Peter Grimes* with the ironical peccant-preacher theme also handled in *Thaïs* and *The Scarlet Letter.* But Susannah's offense, unlike Grimes's or Hester Prynne's, is so slight that the community's behavior will seem stagy, insufficiently motivated, a conventional donnée, unless the reasons for it are vividly shown: the women's resentment of her youth and beauty, the men's lust for her in conflict with their piety, the anger of the chief elder and his wife that their son should be in love with her.

To show these vividly is the director's task. A great opera composer can make us believe anything. The music of *Peter Grimes* sufficiently covers the awkwardnesses revealed by a cool analysis of the libretto, for music—as in the final scene of *The Ring*—can "say" the things that the librettist has not been able to find words for. But Floyd's music is not of this kind. His score, like his libretto, is a construction: facts and emotions are stated, not brought to life by the very way the notes move and sound. It is well-written music, fluent, honest, and effective. The amalgam of square-dance tunes, hymn tunes and folk tunes new written in hymn harmonies and folk modes, and Puccinian (or now lingua-franca) orchestral emotionalism is skillful and individual. And the word setting is natural: Floyd's ability to match vernacular modern speech and operatic melody is a considerable and uncommon gift. But most of the time the music is an accompaniment to the drama, not really dramatic in itself. To justify that charge, I'd point (as I did when writing about *Bilby's Doll*) to the reluctance of the harmonies to move, to impel and not merely follow the drama; and also to the way that Floyd, when he gets hold of a good idea, works it out thoroughly, doggedly, without the flights of imaginative fancy that suggest the music has taken on a life of its own. Floyd has said that when he composed *Susannah* he was still "virtually illiterate where opera was concerned," and that his careful study of *Peter Grimes*—the twentieth-century opera he admires most—preceded the composition of *Of Mice and Men* (first performed in 1970). But *Grimes* was surely the inspiration for much of *Susannah*: the onstage dance; the witch-hunt chorus heard both advancing from the distance and onstage in full cry; the treatment of the tenor, Sam, as an "uncomprehended poet," violent when "the one thing of beauty left in his life is attacked." Perhaps it is just coincidence that the Reverend Olin Blitch's entrance music echoes the big rising ninth (dominant to submediant) followed by a stepwise descent of Peter Grimes's principal motif. But if one of Floyd's aims was to write "an American *Grimes*" (rather as *Grimes* itself is in some ways "an English *Wozzeck*") it was an ambitious and honorable aim, and success certainly attended it.

The City Opera production was disappointing. Mr. Lee's scenery was neither realistic nor evocative of a real place where people lived; it seemed to be the décor for some Oriental fairy tale. Set down in it were not real people dancing, gossiping, singing but a group of choristers and soloists keeping a wary eye on their conductor while they went through prescribed "blocking." Although *Susannah* is often performed by students, its vocal demands are not light: the three principal roles call for, in effect, a Butterfly voice in the frame of an eighteen-year-old, a powerful bass-baritone Scarpia, and a young Pinkerton. The vocal requirements were met in the Cincinnati performance by what the composer in an intermission talk described as "the most ideal cast over all" his opera had had. Patricia Craig was Susannah, James Morris was Blitch, Jon Garrison was Sam, and James Hoback was keen in the small role of Little Bat. But Miss Craig, instead of letting "The trees on the mountains" flow like a folk song, made a meal of it, molto espressivo. So did Faith Esham in the City Opera performance. Miss Esham, hardly a lirico-spinto yet, seemed miscast, and in the louder passages the voice was forced, pressured, not limpid. Samuel Ramey, as Blitch, sang bravely, and John Stewart, as Sam, sang agreeably. But none of the three moved easily, naturally, or convincingly. They stood or sat about in studied, mannered postures. The opera depends a lot on its acting. In elaborate rubrics, Floyd spells out what his music alone does not convey. For example:

> Blitch fixes his gaze upon Susannah. Slowly into his eyes and face comes an expression of intense desire bordering on lust. His voice also reflects what is happening inside him.... Susannah moves slowly into the aisle and trance-like walks toward Blitch, a confusion of fear, bewilderment and protest on her face. The only sign of life about her is the periodic shaking of her head from side to side in weak dissent.... A smile of triumph comes over Blitch's face as Susannah comes abreast of him and the change of expression in an instant shatters the spell for Susannah. She immediately comes to life and looks around her as if trapped.

Now, unless that or something like it happens—and it didn't at the City Opera—the action seems stagily abrupt. Similarly in the very tricky scene of Susannah's seduction by Blitch, where her "I'm so tired"—a common excuse for rejecting an importunate but unwanted lover—must be accepted as the reason for her submission. The smaller parts were played either from stock or amateurishly; the company that gave so accurately detailed an account of Kurt Weill's *Street Scene* was barely recognizable. Mr. Ferden's accompaniment was carelessly balanced—even Mr. Ramey was drowned at times—and his pacing of the score was less eloquent than Mr. Keene's in Cincinnati. The strings sounded thin.

When *Susannah* first came to the City Opera, in 1956, Winthrop Sargeant greeted it in *The New Yorker* as "a very important artistic experience," and continued, "To my mind, *Susannah* is probably the most moving and impressive opera to have been written in America—or anywhere else, so far as I am aware—since Gershwin's *Porgy and Bess,* and in many ways it is a more genuine opera than that justly celebrated but slightly uneven work." True, it had faults, which he mentioned ("lest you think my unaccustomed enthusiasm is running away with me"), but they were

> insignificant in view of *Susannah's* dramatic sweep and the heartening sincerity of its musical style. This style owes a great deal to the homely idioms of rural American religious and folk music, but Mr. Floyd's work is by no means the dreary essay in musical ethnology that American "folk operas" have usually turned out to be. The language he employs in telling a story that moves for-

ward with enthralling intensity is clearly his own, and he uses it with the intellectual control and the theatrical flair that bespeak both the serious composer and the born musical dramatist.

There are operas both American and European written between 1935 and 1956 that I find more moving and impressive than *Susannah*, but otherwise I would echo those sentences.

The *Susannah* broadcast was one of National Public Radio's World of Opera series, which WNYC broadcasts on Friday evenings. It provides valuable chances for hearing and rehearing, and for enabling listeners to travel the country without leaving their armchairs. Alva Henderson's *The Last of the Mohicans* (from Lake George), Ned Rorem's *Miss Julie* (in New York), Conrad Susa's *Black River* (from Minneapolis), and the first production of Menotti's *La Loca* (from San Diego) have been other recent offerings. But the WNYC Program Guide listings are summary and sometimes strange. The star of the San Diego *Hamlet*, it seems, is Robert Hale in the role of Claudius. Mr. Hale was certainly a good Claudius, but it is not a big part. Noting that Sherrill Milnes sings the title role and Ashley Putnam sings Ophelia might have made this broadcast of Ambroise Thomas' opera more attractive to potential listeners. Another complaint, which applies equally to most television broadcasts that are not "live": to present long operas without intermissions between the acts is an inartistic thing to do, and to have short intermissions filled with related matter claiming a listener's attention is almost as bad. Composers meant us to have a break between the acts, not give them our unfaltering attention for anything up to three hours.

FIDELITY

April 19, 1982

ONE OF the concert series presented this season at Merkin Hall—a 426-seater and, on the whole, the city's best chamber for public chamber music—is entitled Haydn on Original Instruments. Its first two programs provided evenings of delight. At the first of them, Malcolm Bilson played Haydn on his fortepiano modelled after the 1780s Anton Walter instrument that Mozart once owned. (It was built in 1977, by Philip Belt; "apt" might be an apter epithet than "original" in the series title.) One must be a Horowitz to bring Haydn's keyboard sonatas to full, detailed life on a modern iron-framed monster. When Horowitz plays Haydn on his Steinway, the textures are clear, the timbre is light, and the composer's marvellous inventions hold one spellbound. So they do when Mr. Bilson plays Haydn on his Belt-Walter. It is a different experience and no less enthralling, for Mr. Bilson is not just an accomplished player. He combines very good fingers with intellectual and structural command, wit, fancy, and exuberance. Mind, ear, and muscles work as one, and his piano works with them, stating, singing, sighing, and turning into shapely yet thrilling sound tempestuous ideas that—unless one is a Horowitz—must on a modern instrument be either coarsened or played down. (During the intermission, one of New York's celebrated piano teachers remarked to me, "How vulgar this makes a Steinway sound!") Mr. Bilson played three great sonatas (Nos. 49, 34, and 52), the F-minor Andante and Variations, and the C-major Fantasy.

The second concert was given by varied consorts. Mr. Bilson accompanied the soprano Susan Robinson in a group of Haydn's English canzonettas. Miss Robinson has a voice of uncommon purity and steadiness. "The Mermaid's Song" showed her fluency in divisions, "She never told her love" a most beautiful molding of expressive line, and "Sailor's Song" a meetly Haydnish exuberance and musical humor. Voice and instrument were a balanced duo; the turbulent accompaniment of "Fidelity" ("While hollow burst the rushing winds") could surge forth without drowning the singer. John Hsu, a virtuoso performer on the baryton—that recondite instrument that presents to the world a viola-da-gamba front of bowed strings while the player's left thumb reaches in from behind to pluck, harplike, a second set of strings—joined David Miller, viola, and Fortunato Arico, cello, in two of Haydn's 126 baryton trios. (Haydn's employer, Prince Nikolaus Esterházy, played the thing.) The baryton's timbre is a thread of dusky, grainy gold. The charm of the sound, Grove warns us, wears thin after a while. An "integral" recording of all 126 trios would be daunting. But just two of them left one eager to hear more. Haydn made jokes (which Mr. Hsu sounded with quiet elegance), and even while making them he wrote music of rare beauty, poetry, and finesse.

Haydn's 250th birthday—does anyone still need telling?—fell last month. The March *Musical Times* is a Haydn number; in its first article, the Haydn scholar Jens Peter Larsen reminds us how much we still have to learn about the composer, recalls his "many-sidedness and richness," and looks forward to the "abundance of new experience and pleasure" that awaits us. At this concert, the canzonettas and baryton trios brought forward aspects of the less familiar Haydn, while two string quartets presented the known master in a clearer, truer light than usual. Opus 54, No. 1, and Opus 77, No. 2—Haydn's last completed quartet, and one of his greatest compositions—were played on eighteenth-century instruments and with eighteenth-century bows by the Classical String Quartet (Nancy Wilson, Linda Quan, Mr. Miller, and Mr. Arico). Merkin Hall tries to provide good program notes, and James Webster's copious notes for these Haydn concerts were exemplary. His statement that "an eighteenth-century violin permits unparalleled lightness, clarity, and subtlety of articulation, greater ease and precision in fast tempi, and less need to depend on vibrato for expressive effect" was demonstrated in sound. But old instruments and a technical command of them are not, of course, enough; the members of the Classical String Quartet—who came together at Aston Magna—are also subtle and penetrating musicians. Since a critic concerns himself with all aspects of a concert, let me deplore just the violinists' decision to sheathe themselves in strident modern colors that swore at the music. The third concert in the series, to be given by the Amadé Trio, is devoted to five of Haydn's piano trios, works that—as Charles Rosen remarks in the recently published *Haydn Studies* (Norton)—are particularly difficult to balance on modern instruments.

The jubilee of Haydn the opera composer—for some fifteen years his principal activity was directing a busy and distinguished opera company—was celebrated in Philadelphia. A visit to that city brought me a theatre, a company, and an opera unseen before. The Arch Street Opera House opened in 1870. It played four decades of light opera, two of vaudeville, and then—renamed the Trocadero—four of burlesque. Now, attractively restored, it is a Chinese movie house but also the home of the Pennsylvania Opera Theater, a company that in its seven seasons has done some adventurous things. *Orlando paladino*, the latest of them, was the last but one of Haydn's Esterház operas, and a success there and elsewhere; in German translation, as *Der Ritter Roland*, it was played in at least twenty cities. Antal Dorati has recorded it for Philips; the modern stagings I know of—Santa Barbara in 1967, Birmingham, England, in 1980, and now Philadelphia—have been in English (three different translations). If stagings have been few, the reason is easy to find: the libretto is apparently a mess. But it's a fascinating piece: a dramma eroicomico that shows Haydn trying new things as he moves from the vein of his earlier comedies toward that of his most successful stage work, the beautiful opera seria *Armida*. Orlando, Angelica, and Medoro provide the familiar basic situation. There's also Rodomonte, King of Barbary, who blusters in again and again wanting to fight everyone in sight. Whenever bloodshed threatens, the sorceress Alcina makes an opportune appearance. In the Act I finale, she drops an iron cage over Orlando. In the Act II finale, she turns him to stone. In Act III, she transports him to the Underworld, where Charon sprinkles him with Lethe water and he forgets his mad love for Angelica. The shepherdess Eurilla provides a soubrette role; Pasquale, Orlando's squire, is an earlier Leporello or Papageno. Comings and goings are arbitrary; nevertheless, I believe *Orlando* could be held together as a chapter of Ariostan adventure and surprises. The characters are consistent. And the music is beautiful.

The Philadelphians did not quite trust the piece. The conductor and the director, Barbara Silverstein and Vincent Liotta (they also made the translation), reshaped it into two acts, and in doing so dismembered the second-act finale, a glorious stretch of connected music. Two minor characters were missing, and with them we lost the introduzione (one of the few ensembles the opera contains) and Charon's aria, "Ombre insepolte," a wonderful number. In fact, the attempt at "sharpening the opera's dramatic thrust beyond the conventions of the eighteenth century" (thus the program note) blunted its special character. Still, there was plenty left to show what *Orlando* might be, and much to enjoy. The sets, by Dean Taucher, were attractive, and the singing and the orchestral playing (on modern instruments) were fairly accomplished. But most of the singers sang far too loud, producing a pressured, modern sound. (The exception was the tenor Glenn Siebert, a delicate and stylish Medoro.) The Cambridge production of Handel's *Orlando,* in a theatre larger than the Trocadero, was proof that in eighteenth-century music light, unforced tones are most dramatic, and allow for more telling projection of the words and subtler phrasing, than voices at full stretch. Moreover, none of the cast showed much skill at recitative. Instead of sentences of dramatic dialogue naturally paced, we heard little clumps of quarter-notes and eighth-notes, sung out, and broken by rests. ("Angelica's devotion. Will at last be rewarded.") Finding a true style for Haydn's operas is as hard as finding one for his instrumental music.

The Met revived its stark, striking production of *Les Vêpres siciliennes* (once again in Italian translation as *I vespri siciliani*), directed by John Dexter. The costumes, by Jan Skalicky, are black and white, with the French forces in gray. The set, by Josef Svoboda, is a broad staircase, flanked by black wings, against a black sky. Some of the stage pictures are arresting, but they have little in common with Verdi's colorful and varied grand opera: the popular outdoor festivities of Act II and the Governor's aristocratic ball in Act III look much the same. The piece —composed for the Opéra in 1855, just after *Rigoletto, Il trovatore,* and *La traviata*—is the most "different" of all Verdi's operas, the most patently Meyerbeerian in the cut of its melodies, its instrumentation, its textures, and its formal procedures. Commentators, I think, make too little of its oddities. There is nothing else in Verdi quite like the two-part cantabile grandioso "Ô noble patrie," in the third-act finale, or the octave theme, "Transports d'allégresse," in the fourth-act finale; there are several things like them in Meyerbeer—and none quite so stirring. Both Montfort's "Et veux pour te sauver," in the duo-finale of Act I, and Hélène's and Henri's "Pour moi/Au ciel rayonne," in the Act IV duo, suggest "Sì, vendetta" (in *Rigoletto*) recomposed by Meyerbeer in a way to place novelty and intricacy before naturalness of melody. Although the Met performance was in the wrong language and incomplete (the ballet and Henri's Act IV mélodie, "La brise souffle," were the largest omissions), and although the staging was wrongheaded and the singing far from grand, the opera held one's interest securely. It is an enthralling piece, the product of a great composer working at the height of his powers in a new medium, French grand opera, that he has determined to master. I wish the Met did it better but am glad that it is done.

The principal characters are Henri and his father, Montfort. Both roles were undercast. The Henri was Wieslaw Ochman, once an elegant lyric tenor, pleasing in Mozart and in *La traviata,* who has acquired force at the expense of sweetness. His timbre was sometimes nasal, strained, and ugly, and his phrasing was blunt. The Montfort was Pablo Elvira, a decent second-league baritone without the grandeur of tone and of presence one expects in a Metropolitan principal. Renata Scotto sang Hélène in tones that verged often on inaudibility. She did not scream loud passages, and that was welcome, but the timbre grew narrow when the volume rose. It was a carefully studied and seriously intentioned performance, sadly mannered in execution. "Ami, le coeur d'Hélène" and the sicilienne were treated in so affected and rhythmically sluggish a fashion that they almost fell apart. At the close, where the stage directions tell Hélène to drop to her knees before Henri in the hope of protecting him, Miss Scotto stood alone amidst a sea of corpses and raised her hands to her brow as if to say "Oh dear, what uncouth behavior!" Ruggero Raimondi was a smooth-voiced but unimposing Procida; James Levine, conducting, did not give him space to register. Mr. Levine began promisingly. There was drama at the start of the overture. But when the big G-major tune sailed in it was not phrased broadly, and most of what followed was treated with the adolescent excitability that can make Mr. Levine's Verdi seem shallow and insensitive. He gets bright, energetic playing from the orchestra, but to respond to the vigor of Verdi's music by driving through it with bravura is not enough. Conductors who feel the long breaths and who allow the singers to stretch and shape their phrases, to emphasize key words, and to slow melodic triplets without losing basic impetus grow increasingly rare.

The Italian translation, which the Met persists in using, is fairly described by Julian Budden, in *The Operas of Verdi,* as "one of the worst ever perpetrated ... full of slack words and phrases which in the original had been taut and striking," and "wildly false" in some of its scansion. Moreover, it was designed to satisfy mid-century Italian censorship: odd to find the word "liberty" suppressed on the American stage in 1982! Sometimes the scansion is right and the tone quite wrong: because the notes to which Verdi set "Hélène" will not fit "Elena," which is accented on the first syllable, the heroine is regularly addressed, even by her lover, as "O donna."

The Met's revival of *Die Entführung* was unsatisfactory. The Konstanze, Edda Moser, sang the role on a worn, frayed thread of tone, rising at times to an acid squeal, and her portrayal was blankly expressionless. All three arias were unpleasant to listen to; the first of them, "Ach ich liebte," with the trickier fioriture simply omitted, was painful. If she was unwell, an announcement should have been made; as it was, it seemed cruelty on someone's part to have put her up before an audience to tackle these exuberant outpourings of Mozart's youthful genius. The Belmonte, Stuart Burrows, was got up as a Victorian grocer in Sunday best, complete with watch chain, and he sang with a prosaicism to match. In his second aria, "O wie ängstlich," the octave falls on "schwanke" ("falter"), which generations of Belmontes have made magical, were bawled as if the word meant "defy the fates," while "Lispeln" "(whispering)" was sung as if it meant "yelling." Mr. Burrows made heavy weather of "Ich baue ganz"—another piece that Mozart wrote for a singer who can sail exultantly through coloratura intricacies. Kathleen Battle was a promising Blonde, even if she took "Durch Zärtlichkeit" too sleepily and "Welche Wonne" so fast that it couldn't be phrased. Her acting was textbook soubrette, not individual, but she has a pretty voice, and she was accurate. Philip Creech, the Pedrillo, has big eyes and a ready grin, but his singing was raw, and his German first-week Berlitz. The Osmin, Martti Talvela, *was* on what one used to think of as a Met level—a fine singer who portrayed a rounded character. Werner Klemperer was a lightweight but, in an understated way, skillful Pasha Selim.

Mr. Levine's conducting had a brisk, active surface and little feeling for the shape and breathing of a phrase. The sets, by Jocelyn Herbert, look like window displays but are effective in throwing the action forward into the enormous house. I liked the championship of the work as Mozart wrote it, without cuts and without reordering—except in Act II when the delaying of Konstanze's second entrance turned Belmonte's "Wenn der Thränen Freude," which should be addressed to her, into a fourth soliloquy for the tenor. (Like so much else in the score—Osmin's three arias, Blonde's two, Konstanze's first and third—this aria is a dramatic "dialogue" in which only one person actually gives tongue.) I did not like the penny-plain reading of the notes, bereft of appoggiaturas, graces, cadenzas, and *Eingänge*—those unwritten but essential "lead-backs" into recapitulations. I did like the plainness of Mr. Dexter's stage direction, but it needed much better acting and some sort of "ensemble" thought, for the deeper themes of the opera remained unsounded. These include contrasts not only of Christian callousness with pagan magnanimity but also of the savage side of Muslim morals with Christian chivalry; the "rights of women," a recurrent Mozart concern; and "the education of Belmonte"—prefiguring Tamino's—from a youth luxuriating in his plights to the mature hero who, strengthened by the love of a heroic woman and enlightened by a wise man, steps forward to lead the finale. These are Mozart's wonderful additions to his sources, distinguishing *Die Entführung* from the stock seraglio operas of the eighteenth century. So are the mirror triangles into which the six characters are grouped, as Konstanze and Belmonte give poetic, romantic voice to plights that Blonde and Pedrillo deal with in active and practical fashion. T' Pasha's last, rueful words to Osmin point the pattern.

Having earlier this year directed an *Entführung* myself, I sh haps, in the politicians' phrase, "declare an interest." B "interested" in *Die Entführung* for as long as I can reme on it in three dimensions—and discovering at first h compromises between intention and practical realization—has not, I trust, made me a biassed critic. Rather, it has sharpened a sense of the opera's richness and of varied possibilities in its execution, and has increased, too, tolerance of what goes wrong and impatience with what can be put right. As Peter Brook says in *The Empty Space*, "the more a critic becomes an insider, the better."

FLUTING

April 26, 1982

LEONARD BERNSTEIN's *Ḥalil*, a "nocturne for solo flute, string orchestra, and percussion" (thus the score, but the orchestra also includes a piccolo, an alto flute, and a harp), was given its New York première last month by the Philharmonic, conducted by the composer, in Avery Fisher Hall. The title is Hebrew for "flute." The piece, which lasts about fifteen minutes, is dedicated "to the spirit of Yadin, and to his fallen brothers;" Yadin Tanenbaum was a young Israeli flutist killed in a tank in the Sinai in 1973. It was played in Israel last May, and the following month in the Vatican. *Ḥalil* is a stretch of music partly elegiac, partly dramatic, and wholly good to hear. In an interview last year, Bernstein said, "A tune came to me that occurred to me as a flute tune—almost a pop song, very diatonic, very simple. I fooled around with it and then found that it led to all kinds of very symphonic things. So before I knew it, I was off and writing a flute piece." The tune itself is a beguiling D-flat melody, andante tranquillo, swaying gracefully between D-flat and A-flat in measures of varied length, but what it rises out of is a troubled, stormy slow passage of violent contrasts and jagged contours in which the solo flute plays a twelve-note theme (enclosing a D-flat triad) forward, backward, then forward again, impressing its shapes on the listener so that their subsequent adventures and transformations can be followed. In a program note, the composer writes of a "struggle between tonal and non-tonal forces" that is waged in much of his music and of a particular sense in this piece of "that struggle as involving war and the threat of wars, the overwhelming desire to live, and the consolations of art, love, and the hope for peace." Bernstein may wear his heart on his sleeve, but he's a composer who does have a heart, and the warm, generous content of his music is something one can respond to as to—well, as to the warm, generous, humanity-loving eloquence of Beethoven. Implying only parallels, not ⟨simila⟩rities, I'd suggest that what Bernstein calls "fooling around" with a ⟨theme⟩ ⟨is⟩ a Beethovenish way of discovering its kinetic potential, while ⟨what⟩ ⟨appe⟩ars in the finished work, after this exploring, is not a merely ⟨state⟩ment of ⟨demo⟩nstration of varied possibilities but a passionate statement ⟨of⟩ be assertion ⟨an⟩d beliefs about the human condition. That can only quisite scoring ⟨mu⟩sical felicities of *Ḥalil* are demonstrable: the exquisite scoring ⟨as⟩ ⟨the⟩ flute leads the soloist toward D-flat or as a solo viola—movingly played in the Philharmonic performance by Leonard Davis—sings duets with him; the drama of the extended cadenza against percussion irruptions; the stroke by which the soloist, apparently silenced, is induced by the alto flute and the piccolo to return and breathe a benediction over the final cadence. Julius Baker, the Philharmonic soloist (other flutists who have played *Halil* are Jean-Pierre Rampal, Uri Choham, Doriot Anthony Dwyer, and Ransom Wilson), was technically adept but emotionally somewhat staid, I thought, in sounding what Bernstein calls the "wish-dreams, nightmares, repose, sleeplessness, night-terrors" of his work.

Walton's Viola Concerto, played in observance of his eightieth birthday, followed, with Sol Greitzer a less than poetic soloist. Then came an incandescent account of Elgar's *Enigma Variations*. Maybe it *was* overdone: the slow movements very slow, the fast movements furious. But I found it overwhelming. The Philharmonic's note writer, Phillip Ramey, seemed to endorse Virgil Thomson's thin approval of the *Enigma* as "an academic effort" and "mostly a pretext for orchestration, a pretty pretext and a graceful one, not without charm and a modicum of sincerity, but a pretext for fancywork all the same." The piece Bernstein conducted was a blazing and beautiful dithyramb to love and friendship, and a zestful celebration of the vagaries and oddities of companions. Emotion is not enough in itself to invest music with eloquence (though perhaps it is what matters most). This performance of the *Enigma*, which is technically a work of formal and instrumental mastery, was technically, too, on a very high level. I have seldom heard the Philharmonic play with such warmth, intensity, and richness.

Leon Kirchner's Music for Flute and Orchestra was given its New York première last month by the American Symphony Orchestra, conducted by Michael Tilson Thomas, in Carnegie Hall. The piece, which lasts about fourteen minutes, was commissioned by and is dedicated to the flutist Paula Robison, who gave the first performance in Indianapolis in 1978 and has played it in Boston, Buffalo, San Francisco, Atlanta, and now New York. Subtitled "Encounters of Another Bird," the work is a stretch of gleaming and physically exhilarating sounds, containing what Miss Robinson, in an interview, described accurately as "wonderful, kind of exotic, flashing and shimmering 'bird' music." But, she continued, "the whole piece really swings; it has a lot of big-band sounds in it. . . . I kept on thinking of Erroll Garner when I heard it." I thought of Villa-Lobos's once popular *Uirapurú*, another piece where seductive, full-throated flute melody assumes incantatory powers and bird-song becomes a symbol of human yearning, and of Kirchner's opera *Lily*, whose music is at once picturesque and visionary. The Music for Flute and Orchestra is rhythmically complicated and texturally intricate; the orchestra is large, and the writing for it is delicate and detailed. Like all Kirchner's music, it combines fastidiousness with largeness of spirit, and complexity with directness of appeal. Miss

Robison, whose full, lustrous tone is not apt for everything she plays, sounded wonderful.

The program was well planned and interesting. Before the Kirchner, there was a "classic" for flute and orchestra, Charles T. Griffes's *Poem*—a late work (1918) and a fine one. Brahms (the *Academic Festival Overture*) began the concert, and Brahms orchestrated by Schoenberg (the G-minor Piano Quartet) ended it. Mr. Thomas is a conductor in whom instinct and intelligence unite. The roster of the American Symphony is a roll call of fine young New York players. But what has happened to Brahms sound? Have those modern orchestral innovations—no portamento, metal E strings, uniform bowing, and, above all, lopsided platform placing—at last put an end to it? Sir Adrian Boult, who learned his Brahms from Fritz Steinbach, Hans Richter, and Arthur Nikisch, will forgive me if I quote some sentences he wrote to a student of orchestral practice. "I hold very strong views and am constantly shocked at the present orchestral arrangement, which makes things a bit easier for conductors and players but gives a crooked picture of the music to most of the audience." "In my boyhood there was hardly any vibrato (but a good deal more portamento)." "I would say that metal strings did not exist in England until sometime like 1914. String tone has never recovered!" "My first experience of uniform bowing...was in 1919 or 1920, and it was several years later that it gradually invaded Queen's Hall....It soon became the fashion, and everyone had to do it." And, again on the matter of platform placing, "I can't believe that the counter-reformation isn't coming: all the critics—or nearly all—favour it, and a number of unselfish conductors who use their ears admit that the orchestra *sounds better.*" Edo de Waart now seats the violins of the San Francisco Symphony in their traditional places, firsts on his left and seconds on his right. Across the Bay, Calvin Simmons has been seating the Oakland Symphony that way for years. Stokowski, the founder of the American Symphony, often tried bold new arrangements. Six of his orchestral ground plans—including one for the American Symphony's 1971–72 concerts—are illustrated in the New Grove; the first and the last show a solid, central foundation of double-basses. I wish one of his successors would now boldly try the old arrangement that Brahms, Rimsky-Korsakov, Strauss, and Mahler wrote for.

I lombardi alla prima crociata, Verdi's fourth opera, is a young composer's epic—vigorous, grand, vastly ambitious, rough in places and beautiful in others, colorful. It must be hard to make it unexciting, but the City Opera production—New York's first since 1847—managed. The combination of Christopher Keene's thin, mean conducting, Mario Vanarelli's depressing, monotonous décor (black curtains around a gray contraption of steps), Gilbert Hemsley's dim light, and Cynthia Auerbach's weak staging proved well-nigh fatal. Ashley Putnam—who a few weeks earlier had been an accomplished Elvira in *I puritani*—was light casting for a Verdi dramatic heroine in a big house. The sustained cantabile of "Salve Maria" and of "Se vano è il pregare" was unsteady (I heard the second performance), but the cabaletta was bright and true, and so was most of what followed. Riccardo Calleo's Oronte had some good and some raw, blared phrases. Garry Grice's Arvino was strained. Justino Díaz's Pagano missed grandeur because he seldom took enough time to sound the phrases fully, but it was a sketch for a considerable performance. None wore their costumes as if they felt proud of them; the spectacle had a village-hall aspect. The famous chorus "O Signore, dal tetto natio," which in Verdi's day would "move the public to frenzy," was received in glum silence. Cuts were few (a verse of Oronte's cabaletta being the largest), but the prelude to the trio was played after the trio. Properly directed, the City Opera artists can do big Verdi with spirit; the splendid *Attila* showed that. But this *Lombardi* was as halfhearted and half-baked an affair as last year's *Nabucco*.

DEDICATION

May 3, 1982

Parsifal should not leave listeners indifferent. In 1887, Nietzsche—who knew the text but never heard the opera in the theatre—described it as "a work of perfidy, of vindictiveness, a secret attempt to poison the presuppositions of life." But the same year, after hearing the prelude, in Monte Carlo, he wrote to his disciple the composer Peter Gast:

> Has Wagner ever done anything better? The very highest psychological con-
> sciousness, and definiteness about what should be said, expressed, communi-
> cated, as briefly and directly as possible; every shade of feeling reduced to its
> most epigrammatic... in the depths of this music a sublime and extraordinary
> feeling, a living experience and an event of the soul...a synthesis of states that
> many people, including our "superior" intellectuals, will regard as incompati-
> ble: an awful severity of judgment "from on high" that issues from an intimate
> understanding of the soul and sees through the soul, piercing it as with knives,
> and hand-in-hand with that a compassion for what has been perceived and
> judged. Only Dante is comparable, no one else.

Wagner conceived *Parsifal* in 1845. Thirty-seven years later, he brought the opera to the stage. Six months later, he died. He had always intended *Parsifal* to be his last opera, and under its spell an enthusiast is tempted to regard *Lohengrin, Tristan, Die Meistersinger,* and the *Ring* as preparations for the final, pure masterpiece—a work composed only when other things that needed saying had been got out of the way, and when the theatre in which it might take shape had been built and a company that could perform it had (in that first *Ring* of 1876) been assembled and tried.

Each month brings new books about Wagner. One I've read with admiration and excitement is Lucy Beckett's *Parsifal*, a Cambridge Opera Handbook. It is a long, thoughtful, and well-organized essay that follows the drama from its sources in Wolfram von Eschenbach, through the rich fields of Wagner's thought over decades as tributary streams join the flow, to the finished work, which is traversed in an eloquent chapter. On again, through the stage history of the piece and a century of what it has meant to philosophers, poets, and sensitive critics. Miss Beckett's own conclusion is anticipated in a sentence of the essay she wrote to accompany Karajan's broad, beautiful recording of the opera (Deutsche Grammophon): "The single word that defines the region of *Parsifal* is 'Christian.'" She rejects modern approaches that would "regard *Parsifal* as interesting but harmless, as an entertainment or *jeu d'esprit* on however solemn a level, a closed system of expertly revolved symbols": Wieland Wagner's psychological patternmaking, Werner Diez's mythological interpretation, Carl Dahlhaus's attempt at "consigning the religious elements in *Parsifal* to a safe aesthetic distance," Michael Tanner's "method of distancing the Christian element" by declaring that "*Parsifal*, rather than being a religious work, is *'about* religion.'" (I began the Nietzsche letter in praise of *Parsifal* quoted above as Miss Beckett begins it, but what Nietzsche wrote to Gast was "As a purely aesthetic question: Has Wagner ever done anything better?") In her closing pages, Miss Beckett cites St. Paul (II Corinthians 5:18-21) and Karl Barth:

> Knowledge of God is not an escape into the safe heights of pure ideas, but an entry into the need of the present world, sharing in its suffering, its activity, and its hope. The revelation which has taken place in Christ is not the communication of a formula about the world, the possession of which enables one to be at rest, but the power of God which sets us in motion.

Not everyone will accept Miss Beckett's challenging, dynamic interpretation of *Parsifal*. It is more comfortable, less disturbing, just to enjoy the wonderful sounds the opera makes than to pay close attention to what—Miss Beckett insists—it specifically and unequivocally says. The Metropolitan Opera performs the work in German, thus opening the aesthetic escape route to anyone who does not follow that tongue and would prefer to leave the world's troubles behind when he passes the house's gilded wicket. But the Met's Holy Week presentation of *Parsifal*, conducted by James Levine, was so earnest, so powerful— one might say so devout—that it could not be taken as mere entertainment. The performers' personal beliefs are probably irrelevant. If—to paraphrase Shaw—Wagner's music is performed with the single aim of making it sound as beautiful as possible, it simply cannot take the wrong expression. The orchestra played for Mr. Levine as if inspired. His reading was broad, long-breathed, eventful, perfectly balanced. The cast was good. Jerome Hines, whose Gurnemanz I heard in Bayreuth twenty-four years ago, commands his role. So does Thomas

Stewart, whose Amfortas I heard in Bayreuth twenty-two years ago. Mignon Dunn's first stage Kundry was strong, passionate, and sensitive. "Ich sah das Kind" needed more beautiful singing, but a touch of vocal unruliness in the desperate outbursts of "Seit Ewigkeiten," while not desirable, can be forgiven. About Peter Hofmann's Parsifal, mixed feelings: he played a self-pleased brat rather than a guileless fool, his bouncy demeanor suggested a principal boy, and the lyrical lines Karajan draws from him in the recording often broke into non-legato, note-by-note singing. But his utterance was clear, carrying, and sure. All in all, this *Parsifal* reached the level of seriousness and intensity that many Met presentations this season have missed.

The Met *Fidelio* I saw was a disappointment: a performance that reduced the great opera to house routine. Bernard Haitink's conducting was, unexpectedly, pedestrian—without tension or dramatic energy. Johanna Meier, stepping in for Shirley Verrett, played a Leonore neither dramatically nor vocally in sharp focus. Edward Sooter's Florestan was approximate. Leif Roar's Pizarro was accurate but lightweight. The production, credited to Otto Schenk, looked like "blocking"—moves made after the book, not from dramatic necessity.

Between the Met's second and third *Fidelio*s, Princeton University held a one-day symposium on the opera, culminating in a production of *Leonore* (by which title one conveniently, if unauthentically, distinguishes Beethoven's opera of 1805 from its 1814 revision as *Fidelio*). The four papers hardly showed Beethovenian clarity, firmness, and polish of structure, but three of them, given by scholars—Alan Tyson, Philip Gossett, and Lewis Lockwood—who have studied unpublished sketches for the opera, were filled with important, interesting observation. (The fourth, Maynard Solomon's, moved from loose psychological speculation to a preposterous likening of the *Fidelio* plot to that of *Oedipus*.) *Leonore*, which was published early this century and again in 1967, is hardly a rarity on the world's stages—in London alone there were two different productions in 1969–70—but the Princeton staging was apparently America's first. It was handsomely and effectively designed, by Alison Carver, to fit into the Richardsonian splendors of Alexander Hall. The absence of a pit insured a more authentic balance than modern opera houses provide. The singing was pretty weak, apart from Alice Helgeson's in the title role (she was got up as Bella Abzug, but her tone was fresh, pure, and direct), and the speaking weaker still. Peter Westergaard's direction was amateurish. Michael Pratt's conducting held as little dramatic tension as Haitink's, but he drew good playing from the University Orchestra.

Leonore—which the City Opera might well do, since the Met has a *Fidelio*—is a stronger piece than was made apparent in Princeton. The best account of the differences between *Leonore* and *Fidelio* is Winton Dean's in a chapter of *The Beethoven Reader* (Norton). He rightly observes that "there is no need to regard the later version as a replacement of the earlier; both are viable." Willy Hess, the editor of a 1967

Leonore score, claims often in his essay "Beethovens Oper Fidelio und ihre drei Fassungen" that the composer by his 1814 revisions spoiled his original design. Dean is more judicious, yet even he, I think, shows too little awe at the marvellous nature of the revisions, which is surely unparalleled. Perhaps in a live performance of *Leonore* it is most fully revealed, as one hears familiar, unaltered measures serve a new function in their different context. The same stone later becomes the headstone of quite a new corner; or by a small refashioning—a changed harmony, a rhythmic elision—it is keyed into a different structure. The Princeton *Leonore* was of absorbing interest to hear.

A recurrent topic of the Princeton symposium was the play of Mozart upon Beethoven. (In London last month, Beethoven's copying out of passages from *Don Giovanni* was sold at Sotheby's for thirty thousand pounds.) The other big influence on *Leonore* was Cherubini, whose *Médée*, a heroic Paris opera of 1797, reached Vienna in 1802. (The German translation was by G. F. Treitschke, later the librettist of the revised *Fidelio*.) In 1815, Cherubini, deeming "the character of the music too severe for English taste," discouraged a proposed London production. *Médée* reached London only in 1865 (in Italian, with the spoken dialogue, which is in verse, musicked by Arditi); Italy only in 1909; and New York only in 1955 (when Eileen Farrell sang the title role in Town Hall). Its early triumphs were on German-speaking stages. In Frankfurt in 1855, Franz Lachner upholstered the severely passionate score with German-Romantic recitatives. At La Scala in 1909, when Ester Mazzoleni sang Medea, these were translated into Italian. At La Scala in 1953, when Maria Callas sang Medea, Leonard Bernstein initiated his own cuts and shuffling. Vito Frazzi and Tullio Serafin have also worked over the score. The Italian *Medea* heard in most modern performances—among them both the City Opera's 1974 production, which had Maralin Niska and, later, Marisa Galvany as its heroine, and its new production, which opened last month—is a very different opera from the *Médée* that Cherubini composed. It moves at different gaits. It alters the context and impact of Cherubini's numbers. It gives prominence to the German recitatives, and when Cherubini's own powerful recitative arrives, to launch the finale, it has been weakened by anticipation. Callas, in a 1961 interview, said that "the strength of Cherubini's opera is not the arias but the *recitativi*"; it was Lachner's strength, not Cherubini's, that she approved. But then Callas (whose Medea I heard in London and in Milan) sang and acted Lachner so well that she made him seem like a great composer. Other interpreters have not exerted this transfiguring power.

One can understand the City Opera's reluctance to perform *Médée* in the original: few of its artists are convincing linguists. But if it is to be translated, why on earth set an American cast to learn an Italian translation? (A bilingual libretto was on sale, but the houselights were extinguished, as if for a Wagner opera.) One can understand the City Opera's reluctance to essay the spoken dialogue: few of its artists speak well into the huge theatre. But if a patchwork is preferred, why not commission some new composer to link Cherubini's numbers in a less plushy way: either with 1980s mock-Cherubini or, boldly, in a manner that keeps the new matter distinct from the original? Added recitatives, unless they are made by the composer himself (as Gounod's were for *Faust)* or by a contemporary (as Guiraud's were for *Carmen),* are as little durable as translations; they soon show their age as patently as fake paintings and sculptures that deceived contemporaries do. (Berlioz's recitatives for *Der Freischütz* are perhaps an exception: if the dialogue of Weber's opera is to be sung, not spoken, it might as well be sung to a great composer's music.) Lachner's recitatives for *Médée* mingle 1850s mock-Cherubini with such things as the augmented triads underpinning Medea's first remarks to Jason, which, though striking, swear at Cherubini's classical harmony. The added matter looms too large. One might as meetly perform *Fidelio* with Balfe's recitatives.

That said, let the performance of the Cherubini-Lachner-Frazzi-Serafin *Medea,* translated by Carlo Zangarini, be assessed. Much of it suggested a concert performance with dramatic touches, for it was played against black curtains, parted back-center to reveal a strip of white. Most of the company were robed in black, and several of them lurked about in the gloom during what should be solo scenes. Medea herself wore a cloak and train so copious that her efforts to move in them caused mirth. Something that looked like a sack of potatoes but was identified in the program as "the head of a shattered Statue of Aphrodite, Goddess of Love," hung on a rope from the flies. No attempt was made to suggest the three décors of the action or the final conflagration. Rhoda Levine's direction had one saucy touch: she spurned Horace's injunction "Ne pueros coram populo Medea trucidet," and this Medea stabbed her children in full view. But since she was *coram populo* throughout the finale, she forfeited her last sudden, tremendous entrance—standing in the temple doorway, brandishing a dagger, and ringed by the Eumenides. The program synopsis was misleading: Medea, whose inopportune arrival in Corinth, in angry pursuit of her husband, is a stroke of high theatre, was made a Corinth resident.

Two of the cast showed stage presence: Master Alistair Thurber, in the mute role of Medea's elder son, and Grace Bumbry, as Medea. The title role, Henry F. Chorley once wrote, requires

a Catalani with a voice, as it were, like a clarion, and a frame of adamant and gold, capable of undergoing the strain and fatigue of such a long display of unmeasured emotion. And, after the compass and lungs of a Catalani are found, we must then ask for Pasta's grandeur of expression, and statuesque bearing, and withering scorn and fearful vengeance, and maternal remorse, ere the creation of the composer can be rightly filled up.

Miss Bumbry probably comes as close as anyone around now can to "filling it up." She looked splendid—erect and beautiful. Her performance was, as ever, carefully prepared: the notes lay in her voice and were powerfully projected. But the soprano extension added to her former mezzo had coolness in its gleam, and the mezzo register had lost some of its sultry luster. Moreover, she lacked her great predecessor's ability to forge eloquent line, to present melodies as emotional gestures, not just sequences of notes, each one accurately sounded. It was an admirably studied and imposing performance rather than a stirring one. The others were not incompetent but were nothing special: James Wagner (a Jason too soft-grained in timbre to sound heroic); Rita Shane (Dirce, or Glauce, as she is called in this version); Diane Curry (Neris); and Boris Martinovich (Creon). The new conductor, Klaus Weise, from Kiel, had not taught them the grandly classical, passionately precise etching that Cherubini's—and, for that matter, Lachner's—music requires. Indeed, he seemed not to have mastered it himself, for he allowed sloppy, rather than chiselled, string articulation and softened the outlines of the stern, energetic drama.

During Napoleon III's Universal Exposition in 1867, Offenbach's *La Grande-Duchesse de Gérolstein*, at the Variétés, won a success denied to Verdi's *Don Carlos*, at the Opéra. It is a livelier, wittier, sharper, more interesting—and better-composed—piece than anyone who first encountered it in the City Opera's new production last month might guess. The villain of the evening was the conductor, Antonio de Almeida, who laid a mortific hand on the score, but his work was abetted by weak or clumsy singing, by Jack Hofsiss's imprecise stage direction (plenty of ideas but few of them relevant to the drama), by Gilbert Hemsley's execrable lighting, and by Lloyd Walser's feeble chorus. John Conklin's open scenes did not help the cast to project an opéra bouffe into the large house. The dancers, in school-of-Balanchine choreography by Christopher Chadman, lent a small touch of verve and elegance to the show. It was a poor idea to reinstate two of Offenbach's "bedides goupures," the little cuts by which he converted a work received on its first night with mixed feelings into a triumph. In his authorized version, Act II ends and Act III begins more brightly.

The first Grand-Duchess, Hortense Schneider, did not, so far as I know, make records. But Offenbach's first Mme. Favart (1878) and Fille du Tambour-Major (1879), Juliette Simon-Girard, did, and her Offenbach recordings, including two airs from *La Grande-Duchesse*, have been collected on Rubini GV 600. (They are coupled with those of Anna Tariol-Baugé, a celebrated Offenbach heroine at the turn of the century.) Mme. Simon-Girard, who was born in 1859, celebrated her hundredth birthday: she had known Napoleon III's Second Empire and de Gaulle's Fifth Republic; she had lived through the Siege of Paris, the Commune, and the Nazi Occupation. Her recordings, made in 1903, are not only precious documents of *Aufführungspraxis* and essential study for singers who aim to acquire an Offenbach style; they reveal the *grâce, esprit,* and *talent de chanteuse* that, Reynaldo Hahn said, "emportait tout." She is at once freer and more vivid in her phrasing than modern Offenbach interpreters (who tend to be conductor-bound rather than chivalrously accompanied in whatever flights they choose to take) and more "classical" in her command of a controlled, shapely line.

PASSION

May 10, 1982

THE BENEDIKTBEUERN manuscript, the "Carmina Burana," is a thirteenth-century compilation of love songs, drinking songs, songs in praise of spring, a gambler's Mass, devout songs, and religious music-dramas. (It was published in facsimile in Brooklyn in 1967.) One of its illustrations, reproduced in Richard Hoppin's *Medieval Music* (Norton), shows two youths playing backgammon while a third youth lifts high a goblet. Some of its secular poems have become familiar through Helen Waddell's *Mediaeval Latin Lyrics* and through Carl Orff's scenic cantata *Carmina Burana*. The longer of its two Passion plays was brought to performance in March by the Early Music Institute of Indiana University, in Bloomington, and the production came to New York, to the Romanesque Chapel of St. Martin, in the Cloisters, for three Lenten performances. Not even the Met's *Parsifal* was a drama more gripping or more moving.

The play is itself evidently a compilation: a liturgical Passion drama, in Latin, together with scenes from vernacular medieval drama and *planctus Mariae* (laments of Our Lady) in both German and Latin. Liturgical plainchant, the "quasi-plainchant" of liturgical drama, "art song," popular song, and *planctus* all are used. In the manuscript, the music is notated in unpitched neumes—runelike squiggles above the words, described by Grove as "a mnemonic aid to long-vanished memories." But because the play is an assemblage a fair amount of its music can be found in other, more precisely notated sources, and words and music for narrative chants of which only the opening phrases are given can be supplied from elsewhere. The reconstruction was by Thomas Binkley, formerly of the Studio der Frühen Musik (whose medieval records are famous), and Clifford Flanigan. The staging was by Ross Allen, the general scenic direction by Max Röthlisberger, and the lighting by Allen White. How the play was first presented no one is sure. (Does it, indeed, represent any play that was actually performed or some monkish scholar's grand composite of available material?) Generally, it seems, liturgical drama was played in church, and vernacular drama out-of-doors. The Benediktbeuern play combines elements of both. There is nothing quite like it, though there are parallels for its various components. The preface to a *planctus* from Bordesholm, in Saxony, specifies performance on a platform in the church, "or outside the church if the weather is fine," by a cast of five: a devout priest as

Christ, a priest as John, and three youths as the Virgin, the Magdalen, and the mother of John. "When it is done by good and sincere men... it truly arouses the bystanders to genuine tears and compassion." It has elaborate performance instructions. A fourteenth-century *planctus* from Cividale del Friuli has phrase-by-phrase acting directions: "Here shall she turn to the men with arms outstretched"; "Here shall she wring her hands"; "Here shall she point to Christ with open palms"; "Here with bowed head shall she throw herself at Christ's feet." A fourteenth-century Visitation play from Essen, whose collegiate church had both canons and canonesses, was played by a mixed cast—the three Marys by women, the angels by men. This seems to have been an uncommon practice, but in the fourteenth-century Avignon Presentation play "a very beautiful little girl" took the part of the Virgin, and two young men played instruments. Instruments are implicit in the well-known "Play of Daniel" (though they are not called for as often as they were played in the New York Pro Musica's 1958 production). Expressive indications for singers are common: "in a medium voice, sweetly"; "in a low voice as if speaking into his ear"; "vociferously." John Stevens's long Grove essay on medieval drama (from which these examples are culled) provides a vivid picture of, on the one hand, ideas about music-drama that thirteenth- and fourteenth-century Christendom had in common—favorite episodes for representation, poems and tunes that conquered in every country—and, on the other hand, local, particular plays and practices. Apropos of the acting directions in the Cividale *planctus,* Stevens says, "The gestures and movements must surely have been... not subtle, shaded, infinitely expressive, but immediately recognizable, demonstrative, and impressive." Apropos of the vocal directions and the "unexpected dimension of psychological realism" they introduce, he says, "The problem is how the implications of these rubrics can be squared with other indications in the plays of formality, impersonality, and emotional restraint." By extension, that "problem" concerns all aspects of performing a medieval religious drama today. Bloomington's solutions to it were carefully judged, precise, and convincing. But those are cool epithets. What we heard and saw was a drama that "truly aroused the bystanders to genuine tears and compassion." It was passionate, piercing, overwhelming —one of those performances not often encountered that pour the past into the present, that leave listeners for hours afterward all but speechless and make hard the return to mundane life.

Of course, the subject matter—the libretto—has much to do with it. The deaths of Mimì and Madame Butterfly draw tears, but they are dramatic representations of events less tremendous than the death of a god, crucified by the men among whom he has come to dwell. Whatever a Westerner's personal beliefs may be, he is conditioned from childhood to respond to this Passion history. His art is founded on it. His music has its roots in the movements through pitches, time, and space of plainchant. Those are deep matters. Let me turn to the manner of the Bloomington presentation. Indiana University, like the Essen collegiate church, is a mixed-sex institution: the female roles were taken by young women, the male roles by young men, and in all respects the performance represented a skillful, sensitive, and artistic combination of historical insight and present-day reality. As the Bloomington program note said, "a twentieth-century audience cannot pretend to be a thirteenth-century one." Mr. Binkley had taught his cast to use an open, natural, direct way of singing—unstrained, unmannered, at once grave and alert. Mr. Allen's direction squared those requirements of formality and realism. His groups and gestures had evidently been inspired by medieval iconography; the result was at once stylized and lively. (The scourges, for example, were left to the imagination, but Christ's flinching beneath their mimic blows was naturalistically enacted.) The play itself, dealing with. God among men, blends the hieratic and the human, and it is carefully constructed. The action opens with Christ before Pilate, a scene ritually presented in the Palm Sunday response "Ingressus Pilatus." Then events that led to the confrontation are shown in a series of dramatic flashbacks, until we reach the trial again; now it proceeds in tense dialogue. Before it, the Entry into Jerusalem has brought a large choral scene, sounding the recurrent theme of the play: Christ as King. Mary Magdalen, singing gay German songs to harp, lute, and vielle accompaniment, has bought cosmetics from a merchant and has attracted her lover of the night; and she has hearkened to the voice of an angel breaking into the soft night hours and calling on her to repent. Lazarus, gaunt and alarming, has stepped from his tomb. The Agony in the Garden, with its recurrent refrain, has been poignantly reënacted. The drama proceeds to its climax. Mary is not the gentle Madonna of popular imagery but a forceful, mature woman pouring out her grief as she watches her son die in torment before her. The last, despairing cry from the Cross rings out: a god asking why God has forsaken him. There is a brief, quiet coda: Longinus' awed "Vere filius dei erat iste," repeated in German; an echo from early in the play, "He has done a miracle on me," from the blind man whose sight was restored; and, with an oddly modern distancing effect, casual comments from three indifferent bystanders.

Richard Morrison, as Jesus, and Karen Young, as Mary, gave beautifully judged and admirably sung performances. Eileen Moore's tangy, lithe soprano, used not Carmen-like but with the style and tact that informed the presentation, made her a vivid Magdalen. All the large cast, it seemed to me, performed as if inspired—handling the sensational matter with gravity and restraint, singing both the jubilant and the tragic music with seemly ardor and uncommon technical skill.

There were at least three performances in New York this year of Bach's St. John Passion accompanied by Baroque instruments: in Corpus Christi Church, in Alice Tully Hall, and in St. Thomas Church.

I heard the second, presented by the Muse of Eloquence, Inc., and sung by the New Calliope Singers, conducted by Peter Schubert. In the large, unresonant hall, the little orchestra sounded weak, and possibly it was underrehearsed. The clarity of the textures, however, was a pleasure, and there were some fine passages of individual playing. There seem to be two opposed schools of Baroque interpretation: the "express the words" group and the "feel the dance rhythms" group. Mr. Schubert evidently belongs to the latter. There was no plodding, no heaviness. On the other hand, "Bist du nicht seiner Jünger einer?" (the Passion was sung in German) emerged as meaningless syllabic chatter, not a pointed question. The punctuated line "Ach, grosser König, gross zu allen Zeiten," which opens the first verse of a chorale, was given exactly the same phrasing, stresses, and articulation as the continuous "Ich kann's mit meinen Sinnen nicht erreichen," which opens the second verse. The mob cried "Kreuzige, kreuzige!" in dainty, tripping measures. One might describe it as a determinedly secular performance. (A little positif organ, not the hall organ, was used; the latter should at least have been revealed, to make an apter backdrop for the music than bare wooden screens.) One might say that Mr. Schubert aimed at—and achieved—purely musical effects. But such Bach without words—without the words' sense being felt and expressed—is Bach diminished. The music, too, loses its power. The most satisfying Baroque interpreters are both rhythmical and eloquent.

In Weimar and again in Leipzig, Bach prepared performance material for Reinhard Keiser's St. Mark Passion. Parallels between it and his own Passions have been detected. Recently, however, it has been suggested that Keiser's most Bachian episodes are in fact interpolated composition by Bach himself. The Brooklyn Philharmonia Chorus, conducted by Alexander Dashnaw, sang Keiser's Passion in Merkin Hall in March, but it wasn't much of a performance. Mr. Dashnaw neither "danced" nor got his singers to express the words. The result was unphrased, dull. The brief operalike arias that form the work's main attraction were generally shorn of their da capos.

MONUMENT

May 17, 1982

TEN YEARS ago, the British composer and critic G. W. Hopkins remarked that Jean Barraqué's Piano Sonata had "in the twenty years of its existence ... acquired a special and formidable reputation as a modern classic, a work standing on a plane apart from the avant-garde productions of the Fifties and Sixties." Barraqué himself became a kind of legend. He was born in 1928 and died in 1973, leaving incomplete an immense composition founded on Hermann Broch's *The*

Death of Virgil—a composition that, according to Barraqué's champion André Hodeir, was planned to be much longer than the St. Matthew Passion and *Parsifal* combined. (Individual sections of it have appeared.) Hodeir's championship, most ardent in his book *Since Debussy* (1961), brought Barraqué notoriety—as "that French composer who has been called the new Beethoven." The advocacy was indeed strong: Schoenberg, Webern, Messiaen, and the young Boulez had fine, rare musical minds, but

> the real descendant of the great masters of the past is the artist who, taking stock of his own powers, feels strong enough to discard the relics of a dead language and sets about re-creating the stuff that masterpieces are made of. There has been only one great twentieth-century disciple of Beethoven, and his name is Jean Barraqué.

And Barraqué himself did not exactly reject the proffered mantle, in such a statement as

> Whether I am the musician that some think, and I think, will be revealed half a century hence. In my opinion, my Concerto [first performed in London in 1968] goes beyond the Late Quartets. . . . I know there is room now for only one great musician. . . . Whether I am he, I do not know. But I know well that there cannot be two. The rest will crumble away, I am sure. But I cannot say: he will be I.

Hodeir, like Stockhausen, Boulez, and Barraqué, studied with Messiaen, and his *Since Debussy* (which has been reprinted by the Da Capo Press), an unbalanced but fascinating book, gives a vivid picture of the intellectual excitement generated in those first heady days of postwar serialism. Boulez's Second Piano Sonata was published in 1950. Barraqué's Piano Sonata, composed in 1950–52, was published only in 1965. (The score is distributed in this country by Margun Music.) There have been at least two recordings of it—an early one by Yvonne Loriod, and one by Roger Woodward on Unicorn. What was billed as the American première formed the second half of Robert Black's recital in Merkin Hall in March.

The Barraqué sonata, like the Boulez, is a mid-century monument and a twenty-three-year-old genius's ambitious, assured attempt to create, as it were, a new "Hammerklavier" for our times. Boulez's amazing score was by intention the more iconoclastic: "It was probably the attempt of the [Second] Viennese School to revive older forms that made me try to destroy them completely." Barraqué's is some forty minutes of extremely demanding, sustainedly intense music. Essentially, it is a long fast movement followed without break by a long slow movement, each of them containing alternations of four basic tempi and many gradations between them. There is no regular, perceptible meter or pulse but, rather, an observable growth and development— now slow, now rapid—of rhythmic "cells." The rhythmic complexity is great. The sonic, or linear, textures are generally spare, but the lines span the keyboard as boldly as if its whole range lay at once under a giant pair of hands. Technical writing about this composition I have found of little help toward entering it. Its emotional power cannot be missed. Hodeir likened it to a mortal struggle between Music and Silence. An active, exultant celebration of sound in action is invaded by silences—missing notes, phrases abruptly cut short, and then irrational, alarming cracks in the music, as if the world were falling apart. "The finale attains a summit of agonizing grandeur.... Whole slabs of sound crumble and vanish beneath the all-engulfing ocean of silence, until only the twelve notes of the row remain, and even these are plucked off, one by one."

Mr. Black is a pianist who unites good fingers with a warmth of musical personality and an eagerness to communicate that are missing in some capable but chiller exponents of the modern repertory. I don't know the sonata nearly well enough to appraise his performance (rough impressions: less "lucid" and expository than Miss Loriod's recorded version; more emotional, if also a shade less rhythmically accurate, than Mr. Woodward's), but I do know that it provided an immense, extraordinary adventure. Dane Rudhyar's neo-Lisztian *Epic Poem* (1979), in its New York première, and Miriam Gideon's carefully fashioned Piano Sonata (1977), in its world première, were dwarfed by it.

Similar qualities of warmth and communicativeness inform the playing of the New York New Music Ensemble, founded and conducted by Mr. Black. Its Carnegie Recital Hall concert last week closed with a moving performance of Peter Maxwell Davies's *Ave Maris Stella*. This radiant, readily approachable work, written seven years ago, is perhaps the easiest pathway into Davies's later instrumental style. (There is a fine recording, made by the Fires of London, for whom the piece was written, on Unicorn-Kanchana; the score is published by Boosey & Hawkes.) Technical writing about *Ave Maris Stella* can help the listener to hear more and more in it. A chapter of Paul Griffiths's skillful, perceptive monograph on the composer (Robson) discusses the nine-by-nine magic square that yields the work's pitches and note values; Stephen Pruslin's study in the Boosey & Hawkes collection of essays on Davies discusses its form in relation to Beethoven's late quartets. The analyses help because the procedures and the structures are audible: the magic square, Davies has said, "gives very, very simple results which you can learn and work with—like triads—and very simple rhythmic values, too," and "the harmonic movement, from the beginning right through to the end, is very clear." Yet, at the last, both analysts turn from facts to metaphor: Griffiths writes of "frozen violence" and "intense luminosity," Pruslin of a "spiritual programme" and of progress from "a luminous dawn" to "the Hour of the Wolf—the symbolic time between night and day when nocturnal sounds have ceased and the sounds of dawn have not yet started." Perhaps one can also sense a seasonal progress from brave, strong stirrings of spring to a piercing midwinter cry—of death, of birth?—that holds the promise of a new spring. That cry, Mr. Pruslin says, "has never yet failed to leave players and listeners drained and silent." New York is a city where it is easy to spend a whole day, even days on end, without once setting foot on naked, living earth. *Ave Maris Stella* is comforting, in the old, fortifying sense of that word, and inspiring. Techniques of great subtlety and refinement have not lost touch with the natural rhythms of life.

The program included two premières: Tobias Picker's *The Blue Hula* and Milton Babbitt's *Playing for Time*. *The Blue Hula,* a ten-minute sextet for the same forces as those of *Ave Maris Stella* (the *Pierrot Lunaire* quintet—flute, clarinet, violin/viola, cello, and piano—plus percussion), left the impression of a fluent young composer with nothing urgent to say. After his richly promising start, Picker seems to have lost his way for a while. I hope something important to him soon engages his attention and focusses his skills. *Playing for Time,* a piano piece, brief and brilliant, was followed by one even briefer and equally brilliant—the *Minute Waltz* that Babbitt composed in 1977 for Roger Sessions's eightieth birthday. Davies, in conversation with Mr. Griffiths, remarked that he found Babbitt's language "very hard to penetrate," but these taut, witty miniatures are hard only for the player. Alan Feinberg gave exhilarating performances.

Davies's Brass Quintet, composed for the Empire Brass Quintet, was given its first performance at an Empire recital in Town Hall in March. It is a substantial work—lasting thirty-two minutes—and serene, strong, and beautiful. A nine-note melody, played at the start by the horn while a soft C from the second trumpet provides a horizon against which the contours rise and fall, runs through the three movements, inspiring a fugato in the last of them. In the adagio of the first, two-tempo movement, the three lower instruments sing lyrically while the two trumpets, muted, touch in a soft, poetic commentary, often trilled. A cadence is reached on C and F; the trumpets take off their mutes and take on a fiery, impetuous character in the volatile allegro that follows. The middle movement is an adagio; a soft-swelling, richly harmonized introduction leads to a set of variations with long accompanied solos for horn, trombone, and tuba. The finale is an allegro vivace of incisive rhythms, closed by some grave paragraphs in which the note values grow long, and an exuberant final cadence springing from a wild horn flourish. C and F are recurrent fixed points, oft sounded, but D becomes insistent, too, and the quintet ends on C and D at once.

A composer is unlikely to write many brass quintets during his career. Davies has poured into this one a wealth of sounds specific to the medium: cantabile melodies, ceremonial intradas, bright signals, romantic echoes as if from the distance. The textures are varied, and there are sonorities I had never before heard from a brass quintet— finespun traceries, mistily "atmospheric" effects. The two trumpets are usually treated as if they were brothers, handled in duo. The horn is the principal singer. The music is not "top line and bass" but shows, more easily than the rich, complicated pages of Davies's two symphonies do, his increasing command of a harmony growing both upward and downward around a central "tenor." Sometimes the instruments are five very distinct characters; in one beautiful episode they cluster close, as if trying to match their voices. Rolf Smedvig, the Empire's first trumpet, and David Ohanian, its horn, were in the Boston Symphony when it created Davies's Second Symphony, early last year, and there the composer must have learned their virtuosity of technique and quickness of temperament. The performance was brilliantly accomplished. Once or twice, the balance of lines in the slow movement was perhaps not quite ideal, but the poetry, the power, and the shapeliness of the work were all apparent.

TESTIMONY

May 24, 1982

THE FITZWILLIAM String Quartet in a series of five concerts, spaced through a fortnight of April and May, played Shostakovich's fifteen string quartets, in Alice Tully Hall, and provided New York with a rare and wonderful musical event. The complete series has been played only once before in this country, it seems. (The Fitzwilliam's cycle was billed as "United States Première," but the day after its opening concert the Bakken String Quartet, in Minneapolis, completed a Shostakovich cycle.) The presentation of complete cycles, *intégrales,* can sometimes smack more of packaging than of artistic planning. In 1976, the Philharmonic played Mahler's nine symphonies within a month, and that was surely too much of a good thing. But string quartets lend themselves more amenably to such gathering. They generally represent a composer's more private, intimate thoughts—combining elements of diary, autobiography, progress-record of musical developments, and finely worked lyric poetry. Listening to a string quartet is an experience closer to that of reading a book than is listening to a symphony or to a concerto. One can read on and on, enthralled, if the author is a great one. And, I think, it brings one even closer to a composer than listening to a piano sonata does, for, however personal piano writing may be, a public performance of it is like being read to aloud: another voice, another personality, an interpreter, intervenes. Whereas, in the best quartet-playing, four instruments seem to speak to the listener in the composer's own voice. Some years ago, I described how hearing Ernst Krenek's seven string quartets, played by the Thouvenel String Quartet, within six days had led one from an energetic young modernist musing on Beethoven's Opus 132 (in No. 1, of 1921), through his neoclassical and neoromantic explorations, to a forceful, eloquent twelve-note conqueror (in No. 6, of 1937), and thence to the serene, active master who in America has come to terms with himself and the world. (I called No. 7 "Krenek's Opus 135, as it were," but since then an Eighth Quartet has appeared.) To hear these quartets was not only to traverse, in live sound, an extended and important chapter of musical history—though *intégrales* do have their educational side, and valuable it is. It was also—such is the nature of the medium—to become the intimate of a questing, questioning, well-informed, and fruitful mind and to share with it, through decades, the excitements of discovery and new creation.

And so with Shostakovich. His fifteen symphonies are public utterances, to be taken one at a time. The voice in them is personal, but—such is the nature of the medium—it is a voice lifted to address a large audience, even in those three last, beautiful symphonies, which are in turn boldly, bleakly, and despairingly defiant. ("Public utterances"—need it be said?—does not imply criticism. The Eroica and the Choral Symphony are public utterances.) Shostakovich turned late to the string quartet. His First Quartet was written in 1938. It seems to be an essay in uncomplicatedly pure music after the heroic rigors of the Fifth Symphony—the work that returned its composer to official favor after Stalin's denunciation of *Lady Macbeth of Mtsensk*. Six years passed before the Second Quartet appeared, after the "war" symphonies—the "Leningrad" and No. 8. (It was played by the Beethoven Quartet, which gave the first performances of all but the first and last quartets, and had No. 15 in rehearsal when its cellist died; six of them are dedicated to it or to one of its members.) Four string quartets, Nos. 9 to 12, appeared in the six-year gap between the Thirteenth ("Babi Yar") Symphony and the Fourteenth. Solomon Volkov, in his book *Testimony: The Memoirs of Dmitri Shostakovich* (Harper & Row), quotes the composer as saying, apropos of reports that he had embarked on an opera based on *And Quiet Flows the Don*:

I never started it.... You say that you're planning such-and-such a composition, something with a powerful, killing title. That's so they don't stone you. And meanwhile you write a quartet or something for your own quiet satisfaction. But you tell the administration that you're working on the opera *Karl Marx* or *The Young Guards*, and they'll forgive you your quartet when it appears.

There is a view that in the quartets we hear the "real" Shostakovich —in, for example, the Seventh Quartet (1960) rather than the two revolution-celebrating symphonies, No. 11 ("The Year 1905") and No. 12 ("The Year 1917"), that flank it. Boris Schwarz in his Grove article on Shostakovich seeks to provide a corrective to that view. "No outside pressure was needed to make him write 'facile' music; he enjoyed it; it was part of his multi-faceted personality." "As a creative artist, he was attuned to the needs and responses of his audiences." "The few setbacks in his career were more than counterbalanced by decades of unparalleled recognition, both national and international." Commentary on—and, for that matter, listening to—Shostakovich's music has ever been mixed with speculation about his political convictions, and that is inevitable. In recent years, the sorrow and despair that fill the final works—the last three symphonies, the last quartets, the Viola Sonata—have cast new shadows backward, and have thrown into question even what once seemed affirmatively untroubled or unambiguous. The authenticity of the Volkov memoirs is unestablished, but several of the composer's reported declarations—that the Seventh Symphony is "not about Leningrad under siege, it's about the Leningrad that Stalin destroyed and that Hitler merely finished off," that "the majority of my symphonies are tombstones," and that the Eighth Quartet (composed in Dresden in 1960, "in memory of victims of Fascism and war") is autobiographical, especially in its quotation of the song "Languishing in Prison" followed by a theme from the banned opera *Lady Macbeth*—chime with the emotional content of the final works. It seems to me not improbable that Shostakovich in his last years (from which Volkov dates the memoirs), disillusioned, weary, dying, looked back on his life with embittered and despairing eyes and on his life's works with attention to but one facet of their "multi-faceted" nature. That provides a way of reconciling the portraits by Volkov and by Schwarz, and of reconciling the ardent assertions in so many earlier works—not the music of a cynic or a time-server—and the tragic repudiations, at first scornful, finally resigned, in the last works. Hugh Ottaway, in his admirable little monograph on the Shostakovich symphonies (one of the BBC Music Guides), is surely right in saying, "All the evidence shows that the young composer identified strongly with the new, revolutionary order in which he had come to manhood." Ottaway continues, "He remained an individual, but one whose commitment to a revolutionary socialism can hardly be questioned." But whether that commitment lasted can be questioned. Shostakovich would not be the first Soviet composer whose belief in the idea was eroded by the reality, and now that all his work lies before us it is harder than ever to trace any simple patterns in his thought and his development. In the Fourth String Quartet (composed in 1949 but not made public until after Stalin's death, in 1953), a lucid and radiant composition, the Jewish inflections of some of its melodies once seemed no more than a touch of exotic color. To listeners who have since heard Shostakovich's "Babi Yar" Symphony (1962), they become ominous and disquieting.

The last Shostakovich quartet cycle I had heard was in June, 1968, in London, when there were only eleven quartets. (No. 12, a turning point in Shostakovich's style, appeared later that year.) They were played by the Borodin Quartet, masters of sweet, luminous tone and exquisite detail. The ear was ravished, enchanted. The music lived along the lines; one followed the movements of the notes with bated breath. Eleven years later, the Borodin played Nos. 8 and 15 in the music room of the Frick Collection and again held its listeners spellbound. But it "Borodinized" those tragic compositions—played them, as I wrote at the time, "with a beauty of tone and inflection which would remove the pangs, the keenness, the bitterness, if anything could." It was the Borodin Quartet that most prominently brought Shostakovich's quartets to the Western world, and its recordings stayed in the catalogues while those of the Beethoven Quartet disappeared. In 1972, another ensemble took the lead in introducing the later works. Alan George, the viola of the Fitzwilliam Quartet—four young men who had played together as Cambridge undergraduates and after graduation went on to become quartet-in-residence at the University of York—wrote to the composer and asked if they might give the Western première of his Thirteenth Quartet. Shostakovich not only sent the music and his blessing but came to York himself to hear the performance. Later, he sent them the music of the Fourteenth and Fifteenth Quartets. He kept in touch, wrote often, and invited them to come to Moscow to work with him, but died before the visit could take place.

Gradually, the Fitzwilliam mastered all fifteen quartets, and it recorded them (on prize-winning, Oiseau-Lyre discs) in the space of seven years. It gave a complete Shostakovich cycle in London in 1979, another in Montreal the following year. Also in 1980, it made its New York début, in Carnegie Recital Hall, playing Nos. 4, 8, and 12. For the New York cycle this year (which was sponsored by Bucknell University, in Pennsylvania, the quartet's regular American host), Tully Hall was only about half full, but it was half filled with attentive, appreciative listeners who at the end of each concert rose to their feet and cheered. Tully Hall is large for chamber music. The Borodin Quartet played its London cycle in the Goldsmiths' Hall, on a shallow platform surrounded by listeners, all in a chamber together. The Fitzwilliam played its London cycle in the Wigmore Hall, which holds 550 people. Tully, high and wide, holds twice that number in perhaps four times as large a space. The acoustics are dry. The performances were sometimes disturbed by a soft, high electronic whistle in the roof. In the closing measures of No. 15, a small dog that its mistress had brought along in a canvas bag grew impatient, popped its head out, and yapped. Sundry beeps, from those electronic watches that mark the hours, sounded at times, and in the softest passages the hall's ventilation system could be heard adding its continuo to the music. Nevertheless, these five, shared concerts provided an adventure complementary to that of listening to the records at home.

The Fitzwilliam is a quartet on the highest level. Its tone is less sweet than the Borodin's, less vibrantly lush than the Guarneri's. It is something even better. The first concern is for the musical sense, not for richness and ripeness of sound: the tone is protean. While it can be forceful, it never sounds forced. The quartet dares to play long soft passages—there are many in Shostakovich—with a softness that makes listeners still and intent; hundreds of people become a hushed, intimate handful. The fine-grained interpretation is founded on scrupulous attention to the composer's markings: his precisely judged metronome figures, his careful indications of balance, phrasing, and accent. In "free" passages—the mimetic recitatives that Shostakovich began to write as early as the Second Quartet—the balance between rhetoric and confidential, though urgent, discourse was justly found. In general, the Fitzwilliam showed a sure instinct for the composer's distinctive, elusive compound of reticence with explicitness. (I met Shostakovich only once, at the 1962 Edinburgh Festival, where his Fourth and Twelfth Symphonies had their Western premières; the composer of those assertive pieces was not recognizable in that shy, friendly, yet frightened-seeming figure, but the composer of the quartets was.) Rhythm was unfaltering, at tempi fast or slow. To sustain the six consecutive adagios that make up the Fifteenth Quartet needs control to match the composer's own. And the special Shostakovich sound that keeps returning—a veiled, often vibratoless cry from muted strings, sometimes in long, musing, quasi-improvisatory melodies, sometimes in chords—is something the Fitzwilliam understands perfectly.

The playing was technically accomplished, emotionally keen, musically intelligent and compelling. Even Shostakovich's warmest champions can see substance in such charges against his music as those brought by Robert Craft (in a review of Volkov's book): that it "does not exhibit a wide range of emotions, but depends on simple contrasts of the lyrical and the dramatic, the elegiac and the grotesque, the solemn and the 'impudent'"; that "ideas are worked to death, the forms, with their clichés of crescendo and climax, tend to sprawl, and the substance is thin"; that "the music lacks rhythmic invention." Much of that can be admitted, more readily of the symphonies than of the quartets, and then balanced against merits of eloquence (Craft tells also of "intensity of feeling and concentration" in some works), directness, individuality, and—something hard to express—the way the composer makes us present-day heirs of, in the quartets, Haydn, Beethoven, Mahler, Berg. A twelve-note theme, resolving into D-flat major, opens the Twelfth Quartet. A twelve-note theme opens and closes the one-movement Thirteenth, in B-flat minor. The Fitzwilliam performances (which were given in an order not strictly chronological but with chronology tempered to yield five shapely programs) revealed, on the one hand, continuity from work to work—a steady progress both in the handling of the instruments and in the ways of "thinking in the medium"—and, on the other hand, the individual shape and character of each quartet. In the long series, there was no monotony.

The scores are published in two handsome volumes, Nos. 35 and 36 of the Russian State Music Publishers' Shostakovich edition, distributed in this country by G. Schirmer.

ATHENIAN PURSUIT

May 31, 1982

THIS IS a roundup of some contemporary-music concerts—notes on a few of the new or newish compositions I heard during the latter part of the season. The fare was rich and varied. No general conclusions emerge. The recurrent name is Schoenberg: the influence of that powerful mind and that vigorous music remains strong.

The players of the Emmanuel Wind Quintet—named for Emmanuel Church in Boston and its busy music program—came together six years ago to perform Schoenberg's Wind Quintet. Last year, the Emmanuel won a Naumburg Award, and its Naumburg concert this year, in Alice Tully Hall, opened with the Schoenberg—an important, arresting, but ungainly composition. The ungainliness lies in the sound. The substance of the Quintet—Schoenberg's first large essay in filling classical forms with twelve-note music—is enthralling. Its four movements are shapely. The themes, as John Harbison wrote in the program note, "are always clear, sometimes immediately attractive." But the writing for the instruments is ruthless. Arnold Whittall, in the BBC Music Guide on Schoenberg's chamber music, calls the Quintet "an impressive and often entertaining achievement, full of ideas about how serial technique may be explored, but not a completely satisfying musical experience." What looks lucid and graceful on the page becomes lumpy in performance. The piece proves intractable even in as finely pointed, carefully balanced, and spirited an account as that of the Emmanuel, whose members are as cogent and accomplished champions as one could hope to hear.

Two Naumburg commissions followed: Fred Lerdahl's *Episodes and Refrains,* given its first performance, and Harbison's Wind Quintet. The Harbison, composed in 1978 for the Aulos Wind Quintet, a Naumburg winner that year, has achieved some popularity (and a fine CRI recording, by the Aulos)—deservedly, for it is both engaging and poetic. Since flute, oboe, clarinet, horn, and bassoon are not, Harbison wrote, "a naturally felicitous combination of instruments, such as a string quartet," he decided to work with mixtures of timbres rather than with counterpoints. Perhaps he had been listening to the busily contrapuntal Schoenberg; nothing could sound more natural and felicitous than the combination as Carl Nielsen used it in his idyllic Wind Quintet, of 1922 (composed two years before Schoenberg's). Nielsen, one is told, had been listening to the Copenhagen Wind Quintet rehearsing Mozart. (What Mozart? The quintet for piano and wind quartet? Did anyone write wind quintets before Reicha and Danzi, in the second decade of the nineteenth century?) In any event, Harbison's quintet, now romantic, now dapper, is closer both in temper and in timbres to Nielsen's than to Schoenberg's. Lasting about twenty-two minutes, it is, in effect, a five-movement suite, none of whose movements outstay their welcome. An admiration for Stravinsky, salutary and unconcealed, mingles with a lissomeness most easily, if loosely, described as "French." In the finale, a perky tune is launched from a paraphrase of the start of *Siegfried*. Both the ideas and the sounds are winning.

One of the sounds is that of the five instruments in unison—a complicated, composite timbre that varies as the melody rises and falls and the constituent instruments change register. Lerdahl uses the sound more extensively in his twelve-minute *Episodes and Refrains*. The piece opens and closes with a refrain that is a monody for the full ensemble. From its melody, three episodes and two other refrains are derived. Lerdahl is a more schematic composer than Harbison. His planning is clear, his thought distinguished, and his execution masterly.

The New Music Consort's last concert of the season, in Carnegie Recital Hall, opened with Schoenberg's buoyant, catchy cabaret song "Nachtwandler" (for voice, piano, trumpet, fife, and drum), composed in 1901 and performed at the Überbrettl cabaret, in Berlin, where Schoenberg succeeded Oscar Straus as music director. It brought the première of Joseph Ness's *When Orpheus Last Sang*, a winding instrumental sextet, and the New York première of Conrad Cummings's pretty *Summer Air*, a nonet for three woodwinds, three strings, and two percussionists and harp. Although the program books arrived only after the concert, the picturesque content of Cummings's music was plain even without his reference, in a program note, to "the lush mid-May New Hampshire woods" and "the almost palpable heavy sweetness of the air" around the MacDowell Colony, where the piece was composed. "Has Conrad no sense of shame?" a composer of rather more rigorous bent was heard to murmur, but there was nothing to be ashamed of in this deft, delicately scored, and beguiling work. Charles Wuorinen's Second Trio, of 1962 (for flute, cello, and piano), brilliant and energetic, was revived. And Elliott Carter's Elizabeth Bishop cycle, *A Mirror on Which to Dwell*, for soprano and nine instruments, was given a bewitching performance. A critic sometimes approaches with apprehension a work that at its première he made much of, as I did of *A Mirror* six years ago. But after this performance—conducted by Harvey Sollberger, with Lucy Shelton a precise and sensitive soloist—I thought I'd made too little of it then.

Similar reassurance, this time that enthusiasm for Carter's *Night Fantasies*, for piano, had not been excessive, was provided by that work's New York deuxième, played by Ursula Oppens at her Metropolitan Museum recital earlier this season, and again when WNYC broadcast tapes of both her performance and Paul Jacobs's—hers more lyrical, his more incisive, and both authoritative.

Matthias Kriesberg's exhilarating piano recital last month for the Guild of Composers, in the McMillin Theatre, on the Columbia campus, was packed with local premières and ranged the world. The first New York performances were given of Valentin Silvestrov's *Elegy* and Edison Denisov's *Signs in White,* from the Soviet Union; of the Piano Sonata No. 4 by Rodrigo Asturias, Guatemalan-born and Paris-trained; and of Kriesberg's own *a3520*. Milton Babbitt's glittering *Tableaux,* composed in 1973 but first played in 1980, by Mr. Kriesberg, was the nearest thing to familiar fare. All five pieces treat the modern piano in the modern way—as a pitched percussion instrument of exceptional clarity and definition, wide dynamic range, and versatility of timbres, and one able to stutter or sustain at will, to mix singing and staccato tones as no other instrument can, and to cast clouds of romantic resonance over sharpdrilled thematic statement.

Asturias's sonata, the largest piece on the program, was written in 1967 and, in 1980, won the Stockhausen Competition for Musical Composition. It is the third part of a five-sonata *Livre pour piano,* an ambitious work whose twelve related movements at the same time (in the composer's words) "develop twelve prototypes of piano writing" and—though each sonata can be played separately—amount to a single, giant five-movement sonata. No. 4 is a toccata-like set of variations, in three movements. Long lines soar above iridescent, adamantine patterns. Complicated, bell-like harmonies are built, touched in tone by tone as animated figuration ranges the keyboard. It is a fascinating piece, surely and strongly made.

Silvestrov, a vanguard Kiev composer, was attacked in Tikhon Khrennikov's notorious address to the 1968 Congress of Soviet Composers. The next year, the author of an article expounding the composer's artistic credo was committed to a mental hospital. According to Grove, Silvestrov has in later works "consciously confined himself to traditional methods, but in an allegorical manner...employing the genres and stylistic norms of the seventeenth to nineteenth centuries." His *Elegy,* of 1967, is "traditional," too, but not in any way that Khrennikov would accept. It is a late fruit of the Second Viennese School. The vocabulary is Webernian, but the gestures are personal and unreticent. Denisov's *Signs in White* (1974) is a very quiet piece; the dynamic range is *pppp* to *pp* with an *mp* climax, until at the end a few notes marked *mf* or *f* ring out like thunderclaps. It is gentle meditation on the friction between adjacent notes, on what happens to piano sound as the vibrations in the strings die down or when particular frequencies are lightly reactivated, picked out in a high treble tracery. At first, I was tempted to deem it no more than one of those exercises in listening intently, healthful to glutted ears but more useful than nourishing. At a second hearing via a tape recording of the recital, I thought it poetic.

Kriesberg's *a3520* (1980), named for the frequency of the highest A on the keyboard, struck me as rather clattery, cluttered, and insistent —particularly after the Denisov. The piece is elaborately and thoroughly constructed. Every note bears its separate dynamic indication.

While I'm sure there is a sound structural reason for each note's being what it is, I had that not uncommon philistine reaction that from a listener's point of view any other note might have done just as well. What did come across was a sense of boldness and vitality—the purposefulness that, united to good fingers, enthusiasm, and a strong, clear mind, makes Mr. Kriesberg an arresting interpreter.

The Group for Contemporary Music's last concert of the season, in the Borden Auditorium of the Manhattan School of Music, brought the première of Susan Blaustein's *Ricercate,* a long, carefully composed five-movement string quartet designed as an essay in "nested" sonata forms, a piece in which—as in Schoenberg's First Quartet, its inspiration—each recapitulation takes account not just of the movement in which it occurs but of all preceding movements as well. The composer likens it to "a river whose size and momentum increase as it picks up the bits of mud and stone in its path." An ambitious, serious, and well-sustained piece of writing. Dean Drummond's *Columbus* explored a division of the octave into thirty-one steps, which makes possible truer consonances than our familiar twelve-step compromise division. It is scored for flute (played by Stefani Starin, who has mastered microtones) and zoomoozophone—rows of tuned aluminum tubes played upon by mallets.

The concert began with Richard Hervig's *An Entertainment* (1978), a duo for clarinet and marimba/vibraphone, which left me glum. It included revivals of Sollberger's animated *Riding the Wind* pieces (1973–74), for amplified solo flute, played by the composer, and of Nicolas Roussakis's slight but clever *Night Speech* (1968), for voices that click, hiss, etc., and percussion. It ended with Lukas Foss's *Thirteen Ways of Looking at a Blackbird* (1978), the Stevens poems retraced for soprano (Susan Belling, sweet and limpid), flute, percussion, and piano.

At the American Composers Orchestra's final concert of the season, in Tully Hall, conducted by Gunther Schuller, Ellen Taaffle Zwilich's Three Movements for Orchestra had its première. It is an unabashedly romantic composition, lushly Straussian in sound, enjoyable to hear. David Diamond's Fourth Symphony (which Leonard Bernstein conducted with the Boston Symphony in 1948) was revived. George Perle's Short Symphony and Schuller's own Contrabassoon Concerto had their New York premières. The Perle, which I thought so striking when it was broadcast from Tanglewood, in 1980, now seemed a less inventive piece than most of his work, trim but dry. As for the Schuller, the composer's confidence was not misplaced when, in a program note, he wrote, "I am quite sure that my Contrabassoon Concerto will not automatically convince everyone of the instrument's potential for "beauty" and 'good.'"

Perle at his most captivating graced Richard Goode's piano recital in Tully Hall, with a new ten-minute Ballade in which Chopinesque piano writing, including chains of thirds, and the composer's own brand of "twelve-note tonality" are happily wed. Like Perle's earlier Six Études, the Ballade is piano music at once traditionally "pianistic," accessible, thoughtful, and new.

APOLLONIAN PURSUIT

June 7, 1982

THE LONG preface to Marco da Gagliano's *Dafne,* one of the earliest operas, performed in Mantua in 1608 and published in Florence that year, is a veritable production book containing detailed instructions for the "blocking" and gestures, specification of the choral forces, hints for the props man (how to prepare a laurel bough that can be twined without awkwardness into a wreath), notes on how to seat the orchestra, and much else. Opera was still young. The first opera is reckoned to be Jacopo Peri's *Dafne,* which appeared in 1598, or (by those who consider *Dafne* an experimental precursor) Peri's *Euridice,* which appeared in 1600. But already Gagliano finds it necessary to warn opera singers against misplaced or excessive vocal display. He indicates those numbers in which virtuoso adornment can fitly serve expression—"but where the tale does not require it, leave all ornamentation aside, so as not to be like the painter who, being a master of painting cypresses, painted cypresses everywhere." The singers' chief aim must be to make the words intelligible, for "true delight is born from an understanding of the words." (The words of *Dafne,* by the excellent poet Ottavio Rinuccini, are worth understanding.) Nevertheless, the spectacle is also important. Ovid provided the subject matter for the first two decades of opera, and the *Dafne* libretto is drawn from the first book of the *Metamorphoses*—from the pages telling of Apollo's slaying of the Python, his taunting of Cupid, Cupid's revenge, Apollo's pursuit of Daphne, and her transformation into a laurel. The vegetable metamorphosis is not scenically represented but happens offstage; the shepherd Thyrsis describes it in music hardly less eloquent than Richard Strauss's for the same event. But the Python does appear. "The serpent should be large, and if its designer knows how (as I have seen) to make it flap its wings and spit fire, it will be a finer sight still if it snakes along—the man inside it putting his hands to the ground—on all fours." The Python had already made a spectacular appearance in a 1589 Medici entertainment, designed by Bernardo Buontalenti—in its third intermezzo, which had words by Rinuccini and music by Luca Marenzio. (Buontalenti designs and an Agostino Caracci engraving of the scene survive; so do descriptions of the monster's mirror-spangled wings, its gaping jaws set with three rows of gnashable teeth, its glowing tongue and fiery breath, the inky blood gushing from the wounds Apollo inflicted.) A few years later, Rinuccini, "merely to make a simple test of what the song of our age could do," recast his piece for dramatic singing—retaining just a line or two of the original, and adding the Daphne sequel. And from this initiative opera was born. Peri's *Dafne* was first given with small forces in a small room. For Gagliano's *Dafne*, a decade later, Rinuccini amplified his libretto, enlarging the chorus's role (perhaps on the model of Monteverdi's *Orfeo*, which had meanwhile appeared, in 1607) and adding not only the piece that describes and accompanies Apollo's fight but, later, a narrative replay of the contest, recounted for Daphne's benefit. (Since Apollo would be out of breath after his exertions and unable to sing his victory song, Gagliano, ever practical, prescribed two identically dressed performers, one to fight and one to sing, and indicated when the substitution should take place.) Exactly where in Mantua this *Dafne* was first performed we are not sure. Presumably not in the large wooden theatre (its capacity variously estimated as four thousand and six thousand) used later that year for Monteverdi's *Arianna*. But the nature of Rinuccini's additions and of Gagliano's stage directions suggests that their *Dafne* may have been the first attempt to inject a spectacular element into the new genre. The earlier operas—Peri's *Dafne*, his *Euridice* and Giulio Caccini's, and (although its music is far more graphic) Monteverdi's *Orfeo*—contain nothing as scenically exciting as the Python, while Caccini's elaborate *Il rapimento di Cefalo,* to judge by the libretto and contemporary descriptions, was closer to a vast theatrical pageant than to the Rinuccinian idea of opera.

Gagliano's *Dafne* is no *Orfeo*. The music does not have that work's richness, invention, or affecting power, and the plot is less shapely. But it is a fascinating piece: the first opera remodelled and, by an able composer, reset under the influence of the Monteverdi masterpiece that its earlier version had influenced; one of the early, still eloquent essays in harnessing poetry, drama, singing, playing, acting, dancing, scenery, and lighting effects to a single end. All the "problems" that have always beset and still give life to opera—the tensions between words and music, spectacle and music, star singers and composer, singers and orchestra, acting and singing, solos and ensembles, straight-line narrative and formal pattern—were from the start identified and explored. Since Monteverdi and his contemporaries, opera has increased its arsenal of affective weapons, but its essential ways of working upon audiences are hardly altered. In *Dafne*, the solo-and-chorus exchanges in the opening scene, bewailing the devastation the Python has spread, and those in the closing scenes, where Daphne's companions lament their loss of her, have a Gluck-like quality. Thyrsis, like Sylvia, the comparable messenger in *Orfeo*, is a forerunner of Waltraute in *Götterdämmerung*.

In our day, this *Dafne* has not been neglected. The 1608 score has been published in facsimile. The New York Pro Musica Antiqua staged *Dafne* at Hunter College in 1974, and there have been at least three recordings (the best of them was a Musica Pacifica performance on ABC Command). Last month, the Mannes Camerata presented *Dafne*, its inaugural production, in Christ Church, on Park Avenue at 60th

Street. The church, an expensively columned, marbled, and mosaicked neo-Byzantine late work (1932) by Ralph Adams Cram, which is described in the AIA Guide as a "stage set for well-to-do parishioners," lends itself to drama. The Camerata is the performing group of the early-music program at Mannes College. Its production was ambitious in aim while modest in scale, and very pleasing—intelligently and stylishly conceived, carefully rehearsed, sung, and acted by a young cast who had striven to master both the text and ways of singing and moving apt to the music. The band was ten strong (twice as many as the Pro Musica used, a third as many as in the rather heavy Hamburg performance recorded on Archiv). The ritornelli were played by a recorder consort, because the Camerata is still short of strings. Besides Daphne, Apollo, Cupid, and Venus, there was a chorus of five and a dance group of six—the Minstrel Tapestry Dancers, directed by Dorothy Rubin, a re-creator of High Renaissance dance. But since the dancers could sing and the singers could move, pastoral life and high adventure on Parnassus' slope were neither underpopulated nor undervoiced. The design was simple: a dapple of light, the Castalian spring pouring out over the altar on a painted frontal, a sprightly Python represented Kabuki-style. The notable singers were the young baritone Toshiaki Kunii—the only professional in the cast—as the Second Shepherd, and the light tenor Gregory Purnhagen, a Thyrsis who, like il Brandino, the creator of the role, not only made his words understood by clear diction and graceful singing but enhanced them with well-judged gesture and action. Elsewhere, there were a few patches of errant pitch, but in general the singing was light, clear, and steady. Paul Echols, the sapient, gifted, and dedicated director of the Camerata, himself played Ovid, who delivers the Prologue—with majesty gradually tempered by friendliness, as Gagliano required—and then sat in a front pew to supervise the progress of his show. In an attempt to "strengthen the individuality of some roles," Mr. Echols added three extra pieces, from elsewhere in Gagliano—wrongly, I think, to so carefully planned a work. A bilingual libretto was provided, but the light in the church was rather dim for following both text and action with ease. The Mannes Camerata plans a production of Peri's *Euridice* next spring (see page 441).

In Merkin Hall last month, the Florilegium Chamber Choir, accompanied by a Baroque string quintet and a harpsichord, gave a concert performance of Purcell's masterpiece *Dido and Aeneas*. The Belinda, Marjorie Patterson, was charming. The Dido, Bernadette Fiorella, and, even more, the Aeneas, Joseph Penrod, tended to sacrifice lightness, accuracy, and telling verbal inflection to volume of tone. The conductor, JoAnn Rice, beat time through continuo-accompanied airs (which is rather like conducting a singer and a pianist in a lieder recital). It was a presentation not fully worked out and, even in concert terms, insufficiently dramatic. The chorus's contributions, however, were well prepared, and on the whole it was an enjoyable enough show. An interesting effect—one I'd not heard tried before—was obtained in the echo chorus by sustaining, very softly, the main body's final chords through the echo phrases. It evoked the acoustics of a witches' cave. A libretto, a (revised) facsimile of the sole surviving seventeenth-century copy, was provided—but, again, the light in the hall was feeble. If singers don't know how to pronounce names like Aeneas and Actaeon, they should look them up in Webster instead of guessing and getting them wrong.

Merkin Hall is unresonant for choral music, but the Heinrich Isaac concert given there last month by Pomerium Musices, directed by Alexander Blachly, was memorable. The big work was Isaac's *Argentum et Aurum* Mass. The title may recall Franz Lehár's famous *Gold and Silver* waltz, but this fifteenth-century Mass is a large, brilliant, and beautiful composition—it suggests a composer rejoicing in his strength—based on the chant for the Feast of Saints Peter and Paul: Peter's "Silver and gold have I none; but such as I have give I thee" set to a very striking melody. Between its movements, Pomerium sang choral songs, mostly secular, by Isaac and his contemporaries, which formed a pendant to the revelation of Isaac in all his grandeur provided by the Mass and by Cappella Nova's Isaac concert in St. Joseph's Church two years ago. The Pomerium's singing is as clearly defined, as well tuned, and as rhythmical as the Cappella's, yet quite different in effect. One might describe it, perhaps, as more "instrumental"—less concerned with varying the tone and with coloring and expressing the words, and less flexible in tempo. The sound is very strong, exciting in timbre; the phrasing is crisp and firm. The choir was accompanied—where accompaniment was apt—by a trio of cornett and two sackbuts, with Ray Mase a cornett player to end doubts about the instrument's ability to stay in tune, and to justify that seventeenth-century likening of it to "a ray of sunlight."

GENIUS OF A KIND

June 14, 1982

ROSSINI CALLED Offenbach "the Mozart of the Champs-Élysées." Wagner in early days likened the warmth of his music to that of "a dungheap on which all the swine of Europe wallowed" but in 1882 was ready to allow him a resemblance to Mozart. Offenbach is a composer who has been received with delight, with contempt, with praise now extravagant, now tempered. The fifth edition of Grove ranked him below Johann Strauss for sentiment and below Sullivan for craftsmanship. The New Grove calls him "the composer of some of the most exhilaratingly gay and tuneful music ever written." His merits and his methods await scholarly examination. He had genius of a kind, and the materials for assessing it are at last being assembled. The music publisher Belwin-Mills has announced a detailed thematic catalogue of Offenbach's works, compiled by Antonio de Almeida. *[Five years later, we are still waiting for it.]* Volume II—the critical report—of Fritz Oeser's careful new edition of *Les Contes d'Hoffmann* has recently been published. And Belwin-Mills has also announced a complete reissue in piano-vocal score of Offenbach's hundred-odd *oeuvres scéniques*, with Mr. Almeida as their general editor. A few volumes have appeared. They are clarified and corrected reprints of French vocal scores, amplified by an English translation and by bilingual appendices containing the spoken dialogue. The gatherings of pages are glued, not sewn, into their paper bindings. I hope they don't come apart—as my paperback Fifth Grove has done—when the volumes are put to use. I hope they will be put to use. The music is exhilarating. But a performing style for it needs to be found. Offenbach's wit, grace, and sparkle often escape Anglo-Saxon performers—opera singers and conductors alike. In the last decade, only one of the Offenbach revivals I have seen has been intoxicating: the Bronx Opera's *Ba-Ta-Clan*, in 1975. The same director, Lou Galterio, laid a heavier hand on *Le Mariage aux lanternes* when the Manhattan School of Music mounted it in April. The show wasn't bad. It wasn't as crude as the City Opera's unhappy *Grand Duchess of Gerolstein*. But the execution was workaday. John Crosby's conducting was sedate, not springy. The young performers lacked lightness and charm. None of them was debonair.

Marriage by Lantern Light was done in English, on a double bill with the American première of Alexander Zemlinsky's *Eine florentinische Tragödie*, first performed in Stuttgart in 1917. The libretto is an abridged German translation of Oscar Wilde's *A Florentine Tragedy*—an overwritten, overripe costume drama cast in purple blank verse indebted to Webster and Marlowe. Zemlinsky's music is a rediscovery of our day. Two years ago, I told of my delighted encounter with his Second String Quartet, recorded by the LaSalle Quartet for Deutsche Grammophon. His name turns up in operatic reports from Europe, and there are three recordings of his Lyric Symphony. *Eine florentinische Tragödie* is composed and scored with his habitual mastery, but the libretto is distasteful. In Renaissance Florence, a hardworking merchant surprises his young wife with a rich, noble lover, taunts him, tricks him into buying his costliest goods, duels with him, disarms him, strangles him, and then turns to his wife. She, formerly disdainful, now "comes towards him as one dazed with wonder and with outstretched arms," saying "Why did you not tell me you were so strong?" He replies, "Why did you not tell me you were beautiful?" and kisses her on the mouth. Curtain. A distasteful libretto needn't stop an opera from being a masterwork; after all, there is Strauss's *Salome*. Puccini contemplated setting *A Florentine Tragedy* in 1906 (after *Butterfly*) and again in 1912 (after *La fanciulla del West*), deeming it potentially "a rival to Strauss's *Salome*, but more human, truer, closer to the feelings of the common man." (That was in a letter to his publisher, Giulio Ricordi.

Ricordi sent a curt telegram to Puccini's librettist, Luigi Illica: "Absolutely necessary for future good of Doge [Puccini] to throw Florentine stupidity into fire.)" The dramatic world is that of Max von Schillings's *Mona Lisa* (1915), Erich Korngold's *Violanta* (1916), and Franz Schreker's *Die Gezeichneten* (1918), all once widely performed on German stages. Schillings conducted the first performance of *Eine florentinische Tragödie*. Schreker wrote the libretto of *Die Gezeichneten* for Zemlinsky but then decided to set it himself. There was a vogue at the time, especially in Germany, for charged Italian costume drama, sensual, violent, and satined—for *cavalleria* not *rusticana* but *cortigiana*. Prokofiev's *Maddalena* represents a Russian variant; Italo Montemezzi's *L'amore dei tre re* (1913) and Riccardo Zandonai's *Francesca da Rimini* (1914) are earlier Italian examples. Most of those pieces seem dated now unless they are sung by potent and passionate singers. Then they can still grip an audience. I wasn't exactly gripped by the *Florentinische Tragödie* at the Manhattan School but was glad of the chance to see and hear it. So, I imagine, were most of those who care about opera. Schools and universities do well to fill the gaps in our live experience of operatic history. (The Manhattan School's productions of Humperdinck's *Königskinder* and Hindemith's *Neues vom Tage* and the Juilliard School's productions of Mozart's *La finta giardiniera* and Chabrier's *Le Roi malgré lui* are shining examples.) And sometimes they come up with a revival of a piece that goes on after a school showing to join the international repertory. (The Oxford University Opera Club's *Idomeneo* and *Les Troyens* helped to relaunch those operas.) I shan't urge *Eine florentinische Tragödie* on the Met or the City Opera, but the decent school performance left me eager to hear again the *music*, at least, with someone like Dietrich Fischer-Dieskau or Sherrill Milnes in the leading role. (The opera is almost a monodrama for the husband.) Manhattan's very able baritone Allan Glassman revealed how much might be made of the part. In a concert performance, the music would take precedence of the trite, gaudy play. The score is worth hearing. Zemlinsky's one-acter could well form the second half of an orchestra program. [*The opera was taken up, on a double bill with Zemlinsky's* Der Zwerg, *by Santa Fe, Hamburg, and Covent Garden.*]

Concert performances provide another way of hearing works that for one reason or another the regular opera companies are shy of. Without the concert performances of Eve Queler and her Opera Orchestra of New York, the city's operatic life would have been duller in the last decade. Miss Queler's latest venture, in Carnegie Hall in April, was the American première of Arrigo Boito's *Nerone*, the grandiose opera Boito worked on from the 1860s until his death, in 1918. He left *Nerone* incomplete. Toscanini and Vincenzo Tommasini brought four of its five acts to performance at La Scala in 1924. The production was spectacular (there is good reason for opera companies to be shy of *Nerone;* its scenic demands are immense), but the music, it seems, was found rather dull. It is rather dull. Back in 1877, after *Mefistofele*, Verdi, in a letter to a friend, set out a sage, measured opinion of Boito:

> It is difficult at the moment to say whether Boito will be able to provide Italy with masterpieces. He has much talent, he aspires to originality, but the result is rather peculiar. He lacks spontaneity, and he lacks *il motivo* [a term Verdi uses to describe incisive, eloquent melodic inspiration]. He has many musical qualities. With those attributes, he can succeed, more or less, in subject matter as strange and theatrical as that of *Mefistofele*. It will be more difficult with *Nerone*.

The world holds Boito in esteem, and rightly, for without him it would not have Verdi's—and his—*Otello* and *Falstaff*. Boito was learned, cultivated, and influential. He had an aspiring and wide-ranging mind. He recognized genius and was eager to associate himself with it. He once wrote, "I offer Wagner everything I have, even my legs," and he translated *Tristan* for its Italian première, in 1888. In *Otello* (1887), he made of Verdi the "Italian Wagner" that he perceived Verdi could be, cunningly drawing out the old master's strengths. In *Falstaff*, he led Verdi to create an Italian answer to *Die Meistersinger*. But he hankered for more. In his own *Mefistofele*, he had tried to show that an Italian composer could rise to Goethe's heights; his unrealizable *Nerone* was planned as a yet greater *Faust*, richly wrought, intellectually intricate, a consummation of Italian art. The *Nerone* libretto Boito wrote is enthralling, not at all dull: a mingling of mythical, classical, and Christian history, and of love pure with love polluted and perverse. The contrasts are violent. Extremes of passion, piety, and cruelty are explored. The panoplies of church and state—high spectacles of temple, circus, theatre, and civic assembly—become metaphor. What is real, what illusion? Nero makes his first entry screaming in terror, bearing his mother's ashes, and believing himself pursued by the Furies. The last, uncomposed act out-Freuds Freud as, in a theatre amid a Rome ablaze, Nero plays—and seems to become—Aeschylus' Orestes.

Alas, Boito was not composer enough to find the music for this. Ernest Newman once declared him possessor of "a semi-musical gift that rarely rises above the mediocre and generally dips a point or two below it." If transcendent capacity of taking trouble could produce a masterpiece, *Nerone* would be one. But Boito lacked *il motivo*. The one per cent in Edison's famous formula was missing, and without it Boito's music remains lifeless. *Nerone* was an opera I'd wanted for decades to hear; now, a few weeks after hearing it, I find that almost none of its music has stayed with me. I return to the score and see careful planning, careful workmanship, thoroughness—Verdi's "many musical qualities"—and nothing more. No fault of Miss Queler's. The performance was good. There was a strong international cast. Krunoslav Cigoj, a Yugoslav tenor, made his New York début in the title role. The other principals were the Mexican soprano Rosario Andrade (Asteria), the Hungarian contralto Klára Takács (Rubria), in her American début, and, more familiar, Pablo Elvira (Phanuel) and James Morris (Simon Magus).

Another piece heard in concert in Carnegie Hall in April was Tchaikovsky's last opera, *Iolanta*, brought from Washington by the National Symphony Orchestra. It is a sweet, charming short opera, composed to form a double bill with *The Nutcracker*. Galina Vishnevskaya was the heroine, and she was in admirable voice, sounding pure, true, and unworn. Nicolai Gedda (Vaudemont), Chester Ludgin (Duke Robert), John Shirley-Quirk (the Moorish Physician), and Dimiter Petkov (King René) made up a distinguished team of principals. Mstislav Rostropovich conducted with enthusiasm and emotion but missed the grace of the score. I would have enjoyed the evening more if memories of the captivating Mannes College production, staged in 1977, had not been so strong. Performed by young, fresh singers, *Iolanta* was more poignant and more beautiful.

SERIOUS MATTERS

June 21, 1982

IN SYMPHONY Space last month, a group of distinguished American musicians—among them Earle Brown, Alvin Curran, Shem Guibbory, Ursula Oppens, Frederic Rzewski, and Christian Wolff—gathered to give a memorial concert for the British composer Cornelius Cardew, who was killed in London last December, on his return from a political meeting, by a hit-and-run driver. The program book contained the text of a memorial lecture on Cardew delivered in London by the pianist John Tilbury and Cardew's long obituary in *Worker's Weekly*. In a foreword, Wolff declared that "to a remarkably large number of us" Cardew was "the most important composer in England, because of the quality of his music, because of his organizing, because of his thinking, speaking, and writing." Born in 1936, he had a conventional training, as a Canterbury Cathedral choirboy and then at the Royal Academy of Music. At the Academy, he and Richard Rodney Bennett gave a performance of Boulez's *Structures* which is still remembered. Bennett went on to study with Boulez. Cardew went to Stockhausen, in Cologne, and helped in the creation of *Carré*. Then John Cage and David Tudor left their mark on him, as on so many young European composers. He returned to London in 1961, and the *Musical Times* (which I was editing) published his *Octet '61*. It was the first piece of his to see print, and it ruffled the establishment. The octet, which is for any number of players, on any instruments, is a sheet of sixty signs, or "events." The *Sunday Times* critic likened them to "the labyrinthine curlicues that proceed from the mouths of the people in Steinberg's drawings." Starting anywhere, proceeding either forward or backward,

adding other notes at will, omitting parts of the signs at will, the performer or performers are invited to turn the signs into whatever
sounds they suggest. As such things went—they went far in those days,
when black beetles crawling over music paper, or fish swimming in a
staff-ruled glass tank, or the star maps of Cage's *Atlas Eclipticalis,* for
from one to eighty-six players, could provide "scores"—*Octet '61* was an
elegant and comparatively disciplined piece. At the least, it supplied
creative therapy for performers, set their wits to work; the best performers made music from it worth listening to. Cardew proceeded to
Treatise, a long graphic score. Sections from it were heard all over the
world, and the first complete performance, in London in 1967, was a
musical adventure comparable to adventures Stockhausen later provided in his *Aus den sieben Tagen* cycle. That year, Cardew became a
professor of composition at the Academy. *Treatise* was followed by *The
Great Learning*—the Confucian classic set for many performers,
trained or untrained, and dedicated to the Scratch Orchestra, which
Cardew had founded: a body of musicians several of whom had had
no formal training. The Scratch Orchestra, whose repertory included
Cage, Wolff, Terry Riley, La Monte Young, Rzewski, and pop songs,
played for farm workers, for industrial workers, for festival audiences
on the Continent, and for concert audiences in London. I heard it play
in the Royal Festival Hall, and I heard it play under a flyover north of
Notting Hill Gate at a kind of super-block party, a neighborhood "festival," that ended in racial brawls. For about two years, the orchestra
flourished. In Mr. Tilbury's words:

> Despite the ultra-democratic procedures the Scratch Orchestra had evolved
> for every aspect of its activity, Cardew was very much the unproclaimed au-
> thority, a father-figure to whom people looked for guidance and inspiration.
> The Scratch Orchestra bore his stamp, and in fact it was the embodiment of
> the ideas he had formulated about musical life over the years.

The anarchical group sought support from the establishment—the
Arts Council, the BBC, the bourgeois concert-giving organizations—
and inevitably a crisis arrived. At an orchestra meeting, it was defined
by references to sentences in Christopher Caudwell's essay on D.H.
Lawrence:

> The commercialization of art may revolt the sincere artist, but the tragedy is
> that he revolts against it still within the limitations of bourgeois culture. He
> attempts to forget the market completely and concentrate on his relation to
> the art work, which now becomes still further hypostatized as an entity in
> itself. Because the art work is now completely an end-in-itself, and even the
> market is forgotten, that art process becomes an extremely individualistic rela-
> tion. The social values inherent in the art form, such as syntax, tradition,
> rules, technique, form, accepted tonal scale, now seem to have little value, for
> the art work more and more exists for the individual alone.

The dilemma confronts all sincere artists, whatever their musical
and social beliefs, who would do more than supply a "product" for

market consumption. Each composer must find his own ways of working within or without the system and of accepting it (however uneasily and regretfully) or attempting to alter it. (There are two good essays on music and the market, by Gunther Schuller, in the May and June issues of *Keynote*.) Cardew at first repudiated his earlier works and all they represented (his manifesto *Stockhausen Serves Imperialism* was published in 1974), but later decided they were not irredeemable. At the 1972 Proms, the performance of a paragraph of *The Great Learning* was justified by a sentence from Mao: "Works of art that do not meet the demands of the struggle of the broad masses can be transformed into works of art that do." In the mid-seventies, he joined, and later was elected to the central committee of, the party now known as the Revolutionary Communist Party of Britain (Marxist-Leninist). When I came to America, I lost touch with his work. I reëncountered it at a 1975 Kitchen recital and was distressed to find his rare musical intelligence now spent on simple arrangements of Irish and Chinese songs. But at the Symphony Space concert there were some later, larger compositions that are a more substantial result of what Hanns Eisler called "a difficult and contradictory exercise, but the only worthy one for artists of our time...to write music that serves Socialism." The first half of the concert was a retrospective: *Memories of You* (1964), which I've always thought a silly piece, like a Cage parody, and interesting only to its performer; the exhilarating *Volo Solo* (also 1964), for two pianos (played by Miss Opens and Mr. Rzewski); and excerpts from *Treatise* and *The Great Learning* too brief, I thought, to mean much to any members of the largely young audience unfamiliar with those long works and the thinking they represent.

In my own life, Cardew—eight years younger than I—was a disturbing, challenging musician; a quester; a questioner of any comfortable reliance on history, musicology, and tradition; and a shaker of ivory towers both ancient and vanguard. The Symphony Space concert was disturbing to anyone who might have chosen, as Mr. Tilbury harshly put it, "to settle for an existence of comfort, smugness, complicity, and self-deception." The lecture ended with a last memory of Cardew at a concert he had organized a week before he was killed:

> He was playing the piano, accompanying and singing to a packed audience in a community hall in Camden [a London borough]. Many members of London's ethnic groups were in the audience and participating. It was a far cry from the international festivals of contemporary music where he had begun his career, but it was the path he had consciously chosen, to force his music into life in a way that would inspire any young composer for whom composition is something more than the manipulation of sound.

At the first New World Festival of the Arts, in Miami—a moist, muggy, mosquito-ridden June city—Robert Ward's latest opera, *Minutes till Midnight,* has had its première. Its subject matter is serious and topical.

Emil Roszak, a physicist who worked on the atomic bomb, is on the verge of completing a formula for the use of "cosmic energy...a new power, a source of energy that would dwarf anything known." There's just a gamma-ray problem to solve. Roszak's assistant, Chris, envisions cosmic energy as bringing "the banishing of disease, the power to make the deserts bloom, and to roam the galaxies in giant gondolas." Roszak says to him, "Perhaps you're right, Chris, perhaps some will choose to use it to remake the world, but for others it will only mean new profits...new ways to rule the continents and seas." He is summoned to the White House and asked to produce a "cosmic bomb," since "the enemy" is apparently at work on one. Back in his lab, he sings an aria—

> Oh, cosmos with your myriad stars
> afloat in the mystery of space,
> let your mantle of peace descend
> on this tormented place—

completes the formula, and has a vision of the world destroyed by his bomb. Chris is shot in an anti-bomb demonstration. Roszak decides to publish the formula in the *International Physicists Journal.* "The whole world, people everywhere must decide their fate." He joins with his wife, Margo, and Chris's fiancée, Julie, in an optimistic final trio, "There shall be a better tomorrow." The late Daniel Lang, the librettist of *Minutes till Midnight,* thought and wrote with concern and distinction about the issues presented in the opera, but he has dramatized them in soap-opera style. The characters talk in clichés. Ward's music—melodious, fluent, eclectic, made from memories of Puccini, of Richard Rodgers, of Kurt Weill—is undistinguished. The performance—put on by the Greater Miami Opera in the Dade County Auditorium, a large, rather bleak modern house—was good. Thomas Stewart, in the principal role, strove to give seriousness and depth to the physicist's plight. Evelyn Lear worked almost too hard to vivify the part of Margo. (She has an aria to the words "Run, run, run...always on the run.") Henry Price was Chris, and Richard Cross was Amory Dexter, the Secretary of Science. Claudia Cummings was a bright Julie. Günther Schneider-Siemssen's scenery was efficient, and striking in its effects. Although revolving stages soon become tiresome to watch, *Minutes till Midnight,* which has nine scenes (divided into three acts in the printed libretto but here played in two), probably needs one. Eight Pani projectors, the theatre's latest light marvels, created interiors at the touch of a switch; made galaxies twinkle; transformed a symbolic budding tree, at the close, into a heaven-tree of stars; and portrayed the destruction of mankind by an atomic bomb—Roszak's vision of "unimaginable human suffering"—so picturesquely that the audience broke into delighted applause. Emerson Buckley conducted. Nathaniel Merrill directed.

The message of the opera seems to be that anyone with access to classified information about nuclear weapons should forthwith make that information internationally available. The thinking is unclear. Roszak's decision is preceded by this exchange with the Secretary of Science:

> DEXTER: Look, Emil, weapons aren't all bad. The mightier our weapons, the less likely that there will be war. Weapons buy us time to find new paths to peace.
> ROSZAK: Not paths to peace, Amory, not paths to peace but a speedway to obliteration. That is what they buy us. A single false move, one miscalculation and all may be lost forever.

Minutes till Midnight was the largest première in an ambitious new twenty-three-day festival of operas (Carlisle Floyd's *Of Mice and Men* is the other production), concerts, plays, dance, films, and exhibitions. Miami wished to show that it is more than beaches, the drug-running capital of the country, and the city with the highest homicide rate. It is not a festival city like Edinburgh, Amsterdam, Salzburg, Spoleto, or (the other new summer-festival city in America) San Francisco, traversable largely on foot, with convenient public transport to outlying festival sites. Most of the Miami sites were widely separated, and even between those that were not, one was advised not to walk.

HALL OF SONG

July 5, 1982

MENDELSSOHN'S D-MAJOR Te Deum, written in 1826, when the composer was seventeen, is not an early work: thirteen symphonies, several operas, the *Midsummer Night's Dream* Overture, and much else had preceded it. It is a large-scale setting in twelve movements—the last a reprise of the first—for double choir, double solo quartet, and continuo. The continuo bass line is often independent of the voices. Mendelssohn composed it for the Berlin Singakademie, which he and his sister Fanny had joined in 1820; it was published only in 1977; and it had its American première last month in Merkin Hall, given by the Pro Arte Chorale, conducted by Roger Nierenberg. The program note went too far in describing the Te Deum as "an intricate filigree of sound that seems to vanish into some other dimension of being the moment it is sung—like the alleluias of an angel." It is, rather, an effortlessly assured, substantial, and well-sustained essay in the Handelian manner, neither flighty nor ethereal. The themes, like those of Handel's "Utrecht" and "Dettingen" Te Deums, are conventional. The part writing in the fugal sections is exemplary. Some smooth, sweet chromaticisms—in, for example, the "Te ergo quaesumus," for solo quartet—make the identity of the composer apparent. The "Dignare, Domine," which looks to Bach rather than Handel, is a remarkable movement: the four male soloists and the continuo weave a sombre five-part texture; the other soloists steal in with a four-note motif on "miserere," spanning a ninth; the two choruses take it up voice by voice; and at the climax the first sopranos expand the motif to span a thirteenth. The Pro Arte was in good form—firm and rhythmical, bright and full but not forced in the big D-major cries of praise. In the principal solo quartet, the tenor, Mark Bleeke, was outstanding; the soprano, Diane Durand, etched her line with a rather bitter tone not unattractive in itself but too unusual to blend easily. The other quartet was drawn from the choral ranks. The concert began with motets by Alessandro Scarlatti, Giacomo Antonio Perti, and Monteverdi, followed by an attractive group of Elgar choral songs.

Jane Bryden's Merkin Hall recital, the previous day, had been a mixed affair. She sang in five languages, and pronounced them all clearly, but was eloquent only in the Spanish of Luigi Dallapiccola's *Four Machado Songs* and in the English of Andrew Imbrie's *Roethke Songs* (which had their New York première). In an introductory Dowland group, accompanied on the lute by Stanley Charkey, her tone was pallid and her rhythms were too strict. The words did not come to life. Cantatas by Rameau *(L'Impatience)* and Handel ("Nel dolce dell'obblio"), accompanied by harpsichord and gamba, with a Baroque flute in the Handel, were similarly constrained. Then, in the Imbrie cycle, Miss Bryden suddenly broke free. High notes that she had hitherto sounded warily now poured out exuberantly. Her combination of chaste timbre and passionate expressiveness was well matched to the work. The vocal lines seemed more singable, more natural, less angular than they had at the work's première, in San Francisco last year. This is a strong, refined, and moving composition. Miss Bryden brought the same qualities to the glowing Machado cycle. A final Hugo Wolf group had moments of true animation, but some passages sounded merely studied. Miss Bryden's platform demeanor was awkward, almost gawky; her musical style lacked something of ease, grace, and confidence. Perhaps Peter Sellars, who directed her fine-drawn, communicative Angelica in Handel's *Orlando,* for the American Repertory Theatre, in Cambridge, should work with her on song presentation. The voice is not big, but, after a nervous start, it ran sweet and true. Her musicianship is keen. At this recital, she hardly seemed to be making the most of her considerable gifts. The alert pianist in the Imbrie, Dallapiccola, and Wolf songs was Robert Merfeld.

EAGLE AND NIGHTINGALE

July 12, 1982

IN THE vast, resonant spaces of the Cathedral of St. John the Divine, Berlioz's Requiem has an apt setting, and the performance given there in May, in the Cathedral's Music for a Great Space series, was stirring and noble. The composer suggested forces of something over four hundred, divided equally between singers and players. Richard Westenburg, who conducted the Cathedral performance, had about half that number, but his professional choristers made a brave, brilliant sound, and distinguished players appeared in his orchestra. It is not just the loud passages—the thunder of massed kettledrums, the four brass bands, the chorus in full cry—that flourish in space. The grave two-part and one-part writing of the "Quid sum miser," the unaccompanied string melodies that open the Offertorium and the Sanctus, the lines of the solo flute (John Wion) and the solo tenor (Vinson Cole, sweet, full, and fervent) and the dusky glow of the divided violas in the Sanctus, the soft drum chords in the Agnus Dei—these, too, were awesome and beautiful as they stole out into the huge building and set it gently sounding. The far-flung harmonies of the Hostias—three high flutes floating over a low trombone pedal—which can seem merely peculiar in a concert hall, became wondrous. In his *Memoirs*, Berlioz writes of "the scale of the movements, the breadth of style, and the formidably slow and deliberate pace of certain progressions, whose final goal cannot be guessed," which give to his "architectural" compositions—the Te Deum, the Requiem, the Funeral and Triumphal Symphony, and the cantata *L'Impériale*—their "gigantic" character and "colossal" aspect. Mr. Westenburg's reading of the Requiem was broad, majestic, energetic, and ardent—paced with a fine command of the music's architecture, and carefully balanced and "placed" within the church's actual architecture. It was a performance responsive to what Berlioz in his writings and in his music asked for.

Admission was free. A very large audience, estimated at four thousand, attended. The event drew people together in an inspiring musical celebration. The performance was dedicated to the late René Dubos, scientist and humanist, whose last essay was printed in the program book:

> Unclear values allow us to accept the possibility of nuclear war for reasons of national prestige when every sensible person knows that the inevitable result of nuclear warfare would be not only immeasurable damage to every living and inanimate thing on earth but also the virtual collapse of Western civilization.

The Requiem formed a prelude to the Cathedral's Peace Sabbath Weekend—held in conjunction with the United Nations Special Session on Disarmament—when people of many faiths gathered ecumenically in the church to pray for peace. The film *Hiroshima Nagasaki 1945,* made shortly after the bombs were dropped on those cities, and chronicling a *dies irae* of man's making, was shown daily.

Berlioz was a good critic. As the predominant features of his own music he discerned "passionate expression, inward intensity, rhythmic impetus, and a quality of unexpectedness"—adding a rider that it might well be gentle, tender feeling or profound calm (as in the Sanctus of the Requiem) that was being passionately expressed. His public music is grand and elevating; his autobiographical music is vivid. As the climax of a Smith College international conference on Music in Paris in the Eighteen-Thirties, Berlioz's autobiographical diptych, the Symphonie Fantastique followed by *Lélio, or the Return to Life,* was played by the Springfield Symphony, conducted by Robert Gutter, in the handsome neoclassical Symphony Hall of Springfield, Massachusetts. The symphony and the monodrama were first played together, in Paris, on December 9, 1832. That concert brought Berlioz renown. The critic of *La France Littéraire* wrote, "Before Sunday's concert, M. Berlioz was nothing but an eminent composer; today he is our musical glory." And in the audience there sat an Irish actress, Harriet Smithson, who suddenly realized that she was the beloved being apostrophized by the actor playing Lélio. In Berlioz's words:

> "God!" she thought: "Juliet—Ophelia! Am I dreaming? I can no longer doubt. It is of me he speaks. He loves me still." From that moment, so she has often told me, she felt the room reel about her.

Ten months later, she became Berlioz's wife.

There are commentators who urge us to approach Berlioz's compositions as "pure music"—to forget, for example, the picturesque, dramatic program of the Symphonie Fantastique as we listen, and to hear the piece simply as structured sounds. That approach diminishes appreciation of it, I think. The commentators' point is taken once the listener admits that the symphony doesn't *need* a program. As "pure music" it is potent. But when it becomes simultaneously a magnificent musical structure and an enthralling autobiographical chapter the listener's delight is surely keener still. Berlioz's *Memoirs* is perhaps the most arresting autobiography ever written. (What are the runners-up? Wagner's? Benvenuto Cellini's?) The Symphonie Fantastique—memoirs turned into sound—may not need bolstering by written words, but *Lélio* does. Its unity is personal, not formal. An assemblage of earlier pieces, it is often dismissed as a gallimaufry. In Jacques Barzun's Berlioz biography, a defensive index entry refers to Berlioz's "SANITY (even while composing *Lélio*)." But anyone who knows the *Memoirs* must find *Lélio* a thrilling attempt to relate the varied forces that played upon a susceptible and capacious mind: Goethe, Shakespeare, Italy, and the attractions of three very different women (Estelle Duboeuf, Harriet Smithson, and Camille Moke). Anyone who tries to "make sense" of life's puzzles, posed by the past and by the present, must respond to *Lélio*.

In Paris, the Fantastique-plus-*Lélio* bill had a concert performance. In Weimar, in 1855, it was given the "dramatic" performance suggested by the instructions of the *Lélio* score—the chorus and orchestra concealed behind a curtain until the last number, the *Tempest* fantasy. In Springfield, there was a "semi-dramatic" performance. The chorus and orchestra were behind a gauze curtain; but since they were brightly lit when performing, while the auditorium—in the modern American way—was plunged into darkness, the gauze might as well not have been there. The *Lélio* soloists—actor, tenor, and (a small part) baritone—were conventionally rather than carefully chosen. (Eve Queler's 1975 *Lélio* cast in Carnegie Hall was more impressive.) A modern, instead of a nineteenth-century, seating plan unbalanced the orchestral timbre. But Mr. Gutter is an excellent Berliozian. The Springfield Symphony—drawn from the Springfield region, Boston, and New York—is an accomplished orchestra. And so the evening *valait la visite*. It was enriched by a revival of the final passage—all that survives—of Berlioz's 1830 Prix de Rome cantata, *Sardanapale:* a colorful piece, its best melody familiar from its reappearance in *Roméo et Juliette*.

HEART OF GRACE

July 19, 1982

AT SAN DIEGO'S Verdi Festival this summer—the fifth in a series that aims to present all Verdi's operas—the unfamiliar work was *Il corsaro*, and the familiar *Un ballo in maschera*. *Il corsaro*, Verdi's second Byron opera, is (as I noted after its American première, last December in Stony Brook [see page 189] among the most audacious and arresting of his early works. Conceived before *Macbeth* and *I masnadieri*, it was completed after them and after the adventure of composing the grand opera *Jérusalem* for the Paris Opera. The plot, related in that earlier review, is slender but not uneventful. It contains a touch of *Tosca*, and a touch of *Tristan*. There are two type figures of Romanticism, both vividly drawn. One is Conrad the Corsair, a Byronic hero, kin to Karl in Schiller's *Die Räuber* (which furnished the matter of *I masnadieri*) and to Jaromir in Grillparzer's *Die Ahnfrau* (which Verdi often thought of using for an opera), "lone, wild, and strange," a hero whose "heart was form'd for softness—warp'd to wrong." The other is Medora, the gentle, tender maiden who loves him. And then there is one unusual figure, Gulnare, the slave girl who steels herself to commit murder—forced into one of the unusual, extreme plights that regularly stirred Verdi's imagination. The fourth principal, Seyd, is a conventional vigorous baritone. Most of Verdi's chosen subject matter contains autobiographical elements. Julian Budden has attractively suggested that there may be features in Medora of Verdi's first wife, the pure, gentle Margherita, and features in Gulnare of the active, experienced, adoring woman, Giuseppina Strepponi, with whom Verdi had begun to live.

Gulnare was first played by Marianna Barbieri-Nini, Verdi's Lady Macbeth. The long, detailed letter he wrote to her (published in 1906 but unnoticed by Verdi scholarship until Marcello Conati republished it in 1980) about the interpretation of Gulnare's four numbers—a cavatina, two duets, and the trio—should be enough to dispel the old, oft repeated view that *Il corsaro* was undertaken as a piece of hackwork, composed without much care in order to fulfill an irksome contract with a publisher, Lucca, whom Verdi disliked. In any case, that view could not survive the Long Island performance or the San Diego production (the first American staging). We should be hearing more of *Il corsaro*. While hardly a "chamber" opera, it would suit a company that cannot muster the large forces, the spectacle, and the rehearsal time that such a piece as *I lombardi* calls for. *Il corsaro* is terse. The music, uncut, lasts little more than ninety minutes on the Philips recording. (Verdi recommended that the piece should be done with only one intermission, after the second of its three acts.) The libretto is not a well-made play. Much is abrupt, much is left unexplained. It has an existentialist quality. It is a defiantly unconventional drama of characters in action. Old-style opera is pared. *Macbeth* has taught Verdi to write psychologically penetrating music (especially in the two duets of Act III). His imagination takes wing, and his technique is sure. Some old-style numbers—jaunty cabalettas, traditionally picturesque choruses—remain. *Il corsaro* is not as grandly pondered or sustained an achievement as *Macbeth*. But the almost arrogant juxtaposition of new and old makes a heady mixture, and the flow of invention never falters. The laconic note with which the composer ceded all rights in the piece to Lucca has a take-it-or-leave-it quality—rather as if he were saying, "You insisted on wringing an opera from me. Here's something odder than you bargained for; make of it what you will."

In San Diego, Medora was sung by Rosalind Plowright, a Donna Anna and Aida, and Gulnare by June Anderson, a Lucia—reversed casting on the face of it, but it worked. Miss Plowright, in her American stage début, added to a fast-growing reputation. To a world short of Verdi sopranos she is a shining addition. The voice is lustrous, darkly mezzo in timbre but fully soprano in compass, passionate in its emotional colors. The exotic arabesques of Medora's romanza, "Non so le tetre immagini," were delicately traced. Miss Plowright is tall, beautiful onstage, theatrical in appearance (Byron's Medora is blue-eyed and fair-haired; Miss Plowright's was rich-hued, with dense jetty ringlets), and a moving actress. Miss Anderson sang Gulnare with her wonted steadiness, accuracy, and brilliance. Like most of Verdi's early heroines, from Abigail onward, Gulnare must command both coloratura and *canto d'azione*—a declamatory manner of sudden, violent contrasts and wide leaps. Miss Anderson does, but there were moments when, in the large San Diego house, she sacrificed purity of tone to power. The Conrad was Alfonso Navarrete, a useful Mexican tenor, neither remarkable nor displeasing. Patrick Raftery, the Seyd, pushed his fine young baritone too hard, trying to achieve by volume and bluster what could more effectively have been won by energy and accuracy of accent.

Edoardo Müller was a secure, stylish conductor. Miss Anderson began her aria lying prone—something I bet Barbieri-Nini was not asked to do—but otherwise Tito Capobianco's staging was precise, direct, theatrical, and unfussy. It was well matched to the work. So were Bill Gorgensen's simple, striking décor and lighting.

Ballo is the most shapely of Verdi's operas, and (like *Il corsaro*) one of the few for which there is no alternative or extra music. All a conductor and a director must decide is whether to set it in the eighteenth-century Stockholm of the original story, the seventeenth-century Stettin of the version Verdi composed, the seventeenth-century Boston used at the first performance and in the published score, or some other time and place. San Diego settled for "a northern European kingdom" in 1792 (the date of Gustavus III's assassination), but its king was addressed as "Conte" by the inhabitants of "a virgin country" and died bidding farewell to "beloved America"; the fortune-teller Ulrica, though got up as a chalk-white Miss Havisham, was described as being "of unclean Negro blood." Textually, we were in Massachusetts; visually, at some unspecified eighteenth-century court. (Zack Brown's décor was handsome but—it was borrowed from Washington—looked somewhat travel-worn.) The detail of Michael Rennison's staging was in those respects careless and in other respects ineffectively overelaborated. No great harm was done by the mute introduction of the painter Roslin and the sculptor Sergel, who figure in Scribe's *Gustave III* (the libretto from which that of *Ballo* is drawn) and again in the first drafts for *Ballo*. On the other hand, the artists serve no purpose except in a historical, Gustavian presentation. Verdi deliberately cut the clutter, pageantry, and local detail of the Scribe original. His *Ballo* moves swiftly without a superfluous incident or personage. Harm *was* done by reintroducing Scribe's Dancing Master and setting him to teach the King the steps of a hornpipe—enthusiastically taken up by some of his courtiers—in the stretta of the first scene. The first-act curtain was dominated by a minor character, the Lord Chief Justice, as he joined the conspirators' party. The final curtain was dominated by Miss Ulrica-Havisham, tottering Norn-like into the ball to be present at the fulfillment of her prophecy. Otherwise, it was not a wholly perverse production: it was not presented as Oscar's Dream; it was not set in Dallas. But the action was embroidered with fiddly bits of business— jejune little glosses and explications unneeded by anyone who knew the opera, confusing to anyone who did not, and, in sum, revealing too little faith in Verdi's precisely calculated dramaturgy. What the show lacked on the directorial side was a forceful, fiery presentation of the principal themes: the responsibilities of a ruler, the tensions of trust and betrayal, the inevitability of unmasking after an attempted masquerade—a dramatic metaphor used in every act, not just in the final scene.

Nevertheless, *Ballo* proved gripping. It always does. The strengths of this performance were Michelangelo Veltri's well-judged conducting and, above all, Josephine Barstow's Amelia. How should one describe Miss Barstow? Perhaps as a Pauline Viardot of our day? A champion of the contemporary repertory—Tippett's Denise and Gayle, Prokofiev's Natasha, Penderecki's Jeanne, Henze's Autonoe—such as composers dream of finding. An interpreter of the old repertory—Leonore, Salome, Aida, Violetta, Lady Macbeth, and now Amelia—who as if by instinct finds her way to the precise sense that a composer intended. Of soprano roles—Monteverdi's Poppea, both Purcell's and Berlioz's Dido, Gluck's Alceste, Bellini's Norma, Janáček's Jenůfa, Kát'a, and Emilia Marty, even (in a small theatre) Isolde and Brünnhilde—there is scarcely one that I would not gladly go to hear Miss Barstow sing. Does this sound excessive? She is no Flagstad, Welitch, Tebaldi, Los Angeles, Freni, Caballé—a short-list of the sopranos who have consistently made the most beautiful sounds I have thrilled to in a theatre. Miss Barstow cannot set a Verdi arch soaring out into a large house in glorious sound as Milanov could. The voice is limited, even constricted. It does not flower into full-throated, effortless radiance. I would not describe it as "beautiful." But the artistry is intense and beautiful, and it seems limitless. One does not censure Alfred Brendel's performances for lacking the pianistic allure that informs those of Horowitz, or Horowitz's for lacking the intellectual depth of Brendel's. The rewards are different. A listener responds to special, wonderful things that an individual performer offers, and to feeling that stirs his feelings. I have no quarrel with those who protest that Miss Barstow does not have "a true Verdi voice." I can only report that her timing, her weighting, her phrasing, her coloring of the music brought Amelia to life as I have never heard before. That she is a superlative actress, expressive in every glance, pose, gesture, and slow or sudden move, is not in question.

San Diego's Verdi Festival matters both for its repertory and for its introduction of artists (Miss Plowright, Mr. Müller) and performances (Miss Barstow's Amelia) new here. Adriaan van Limpt, the Riccardo of *Ballo,* is a Dutch tenor who has been winning good reviews in such Verdi roles as Ernani (for the Welsh National) and Zamoro, in *Alzira* (in Holland). I wanted to hear him and enjoyed hearing him. His sound was sterling—bright, clean, ringing, perfectly steady, and effortless through all the range. He was a cut above much Met second-cast casting. His interpretation was well schooled but somewhat stodgy, lacking in individuality. His Italian was clipped and faulty. But he made exciting, "authentic" sounds. The Renato, Cornelis Opthof, was violent—ever ready to force his voice into a barked declamato that missed the notes and spoiled the phrases. Ulricas—powerful, steady dramatic contraltos—do not seem to exist anymore (perhaps Jessye Norman, who has the necessary range, power, and steadiness, will take up the role), so one can hardly blame Mr. Capobianco, who directs the company and the festival, for not having found one. Oscar, dressed as the Blue Boy (authentically, it seems, for we are told that Gustavus modelled his pages' liveries on Gainsborough's picture), was Janice Hall. She was bright, true, not quite sparky enough in musical manner, and content to stick to the written notes instead of—as Verdi surely intended—enlivening them with trills, cadenzas, and sudden surprises. Two good basses, John Seabury and Kenneth Cox, made a formidable pair of conspirators, Sam and Tom. (The Ermanno and Manuel of the Stettin version gained those avuncular names when the setting was moved to America.) Carlos Chausson was a spry Silvano.

CHALLENGE

July 26, 1982

ROUGHLY SPEAKING, there are two ways of approaching Handel's operas. They might be called the historical and the dramatic. The first was favored by Charles Burney, who in his *History* treated the operas as strings of individual airs—one tune after another, assigned to singers, not to characters—and was practiced by Mario Bernardi and Frank Corsaro as conductor and director of a *Rinaldo* staged this summer at the Ottawa Festival. The dramatic approach has been championed notably by Winton Dean, whose *Handel and the Opera Seria* provides recurrent texts for any writing and thinking on the subject, and by Peter Sellars in the celebrated production of *Orlando* that ran for forty performances in Cambridge last year and this. It starts in the conviction that Handel, as Dean puts it, "was not only a great composer; he was a dramatic genius of the first order," and that "the music of no other dramatic composer comes closer to Mozart in its detached but penetrating insight into human nature, its capacity to make a profound statement in a frivolous or comic situation, and its peculiar mixture of irony and pathos, solemnity and grace, tragedy and serenity." Alan Kitching, who staged fifteen Handel operas in that belief, between 1959 and 1975, mostly in the little Unicorn Theatre, in Abingdon, England, has chronicled the adventure in *Handel at the Unicorn*, wherein he formulates a "credo by negatives" that begins "The operas are *not* all alike" and mounts, clause by clause, to "the plots...are *not* any more absurd than Shakespeare's."

When Burney defended the Italian opera against the taunts of Addison and Steele, it was as music with trimmings:

Let it be remembered by the lovers of Music, that opera is the *completest concert* to which they can go; with this advantage over those in still life, that to the most perfect singing, and effects of a powerful and well-disciplined band, are frequently added excellent acting, splendid scenes and decorations, with such dancing as a playhouse, from its inferior prices, is seldom able to furnish.

It can hardly be denied that most men of Handel's day viewed opera thus, giving their first attention to the singers and the spectacle. So Mr. Bernardi and Mr. Corsaro can claim period authenticity for their un-dramatic treatment of *Rinaldo*. In Ottawa, excellent acting was in short supply, but there were some accomplished singers, a powerful and well-disciplined band, scenes and decorations of uncommon splendor, and such dancing as a playhouse is seldom able to furnish. More: on scholarly grounds the pair can claim Handelian precedent for chop-ping up and rearranging the score and for throwing in numbers from other operas. Handel himself did so through a series of *Rinaldo* re-vivals, until twenty years after the première he put on a version that Dean calls "a monumental example of the artistic vandalism Handel often practiced on his own works after the ardour of composition had cooled." The Ottawa vandals simply took things a stage further.

Still more can be conceded: that *Rinaldo*, Handel's first opera for London, is not one of his strongest or most consistent dramas. Its scenarist and producer, Aaron Hill, had "resolv'd to frame some Dramma, that, by different Incidents and Passions, might afford the Musick Scope to vary and display its Excellence, and fill the Eye with more delightful Prospects, so at once to give two Senses equal Plea-sure." He subordinated character and plot to spectacle. Armida makes her entrance "in the Air, in a Chariot drawn by two huge Dragons, out of whose Mouths issue Fire and Smoke." Act III has three battle scenes, the first waged on a magic mountain "horridly steep, and rising from the Front of the Stage, to the utmost Height of the most back-ward Part of the Theatre; Rocks, and Caves, and Waterfalls, are seen upon the Ascent, and on the Top appear the blazing Battlements of the Enchanted Palace, guarded by a great Number of Spirits." Except in the grove scene of Act I, where a flageolet and two recorders warble deliciously in accompaniment to Almirena's "Augelletti," the scene painting was scarcely reflected in Handel's music. *Rinaldo* was com-posed—and in large measure compiled from hit numbers in earlier compositions—chiefly to display the versatility and prowess of the composer and his cast and the scenic resources of the theatre. That is accepted opinion. I try to think it true. But the more I contemplate the original, 1711 score of *Rinaldo* the more I find that Handel, if less consistently than later, already practiced his rare dramatic virtues. *Ri-naldo is* shapely. Its scenes are coherent. It has a plot. Crusader and pagan forces are ranged. Personal intrigues (as in Tasso) then distract the captains from their great enterprise: the liberation—or, in the other camp, the defense—of Jerusalem. The characters live and grow, moving through trials and adventures toward the last battle, when the

Holy City is won, and Armida (as in Tasso, but here with unhappy abruptness) becomes a Christian.

I wait to see a production of *Rinaldo* conceived on those lines. Perhaps the Metropolitan Opera will present it when, in January 1984, the Ottawa *Rinaldo* comes to New York, as a gift from the Canadian people to mark the Met's hundredth anniversary. *[Vain hope! The production came to New York essentially unaltered.]* Physically, it is a handsome gift indeed. America has already seen one beautiful, spectacular staging of *Rinaldo*—Houston's, in 1975. Ottawa's, designed by Mark Negin, a stage artist well known in Canada and in Britain, is more beautiful and more spectacular still. The costumes—cut, sewn, embroidered, painted, and plumed by the Toronto firm of Malabar—are eighteenth-century extravagances brought luxuriously to life. The sets combine old techniques of sliding wings and aerial entrances with modern trucking, and (except once in Act III) fulfill the Handelian requirement that a front curtain should not fall between scenes.

From spectacle, rather than from the score, the plot, or the singers, Mr. Corsaro took his cue. His principals were a corps of dancers and tumblers. During the overture, they practiced sword drill. Then two of them changed into hippogryph costumes to draw in Argantes' chariot, and Samuel Ramey, the Argantes, sang his "Sibillar gli angui d'Aletto" to accompany their preening and prancing. (He had a formidable whip in his hand; it was good-natured of him not to use it to whip the steeds into stillness, so that the audience could pay attention to *him.*) Then all donned gryphon garb, to reel, writhe, and faint in coils around the singers of the subsequent airs. (Handel's score was choreographed by Eugene Collins.) They changed back into decorative military gear for the final battle: eight golden, near-naked Christian warriors engaged with eight blue-clad Paynims while Marilyn Horne, the Rinaldo, stood aloft on one side to sing "Or la tromba" as an accompaniment to their exuberant display of leaps and somersaults. Perhaps modern operagoers do care more about the show than about the score, the plot, and the singers: the Ottawa spectators did not hesitate to clap their hands together and drown the music when anything delighted their eyes. It was fun, but it was not enough: not for anyone who expects more of opera than "the completest concert"; who believes that Handel was a dramatist; who discerns a touch of *Così fan tutte* in Armida's feelings for Rinaldo and Argantes' for Almirena, and a touch of *Fidelio* in Rinaldo's heroic constancy; who thinks that *Rinaldo,* precisely because of its slightly shaky dramatic structure, calls for even more sensitive dramatic direction than the later operas do.

The edition used was that prepared by Martin Katz for Miss Horne and Houston, improved in Ottawa by the restoration in Act II of an original Argantes air in place of the *Lotario* alto air that Handel dropped in one season when Francesca Bertolli sang Argantes. The original *Rinaldo,* published by Chrysander, contains thirty-one airs and three duets. In Ottawa, fourteen airs were done complete, and one was done nearly complete. Three more were represented by first sections only. Both sections of Armida's "Ah! crudel!" were heard, but not consecutively and without da capo. An air from *Partenope* was added for the hero (replacing Rinaldo's celebrated "Il Tricerbero humiliato"). Two of the duets were complete, the third was abridged, and a fourth duet, from *Admeto,* was added. The oddest feature of this edition was the dismemberment (even if in 1731 Handel set some precedent for it) of the scene generally deemed the finest of all, which closes Act II. If I go into this in some detail, it is to show that Handel knew what he was about and wrote long dramatic sequences, not a haphazard collection of numbers that can be shuffled at will. Armida, her amorous siege of Rinaldo repulsed in a resolute duet and G-major air, breaks into a passionate accompanied G-minor recitative. She meant to bewitch him and then scorn him; instead, she has fallen victim to his beauty. She mourns the impotence of her charms, meditates fearful revenge, breaks off with a cry of "Ah! no, he is too fair," and sings the slow, lovely G-minor "Ah! crudel!," which is wound through with oboe and bassoon obbligati and cradled in six-part strings. Its central section is a presto in violent contrast. Armida then assumes Almirena's form, so that if Rinaldo returns he will embrace her. Her plan misfires. Argantes enters, and Armida is further humiliated: she discovers that he—the king who owes everything to her mighty aid—also loves Almirena. She closes the act with a brilliant G-major air, "Vo' far guerra," swearing vengeance on those who wrong her. (Handel used to adorn it with improvised harpsichord episodes, some of which were subsequently published.) The great sequence (shorn of a "Vo' far guerra" da capo) can be heard on the CBS recording of *Rinaldo,* with Jeanette Scovotti as Armida. In Ottawa, Armida's "Ah! crudel!," as mentioned, was broken into two, and its bits were dropped into Act III. "Vo' far guerra," the finale, did not end the act, which continued with the Rinaldo-Armida duet and then with Rinaldo's "Cara sposa." Now, "Cara sposa," which Rinaldo should sing in Act I, when Armida and her horrible monsters have carried off his bride, is a beautiful air. Handel himself thought it one of his two finest (the other being "Ombra cara," in *Radamisto*). But it is not a finale. It is the E-minor centerpiece of another tonally coherent, dramatically dynamic sequence: one that begins with Almirena's "Augelletti," continues with a love duet for Almirena and Rinaldo, and—when Armida has struck, and bliss has changed to lament ("Cara sposa") and then to resolve—ends with Rinaldo's whirlwind "Venti, turbini," the first-act finale. (The outer airs of the sequence are both in G, but Miss Horne, adopting a transposition Handel made in 1731 for Senesino, sang "Venti" in F.)

The campaign for Handel, Dean wrote, "will not be finally won ... until our professional opera houses at last get down to tackling his operas in productions that do justice to their large-scale design, involving music, drama, scenic spectacle, and sometimes ballet in a comprehensive unity." I have not seen Britain's latest fully professional productions: the English National's *Giulio Cesare,* the Welsh National's *Rodelinda* (soon to be followed by a *Tamerlano*), Kent Opera's *Agrippina,* all of which play in repertory. Ottawa's *Rinaldo,* like Houston's, had plenty of scenic spectacle. Like Houston's, and like the City Opera's *Giulio Cesare,* it wrecked the large-scale design. Music and such drama as there was formed no part of a comprehensive unity.

The role of Rinaldo was composed for Nicolini, whom Addison, no friend to castrati, called "the greatest Performer in dramatic Music that is now living, or that perhaps ever appeared on a Stage." Steele, otherwise an enemy to opera in Italian, found Nicolini intelligible, since "every Limb, and every Finger, contributes to the Part he acts, insomuch that a deaf Man might go along with him in the Sense of it." I doubt whether a deaf man could have gone along with the sense while watching Miss Horne's impersonation, for in breeches roles, at least, she seems to have renounced any aspiration to act. Her Met Rosina last season had character, but Rinaldo was a beplumed, self-propelled sound-making machine. Miss Horne strode onto the stage, planted herself firmly, and uttered. The sounds were remarkable for their fleetness, their accuracy, and their power. The dark, admirably steady, sometimes almost ventriloquial timbre was fascinating, but on occasion a Billingsgate quality got into it. Singers of the eighteenth and nineteenth centuries were commonly appraised as much for their acting as for their vocal prowess. Must we of the twentieth century be less exigent?

The Almirena was Benita Valente. Her singing was sweet-toned and attractive, if not quite pure or true enough. Her musicianship was faulty. The da capo of "Bel piacere" (a pretty Act III piece, light relief before the rigors of the final battle, but here displaced to serve as Almirena's entrance air) was not so much decorated as recomposed; the unison line became a two-part invention. In the da capo of "Lascia ch'io pianga," Miss Valente produced not an adorned version of the lovely melody but a dull descant to it. "Augelletti" was prettily sung, but Mr. Corsaro drained the charm and destroyed the drama of the scene by bringing three costumed recorder players onstage and turning Almirena's rapt soliloquy into a cute little concert number. As in Houston, Noelle Rogers was Armida, and Mr. Ramey Argantes. John Alexander was Godfrey. (The role, composed for a woman, is better taken by one.) A blunt assertion that the cast had little idea of Handel style must be qualified by the observation that it was evidently doing, with efficiency and accomplishment, what the director, the conductor, and the editor had set it to do. Recitatives were sluggish, sung "oratorio-style," in full voice, with protracted vocal cadences and espressivo delays. The instrumental cadences hung fire in the now discredited manner. An amplified harpsichord worked overtime to fill the holes between phrases with arpeggio rolls. The orchestral playing, on modern instruments in a deep modern pit, lacked clarity of texture, sharpness of articulation, and liveliness of line.

There is, fortunately, plenty of time before the show comes to New York for all concerned to think harder about *Rinaldo* and treat it rather more seriously. Time to prepare a more faithful and more effective edition, closer to the 1711 drama: an edition that—even if modifications are introduced to show off individual singers—preserves the dynamic movement of the original and sets the great airs in their dramatic contexts. Time to study a more convincing, less Victorian manner of Handel performance in such recordings as Sigiswald Kuijken's of *Partenope* (Harmonia Mundi), Jean-Claude Malgoire's of *Rinaldo* and *Serse* (CBS), Alan Curtis's of *Admeto* (EMI). Time for the Met orchestra to consider Baroque orchestral practice and discover a compromise by which something of its spirit and style can survive performance on modern instruments. The Ottawa artists seemed to have blundered like strangers into Handel's realm of enchantment, emotion, and pageantry. They responded with enthusiasm and with their own skills to the marvels they found there, and what they did, despite the misunderstandings and the mishandlings, was enjoyable. The public thrilled to it. The 1966 City Opera public thrilled to *Giulio Cesare*. Handel's operas are strong enough to take a battering and come to port in triumph. But for how long will our big companies leave unlearned lessons that decades of dedicated Handelians have taught? Was the Cambridge *Orlando* staged in vain?

Ottawa is an attractive summer city. The halls, terraces, restaurant, and café of the National Arts Centre, beside the sunny Rideau Canal, make a good festival place. This year, Szymanowski's centenary was celebrated in recitals and concerts. The other operas staged were *Die Entführung* and *Lucia*. The Mozart was pleasingly done by a young cast. Mr. Bernardi, conducting, and David Alden, directing, approached the masterpiece with confidence in the composer. It was given almost uncut (a few bars fell from the Act III duet) and in the right order. More dialogue than usual was retained, and in clear German it was tellingly spoken. The richness, the freshness, the seriousness, and the humor were done justice to in a poised, intelligent, and loving presentation. (Blonde's "Durch Zärtlichkeit" became an "ironing" aria, but that was the only lapse into stock business.) On the first night, Erie Mills, the Blonde, and Michael Myers, the Belmonte, pushed their characterizations a shade too insistently, but both gave promise of relaxing into elegant, stylish performances. Costanza Cuccaro's soprano flowed freely, accurately, and purely through the intricacies of Konstanze's music. Some of her rhythms needed firming. Her demeanor, hampered, perhaps, by a hot-looking voluminous black velvet dress, was less than aristocratic. But she was affecting. Bernard Fitch, who sang small parts at the City Opera a decade ago, was a delightful, unconventional Pedrillo. He shaped phrases with precision, individuality, and wit, in a tenor small and true. A new bass, Gunter von Kannen, from the Zurich Opera, was a sonorous and lively Osmin. Donald Bell was a grave, dignified, yet formidable Pasha. The Met's ugly scenery, with its absurd sliding doors, had been borrowed, and it sat awkwardly on the Ottawa stage. The performance was dedicated to the memory of Robert Prévost, a distinguished Canadian stage designer, and an obituary note in the program cited a remark of his that bears thought: "If the audience applauds the moment the curtain goes up...then the design is a failure."

AMERICAN VERISMO

August 2, 1982

STEPHEN PAULUS'S second opera—a full-length work commissioned by the Opera Theatre of St. Louis, which three years ago presented his first opera, the one-acter *The Village Singer*—is *The Postman Always Rings Twice*, with a libretto by Colin Graham after the James M. Cain novel. Cain (who was managing editor for a while of *The New Yorker*) is a writer difficult to assess. *Postman* (1934), his first book, is a classical tragedy played out in Glendale, near Los Angeles. The characters are Nick Papadakis, owner of "a roadside sandwich joint, like a million others in California"; his wife, Cora, born in Iowa, an ex-waitress; and Frank, a young vagrant. The tale is recounted with the laconicism of a theorem. The prose is lean, careful, and deliberate. Emotions, if not exactly understated, are *plainly* stated (though there are some sudden hyperbolic flights). The setting, the persons, and their passions come to life. There is more to the *Agamemnon* than "WIFE SLAYS RE-TURNING WAR HERO; DEED PLANNED BY HER LOVER." There is more to *Postman* than "WIFE AND LOVER SLAY HUSBAND." For one thing, the plot continues. Wife and lover, chained by mutual vul-nerability, live on in something like hatred until Fate, which let them get away with the murder, "rings" again: Cora is killed in an accident, and Frank, who was driving, is hanged for murdering her. It's very neatly worked out. So is Cain's next novel, *Double Indemnity* (1936), the exposition of a closely related theorem: again the Glendale setting; the murder by wife and lover, and their falling out ("I had killed a man to get a woman...and I never wanted to see her again"); a first-person narrative in the form of a written confession; a car-over-cliff crime; intricacies of insurance practice that are important to the plot. Cain worked his motifs hard. *Mildred Pierce* (1941), another Glendale ro-mance, opens in almost the same "set" as *Double Indemnity* ("crimson velvet drapes, hung on iron spears...a crimson velvet coat of arms"; "red velvet drapes that run on iron spears...red velvet tapestry"). It picks up from *Postman* a neon-sign motif. It amplifies with detailed— and not uninteresting—information Cora's references to the lot of a waitress in a Hollywood hash house. ("Two years in a hash house" is the burden of a song in Paulus's opera.) In a later novel, *The Institute* (1976), two episodes of a young woman's taking an older one by the wrist and forcing her backward to a seat sound a plain echo from *Mildred Pierce*. Those four novels are the extent of my Cain reading. No doubt there are dissertations that deal with recurrent imagery in all eighteen of his books, and perhaps studies on such subjects as the significance of the cat motif in *Postman*. A gray cat, a stray, aborts the first murder attempt; the gift of a gray puma kitten accompanies the final crisis; Frank calls Cora a hellcat; his defense lawyer is named Katz, and his prosecutor is named—a sort of sonic anagram—Sackett. And what that amounts to beyond a literary embellishment I have no idea. Nemesis stalks through Frank's life in various cat forms? There is a literary-exercise aspect to Cain's books. The sex scenes recall those of trashy novels. In Boston, *Postman* was prosecuted for obscenity. But it's not just a violent, sexy thriller. And it's not just—in fact, it's hardly at all—a "mystery," although categorized as one in a paperback reprint. (My local bookshop shelves Cain under "Mystery," not "Literature.") It's a bold attempt to make elements of cheap sexy romance, popular murder mystery, and tough-guy fiction serve a more elegant and ambitious purpose. By *Times* critics, his stories have been hailed as "the stuff of American mythology," and *Postman* and *Double Indemnity* as "a pair of native American masterpieces." There's something about the exercise at once arresting and disconcerting. The physical and emotional violence, characters everyday and credible yet as monstrous as Clytemnestra, and construction as trimly calculated as that of a crossword make a strange mixture. *Mildred Pierce*, in conventional narrative form and twice as long, is more disconcerting. Long passages stay on a level that Cain, I suppose, aimed to start from and then transcend. The sentence blazoned on the paperback's cover—"No one has ever stopped in the middle of one of Jim Cain's books"—held true, but was I, I wondered, held by a classical tragedy played out in an exotic setting of Californian suburbia or by a housemaid romance with literary trimmings?

Graham—who chose *Postman* as an operatic subject, urged it on Paulus, and directed the first performance, in St. Louis this summer—made it clear in a program note, by his libretto, and then in his production what had attracted him: "the driving passion of the plot and its roots in classical tragedy" and "the fact that page after page (as in so much of Cain's writing) is full of music—whether literally, as in Nick's guitar songs, or figuratively, in the unselfconsciously lyrical outbursts of the two doomed lovers." He likens Cora to Wedekind's Lulu, but not without noting that Cora matures. (Lulu never changes.) St. Louis, I understand, wanted an opera with a contemporary American subject. Cain's *Postman*, half a century old, is not exactly that but close enough. Librettist and composer were faced with what might, after a line in *Butterfly*, be called the "milk-punch or whiskey?" problem: finding apt words and music for contemporary vernacular dialogue in a formalized medium that has more often than not set its subjects in the past. Both Graham and Paulus solved it. The words of the libretto are in large part drawn from those of the book, with little cuts, alterations, and repetitions that rhythmicize them. The amplifications needed for songs, arias, and other set pieces are deftly written. Cain's action is, by someone who knows his *Pelléas*, *Wozzeck*, *Lulu*, and *Peter Grimes* skillfully compressed, and shaped into twenty "numbers" (ten in each of the two acts), three of them instrumental interludes. (The first act lasts about sixty minutes, the second about seventy.) A few loose ends are left: the mute role of First Cop may be meaningless to anyone who has not read the book; Cora and Frank's marriage is omitted, and with it goes the motive that landed Frank with a murder charge. Maybe such things don't matter: opera can jump gaps, and, in any case—some may argue—opera audiences, happy to attend dramas in tongues they don't understand, seldom follow opera plots in detail. Maybe they do matter. Cain's plots are as precise as balance sheets (sometimes he cooks the book with coincidences, but at least everything is thereby accounted for); any item omitted upsets the total. He once declared that "suspense comes from making sure your algebra is right."

Loose ends or not, Graham's libretto is the work of an operatic expert. In his best productions—among them the Santa Fe *Lulu*, the Met *Traviata*, the English National *House of the Dead* and *War and Peace*, the premières of Britten's church parables—he has combined theatricality with a larger spiritual vision and a feeling for the special significance of each individual work. The idea of using *The Postman Always Rings Twice*, he says, "came in a blinding flash." In his operatic working of it, technique and emotion conspire. It has the raw effectiveness of *Cavalleria rusticana* and the mythic, poetic quality of *Lulu*.

Paulus is not a Mascagni or an Alban Berg. An adverb in the program note suggests that he needed persuasion to tackle the subject; Graham says that Cain's "lyrical quality transfigures what could otherwise be a tawdry tale, and it eventually hooked Stephen on the novel as a subject for his opera." The best operas, music history suggests, are made when the composer is suddenly and irresistibly seized by a subject—one that comes to him "in a blinding flash," seems positively to choose him, and, as Verdi once put it, drives him to cry "That's it! That's the one!" and rush to set down notes without delay. *Postman* does not have this inspired quality. *The Village Singer*, I thought, did. But, like its predecessor, the new piece shows that Paulus is an uncommonly gifted opera composer. His vocal lines sing naturally. Vernacular inflections are made lyrical. His stage timing is effortlessly sure. His musical forms are shapely. His orchestra (a fairly small one, with six woodwinds and five brasses) is deftly handled. He brings Act I to an effective climax. The scene is strong in itself: Nick is murdered while carolling exuberant vocalise toward an echoing cliff ("He had a tenor voice, not one of these little tenors like you hear on the radio, but a big tenor, and on the high notes he would put in a sob like on a Caruso record"); suddenly the dead man's voice rings back to his murderers in echo. Paulus's music makes the scene stronger still. Nick's earlier, guitar-accompanied song seems to me miscalculated—too operatically intricate, not catchy enough, insufficiently a sung song within a sung drama. The nonrealistic handling of the lawyers in Act II—in a cabaret duet, and a cabaret aria for Katz—is very effective, and suggests that Paulus might profitably (and Cain-like) have drawn still more freely on a wider range of popular idioms than the neo-verismo manner used for most of the piece. The Cora-Frank duets of Act II, which should carry the emotional burden of the drama, don't really get off the ground. Their music is aspirant but thin. There is too much reliance on ostinato figures and passacaglia basses. But it is intelligently and carefully worked, with a neat recurrence of characterizing themes. All in all, *Postman* is an impressive new opera, an excellent essay in American verismo, that difficult vein which Menotti, Carlisle Floyd, Robert Ward have worked in their different ways. I don't know what Paulus plans next but am eager to hear it, whatever it is. I still wish *The Village Singer* could be made the central panel of an American *Trittico*.

The St. Louis performance, conducted by William Harwood and designed by John Conklin, was first-rate. Although the principals were cast against physical type—the Cora, Kathryn Bouleyn, was not Latin-looking, sultry; the Frank, David Parsons, was not lean and hard—they had the voices and the presence to suggest the sexual passion that makes them, like Isolde and Tristan, oblivious of right and wrong. Miss Bouleyn has become a radiant lirico-dramatic soprano—powerful, beautiful, and accurate of voice and eloquent in her phrasing. Michael Myers's Nick was fine. Carroll Freeman's Katz was brilliantly neat and witty. Mr. Graham's direction was masterly.

St. Louis in its seventh season maintained (on the whole) its high reputation for freshness, adventurous repertory, admirable young casts, and carefully rehearsed productions—all brought together in an atmosphere uncommonly cultivated, artistically serious, and enjoyable. It offers a true summer festival. Besides the première of *Postman*, there was the American première (and world stage deuxième) of Prokofiev's *Maddalena*, done on a double bill with Tomás Bretón's zarzuela *La verbena de la paloma;* a new production of *Così fan tutte;* and an *Elisir d'amore* put on in sets borrowed from Washington. Not everything was good. The zarzuela was wretched. The *Elisir* was by St. Louis standards pedestrian, so-so, except in the pretty singing of Maria Spacagna as Adina. Nemorino's sporting a villainous scruffy beard was a new nastiness.

Maddalena is early Prokofiev. He composed it in 1912 but orchestrated only the start. In 1913, he began but did not complete a revision. He may have tinkered with it again later. In 1934, he left the score behind in Paris when he returned to Russia, and there it remained. A few years ago, Prokofiev's widow brought *Maddalena* to the attention of the conductor Edward Downes. He orchestrated the scenes Prokofiev had not ("some three-quarters of the whole," Downes says), translated it, and brought it to performance for the BBC. In

1979, it was broadcast, first in Russian and then in English. Last year, it was staged in Graz. It was well received. And *Maddalena* may perhaps be a stronger work than the St. Louis production suggested. There a new, smaller orchestration was used. The staging, by Lou Galterio, was tame. The libretto, written by "a young society lady more pleasant in her social behavior than talented in dramaturgy" (thus Prokofiev in his memoirs), is tushery influenced by Wilde's *A Florentine Tragedy*. Stephanie Sundine, a pure, shining young Ariadne at the City Opera last season, seemed miscast as a voluptuous Venetian heroine. James Schwisow, as her husband, looked and sounded handsome but acted woodenly. Given Straussian richness of sound, glamorously uninhibited principals, and more energy and verve than the St. Louis conductor, Bruce Ferden, lent it, *Maddalena* might be effective. On this showing, I thought it only just worth exhumation.

Così directed by Jonathan Miller and conducted by Calvin Simmons, was sung—for the most part—in my translation, and so decorum prevents me from saying much about it. To say nothing would be hard on a remarkably well-balanced young cast: Ashley Putnam and Patricia McCaffrey as the sisters, Jerry Hadley and Thomas Hampson (a new baritone we must hear more of) as their lovers, Ruth Golden as Despina, John Stephens as Alfonso. It was a serious—unjokey but not unwitty—production, and the most emotionally precise I have seen.

A FRAIL BARK

August 16, 1982

REFLECTING ON Melville in *The New Yorker* a few months ago, John Updike called the last novel, *The Confidence-Man*, a "crabbed and inert work," "suffocatingly difficult to read," and one that "has the texture of gnashing teeth." I gritted my teeth and read it, in preparation for George Rochberg's first opera, *The Confidence Man*, which had its première at Santa Fe last month. After a while, the going proved not too hard. Melville's networks of motif, allusion, delayed development, and varied restatement soon fascinate anyone accustomed to tracing such things in Wagner or Berg. The transformation of sources to serve new ends also has operatic analogues. The progress once made by Bunyan's Pilgrim and, in a later age, by Hawthorne on "The Celestial Railroad" evidently suggested Melville's metaphor of an April 1st journey down the Mississippi from St. Louis. In the first scene of his book, a mild, lamblike, mute figure joins the embarking throng, bearing a slate on which he proclaims texts from I Corinthians: "Charity believeth all things," "Charity never faileth." Meanwhile, the boat's barber starts the day by hanging over the door of his shop a sign that reads "No Trust." In various motleys—but settling at last into the role of a cosmopolitan —the Confidence Man converses with one passenger after another.

That he is an incarnation of the Devil, moving among the men on this bright, busy Ship of Fools, is made plain by the imagery that clusters around him. But what he preaches is, in effect, from a famous sermon: "Give to every man that asketh of thee; and of him that taketh away thy goods ask them not again." No wonder the harder-headed passengers scorn his counsel and close their purses; they are tuned to a Benjamin Franklin text, "In the affairs of this world men are saved, not by faith, but by the want of it." In the final scene, the Confidence Man accosts a good, pious, robed old Christian, his snowy head haloed by the glow of a "solar lamp" as he reads the Bible; wins his confidence (with the help of a glittery, smoky imp accomplice, an urchin peddler); replaces the Bible in the believer's hands with a closestool as an infallible life preserver; extinguishes the light; and "kindly" leads him out into the darkness. It is a charged, powerful, and moving scene—black, blasphemous, yet also comic and curiously tender.

Even the closest student of *The Confidence-Man*, Elizabeth Foster, whose 1954 edition of the novel clarifies connections, identifies sources, analyzes allegory and satire, and solves many riddles, remarked that the book "still keeps many, or most, of its secrets." Much critical and analytical study has been made of it; an extended bibliography appears in the Norton Critical Edition. It has long been recognized that the book is more than—as Hershel Parker, the editor of that Norton edition, put it—"merely a picaresque satire on the hazards of Western travel and the peculiarities of American manners and morals." The protagonist has been variously identified: as Uncle Sam, Orpheus, Christ, the Devil. "Emerson is the confidence man," Carl Van Vechten said in 1922, "Emerson who preached being good, not doing good," and Melville's book is "the great transcendental satire." But a contemptuous limning of Emerson has more plausibly been discerned in Mark Winsome, the "mystical master" of Chapters 36 and 37. Winsome's disciple Egbert is presumably Thoreau. Poe makes a fleeting appearance. Fanny Kemble is unkindly parodied in one of the tales told during the journey. *The Confidence-Man* is a work rich and dense; it moves on many levels, some of them deep. It is as carefully and consciously—though not nearly as well—written as *Billy Budd*, or as Thomas Mann's *Death in Venice*, both of which yielded librettos that then needed music for their completion. Those two novellas, like *The Confidence-Man*, are allegorical and allusive, and are composed with recurrent motifs and imagery in ways that musicians respond to. Unlike *The Confidence-Man*, they also have what an opera needs: characters and a plot. *The Confidence-Man* is made of discourse punctuated by description. One was curious to discover what the Rochbergs—the composer's wife, Gene, is the librettist of his opera—could possibly do with it.

What they did was to choose as their main matter one of the tales told during the trip: Chapter 40, "The Story of China Aster." It is told to, not by, the Confidence Man, and is told by Egbert-Thoreau, but in the manner of Emerson (or perhaps Franklin). In fact, it is rather more complicated than that: the Confidence Man and Egbert are, for the purposes of argument, here assuming the roles of Frank and Charlie, bosom friends since childhood—Frank seeking a loan, and rich Charlie refusing to grant it. (To make things yet more complicated, in an earlier chapter the Confidence Man, calling himself Frank Goodman, has sought a loan from another Charlie, whom Winsome-Emerson then denounces to the Confidence Man as a confidence man. This stretch of the book is one of dizzying sudden "modulations.") Well, Egbert-Thoreau-Charlie, after apologies for sliding into the diction of the master who has "tyrannized" over him, tells the story to illustrate why he will not even accept loans, let alone offer them. China Aster, a poor candlemaker, accepted a loan from a rich friend, Orchis, became destitute trying to repay it, and died in misery, having prepared his epitaph: "He was ruined by allowing himself to be persuaded, against his better sense, into the free indulgence of confidence." (Another "level" may be found in the possibility that China Aster, the light-bringer, and Orchis, the successful friend who gives bad counsel, are reflections of Melville himself and Hawthorne, and that the tale parodies Melville's own disastrous literary career.)

It's a slender plot for an opera. The Rochbergs have made the Confidence Man himself its teller (even though it is a tale against confidence), dramatized it, and padded it out with a long prologue and some other episodes drawn (out of context) from the book, and with an irrelevant minstrel show as a divertissement. After China Aster's epitaph has been sung, the entire cast assembles to pronounce an envoy:

> *Trust! Trust!*
> *What trust can you put in men?*
> *Why, what else*
> *But the trust of perfect*
> *CONFIDENCE!*

One assumes at first that it is intended as a wryly ironical moral. But no, the musical setting proves to be perfectly straight, and in program notes the creators say that "the theme of our work" is indeed "faith and trust in mankind," "the idea that trust in each other is essential to life." An odd moral to draw from the tale of China Aster, who trusted and was destroyed by his trust! The opera doesn't make sense. It seems to me an amateurish piece of dramaturgy, intellectually weak and theatrically inept. The complaint is not that the authors have altered Melville. Effective operas—Tchaikovsky's *Eugene Onegin* and *Queen of Spades*, Puccini's *Madama Butterfly* in its familiar, revised version—have been composed to librettos that keep the incidents of an original source but drastically alter the tone. In this opera, the Rochbergs have altered Melville's *The Confidence-Man* without putting anything coherent or effective in its place.

The music is all but worthless. (The orchestration is adept, and the vocal lines sing freely.) Lest that seem too harsh a judgment, let me admit to prejudice: against music that encourages the bourgeois middlebrow who "knows what he likes and likes what he knows" to turn that apologetic disclaimer into a proud assertion. Prejudice, too, against the glib trivialization of a strenuously earnest, aspirant work of art. Rochberg has adopted eclecticism and pastiche as an article of faith. At a Santa Fe symposium on "Historical Issues in Twentieth-Century Music," he declared that modern music had died in 1965, dismissing by implication all that Roger Sessions, Elliott Carter, Milton Babbitt, Peter Maxwell Davies—to name but four, very different modern composers—have achieved since then. When his three "Concord" Quartets—a survey of musical styles from Pachelbel to Schoenberg, now available on an RCA album—appeared, in 1979, I heard them with a sympathetic ear and was not bored: they contained much that I knew and liked. They seemed to ask, and to search for answers to, urgent questions: What do the varied musics of the past mean to a modern listener? And what the varied musics of the present? Is that listener being promiscuous or healthily "pluralistic" when he can respond with enthusiasm to many discrete manners? But the seriousness and urgency have in *The Confidence Man* degenerated into mannerism and routine. Rochberg has settled for easy answers. Plainly, he has a retentive memory, and the music of the opera is largely a reworking of ideas that other, better composers—Walton, Britten, Kurt Weill, Stephen Foster, Mozart, Menotti, Mahler, Sigmund Romberg, Pierre Boulez—have put to more effective and, generally, more responsible use. (Romberg, laced with accompaniment from Walton's *Façade*, appears in an irrelevant waltz drinking song; Boulez's manner of high-soprano writing is crudely caricatured in two apparitions of an Angel of Bright Future.) The result is at once vulgar and boring. Sometimes the music is short-breathed: a nifty little ensemble in the minstrel show which would bear repetition was heard only once; the protagonist's mock-Italian arias in Act II petered out soon after they had started. Sometimes it is garrulous: short motifs are played over and over again —worked to death. The first act lasted about eighty-five minutes, the second about seventy-five, and they seemed interminable. Some cuts had been made before the première. More could easily have been made, anywhere, since nothing seemed necessary.

The Santa Fe execution was admirable. William Harwood, conducting, had the chance to show his mastery of a wide variety of operatic styles, and he did all he could to invest the proceedings with life, color, and continuity. The orchestra played well. The choral sound was excellent. Richard Pearlman's direction and John Scheffler's décor were conventional but lavish and competent. As the protagonist, China Aster, Neil Rosenshein sang in clear, true, telling tones; he is moving into the front line of young American tenors. Brent Ellis gave a strong performance in the title role, which loses importance once the long prologue is done. Among the others were Sunny Joy Langton, as Aster's wife; Deborah Cook, as the Angel; Michael Fiacco, as Orchis; Carolyne James, as Mrs. Orchis; and Joseph Frank, as the Barber. The cast list is long. There were solo opportunities for seventeen young artists in Santa Fe's apprentice program, which has been as abundant a supplier of America's operatic artists as the Glyndebourne Chorus has been of Britain's. Santa Fe, having undertaken *The Confidence Man,* did it proud. Sad that much talent and energy were expended on undeserving material.

At a concert of the Santa Fe Chamber Music Festival, three days before the opera's première, Rochberg's String Quintet was played by the Concord String Quartet and Nathaniel Rosen, cello. Composed last year, it draws some of its material from *The Confidence Man.* The concert began with Dvořák's F-major Quartet, of which the Concord gave a vigorous, ill-tuned, and unshapely performance. It ended with Shostakovich's Piano Quintet, played with conviction by five of the young artists who gather to form Santa Fe's resident chamber ensemble during the festival: Daniel Phillips and Ani Kavafian, violins; Geraldine Walther, viola; Carter Brey, cello; and Edward Auer, piano. An extraordinary program note accused Shostakovich of insincerity in the opening movements. In fact, his passionate, powerful, and individual Quintet, heard after Rochberg's piece, made that work seem like a fake exposed by confrontation with "the real thing." No one questions Rochberg's sincerity. After the "Concord" Quartets, I wrote that I could "respect a creator who genuinely feels that clothes of the past are more comfortable and more expressive garments than those of today." And now? In the recent works, the borrowed plumes seem to be more complacently, less modestly worn. The sense of exploration, of testing a new-old style, is gone. Of course, the composer's pronouncements— such things as his reference to "the cultural pathology of my own time"—must not be allowed to color appraisal of his music. It's the music itself that I found distasteful. Moreover, the effect of this music can perhaps be pernicious. It was disturbing to hear Mr. Phillips, one of our abler young violinists, remark at a symposium that he would rather play good Amy Beach than bad Elliott Carter. (Is there any bad Elliott Carter?) Rochberg writes reactionary stuff—music whose appeal is to closed, unadventurous minds. I know nothing of his extramusical beliefs, but his works could become cultural fodder for the New Right: Down with progressive thought! Down with progressive music!

Ten years ago, Rochberg wrote—in a note accompanying the Nonesuch recording of his Third String Quartet—of "an effort to rediscover the larger and more sweeping gestures of the past, to reconcile my love for that past and its traditions with my relation to the present and its often-destructive pressures." Many composers have made that effort, and it has led the best of them to write not pastiche but vital new music rooted firmly in and drawing rich sustenance from the past.

Roger Sessions comes to mind. And Peter Maxwell Davies—by Rochberg reckoning surely a "modernist"?—who in many radiant, uncompromisingly "modern" compositions has not found it "virtually impossible to express serenity, tranquillity, grace, wit, energy." In Davies's two recent symphonies, plainchant and Sibelius both play a part. Between the symphonies, he composed the ballet *Salome* (1978), his longest and one of his most important orchestral scores. It contains about two hours and twenty minutes of music. It has been recorded (EMI), and a study score is published by Boosey & Hawkes. *Salome* was written for Flemming Flindt's Circus Company (named after the Circus Building in Copenhagen, where it played) and was given there with sensational success for a two-month run. (The fact that Salome's long dance before Herod was performed naked, by Vivi Flindt, did nothing to hurt the publicity.) In Copenhagen, the score was tape-recorded. Flindt is now the artistic director of the Dallas Ballet, which brought *Salome* to Santa Fe and there gave the piece its American première, its hundredth performance, and the first to be danced to more or less live music.

The scenario, essentially Flindt's—according to a remark in Paul Griffiths's valuable little monograph on Davies (Robson)—is a rather naïvely politicized transformation of the Salome tale. Salome "is portrayed as the overindulged daughter of rich materialistic parents, who is driven to revolutionary desperation by their power-hunger and crassness." And "the parallel with the modern girl terrorists should be made quite clear ... the same morass of opportunism and degradation which is their social background, the same clash with a deformed and corrupt petit-bourgeois that is the element of power, the adolescents in conflict with the parents, the erotic attraction to the men who will be the tools for their revenge." John the Baptist is a pacificist leader. The ballet opens with the greening of Israel by John and his followers: a folksy work dance; a "liberty theme." Then Roman invaders march on and enslave the Jews; the land becomes desolate again. The brothers Philip and Herod struggle for the crown of the puppet state. Philip's wife, Herodias, helps Herod to murder Philip; Salome, her daughter, watches with revulsion. And so on, until—after the dance with no veils (but in Santa Fe Mrs. Flindt was chastely sheathed in a body stocking), the beheading, and the kissing of the head—Salome and John achieve an apotheosis, dancing on a field of pure white. "United, they step up toward the stars ... and during the transformed liberty theme, John's disciples follow from earth this rising to an inalienable freedom."

It might be stirring were Flindt's choreography (Bournonville polluted by Béjart) not pretty trashy. What matters is the music—rich, colorful, and eloquent. It is based, often audibly so, on a plainchant for the Feast of St. John the Baptist; the chant is closer to the surface than in many Davies pieces, recognizable through the dance rhythms it assumes. Not with simple schematicism but subtly and eloquently, the contrast between innocent, industrious, pastoral mildness and fierce, jewelled, chromatic corruption is made. There is fervor in the score. There are bright, entertaining divertissements: an Arabian dance and a tumbling display at Herod's feast. Above all, perhaps, there is a sense of joy, energy, and exuberance in creating free, copious theatre music. For Santa Fe, the composer had prepared a "version for small theatre orchestra." Not very small: double woodwinds, double brasses, four percussion players, harp, celesta, and strings (a reduction of two horns and two percussion players on the original). So far as one could judge, the musical performance—some of the players came from Dallas, others were members of the New Mexico Symphony, and Anshel Brusilow conducted—was less than fully assured. But it was hard to judge, since the sound was loudly amplified, in a gym-type auditorium with a noisy ventilation system.

MUSIC OF TIME

August 23, 1982

AMONG THE matters discussed by composers, performers, critics, and the public at the symposium of the Santa Fe Chamber Music Festival were "authenticity in performance: the impact of historical research on present-day musicians and audiences," "the place of cultural chauvinism in the United States" (the charged word "chauvinism" was at the meeting amended to "pride in and promotion of national achievements"), "historical issues in twentieth-century music" (or "Does Schoenberg still matter?"), and "American composition today: coexistence between mainstream American composers and experimentalists." Much well-trodden ground was trodden again, but not, I thought, dully or doggedly. Although the old questions recur, it is of new kinds of music that they are asked. The discussions bore closely on the Santa Fe programs and their performers; and Santa Fe in summer is a festival town where opera, chamber music, dance, and drama abound. Outside the concert halls and the discussion halls, New Mexico's mesas and canyons place our cherished urban arts in a wider, wilder perspective. One can walk there for hours and miles meeting only rocks, trees, birds, and beasts. "Ah, how fleeting, ah, how ephemeral is a man's life!" Bach sang at the start of his Cantata No. 26, and, at the end of it, "Ah, how fleeting, ah, how ephemeral are men's concerns!" At Pecos, a seventeenth-century church has crumbled into a historic ruin. At Kuaua, the walls of the once-flourishing pueblo beside the Rio Grande which Coronado invaded in 1540 were crumbling before one's eyes—in a rainstorm—into the dirt from which they were built. Indian culture all around stamps the white man's art as an exotic, even if it has put down strong roots and drawn sustenance from the new soil. Then the long-deserted cliff palaces and apartment blocks at Puye and Bandelier make the old Indian achievements seem ephemeral—passing traces left on nature by the immigrants from Asia. But those cliffs themselves are not old, not by geological time: merely Pleistocene, and little older than modern man. Reflections on time— whether seconds subdivided, tempi ticking by at different paces, or centuries of thought and millennia of evolution playing upon a present work—arise often enough in our concert halls: after Elliott Carter's First String Quartet, conceived in the Arizona desert, where animals and plants learned through long ages to adapt to the rigors and sudden bounties of nature; after Peter Maxwell Davies's Orkney compositions, where rocks and ocean, memories of old civilizations and opposition to modern commercial menace mingle. The play of the past upon the present was a recurrent theme of the Santa Fe symposium, and the setting gave it vividness. In a "keynote" address, delivered at the close—aptly so at a festival where most of the works closed on a clear tonic chord—Robert Morgan traced the current abandonment of the "stick-to-the-work-itself" school of criticism and the return to an "only-connect" approach. During the symposium, most of the participants had been making connections.

Live illustrations to the authenticity discussion were largely lacking. The resident and visiting ensembles played modern instruments in the modern conservatory manner, which suits twentieth-century music— there was Prokofiev and Shostakovich, and there were new or recent works by John Harbison, Ned Rorem, George Rochberg, and William Schuman to be heard during the symposium days (and works by Britten, Poulenc, Copland, Richard Wernick, and Yehudi Wyner before or after them)—and suits not much else. Haydn trios were played, unbalanced and out of style, on vibrant modern violin and cellos, a fat modern flute, and a thick, powerful modern piano. The solo part of Falla's Harpsichord Concerto, on the other hand, composed for Wanda Landowska's strong twentieth-century instrument, was played on an eighteenth-century replica, which was often inaudible against the (authentically) modern quintet that constitutes the "orchestra." Brahms and Dvořák were played with the modern eschewal of Romantic string portamento. In short, the performers lagged behind their listeners in the appreciation of the diverse sounds and styles, accents and inflections of different centuries. At the touch of a switch in their homes, and increasingly in our concert halls, those listeners now hear the musics of the past done "properly"; and, increasingly, that's the way they want to hear them. The old ranging-through-the-centuries kind of program now favored by most pianists, violinists, string quartets will, I believe, start to disappear, to be replaced by more consistent programs played on the right instruments, in the right style, and in halls of suitable size.

The Santa Fe Opera's production of Ambroise Thomas' *Mignon* was also troubled by problems of style. Much was right about it—notably Allen Charles Klein's realistic, pretty décor and Bliss Hebert's straightforward staging—but the music didn't move in ways to captivate us.

I'm old enough to have known the Opéra-Comique in the days when its traditional repertory—*Carmen, Les Pêcheurs de perles, Mireille, Manon, Werther, Les Contes d'Hoffmann, Pelléas*—was still played, by a company steeped in the style. Today, thanks to the abundance of record reissues, there is no reason that young singers and young conductors should not be coached by and conversant with artists superior to those of the fifties—by Emma Calvé, Ninon Vallin, Germaine Cernay, Edmond Clément, David Devriès, and many others. As the heroine of the Santa Fe *Mignon*, Frederica von Stade was careful but strangely charmless, characterless, dull. And she sang "Connais-tu" so slowly that it became a dirge. Gianna Rolandi's Philine was rather coarse in tone and in manner. A spirited artist, with a fleet, bright voice, she lacked refinement. Barry McCauley, the Wilhelm Meister, was a gauche creature onstage, but he has the voice for French opera—a tenor plangent, firmly focussed, both dulcet and ringing. If he took lessons from Clément, Devriès, Fernando De Lucia, Tito Schipa, he should shine in this repertory. Claude Corbeil was a fuzzy, imprecise Lothario. Kenneth Montgomery conducted the overture and the entr'acte that opens Act II with grace and verve. The dialogue was sung, not spoken—preferable when an American cast performs the piece in French. Of the various alternative endings, a happy one, Philine-less except for a snatch of offstage song, was chosen.

Richard Strauss's penultimate opera, *Die Liebe der Danae*, is a glowing, golden composition, often underrated by the Strauss commentators. I loved it at its première, in Salzburg in 1952; again when the Munich company brought it to London, a year later; and again at its American professional première, in Santa Fe last month. But the Santa Fe production was the least good of the three. Rouben Ter-Arutunian's set was an inappropriate and horrid affair of serpentine Mylar walls, reminiscent of a steam room. Colin Graham's production treated much of the "merry mythology" as low camp, and made fun, not glory, of the Wagnerian reminiscences. John Crosby, conducting, slogged through a score that needs a touch now light, now magisterially expansive. Nevertheless, much came through, even though the casting was odd. Ashley Putnam felt the force of the title role. She acted it well and sang it confidently, but the sound of her voice was unsuited to it. The heroine's music needs the spin and shine of a Rysanek or a Schwarzkopf —a full, warm radiance that Miss Putnam does not command. Dennis Bailey, the Midas, sounded urgent but strangled. Victor Braun, the Jupiter, seemed a second-league baritone in a role written for a Wotan. Hans Hotter sang it at a 1944 dress rehearsal (after which Germany's theatres were closed), and Paul Schöffler at the 1952 première.

Die Liebe der Danae, the New Grove rightly remarks, "requires a producer and conductor who can bring its extraordinary luminosity to full life in a manner to match the old composer's touchingly noble and festive celebration of all that the Greek classical tradition had meant to him." Its performers should know *Die ägyptische Helena* and *Daphne;*

should have followed Strauss's exchanges with Hofmannsthal (who first thought to combine the legends of Jupiter's golden shower and Midas' golden touch in a single plot) and with Josef Gregor (who, under the composer's careful supervision, wrote the *Danae* libretto) about treating mythology on the modern stage; and should have the sound of rich, glamorous German singers in their ears. *Danae* is a noble, romantic opera. Strauss still had the conversation piece *Capriccio* to write, and at the last he took leave of the world and of music in the glowing envoy of the Four Last Songs. But *Danae* was already a conscious farewell. While planning it, Strauss called it his "posthumous" opera. It closes with Jupiter's long *Maja-Erzählung*, the god's account of his attempt to seize the elusive, lovely goddess of spring. It was the composer's own addition to the dramatic scheme and is his moving farewell, serene yet rapturous, to love, desire, tenderness, and illusion. The goddess escapes Jupiter's grasp, but she vanishes amid flowers and fragrance that each year return to give delight. Few operas of our time are so continuously beautiful, so ardent, or so tender.

PART III

1982–1983

SOUNDS AND SWEET AIRS

September 20, 1982

THE SEASON starts with new or renewed halls opening all over. There are big new halls in Baltimore, Colorado Springs, Eugene, Peoria, and Toronto, and in New Orleans the Orpheum, formerly a vaudeville house, has been refashioned as the home of the New Orleans Philharmonic. [For more about those halls, see page 318.] Here in New York, the City Center has been refurbished, and its notorious sight lines have been corrected; Symphony Space has a new stage; and the New York State Theater has been done over, at a cost of more than five million dollars, under the sonic supervision of Cyril Harris, the man who gave to Kennedy Center and to Minneapolis's Orchestra Hall their fine sound and did much to improve the acoustics of Avery Fisher Hall. In this revised State Theater, the New York City Opera has a chance to flourish again. True, the place, like most American opera houses, is large for really effective, "house-filling" opera (it seats over twenty-seven hundred, while Europe's grandest grand-opera houses—in Milan, London, Vienna, Paris, Munich—are all closer to two thousand), but there was nothing Mr. Harris could do about that, short of recommending demolition and rebuilding. There was, however, a great deal he could do to improve the sound within the existing structure. And he has done it. The season there began with a *Merry Widow* that sonically, at least, was a success for the theatre.

Popular report has it that the State Theater, planned in the first place as a home for the New York City Ballet, was so designed that as little sound as possible made onstage would reach into the auditorium. That's fine for dance, where the squeak of rosined slippers, the cracking of knee joints, and the thud of an occasional heavy landing are noises unneeded. It's not at all fine for opera. Singers must be both heard and seen. And—whether popular report is true or not—singers were not heard to advantage in the State Theater. That became especially clear when they sang in other houses: when, for example, in the fall of 1974, Maralin Niska sang Puccini's *Manon Lescaut* for the City Opera and then *Tosca* for the Met. In the larger house (the Met seats a thousand more than the State Theater), Miss Niska's voice actually sounded larger, fuller, more substantial. (The Met acoustics are another of Mr. Harris's successes.) Critics learned to compensate when

301

assessing voices, making allowances for the State Theater acoustics, and, by trial and error, to discover the seats where the sound was best. (I settled for being well forward, violin-side, and not too far from a reflecting side wall.) But critics are privileged. Through much of the enormous house, the sound was peaky, erratic, and, in general, lacking in body. The orchestral tone often seemed thin, even though the personnel list in the nightly program book contained the names of players admired in other settings.

Mr. Harris's work of sonic reconstruction began last season, and the work-in-progress sometimes made things even worse: when the hiss and hum of the ventilation system in a temporary state rose to fill silences, and even to drown the softest musical passages. This is now righted; the background noise of air-conditioning—curse of many modern halls—has, in the words of the fact sheet issued by Lincoln Center, been "quietened significantly." Last season, too, a start was made on breaking up the smooth concave curve of the auditorium's enclosing wall—an acoustic reflector that focussed sound on particular spots and left the rest of the house unnourished—by bastion upon bastion of convex, polycylindrical wooden pilasters, rising through every level, to scatter the sound equably. (And last season it became plain that as a result of these reflectors the singers and their words could be heard more clearly.) Overhead, work was also being done. The State Theater ceiling was a gilded grille that allowed sound to leak up through it and be lost in the spacious attic. Now, directly above the grille, a solid plaster ceiling has been added, so that rising sound is returned to the listeners.

When the spring season ended, and the theatre was dark for two months, further reconstruction, the work that could not be done without disrupting performances, was put in hand. The proscenium—the frame through which one watches and hears—was demolished and rebuilt. Its formerly concave surfaces—partial and inefficient reflectors—are now plane, and its height has been reduced. Above it, a lumpy reflecting cornice, ugly but apparently effective, juts out over the orchestra pit. (The new proscenium, hung with gilded chain mail, was designed by the theatre's original architect, Philip Johnson, and his partner, John Burgee.) The orchestra pit, once cramped, has been enlarged and, at the sacrifice of a row of seats, brought forward into the house. It can now hold more players or hold the old number more comfortably. And there are new seats for the audience, seats with "better acoustical characteristics."

All this should make a great difference. But since I attended *The Merry Widow* in my usual "good" seat, where the sound was already acceptable and undistorted, I so far have nothing particularly striking to report. However, at an open dress rehearsal, when the critics were invited to sample the new house from various vantages, there was evident a general increase of vocal clarity and body, and a fuller, freer, richer orchestral sound. Further comment must await the production of some real operas.

"A constant delight" was Ernest Newman's phrase for Lehár's operetta: "The man in the street may love *The Merry Widow*, but the musician, in addition to loving it, admires and wonders at it, so fresh and varied is the melodic invention in it, so deft, for all their economy, the harmonization and the scoring." His remarks accompanied a recording of the piece, with Elisabeth Schwarzkopf as its heroine, which is indeed a performance to excite admiration and wonder. In the theatre, however, the *Widow* seldom fares so well, and the City Opera's new production, the company's third, is hardly stylish or graceful. Charm it did have in the person of Elizabeth Hynes, its heroine (the first of the season's four Widows). This young ingénue, the company's Susanna and Pamina, is piquantly pretty. Her voice is sweet and true. Her manner is delicate. But she was miscast as the mature, glamorous Hanna Glawari. The role was understated (which is at least preferable to overstatement). Wit, temperament, a strong, sudden flash in the timbre (for the "Heia, Mädel" duet), a richly Straussian swell (for the Vilja-Lied) were missing. Miss Hynes was enchanting but too consistently gentle. Danilo, as often nowadays, was assigned to a baritone. That need not matter when the baritone is dapper and dashing both of presence and of voice, but Alan Titus's voice has been growing darker, heavier, and fuller, and he was rather dull. Susanne Marsee was an edgy Valencienne (she should study Fritzi Massary), and Joseph Evans, as the suave, aristocratic Camille de Rosillon, was blank. The comics— Jack Harrold as the Pontevedrian Ambassador and James Billings as Njegus—were broad. I use the familiar names for the characters, but in fact the City Opera (which in its last production employed new lyrics by Sheldon Harnick) has now reverted to the old 1907 London version, with lyrics by Adrian Ross. This changes names, relocates the third act, and assigns Valencienne's Grisetten-Lied to a grisette. Njegus's song, in Act III, which Lehár added for the London production, was omitted, and in its place Danilo sang a sentimental number from Lehár's last operetta, *Giuditta*.

The City Opera—at any rate, during my ten years' experience of it—has seldom been much good at operetta, whether Viennese, French, British, or American. The new show is the mixture as before. By comparison with, let's say, something as fresh, lively, energetic, professional, carefully paced (and skillfully amplified, so that nuances tell) as Tony Tanner's production of Andrew Lloyd Webber's dramatic oratorio *Joseph and the Amazing Technicolor Dreamcoat*, farther down Broadway, this *Widow* seems dowdy, draggy, and not especially competent. Operetta, of course, calls for talents that not all opera singers command. (Hofmannsthal made the point strongly in a 1923 letter to Strauss: "When I see someone like Massary on the stage, whose intelligence, versatility, and richness of nuance match on the inmost level my own creative aspirations, and then think of opera singers, it is as if I were snatched away from a celestial banquet table decked with ambrosia to some dirty pot-house table laden with the coarsest victuals.") There were gifted opera singers here. They needed more stylish direction. The scenery, by Helen Pond and Herbert Senn, was unattractive. The staging, by Bill Gile, was stale routine. The conducting, by Scott Bergeson, was unidiomatic.

PASTORAL

September 27, 1982

JOHN GAY's Newgate pastoral, *The Beggar's Opera*—that high-spirited play-with-songs about highwaymen, whores, thieves, corrupt officials, and two loving young women—has attracted the attention of composers for two and a half centuries. It appeared in 1728 and caught on at once. On British stages, it was played most years until the late nineteenth century. Jamaica saw it in 1733, New York in 1750. A London revival in 1920 ran for 1,463 performances, setting an operatic record, and it is unlikely that a year has passed since without a *Beggar's Opera* somewhere. Its latest triumph has been in Clarksville, Missouri—a small Mississippi town about sixty miles upstream from St. Louis, where it has been playing in a large barn, the Apple Shed, in a brilliant presentation by the Opera Theatre of St. Louis.

The first published edition of *The Beggar's Opera* contained just the melodies of sixty-nine popular tunes to which Gay had written new lyrics. (It has been claimed, not improbably but without strong evidence, that Swift contributed three of the poems and Lord Chesterfield another.) In the third edition (1729), these melodies were provided with basses by Johann Christoph Pepusch, and Charles Burney, in his *General History of Music* (1776–89), declared that the German composer, Handel's colleague at Cannons, had "furnished the wild, rude, and often vulgar melodies, with basses so excellent, that no sound contrapuntist will ever attempt to alter them." Burney was wrong. In 1759, Thomas Arne had already worked over the score of *The Beggar's Opera*, for Covent Garden. In 1777, Thomas Linley brought out his version, at Drury Lane. And these are but the first in a list of *Beggar's Opera* realizations which now runs to perhaps a hundred or more. Among the more celebrated of them are Frederic Austin's (1920), which launched the modern revival and is highly attractive, though some deem it dainty for the subject matter; Edward J. Dent's (1944), an amusingly "learned" version with much neat counterpoint; Benjamin Britten's (1948), fairly described by the conductor Norman Del Mar as "the conversion of a folk piece into an operatic work on the highest artistic level"; and Arthur Bliss's (1953), a lusty full-orchestra version made for a film starring Laurence Olivier as Macheath. (Kurt

Weill's *Dreigroschenoper* stands apart from these, since it uses only one of Gay's tunes and is otherwise an original composition.) The list of distinguished singers and actors who have appeared in *The Beggar's Opera* over the centuries is longer still. It includes Peg Woffington, Kitty Clive, Mrs. Cibber, Mrs. Billington, Mme. Mara, Catherine Stephens (the first English Susanna), Mary Anne Paton (Reiza in the first *Oberon*), Janet Baker, and Heather Harper; and, as Macheath, Handel's tenor John Beard, Mme. Vestris, John Braham (Sir Huon in the first *Oberon*), Sims Reeves (the first English Faust), Charles Santley, and Michael Redgrave (in a 1940 Glyndebourne production, directed by John Gielgud). The latest recording of the piece, on London, has Dames Joan Sutherland and Kiri Te Kanawa as the rival heroines and the Met's James Morris as Macheath.

Most *Beggar's Opera* arrangements have been tailored to a particular company's available resources. Austin's followed hard on and used singers from a Beecham *Figaro* at Covent Garden. Britten's was composed for the skillful soloists and twelve-piece instrumental ensemble of the English Opera Group. (Rose Hill, the dear Miss La Creevy of the Royal Shakespeare Company's *Nicholas Nickleby*, was its first Lucy.) The London recording has a gaudy score by Richard Bonynge and Douglas Gamley, for full symphony orchestra, replete with Straussian and Prokofievian device. At a pole from it is Denis Stevens's edition, recorded by the Accademia Monteverdiana on ABC, which departs from Pepusch only where he was clumsy, and limits itself to eighteenth-century resources. Each arrangement makes a different effect in performance. Britten's, which had Tyrone Guthrie as its librettist, flows like an opera in which the recitative happens to be spoken; the treatment of the songs varies from what Del Mar calls "straight settings" to "settings in which the air is worked into an elaborate, but formally concise, musical scheme" and "settings embodied in larger musical designs." In the Bonynge-Gamley version, each number becomes a separate aria; there is plentiful elaboration and repetition, with interpolated sustained high notes to produce applause-catching cadences. Dr. Burney would not approve. He complained that

> either from the ambition of the singer, or expectations of the audience, music
> is not suffered to remain simple long upon the stage; and the more plain and
> ancient the melodies, the more they are to be embellished.... The tunes in *The
> Beggar's Opera* will never appear in their original simple garb again.

The St. Louis troupe used a score by Raymond Leppard made originally for the Royal Shakespeare Company, in 1963, when Dorothy Tutin was the Polly, Virginia McKenna the Lucy, and Derek Godfrey the Macheath. It is an actors' version, not an opera singers' version. It flows like a play in which some of the speeches happen to be sung. For the Clarksville production, Colin Graham, who directed, made his own abridgment of the Gay text. Almost all the songs were included (which seldom happens in *Beggar's Opera* performances). The actors dropped into them with often no more prompting than a soft tuning note from the instrumental ensemble, sang them through simply, and slipped back into speech. Speaking, singing, and spectacle were ingredients not disjunct but combined in a lively dramatic adventure. Brecht, Japanese theatre, and *Nicholas Nickleby* probably played a part in inspiring Mr. Graham's imagination. The result was at once true to Gay's spirit and dazzling as a piece of modern theatre to interest the historian, please the musician (for Leppard's touch is light and wonderfully ingenious), and exhilarate players and audience alike.

In introducing his opera, the Beggar declares it, in effect, a parody of Handelian opera seria, with its abundant simile arias, its prison scene ("which the ladies always reckon charmingly pathetic"), and "such a nice impartiality to our two ladies, that it is impossible for either of them to take offence" (as in the operas Handel composed wherein both Faustina and Cuzzoni appeared). It is frequently and too flatly said that *The Beggar's Opera* dealt a death blow to the Italian opera. It didn't. It merely checked for a while the latter's triumphal progress. (It is a pleasant irony that Covent Garden, now London's international opera house, was built from the profits of Gay's piece.) The town flocked to *The Beggar's Opera*. The champions of opera in English, who not without reason thought it ridiculous for English-speaking audiences to attend dramas declaimed in a foreign tongue, rallied around it. But parodies are perhaps most keenly enjoyed by those fond of the thing parodied, and I believe that *The Beggar's Opera* then, as now, pleased people who also delighted in and rightly valued the very genre it mocked. In any case, operatic parody plays a smaller part in it than the Beggar's introduction would suggest. And several of the simile airs function just as they might in "real" opera. Polly's lament when Macheath must leave her—

> The boy thus, when his sparrow's flown,
> The bird in silence eyes:
> But soon as out of sight 'tis gone,
> Whines, whimpers, sobs, and cries—

is very tender. Macheath's extended prison scena, in which strains from ten popular ditties are strung together, has something in common with Peter Grimes's mad scene.

The work is also a social and political satire. Its theme is sounded in the first song, sung by Peachum, the thief-master, a recognized portrait of the Jonathan Wild who efficiently organized London crime until he was hanged, in 1725:

> Through all the employments of life,
> Each neighbour abuses his brother;
> Whore and rogue, they call husband and wife:
> All professions be-rogue one another.
> The priest calls the lawyer a cheat:
> The lawyer be-knaves the divine:

And the statesman, because he's so great,
Thinks his trade as honest as mine.

And at the close of this drama about dishonor among thieves the Beggar returns to observe that "through the whole piece you may observe...a similitude of manners in high and low life"—but with this difference: that while "the lower sort of people have their vices in a degree as well as the rich," only the former "are punished for them." Mr. Graham, in a program note, calls Gay's opera "the strongest piece of social satire that had yet appeared in the theatre" and declares that "its social significance is no less now than it was in those days." No less, indeed, when our papers tell daily of corrupt politicians, venal clergymen, new Wilds, and convicted criminals who cling to public office. But political cabaret, of which *The Beggar's Opera* can be counted an early example, is a curious genre. It flourishes—as it did in London then, as it has in Poland and in Iran more recently—when those attacked are also amused by it. By fond laughter it is disarmed. When it becomes too keen, it is banned. *The Beggar's Opera* is hardly bitter. Frank Kidson, in his elegant little study of the piece (1922), suggests that the adherents of one political party may have been disappointed by satire so good-tempered, and those of the other party no less vexed that there were no clear grounds for suppressing the show: "Everybody knew that the Court and the Governing Party were corrupt, and the mere generalisation of this was nothing to complain of." To the common audience, "the brilliant dialogue, the wit, and life-like conception of the whole story appealed...in a far greater degree than any flings at Court or Government."

The Beggar's Opera is also a love story, a *Don Giovanni* with a happy ending, in which the picaresque rogue-hero joins hands with the Donna Elvira figure, Polly, to lead a final dance. (In real life, the first Polly, Lavinia Fenton, became the Duchess of Bolton.) It has even been considered immoral. Sir John Hawkins in his *History* declared, "The effects of *The Beggar's Opera* in the minds of the people have fulfilled the prognostications of many, that it would prove injurious to society. Rapine and violence have been gradually increasing ever since its first representation." But Dr. Johnson's comment is surely sounder: "More influence has been ascribed to *The Beggar's Opera,* than it in reality ever had; for I do not believe that any man was ever made a rogue by being present at its representation." It has not passed uncensored. In an 1854 Boston libretto, made for the Pyne-Harrison company, the text is "revised by Mr. Harrison and the objectionable dialogue expunged." In Sir Malcolm Sargent's recording, the bold language is toned down.

Mr. Graham's production was true to the original in its precise balance of political comment and operatic parody with witty entertainment. The piece was neither prettified nor didactically overpointed. The characterizations were fearless—now funny, now fierce, and sometimes touching. Human behavior was accurately observed. The merits that have secured the work's longevity were made plain.

The Clarksville Apple Shed is a long, rambling barn, divided from the Mississippi by a railroad track. (Plans to run an Opera Special, the Super Thief, from St. Louis were frustrated by Amtrak bureaucracy.) It has something of the feel of the medieval Grange de Meslay (which is seven centuries older), chosen by Sviatoslav Richter as the site of the Fêtes Musicales en Touraine; and, with its vistas of river and field, something of the feel of the Maltings, that Suffolk brewery refashioned as the principal hall of the Aldeburgh Festival. But it is more informal than either. At about its center, an open loft has been built into the rafters. This provided the troupe with a two-level acting area, around which an audience of some three hundred clustered, for seven performances. The Opera Theatre and the Raintree Arts Council, which runs the Shed and fosters the arts in Pike and Lincoln Counties, joined in the presentation. This was fully community opera. The performers were housed locally; willing helpers built scenery and sewed costumes; church and social groups vied to feed the visiting troupe. An essay in Hans Werner Henze's *Music and Politics* (a collection of his writings just published by the Cornell University Press) recounts his endeavor to involve a whole community in an artistic enterprise, the Montepulciano Cantieri. The Clarksville *Beggar's Opera,* though less polemical in intent, had something of the warm Politian spirit about it.

There were twenty-three singing actors and eight instrumentalists, and (as in *Nickleby*) every one of them told. Elaine Bonazzi, doubling as Mrs. Peachum and Mrs. Diana Trapes, gave two rounded, ripe but admirably disciplined, perfectly inflected performances. James Daniel Frost, doubling as the Beggar and Filch, was alert, accurate, and endearing. Herbert Beattie, doubling as the Player and Peachum, was splendid. David Parsons was a bonny Macheath, even if, like the Polly and the Lucy, Stephanie Friede and Melanie Sonnenberg, he did at times become a mere opera singer. Over all three, an occasional shadow of a singing teacher seemed to pass; words and sense became subordinate to tone. But not often, and not so as to disturb enjoyment of the swift-moving, captivating show. Leppard's arrangements are economical: Peachum's "Through all the employments" has only a bassoon obbligato; Mrs. Peachum sings "If any wench" to tambourine accompaniment. They are filled with deft musical devices that charm but do not distract the ear—piquant little surprises, rhythmic ingenuities. They have variety of color and of texture, and the few numbers more elaborately and extensively treated are cunningly placed and exquisitely wrought. All in all, an ensemble production skillful on every level. And the happiest, liveliest operatic presentation I have encountered since—well, since St. Louis's *Così fan tutte* a few months ago.

UNDER WAY

October 4, 1982

MERKIN HALL —whose various concert series promise fare from Bala-
kirev, Biber, and Byrd to Wuorinen, Zelenka, and Zwilich—began its
season with one of Gerard Schwarz's Music Today concerts, each program of which contains a "modern classic" as well as new pieces. Eighteen expert young players had been assembled—largely wind players,
for the classic was Berg's Chamber Concerto, for violin, piano, and
thirteen winds. The violinist was Mark Kaplan, the pianist David
Golub, and with Mr. Schwarz and his ensemble they conspired to give
a performance at once polished and uncommonly emotional. The climaxes took the hall to its sonic limits but not beyond them, and it was
exciting to hear the concerto in intimate surroundings. In larger halls,
the *pp* and *ppp* lines can sound softer, but the warmth and directness of
this performance were very taking.

The concert opened with two of Percy Grainger's folk-song settings
—"Spoon River" and "The Power of Love"—that have "elastic" scoring. In the preface to the score of "Spoon River," the composer wrote,
"I do not care whether one of my 'elastically scored' pieces is played by
four or forty or four hundred players ... I do not even care whether
the players are skilful or unskilful, as long as they play well enough to
sound the right intervals ... as long as they play badly enough to *still
enjoy playing* ('Where no pleasure is, there is no profit taken'—*Shakespeare).*" Grainger misquoted the *Shrew,* but the sense is there, and for
players and listeners alike the works made a good warmup to an evening mainly of pleasure and profit. Nicholas Thorne's *From the Dying
Earth: Three Tales for Eleven Players* left, I regret to say, little impression,
although in a program note the composer wrote that he "wanted to
create something unimaginably beautiful and strong, something with a
sense of personal, poetic vision." Leonard Rosenman's Chamber Music
V, written in 1979 for the Collage Group of Boston and here receiving
its New York première, was more beautiful, stronger, more poetic. It is
a small-scale concerto, lasting about twenty minutes, for piano and an
ensemble of flute, clarinet, violin, cello, and two percussions. The ideas
and their working are deft, and the form is shapely. Christopher Oldfather was the refined soloist.

In Alice Tully Hall, the Aston Magna Foundation for Music celebrated
its tenth anniversary with a concert of Handel, Vivaldi, and Mozart,
played by a band of eighteenth-century size and on eighteenth-century
instruments or modern replicas of them. Aston Magna's care is not
simply for authenticity and historical replication; under Albert Fuller's
inspiring artistic direction, it explores—in its Great Barrington sum-

mer academies and in concerts both private and public—the whys as well as the hows of seventeenth-century and eighteenth-century music and its contemporary performance. In a brief, civilized speech of welcome before the concert, Mr. Fuller recalled that the founding of Aston Magna was influenced by the moon landing: man's farthest reach outward into the unknown chimed with and affected the musicians' inner search for perspective and significance. And in a program note he wrote of "our inquiry into the meaning of musical art—what it has to do with our behavior, how it touches and alters our lives, what we have inherited through it from the past, and where we might be going with it." If the Tully Hall concert raised as many questions as it answered, they were questions of a kind that Aston Magna is passionately and practically concerned with: Whom was this music meant for? Whom is it meant for today? Where, how, and to whom should it be played?

Answers are still being sought. Aston Magna has abandoned the Grace Rainey Rogers Auditorium, in the Metropolitan Museum—its former New York showplace—as being acoustically and architecturally unfriendly. But for early music Tully Hall is only a little better. True, at the Aston Magna concert it looked less bleak than usual, since the handsome organ stood revealed—not to be played but, as Mr. Fuller said, only to provide a striking backdrop. The acoustics, as dry as ever, drained the bloom from eighteenth-century string tone, and the little band could not bring the vast space to life. The program ended with Mozart's D-major Symphony, K. 250—one of the five D-major symphonies extracted from Salzburg serenades. The performance was directed by the concertmaster, Jaap Schröder. He is also the concertmaster of the K. 250 played by London's Academy of Ancient Music in Volume V of the complete recording of Mozart symphonies from Oiseau-Lyre. That performance was recorded in resonant acoustics. When chords are cut off by the players, they do not "drop dead," as chords did in Tully, but linger on for a moment in reverberant space. And the music lives in a way that the Tully acoustics precluded. (Aston Magna played just four of the five serenade movements that went into the symphony. The second minuet, which calls for two flutes, was omitted; there were no flutes in the Aston Magna ensemble. Mozart's oboists could evidently double on flutes; in our day instrumentalists have tended to specialize—although some Aston Magna players are acquiring an eighteenth-century versatility.)

The pleasure and profit of hearing Mozart's music with timbres, balances, and phrasing that he would recognize scarcely need stressing today. The Oiseau-Lyre albums make the sounds available to all, and in successive issues the style of the London players has become surer, more graceful, and more poetic. For Aston Magna, Mozart has also been a goal achieved—led up to by fiddling, singing, and dancing through the musics of the previous century. And yet this New York performance of music originally written to be played at Elisabeth

Haffner's wedding party was by Aston Magna's own standards a trifle staid. The players had donned the formal uniform of urban concert giving. No harm in that—but it was rather as if along with the old soup-and-fish they had put on an earnest manner, unsuited to the score. The Academy of Ancient Music—as photographs of the sessions included in the record albums make plain—records Mozart in its shirtsleeves. In Great Barrington, garb is informal. The appearance of a concert does matter; to prescribe, on the ground of historical authenticity, the slovenliness of dress—or the bibulousness—that, Mozart wrote, the Salzburg court musicians were prone to would be carrying things altogether too far. (Or would a touch of drunkenness in wedding-feast music be apt?) It matters most when the music itself seems to be affected. Whatever the reason, at this formal concert the players had evidently forgotten some of what Great Barrington teaches them about dancing, singing, and enjoying themselves in a way to fill their listeners with shared happiness. Not Mr. Schröder: his direction was an invitation to delight. His colleagues produced exquisitely shaped, delicately balanced, and technically accomplished playing, but they remained grave.

Vivaldi's Two-Violin Concerto in D, RV 511, flowed more freely. The soloists were Mr. Schröder and Stanley Ritchie, a well-balanced yet fascinatingly different pair—one a quirky, attractive, unpredictable blend of poet and pedant, the other an exquisitely sane, polished performer. The account of Handel's Grand Concerto in D, Opus 6, No. 5, which opened the program, was oddly lumpy, and three of Cleopatra's airs from Handel's *Giulio Cesare*, which followed, were unaccountably undramatic. "Unaccountably" because they were sung by that accomplished young soprano Elizabeth Pruett, whose Violetta for the City Opera's touring *Traviata* was vivid, and whose Donna Elvira at Glyndebourne this summer was much admired. "Tu la mia stella," "V'adoro, pupille," and "Da tempeste" were tamely done—sweetly, truly, but tamely. On accessory levels, the soprano's coiffure, costume, and constricted stage demeanor and the rude lighting that shone on her nose and her hands but left her eyes and her lips in shadow further dimmed the portrait of Cleopatra. Separation of the two bands in "V'adoro"—a nine-strong ensemble of Muses set apart from the full-orchestra interjections—was not attempted. The words of the airs were printed in the program book but in an italic type too small to be followed at a glance.

The first program of the New York Philharmonic's subscription series, in Avery Fisher Hall, began with two American compositions: Charles Ives's *Decoration Day* and Steve Reich's *Tehillim*. Zubin Mehta conducted. *Decoration Day* is the second of the four pieces that make up the *Holidays Symphony*—each movement, Ives said, being "based on something of the memory that a man has of his boy holidays." The composer allowed that any one of them might be played independently but foresaw a danger that it might then be received as "just an emasculated piece of nice embroidery!" There is also a danger that *Decoration Day*, which lasts eight or nine minutes, and has been much played by the Philharmonic, may be used to provide too easy a token representation of Ives for audiences unprepared to grapple with his large-scale visionary music. The *Holidays Symphony*, which the Philharmonic has never played as a whole, is greater than the sum of its parts; the "attempts to make pictures in music of common events in the lives of common people (that is, of fine people), mostly of the rural communities," culminate in a transcendental finale, *Thanksgiving*, which "has some religious significance." *Decoration Day* was fairly well done, and the program note did give the audience a context within which to listen. But its scenes—the dawn flower-gathering; the Town Hall assembly; the solemn march to Wooster Cemetery; the brassy quickstep return, its jaunty strains shadowed by sombre reflections—were less passionately and picturesquely evoked than they can be.

Tehillim, Reich's setting of four Psalm texts, had a poor performance. The sparkling, dancing composition heard at the Metropolitan Museum in March (see page 220) was dulled. The Philharmonic played the full-orchestra version, which calls for twelve woodwinds instead of the six in the chamber version, and full strings instead of an amplified string quintet. Mr. Mehta and his players seemed to approach the piece as if its performance were a duty rather than a joyful celebration. The amplification of the vocal quartet, through loudspeakers on the edges of the platform, was tinny. *Tehillim* probably dances and sparkles more readily in the chamber version. Steve Reich and Musicians have recorded it on the ECM label.

The American Philharmonic's first concert of the season, in Fisher Hall, was an old-fashioned Wagner program, distinguished by the presence of Birgit Nilsson as the soloist. Miss Nilsson sang Isolde's Act I narrative, Elisabeth's Greeting, and the Liebestod. She has been just about the only singer of our day able to set the Met spaces ringing, and last week she set Fisher Hall ringing, too. That was exciting. She is sixty-four. Her best notes had lost none of their old power or burnished brilliance, but the control of the voice was less secure than before: there were moments of unsteadiness and others of untrue intonation. I was glad to hear her Isolde again: she has a fine concert presence and the ability to make excerpts from an opera seem not just concert numbers but parts of a complete and intently imagined performance. Rohan Joseph, the founder and director of the American Philharmonic, conducted. His young orchestra was large and rich in tone. An ambitious series of eleven further programs, containing much of interest, has been announced, but the orchestra's president told us that unless more subscriptions were forthcoming the Wagner concert would be the orchestra's last. [*And so it was.*]

OPERA IN EARNEST

October 11, 1982

THE METROPOLITAN Opera season opened with a revival of *Der Rosen-kavalier*, a long opera about rather little. Strauss, as that sage critic Richard Capell once remarked, treats a theme of sensual frivolity with the thoroughness of a German encyclopedist. (The result is a master-piece, Capell swiftly added.) It was the company's 218th performance of the work, and the latest in the long list of Met Marschallins—which opens with Frieda Hempel, in 1913, and includes most of the role's famous interpreters—is Kiri Te Kanawa (who essayed the part for the first time last year, in Paris). She looked beautiful, and even discon-certingly younger than the Octavian, Tatiana Troyanos, and the So-phie, Judith Blegen. The composer described his heroine as "a young, beautiful woman of thirty-two at the most," and Dame Kiri is only six years older. The model for her interpretation seems to be Elisabeth Schwarzkopf, not the more spontaneous and lovable Lotte Lehmann, but she was less individual and specific than either. Cool, gracious, and dignified, maintaining an all-purpose, enigmatically rueful half smile, she glided exquisitely through the opera. There were some lovely sounds, others that were murmurings rather than Hofmannsthal's words given precise and poignant utterance. She has the physical and vocal capacities for the part, and perhaps she already feels it keenly and intricately. Time will show whether she learns to make her lis-teners feel it with her.

Miss Troyanos's Octavian and Miss Blegen's Sophie—carefully stud-ied and capably sung—are familiar impersonations. Kurt Moll's Baron Ochs began well but as the evening progressed grew broader and coarser. He may have been tempted to play up—play down—to an audience on whom subtleties of merely verbal inflection were likely to be lost. *Der Rosenkavalier* is a wordy opera and needs to be followed word by word. The first volume of the Metropolitan Opera Classics Library (Little, Brown), a new series, is devoted to *Der Rosenkavalier*, and in a frank foreword the Met's general manager, Anthony Bliss, writes:

> The use in opera of...languages other than our own narrows rather than expands their immediacy and their hold over us. We are all aware of having to "read up" on the story of an opera before attending a performance—or, drearier still, of having to sit through three or four acts without ever really knowing who is saying what to whom. Far too often the drama is lost com-pletely, and the whole opera itself becomes clouded over, dusty like a museum piece.

The volume contains a synopsis and a libretto with facing English translation (not literal but the old Alfred Kalisch singing version, slightly revised), and also "the story of the opera" retold by Anthony Burgess as a novelette—not quite accurately, and in tones that would surely make the fastidious Hofmannsthal wince. There are illustrations, two essays, and interesting but incomplete Met statistics. As an introduction to the work, the English National Opera Guide to *Der Rosenkavalier* (published here by Riverrun, at $4.95, as against $16.95 for the Met volume) is a better value: its essays are fuller and more interesting, there is more about the music, and the Kalisch translation is extensively revised.

The Met production—Nathaniel Merrill's of 1969, designed by Robert O'Hearn—has been carefully maintained. It was not dreary or dusty. In Act I, the Marschallin's bed is on the wrong side—stage left instead of stage right—and this produces some novel, if finally unconvincing, sonic effects: the lovers' voices are separated from the violins. In *Richard Strauss: The Staging of His Operas and Ballets* (Oxford)—a fine album of sets, scenes, and commentary—Rudolf Hartmann reproduces the Met's Act II with the remark "Too many decorative details crowd the room." Act III works well in the main, but the Marschallin's grand entrance is muted, and the scenic echoes, surely deliberate, of Act I are not sounded. James Levine conducted. The three preludes were rather noisy, bangy, and vulgar, but then there was refined playing, care, and eloquence.

La forza del destino is a long, turbulent opera about many matters, foremost among them Verdi's belief that in this world it is vain to hope for untroubled happiness—that for a person of sensibility and spirit retreat into a cloister or ivory tower provides no serene refuge. The opera chimed with the composer's attempts to renounce the hurly-burly of theatre life and with his experience as a member of the first Italian parliament. Donna Leonora and Don Alvaro enact his theme against a background of popular, religious, and martial activity; the consolations no less than the confinements of the Church and the exhilarating splendors no less than the miseries of a war in a just cause are vividly portrayed. The Met's revival of *Forza*, directed by John Dexter, was well conceived, although its execution was of mixed merit. The edition used was Verdi's 1869 revision, with its tacked-on Christian ending in a spirit of Manzonian resignation to fate. Antonio Ghislanzoni wrote the words for it, and the scene resembles one in his *Promessi sposi* libretto for Errico Petrella. The very fact that this trio-finale, fine music though it be, sounded glib, false to what had gone before, showed that the performance had caught the spirit of Verdi's original intention. And Act III had been reshaped in its spirit. In 1862, the act consisted of: Alvaro aria; Alvaro-Carlo duet, Carlo aria; Scenes of military life; Alvaro-Carlo duet, Alvaro aria. In 1869, Verdi removed the final aria; placed the second duet earlier, dividing it from Carlo's aria by a new little *ronda*, or dawn patrol; and ended the act with the scenes of military life. The Met, omitting the *ronda,* restored the original order but not the aria-finale. When it first tried this arrangement, in 1975, I was dubious, but since then I have got to know and admire the original, unrevised *Forza* in the theatre. The Met solution is more shapely and more dramatic than the revision, and preserves the pattern of partings and reunions. (Heroine and hero meet only in the first and last scenes of this unconventionally but excitingly constructed opera.) If four minutes more running time can be allowed, and if the tenor is up to it, perhaps the aria-finale could be restored; the act now ends abruptly—though not ineffectively—with recitative cut short by a cadence that Verdi didn't write, and it ends in the wrong key.

Leona Mitchell sang her first Leonora in warm, full tones that flowed evenly without any forcing. It was not a temperamental performance, but it sounded good and was accurately phrased. The two baritones were fine—Sherrill Milnes an alert, trenchant Carlo, and Gabriel Bacquier a rounded, fervent, entertaining, and unclowned Melitone. The Alvaro, Giuseppe Giacomini, was crude. The Preziosilla, Isola Jones, squawked her higher notes. The Father Guardian, Bonaldo Giaiotti, was dull. Mr. Levine's conducting was at once committed, energetic, and ponderous; the score seldom moved at convincingly natural paces or sounded as if the singers' declamation and phrasing had determined the accompaniment. Nevertheless, this was a serious attempt to show that the great drama is far more than a sequence of good musical numbers in picturesque settings.

The Met's *Boris Godunov,* rich yet sombre in its staging, directed by August Everding, has the same integrity and coherence. This season's revival is conducted by James Conlon and is his finest achievement: broadly paced, grand, yet poetic and emotional, with instrumental lines and colors direct in their eloquence. The edition used is a conflation of Mussorgsky's first and second versions, containing more music than the composer ever intended to be played in a single evening. The result could be unwieldy but proves not so, because Ming Cho Lee's scenes change swiftly and the "dramatic iconography"—in which Gil Wechsler's lighting has an important part—is striking. But unless a Princess Marina smoother and more seductive of voice than Mignon Dunn was and a less boring Rangoni than John Darrenkamp can be found, the Polish act—Mussorgsky's afterthought—might as well be omitted. The time gained could be used to restore passages missing from the study scene. The Kromy Forest scene is this season played without some cuts that disfigured it before.

Martti Talvela is a Boris without the bite of his great predecessors, but in his slightly soft-grained way he is imposing. His histrionics looked calculated; one noticed him preparing to overturn the heavy table, claw down the curtains, take a spectacular final tumble. Wieslaw Ochman was a strong, fine-drawn Grigory, though the fountain duet needed a sweeter timbre. There were good performances from Robert

Nagy (Shuisky), Paul Plishka (Pimen), Donald Gramm (Varlaam), and several others. James Atherton's Simpleton should have been more simply played and sung. The chorus's curious log-rolling exercises in the final episodes suggested that rehearsal time had run short. But, all in all, this was a noble and stirring account of the piece.

Any weaknesses in the performance of the three long, difficult operas were those of individual artists. The aim was earnest. The composers were served. But a fourth long, difficult opera, *La gioconda*, which completed the repertory of the Met's opening weeks, was less scrupulously treated. It seemed to have been shovelled onto the stage: choruses lined up in V-formation to stand and sing; lighting was largely by jerky follow-spots; the soprano's and the tenor's chief concern was apparently for volume; and the strange, special quality of a fascinating work was scarcely apparent. Boito's unconventional libretto is in many ways a sketch for his *Otello*, while Ponchielli's score is a bid for the popular success that his *Promessi sposi* and *Lituani* had nearly but not quite won. After beginning work on the piece, the composer confessed to a friend that he had "no faith in the libretto," with its "frequent high-flown conceits," elaborate metrics, and "involved expression in which I cannot find the ideas I want." (There were many revisions, but in the final version the third-act finale is still launched with the general cry "A fatal vampire's hand passed over us, and to a funerary brand transformed every torch;" in the fourth-act duettino, Enzo calls Gioconda a "furibund hyena.") *Cavalleria rusticana* was fifteen years in the future, and *La gioconda* is reckoned a pre-verismo opera, but the composer had to struggle to keep it one:

> In Gioconda's role, all is rage, suicide, jealousy, poison, and the hell that these exaggerations have introduced in recent times, whereby the singer is held to *the word and the note*, with the straining of throats that must continually declaim or croak. We are off the track, dear friend. Verdi, who says "Let's go back to the old ways," should set us an example.... The public wants smooth, clear things, melody, simplicity; and we do all we can to shroud ourselves in confusion and complexities. Boito is forcing me in that direction. But I hope I'll have enough common sense to keep clear of the abyss.

Otello, on both Boito's part and Verdi's, triumphantly combines verismo and traditional ideas. *La gioconda* shows them in arresting conflict. Compare Alvise's rhetorical iteration of the line "La morte è il Nulla, è vecchia fola il ciel," in the second edition of *La gioconda*, and Iago's terse, chilling utterance of the same line at the close of his Credo.

It is a mistake to think that verismo opera—let alone *La gioconda*—should be bawled. Fernando De Lucia, the most elegant and exquisite of the "old-style" tenors, turn-of-the-century successor to Giuliano Gayarré, the first Enzo, and to Roberto Stagno, the first Turiddu, was a favored interpreter of the verismo composers. Eva Marton, the Met's new Gioconda, set about the part like a provincial Santuzza, and there was little "music" in her voice. In an unrefined way, her vigor and loudness were exciting and not without effect. Abuse of the chest register, as Manuel Garcia remarks in his classic treatise on singing, will "in a comparatively short time injure the whole instrument and reduce it to the state of a 'broken voice.'" Miss Marton's strong voice still holds together, just, but she seems bent on tearing it to tatters. Placido Domingo's first Met Enzo was disappointing, without bloom or freshness to the tone, without poetry in the manner. The timbre had a rough edge; the style was forceful, manly, but unromantic. Cornell MacNeil's Barnaba, on the other hand, was admirably sung—purely, fully, with every note and every word in place. But there was no dramatic projection of the character. (I attended the second performance, when Mr. MacNeil, unwell, retired after Act III; Richard Clark finished the role.) The new Alvise, Ferruccio Furlanetto, was a cipher. The new Cieca, Patricia Payne, was a wobbler. The Laura, Bruna Baglioni, was poised, patrician, clear and steady in tone, and altogether admirable. Giuseppe Patané was a sound conductor. *La gioconda* offers as many textual variants as *Boris, Forza,* or *Don Carlos.* The Met sticks to the fourth, final version.

The San Francisco Opera season opened with a revival of *Un ballo in maschera.* I saw the sixth performance, by which time the first-night Amelia, Riccardo, and Renato, who were Montserrat Caballé, Luciano Pavarotti, and Silvano Carroli, had been replaced by Rebecca Cook, Vasile Moldoveanu, and Pablo Elvira. Miss Cook is a promising young soprano, a bright graduate of Kurt Herbert Adler's "academy," which has nurtured operatic talent through big roles with his small companies and small roles with his big one. Next year, she becomes a leading soprano in Mannheim, which has a thousand-seat house. The voice was not really ample enough for a big-house Amelia, but as a "cover" performer she won admiration. Her manner was confident, the sound was often shining, and she has a natural feeling for the swell of a Verdi phrase. Mr. Moldoveanu—a Met Don Carlos—is among the more distinguished Verdi tenors of our day. The timbre may not be glamorous, but it is sterling, unforced, and true. His phrasing was sensitive and well molded, his portrayal sharp-cut and aristocratic. (San Francisco uses the royal Stockholm setting for the drama, although the courtiers sang the opening chorus to the Massachusetts text.) Mr. Elvira was a correct and satisfactory Renato. Ruža Baldani was the first Ulrica I have heard in many years who sang the satanic invocations firmly, potently, and with dramatic imagination. Kathleen Battle was a perky, pretty Oscar, despite the slow tempi set for her songs and her tame adherence, except once, to the letter of the text. There were striking performances from Kevin Langan, as Samuele; Thomas Woodman, as Silvano; Jeffrey Thomas, as the Judge; and Peter Kazaras, as Amelia's servant, who has only one F-sharp and twenty-eight B's to sing but was given further appearances in Sonja Frisell's production. Miss Frisell's work was no more than "functional"—and less than that in the unreal, arbitrary maneuvers of the love duet. Mr. Adler's conducting had scope and sweep; his visionary grasp of the whole drama more than made up for some passing moments of ragged detail. John Conklin's rich décor is well scaled to the scenes, is apt for the action, and provides a *Ballo* setting of uncommon beauty.

San Francisco's *Norma* revival brought back Joan Sutherland in ringing, powerful voice and Marilyn Horne in brazen, brilliant cry. And both ladies acted conscientiously. But *Norma* needs more—the sort of dramatic genius that once led London critics to acclaim Giuditta Pasta in the title role (which Bellini had composed for her) even when she sang so flat that the winds gave up trying to accompany her. The San Francisco Pollio, Ermanno Mauro, was clumsy at first, fairly decent in the final scene. The Oroveso, Ezio Flagello, sounded threadbare. Richard Bonynge conducted crisply, sometimes with a briskness that verged on the perfunctory. Should the noble and, in recent decades, much-performed opera perhaps be shelved again until some new Lilli Lehmann, Ponselle, or Callas arrives to take up the druidess's mantle? Lehmann deemed the title role ten times more exacting than Beethoven's Leonore. And Mr. Bonynge introduced Dame Joan's recording by remarking that "the singer who can be a complete Norma probably has never existed."

HOW IT PLAYED IN PEORIA
(AND ELSEWHERE)

October 18, 1982

IN THE space of a September fortnight, five large concert halls opened in this country and one in Canada: in New Orleans, Baltimore, Peoria, Eugene, East Lansing, and Toronto. Later this month, a seventh new hall opens, in Colorado Springs. I attended five of the six September openings (not East Lansing's). What follows is acoustical and architectural impressions gained from a single concert in each hall. Four of the five halls have built-in "tuning devices"—architectural, electronic, or both—and the fifth (New Orleans) has an adjustable orchestral shell; their acoustical characteristics may well be altered and improved. Two of them (Baltimore and Toronto) are "pure" concert halls; two (Peoria and Eugene) are theatres capable of presenting grand opera and large-scale ballet as well as symphony concerts; the fifth (New Orleans) can house small-scale opera and dance. Four of them are brand-new and were designed by celebrated architects; the fifth (New Orleans) is a renovated 1920s vaudeville house. Their seating capacities range from around two thousand (New Orleans and Peoria) to twenty-eight hundred (Toronto). Their cost ranged from $3 million (New Orleans) to $39 million (Toronto). The orchestras I heard in them ranged from the high-powered, virtuoso Chicago Symphony (Peoria)—this orchestra also opened the East Lansing hall—and the warm, fresh Baltimore

Symphony to the modest, low-powered Eugene Symphony. Wilhelm Furtwängler once remarked that "the hall with the best acoustics is the hall with the best performers in it." Last year, I discovered that the acoustics of San Francisco's new Louise M. Davies Symphony Hall were "improved" overnight when the Boston Symphony came to play there. In all acoustic commentary, there are more variables than where the critic sat and what he had for dinner. Aspirin, a doctor once told me, cuts its taker's response to high frequencies; flying, another explained to me, can shift eardrums for days. I heard these concerts undrugged but flew to all the cities except Baltimore. With those caveats, I continue.

The New Orleans Orpheum, at the northwest corner of the city's French Quarter, opened as a vaudeville house in 1921. Then it became a movie house. Now it houses the New Orleans Philharmonic. Wider than it is deep, the Orpheum stacks an audience of two thousand close around the stage, on three levels, insuring the intimacy and audibility that live-theatre performers needed in days before miking. The architect was G. Albert Lansburgh, who worked on San Francisco's great Opera House. It is a dignified and attractive place, decked in ivory and turquoise, with some gilded detail, and unpretentious—not a splendid palace, like the Rapp & Rapp theatres that now house the Pittsburgh and the St. Louis orchestras, or Timothy L. Pflueger's Paramount, now the home of the Oakland Symphony. (In passing, an exclamation of wonder at C. Howard Crane's "fabulous" Fox, also in St. Louis—a new Persepolis lovingly restored!) The Orpheum façade is Beaux-Arts in glazed ivory terra-cotta, spanned by a tinted Donatellesque frieze of music-making putti. It is cumbered at the moment by a heavy, hideous marquee; there are plans to remove this and hopes that the original, elegant canopy survives inside it. The lobby is tiny; on opening night the street outside was closed to traffic and became an open-air foyer.

The program was Tchaikovsky's Violin Concerto (Itzhak Perlman the soloist) and his Fourth Symphony, conducted by Philippe Entremont. I sat in various parts of the first balcony and found the acoustics of the house ideal. Warm, full, rich, clear, alive—all the musician's epithets of approval were apt. A colleague downstairs was less happy, but when he moved upstairs he was similarly impressed. (Is there a house in the world where "the higher you sit, the better the sound" does not apply?) The orchestra plays in a wooden stage shell designed by Christopher Jaffe.

When a hall's seating capacity goes much above two thousand, acoustics become tricky. Of the European orchestra halls famous for good sound, Vienna's Musikvereinssaal (1870) holds only 1,680, and Amsterdam's Concertgebouw (1888) 2,206. Leipzig's Neues Gewandhaus (1884, destroyed by bombing in 1943) held only 1,560. But two nineteenth-century American halls built roughly on the Leipzig model, Baltimore's Lyric Theater (1894) and Boston's Symphony Hall (1900), were made much larger; each holds around 2,600. Augmentation did not necessarily mean poor acoustics: Boston is the proof of that, and so, in Toronto, is Massey Hall (1894), which originally held nearly four thousand and was hailed as one of the world's best. Other shapes than a rectangle were tried with success: the round-balconied Carnegie Hall (1891), which holds 2,760; Philadelphia's horseshoe Academy of Music (1857), patterned after La Scala but with 2,984 seats as against La Scala's 2,289; Louis Sullivan's elliptically vaulted Chicago Auditorium (1889), which originally held 4,237. The Boston acoustics are generally deemed great, and those of the other American halls mentioned are deemed good. It is against them that musicians assess our modern halls of comparable size. The best of these that I have encountered is Orchestra Hall in Minneapolis; the next, perhaps, the Concert Hall of Kennedy Center. But there are several I have not yet visited; Symphony Hall in Salt Lake City is one for which I have heard nothing but praise. Minneapolis seats 2,573, and Washington and Salt Lake City each about 2,800. All three are acoustically the work of Cyril Harris.

Mr. Harris uses prescriptions of proved efficacy: an "open," basically rectangular hall with the orchestra elevated at one end and balconies along the three other sides; walls and ceilings broken by ornament to provide well-distributed sound; reflective surfaces of wood and plaster. Vienna, Leipzig, and Boston set this pattern. As hall after hall built to different formulas—in fans or ovals or circles, with surfaces of concrete or plastic—proves musically unsatisfactory, musicians wonder why it is ever departed from, why millions in public money is risked on monumental experiments that may or may not succeed. Minneapolis, an exhilarating building by Hardy Holzman Pfeiffer, is proof that adherence to sound acoustical principles need not inhibit architectural adventure.

The Cambridge acoustical firm Bolt Beranek & Newman seems to pin its large-hall hopes to "clouds"—adjustable reflectors hanging down from the ceiling which direct the "acoustical energy" toward the listeners in a precisely controlled fashion. BBN's reputation, in fact, is still beclouded by the fiasco of New York's Philharmonic Hall in its first state (unfairly, it has been claimed, but I won't go into that old wrangle again). San Francisco's Davies Hall (which seats over three thousand), Toronto's new Roy Thomson Hall, and Baltimore's new Joseph Meyerhoff Symphony Hall are all acoustically designed by Theodore Schultz, of BBN. In all three, "clouds," or "flying saucers" (of clear acrylic in San Francisco and Toronto), hover over the platform and the front part of the "stalls." (That British term for the ground-level seating avoids the ambiguity of American usage: "The orchestra sounded good in the orchestra.") All three halls are shaped in plan like—well, it's hard to describe: a Chinese ginger jar with a slightly elongated neck; a plump, snub pear; a squarish circle with a bulge for the orchestra platform. (The basic shape changes from level to level.) San Francisco and Toronto both have arrays of retractable sound-absorbent banners hanging down from the ceiling. In neither did I care much for the sound. In both, it was strong, clear, "positive," immediate—but not warm, rich, cohesive, expansive, or lovable. One didn't feel the hall coming to life (as Boston and Carnegie and Minneapolis do), reverberating with music, but was conscious, rather, of "acoustical energy" efficiently projected. San Francisco, after two years, is still being worked on, and improvements there and in Toronto are promised.

Massey Hall grew shabby. The windows (God's light is a pleasure rarely encountered today at concerts; the outside world has grown noisier, and new halls are wombed within outer structures) were blocked. The dignified classical exterior has been scrawled over by fire escapes. The original bold, bright Mauresque interior has been much altered. The sound in the hall remains very good, I think whenever I visit it, but for the performers, it seems, it is not. The Toronto Symphony and the Toronto Mendelssohn Choir wanted a new home. In 1972, Mr. Schultz was engaged to create its acoustical design, and Canada's foremost architect, Arthur Erickson, was chosen to implement it. Mr. Erickson's first sketches, revealed in 1977, for a huge tent of sparkling, many-faceted glass, unmullioned, hung freely over the auditorium within, were exciting. But, we are told, technical and financial objections dulled the realization of that idea, and the hall is now more regularly glazed—a circular greenhouse set on a rectangular concrete podium. In a city of soaring mirrored towers, it seems oddly squat, and on opening night its panes refused to catch light from the evening sky and remained leaden, sullen. As in Davies, lobbies ring the auditorium on linked levels, but here they are more spacious. All is concrete, glass, mirror, stainless steel, and silver-gray carpet, within a cage of white-painted tubular girders crisscrossing beneath the glass outer skin. The play of the terraces is intricate and perhaps a shade fussy. Inside the hall itself, concrete, silver-painted plaster on the lowest tier, gray seats, gray carpet, and gleaming organ pipes make an effect of restrained opulence. High above, there hangs a great glittering wheel of light, descending from a polychrome thicket of felt tubes and banners. Two balconies broken into "paddocks," or deep, steep boxes, ring the hall, dipping down toward the platform; above the platform they can serve as chorus seats.

At the opening concert, the Toronto Symphony, conducted by Andrew Davis, played Raymond Luedeke's *Fanfare,* composed for the occasion; Poulenc's Organ Concerto (Hugh McLean the soloist); and Ravel's second *Daphnis and Chloe* suite. The Mendelssohn Choir, conducted by Elmer Iseler, sang Murray Schafer's *Sun*—commissioned for the occasion and a rich, imaginative composition—and Ernest MacMillan's *Blanche comme la neige.* They joined in Walton's cantata *Belshazzar's Feast.* I sat in various places. From one, an upper side box, only half the orchestra was visible, and only that half could be clearly heard.

(But the unaccompanied choristers, part visible and part not, all sounded fine.) In the first balcony, the sound was clear and strong but not warm.

The cost of Roy Thomson Hall was about $39 million: $9.4 million-came from the Canadian government, $13.3 million from the government of Ontario (raised largely by lotteries), $5 million from the city of Toronto, and $16.4 million from corporations, foundations, and individuals. (The family of Roy Thomson, the newspaper baron, gave $4.5 million.) That leaves some $5 million over. Massey Hall still stands and is still being used.

Meyerhoff Hall, in Baltimore, cost $22 million, which was provided by the city, by the state, and—$10 million of it—by Mr. Meyerhoff, the Baltimore builder and philantropist who has been president of the Baltimore Symphony since 1965; he also presented the site. (To the extent that private contributions to good causes represent taxes remitted they should, I suppose, really be reckoned as public funding directed in accord with private inclination.) The principal architect was Pietro Belluschi. The hall seats 2,467—150 fewer than Baltimore's Lyric Theater (where the Baltimore Opera will continue to play). It is built of glazed brownish brick. A tall oval drum with a slanting roof rises from an egg-shaped construction housing offices and a lean-to lobby of glass, steel, and white-painted roof ribs. Inside, there are wooden walls around the platform, wooden seats upholstered in rust red, a wooden floor, and burnt-orange carpets down the aisles. The walls, white-plastered, are nowhere flat; they are cylindrical sections, of various widths and heights. Two balconies, broken into boxes with pointed prows, run round the sides and the back; their snouts are of plaster. Eighteen of Mr. Schultz's saucers, made of fiberglass-reinforced plaster veneered in wood, hang over the platform; and the ceiling, of concrete, is studded with fifty-two large, fixed concrete "buttons," painted white, and each weighing over a ton. From without, the hall might be taken for some kind of specialized hospital building. Inside, it is quirky and not exactly festive, but the assemblage of geometrical shapes is not unlikable in an "old-fashioned modern" way.

The Baltimore Symphony, conducted by Sergiu Comissiona, played Morton Gould's *Housewarming*, commissioned for the occasion; Franck's Symphonic Variations (which brought Leon Fleisher's much-welcomed return to the platform as a two-handed pianist; for sixteen years he had played only left-hand music in public); and Strauss's *Ein Heldenleben*. Like just about every hall I know, Meyerhoff sounded better when empty. At a rehearsal, the Strauss was broad, full-toned, and expansive. At the concert, the bloom had gone off it; it was hard and bright. Mr. Schultz had announced an average reverberation time of 2.4 seconds in the empty hall, of 1.9 in the full. Good halls vary widely, from (when filled) Vienna's 2.1, through Boston's 1.8, to Philadelphia's 1.4. Reverberation is but one of the many factors that make for pleasing musical sound. The conductor Denis Vaughan considers the desirable qualities, and ways these have been achieved, in a fascinating three-part *Musical Times* article, "Orchestral Sound in Concert Halls" (January to March, 1981). Richness, density, clarity, intimacy, weight, warmth, and singing tone are what he prizes. I cannot scientifically appraise his analyses and propositions but find most of them persuasive, because what he says matches the behavior of the halls I know. Particularly suggestive in his stress on the angling of primary reflections: the ear, a more selective receiver than an engineer's instruments, hears better musical quality in lateral than in overhead reflections, and so Mr. Vaughan pleads for narrow halls or halls narrowed by balconies. (Avery Fisher Hall is shaped roughly like Boston's, but it is significantly wider.) Can it be that Mr. Schultz's saucers transmit signals ill-angled for satisfactory reception?

Peoria, an attractive town beside the Illinois, has an unemployment rate above the national average. Its new Civic Center cost $64.2 million: $20 million came from the state, and $1.3 million from private donations; the rest, raised by the city, was underwritten by a three-percent hotel tax and a two-percent tax on restaurants, taverns, and profitable entertainments. It comprises a vast arena for sport and mass entertainment, a large exhibition hall and convention center, and a 2,187-seat theatre. (The cost of the last is estimated at around $18 million.) Philip Johnson and John Burgee were the architects. Their three linked buildings open off a lofty cloister walk, clad in reflecting glass, which traces an L around the Flemish-Renaissance City Hall (1897) and forms courtyards with it. Within the cloister, between the buildings, there are other exciting enclosed spaces—a Johnson/Burgee specialty. The theatre, a rectangle in polychrome fire brick, has an attached semicircular lobby rising to the full height of the building, one quadrant made of mirror glass. The design, like that of some other Johnson public buildings, is a puzzling mixture of high, bold invention and heaviness, of exuberant elegance and coarse, clumsy detail. The lobby, of brick, concrete, and glass, is a place at once impressive and uninviting; its semicircular upper ambulatories are oddly thick. The hall itself, roughly rectangular, is plain with gaudy touches. There is a triple-frame proscenium in wood. The walls are painted brown, and the seats are upholstered in mustard. There are two rear balconies and two tiers of boxes down the sides, with a row of dummy box fronts above them. All the box fronts are of coarse gilded grillework, studded penny-arcade (or Fisher Hall) fashion with naked light bulbs. From the ceiling, five "reverse barrel vaults" of gilded chain mail hang down, parallel to the stage.

The theatre is "multipurpose," and it opened with a triple bill: the finale of the Choral Symphony, played by the Peoria Symphony and sung by local choirs; scenes from *The Sleeping Beauty*, danced by the Peoria Civic Ballet; and Act II of *La traviata*, done by the Peoria Civic Opera. I attended a concert ten days later, at which the Chicago Symphony, conducted by Reynald Giovaninetti, played the Weber-Berlioz

Invitation to the Dance, Haydn's Symphony No. 85, and Berlioz's Symphonie Fantastique. For this concert, an orchestral shell enclosed the stage, with overhead panels reaching out into the house. While the halls in New Orleans, Toronto, and Baltimore are intended specifically as homes for orchestras, those in Peoria and Eugene will house "attractions" of all kinds: rock groups, amplified Broadway musicals, grand opera, ballet, concerts. The acoustician of both, Mr. Jaffe, has therefore given them what might be called "neutral" basic acoustics—dry enough to accept amplified events without mushing, clear enough for opera, reasonably acceptable for symphonic music. But Mr. Jaffe has also provided them with "electronic enhancement," designed to invest classical music with the warmth, fullness, and bloom that musicians desire. At the Chicago concert in Peoria, however, it had been decided not to use the electronics but to let the orchestra play in the hall's natural acoustics. The sound was loud, bright, clear, and immediate, but—I sat in two parts of the stalls—it remained obstinately "frontal"; there was no satisfying sense of being surrounded by music. There are people who maintain that the better recordings of the thirties and forties sound more like "the real thing" than do the super-brilliant, meticulously defined hi-fi recordings of today. And I can hear what they mean. Many modern concert halls—and also, perhaps, some modern conductors and orchestras—seem to aspire to make the real thing sound more and more like a hi-fi recording.

Some regard "electronic" acoustics as immoral. I cannot. I lived long in London, where the acoustics of the Royal Festival Hall, built in 1951, were for thirteen years clear but bleak—in Claudio Arrau's words, "a little antiseptic." Then an electronic system of "assisted resonance" (many linked microphones, amplifiers, and loudspeakers, each set tuned to a particular frequency band) began to be installed—secretly and invisibly. Musicians, not knowing why, commented on the improved sound. After a Berlin Philharmonic concert, Herbert von Karajan declared that "the wood in the Festival Hall was adapting itself more and more to music, like an old violin." Then we were told what had been done. It was too late for indignation: the musical merits of the system had been proved and approved. Festival Hall performers and audiences have long since stopped remembering that what they listen to is electronically "fudged." Is it a moral matter? I think not. Electronically assisted resonance is not crude amplification but merely one of the more effective (and less costly) ways—other ways being the deployment of flying saucers, banners, reflective panels, whatever—of making a large hall as acoustically admirable as possible.

The system, developed by the British firm AIRO, is employed in the Concord Pavilion, outside San Francisco; in the Scottsdale Center for the Performing Arts, in Arizona (to render a dry spoken-word theatre resonant when music is played there); and, on music nights, in Kansas City's multi-purpose Music Hall. Mr. Jaffe has installed it in the Silva Concert Hall of the Hult Center for the Performing Arts, in Eugene.

He has also installed there his own electronic reflected-energy system, or ERES, which is not, he stresses, a sound-reinforcement system but one that "uses pre-amplifiers, amplifiers, speakers, an analog computer, and other electronic components to simulate the reflections of sound waves from the architectural surfaces that would be most desired for specific performances." By the use of it, he claims, he can—sonically—make a wide hall as narrow as Mr. Vaughan might desire, lower or raise ceilings, turn a dry studio into a resonant cathedral, and enclose an open field with a reflecting roof and walls. On *Idomeneo* nights, a huge place like the Met or the State Theater could at the push of a button marked "Mozart" be made acoustically intimate; on *Parsifal* nights, a push of the "Wagner" button would insure Bayreuth sonority. It sounds wonderful. In Eugene, it did sound wonderful at rehearsals, when we heard demonstrations of AIRO and ERES, separately and together, on and off while music was playing. In the 2,450-seat hall, a piano quintet seemed acoustically to be in a chamber. (There was an initially disturbing effect of aural propinquity and visual distance.) At the opening concert, however, the controls, untried before in a filled house, were imperfectly adjusted. The Eugene Symphony, conducted by William McGlaughlin, played Thomas Svoboda's *Eugene Overture*, commissioned for the occasion; a *Rosenkavalier* waltz sequence; and Beethoven's Fifth Symphony. Marilyn Horne sang assorted arias. And—I tried both the stalls and the first balcony—everything seemed frontal and far away: distinct, well defined, and perfectly audible, but more overheard than "shared."

Eugene, like Peoria, has been hard hit by the recession. Its Performing Arts Center, which cost $26.7 million (raised by the city, from a bond issue and private contributions), is a deed of civic renewal. It stands downtown, beside a new convention center and an agreeable Hilton. Its architects are Hardy Holzman Pfeiffer, and they have produced the most lively and individual of the five halls here considered. They are no doctrinal or predictable trio. Their Orchestra Hall in Minneapolis—high adventure within a traditional acoustic frame—has already been mentioned. Into their Civic Center in Madison they incorporated the old Capitol Theater as the town's concert hall and a Montgomery Ward store as its art gallery. Their Eugene building has a poured-concrete exterior with a lively surface; its P shape is swelled to a rectangle by a lobby made of nine lofty, lapped gables—metal-roofed, glass-fronted with some courses colored and some clear—soaring one above the next, to eighty-five feet. One enters onto a meadow of flowery carpet traversed by apple-green tiled paths; towering shafts of squared natural fir lift the eyes to a skywalk high above. All is light, lively, and colorful. Two halls open off this lobby: the Soreng Theatre, a 515-seater, for plays, chamber opera, and recitals, a richly designed, dramatic, fanciful, yet very usable place; and the Silva Concert Hall, for symphony, opera, ballet, and other large shows. One gasps on entering the concert hall. Something so curvy, so unsolemn, so rococo and modern at once would be less surprising in Barcelona or in Prague. Then the eye lights on a proudly American feature: the curve of the proscenium arch surely echoes Sullivan's Auditorium, as does the way that shape is continued into the hall itself, where side-walls and ceiling merge into one embracing arc. Its surface is apparently woven, on the diagonal, of broad cream-colored slats banded in pale jade green and gold. The seats are wooden, with jade-green upholstery and curiously high wooden backs. The floor is covered by dark-green linoleum, with mushroom carpets down the aisles. There are two balconies—or maybe three, since the rear stalls rise up and sweep forward down the sides of the hall.

HHP are architects at once high-spirited, playful, and practical. (There is one practical flaw in their design—an inconspicuous step in the otherwise smooth slope of the stalls aisle. On opening night, one or two scurrying people took a tumble.) As one prowls around the elegant building, delighted by the opening of each new vista or by some inspired detail, one finds a pleasing sublimation of mundane materials: the delicate grilles are commercial granite-sifting screens, and the robust ones New York subway gratings; the roof above the apparently weightless (but acoustically reflective) basketwork is carried on precast highway girders. A posse of Oregon artists has contributed glass panels, tile friezes, ceramics, bronzes, highly wrought wooden railings to beguile the eye and seduce stroking fingertips. Margaret Matson and Mollie Favour's charming house curtain, forty feet by ninety, is hand-printed with an airy row of blackberry vines beneath a shower of glassy raindrops. This is a delightful and thoroughly civilized building, substantial and serious, yet executed with a light touch. Perhaps the word for it is Mozartian. If AIRO and ERES do their stuff properly, lucky Eugene!

ARISTOCRATS

October 25, 1982

POMERIUM MUSICES, a nine-voice chorus directed by Alexander Blachly, who sometimes adds his own bass voice to the ensemble, provided an evening of unalloyed, intricate delight at a packed Merkin Hall recital this month. The program bore the general title "The First Flowers of the Renaissance." Guillaume Dufay, who dominated European music in the fifteenth century, supplied most of the music. The Kyrie, Gloria, and Sanctus of his *Ave regina celorum* Mass made a framework around which rondeaux and motets by Jacques Vide, Johannes Ciconia, Baude Cordier, Beltrame Feragut, Gilles Binchois, Leonel Power, and Dufay himself were spun. These included Dufay's lament for Constantinople fallen into the hand of the Turk (1453 is the schoolboy's starting point for the Renaissance; for musicians and art historians it begins rather earlier) and ended with his motet on the Mass chant—the motet Dufay asked to hear during his last moments on earth. The Pomerium is a virtuoso Renaissance ensemble: smooth, fluid, supple, carefully balanced, exquisite but not arty in timbre, sure-footed in rhythm. Its recording of Dufay's *Ecce ancilla domini* Mass (Nonesuch) is beautiful. At this recital, I thought it reached new heights of achievement, treading one rhythmic maze after another with the serene swiftness or slowness of Balanchine dancers, with skill and confidence that were never merely dapper. Eugene IV and the Este, Malatesta, Medici, Savoy, and Burgundian dukes—Dufay's connections were wide—would surely have approved. Some New York ensembles can silence criticism. Speculum Musicae (now resident at Columbia University) is one, and on the strength of this recital Pomerium Musices is another. Everything was right. (Beckmesser's chalk hung over the slate at a moment of questionable lower-voice intonation but withdrew as the harmony swiftly cleared.) The music ranged from the secularly captivating to the sublime. On subsidiary but not unimportant levels, there were well-planned program notes, texts and translations, and light to read them by. The choristers looked clean and attractive, with tidy, well-brushed hair. The "staging"—platform disposition, grouping for the varied textures, moves on and off, general demeanor—was unobtrusively deft, both friendly and decorous. Most important, Dufay's sheer musical mastery shone forth.

The City Opera season continued with new productions of Ambroise Thomas's *Hamlet* (Sherrill Milnes in the title role, Ashley Putnam as Ophelia, and a set borrowed from San Diego); *The Magic Flute* (newly directed by Jay Lesenger in the 1966 Beni Montresor scenery); Gluck's *Alceste*; and Leonard Bernstein's *Candide*. *Hamlet* and the *Flute* were done in English—in my English, so I won't review them. *Alceste* was a rather dismal affair; Gluck's noble opera seems to be cropping up all over, and I'll hold a review until I have seen the Kentucky Opera production later this month. *Candide* on its opening night was coarse, heavy, and clumsy. Only David Eisler, in the title role, could be admired.

There were also revivals of three of last season's unhappy new stagings. Montemezzi's *L'amore dei tre re* was as dull as before: the soprano, the tenor, and the baritone were inadequate to their roles; only the bass, Samuel Ramey, was good. The Cherubini-Lachner-Frazzi-Serafin *Medea* (the City Opera persists in using an Italian translation of a German *Bearbeitung*, further worked over by two Italians, of Cherubini's French opera *Médée*) had a fiery heroine in Marisa Galvany and an able Neris in Susanne Marsee. Rita Shane was assured but miscast as the vulnerable Dirce. James Wagner was a stolid Jason. Harry Dworchak, new to the company but familiar elsewhere (I admired his Timur in Newark eight years ago), made a potent Creon. Klaus Weise's conducting was weak.

One performance eagerly awaited was Carol Vaness's Violetta, in the revival of last season's *Traviata* production: Miss Vaness is one of our most exciting young sopranos, with a voice that can carry the emotional colors of tragedy, triumph, rapture. Her Donna Anna at Glyndebourne this summer was highly praised. I wish she could have been the First Lady of the *Flute* (a role Ternina, Lilli Lehmann, and Frida Leider used to sing) and the heroine of *Alceste*. Her first Violetta began affectingly. The timbre was rich, dark, and lustrous, the phrasing delicate. But she was unwell: toward the end of "Ah fors'è lui" she faltered, and at the close of it she retired. Miss Putnam, who happened to be in the house, finished the show with accomplishment and aplomb, despite the fact that the staging was new to her. Miss Vaness's complete Violetta a fortnight later left me with mixed feelings. It was hugely promising but in need of musical and dramatic discipline. The singer seemed to have forgotten that Verdi's frequent dots-under-a-slur indication, as on the "unico" of "unico raggio di bene," in the Act II duet, does not mean stabbed staccatos; that rests between notes, as at the start of "Ah fors'è lui," mean a cessation of tone but not piqué staccatos (Gemma Bellincioni, a Violetta whom Verdi admired, simply sang through the rests); that plain slurs between notes often mean—if we can trust the recorded evidence of singers Verdi worked with—a portamento joining of note to note. Dramatic silences were exaggerated to a point where one expected a prompter's voice to remind the singer what came next. The soaring arches in the second-act finale, on "Ah perchè venni, incauta," and then twice on "Che fia? morir mi sento," were uttered note by note, not as smooth spans. At "Alfredo, Alfredo," which Verdi marked to be sung "con voce debolissima," Miss Vaness thinned the sound to a sickly croak. She has it in her, I feel sure, to be a great Violetta. She has the voice for it. And "she has a beautiful face, spirit, and theatrical presence—the best qualities for a Traviata" (Verdi's description of Rosina Penco, who he hoped would first sing the role). From the City Opera production—which is dowdy, and difficult to sit through to the end (the Act II finale, divided from the preceding scene by an intermission, is almost a collector's piece of operatic awfulness)—she received little support. Jon Garrison, the Alfredo, gentlemanly in an anyone-for-tennis way, was passable, and so was William Stone, the Germont, although by failing to elide consecutive vowels he sang several notes that Verdi did not write. Bruce Ferden conducted.

Last season's general pattern is not yet decisively broken: an adventurous and interesting repertory; a roster of young artists which any company in the world might envy; much ill-conceived staging, crude lighting, and feeble chorus work; all too often, mediocrity on the podium; and some odd casting.

David Tanenbaum, a poetical and musical young guitarist, gave a brief, pleasing recital in Merkin Hall last month. It began with two Mozart pieces billed as Larghetto and Allegro, K. 229, arranged by Julian Bream; they proved to be two movements from the five woodwind-trio divertimentos deemed dubious by Köchel and banished to the appendix of his catalogue, as K.-Anhang 229, but reinstated by Einstein as Mozart's work, K. 439b. Mr. Tanenbaum played them with poise and grace. Then there was Bach's A-minor lute suite, exquisitely shaped, and William Walton's elegantly wrought Five Bagatelles (composed for Mr. Bream in 1971, and five years later reworked as the *Varii Capricci* for full orchestra). The second half was Hans Werner Henze's *Royal Winter Music,* composed in 1976 for Mr. Bream, in answer to his request for "a guitarist's Hammerklavier," and played by him in Town Hall six years ago. It is a substantial suite in six movements: Gloucester; Romeo and Juliet; Ariel; Ophelia; Touchstone, Audrey, and William; Oberon. Composers' responses to Shakespeare, in whatever medium, are ever arresting. Henze's character sketches are drawn with swift, sure strokes.

Mr. Tanenbaum has the gift of making listeners hang upon lines and attend keenly to discourse. At this recital, he eschewed virtuoso panache of the kind that suddenly can fire Mr. Bream's playing, although he, too, commands it, I know: he displayed it as the guitarist of Henze's *El cimarrón* in San Jose's New Sounds festival last year. At this New York recital, he seemed to be on his best behavior, concerned above all to show the guitar as a serious and subtle classical instrument. In that he succeeded. It was an evening of refined, aristocratic music-making.

HOW TO LIVE IN GRACE

November 1, 1982

IT WOULD be hard to justify the pouring of so much public money into the performance of opera if its composers were not among the unacknowledged legislators of the world. On consecutive October nights, at the State Theater and at the Metropolitan, there were new productions of operas that could move their listeners to more than pleasure in the singing, the scenery, and the sound of the orchestra. At the Met, Arbaces, King Idomeneus' minister, cried, "Unfortunate Sidon, I see death all around you...Sidon no more, but the city of grief." Although it was a Cretan, not the Lebanese, city he mourned, the sentence rang out strongly: Mozart's *Idomeneo* is an opera about, among other things, an individual's responsibility for public suffering and his readiness, after long reluctance, to resign power when his policy has proved disastrous. The City Opera production was of Leonard Bernstein's *Candide,* which is based on a 1759 book so topical that illustrations to its chapters can be seen in any television news program. Neither opera was given a narrowly didactic, politicized, or modern-dress staging. Neither requires it. They are poetic parables, not tracts. Applicability should not be confused with allegory; musical discourse about despair or hope, confusion or order is easily obscured by a director's added imagery. All that the works require is lucid, sympathetic, accurately styled execution. *Idomeneo* was seriously performed. *Candide*, alas, was not.

I first saw *Candide* in 1959, in London. Mary Costa, soon to be a San Francisco Violetta and Gilda, sang Cunegonde; Denis Quilley sang Candide; Edith Coates, a Covent Garden Fricka and Amneris, sang the Old Lady. Osbert Lancaster designed bright scenery. Since then, like many other admirers of the piece, I have been waiting for regular opera companies to take *Candide* into the repertory. It is a work at once witty, intelligent, and entertaining, and one that bears repetition. Lillian Hellman wrote the libretto. Richard Wilbur wrote most of the lyrics; John Latouche, Dorothy Parker, Miss Hellman, and the composer contributed others. Like *The Magic Flute*, *Candide* is a "musical" created by a team of inspired collaborators, and a popular entertainment that deals with important matters. Voltaire's *Candide*, André Maurois said, "represents one of the attitudes of the human mind, and perhaps the bravest." It is "admirable as a work of art." In it, "the wild chaos of the universe is . . . expressed and controlled by a rhythm. Over every page stream unforeseeable cascades of facts, and yet the swift movement, the regular recurrence of Pangloss's optimistic themes, Martin's pessimistic themes, the Old Woman's narratives, and Candide's refrains afford the mind that troubled, tragic repose which is given only by great poetry." Much the same—read "unforeseeable cascades of buoyant musical invention"—can be said of Bernstein's *Candide*. At its close, the composer, more generously optimistic than Voltaire, swells the small, rational consolation of "Il faut cultiver notre jardin" to an exhortatory C-major affirmation.

Candide was first performed in Boston, in October, 1956. It was directed by Tyrone Guthrie and designed by Oliver Smith. Robert Rounseville, Barbara Cook, and Irra Petina sang Candide, Cunegonde, and the Old Lady. That December, the production came to the Martin Beck Theater, on Broadway, where it ran for seventy-three performances—a figure most contemporary opera composers would be glad to achieve but one not high enough, it seems, for a Broadway success. The music—to judge by the original-cast recording (Columbia)—was not well executed, except by Miss Petina. The book was criticized for pretension. *Candide* reappeared for a night in Philharmonic Hall in 1968, provided with a revised book, by Michael Stewart and Sheldon Patinkin, and with some songs not sung in the original production. In 1971, another production, with further reworking, expired on tour, in Washington. Then in 1973 *Candide* was revived at the

Brooklyn Academy; the show came to the Broadway Theater, and it ran there for seven hundred and forty-one performances. This was not, however, the original Hellman-Bernstein *Candide;* it was an abridged, one-act reworking of it. There was an altogether new book, by Hugh Wheeler. The musical numbers were disordered; some were assigned to the wrong characters, and several were placed in a wrong setting. There were one or two new songs, with lyrics by Stephen Sondheim. The piece was rescored, by Hershy Kay, for a thirteen-piece ensemble. Harold Prince directed it on what he describes (in a foreword to the libretto-cum-vocal score of this edition, published by Schirmer) as "an intricate network of platforms, stages, runways, ramps, and drawbridges all around and through the audience." I did not see the production, but I have heard it (on the original-cast recording, also Columbia), and I do not like what I hear. The singing is wretched, the dialogue slow, and the orchestra scrawny. Worse: the new book cheapens and confuses the original. Admirers of *Candide* clung to the 1956 recording, the original vocal score (Amberson/ Schirmer), and the original libretto (Random House; republished by Little, Brown in Miss Hellman's *Collected Plays),* and waited on for an opera company to rescue the piece from Mr. Prince's and Mr. Wheeler's attentions.

The City Opera, which performs yet a new edition, billed as the "opera house version," has not rescued it. The director is again Mr. Prince. The book is again by Mr. Wheeler, and not much altered from his earlier effort. On the credit side, there is a proper orchestra, and the musical supervision is in the hands of the Bernstein scholar and champion John Mauceri, who also conducts (very well). The scoring is by Bernstein, Mr. Kay, and Mr. Mauceri. Mr. Mauceri has restored musical integrity to some numbers that were mangled in 1973. Moreover, five good numbers that were dropped in 1973 have been reinstated. But they appear now in irrelevant contexts, to new texts, and their effectiveness is thereby diminished. The Paris Waltz is danced in the New World. The Eldorado ballad, shorn of its Hellman text, is sung in mid-Atlantic. The Act I quartet-finale is shifted from Buenos Aires to Cadiz, and "Quiet" from Buenos Aires to an Atlantic island. (In Mr. Wheeler's book, Cunegonde never reaches the New World, and her Périchole-like passages with the Governor are distributed, awkwardly, between Maximilian *en travesti* and Paquette.) "What's the use?," the casino waltz quartet, is shifted from Venice to Constantinople. The last three pieces are sung by the wrong characters. Two strophes of "Dear boy," Pangloss's only solo, are also restored. (The song dates from 1956 but was dropped from the original production.) It is good to hear all this music again, but dramatically the process that began in 1973—converting a coherent and shapely work of art into a piece of low, brash flummery—is continued. The clear scheme of the original—its scenes laid in Westphalia, Lisbon, Paris, Buenos Aires,

Venice, Westphalia again, and each with a distinct musical character—becomes a muddle. A musically integrated score is dismembered. The networks of development and allusion are rent.

The new staging, like the new book, replaces polished Voltairean wit with stock gags and routines. Of Voltaire's and Bernstein's point and purpose nothing remains—except in the performance of David Eisler, as Candide, who somehow rises above the clutter and rubbish all around him to find the poetry, the romance, the honest emotion, and the small bright beam of reasonable hope, making life's tragedy endurable, that shine in both the book and the original opera. Mr. Eisler's tenor is sweet and true. His phrasing and acting were sincere and unaffectedly eloquent. Erie Mills, the Cunegonde, stood no chance against the production; she was directed as a shrill, pert little floozie. John Lankston, as Voltaire, Pangloss, etc., fell back on a series of funny voices. Muriel Costa-Greenspon, as the Old Lady (got up as a parody of Beverly Sills), made no more of her than a stage-joke émigrée, and she sang atrociously. The company that performed Kurt Weill's Broadway opera *Street Scene* so accurately, so sensitively, so movingly was unrecognizable; everyone but Mr. Eisler was a two-dimensional comic cutout. Clarke Dunham's décor was drab, and Ken Billington's lighting rudimentary.

When the Birmingham Repertory Theatre brought the 1973 *Candide* to the Edinburgh Festival last year, a colleague, loving Bernstein's score and deploring Mr. Wheeler's book, expressed (in *Opera*) the hope that "this airing may encourage one of our opera companies to tackle the piece in its original, operetta form, Hellman book and all." After the City Opera airing of *Candide*, I say the same. But what we need is a critical edition containing all the music that Bernstein has composed for the piece, even though sorting it out may prove to be a harder task than sorting out Verdi's *Don Carlos*. The composer, I am told, has boxfuls of *Candide* material, used and unused. The Public Library, I discover, holds two preliminary Wheeler drafts, entitled *Dr. Voltaire's Candide*, for the 1973 version. On the first night, a typescript libretto (subsequently withdrawn) not corresponding to the City Opera performance but apparently representing a transitional stage between the Broadway and the opera-house editions was on sale. (It contains a long, tedious spoken prologue, and several numbers bear the rubric "Lyric to be rewritten.") Each production of *Candide* has included musical numbers not heard in others: among them, in 1959 the Cunegonde–Old Lady duet "We are women;" in 1968 Pangloss's "Ring-a-round-a-rosy" (an alternative to his "Dear boy"); in 1971 Martin's "Words, words, words." The duet "One hand, one heart," familiar from *West Side Story*, was originally composed for Candide and Cunegonde, and should perhaps be restored to them. Whatever music is used, it should be used in its proper place and assigned to the characters it was composed for. The debased City Opera *Candide* merits no

332

further currency [*but has received it in the form of revivals and a New World Records album*].

Of *Idomeneo* we do have a complete critical edition, made by Daniel Heartz for the Neue Mozart-Ausgabe. In his main text, Mr. Heartz includes both the opera as Mozart first brought it to the stage, in Munich in 1781, and the new music that he composed for it five years later, for a concert performance in Vienna—two authorized versions, the first with a soprano and the second with a tenor Idamantes. To an appendix Mr. Heartz relegates the music that Mozart cut before the Munich première: passages of recitative, and three arias in Act III. The composer's cuts were drastic, and few Mozartians have been able to bring themselves to accept them. From Munich, Mozart reported that those who had got to know the jettisoned arias sighed at their loss but "one has to make a virtue of necessity." Mr. Heartz himself restores in full to the main text two solo-with-chorus prayers in Act III which Mozart reduced to their first strophes. He opines that their abridgment was due "more to the special circumstances of the Munich première than to general musico-dramatic necessity." (He does, of course, indicate clearly where the cuts were.) In the assembling of any performing edition of *Idomeneo,* special pleading and specific circumstances are likely to play a part. Mozart cut recitatives for Idomeneus and Idamantes, it is said, because his first performers of the roles sang recitative monotonously; the former, he told his father, was wooden, and the latter inexperienced, and they were "the worst actors that ever trod the stage." So, people argue, if good actors can now be found, should not the recitatives be restored? A composer's letters must be read in full context before phrases from them are used to bolster artistic decisions. The strong remarks about the original performers' incompetence were made in self-justificatory reply to Leopold's insistence that the crucial recognition should not be cut but, if anything, lengthened; and his letter was occasioned by Wolfgang's having earlier declared that the scene in full "would certainly bore the audience." In general, the Met follows the Munich text, but two of the discarded arias have been restored: Electra's "D'Oreste, d'Aiace" and Idomeneus' "Torna la pace." Neither of them bores the Met audience. The former, indeed, brings the house down, stops the show—which is possibly why Mozart removed it from a score carefully planned to proceed with as few audience interruptions as possible. However, if "D'Oreste, d'Aiace" is to be included then "Torna la pace" should also be heard; otherwise the last extended utterance comes from a character who retires from the action, and the resolution seems perfunctory, especially when the clinching celebratory ballet is omitted (as it is by the Met). In theory, one wants to hear and see the ballet. In current opera-house practice—given the kind of dancing offered by, for example, the Covent Garden and the City Opera productions of Gluck's *Alceste*—one is glad to be spared it. The most serious objection that can be offered to the Met edition is that Electra sings both her aria and, before it, the fiery recitative that Mozart composed to replace it. That is an artistic misjudgment. One or the other, not both!

As a large-scale mass-audience introduction to the greatness of *Idomeneo*, the Met production, the company's first, serves pretty well. Although there is more to the *dramma eroico* than is revealed here—subtleties of sound and sense that only a refined performance in a smaller house can discover—the vigor and the richness of the piece come across. Jean-Pierre Ponnelle has designed and directed it in a large, romanticized neoclassical setting, a revised edition of a staging that has been seen through Europe and in San Francisco and Chicago. The drama is again played against a huge masonry mask of Neptune —his mouth, Bomarzo-fashion, squarely opened to make a doorway— but the design is much improved. It is now a stern, menacing classical mask, freed of the rococo marine trimmings—starfish, whelks, cockles, cods—that formerly cased and prettified it. In the Met edition, neoclassical painted curtains, representing a temple, a pleasant landscape, a public square, mask the mask until someone sings "Nettuno" (as someone often does); then the curtain becomes transparent and Neptune's face glowers through. As an emblem of the *numi implacabili* that rule human existence and hold Idomeneus to his vow (like Jephthah, he rashly promised to sacrifice the first person he met, and met his own child), it is striking. But it does not allow for a final transformation to a new order—a New Testament gospel, as it were, replacing the inexorable decrees of the Old: the triumph of love and self-sacrifice over retributive justice (as in Wagner's first, optimistic close to the *Ring*). The scenery is very well painted. The handsome costumes are eighteenth-century, except Ilia's; she, the Trojan princess, wears classical Greek dress.

The cast is headed by Luciano Pavarotti, in the title role. He gives a serious and dignified performance, confident and committed as his Idamantes at Glyndebourne eighteen years ago was not, and he makes more of the Italian text than anyone else. Frederica von Stade is an accurate, tasteful, but slightly pallid Idamantes. Hildegard Behrens, got up in a large black dress and a red wig, is a passionately overheated, excitable, and impressive Electra, if sometimes histrionic to the point of parody. Her voice comes and goes. Neither she nor, in a different way, Ileana Cotrubas, the Ilia, seems in easy, flowing command of all her music. John Alexander, the Arbaces, sings incisively but in worn tones. They are all intelligent and experienced singers. Mr. Ponnelle's production presents high emotions enacted on a large scale. From earlier versions he retains his fondness for eavesdroppers: during Ilia's first aria, a soliloquy, Idamantes and Electra are prominent; during her second, Idamantes plays peekaboo behind a pillar; and during her third he lies upstage doing arm-lifting exercises. The second-act trio becomes a visual quartet; and so on. The treatment of the famous dispersal chorus at the close of Act II, "Corriamo, fuggiamo," prompts the comment "Yes, but you *don't* go," and the hero's sentimental exit at the close of Act III seems to call for "Adieu, Idoménée; on t'aimait." However, the issues at stake are clearly presented. The drama moves powerfully. The style chosen combines directness and romance with due formality. *Idomeneo* can be seen and heard as what David Hamilton's program note calls it, "arguably the greatest serious opera of the eighteenth century."

James Levine's conducting is strong, energetic, a little insistent. One senses him beating the time to his soloists on the stage and in the pit. Many necessary appoggiaturas are missing. Even if the singers and their conductor have not learned to read eighteenth-century musical notation, they can find its conventions spelled out above the staff in the Heartz edition. Frederick Neumann, in an article in the spring *Journal of the American Musicological Society*, declares that the Neue Mozart-Ausgabe editors introduce too many appoggiaturas, and some of a wrong kind, but even within his guidelines—more narrowly drawn than mine—the *Idomeneo* cast introduces too few. Robert Donington, in his latest handbook, *Baroque Music: Style and Performance* (Norton), is forthright: "The addition of the ornament is not optional, but an obligatory correction of misnotation recognized by every trained musician.... It is of paramount importance, for example, in the recitatives of Mozart." The Met sells (for $3.50) an Italian/English libretto wrongly lineated and with the stage directions missing.

SAINTLY SHOUT AND SOLEMN JUBILEE

November 8, 1982

THE VOLUMES of the New Grove are as seductive and time-consuming —if not always as elegantly written—as those of the eleventh Britannica. Consulting them on one topic, one strays to the next, and reads on. My Volume VIII, "H to Hyporchēma," usually falls open now at Anthony Hicks's careful Handel work list, but the other day the reproduction of a page of Hildegard of Bingen's *Symphonia armonie celestium revelationum* caught my eye and led me into Ian Bent's fascinating columns about Hildegard, a twelfth-century abbess who was known as the Sibyl of the Rhine, who was consulted by popes and emperors, and who wrote accounts of her visions, biographies, scientific and medical treatises, much lyrical poetry ("laden with brilliant imagery"), and the psychoanalytical drama *Ordo virtutum.* Her poetry and the play survive in musical settings, and what Mr. Bent says about the music made me eager to hear some of it. A few days later, I did. Andrea von Ramm was going to give the second recital in the Music Before 1800 series in

Corpus Christi Church, on 121st Street. I went along blind, as it were —no details of the program had been announced—but hardly deaf, for Miss Ramm, a member of Thomas Binkley's fine Studio der Frühen Musik during its eighteen years of existence (1960–77), is someone not to be missed; and she sang a long sequence from Hildegard's *Ordo*. It was gripping, beautiful—a patterned discourse urgent yet serene. It would have been more gripping still had one known precisely what Miss Ramm was singing about so eloquently. Several composers —among them Monteverdi, Mussorgsky, and Janáček—dreamed of setting words in a musical language so explicit that their meaning would be internationally intelligible even though the actual words were not understood. It remained a dream. One still needs to hear and understand the words of a song; sounds alone can be disconcertingly protean. When Rossini revised his Neapolitan opera *Mosè in Egitto* as the French opera *Moïse*, he assigned the music he had composed to express the despair of "Tormenti! affanni! smanie!" to the joyful outburst "Qu'entends-je? ô douce ivresse." In the City Opera's *Candide*, Candide sings "Life is happiness indeed: mares to ride and books to read" to the gavotte Leonard Bernstein composed for Dorothy Parker's lyric "I've got troubles, as I said. Mother's dying, Father's dead." Miss Ramm illustrated the point by devoting her second group to "the French original and the German contrafactum." The minnesingers, as every music student knows, wrote new German verses to trouvère melodies. Miss Ramm sang first trouvère and then minnesinger versions of four songs, and although—insofar as someone unable, without a text, to follow every turn of sung medieval French and sung medieval German could judge—the differences of verbal content were less extreme than in the Rossini and Bernstein examples, they were still striking.

The recital had the general title "Monophony, Machaut, and Minnesang." (The previous concert in the series, given by the Folger Consort, was also devoted in part to Machaut.) Miss Ramm brought pages of medieval history to life with the famous Carolingian "Lament of the Swan"; with the one surviving tune from the hymnbook Abelard wrote for Héloïse; with "the wild Alexander"'s surrealist fantasy "Hie vor dô wir kynder wâren,"; with a song by the adventurous Oswald von Wolkenstein, whose portrait, perhaps by Pisanello, eye-catchingly adorns another page of Grove. The listener's mind, without leaving a New York where runners in Central Park were recalling the check to Darius' advance upon Athens, or leaving a church planned by its builders to reflect tradition while serving the needs of a New World, could range the centuries and ponder on forces that have shaped our history and our art. Miss Ramm accompanied herself now on a medieval harp, now on an organetto, now with clapsticks. Her voice is steady yet wonderfully colorful. She used the architecture to enhance the music, laying her song out through its spaces. Her presence is inspired. Bespectacled, wearing a gray sweater of subtle weave, she occasionally

336

turned eyes and voice to heaven and was transfigured to a St. Cecilia who might well draw an angel down. Saint melted into seductive woman in a final group of Machaut virelais, when the accents of Carmen, of Manon, of Cunegonde filled the church. And, finally, the accents and timbre of Edith Piaf, in Machaut's complainte "Tel rit au main," which Miss Ramm sang in alternating verses of English translation and French. Her English was accented, but—like Elisabeth Schumann's, Conchita Supervia's, Caruso's—it was vivid. All one had missed before by not being able to hang on words as well as sounds was made clear.

The Berlin Philharmonic Orchestra, which last month gave four concerts in Carnegie Hall, is a hundred years old. Like several European orchestras, it is supported by public funds but is self-governing, and it chooses its own conductors. Hans von Bülow was its chief conductor from 1887 to 1894; he was followed by Arthur Nikisch (1895–1922), Wilhelm Furtwängler (1922–54), and Herbert von Karajan (from 1955). To mark the centenary, Deutsche Grammophon has issued six handsome record albums. The first volume contains early Berlin Philharmonic recordings, including a Beethoven Fifth conducted in 1913 by Nikisch. The second, devoted to Furtwängler, includes a Fifth recorded at a 1947 concert. Volumes III (with a 1977 Fifth) and VI are conducted by Karajan. Volume IV is a concerto anthology, and Volume V presents the orchestra under guest conductors—Karl Böhm, Claudio Abado, Rafael Kubelik. Generalizations about an orchestra's particular character are perhaps too easily made, and yet in a strange way some of our long-established great orchestras do seem to maintain a basic character even while bearing the individual stamp of their successive conductors. Recordings made over the decades prove it. The Amsterdam Concertgebouw, the Leningrad Philharmonic, the Philadelphia, the Vienna Philharmonic, the Czech Philharmonic— each has its recognizable timbre, gait, and manner. The Berlin Philharmonic has perhaps the longest, firmest "breath" of any orchestra (though some might wish to claim that for Dresden). Its tone is broad, deep, and full. By comparison with the Vienna Philharmonic, it is an unemotional orchestra—less heart-on-sleeve, readier to "state" than to "sing," less rapt in the sheer beauty of its tone. It never sounds febrile or forced but always grandly and proudly confident, massive in full ensemble, and unhurried even at prestissimo.

Those are the generalizations, the constants. Under Furtwängler, the orchestra took on a rather more vibrant, free-flowing, rapturous quality—although Furtwängler's Beethoven with the Berlin players remained more "classical" (but not less poetic) than his Beethoven with the Vienna Philharmonic. Karajan then added a new virtuosity. He cast his recruiting net wide and brought in more players from abroad— James Galway as first flute, for example. Mr. Galway's autobiography contains lively chapters on his six years with the Berlin Philharmonic and Karajan. He stresses both the intense competitiveness—"I was playing with an orchestra where every member hopes to outshine the others"—and the sense of communal achievement:

> Its strength does not lie in the exceptional work of one or two outstanding players. In Berlin, by a process of careful selection and by paying the highest salaries, only the best musicians eventually appear on the Philharmonic platform. The man on the back desk of the second violins is likely to be the equal of the best in Europe.... In the last analysis, though, it is the way the whole orchestra has been welded into a team...that makes it, in my view, the finest orchestra in the world.

The personnel list in the Carnegie program included famous names but was manifestly incomplete. Who was the remarkable first clarinet at the opening concert? I hardly believe she is called Karl, Peter, Herbert, or Manfred. [*In fact, she was Sabine Meyer, on probation with the orchestra; and the following month there was a much-publicized disagreement between Karajan and the Berlin Philharmonic. Karajan wrote to the players: "You decided not to secure the talents of Ms. Meyer.... It is your right, contractually, to decide upon either a positive or negative recommendation vis-à-vis a candidate. On the other hand, however, I find my judgment and that of the orchestra are in this instance diametrically opposed."*]

Karajan put a high tonal gloss on the solid Berlin virtues. His orchestra learned to outplay the best French players in *La Mer* or the *Symphonie Fantastique*, to outplay the best Russians in Tchaikovsky ballets or Shostakovich symphonies. The sound became matchless—smoother, more luminous, more beautiful, more exquisite in pianissimi, more rounded at climaxes than anything one had ever heard. As a conductor, he declared, he aimed to combine "Toscanini's precision with Furtwängler's fantasy." As a conductor he seldom won the fervent, wholehearted surrender accorded—by many, not by all—to Toscanini and Furtwängler. All succumbed to the tonal beauty and splendor of his performances. David Cairns, who writes so eloquently about Furtwängler in the New Grove, has produced one of the closest accounts of a Karajan performance in a 1958 essay reprinted in his *Responses* (Da Capo); the book also includes a fine chapter on Furtwängler. After the Berlin Philharmonic's last New York visits, in 1974 and 1976, I tried to define the baffling mixture of admiration and reservations which Karajan inspired. I'm older now, and perhaps mellower, less critical, readier to be grateful for glorious sound and flawless execution. And Karajan is certainly mellower. The October concerts reached a new summit. Two of them, at least—the first and the third—seemed to me "never-to-be-forgotten" events, to be recalled with, if not ranked beside, a Furtwängler Beethoven cycle that in student years changed my life. Moreover, the Carnegie concerts cast a retrospective glow over the many Karajan-conducted operas and concerts I have heard in three decades and more: in London, Salzburg, Vienna, Milan, Berlin, New York. Musicians' memory is an odd, living, developing thing, played upon by time and experience, not an unalterable "tape" that reruns each time with the same sounds.

The first concert began with Stravinsky's *Apollo*, in a superlatively rich, lush, supple, Tchaikovskian performance. Then Strauss's huge *Alpine Symphony*, a controversial work. Norman Del Mar, in his Strauss study, considers it in the chapter called "Marking Time," but does not fail to note its "unusual flavour and spirituality" or "the atmosphere of exaltation in the face of Nature's mystery." Under Karajan, it became a vast and elevating adventure—a Mahlerian excursion into a world of grandeur and picturesque beauty which one could enjoy and marvel at untroubled by any of the reflections that struck Shelley or Mahler when they trod similar lofty paths. Perhaps the piece should be deemed an escapist diversion on the highest level: repose for the spirit, delight to the senses, refuge—even during the most graphically depicted of all natural storms—from any storm of the soul. The performance was also a revelation of large-orchestra playing on the highest achievable level; but perhaps that goes without saying.

The second program was Brahms's Fourth and Second Symphonies —one the orchestra had also played on its 1974 visit. And again Karajan provided too smooth a ride, without the grit, the almost painful grinding of cross-rhythms, that is a part of the music. ("So much beauty on the surface and so little music below it" is one of Mr. Cairns's charges.) The new performances, however, were warmer, freer, more personal than those of eight years ago—one would say more Furtwänglerian did that epithet not suggest philosophical levels unplumbed by Karajan. Some tiny flecks on the uncanny instrumental perfection could even be welcomed as signs of grace, of human fallibility, of priorities reordered. The third concert, of Brahms's Third and First Symphonies, revealed the new Karajan at his most lovable, for these were natural, emotional, and—let the word escape at last—profound interpretations: voyages of discovery; loving traversals of familiar, exciting ground with a fresh eye and mind, in the company of someone prepared to linger here, exclaim there; summations toward which many of his earlier, less intimate performances of the works had led. At the fourth concert, devoted to Mahler's Ninth Symphony, some of the old reservations reappeared. The first movement was memorable. In the utterance of the main theme—that "warm singing melody redolent of summer, full of tender longing," as Deryck Cooke describes it—there was a curious inhibitedness, a haltingness, a reluctance to accept easily the consolations it offers, which promised a highly emotional and sharply characterized performance. But the brutality, the horror, the madness in the scherzos that follow were minimized—subordinated to a display of carefully equilibrated, highly wrought orchestral wizardry. And in the finale expressiveness was pushed, with thick, throbbing string tone, to a climax of brute force rather than full-throated passion. The coda, however, was poignant— its brief, simple cello solo heartrending.

In little over a month, New York will have had the chance to hear seven of Mahler's nine symphonies: between October 4th, when the Vienna Symphony, under Christoph Eschenbach, played the First, and November 9th, when the Philadelphia Orchestra, under Klaus Tenn-stedt, is to play the Third. The Second was done by the Boston Philharmonic, under Benjamin Zander, and the Seventh by the Concertgebouw Orchestra, under Bernard Haitink. The Eighth comes from the Canterbury Choral Society, under Charles Dodsley Walker. The Philharmonic played three performances of the Sixth in its subscription series. A fourth performance of the Sixth was given by the Julliard Orchestra, under Jorge Mester, in Alice Tully Hall.

The Philharmonic performances were conducted by the Italian composer Giuseppe Sinopoli, who came to attention a few years ago as a Verdi and Puccini conductor (in Venice, Berlin, Hamburg, Vienna). With the Berlin Philharmonic he has made a good record of Giacomo Manzoni's *Masse: Omaggio a Edgard Varèse* and Schoenberg's Chamber Symphony (Deutsche Grammophon). His account of Mahler's Sixth, the "Tragic," was less than overwhelming. A true performance leaves its listeners shattered, stunned. Mr. Sinopoli's, at a Friday matinée, left me not so numbed as to be unable to face the work again that evening, at the Juilliard concert. His performance was slow, carefully planned, conducted in detail, mannered, lacking in emotional power. Mr. Mester's, with the Juilliard students, moved at more natural gaits, and his young instrumentalists were allowed to play out. There was, at least, the sense—essential in Mahler—of individual voices raised, one after another, in eloquent lament or protestation. Both conductors, incidentally, omitted the third sledgehammer blow that "fells the protagonist." Both reversed the order of the andante and the scherzo—following Erwin Ratz's 1963 edition of the symphony, not Mahler's own practice. Neither sought a return to the platform placing or the string portamento of Mahler's day. Nor did Karajan, in the Ninth. At all three concerts, the second violins were slighted, tucked behind the firsts, and the double-basses were clumped right. (But, effectively, Karajan divided his horns right and left, in the way old conductors divided their basses, to build his climaxes on a broad foundation of horn tone.) On the first of the Deutsche Grammophon albums, the Berlin Philharmonic's string portamento can be heard persisting as a matter of course well into the 1920s as Bruno Walter conducts Mendelssohn and Hans Knappertsbusch conducts Wagner.

DUCAL SPLENDOR

November 15, 1982

DONIZETTI COMPOSED *Le Duc d'Albe* in 1839, for the Paris Opéra. It was not brought to performance, and so the score was not completed. In those days, an opera score became fully fleshed only after rehearsals had begun; once the vocal lines, the bass, and a few significant instrumental cues had been set down, the singers could start learning their roles. (Not only instrumentation was left incomplete; Verdi delayed composing Lady Macbeth's second display aria until the *Macbeth* cast had assembled and he could hear his prima donna in action.) The autograph of *Le Duc d'Albe,* now in that Aladdin's cave of operatic manuscripts the Ricordi vaults, in Milan, is fairly full for two acts and a "skeleton" score (with some limbs missing) for the next two. When the opera was first performed in Carnegie Hall, in 1959, it was in Italian translation and in an edition completed by Thomas Schippers. When it was performed there last month, by Eve Queler's Opera Orchestra of New York, it was again in Italian translation but this time in (largely) the edition made in 1882 by Donizetti's pupil Matteo Salvi. Neither version is altogether satisfactory. Schippers's is closer to Donizetti in orchestration but is a pared-down account of a four-act *grand opéra:* the conductor was reluctant to add anything that Donizetti himself had not at least sketched. Salvi's contains more free composition; gaps left in the Schippers reconstruction are filled. But in many episodes it sounds less like Donizetti. Salvi worked in knowledge of Verdi's *Les Vêpres siciliennes* (1855), which is yet another version of *Le Duc d'Albe,* and, for all his endeavor to remain stylistically within 1840s bounds (his own fourth and last opera, *Caterina Howard,* had appeared in 1847), he had recourse at times to 1880s harmonies and orchestration. At a greater distance, Schippers could feign the original sonorities more convincingly. The Schippers version has held the stage (productions in Modena, Bologna, Ghent, Brussels, Naples, Florence) since its première, in Spoleto in 1959. Meanwhile, the Salvi version has circulated on disc, in a passionate 1952 Italian Radio performance published on Voce. I am happy with either, and would be happier still with a new edition that sought to combine the virtues of both. Miss Queler had compiled an edition combining some of those virtues. The prelude and the passages common to Salvi and Schippers were done in Schippers orchestration. Salvi passages were done either in his orchestration (where it could be found, pinned up or pasted over in a Salvi score adapted to the Schippers edition) or in a new orchestration, by Charles Rizzuto, made from the Salvi vocal score. A few Salvi passages were omitted because new scoring could not be finished and copied in time. Two cabaletta sections and a recitative were cut at the request of the prima donna, Marina Krilovici, who had sung the Schippers version in Brussels; but they were included in the "national" performance, given by singers in Opera Orchestra's Young Artists Program, which Miss Queler had conducted at Long Beach, New York, twelve days earlier.

Part of the fascination of *Le Duc d'Albe* is that of comparing Donizetti's and Verdi's treatment of the same text. Stretches of the *Duc* and the *Vêpres* librettos, which are both by Scribe, are identical. *Le Duc*, in fact, is the better drama. For Verdi, Scribe transferred its action from Brussels to Palermo and its date from 1573 to 1282. The actors lose stature; they lose the historical and literary resonances provided—at any rate to audiences who know their Goethe and Schiller, their Motley and Prescott—by a crisis concerning Alva, his natural son, and Egmont's daughter, caught in a tense (if fictitious) web of conflicting patriotic, filial, and amorous attachments. Moreover, the original dénouement is far more striking, enigmatic, and interesting than that of *Les Vêpres*, where the curtain falls on the three principals about to be wiped out in a general massacre. Donizetti's opera, insofar as one can judge from its incomplete state, made fewer concessions to Paris convention than Verdi's did. (Scribe's autograph libretto, and drafts of it, survive in the Bibliothèque Nationale, along with his successive versions of *Les Vêpres*.) In the later opera, there is more picturesque decoration, scenic and musical (the popular scenes were expanded at Verdi's request); there is a strenuous and conscious determination to out-Meyerbeer Meyerbeer in the cut of the numbers, in novelty of textures, and in the deployment of large forces. *Les Vêpres* contains greater music, but *Le Duc d'Albe*, a composition of Donizetti's mature, confident mastery, effortless and unmannered in a way *Les Vêpres* is not, deserves revival. So do Donizetti's other *grands opéras: Les Martyrs* (April 1840), *La Favorite* (December 1840), and *Dom Sébastien* (1843).

All three pieces have their textual problems. *Les Martyrs* is a reworking of Donizetti's Neapolitan opera *Poliuto*, and *La Favorite* of his unfinished *L'Ange de Nisida*. As for *Dom Sébastien*, his last opera: Camoëns' principal air, "O Lisbonne," was rewritten between the dress rehearsal and the first night, and further large changes were made during the run; for the Vienna première the opera was again revised, by Donizetti; and it was revised again for the Milan première, by the conductor Giacomo Panizza. Then Verdi's former companion and amanuensis, Emanuele Muzio, had a go at it. (Verdi, now occupied, in Paris, with Giuseppina Strepponi, had dispatched Muzio back to Milan and had asked Ricordi to find him some employment.) Muzio described his assignment as "the devil of a job." In the Opéra library a few years ago, I came across alternative versions (sometimes several alternatives) for most of the principal numbers. It would indeed be the devil of a job to assemble a *Dom Sébastien* for performance—and one well worth undertaking. Donizetti's last years (1840–43) before madness clouded his mind were amazingly fertile. Operas in every genre appeared, for

Paris, Vienna, Rome, Milan, Naples: besides the *grands opéras*, there were *La Fille du régiment, Rita, Linda di Chamounix,* and *Don Pasquale;* the less familiar but very fine *Maria Padilla, Caterina Cornaro,* and *Maria di Rohan;* and the patchy but far from negligible *Adelia.* All of them are adventurous and (except for *Adelia*) consistently distinguished compositions.

The Carnegie performance of *Le Duc d'Albe* had a protagonist, Matteo Manuguerra, whose firm, rich baritone was well suited to the part and who declaimed with vigor and command. Hélène, like all the roles tailored for the exigent Rosine Stoltz, a mezzo of wide range, lies awkwardly for other singers. Miss Krilovici tackled it with determination and some dramatic fire, but the actual sound was often ugly. Dalmacio Gonzalez was rather light casting for Henri, a role composed for Gilbert Duprez (who began his career as a *tenore di grazia* but was a *tenore di forza* at the time of *Le Duc*), and he seemed not to have gone very deeply into the character. He made little effect with the crucial cry "Mon père!" (when, to save Hélène from the scaffold, Henri acknowledges the tyrant as his father); Donizetti "placed" it as strikingly as Verdi did. But Salvi's "Angelo casto e bel," composed to replace "Ange si pur" (which Donizetti had carried over into *La Favorite),* was prettily sung. After a somewhat sticky first act, the performance began to move surely. Miss Queler's conducting was both spirited and sensitive.

In pre-phonograph days, players of all kinds, not only pianists, had a chance to get their fingers around the music of a successful new opera. Ricordi published *Macbeth* arranged for flute and piano, for two flutes, for flute solo. He published *Don Carlos* for violin and piano, for flute and piano, for flute solo. And fantasias, capriccios, "reminiscences" or "souvenirs" abounded. At the close of a Merkin Hall recital this month, Jean Kopperud, clarinet, and Cameron Grant, piano, played a *Rigoletto* fantasia by Luigi Bassi (not the baritone for whom Mozart composed Don Giovanni—he died in 1825, twenty-six years before *Rigoletto*—but the celebrated clarinettist). His fantasia made an entertaining, agreeable, and (in the coda) brilliant close to an agreeable and cultivated recital. Over Rigoletto's "Piangi, fanciulla," assigned to the piano, Miss Kopperud's clarinet spun tracery more elaborate than Gilda's. It played "Caro nome" first straight and then with decorations that Rosalia Chalia or Joan Sutherland might envy. It declaimed "Bella figlia dell'amore" with a grace of phrasing few modern tenors achieve.

The recital began with Weber's Grand Duo Concertant, a light but wonderfully deft and delicate piece. It included Saint-Saëns' Sonata, Opus 167, one of his very last compositions and a lovely testament to his belief in purity of form and seemliness of progression as musical elements no less stirring than emotionalism. Louise Talma's *Studies in Spacing,* given its world première, proclaimed a similar belief. Its five brief movements, lasting about ten minutes in all, were gentle and pleasing. Ives's Fourth Violin Sonata sounded good in a clarinet transcription; Miss Kopperud tackled it with mingled fervor and wit. Although her breaths were noisy, and although throughout the evening she played from music (and one of Plunket Greene's rules for singers —"*Memorise it.* There will be no senses to spare for effect, or lilt, or magnetism, or illustration or anything else, if the eye is on the printed page"—should apply equally to instrumental soloists), by her keen phrasing, her dynamic range, and her ready, unaffected responses to sentiment, solemnity, and pleasantry she brought a wide range of musics to life. Mr. Grant, who also played from scores, was more a fluent, sensitive, courteous accompanist than an equal partner. The Weber, the Saint-Saëns, and probably the Ives would have benefitted from a lighter, less plummy piano—one he could have played strongly without danger of drowning the clarinet.

A passionate note was sounded by Ned Rorem's *Ariel,* for soprano, clarinet, and piano. This Sylvia Plath cycle, composed in 1971 for Phyllis Curtin (who has recorded it on Desto), is a strong, lyrical composition: Rorem caught the poet's tone of disciplined desperation, of high emotion forced into controlled imagery. The musical gestures are vivid. The music is nervous, varied, sure, and potently shaped. The soprano was Kristine Ciesinski, a promising singer, bright of presence (even though she, too, read from the score), fresh and clean of tone except when high notes splayed under pressure. (There is hysteria in the music, but it should be a focussed hysteria.) She pronounced the words clearly but did not always inflect them as if she knew what the poems meant. Once more, let me in passing regret the modern practice of printing vocal music beamed and slurred as if it were instrumental. The very look on the page, I'm sure, inhibits some interpreters' response to Rorem's fine, subtle word setting: it tempts them to sing too strictly in time, and with stresses too even.

Miss Ciesinski—and many another singer—could learn much from Paul Sperry, who is a master of words and their inflections and their projection. At a Musical Elements concert this month in the Great Hall at Cooper Union, he sang Robert Beaser's cycle *The Seven Deadly Sins* (1979), for voice and piano, and Jacob Druckman's *Animus IV* (1977), for tenor, six players, and tape. The Beaser, a good piece, is a pithy, indagative setting of seven taut, harsh epigrams by Anthony Hecht. The Druckman cites and comments upon Chabrier's song "Villanelle des petits canards" and Liszt's song "Die drei Zigeuner." It is a stretch of music—about twenty-two minutes—part entertaining and part alarming, brilliant, colorful, and personal, and it has become a showpiece for Mr. Sperry, who gave the first performance, at IRCAM in 1977, and has often done it since. Having heard a few of these performances, I now find myself wishing that he were singing the original songs instead. Commentary, however keen, shapely, and imaginative it may be, seldom proves more durable than its object.

The program was varied, and—once Xenakis's *Anaktoria* (1969), a beastly work, was done—it was enjoyable. *Anaktoria* requires an instrumental octet to screech and growl for a *mauvais quart d'heure*, more or less. Kurt Schwertsik's *Twilight Music* (1976), in its American première, followed as balm. The subtitle is "A Celtic Serenade"; the movements are "Maytime," "To the New Moon," "Secret Love and Jealous Husband," and "At the Fiddler's." A divertimento composed for the forces of the Schubert Octet, it is relaxed, masterly, poignant, captivating. Andrew Thomas's *In Memoriam,* another good piece, for instrumental nonet, had its first performance. It is a set of grave, intense variations, beautifully scored. Daniel Asia and Mr. Beaser shared the conducting.

At the Philharmonic, there was more Druckman to be heard: his popular *Prism* (1980), taken up by six orchestras last season, by four this. The work cites and comments upon excerpts from three Medea operas: by Charpentier, Cavalli, and Cherubini. Again, the commentary is brilliant, colorful, and personal. The scoring, the contrasts, the opposition of rhythms and of timbres in space (Druckman uses a second string-band, seated upstage from the main orchestra) are beguiling. Again, one was left with an uneasy feeling that the commentary did not amount to new composition—especially when original Cherubini cut through the surrealist textures with such force and precision. John Nelson conducted, and the orchestra produced the liveliest, most polished, and most committed playing I have heard from it this season.

In the Philharmonic's third subscription program, token observance was paid to Szymanowski's centenary with a noisy, unrefined performance of an early, uncharacteristic work, his Concert Overture, conducted by Zubin Mehta. It appeared in a skimpy concert where Shirley Verrett, without grace, sang Chausson's *Poème de l'amour et de la mer* and two Massenet arias. In the sixth program, Mr. Mehta produced a clotted account of Schoenberg's *Pelleas and Melisande* and routine accompaniment to Nathan Milstein's fine-drawn, poetic solo in Beethoven's Violin Concerto. I missed Joan Tower's *Sequoia,* in the second program, but caught up with it, via television and radio, at the United Nations concert last month, and enjoyed its colorful inventions.

Maxim Shostakovich made his Philharmonic début conducting two of his father's compositions—the very powerful Eighth Symphony and, with the orchestra's concertmaster, Glenn Dicterow, as soloist, the First Violin Concerto. Mr. Dicterow is no David Oistrakh, for whom the concerto was written; Mr. Shostakovich is no Eugene Mravinsky, to whom the symphony is dedicated, and who conducted (and recorded, memorably) the concerto with Oistrakh; and the New York Philharmonic was no Leningrad Philharmonic. The concerto was poetic but less than heroic. The symphony's images of totalitarian foulness, its poignant threnody for the suffering, its small but unquenchable message of trust in human goodness were softened in outline, handled in rather too restrained a fashion. Mr. Shostakovich seems to be an emotionally reticent conductor. But, understated though both pieces were,

345

they were sensitively treated. I heard the concert twice, in the hall of the C.W. Post Center, at Long Island University, and in Fisher Hall, and was both times stirred by it.

A RAKE AMONG SCHOLARS

November 22, 1982

THE RAKE'S PROGRESS, as Paul Griffiths remarks in the latest Cambridge Opera Handbook, a small, highly intelligent collection of essays about the piece, "must have enjoyed more productions than any other opera composed since the death of Puccini." And in this Stravinsky centenary year most cities of any musical aspiration have revived or remounted the *Rake*. New York, however, has managed only a piano-accompanied Off-Broadway presentation. The Met has neglected the work since 1953; the City Opera, its natural home, has put on four different productions of Carlisle Floyd's *Susannah* and not even once tackled the *Rake*. [*It did so at last in 1984.*] There were new productions this year upstate at Artpark; in San Francisco (an enlarged version of the famous Glyndebourne presentation); and, most recently, at the University of Michigan in Ann Arbor, coincident with the annual meeting of the American Musicological Society and of the American Society for Music Theory, during which two long sessions were devoted to Stravinsky papers.

The Ann Arbor staging was the most spectacular of my dozen-odd *Rake*s. Although there was only one set, it was a vast, intricate construction of scaffolding, ladders, stairs, ledges, and lofts reaching to the flies and peopled by an elaborately costumed cast of about a hundred and thirty (the University Choir and the University Dance Company combined). The scene was billed as "the Bedlam of Hell"—an infernal corner uncharted by Dante, where Nick Shadow was reigning prince, two little demons did his will, a huge caldron steamed, and damned madmen writhed ceaselessly. To the strains of an electronic prelude not composed by Stravinsky and then Stravinsky's own prelude (drowned by shrieking), Tom Rakewell was flung into the seething madhouse, beneath the eyes of a crisply bonneted Anne, who abandoned him there. A "dream" Anne, one of the lunatics, enacted the heroine's role in the subsequent opera until, at the close, the "real" Anne revisited the scene. But she had no comfort for Tom: the "dream" Anne sang the soothing lullaby, and the "real" Anne left him to his fate. Was the drama we watched simply a nightmare passing through Tom's mad brain? A flashback presentation of the progress that had brought him to Hell? A charade presented *Marat/Sade* fashion by the denizens of the place? Nothing made much sense. (Was Nick merely shamming when at the close of the graveyard scene he proclaimed his defeat? Stravinsky's vigorously agonized B-flat-minor aria says no, but in this production Nick later reappeared unscathed, triumphant.) *The Rake's Progress,* its composer once said, "is simple to perform musically, but difficult to realize on the stage. I contend, however, that the chief obstacles to a convincing visual conception are no more than the result of an incapacity to accept the work for what it is." Robert Altman, the director of the Michigan production, showed not so much that incapacity as a failure, it seemed, to have heard, understood—and then perhaps rejected—Stravinsky's opera for what it is. By his own avowal—if he was correctly reported in the Ann Arbor *News*—he cannot read music and has a tin ear. Poor qualifications for an opera director, particularly when the opera concerned "makes sense" through some of the most precise musical statements of our century. On the simplest theatrical level, the piece was weakened by the nonobservance of Stravinsky's carefully planned contrasts between crowd scenes and solo scenes: the thronged auction followed by a cemetery duologue punctuated—as the *Don Giovanni* cemetery duologue is—by just one otherworldly voice; a madhouse first populous, then swiftly cleared to contain a duet, then a solo, before the chorus returns. Literal observance of every stage direction in the *Rake* is perhaps not necessary (though the most successful productions of my experience have essayed it). The opera is strong enough to bear a good deal of directorial distortion and rich enough to allow many variant embodiments. Robert Craft recorded that Stravinsky was deeply moved by Ingmar Bergman's 1961 production, in which much was "at loggerheads with the book." Directorial antics usually afflict first the brothel scene. In Michigan, Tom's catechism was accompanied by a lewd exhibition of monstrously enlarged breasts, bottoms, and other private parts. The pornographic display could be passed over as a childish attempt to be indecorous and to shock a campus audience. More serious was the constant subordination of the score, its sense, and its text to irrelevant theatrical tricks.

The tricks, however, were skillfully executed. Baba's solos in the auction scene, for example, proceeded from an apparently trunkless head lying on the auctioneer's table. (It was done with mirrors, I suppose; one couldn't spot how.) But when the warm, lovable advice to Anne was literally disembodied the character was lost. The whole extravaganza had a Meyerbeerian scale and sweep; it was a thing of effects without causes. Bank upon bank of colored lights in wondrous profusion played upon and vivified the largely white-and-gray décor. (But one fan-cooled lantern slung from the balcony filled the theatre with its hum and murked the music; a director not tin-eared would surely have extinguished it.) The staging had been long and carefully rehearsed, and it was performed with accomplishment. In New York, we seldom see such lavishness and alertness combined. For the students involved, nothing but praise. On the director who led them into their enthusiastic, committed, untruthful, and meretricious presentation of a chamber opera that is a masterpiece of our age, a commination tempered by recognition of his zest, his flair, and his concern that audiences should enjoy the show.

The music director was Gustav Meier, one of America's more distinguished opera conductors. The choral singing was splendidly accurate and intelligible. There were two solo casts. The student voices were light, slight, and clear. Carla Connors, a very steady Anne; Stephen Morscheck, a confident Nick; and Katherine Eberle, a Baba vivacious even after decapitation, were the best performers. Once heard, *The Rake's Progress* (like Monteverdi's *Orfeo*, Handel's *Semele*, *The Magic Flute*, *Fidelio*) "prints" itself on a musical listener as a necessary part of his life. Hearing it again after a year or more's deprivation, he is refreshed, comforted, nourished in soul and spirit. And in an interpretation as acute as Mr. Meier's he discovers riches unnoticed before.

Monteverdi, Handel, Gluck, Mozart, Beethoven, Wagner, and Verdi provide the essential, basic repertory of the past for a serious-minded company. But Gluck's operas, like the *Rake*, are difficult to realize on the stage. Dance is an integral part of them. And the composer's celebrated "noble simplicity" can turn to dullness if the declamation of the actors (in whatever language) is not keen. They must unite emotional force with dignity, in a manner both chaste and passionate. The City Opera's *Alceste*, earlier this season, was feebly done. The set, by Ming Cho Lee, looked as if it had been pulled from stock: rumpled walls against a wrinkled sky. Brian Macdonald's staging suggested eurythmics in a village hall. Heather Harper was an odd choice of heroine. Although she made her début, twenty-eight years ago, in a dramatic role, Lady Macbeth, she has made her reputation mainly in such parts as Anne, Elsa, and Ellen Orford. As ever, she displayed what Grove nicely describes as her "quiet confidence in her own considerable abilities." She sang truly, and with expression. But both her acting and her singing were light for a heroic role among whose noble modern exponents have been Kirsten Flagstad (her Met farewell, in 1952), Maria Callas (at the Scala première of the opera, in 1954), and Janet Baker (her Covent Garden farewell, last year). The performance as a whole was not dull: it took life from Raymond Leppard's strong, stylish conducting. Mr. Leppard commands the feeling for individual lines which turns Gluck's phrases into direct emotion, the sense of proportion which makes the architecture of the acts beautiful and moving, and the long line that seems to run unbroken through the drama. Jon Garrison was a clean Admetus but stolid except in some exchanges before Hellgate. Alfred Anderson, a company débutant, was a good Apollo.

Julian Hope and Roger Butlin, the director and the designer of an *Alceste* presented by the Kentucky Opera in Louisville last month, approached the piece with an urgency and conviction that would have matched Mr. Leppard's conducting well. But the Louisville conductor was Christian Badea, who softened Gluck's firm musical outlines until sometimes his powerful stride became an amble (a matter less of tempo than of accent and articulation). Otherwise, it was a gripping performance. Mani Mekler, a Californian soprano who has been winning praise in Europe, made her American début, as Alcestis. Her voice is not conventionally beautiful: it is colorful, dramatic, incisive; there is an arresting touch of bitterness in its timbre. She is a potent performer, and would have been more effective still had she not addressed so much of her music to the ground. Mr. Hope deliberately eschewed the straightforward appeal of singers who advance to the footlights and lift eyes and voice to the house. He set many of the great speeches fairly far upstage, and he was wrong to do so. Mr. Butlin also designed Covent Garden's *Alceste*—in an eclectic, rather timid mixture of romanticized neoclassicism and modern. His Kentucky décor was stark and bold: elements of a Greek theatre viewed from the back, as it were—through the *proskenion* to a circular *orchestra* filling most of the stage and, beyond and around it, the *kerkides*, or wedge-shaped blocks of rising seats. This *Alceste* was staged in a style recalling that of early Wieland Wagner, and it is not a bad style for Gluck. (I still recall with emotion the solemn, beautiful *Orpheus* Wieland presented in Munich's Prinzregententheater, thirty years ago.) Leo Goeke, a poetic tenor, was the Admetus. His voice—as at Glyndebourne, where he has sung Tamino, Idamantes, Ottavio, and, in three seasons, Tom Rakewell—has an odd way of suddenly fading just when one wants it to ring out strongly. But in Louisville's Macauley Theatre—a resonant fourteen-hundred-seater whose Adamesque architecture suits neoclassical opera—both he and Miss Mekler could be aptly heroic without strain. So could Nicola Fabricci, the émigré Ukrainian baritone, who sang Hercules. Gluck wrote two rather different *Alceste*s, one in Italian and one in French. New York and Kentucky both chose the French version and sang it, more or less, in French. (English would have made more sense.) Both abridged the work, Kentucky more savagely. The City Opera sold a three-dollar French-English libretto not conformable to its performance but prepared for the 1941 Met production, from which the Hercules scenes were omitted. Kentucky sold a five-dollar French-English libretto that was almost complete; a few important lines for Alcestis had been dropped by mistake.

The Louisville *Alceste* inaugurated Thomson Smillie's first season as general director of the Kentucky Opera (founded by Moritz Bomhard thirty years ago and distinguished in its early years by its championship of contemporary pieces). Mr. Smillie is a dedicated young Scot, who worked with Scottish Opera while it grew from an occasional troupe to a year-round company whose commissions have enriched the international repertory; he directed the audacious Wexford Festival for five years; and now he has big plans for Louisville. Among them are plans for productions in houses of the right scale: the Macauley for the medium-sized works, the large and the small theatres in the new Kentucky Center for the Arts (due to open next year) for, say, *Aida* and Monteverdi's *Orfeo*. Artistic standards at New York's two big companies are often compromised by the need to play a very large repertory week in, week out—and seven or eight performances a week—through a long season and in a single house. However, the regularity of that repertory system does bring its rewards, different from and complementary to those of the more flexible *stagione* system—which means concentration on just one or two operas at a time. Between them, they provide America with a rich operatic life. The Kentucky Opera *stagioni* promise to make it richer still.

Most regional companies have their specialties: *grand opéra* revivals in San Diego (more of that next week); nationalist operas in Detroit, where last month the Michigan Opera Theatre played Stanisław Moniuszko's *Straszny Dwór, The Haunted Manor.* (Last year, it did the Armenian opera *Anush,* by Armen Tigranian.) And *Straszny Dwór* (1865) is a captivating piece, one that could be in the City Opera repertory. It is abundantly melodious—even more so than Moniuszko's excellent *Halka*—with points of reference in Weber, Donizetti, and tuneful opéra comique. Like *The Bartered Bride,* its contemporary, it breaks the codified Italian conventions: the scenes are constructed with deft, easy informality; arias turn into ensembles, solos into choruses; tunes pour out in profusion. The plot is slight. A pair of soldier brothers returning home from the war decide to live ladyless, so that there will be no ties when next they are called on to defend their country. An aunt's ambitious matrimonial plan for them is thwarted by the vow of celibacy and, even more seriously, when they visit a neighbor's manor, by their admiration of the daughters of the house, Hanna and Jadwiga. Auntie tells the girls that her nephews are unmanly milksops. The girls play a trick on them: *Ruddigore*-fashion, they animate portraits of their ancestresses. When this fails to scare the lads, a rival suitor for Hanna's hand turns to slander, informing them that the manor is haunted because it was built with the fruits of extortion. Our noble heroes prepare to leave so shameful a place, but the calumny is revealed, and all ends happily. Other episodes concern an enchanted chiming clock and several pretty genre scenes of Polish life. The composition of *Straszny Dwór* coincided with the Warsaw massacres of 1861 and the risings of 1863; Moniuszko sought to console his countrymen, sorely oppressed by Russian tyranny, with an affectionate portrait of Polish chivalry, Polish high spirits, and Polish individuality surviving occupation. Again and again, a patriotic vein rises through the comedy: in the brothers' songs; when the girls' father sings of the brave sons-in-law he hopes for; when Hanna derides the young men's vow, declaring with heroic charm, kin to Isabella's in Rossini's *L'Italiana,* that Polish women, too, can be brave when invaders threaten. After three performances, *Straszny Dwór* was banned by the Russian authorities. The opera is not only romantic and delightful; it is stirring and topical.

Detroit put a Polish team in charge: Jacek Kasprzyk (from the Warsaw Opera) to conduct, Wojciech Haik to direct, and Milosz Benedyktowicz to design. Carol Gutknecht and Kathleen Segar were the sisters, Gordon Greer (at my performance) and Jeffrey Wells the brothers.

The staging was not polished. Nor was the singing—except that of Joseph Warner, who delivered Skołuba's clock song with wit, charm, and lively words. But the performance had verve, and the work is irresistible. There was a new English translation, by Sally Williams-Haik, unrhymed, and less felicitous, I thought, than the translation that J. M. Cembala and Mollie Petrie made for the British première of *Straszny Dwór*, at Bristol University in 1971.

SESSIONS OF STRONG-SOUNDING THOUGHT

November 29, 1982

THE CONCERTGOING public still wants symphonies, and big ones, too: its appetite for Bruckner and Mahler is apparently endless. Roger Sessions is America's greatest symphonist. None of his nine symphonies is long, but all of them are nourishing. He has written a body of works for large orchestra—it further includes three concertos, the Divertimento, the Rhapsody, the recent Concerto for Orchestra—that should figure as regularly in American orchestral programs as the symphonic works of Elgar and Michael Tippett do in British programs. But another New York Philharmonic season is passing without even one of Sessions's symphonies billed, or any of the concertos. However, the Pittsburgh Symphony, under André Previn, is playing the Second Symphony in Avery Fisher Hall in December (see page 377), in the month of Sessions's eighty-sixth birthday, and last week the American Composers Orchestra, under Dennis Russell Davies, gave the New York première of the Seventh Symphony, in Alice Tully Hall.

The Seventh is a beautiful work, and perhaps the most Bergian of the series in its romanticism of melodies and textures and its amalgam of rhapsodic feeling and very clear construction. It was composed fifteen years ago, to celebrate the 150th anniversary of the University of Michigan, and is dedicated to Jean Martinon, who, with the Chicago Symphony, gave the first performance, on the university's Ann Arbor campus. Approachable it is, but, like all Sessions's music, it takes getting to know, on the part of listeners, players, and conductors. Giving, and hearing, a single performance now and again is not enough. Sessions's wise, moving Charles Eliot Norton lectures, published as *Questions About Music* (Norton), should be read by every concertgoer puzzled by other people's enthusiasm for works that he perhaps finds unattractive, even meaningless. In the first lecture, "Hearing, Knowing, and Understanding Music," Sessions considers a listener's encounters with "a new, unfamiliar, or difficult piece":

One's first impression may be a quite negative one; the music may seem opaque, chaotic, crabbed, dissonant.... But if we keep our ears open and will-

351

ing, and listen attentively, we may easily discern, here and there, moments or passages of which we feel the impact immediately, however fleeting this sensation of contact or recognition may be. One may even tell oneself: "This at least is 'striking'—or 'graceful,' or 'amusing,' even 'moving,' 'beautiful,' or simply 'interesting.'" This means that we have begun to recognize features in the work and to sense its character; and if we are interested or patient enough to pursue the matter further, we will find that these moments will grow longer.

And thus a way can be opened not only to that work but to "other works of the composer in question" and "works of other composers whose styles present similar problems."

Such a path to the Seventh Symphony has been cleared by the publication of a recording of it made by the Louisville Orchestra, under Peter Leonard (LS 776 on the Louisville Orchestra First Edition label). The performance is not altogether ideal: Sessions composes with the memory of Carl Muck's Boston Symphony still in his ears; the Louisville strings sound thin, and some of the balance is awry. But it is a lucid, informative, and emotionally committed interpretation that will serve well until Bernard Haitink and the Concertgebouw, Colin Davis or Claudio Abbado and the London Symphony, Klaus Tennstedt and the London Philharmonic, Karajan and the Berlin Philharmonic turn their attention to the piece. The performance by the American Composers Orchestra, a band of expert players, was vivid, cogent, and beautiful. Not every detail had fallen poetically into place, but the long line was drawn surely by Mr. Davies, the balances were just, and the romantic passages were stirring. The composer was present, and at the close the audience cheered him.

The Louisville recorded performance is coupled with Sessions's captivating Divertimento, done by the same forces. Scores of both works are published by Merion Music. A path to the Pittsburgh performance of the Second Symphony can be prepared by listening to Dimitri Mitropoulos' performance with the Philharmonic, reissued on CRI (SD 278)—an old recording of a distinguished interpretation. A study score is published by G. Schirmer.

The ACO concert began with Colin McPhee's *Tabu-Tabuhan* (1936), a toccata for orchestra and two pianos: twenty pentatonic (Balinese) minutes, in three movements, of intricate rhythms within moto-perpetuo pulses, repetitive tunefulness, and glittering instrumentation—romantic, and Steve Reichian in attractiveness. Then came the first performance of Louis Ballard's *Xact'ccé'óyan*, an ACO commission. The title (pronounced, we are told, "Hosh-chay-EE-oh-yon") is the name of a Navajo deity. The composer also goes by the name Honganozhe, Grand Eagle. His program note deserves a place in a collection of "introductory notes that inhibit any strong desire to hear the music":

The opening passage was based upon an Indian rug design converted to a grid which was then overlaid onto an orchestral page where staff lines intersected the lines of the grid. At these points of intersection, notes and rests were pinpointed....

352

But Villa-Lobos once turned the Manhattan skyline into a pretty tune; and, I read somewhere, a computer fed with information from a Bach fugue and then asked, via a mechanical loom, to make a pattern from it wove an attractive rug, in tasteful shades of brown. (A process more or less the reverse of Ballard's.) In fact, the opening theme of *Xact'ccé'óyan* was striking. The dense, busy developments that followed were not. I listened, I hope, with an open, willing, and attentive ear but discerned little to make me "interested or patient enough to pursue the matter further." Life is short, and before following Sessions's advice one needs to be incited either by intuition that there is something there worth pursuing or by trusted advocacy.

The last piece on the ACO program, eclectic and chameleonic, could figure well in a guess-the-composer game. Hindemith? No, the counterpoint is not gritty enough. Vaughan Williams? No, the aspirant earnestness is missing. Not quite Prokofiev, but perhaps a minor Soviet ballet composer (in the lyrical tune of the slow movement)? Copland? But the square-dance effects in the finale are surely "Balinized." American? Probably Californian? Right: the work was Lou Harrison's Third Symphony (1981), in its New York première—a relaxed, agreeable, generous, slightly garrulous composition, with winning concertante episodes.

The Play of Daniel, an opera composed by young people of Beauvais in the twelfth or thirteenth century, was revived this month by the Boston Camerata in the medieval court of the Metropolitan Museum. The production had high aims: in the words of a note by the Camerata's music director, Joel Cohen, "to establish a good and faithful musical text, and an honest and plausible musical style"; "to recapture, insofar as we are able, the spirit of that Beauvais performance seven hundred and fifty years ago"; and to combine pageantry and entertainment with "the opportunity to reflect, as the citizens of Beauvais reflected before us, on the cruelty of the powerful, the extreme fragility of our existence, and the necessity for us to remain just and steadfast even in the worst of times." The libretto of *Daniel* calls for processions, Belshazzar's feast, the writing on the wall, Darius's overthrowing of Belshazzar, the lions' den, the aerial delivery of Daniel's dinner (by Habbakkuk, food pail in hand, whisked by the hairs of his head from Judea to Babylon by an angel of the Lord), and the hungry lions' consumption of Daniel's accusers. (A pity Daniel's early invention of dynamite, fed with explosive effect to a brazen dragon, was not included.) For the music, only vocal lines survive, but the text and one of the stage directions imply the participation of instruments in at least the processions. As W. L. Smoldon observed in the 1954 Grove, "altogether we have a picture of a pageant of the utmost brilliance: a crowded 'stage,' rich costumes, ringing voices, the clang of instruments and the glitter of gold and steel." Smoldon ended his survey of liturgical music drama by remarking that "a modern revival would be a pleasurable and moving experience." Noah Greenberg and the New York Pro Musica's revival of *Daniel,* four years later, was indeed pleasurable and moving, and it established the piece as the best-known of medieval music dramas.

With perhaps too liberal a hand, the Pro Musica decked *Daniel* in bright medieval instrumental colors. The Camerata *Daniel* is also lavishly scored, with medieval fiddles, flutes, a shawm, blasts on a ram's horn, cymbal clashes, bells, and drums (the result is sometimes close to the jaunty medievalism of Carl Orff's *Carmina Burana*), and there are other embellishments. "We have added drones and countermelodies of the kind which were freely improvised and occasionally notated in thirteenth-century France. And we have supplied a medieval dance band to perform the interludes and accompaniments which...most probably complemented and supported the vocal music." The Pro Musica version was threaded with an English narration written by W. H. Auden. The Camerata edition is "troped" with well-chosen prose readings (Mechthild of Magdeburg, Carlyle, Donne, Shelley, Dante) and with nineteenth-century American folk hymns, "which have been included to draw us closer to the spiritual center of the Daniel drama."

The show was directed by Andrea von Ramm, who also took the title role. Roland Guidry's costumes and Don Beaman's scenery found inspiration in Babylonian and Persian art. Carol Pharo's choreography included belly dancing at the feast; her lions were slinky and stylized. Miss Ramm's own performance was wonderful—firm and clear in timbre, sharply projected, enacted with a simple, direct expressiveness of pose and gesture which suggested, without affectation, an instinctive response to medieval sculpture. No one approached her except two countertenors, Kenneth Fitch and Fred Raffensperger, who played Daniel's accusers vividly and sang their music like a pair of keen virtuoso oboes, and the reader, Nicholas Linfield, who, garbed as a rural preacher, delivered the prose passages with tactful eloquence. About the rest there was a touch of arty pageant. The phrase is unkind: the play had been elaborately and carefully rehearsed; the plotting of the entrances, bodily or musical, from different parts of the court was intricate and effective; both the singing and the instrumental playing were accomplished. But the way the artists stood, moved, used their eyes, declaimed their words contrasted unfavorably with the naturalness and easy performer-audience relationship achieved in some other recent non-proscenium presentations of music drama—such things as the Opera Theatre of St. Louis presentation of *The Beggar's Opera* and Indiana University's re-creation of the Benediktbeuern Passion play. A church setting—the Met atmosphere was unnuminous and concertlike—would probably have helped both the sound and the drama, and have furthered the Camerata's serious, skillful endeavor to recapture at once the (in Mr. Cohen's words) "glorious make-believe and student revelry" and the "profoundly questioning and deadly earnest" elements that are brought together in *Daniel.*

• • •

The San Diego Opera is making a specialty of grand-opéra revival: Ambroise Thomas's *Hamlet,* four years ago; Saint-Saëns' *Henry VIII,* due in February; and, last month, Emmanuel Chabrier's *Gwendoline.* Rollo Myers, in his little book on Chabrier, calls *Gwendoline* (1886) "an opera which, though scarcely conforming to the tastes of today, is yet as deserving of revival as many of the faded Italian mediocrities that are resurrected from time to time." On those terms, I'd rank *Gwendoline* above *Adriana Lecouvreur* and *L'amore dei tre re*—but below Moniuszko's *Halka* and *Straszny Dwór* or Chabrier's own *Le Roi malgré lui*—in any general list of pieces deserving more frequent performance. It's a heady, an almost intoxicating opera: in effect, a long, three-act duet for soprano and baritone, richly composed and richly scored in Chabrier's most elevated and original vein—a Frenchman's tender, passionate tribute to *Lohengrin* and *Tristan,* to opulence of colors both sonic and scenic, and to high romantic emotion.

The soprano, Gwendoline, is the daughter of Armel, an eighth-century Saxon lord. The baritone, Harald, heads a Danish raiding party. They fall in love. Armel countenances the match but gives his daughter a dagger and bids her, Judith-like, to murder her lover while he sleeps. She cannot do it. After the wedding feast, the Saxons attack the drunken, unarmed Danes, and Harald is mortally wounded. Gwendoline drives the dagger into her own breast, and, lit by a glare from burning boats, the couple, "happy, proud, magnificent...die superbly, without falling," having sung, "The hour has come to take our flight to fair Valhalla! On a proud steed I/you shall be the cloud-borne Valkyrie with a golden helm. Let us soar together on wings of fire...and mingle forever our bodies, our hearts, our souls in imperishable radiance!"

The San Diego production was brilliantly devised and directed by Tito Capobianco, evidently as an act of loving admiration for the work. Beni Montresor had painted beautiful, strongly colored romantic scenery. Gigi Denda and Bill Gorgensen created curtains, mysterious cones, and firefly enchantments of light to accompany visions, transformations from reality to dream, and the final transfiguration. The large chorus, whose dawn assembly, epithalamium, and battle punctuate the long duet, looked good, moved well, and sang well. The principal roles are written uncomfortably, cruelly high. Neither Rosalind Plowright nor Patrick Raftery sounded untaxed, but she was lustrous and he was ringing. Antonio Tauriello, from the Teatro Colón, obtained sumptuous playing. Joseph Machlis's English translation flinched from the higher flights of Catulle Mendès' original. "O doux yeux! front doré!"—Harald's exclamation on first seeing Gwendoline —became "By the gods! Who is this!" Chabrier is an important composer: a link between Berlioz and Debussy, and an influence on his countrymen. *Gwendoline,* moreover, had a fairly large career in Germany as well as in France. This American première was welcome not only to an operatic historian, however, but in its own right, as a luxuri-

355

ant, exciting, and unusual adventure. Who now has plans for Ernest Reyer's *Sigurd*, Vincent d'Indy's *Fervaal*, Paul Dukas's *Ariane et Barbe-Bleue?*

TOIL AND TROUBLE

December 13, 1982

THE METROPOLITAN Opera's new production of Verdi's *Macbeth* was greeted on its first night with angry booing and mocking laughter; the next morning the *Times* declared that it "may just be the worst new production to struggle onto the Metropolitan Opera's stage in modern history." It represented a bold, resolute attempt on the part of the director, Sir Peter Hall, to see and hear Verdi's opera freshly and clearly and to stage it for a modern audience in a manner observant of its nineteenth-century character. It was a production difficult to assess after a single seeing. I returned to the second performance, which was received with moderate acclaim and no evident hostility.

The witches had caused most of the trouble. So they did to the critics of the first production, in 1847. *Macbeth* was composed, for Florence, as a deliberate essay in the *genere fantastico,* which had captured the Italian operatic imagination after the Italian premières, both in Florence, of Meyerbeer's *Robert le diable* (1840) and Weber's *Der Freischütz* (1843), followed in 1846 by a Florentine revival of *Don Giovanni.* Verdi's first surviving letter about the piece, to the Florence impresario Alessandro Lanari, begins, "Now that we are in full accord that the opera should be in the *genere fantastico...*" He has two subjects in mind, he says, both of them fantastical and both very fine. One was *Macbeth,* the other Grillparzer's wild and whirling *Die Ahnfrau. Macbeth* was chosen, and to his librettist, Francesco Maria Piave, Verdi wrote, "Adopt a sublime diction, except in the witches' choruses, which must be trivial, yet bizarre and original." His thinking about Shakespeare's witches had been formed by a passage in A. W. Schlegel's celebrated *Lectures on Dramatic Art and Literature:*

> No superstition can be preserved and diffused through many centuries and among diverse people without having a foundation in human nature; and on this the poet builds. He calls up from their hidden abysses that dread of the unknown, that secret presage of a dark side of nature and of a world of spirits.... His picture of the witches has a certain magical quality: he has created for them a particular language.... With one another, the witches discourse like women of the very lowest class...When, however, they address Macbeth they assume a loftier tone: their predictions...have all the obscure brevity, the majestic solemnity, of oracles, such as have ever spread terror among mortals.

Schlegel's pages about Shakespeare's *Macbeth* ("this sublime creation") were appended to the Italian translation of the play, by Carlo

Rusconi, from which Verdi worked. We find an echo of them nearly twenty years later when the composer told his Paris publisher, Léon Escudier, who was supervising the première of the revised *Macbeth*, that "the witches dominate the drama; everything derives from them —coarse and gossipy in the first act, sublime and prophetic in the third." Mr. Hall is perhaps the first modern director to attempt the witches of Verdi's description. In the first scene, when they cut the cackle and addressed Macbeth and Banquo I thought their predictions chilling, thrilling; and again in the caldron scene, when, after mixing their horrid soup with frenzied glee, they became earnest creatures of doom in their exchanges with the king. But an audience that had made merry over their livelier antics—aerial riding on broomsticks across a painted pantomime moon, hopping and skipping about with stuffed pussycats and rubber bats—was unprepared to accept their oracular pronouncements with due solemnity. In any case, the execution was in many ways unfortunate. For one thing, there were far too many witches. Verdi wanted eighteen—three covens of six—for the première. A large stage could probably hold a few more without overcrowding: an 1852 Scala production with only thirteen women (including the supers) aroused the composer's ire. But at the Met there seemed to be hundreds of the creatures cavorting about, flying, or keeping watch on the heights; and some of them were lubberly youths in drag. (The posse of cutthroats that mustered to assassinate Banquo was also absurdly numerous; *Macbeth* needs the full chorus only in the three ensemble finales.) There are just three characters in *Macbeth*, Verdi told Escudier: Lady Macbeth, Macbeth, and the chorus of witches. And the chorus of witches, he reiterates, "*is a character*" (his italics). At the Met, this third character became a rout, and the focus grew fuzzy. The three Oracles conjured by the witches were latex dummies that rose from the steaming caldron, itself suspended in midair, and opened their mouths in time to the music. They were ill-designed, Red Groomsy, and did look rather comic. The sprites that tripped on to revive the swooning Macbeth were Giselle and eight of the Wilis, on point and in Romantic tutus. Macbeth, Sherrill Milnes, played Albrecht, trying in vain to seize the elusive sylph. The musical match was exact—strange that Verdi left the lilting *coro ballabile* unaltered when he revised so much else!—but even eyes well disposed to the staging found the divertissement hard to take: the chorus's lewd parody of the ballerinas' dainty poses gave the audience its cue. It had already protested at the apparition of a Hecate wearing nothing but an illuminated tiara; this seemed to me an authentic and beautiful nineteenth-century vision of the goddess, even if it was one embodied in terms that the nineteenth-century stage would not have permitted.

In a preliminary interview, Mr. Hall said, "With singers, the main thing is to persuade them to trust the music. It tells them how to move.... In opera, the meters underlie everything." But he seemed to have misheard some of the meters. His Lady Macbeth, Renata Scotto, was oddly sedentary. She sang the energetic "Vieni! t'affretta!" sitting down; its fierce cabaletta, "Or tutti sorgete," rolling about on the ground; the delirious climax of "La luce langue," when the queen is rapt in the joy of power, again sitting; and the first strophes of the sleepwalking scene not sleepwalking but squatting on the castle floor. This was neither plausible nineteenth-century style nor good modern drama; it simply meant that the arias were projected with less than their wonted force. Miss Scotto's singing was sometimes fined down into inaudibility, sometimes forced and strident. Her care and determination were impressive; her vocal resources and her physical presence were inadequate to a role that, the composer said, calls for "a tragic actress—and tragic to the utmost degree." Mr. Milnes's Macbeth was strong but somewhat stolid. Without apparent emotion, not visibly *attonito* (thunderstruck), he received the news of Birnam wood's advance. His pianissimi were excellently audible, and his singing was scrupulously shaped, but one was conscious of vocalization. Verdi wanted his protagonist to concentrate on expressing the words and let the music come of itself. Ruggero Raimondi was a big-voiced Banquo who advanced centerstage and delivered his aria. Giuseppe Giacomini was a stentorian, thick-voiced Macduff, monotonous and unaffecting in one of Verdi's most poignant tenor plaints. We had neither a drama of living, interacting people, such as Mr. Hall produces so memorably at Glyndebourne, nor even a parade of costumed opera singers singing so vividly that something dramatic could result.

There were other miscalculations. Acts I and II were played, German-style, without intermission between them; so were Acts III and IV. But after every scene the front curtain fell, the houselights came up, and there was a long wait. And so the opera seemed shapeless and episodic. (In Verdi's day, mid-act scene changes were effected on an open stage, and act finales could be felt as such.) John Bury's décor suggested twopence-colored Pollock toy-theatre scenery awkwardly enlarged to the huge Met scale; it was architecturally uneasy and was poorly painted. After ascending the throne, the Macbeths dressed as the King and Queen of Hearts. Banquo's ghost was jacked up and popped down again through a visible trapdoor; what should be a tense moment went for nothing. Gil Wechsler's lighting was consistently tenebrous, without Verdian contrasts. (In Carl Ebert's famous production, the hectic glare of the banquet scene, after the gloom of Banquo's murder, came as a theatrically appropriate shock.) In the light falling across the castle floor from three imagined offstage windows, Macbeth began his dagger soliloquy, and the effect, although at odds with the architecture of the set and therefore distracting, was not unimpressive —until further pools of light appeared as follow spots tracked the principals through the hall.

This was not a personal perversion of the opera, like, say, Jean-Pierre Ponnelle's staging of *The Flying Dutchman* or of *Rigoletto*. It was, I repeat, a serious-minded, ambitious attempt to discover what the composer was about and to present his meanings vividly and enjoyably in a production on a scale larger than any he could have foreseen. For most of what happened, sound reasons could be discerned. The show failed through a mixture of misjudgments (of the house, of the company's capacities, of the audience's openness to contemporary theatrical ideas); inefficient execution (the settings, Stuart Hopps's choreography); and, it must be added, some faulty perceptions and a faulty control of style. Mr. Hall's Glyndebourne productions of Mozart's three Da Ponte operas have been the finest, the most musical, of our day. He works best in intimate surroundings. His Covent Garden *Tristan* failed much as this Met *Macbeth* did. Both were expensive, powerfully interesting, unforgettable flawed visions.

Verdi's 1865 Paris score, uncut and unaltered, was played. (The libretto the Met has on sale is misleading; it is not "the book of the opera" but contains a composite text Erich Leinsdorf used in 1959.) James Levine conducted, with his customary passion and vigor. On the dynamic level, he phrased carefully, but his phrasing in time was rigid, unnatural, unbreathed. Like Riccardo Muti, he brings to mind Giulio Ricordi's strictures on the young Toscanini's Verdi conducting—like "a mastodonic player piano." Timbres and dynamics are sensitively handled, and the rhythms are urgent, but the music is trapped in a grid of regular bar lines.

Oberlin Opera Theater's production of Verdi's *Falstaff*, last month, calls for a review (though I must "declare an interest," since it was sung in my translation), because it contained music unheard since the first performances of the opera, at La Scala in 1893. Verdi grew dissatisfied with two passages, and he recomposed them after the first night and after a vocal score had been published. One was a sixteen-bar lyrical outpouring in octaves from Nannetta and Fenton, behind the screen, in the second-act finale (over patter around the buck basket where Falstaff is stifling, and from Ford's forces), and the other the close of Act III, Scene 1. More than one commentator has regretted the loss of the first, a soaring, ecstatic, harmonically adventurous span of great beauty. Verdi removed it because he feared his finale had become "too much of a *concertato*," and replaced it with six bars of somewhat neutral C-major music. Oberlin restored it in orchestration, from the vocal score, by James Hepokoski (a Verdi scholar who teaches there, and who is the author of the Cambridge Opera Handbook on *Falstaff*). Having now heard this radiant passage in its context, I never want to lose it. The composer was wrong to think that it unduly protracted his finale. Not all his second thoughts were unequivocal improvements: the abridged, Paris finale of Act III of *Otello*, recently revived by the English National Opera, similarly sacrifices wonderful music to dramatic conciseness. But nearly all Verdi's thoughts are worth hearing and worth staging. I urge the Met when it revives *Macbeth* to adopt the stirring 1847 version of the fugitives' chorus and the 1847 ending; they would better match the line of the production.

The other *Falstaff* passage *was* improved. Originally, Verdi ended the scene—the offstage voices calling, the Ford-Caius dialogue overheard by Quickly—to a reprise in fragments of Alice's mazurka. Then he recast the mazurka fragments in 4/4 and spun his "masquerade" motif through them, producing the magical ending we know—in his own words, "a better effect, more fitting, and more musical." The result is pure gain, and not a possible dramatic gain to be measured against a musical loss. *Falstaff* conductors should follow the revision here—as in the caldron scene of *Macbeth,* a similar case.

Listening to *Falstaff* in a small theatre (the five-hundred-seat Hall Auditorium), in a straightforward, sensitive production (by Judith Layng), sung by a talented young cast, and conducted with great delicacy (by Robert Baustian), afforded the keenest delight. The details of the miraculous score told with a sharpness often lost in big-house presentations. Mark Moliterno, the Falstaff, and Katherine Harris, the Alice, are two young singers we should be hearing more of.

The rewards of small-house opera shone, too, in the production of Monteverdi's *L'incoronazione di Poppea* that the New York Lyric Opera has been playing in the Henry Miller Theater—now a disco, and renamed Xenon—on West Forty-third Street. It was an electronic *Poppea:* the singers were amplified, and Monteverdi's continuo accompaniment was realized for piano, synthesizers, drums, bass, and guitar. There was a racy but accurate new English translation of Francesco Busenello's libretto, made by John Haber and Michael Ward, the stage director and the musical director of the show. Where Fortune and Virtue in the Arthur Jacobs translation concede that "'gainst love in vain both men and gods endeavour," and in the Humphrey Procter-Gregg translation that "man would be mad, an angel would be senseless, to defy Love," the Xenon goddesses broke into the catchy number "Love calls the shots." Where Jacobs's Drusilla sings "Be happy, my heart, be no longer repining," and Procter-Gregg's "The heart in my bosom goes light as a feather," the Xenon Drusilla, Kate Phelan, sang "I woke up this morning, and somehow I knew that today would be different." It fits the music precisely.

Love, Richie Abanes, was a cocky rock tenorino. The Poppaea and the Nero, Carolyn Dennis and David Weatherspoon, were soul singers; Miss Dennis had a candid beauty and lustrous presence that recalled the young Gloria Davy. In a regular opera house, unamplified, the performers, most of them from Broadway, would probably not be heard. But they had the advantage over most regular opera singers of today that they sang the words, sang on the words, colored the words, were masters of expressive rubato timing over an unflagging pulse, and flew into astonishing decorative cadences with a virtuosity and freedom seldom heard in opera houses. I must not overpraise the show. Its virtues were complementary, not superior, to those of fine formal Monteverdi presentations, like the *Ritorno d'Ulisse* Mr. Hall produced at Glyndebourne. It was in a different world of eloquence from the tricksy Ponnelle staging or the City Opera's sorry attempt to be fancy and sexy at once. This *Poppea* was warmly and tenderly erotic; the sensuality was expressed by timbres, inflections, and glances, not by striptease and pawing. There was a tenor (not a soprano) Nero, there were cuts, and there was some reordering, but more of the crucial Poppaea-Otho duet was included than in the Leppard edition, and the penultimate Poppaea-Nero duet, missing in Leppard, was sung. It was a straight, honest presentation, dramatically unfrilled—one that trusted in the work and in Monteverdi's ability to hold modern listeners spellbound. The trust was justified.

Two years ago, Indiana University Opera Theatre, in Bloomington, put on a very successful production of *Porgy and Bess* with a double all-black cast. From this came the idea of commissioning a new opera, in conjunction with the university's Office of Afro-American Affairs, to coincide with a conference on Afro-American studies. The conference fell through, but the opera went ahead and was presented in October and November. It is *Soldier Boy, Soldier,* music by T. J. Anderson, libretto by Leon Forrest. Forrest's libretto—poems and poetic dialogue—reads well, but when I first read it I thought that I had the text of just the musical numbers, and that spoken dialogue or narrative would introduce and link them in the theatre, clarifying what seemed elusive and obscure. Not so. The program synopsis provided some general explanation: "The controlling theme of the opera" is "the growing conflict between realism and idealism as symbolized by Clarence Cratwell's private and public adjustment to the values promoted in this country upon his return from Viet Nam." It was hard to discern this theme in an action not very different (except in its dénouement) from that of, say, Moniuszko's *Halka:* a triangle of hero, his new bride, and his former mistress with murder in her heart; or, as a program note from the director, Alan Brody, put it, "standard soap opera stuff —two women, one man, jealousy and ultimate tragedy." But Mr. Brody also called the libretto "deceptive," and went on to explain how more could be found in it: not only concern for the plight of black Vietnam veterans but also consideration of the question "How can we escape the legacy of violence while we are still paying for it?" It is an opera about redemption, he said, with "an astonishing apotheosis through a confrontation with anger and bitterness."

The opera didn't come off, I felt, but it was an ambitious and worthwhile thing to try. Anderson is a composer who has essayed many genres, but *Soldier Boy, Soldier* is his first opera. The pieces in closed forms—songs, hymns—worked best. The sung confrontations lacked dramatic, "gestural" sharpness. The music—even the jazz—might have been written in any country. The jumpy vocal lines did not sing easily; I've never heard a Bloomington cast with so little projection. There was a distinguished and beautiful set, by Max Röthlisberger, but, being "open," it did nothing acoustically to help the singers. Robert Porco's conducting seemed a trifle sedate.

VINTAGES

December 20, 1982

ORLANDO DE LASSUS was a prolific composer: the work list in the New Grove fills eighteen columns of small type. Shortly before his death, in 1594, he published a collection of motets and, introducing them, looked back to the gay, festive works of his springtime and likened them to "arbors covered with new vines, ornamented with a luxuriant growth of shoots and tendrils...more pleasing to the eye than old vines, set out in rows and tied to stakes and props, but with their stocks roughened and split open by age." The young vines bear little, while the old vines, he said, "yield a liquor that is most sweet to mankind." His early works are more likely to please, but he has come to think that the "venerable if less melodious" compositions of his late years "reveal in their sound more substance and energy, and afford a profounder pleasure to the mind and the ear."

It is Lassus' 450th-birthday year, and Cappella Nova celebrated it last week with a "Christmas service" given at St. Joseph's, in the Village. There were Advent, Christmas, and Epiphany motets; the Ordinary was a composite assembled (except for the Kyrie) from Mass movements based on the motets, and the Proper was drawn from items in the *Patrocinium Musices* unpublished since the sixteenth century and newly transcribed for the concert. In a program note, Richard Taruskin, the director of Cappella Nova, suggested that in the year when Stravinsky's 100th and Haydn's 250th birthdays have been widely celebrated, too little attention has been paid to the third birthday boy, who is "every bit the equal of the other two in eminence and significance." Mr. Taruskin and his singers are ardent advocates who turn what they touch into glowing sound. The exclamatory cry that bounds up through an octave at the start of Lassus's "Videntes stellam"; the sudden triadic consolidation, a burst of glory after the voices have been treading mazy paths, in "Multifariam multisque modis"; the polyphony that breaks out like spring flowers, each a new and different delight, from the chant phrases of a Christmas sequence were sung with rare freshness and feeling. They were high points in an evening that never failed to afford profound pleasure to the mind and the ear.

In the July issue of the *Journal of Musicology*, there is an essay by Mr. Taruskin, "On letting the music speak for itself." He takes for his starting point a charge that Cappella Nova performances are "arbitrary and overly personal." What he considers arbitrary is "the flat dynamic and the lack of phrasing, that is, of molding lines to their high points, which characterize so many so-called 'objective' performances of Renaissance music." Because A is wrong, it does not follow that Z is right. I, too, feel that Cappella Nova performances are sometimes overemotional, and do so not on any "musicological" ground (who knows what the Bavarian ducal choir sounded like?) but because the striving for ever more fervent expressiveness can lead to forced tone and, on occasion, impure consonance. Lassus was admired in his day for his rhetorical power; his Penitential Psalms, with their vivid word painting, posit a vividly dramatic performance. But in some of the calmer pieces of the Christmas program a calmer, less tense approach, a suppler play of line against line might have made the music still more moving and beautiful. Yet the fault, if it be deemed one, was a fault on the right side. Everything the Cappella Nova did was alive and urgent. Of Lassus, we seldom get more than a tasting. This was a feast.

About ten years ago, the musical fires in Carlo Maria Giulini seemed to die: the great high tragedian, Callas's collaborator at La Scala, the unforgettable conductor of Covent Garden's *Don Carlos*, *Il trovatore*, and *La traviata*, grew dull. (In comedies—*The Barber*, *Falstaff*—he had always been unsmiling, unsparkly.) His annual Verdi Requiem became tame and mannered. It can happen to conductors. It had happened to Rudolf Kempe, who for three years, 1955–57, conducted Covent Garden's annual *Ring* cycles with increasing mastery and was hailed as the greatest Wagnerian of our day. (Ernest Newman found him "beyond praise.") In two further seasons, his grip on the cycle relaxed, and it was hard—except for those to whom emperors seem always to be wearing splendid clothes—to recognize the conductor whose lyricism and poetry, combined with vigor, large intellectual command, and theatrical flair, had held audiences spellbound. There is a danger, especially in London, that overpraise may be followed by underrating—cracking up to the skies by unfair cracking down. When the British press and public find that an artist can do no wrong, it is said, then in few years' time that artist will be held to do nothing right. But the phonograph provides a check: compare Mr. Giulini's impassioned *Don Carlos* recorded in 1970 (already late) with his dutifully correct *Rigoletto* recorded in 1979, and the point about him is made. I have been unwilling to admit it and have hoped that I was mistaken; no one likes to lose a hero. In the last few years, I have attended Giulini concerts in California, Chicago, New York, London wanting to hear again the musician I once so much admired. Each time, I have been disappointed.

Mr. Giulini and the Los Angeles Philharmonic, of which he has been musical director for four years, came to New York this month to give four concerts, two in Carnegie Hall and then two in Avery Fisher Hall. The last of them began with the *Force of Destiny* overture, and in it there did shine for a while something of the old, brave Giulini. Ezra Laderman's Symphony for Brass and Orchestra, his fourth symphony, followed. It was commissioned to honor Dorothy Chandler, the principal patroness of the orchestra, on her eightieth birthday and was first played in Los Angeles last year. The three-movement work lasts half an hour and can be characterized, without much enthusiasm, as a "well-made" symphony. There is a striking start. The slow movement contains a lush melody whose lyricism is rightly described by its composer, in a program note, as full-blown. Tonality and atonality are conscientiously and skillfully contrasted and reconciled. There is some majestic brass writing.

The second half was Beethoven's Fifth Symphony. It began excitingly: a big, old-fashioned, Romantic performance, with strong emphases, violent contrasts, and heavily expressive phrasing. But the slow movement fell into rhapsodic incoherence and sentimentality; it became a tone poem of passing emotions. The third and fourth movements were episodic, often noisy, and, finally, inflated. "Vulgar" is not an epithet one ever thought might come to mind during a Giulini performance. He is not a vapid, superficial conductor. He tries to do something, to say something, with the music he plays. But the finale of his Fifth was, if not exactly vulgar, at any rate blatant. Another epithet that suggested itself was "Hoffmannesque." Hoffmann's tale about the Fifth Symphony is famous:

Beethoven's instrumental music opens the realm of the colossal and the immeasurable for us. Radiant beams shoot through the deep night of this region, and we become aware of gigantic shadows that, surging back and forth, close in on us and destroy all within us except the pain of endless longing—a longing in which every pleasure that rose up amid jubilant tones sinks and succumbs. Only through this pain, which, while consuming but not destroying love, hope, and joy, tries to burst open our breasts with a full-voiced general cry from all the passions, do we live on, enchanted beholders of spirits in the supernatural realm.

It might be *Tristan*—still half a century in the future—that Hoffmann is describing. As the symphony approaches its climax, it "leads the listener irresistibly onward into the wonderful spiritual realm of the infinite." The reiterated C-major chords of the close are no triumphant affirmation; they are disturbing, destructive of any resolute calm, and "have the effect of a fire that again and again shoots high its bright, blazing flames after one had believed it extinguished."

The wonderful spiritual realm of the infinite is where Mr. Giulini would fain dwell, according to the publicity he has been subjected to since assuming the Los Angeles post. At his concerts, one sometimes has the feeling that he has perhaps entered it and is rapt in Platonic experience while his players and his listeners remain behind in a less than perfect world. They are left with sober blandness of execution, varied by some underlinings of the obvious, and with playing in which precision of attack and purity of wind intonation are counted mundane virtues that need not be strictly pursued. These are hard things to say about a high-minded man whose sincerity and earnestness are not in question. But much of what one reads about Mr. Giulini's performances seems to describe a legend rather than the sounds that were actually made.

The account of the Beethoven Fifth, it should be added, was not fully Hoffmannesque, for the Hoffmann sentences quoted above accompany a careful analysis of the symphony the burden of which is that, while "for many people the whole work rushes by like an ingenious rhapsody"—its movements "linked together in a fantastic way" —what matters most is the apprehensible integrity of the score: "It is particularly the intimate relationship of the individual themes one to another which produces the unity that firmly maintains a single feeling in the listener's heart." The overheated, unbalanced performance was also uncharacteristic of Mr. Giulini's work. The Brahms Requiem done at the first of the Los Angeles concerts was more nearly in the vein of that simply pious, earthbound, prosaic Beethoven Ninth he conducted here three years ago. The Requiem—*pace* Bernard Shaw, who declared that it could be "borne patiently only by the corpse"—is neither gloomy nor dull. It is comforting in the old sense of the word—strong, consolatory, fortifying. In this performance, it slipped by almost without incident.

Santiago Rodriguez, a silver medallist at the 1981 Van Cliburn piano competition, gave an Alice Tully Hall recital last week. A biographical note in the program book began by observing that he "has been called a brilliant, extroverted pianist and a crowd-pleaser by the nation's most respected critics," but the recital revealed an unassertive, gentle, poetic player, untouched by flamboyance, although the possessor of an exceptionally fleet and fluent technique. He began with Bach's Second Partita and gave a delicately poised, sensitively phrased performance. Then came the first two intermezzi of Brahms's Opus 118. The second of them was reticent almost, but not quite, to the point of mildness: a line between modest affirmation and meek understatement was nicely drawn. Alberto Ginastera's Second Sonata, composed in 1981, had its New York première. It is an arresting and attractive ten-minute composition, in three movements, Bartókian in its crisp transformations of folk music. The outer movements are moto-perpetuo toccatas based on Aymara and Quechua dances and songs. In the central slow movement, an ecstatic love song from Cuzco, a *harawi*, frames a *scorrevole* episode that (in the composer's words) "evokes the murmurs of the night in the lonely Andean punas." The singing of the *harawi* by the left hand while the right hand touches in resonances in a not quite parallel line high above, and both hands approach their melody notes through flickering ornaments, is a brilliant piece of ethnic transcription for the modern piano which cunningly creates microtonal illusions on the twelve-note instrument. (Ginastera's Third Piano Sonata, given its first performance last month in Tully Hall, by Barbara Nissman, is a four-minute toccata based on South American indigenous dances; "sonata" is too grand a title, but it is an exhilarating piece.)

The second half of Mr. Rodriguez's recital—three Rachmaninoff Preludes, Scriabin's F-sharp-major Sonata, a Granados Spanish Dance, and Moszkowski's *Caprice Espagnol;* Debussy's *Ondine* and the "cimbalom" final episode of Liszt's Sixth Hungarian Rhapsody as encores—suggested a Horowitz program. It was played without Horowitz panache: not glitteringly, extravagantly, breathtakingly, but with unobtrusive mastery and quiet lyricism. The Rachmaninoff and the Scriabin were beautiful. The Moszkowski, a flashy confection, needed more showmanship; it must be done dashingly or not at all. The second movement of the Scriabin and the Liszt displayed Mr. Rodriguez's self-effacing virtuosity to perfection. There was no piece on the program substantial and sustained enough to indicate whether he is more than a pianist of uncommonly high accomplishment and tenderly romantic instincts, but anyone who uses "gentle" as a term of high praise, and "assertive" as a pejorative, should enjoy him. He played a Baldwin instrument that can be reviewed in much the same terms: it was warm, unbelligerent, responsive, and very pleasing.

GORGEOUS TRAGEDY

January 17, 1982

THE FIRST Covent Garden theatre opened in 1732 with a performance of Congreve's *Way of the World.* Handel's Italian opera company played there from 1734 to 1737 (*Ariodante* and *Alcina* were among the six of his Italian operas that appeared); and thereafter until the year of his death, 1759, he often returned to Covent Garden to give Lenten oratorio performances. *Messiah* had its London première at the theatre, and *Joseph, Judas Maccabaeus, Joshua, Jephtha, Samson, Susanna,* and *Solomon,* among others in the great series of English music dramas, had their premières. In 1744, Handel turned to a secular subject: his setting of Congreve's opera libretto *Semele* was performed at Covent Garden "after the Manner of an Oratorio." Two theatres later, in a 250th-anniversary celebration, the Royal Opera has paid tribute to Congreve and Handel by mounting a fully staged production of *Semele.*

It is at least the sixth production in London alone since 1954 of a work that the Victorian music historian W. S. Rockstro declared "could never, by any possibility, have been tolerated upon the English Stage." Today, the reputation of *Semele* stands high. Washington staged it two years ago. It has been thrice recorded. Winton Dean, in his wonderful book on Handel's dramatic oratorios, remarks that "Handel's joy in the creation of *Semele* is manifest in the exuberance of the invention and the variety of technical and structural resource" and that "all the richest layers of his imagination seem to have been simultaneously exposed." Few who know *Semele* would disagree. Yet it was the only one of the oratorios unrevived by the composer after the year of its first production. Its secularity probably told against it. Charles Jennens, the

366

librettist of *Messiah,* declared it "no oratorio, but a bawdy opera." Semele's lovely air "Oh sleep, why dost thou leave me? Why thy visionary
joys remove?" became popular with sopranos unaware that in context
it expresses the heroine's reluctance to wake from the beguilements of
an erotic dream. In the nineteenth-century vocal score such words as
"fruitful," "bed," and "desire" were expunged.

Among Handel's music dramas, *Semele* holds a special place. It is at
once a classical tragedy, a rapturous celebration of sensual delights,
and a psychological play in which, not without touches of humor, two
women are keenly and vividly portrayed and the feelings of those
around them are eloquently voiced. *Semele* tells of a beautiful, plea-
sure-loving young woman who is installed in luxury as the mistress of a
man of high social station; for this rich, exciting lover she has abandoned the respectable but slightly dull young man she was meant to
marry. In her gilded love nest, she grows bored and ambitious. Her
lover invents distractions for her, but in vain: she insists on being taken
to move in the circles he moves in—on being treated as an equal, not
as someone to be visited on the sly. The man's wife, jealous, vindictive,
and clever, furthers the ambition, knowing that it must end in disaster
for her rival. Claude Autant-Lara's film *En Cas de malheur,* with Brigitte
Bardot, Jean Gabin, and Edwige Feuillère, is a modern version of the
story. Congreve set it in the resonant world of Greek myth, in Thebes
and on Mount Cithaeron (where Actaeon and Pentheus met their
fates, where Oedipus was exposed); on the summit Jupiter has erected
for Semele the pleasure palace where cool gales fan the glade where'er
she walks.

In 1732, the Bishop of London banned a scenic representation of
Handel's oratorio *Esther,* and therby changed the course of Handel's
career and the history of English music. Handel's subsequent oratorios
are written as if for an ideal theatre in which the stagecraft knows no
limits. Scenic directions remain in the librettos, and the composer's
imagination remains pictorial, but, liberated from any dependence on
painted canvas or on the mechanics of choral assembly and dispersal,
Handel composes with the freedom of a movie director. He shifts
scenes in the twinkling of a harmony; musters bands of revellers or
warriors at will; makes his choristers now Hebrews, now Philistines (in
Belshazzar, the most spectacular of the series, now Babylonians, now
Medes and Persians, now Hebrews), without needing to allow time for
costume changes, and employs them to point a moral, sound a warn-
ing, or crown a musical sequence without having to determine whether
they are onstage or offstage, or what characters they are supposed to
represent. Consider the second scene of *Belshazzar.* It is headed "The
Camp of Cyrus before Babylon. A view of the City, with the River
Euphrates running through it. Cyrus, Gobrias; Medes and Persians.
Chorus of Babylonians upon the Walls, deriding Cyrus, as engaged in
an impracticable undertaking." After the Babylonians have sung their
jeering chorus, the camera closes in, as it were, on Cyrus and Gobrias,

discussing a strategy by which the city may be taken. Cyrus prays ("Great God!...Support me still") and then turns to his men: "My friends, be confident, and boldly enter upon this high exploit." The ensuing chorus, "All empires upon God depend; Begun by his command, at his command they end," is at once their response and a gnomic commentary to close the sequence.

The flexibility that freed Handel's dramatic genius from the confines of opera seria and inspired works that have been likened to the *Oresteia* and *King Lear* challenges the director who would now give them theatrical dress. Whether or not they should be staged has been debated since Handel's own day; the clinching argument for staging them is the power and beauty of those modern productions in which the challenges have been bravely and sensitively met. The Handel Opera Society mounted *Hercules* in 1956; its *Theodora*, in 1958, inaugurated a series of annual oratorio productions. Through a quarter century, many approaches have been tried; most of the possible mistakes were made early, and several ways toward effective inscenation have been found. During these years, the regular British companies did less well. They imported foreign directors ignorant of what the Handel Opera Society had revealed. For Covent Garden's *Samson* in 1958, Herbert Graf resorted to a static, tiered chorus; the drama—Jon Vickers its impassioned hero—was enacted within an oratorio frame. At Glyndebourne in 1966, Günther Rennert presented *Jephtha* as a costumed concert (and ruined the work by adopting an edition that mangled the musical architecture and omitted the tremendous statements—the opening words and the second-act finale—that proclaim its theme). For the Sadler's Wells Opera in 1970, in the Coliseum, Filippo Sanjust turned *Semele* into a royal romp: Juno was Queen Caroline angrily pacing the gardens of St. James's Palace while her lady-in-waiting Iris reported that the establishment of George II's latest mistress had been located; there not Loves and Zephyrs but a staff of discreet liveried servants attended upon Semele. None of these three short-lived productions lent much support to the Handelians' claim that the music dramas should be a cornerstone of the national operatic repertory; for a *Saul* of tragic grandeur we pleaded in vain.

About Covent Garden's new *Semele,* directed by John Copley, I have mixed feelings. It is a very lavish show, staged and dressed as if by Veronese in his most opulent vein. There are acres of painted canvas, columns, clouds, aerial cars, and sumptuous costumes, all glowingly lit. (The sets are by Henry Bardon, the costumes by David Walker.) The drama is all but swamped by the décor. The Royal Opera can bring to Handel scenic, choral, and dance resources not commanded by the Handel Opera Society (which performs in Sadler's Wells); but *Semele* does not really demand what its heroine demanded of Jove—"no less than all in full excess." Covent Garden might answer its critics with another of Semele's lines, "You always complain!" There is cause for complaint if decorative values take precedence of drama, if directness and subtlety are drenched in frippery. Admittedly, the Royal Opera House of today (built in 1858, and seating 2,250) is very much larger than the 1732 theatre Handel knew, and big-house Handel is hard to bring off. Yet a strong, simple staging might have worked better than this highly elaborated one. Musically, things were also less than ideal. Sir Charles Mackerras, who in 1970 conducted a poised, buoyant account of the score for the Sadler's Wells Opera, had not induced the Covent Garden orchestra to play for him lightly, liltingly, freshly. Number after number seemed to move ponderously and a shade slowly. (The 4/4 andante of the duet "Obey my will," for example, sounded as if there were eight beats in each measure.) Valerie Masterson, the Semele, was clear and fluent in divisions but less sweetly attractive of timbre in the lyrical episodes, and less piquant in her pouting exchanges with Jupiter, than some of her London predecessors have been. Kathleen Kuhlmann made a good Covent Garden début doubling the mezzo roles of Ino and Juno; without banishing memories of Monica Sinclair and Helen Watts, she was forthright and effective. Marie McLaughlin, the Iris, was delightfully bright, fearless, and true. Robert Tear was a conscientious and intelligent Jupiter, but his tones lacked charm. There was an abundance, sometimes a surfeit, of vocal embellishment, and most of it sounded learned from a score rather than exuberantly improvised.

In this country, Handel's dramatic oratorios are given mainly in concert performances. (Peter Sellars's staging of *Saul*, at Harvard in 1981, was an exception.) Kennedy Center has a *Hercules* in concert later this month, a *Theodora* in concert in April. Two organizations have plans for presenting the complete series of sixteen: the Maryland Handel Festival, which is held annually on the College Park campus of the University of Maryland, outside Washington, and the Sine Nomine Singers, who perform in Merkin Hall. Maryland began at the beginning, with Handel's first oratorio, *Esther*, and has announced his second, *Deborah*, for next year. Sine Nomine began at the end, with his last oratorio, *Jephtha*, in 1981 and his last but one, *Theodora*, this season. A continuation *motu recto et contrario* would lead to *Hercules* at a crossroad in 1989. [*In fact, Maryland reached* Saul *in 1987, having broken the strict sequence with a* Messiah *in 1985, and in 1983 Sine Nomine jumped straight to* Hercules.] Handelians were dismayed when they discovered that the Maryland *Esther* and the New York *Theodora* were billed for performance on the same November afternoon; to make things worse, there was also a New York *Esther*, in Carnegie Hall, on the first day of the Maryland festival. This was poor planning.

Esther was the only one of Handel's oratorios staged in his day—possibly at Cannons in 1718; then in London in 1732, before the Bishop's ban. It is one of the last to have been staged in our day: the Handel Opera Society mounted it only in 1980. The libretto depends from Racine's play-with-music *Esther*, written—like his *Athalie*, which Handel also took up—for the demoiselles of Saint-Cyr. In the English reworking, the plot is not without incident but lacks inner conflicts: Haman, Xerxes' henchman, plans a "holocaust"; Xerxes' Jewish queen, Esther, asks her husband to countermand it; he does so, and the Jews rejoice. Several numbers were borrowed from the Brockes Passion. Haman, a bass, has the liveliest music. He starts things off with a fierce recitative ("It is decreed, All the Jewish race shall bleed") and air, enthusiastically seconded by an officer ("Our souls with ardour glow, To execute the blow") and a chorus. Xerxes (Handel, following Racine, called him Assuerus, and later Ahasuerus) is less a mighty ruler than a love-smitten tenor—or, in Handel's 1732 revision, alto. Esther is a soprano. Her uncle Mordecai is a tenor (in 1732, a contralto). There are solo episodes for unnamed soprano, alto, and tenor Israelites. Most of the drama resides in the Jewish choruses—especially the lament "Ye sons of Israel, mourn" and the sustained D-major jubilation of the finale. But there is also a tense scene when Haman, on hearing his death sentence pronounced, falls to his knees and addresses Esther ("Turn not, O Queen, thy face away"), and she remains inflexible, cutting contemptuously, unaccompanied, into his final cadence with her "Flatt'ring tongue, no more I hear thee."

Maryland used the original, 1718 version. Paul Traver, who conducted, has an admirable feeling for the dance rhythms that underlie many of Handel's movements. Where Handel conductors often plod, his gait is light. But—the never satisfied critic can always find a "but" —in gravely forceful episodes Mr. Traver still tends to dance, and to leave the musical phrases uncolored by the sense of the words and the mood of the scene. It is a happier fault than leaden earnestness. Bernard Shaw wanted to hear *Messiah* sung by "a choir of heathens, restrained by no considerations of propriety." Edward Fitzgerald called Handel "a good old Pagan at heart." But in this *Esther* Mr. Traver sometimes missed the weight of emotion that should mark the piece. The choir, the University of Maryland Chorus, was adept—sixty young, fresh voices, fluent, flexible, and vigorous. They plainly enjoyed their music, and imparted that enjoyment to the audience. The finale was splendid. But they did not make us share in the plight of a people condemned to extermination. In general, the performance was insufficiently operatic, too oratorio-like. There were pauses between numbers during which the action hung fire. The Esther, Benita Valente, seemed to be tied to her book—rendering the notes but not phrasing as if the fate of thousands turned upon her utterances. The Haman, Donnie Ray Albert, was fierce and powerful, but his voice lost quality when not used at full force. There was one true Handelian in the cast, René Jacobs, who sang the alto solos (which include the poignant "O Jordan, Jordan, sacred tide") vividly and affectingly. Although the orchestra was modern, it included Smithsonian players versed in Baroque music and able to modify the modern style in Handelian directions. (At an earlier festival concert, two of the Opus 3 concerti grossi were played on Baroque instruments; a chorally brilliant Dettingen Te Deum followed.) Handel revived *Esther* often between 1732 and 1757, recasting the score, adding numbers (sometimes in Italian), omitting numbers. Through all the "convulsions" (Dean's word), the essential plot and the vital scenes of 1718 survived. It was a popular work. The Maryland performance showed why.

I caught up with the Sine Nomine *Theodora* by means of a tape recording, and was glad to hear it. Handel's last two oratorios are marked by a rare spiritual beauty, to which the performers, conducted by Harry Saltzman, seemed finely responsive. There was a good cast. Bernadette Fiorella's singing of the title role was ardent, limpid, and pure. Jeffrey Dooley's declamation, as Didymus, was keen. Marianna Busching was a moving Irene. Mr. Saltzman had restored several passages of recitative missing in the standard scores, the lack of which had obscured characterization and led to patches of grammatical nonsense. He used a Baroque orchestra, whose timbres gave fresh eloquence to Handel's carefully judged scoring. There was some sensitive wind playing. In Merkin Hall, I'm told, the soloists made entrances and exits as the libretto prescribes, and different parts of the platform were used to suggest the different scenes of the action; the effect of this could not be judged from a tape recording, but the idea is a good one. In some musical ways, the performance could have been more dramatic: sometimes the bass lines trudged, unphrased; the gleeful chorus of sexy Roman soldiers, excited that Theodora is to be made over to their lusts, was rather sedately sung; again and again cadences that should clinch recitatives briskly were delayed and protracted. By the time of *Theodora*, Handel's setting of English was sure and subtle. The singers sometimes spoiled it by observing bars and beats instead of natural inflections: "*and* thy thunders roll around," "by *an* unhappy constancy." But on the whole this was an affecting performance of Handel's radiant late masterpiece, his only oratorio (apart from *Messiah*) on a Christian subject.

QUEEN IN BABYLON

January 24, 1983

Semiramide, Rossini's thirty-fourth, last, and longest Italian opera, written for La Fenice, Venice, in 1823, when its composer was thirty, is a glittering, impressive monster—an opera apt to inspire conflicting feelings in those who see, hear, or study it. I first encountered it at La Scala twenty years ago, in the production—Joan Sutherland its heroine—that restored the opera to the contemporary stage. Giulietta Simionato was the Arsaces. It was a large, handsome production, with battalions of choristers and supers. (Nicola Benois's scenery was based on Alessandro Sanquirico's designs for the Scala première of *Semiramide*, in 1824.) The show lasted five hours; the score was heavily cut, but the two-act opera was divided by three long intermissions. *Semiramide* had been waiting for a soprano with Miss Sutherland's brilliance, fleetness, power, stamina, and stature. In 1964, she repeated the title role in Los Angeles and in Carnegie Hall, joined both times by Marilyn Horne as Arsaces; around the world other productions and concert performances followed. Miss Sutherland and Miss Horne recorded the opera in 1966, for London Records. The next soprano of note to undertake the title role was Montserrat Caballé; a 1980 Aix-en-Provence production, with Miss Horne as Arsaces and Samuel Ramey as Assur, was highly praised, and launched a new international round of revivals and concert performances. One of them starring the Aix principals was due in Carnegie Hall last week; but Mme. Caballé, after singing the rehearsals, withdrew, and in the event the title role was taken by June Anderson, who has been doing the part at the Rome Opera. Since the Spanish conductor originally billed, Jesús López-Cobos (who had conducted the Aix performance), had also withdrawn and been replaced by Henry Lewis, this was an all-American *Semiramide*, sung in Italian.

The opera is at once Rossini's most florid and his most austere composition—strange combination. (I should add that the Victorian music critic Henry Chorley deemed Rossini's preceding opera, *Zelmira*, even more "gorgeously florid," especially in its writing for the male voices.) There are several ways of viewing the work. One is as a link between *The Magic Flute* and *Aida*. The allegro theme of its overture may be based on Mozart's; the solemn priestly musters in which the hero is morally girded for trials ahead recall those of the *Flute*. In the other direction, *Semiramide* seems to leap forward over Donizetti and Bellini (despite the traces it left on *Norma*) and point toward Verdi. Assur's accents anticipate those of Macbeth and of Rigoletto. Other things adumbrate *Aida:* the very start, with its recitative utterances for the High Priest over imitative string writing; the splendid assembly with successive processional entries, in the vein of the *Aida* triumph; the dedicatory temple scene in which the hero is invested with a *sacro brando;* the subterranean tragic finale. *Semiramide*, like *Aida*, is a large-scale work of consolidation built on a rather formal libretto—masterly and grand, in some ways less adventurous than its predecessors.

Other forces played upon it. In Naples, in 1820, Rossini had revived Spontini's *Fernand Cortez;* he was familiar with the high heroic French manner. Gluck's *Iphigénie en Tauride* and Cherubini's *Lodoiska* were also performed in Naples, with Isabella Colbran their heroine, while Rossini was music director there. In 1822, he had visited and been fêted in Vienna and had heard Weber's *Der Freischütz* (which left no evident mark on *Semiramide)* and a fair amount of Beethoven, including the Eroica. Meyerbeer's earlier Italian operas may also have been an influence. I don't know them; but while the librettist Gaetano Rossi was at work with Rossini on *Semiramide* he told the German composer, in a letter, that they had devised for it an "*Introduzione alla Meyerbeer*—an imposing scene of pomp and spectacle." In 1819, Rossi had reworked Metastasio's much-set *Semiramide* libretto for Meyerbeer. (In 1824, his and Meyerbeer's *Crociato in Egitto*, composed for La Fenice, was an evident attempt to outdo his and Rossini's 1823 opera for that theatre.) *Semiramide* came at a turning point in Rossini's career. He had resolved to leave Italy and conquer in person that wider world where his works had already carried all before them. He had just married Colbran, the prima donna of his Neapolitan operas, and he now composed for her her most stupendous role.

Rossi based the libretto on Voltaire, not on Metastasio. In the latter, Semiramis, great Ninus's widow, has donned male attire and, with uncommon success, ruled Babylon, passing herself off as young Ninus, her son—"aided in that imposture [as Metastasio tells in his preface] by the facial resemblance and by the confinement in which Asiatic women lived unseen." Only in the final scene does she disclose her true identity and thereby unravel several amorous and political tangles. Voltaire's, Rossi's, and Rossini's Semiramis, on the other hand, is a tragic heroine in whom elements of Clytaemnestra, Phaedra, Jocasta, Gertrude, and Lady Macbeth are brought together. She is the splendid Queen Mother and Regent of Babylon, superbly imperious in all her utterances. She is a haunted, guilty widow who has conspired with her lover to murder her husband and mount his throne, and who is slain at last by the hand of her son. She is a passionate, jealous, beautiful woman radiantly in love with an officer young enough to be her son. And when it transpires that he *is* her son she is a tender, remorseful mother. In giving expression to all these aspects of his heroine, Rossini combined formal heroic utterance with warmly romantic strains, and from all the styles he commanded or had studied he created a character more classical, brilliant, and imposing than any he had created before. Colbran, who had made her Scala début at the age of twenty-three (thirty-nine performances as Volumnia in Giuseppe Nicolini's *Coriolano*, thirteen as Gluck's Iphigeneia in Aulis), excelled at pouring out lava streams of fiendishly difficult roulades. In his later Neapolitan operas, Rossini had begun to contrast these pyrotechnical displays with smoother, gentler melodies, lit by sudden traceries of delicate embellishment. There are a few such passages in *Semiramide*—notably the brief preghiera in the last scene, when Semiramis implores the shade of Ninus to guard their son—but for the most part the role is unrelentingly florid. It can be claimed that the sheer virtuosity is turned to dramatic virtue, that the enormous stretches of intricate, rather automatic figuration take on a hieratic quality. Whether the claim seems reasonable or not depends on the soprano who sings the music. (Similarly, a particular interpreter of Mozart's Donna Anna may support or confute Berlioz's characterization of her coloratura at the end of "Non mi dir" as "a shocking impropriety...an odious crime against passion, taste, and common sense.")

The only Semiramis I have seen in the theatre has been Miss Sutherland. I have not heard Mme. Caballé in the part; nor Lella Cuberli or Katia Ricciarelli, two others who have tackled it recently. Miss Sutherland—the recording and later concert performances confirmed it—was brilliant, vigorous, commanding, irresistible; Semiramis has been one of her best roles. Miss Anderson burst on City Opera audiences a few seasons ago as Dame Joan's destined successor and then went into international orbit. In Carnegie Hall, there were murmurs and shouts of disapproval when Mme. Caballé's defection was announced; there were cheers after Miss Anderson had sung. Her voice is most easily described as being like that of a young Sutherland: effortlessly powerful; swift and vivid in attack; capable, too, of spinning long melancholy lines, of swelling or tapering, of lingering hawk-like over a final tonic and suddenly pouncing on it dead center. Most American sopranos d'agilità in recent years have been "school of Sills," with light voices. By skill and artistry, the best of them have compassed the pathos and passionate despair of Donizetti's Lucia, Bellini's Elvira. Miss Anderson is an acolyte in a grander, more substantial tradition. She has a strong frame, a sound wind, and a large, ductile voice that seems thoroughly secure and healthy. Rossi, in that letter to Meyerbeer, noted that Colbran herself would figure in the *introduzione:* the prima donna of *Semiramide* is first heard as the second voice in a canon-quartet (an unusual procedure, for which Beethoven's Leonore provides the precedent). Miss Anderson sang her line smoothly and sweetly, and launched the subsequent allegro, "Trema il tempio," with spirit. In her aria, the famous "Bel raggio lusinghier," the low notes were weakly formed but the high ones showed her voice's wonderful ability to glow and blossom as it rises. Thus far, her artistry was correct rather than individual. She gave the impression of having learned to pronounce Italian but not yet to command it; without spirited words, singing, however exciting the sounds may be, is not truly alive. Then Arsaces, in the person of Miss Horne, joined Semiramis, and a sense of drama began to fire their recitative exchanges and the subsequent duet. The two ladies, singing without book, worked well together. The two-part cadenzas of their second duet, sweetly tuned and subtly timed, suggested a long stage partnership rather than a team paired for the first time on the day of the performance. Miss Anderson's notes soon filled out through the whole of her wide range, and she ended the evening in triumph.

For close on two decades, Miss Horne has been singing Arsaces, and singing it ever more richly and grandly. In the theatre, I have sometimes been less than stirred by her portrayals. She is no actress; she is often ill-costumed; she strides on, a chunky sound-making device, and delivers—brilliantly. But at this concert *Semiramide* I soon became as uncritical an admirer as any of those fans who maintain Miss Horne can do no wrong. She sings Arsaces' first aria, "Ah, quel giorno," very well; she sings his second, "In sì barbara sciagura," bewitchingly. Almost alone among contemporary artists she has the imagination, wit, and insight to "interpret" Rossini's music as we know the artists of his day used to, and the technical resource to bring off the most daring flights of bravura without any smudging or fudging. Before resolving a sequence, she may pause an instant and leave listeners uncertain in which of three possible octaves the next note will be sounded. Maybe she knows in advance; but we don't, and so the effect is utterly spontaneous. The zestful, exuberant re-creation of the music is apparently determined by how things are going, and how the voice is flowing, at the particular performance. When Miss Horne sings, Rossini's florid writing doesn't sound automatic, and not only because it is embellished and made even more florid; piquant unpredictability enlivens both the musical text and her delivery of it. Moreover, her concert presence is warm and winning. She seems far more attractive, far more dramatic, more of a character, than when in boots and plumed helmet she stomps around and gesticulates on the stage.

Assur, the villain of the piece, is a role taken sometimes by basses, sometimes by baritones. In recent years, Mr. Ramey has made it his own, for he can achieve most of its coloratura. Even in the nineteenth century, Chorley tells us, Assur's mad scene was commonly omitted: the singers could not manage it. Mr. Ramey sang it all, and sang it impressively. There were moments when he produced more sound than he needed to, as if to wow groundlings by volume rather than to delight musicians by finespun line, but all in all it was a majestic performance. Idrenus, the tenor, is incidental to the plot. He does not appear in Voltaire's play; Rossi imported him from Metastasio but altered his function. In Metastasio, he pairs off, in the happy ending, with Semiramis; in the opera, he is an Indian prince, Arsaces' rival for the hand of Princess Azema (a character important in Voltaire but by Rossi reduced to a cipher). In fact, Idrenus could be omitted altogether without affecting the action, but the composer needed a tenor line in the ensembles, and for the tenor he also composed two very difficult arias; John Sinclair, the original Idrenus, must have been a remarkably accomplished singer. At La Scala in 1962, both arias were omitted. One is restored in the recording. I heard both in a London concert performance in 1969, when Anastasios Vrenios cadenced the second from an astonishing high E. In Carnegie Hall, both were sung, by Douglas Ahlstedt. He got through them, but in tones that grew tight and unattractive above the staff; a sustained high C-sharp at the close of the second, however, rang out full and free. Eric Halfvarson was a deplorable Oroes, the High Priest, roaring and bawling in the approximate vicinity of Rossini's notes. Stephanie Friede sang Azema's few phrases in tones darkly lustrous except when she pushed too hard. Walter MacNeil's account of the even smaller role of Mithrates was clear and well judged.

Few composers have poured out melody with (in Chorley's phrases) "such luxury of beauty," "such delicious abundance," as Rossini did. *Semiramide* contains about four hours of music. Immediately after the

Venice première, we are told, it was shortened. When Giuditta Pasta sang Semiramis in Paris, in 1826, the curtain rose at eight-ten and fell at eleven-thirty; so Stendhal reports, and he recommended cutting half an hour more of music. The Carnegie Hall performance, which was lightly abridged, began at seven-thirty and ended at nearly midnight; about three hours and thirty-five minutes of music was heard, and this was surely the fullest account of *Semiramide* in modern times. It was no doubt because the piece had already become so long that Rossini closed it in a brisk, almost perfunctory manner—a few exclamations and a brief chorus, where a grand finale dominated by the dying heroine seems to be needed. Voltaire provided matter for a possible aria ("Mon fils...je te pardonne") and cabaletta ("Vivez, régnez heureux"). Rossini later set some of this, in recitative, for Paris, but elsewhere the brisk ending remained standard; in the autograph (which has been published in facsimile by Garland) there is even a paste-over that makes it more abrupt still.

This concert *Semiramide* was strongly cast and textually ample but in some ways did less than a concert performance can to suggest the full scale and splendor of a spectacular grand opera. The Sacred Music Society's concert presentations of Rossini's *Mosè in Egitto*, in 1978, and Meyerbeer's *Il crociato*, in 1979, and the Opera Orchestra of New York's concert presentation of Wagner's *Rienzi*, last year, had more sweep, more grandeur, and larger forces. They were more theatrical. *Semiramide* was rather modestly accompanied by members of the American Symphony, and the orchestra sounded top-heavy: there was a small covey of double-basses somewhere over on the right—not the solid bass foundation on which the Sacred Music Society performances were built. There was no *banda*—whereas *Il crociato* had a military band from West Point, forty strong, whose martial snap made a fine contrast with the classical orchestra. The chorus, the Orpheon Chorale, was less than fiery. From a "production" point of view, more could have been done to suggest who was onstage in any scene, who not, and where the scenes began and ended. Since Miss Anderson and Miss Horne were not depending on scores, it seemed a pity that their duets were enacted behind a rampart of unneeded music stands. True, a libretto with translation was provided; the hall was lit just enough for it to be legible, not enough to make glancing between the pages and the platform easy. Finally, Mr. Lewis's conducting seemed to me weak, pallid, and unrhythmical.

AMERICAN SYMPHONISTS

January 31, 1983

IT IS tempting to essay contrasts or comparisons between Roger Sessions and Walter Piston: near-contemporaries (Piston was born in 1894 and died in 1976; Sessions, born in 1896, was eighty-six last month), both New Englanders, both Harvard graduates (Sessions was there a decade earlier), and both teachers of uncommonly diverse pupils (the list of those who studied with Piston, extended only to C, includes Arthur Berger, Leonard Bernstein, and Elliott Carter; a Sessions list extended to D includes Milton Babbitt, Peter Maxwell Davies, and David Del Tredici). A chapter of Aaron Copland's *Our New Music* (1941) is headed "Sessions and Piston," since it seems "natural to couple the names," but the two coinhabit only the first two paragraphs, likened there as being different from the Californian Roy Harris—the subject of the preceding chapter—in that there is "nothing unfinished or uncouth" about their music ("It comes out of a section of the United States that has had from the first a profound feeling for the things of the spirit"), and as being scholarly by nature, no enemies of tradition, and celebrated teachers. Then each is considered quite separately, "for both men are very much individuals in their own right." Sessions's career and Piston's took on a new parallel when the former composed seven symphonies, Nos. 2 to 8, between 1946 and 1968, and the latter composed seven symphonies, Nos. 2 to 8, between 1943 and 1965. But the passing of years has made ever more apparent the differences between them—differences of style and technique, which can be demonstrated, and profound differences of intention and aspiration, which are more easily felt than described. A New World Records coupling (NW 302) of Sessions's First String Quartet, composed in 1936, and Piston's Second String Quartet, composed in 1935, makes plain to ear and spirit what is hard to put into words. So did recent New York performances of two near-contemporary symphonies, Sessions's Second and Piston's Fourth.

Sessions's Second Symphony had its first performance, given by Pierre Monteux and the San Francisco Symphony, in 1947. The next year, it was played at the ISCM Festival, in Amsterdam. In 1950, Dimitri Mitropoulos and the New York Philharmonic played it here, and recorded it. In 1951, Adrian Boult and the BBC Symphony introduced it to London, and Jean Morel and the Juilliard Orchestra repeated it in New York. Thereafter, the list of performances grows thinner (a Gunther Schuller performance at Tanglewood in 1977 was by all accounts memorable), but the Mitropoulos recording—originally Columbia, now reissued on CRI—kept the piece before interested ears. After three decades, it returned live to New York last month:

André Previn and the Pittsburgh Symphony played it at the C. W. Post Center of Long Island University, and the next day in Avery Fisher Hall. I heard the Long Island performance. It was not ideal—the rich details of the large-orchestra texture had not all fallen into place in the seemingly inevitable way that Sessions's music requires—but it was enthusiastic and colorful. In the Mitropoulos performance, the long line of the music is often easier to follow, even though the recorded sound is shrill and sometimes murky, and though breaks of the original issue (which was on seven 78-r.p.m. sides) are not always smoothly joined. The symphony has worn well. At each hearing, there seems to be more to discover, not only in structural niceness but, more important, in expressive content. Except in the scherzo, whose trim, alert tune and developments suggest a latter-day Haydn, it is an emotionally charged work. There are drama and mystery in the first movement. The long melodies of the adagio are beautiful. The brash, banal rondo theme of the finale yields both Ivesian celebration and Mahlerian tragedy; the hard-won D-major close is a disturbing, truthful mixture of assertion and uncertainty.

In London last month, in the Royal Festival Hall, Sessions's latest work, the Concerto for Orchestra (see page 150) had its European première. It was done by John Pritchard and the BBC Symphony, and differed considerably from the Boston première. There Seiji Ozawa had taken sixteen minutes over the piece, and the fast sections had not been brought up to the speeds prescribed by the metronome markings of the score. In London, Sir John took less than twelve minutes—a very big difference in this fairly short piece. The ticktocking of time, sounded by a recurrent xylophone motif, was far more rapid. There was an exuberance that had been missing in Boston, but some of the long-breathed wind solos seemed a shade hurried. The two performances—one scrupulous and affectionate but uninspired, the other marked by flair and an almost improvisatory zest—were complementary. We must now hear others, neither too slow nor too fast, of this vigorous and vital composition.

In Carnegie Hall last week, David Effron and the Eastman Philharmonia—the senior orchestra of the University of Rochester's Eastman School of Music—played Piston's Fourth Symphony, composed in 1950. Like all Piston's music, it is cleanly and expertly written, decorous, direct, and lucid. His merits are well known and are generally and genuinely admired. Aaron Copland, in that chapter of *Our New Music,* and Elliott Carter, in a 1946 essay reprinted in his collected writings, concurred in their appraisals and their praise, with just one disagreement: "There is nothing especially 'American' about his work" (Copland); "Certain qualities mark the music as distinguishably American" (Carter). In 1941, Copland had said, "Piston is not adventurous enough. One would like to know less surely what his next piece will be like." Five years later, Carter detected the stirring of a new venturesomeness in the later pieces and remarked that "it is much harder to predict Piston's future than it was in 1940." But in 1967—seven Piston symphonies later—Copland, in a postscript in a new edition of his book, could not find "anything significant to add" to his former assessment; he hailed Piston's "steadiness of artistic purpose and productivity in the shifting scene of contemporary musical life." They *are* admirable. One hears Piston's music with pleasure, with satisfaction—it is scrupulously made, well worth doing, well worth listening to. But it incites no urgent craving to hear the particular piece again. A British analogue to Piston is perhaps Alan Rawsthorne (1905–71), an excellent composer not much performed. I rate his music high but realize that although I've heard none in a decade I haven't really missed it. Some passages in Peter Evans's Grove account of Rawsthorne pertain equally well to Piston: "So steadfast in his established path and so scornful of 'novelty value'"; "Vocal writing never displaced instrumental as the basis of [his] musical thinking"; "Music that appears 'chromatic' . . . is in fact built from the constant juxtaposition of melodic phrases that individually have clear (but tonally differing) diatonic origins. Their phraseology, though flexible, is essentially traditional . . . often approaching Baroque ideals of patterned figuration"; "That it has failed to accord with fashion does not invalidate the essential qualities of this unostentatious but finely wrought music."

The Piston symphony was part of an all-American evening presented by the Eastman Philharmonia. By an odd coincidence, the symphony's first theme picked up the closing theme of Copland's *Appalachian Spring* (1944), which preceded it on the program: two rising fourths followed by a semitone descent (G–C–F–E in the Copland, a fourth lower in the Piston—a strain that seems to breathe with an essentially American air). The concert began with George Walker's new *Eastman Overture*, a busy, empty confection. The second half was Samuel Barber's justly popular Adagio for Strings (1936) and then Joseph Schwantner's *New Morning for the World ("Daybreak of Freedom")*, a twenty-seven-minute composition for orator and large orchestra, composed expressly for the Eastman tour. (The concert was given on consecutive days in Washington, Philadelphia, New York, Pittsburgh, and Rochester.) The orator's texts are by Martin Luther King, Jr.—an anthology drawn from his more stirring and celebrated sayings and writings: "There comes a time when people get tired—tired of being segregated and humiliated"; "Before the pilgrims landed at Plymouth, we were here"; "*Now* is the time to make real the promise of democracy"; "We're on the move now"; "I have a dream." The ambitious piece is not a success, for at least four reasons. One is that the combination of speaker and orchestra has ever proved intractable. (Poignant spoken moments over or amidst music in the lyric theatre—the dungeon scene of *Fidelio*, the Empress's heroic decision in Strauss's *Die Frau ohne Schatten*—are an exception. Sustained melodrama, for all Mozart's admiration of Jiří Benda's essays in the genre, swiftly palls.) When Robert Craft asked Stravinsky, "What is your feeling now about the use of music as accompaniment to recitation (*Persephone*)?," he replied, "Do not ask. Sins cannot be undone, only forgiven." Words-become-music—song—is perhaps the most eloquent form of utterance known to man, but background music seldom enhances spoken prose. In the final section of Copland's *Lincoln Portrait,* the music takes a back place when the speaker begins; at last it becomes insistent, forcing its way through the Gettysburg Address, and then the repeated four-note theme, crescendo, seems a conventional and inadequate gesture. (The great Lincoln portrait in music is Whitman's *When Lilacs Last in the Door-Yard Bloom'd* become music in Sessions's setting.) Second, only a great, inspired composer can hope to provide music to match important oratory. One sympathizes with anyone who, moved by some strong saying, feels he must lift his own voice to accompany it, but when his music "backs" a noble speech it is apt to seem redundant, and even to have a coattails impertinence. (Copland tried to avoid the awkwardness by making the narrator of his *Lincoln Portrait* not Lincoln but an ordinary man reporting him: "That is what he said, that is what Abraham Lincoln said.") Vincent Persichetti's *A Lincoln Address,* for speaker and orchestra—commissioned for a concert to celebrate the start of Richard Nixon's second term but then deleted from the program—added to the simple grandeur of Lincoln's Second Inaugural Address little more than some movie-music effects. Third—this is tricky ground—I felt there was something almost unseemly, in *New Morning for the World,* about the white composer's first-person identification with Dr. King's repeated "we" ("We're on the move now... neither the burning of our churches nor the beating and killing of our clergymen will stop us"). Fourth—and enough in itself to make the other points unimportant—Schwantner's music is undistinguished: repetitive and conventionally gestural, except at the close. There the players softly sound an open fifth while celesta, glockenspiel, vibraphone, harp, and piano touch in iridescent harmonies—a beautiful device.

Willie Stargell's recital of the text was magnificent. The former Pittsburgh Pirate has an impressive, quietly commanding presence; a dignity of manner; a deep, clear, resonant voice. There was no taint of the actorish inflections that speakers on the concert platform often resort to, no forced magniloquence. Nor was there understatement such as makes, for example, Henry Fonda's account of the *Lincoln Portrait* (in a Columbia recording) too light. The oratory was full, grave, sincere, and stirring—perfectly judged. (Mr. Stargell was skillfully and unobtrusively amplified.) The orchestral playing at the concert had the warmth of tone and the alertness that mark fine student ensembles but was not quite on the highest level. Orchestras, like pianos, can be shaken out of tune by travel, and the strings' intonation in *Appalachian Spring* was not pure. In Schwantner's piece, the general pitch seemed to have risen above that of the fixed-pitch percussion; glockenspiel tings that should have crowned soft chords sounded flat. Mr. Effron is a careful but hardly a romantic conductor. The tan-faced-prairie-boy charm of Copland's open-air music, the easy lilt of its gait in episodes fast or slow, the free lyricism of its wind solos escaped him. In Barber's Adagio, the dynamics and the rhythms were controlled with a literalness that reduced the ardor of the music.

Three days after the Eastman concert, WNYC, New York City's radio station, broadcast Piston's Second (1943) and Third (1947) Symphonies. For some months now, WNYC has committed itself ever more fully to American contemporary music. Quite how fully I had not realized until I pulled some totals from the January WNYC *Program Guide*. This month, sixteen works by Ives, twelve each by Barber and Copland, nine by Bernstein, six by George Rochberg. And six works by Charles Wuorinen; five each by Sessions and Carter (with a repeat of the Cello Sonata); four by George Crumb; three each by Babbitt (with a repeat of the Second String Quartet), Stefan Wolpe (with a repeat of the Chamber Piece No. 1), and Leon Kirchner (with a repeat of *Lily*). Earlier generations—Charles Griffes, Carl Ruggles, Wallingford Riegger—are not neglected. The policy of repeats is welcome; one often wants to hear again a work one has enjoyed or not quite grasped, or both. On the air, the verbal presentation is sometimes inadequate, omitting minimal information: how many movements the work to be heard next contains. But the musical fare is rich.

RIPPLES

February 7, 1983

IN THREE consecutive Philharmonic programs last month, there was contemporary or near-contemporary music: an all-Lutoslawski evening, given in celebration of the Polish composer's seventieth birthday and consisting of his Concerto for Orchestra, Cello Concerto, and *Novelette;* Elliott Carter's Variations for Orchestra and Leonard Bernstein's *Jeremiah* Symphony, the next week; and Bruno Maderna's *Biogramma*, in its New York première, the week after that. *Jeremiah* is early Bernstein, composed in 1942. The other pieces spanned a quarter century: from 1954, when Lutoslawski completed his Concerto for Orchestra and Carter was working on his Variations, to 1980, when *Novelette* had its première, in Washington. *Novelette* and *Biogramma* were both written to American commissions, and beneath each there lies the influence— not patent but traceable—of an American composer: John Cage. What Cage poured into the European musical mainstream is a matter of history. That history reveals the forties, once the war was over, as a time marked by the pursuit of ever stricter serialism, and the fifties as a decade marked by increasing reluctance to heed the stern call to order and by surrender to the siren blandishments of chance and last-minute choice. The crossover year, 1951, produced (as Paul Griffiths notes in his *Concise History of Avant-Garde Music*), on the one hand, Pierre Boulez's *Structures I* and Karlheinz Stockhausen's *Kreuzspiel*—serial Thules whose pitches, dynamics, and durations are predetermined by rows—and, on the other hand, Cage's *Music of Changes*, which was concocted by Cage, the I Ching, and the tossing of coins, and his *Imaginary Landscape No. 4*, which is performed by twelve radios (with twenty-four players to twiddle the knobs) and varies from performance to performance according to what the local stations are offering. Cage's European tours in 1954 and 1958—and especially his presence in Donaueschingen and Darmstadt, the centers from which musical ripples ran through Europe—were determinant. In Darmstadt in 1957, Maderna publicly analyzed Cage scores. His actual music ("if you can call it music," I'm tempted to add) was largely derided. But dozens of logical Frenchmen, mystical Germans, and mellifluous Italians were inspired in their differing ways to incorporate ideas of liberty it suggested into their own more disciplined ways of thinking. Essays in limited choice and circumscribed chance fill the music of the fifties. ("Take these events in any order." "Make up your own melody from any or all of the notes that follow." "Play this in free time quite unrelated to the beat or to what the others are doing.") Later, Stockhausen composed *Kurzwellen*, for four radios, four instrumentalists, and a controller. It might all have happened without Cage. Boulez cites Mallarmé as his aleatory mentor. Stockhausen declares, "What they say Cage did with the I Ching, I did at the same time... with scientific processes and devices." Artistic openness of all kinds was in the air, and it was the music of Charles Ives, exploding late in Europe, that encouraged many composers to set unrelated melodies moving through space and discover what might result. Mallarmé's pregnant, difficult line "Un coup de dés jamais n'abolira le hasard" and the beautiful, difficult poem he built on it (published in 1897) had foreshadowed much of what was thought and composed in those years, whether the management of chance was effected by a dice throw, by the operation of serial rows, or—an extreme but true example—by the crawling of black beetles over a sheet of staff-ruled paper. But the historical fact is that Cage *was* there, along with other Americans—David Tudor, Earle Brown, Morton Feldman, Christian Wolff—who, like the visual artists Jackson Pollock and Alexander Calder, had found new virtue in indeterminacy. And there is abundant testimony to Cage's direct influence. In 1960, Witold Lutoslawski heard over the air some of Cage's Piano Concerto, a work so written that it is inevitably different at each performance. (Merce Cunningham conducted its première, at Town Hall in 1958.) Lutoslawski said:

> Those few minutes were to change my life decisively. It was a strange moment.... I suddenly realized that I could compose music differently from that of my past.... I could start out from the chaos and create order in it, gradually.

It was a matter not of copying Cage but of "listening to something and at the same time creating something else." The first fruit was *Jeux Vénitiens* (1960–61), in which collective ad-lib episodes alternate with measured music. In his later works, Lutoslawski has continued to compose passages where pitch content, timbres, even melodic sequences and rhythmic patterns are specified but not precisely located in time. Maderna's *Biogramma* (1972) uses similar techniques. Hundreds of works do. Britten's music from *Curlew River* on employs his "curlew" sign (a child's pictograph of a bird in flight), designating gathering points after individual excursions, so regularly that in the score of his Third String Quartet its significance is not even defined.

The January Philharmonic concerts brought forward freshly the extent to which in orchestral works with ad-lib elements the composer, the conductor, and the individual players must be collaborative creators if such passages are to be turned into living music; and also—but perhaps only because the performances were less than wholly convincing—a suggestion of yesterday's fashionableness in the extensive use of the technique. Stockhausen has said:

> This freedom is very difficult to handle because it demands mutual understanding and respect and love. You have to train rather than just be free.... You can start only with small groups and with people who are on the same level and are spiritually prepared.

I doubt whether the Philharmonic rehearsal schedules had allowed the players enough time for preparations both spiritual and technical—for listening to and learning not just their own parts but everything else that is happening, for reflection and invention, for becoming co-composers. At any rate, Lutoslawski's Cello Concerto, which had Roman Jabloński as soloist and Mr. Lutoslawski himself as conductor, and Maderna's *Biogramma*, which had Giuseppe Sinopoli as conductor, were neither of them as musically satisfying works as they are in recorded performances made with the same soloist and the same conductors—but with the Polish National Radio Symphony in the Lutoslawski (EMI) and the North German Radio Symphony in the Maderna (Deutsche Grammophon).

Should one draw a moral that the hard-worked Philharmonic might well become a specialist orchestra—a Romantic orchestra committed to Brahms, Bruckner, Strauss, Mahler, Schoenberg, Shostakovich, early Stravinsky, as Baroque orchestras (with Baroque instruments and techniques) are committed to Bach and Handel, and Classical orchestras (with Classical instruments and techniques) to Mozart and Haydn? It would be in tune with our age, which listens to the music of more centuries than any previous age has, and extends its demands for accurate performance practice ever closer to the present. It would please the Philharmonic subscribers who stomp from the hall soon after any contemporary work has started. It would be acceptable if, let us say,

Philharmonic concerts in Fisher Hall alternated with concerts given by the American Composers Orchestra, which is committed to contemporary music. The arguments *against* such specialization—especially while the Philharmonic is the city's only full-time symphony—hardly need stating. Consideration of the many roles the orchestra is required to undertake can check much chiding of it for essaying contemporary music too seldom and then, sometimes, less than wholeheartedly. (Old-music and new-music specialists are not reproved for sticking to their lasts.) Confused feelings: if not blame, at any rate regret when Philharmonic performances of contemporary music are lackluster and underrehearsed. Are poor accounts better or worse than none—when accomplished performances are abundant on records and on the radio waves? No general answer: it depends on what music, and on how it's played.

Lutoslawski's concerto was composed for Mstislav Rostropovich, who first played it, in London, twelve years ago. He makes a heroic and generously emotional protagonist. Mr. Jabłoński, an aristocratic and arresting young performer, plays it with less rhetoric but not with less poetry. This was his Philharmonic début. His tone is pure and proud, his lyricism intense, his wit graceful. He is an artist who holds one on every thread of his discourse. The concerto is a highly dramatic stretch of music—thoughtful, imaginative, and refined in its workings. But in the ad-lib passages, when the conductor simply signals the moments for shifting to a new set of options, the players' contribution was tame; the effect was rather as if Mr. Lutoslawski were merely changing slides behind the soloist's monologue. *Novelette* was also conducted by the composer. It is an attractive work—three Events set between an Announcement and a Conclusion—that breaks no new ground. The early Concerto for Orchestra wears extremely well. During Poland's dark Stalinist years—before new music and new ideas poured in from the West, and Polish composers took them up with a readiness that in a less charged situation might be deemed almost unseemly—Lutoslawski created from folk materials a work so rich, so chivalrously cultivated, so intelligently and finely musical that in the history of nations written by their composers his pages can stand beside pages of Chopin, Moniuszko, and Szymanowski. The Philharmonic first played the Concerto for Orchestra in 1960, under Stanislaw Skrowaczewski, and waited twenty-two years to repeat it. (Few are the new works that have won sustained Philharmonic advocacy.) The revival was conducted by Zubin Mehta, who stays on the surface of most music he touches but has a clear beat and a simple, obvious responsiveness to lyricism and orchestral color. The merits of the Concerto could be perceived.

A fortnight later, Maderna's *Biogramma* received so feeble and incoherent a performance that it might as well have been left unplayed. (The Philharmonic gives each subscription program four times, and I heard the first of the set; perhaps the subsequent accounts were better.) Mr. Sinopoli's program was originally billed to begin with the

American première of a suite from his 1981 opera *Lou Salomé*. Without explanation, this was changed first to Sylvano Bussotti's *il catalogo è questo I* [*Opus Cygne*], which would also have been new to America, and then to *Biogramma,* which was first played, at the Eastman School of Music, eleven years ago. After the Philharmonic's account of it, I returned to the Deutsche Grammophon record, to discover why Mr. Sinopoli had thought *Biogramma* worth revival. Maderna's compositions were shadowed in their day, and still are, by the more forceful compositions of compatriots—Luigi Nono, Luciano Berio, Franco Donatoni —whom he, as both conductor and teacher, so eloquently championed. His own music was avowedly modest in aim—intended, he said in a foreword to the score of *Quadrivium* (1969), "to entertain and to interest." It was also masterly. The Sinopoli record, which contains *Aura* (composed in 1972 for the Chicago Symphony) and *Quadrivium* along with *Biogramma,* suggests that we may have underrated him—that there is more to his music than lyricism; an open-minded, easy command of techniques serial, aleatory, and spatial; and entertaining, interesting demonstrations that new music need not be difficult to approach. His place in musical history is secure. And among his memorials are Boulez's *Rituel,* Brown's *Centering,* and Berio's *Calmo.* The Philharmonic has played the first two, and also *Quadrivium.* Gathered, with *Calmo* (for singer and twelve instrumentalists), in a concert commemorating the tenth anniversary of Maderna's death, in November, they would provide a moving, musically diverse, and rewarding program.

David Schiff, in his long-awaited monograph *The Music of Elliott Carter* (Da Capo), calls Carter's Variations for Orchestra "the most important orchestral work written in the United States in the fifties." It was composed for the Louisville Orchestra, which played and recorded it in 1956. The next year, it reached Donaueschingen. The Philharmonic, under Lorin Maazel, played it in 1972. Solti and the Chicago Symphony took it up in 1969 and have now played it in twelve cities, here and abroad, with virtuosity, precision, and brillance that make most other performances seem pale. The Philharmonic's January revival was conducted by Larry Newland, the orchestra's assistant conductor. His first performance was scrupulously fashioned, neatly laid out, intelligent. His second, the following afternoon, was freer, more expressive, and far more exciting. Carter fits no easy pattern. Mr. Schiff, in a foreword, disavows any attempt to "place" him. The closely argued and generously illustrated chapters provide detailed support for the epitome in Grove: "At best his music sustains an energy of invention that is unrivalled in contemporary composition."

WHAT? WHEN? HOW?

February 14, 1983

IN A summary history of modern music (as I remarked last week), 1951, the year of Pierre Boulez's *Structures I* and Karlheinz Stockhausen's *Kreuzspiel*, of John Cage's *Music of Changes* and *Imaginary Landscape No. 4*, brought both the apogee of total serialism and the first international stirrings of an aleatory flood. History falls handily if not quite precisely into decades. The next landmark is 1960, and specifically the 1960 ISCM Festival, held in Cologne, at which some practices of the fifties found consummation and some new compositional means still with us were first tried. It happens to be also a landmark in my own musical life—not only because of what I heard there but also because conversations with Roberto Gerhard, Hans Keller, and Mátyás Seiber and brief encounters with Boulez, Stockhausen, and Sylvano Bussotti suggested ways of hearing and thinking which have remained with me ever since. At New York's modern-music festivals—there were two of them last month: twenty concerts of Lovely Music Live at the Marymount Manhattan Theater, and the Juilliard School's five-concert Festival of Contemporary Music—one misses easy, frequent informal intercourse between composers, performers, and the audience before, between, and after the rehearsals and the concerts. Should not the Philharmonic designate a "festival club" for such meetings, over food and drink, during its June celebration of contemporary music?

In Cologne, there were new works by Luciano Berio, Boris Blacher, Boulez, Niccolò Castiglioni, Peter Maxwell Davies, Mauricio Kagel, Luigi Nono, Oedoen Partos, Stockhausen, Bernd Alois Zimmermann. Wlodzimierz Kotoński represented musically liberated Poland. Fresh from America there were Stravinsky's *Movements*, Roger Sessions's Fourth Symphony, Darius Milhaud's Eighth Symphony, Gunther Schuller's *Spectra*, Karel Husa's *Poem*, Arthur Berger's String Quartet. When the official concerts were done, we visited the festival fringe: into Mary Bauermeister's studio, which twenty people could comfortably have filled, some two hundred people packed to hear Bussotti's graphic compositions *Five Pieces for David Tudor* and *Pearson Piece*, his do-it-yourself percussion event *Cœur*, his *Per tre* played by Aloys Kontarsky, Cornelius Cardew, and the composer; to hear Nam June Paik's *Hommage à John Cage*, during which, while three tapes played, the composer chucked eggs at a mirror, flung a rosary at the audience, and ferociously attacked a piano with a pair of long-bladed scissors. (A motorbike figured in the original version, but by the time of my performance the threat of two hundred asphyxiates had caused its deletion from the score.) Stockhausen was perched on high in a loft, his eyes kindling to a wilder glow the more extravagant the manifestations became. Bussotti's battery included a gong dipped in water; in the hot, crowded room, as the evening wore on, one began to envy the gong. Mocking is easy. But for two decades now the memory of those concerts has stayed strong. In its wild way, Paik's enactment of bitterness and anger, mounting until they cannot be borne and then exploding into violence, silenced scoffers. The baritone William Pearson's utterance of the single word "cotton"—broken into syllables, into single letters, in Bussotti's *Pearson Piece*—was a sonic emblem of black resentment and hate which makes me shudder still when I recall it.

The concert hall of the radio station was ringed with thirty-two loudspeakers. The veteran pioneer Herbert Eimert set them magically ablaze with the four-track music of his *Selektion I*. In *Kontakte*, Stockhausen brought live and electronic music together. In *Introduzione-Sequenze-Coda*, Bengt Hambraeus provided an early example of live instrumental sounds electronically manipulated during performance. There were several choral pieces. Kagel's *Anagrama* made lively play with spoken phrases, in four languages, built from the letters of Dante's palindrome. "In girum imus nocte et consumimur igni" ("Nu nègre érection inouïe soutien," etc.) while an ensemble played music created by assigning pitches to letters. The piling of new ingenuities upon Dante's ingenious but intelligible line epitomized one activity of the time: pushing possibilities to extremes and beyond intelligibility. Tradition was not forgotten. Schoenberg, Berg, and Webern were played, and there were symphonies by four older composers: Sessions and Milhaud, Karl Amadeus Hartmann and Matthijs Vermeulen. By younger men, the traditional symphony orchestra was untraditionally handled. In a program note to *Spectra*, Schuller declared that "composers think now in kaleidoscopically varied, intricate networks rather than in well-proportioned blocks of tone." Works by Giselher Klebe, Ingvar Lidholm, and Berio seconded his statement. The most influential piece appeared at the final concert: György Ligeti's *Apparitions*, his first work for live instruments since his departure from Hungary, in 1956. It was a stretch of enchanted orchestral music without harmonies, rhythms, or melodies—a static, close-woven structure of colors and densities, vibrant in all its busy details. Years later, Ligeti told an interviewer of a childhood dream of being unable to reach the security of his bed because of an intricate web that filled his room; trapped in it were insects whose every movement increased the complexity of the web's weave. *Atmosphères*, which followed in 1961, at the Donaueschingen Festival, was more spacious, less claustrophobic, but constructed in a similar way. Ligeti had dreamed the music ten years before but had not been able to set it down until work in the West gave him the technical means to notate his "musical hallucination." An aleatory element entered into the precise music simply because there was more happening than the ear could grasp: chance directed the focus of one's attention.

Ligeti's music travelled widely. The Philharmonic played *Atmosphères* in 1964, 1969, and 1978, his *Lontano* in 1975 and 1979. Thousands heard *Atmosphères, Lux aeterna,* and the Kyrie of the Requiem when they appeared (without their composer's consent or knowledge) in the soundtrack of Stanley Kubrick's film *2001.* Directly or indirectly, this music inspired or had links with much else that was written in the sixties and seventies: links with Stockhausen's transcendental compositions (his *Stimmung* a single chord seventy-five minutes sustained, his *Trans* another dream transcription); with Krzysztof Penderecki's popular clusters; with Jacob Druckman's orchestral pieces in which timbres, densities, and textures form the thematic material; with "minimal" music based on the repetition of figures unchanged or in gradual transformation. Ligeti acknowledged the last link—"in homage . . . but at the same time with a nuance of gentle irony," he said—in his two-piano piece *Self-Portrait with Reich and Riley* (1976). He has always had a sportive side. *Poème Symphonique* is composed for a hundred metronomes, ticking away at different speeds, and lasts until the slowest of them has run down. *Aventures* and *Nouvelles Aventures* are intense "imaginary operas," sung to nonsense syllables, that made Boulez smile when he conducted them here. In *Melodien* (1971) and *San Francisco Polyphony* (1974), themes—curls of tune—began to break free of the web and take on a life of their own. In 1965, Göran Gentele had commissioned a work for the Swedish Opera. After much thought and a few false starts, Ligeti between 1974 and 1977 composed *Le Grand Macabre.*

Le Grand Macabre was first performed in Stockholm in 1978. Since then, it has had productions in Hamburg, Saarbrücken, Bologna, Nuremberg, Paris, and London, always in the language of the country. After reading and hearing much about the piece, I caught up with it at last in the London production, which was given in December by the English National Opera; like most, though not all, of those who have written about it, I was captivated and exhilarated by the richness and freshness of its music. Ligeti had first considered writing some extended *Aventures,* but Kagel's *Stattstheater* (Hamburg, 1971), an excursion along those lines, convinced him that for a full-length opera something else was needed. He then sought

a highly-colored comic-strip-like musical and dramatic action. [He cited Saul Steinberg's drawings as an ideal.] Characters and situations would be direct, terse, unpsychological, and startling—the reverse of literary opera. Plot, situations, characters would be brought to life by the music. Stage action and music would be riskily bizarre, totally exaggerated, totally crazy. The novelty of this music-theatre would be manifested not by the externals of the performance but by the inner quality of the music. The musical texture would not be "symphonic." The musico-dramatic conception would be far from the Wagner-Strauss-Berg territory, closer to *Poppea, Falstaff,* and the *Barber* and yet very different, owing nothing, in fact, to any tradition, not even to that of avant-gardism.

He found his subject in Michel de Ghelderode's play *La Balade du Grand Macabre* (1934). Ghelderode—who loved Flemish polyphony and was fascinated by fairground cacophonies; who spoke of music's providing "a deep pedal to the whole of my toilsome existence" and of the "external music...that I want to find again in the best theatre, welling up hidden in dramatic prose, and running beneath it"; whose plays are constructed like scores, with leitmotifs, counterpoints, and rondo refrains—lends himself to operatic handling. Robert Starer's *Pantagleize* (Brooklyn College, 1973) showed it; Alberto Ginastera's *Barabbas*, commissioned by the City Opera some ten years ago, is still eagerly awaited. Some Ghelderode plays also suggest Bruegel paintings dramatized; much of the *Balade*'s imagery appears in Bruegel's "Triumph of Death," in the Prado. Ligeti has cited as influences on or analogues with his *Grand Macabre* Bosch, Bruegel, and Peter Blake, and *Alice in Wonderland*, Kafka, Jarry, and Boris Vian. He and his librettist, Michael Meschke, kept the actions of the *Balade*, more or less, but rewrote the dialogue in brisker speeches or in rough verse, to "Jarry-fy" it. The "Bruegelland, in no particular century," of its setting is, Ligeti says, "our world of today, depicted on another level of reality, on the level of an absurd reality."

The Stockholm production, directed by the librettist, presumably reflected the collaborators' intentions: the costuming was Bruegelish; at start and close the stage was bare. Hamburg resorted to the cliché metaphor of a circus. At the Opéra, the director, Daniel Mesguich, declared the libretto "bad, vulgar, and passé"; the Marx Brothers, Superman, and Greta Garbo enlivened his version. In London, the director and the designer, Elijah Moshinsky and Timothy O'Brien, have rejected the composer's "depiction on another level" and set the piece on the outskirts of London—on the M4 where it crosses the North Circular Road. Nekrotzar (the Ghelderode names are changed in the opera), the Death figure, emerges not from a tomb but, in leather coat and dark glasses, from behind the wheel of a stalled hearse. The young lovers, having no grave handy as a fine and private place wherein to embrace, use the hearse; played in Stockholm (by Elisabeth Söderström and Kerstin Meyer) as the nymph and swain of a passionate pastoral, they are here a lesbian couple strayed from the British television show *Come Dancing*. The ridiculous Prince of Bruegelland, "a plump boy about twelve years old," a puppet in politicians' hands, is played as Prince Charles and has been given an inserted Falklands-inspired speech on which Mrs. Thatcher, as its main author, presumably collects a performance royalty. The goddess Venus, instead of descending cloudborne from a Baroque world, trips on as a high-heeled modern floozy. The audience was amused by the local and topical references, but their effect was cheapening—whatever Moshinsky may have intended. A far-reaching artistic allegory is diminished when, so to speak, prose glosses and footnotes explaining some points, among many, of applicability are presented as if they were the main text. (The Bayreuth *Ring* currently dribbling from PBS is open to the same objection.) Moshinsky's work is always impressively intelligent—his staging of *Le Grand Macabre* was brilliant and sometimes very powerful—but his responses to charm, to romance, and to playfulness are weak. The Moshinsky-O'Brien *Rake's Progress* playing at the same time at Covent Garden was similarly earnest, clean-cut, cold, and uncharming.

Musically, however, the intelligence, the power, the charm, the romance, and playfulness of Ligeti's piece were unmistakable. Elgar Howarth, who conducted—as he did the Stockholm, Hamburg, and Paris productions—was precise, theatrical, lyrical, vivid. The score is filled with affective and wonderful colors. The composer has a superb ear, and everything he writes sounds well. The music, he says, "is not atonal, and yet not a return to tonality; all possibilities can be found in it." The orchestra consists of triple woodwinds, fourfold brasses (plus a bass trumpet), fifteen solo strings, three percussionists commanding a hundred instruments, three mouth organs, harpsichord/celesta, piano, harp, mandolin, small organ. It is used with restraint, delicacy, wit, and occasional wild exuberance. There are "web" episodes, but their textures are diaphanous except in one alarming apocalyptic interlude. There is a dazzling and disturbing collage when an out-of-tune violin plays ragtime, an E-flat clarinet plays "Brazilian-Andalusian" synthetic folk music, a piccolo plays a "Hungarian-Scottish" march, and a bassoon plays a pseudo-medieval hymn (at this performance the four soloists were scattered through the house) while the main orchestra adds layers of cha-chas, marches, and fanfares—all this over a "battered" version of the Eroica bass. There is a bewitching, strictly measured galimatias when dances in many rhythms—among them a minuet in F, a polka in G, a jig in D, a two-step in E, a waltz in E-flat—are neatly and effortlessly superimposed while Nekrotzar holds a vocal pedal. There are snatches of ensemble à la *Falstaff*. There are chorales of bewilderingly unstable tonality, harmonized in elusive fauxbourdon. The prelude is a Monteverdian fanfare sounded on twelve klaxons. There is bel canto for the young lovers, who appear only in the first and the final scene. There is a good deal of spoken and monotoned declamation—rather too much for my taste—especially in the first of the two acts. But because I enjoyed *Le Grand Macabre* so much I hesitate—as some have not—to say that Ligeti underemployed opera's most expressive device: sustained lyrical singing. Every other he commands: force and graphicness of vocal gesture, sureness of timing, variety, contrast, surprise. *Le Grand Macabre*, despite some clumsy episodes in the libretto, is both entertaining and serious. The music is never clumsy. In an age when many new works flounder, some in their endeavor to startle and shock, some in their "neo-Romantic" determination not to, it gathers up two decades of musical discoveries, captures and reshapes them surely for the lyrical theatre, and takes new strides down the path Monteverdi began and Mozart, Rossini, and (despite Ligeti's disclaimer) Berg continued. At my London performance, the fourth of six, the piece drew a full house to the big Coliseum, and at the end the audience cheered. I'm surprised that none of the adventurous big American companies—not Bloomington, Boston, San Francisco, or Santa Fe—has yet taken it up.

The London cast was admirable. Marilyn Hill Smith poured out fleet, glittering coloratura as the Chief of the Secret Police. Piet was brilliantly sung and acted by the tenor Roderic Keating (who also took the part in Saarbrücken, Nuremberg, and Paris). The countertenor Kevin Smith was an adept Prince (a role he also sang in Hamburg and Paris). The baritone Geoffrey Chard, creator of many modern protagonists, was a potent Nekrotzar. The patter of the two politicians, spoken parts played by John Kane and Roger Bryson, was very crisp. But the young lovers lacked purity and precision of tone. About a third of the opera is represented in the suite of "Scenes and Interludes" recorded on Wergo—a Copenhagen concert performance, conducted by Mr. Howarth.

Lovely Music Live was an important event—an extended celebration of music of a kind more familiar in the Kitchen, on campuses, at IRCAM, and on the Lovely Music record label than in New York's midtown concert halls. Most of the twenty concerts had one-composer programs. Some of the composers were celebrated—David Tudor, Roger Reynolds, Pauline Oliveros, Alvin Lucier, Robert Ashley—and some were not. All the concerts but one—Miss Oliveros's evening for voice and accordion—used some form of electronics: for simple (or complicated) amplification, to play tape music either by itself or in conjunction with live performers, to modify live sounds. Sometimes I feel my Kitchen-boy days are over. David Van Tieghem's work, for example, seemed to promise only what Bussotti had provided twenty years ago, and I waited for someone else to report on it. Live encounters with Ashley's music in the past have left me unwilling to seek more; on record, one's own fingers can discipline the volume—and the duration. But the chance of hearing Reynolds's four *Voicespace* pieces in sequence was not to be missed.

Working with words (Coleridge, Stevens, Joyce, Melville, Borges), with virtuoso singers and speakers, and with the sophisticated electronic equipment of the Center for Music Experiment, in La Jolla, Reynolds explores analogues between sound and sense, and, on quadraphonic tape, builds beautiful structures moving through space, enclosing the listeners in a mysterious world where their own poetic and imaginative faculties are sharpened and refreshed. The Philharmonic should bill these pieces—one at a time—for they deserve the widest hearing (and would, incidentally, free rehearsal time for other works on the program). A Lovely Music recording of all four has been published; on disc, the two rear tracks, which should sound behind the listener, have been "folded over" to the front, placed exclusively right and left, while the two front tracks have been slightly centered. The result gives a sense of the original. The Marymount theatre, steeply raked and asymmetrical (columns down one side, not the other), made a less than ideal electronic habitat, but it is an agreeable place, and New York lacks a hall fully and regularly electronically equipped.

Reynolds's latest composition, *Archipelago*, for eight-track tape and thirty-two players, a commission for IRCAM, has four performances this month in IRCAM's Espace de Projection—in four concerts that succeed a four-day series of morning exposés, afternoon round-table discussions, and evening lectures at which Boulez (in an address titled "Quoi? Quand? Comment?"), Berio, Carl Dahlhaus, Charles Rosen, Fred Lerdahl, and others will consider the state of modern music.

Milton Babbitt, whose *Ars Combinatoria,* composed in 1981 for the Indiana University School of Music, had its New York première at the Juilliard Festival, expressed in a program note his "conviction that demanding contemporary works can be performed satisfactorily only under the conditions available at schools of music." But I doubt whether he was satisfied with the Juilliard Symphony's performance of the piece. Cage once said, "I try to arrange my composing means so that I won't have any knowledge of what might happen." Babbitt, who knows precisely what he wants to happen, sometimes achieves the Cagean result by writing music so difficult to execute precisely that chance elements inevitably figure in the performance. I mustn't say more, for I didn't hear the performance of *Ars Combinatoria*—only the final rehearsal—and what happens at rehearsals concerns a critic only insofar as it makes him a more perceptive listener at the resulting concert. But much of what I did hear at the festival concerts seemed to be underrehearsed. The most exciting new composition among them was a solo, played in a masterly fashion by Gary Steigerwalt: Daniel Brewbaker's Piano Sonata No. 2. It is a rich, glittering, confident, ever-interesting six-movement piece, very well written for the instrument—music that Horowitz might enjoy having under his fingers, and would play marvellously.

Two American pioneers, both still composing, have been honored this season: Conlon Nancarrow, who was seventy in October, and Leo Ornstein, who was ninety in December. Nancarrow has found a new champion in Ligeti, who said recently, "His music is totally original, seductive, and constructive, while also being very moving. For me, he is the most interesting contemporary composer." In October, there was a full concert of Nancarrow's player-piano music at the Styrian Autumn Festival, in Graz, given with the composer present, and introduced and analyzed—"with infectious enthusiasm," according to a colleague's report—by Ligeti; and another, in November, at IRCAM. Earlier, at the Y, the Group for Contemporary Music had presented his

String Quartet (about 1945) and, on tape, his Study No. 41, for two player pianos (about 1980). (Nancarrow does not date his compositions.) The quartet is arresting. The study is a shimmering, immense web of "seductive" sound. Easy to understand Ligeti's response! An Ornstein birthday concert in Merkin Hall was less remarkable. The early, "shocking" piano pieces now seem blunt and childish, though William Westney's account of *Three Moods* (1914) was trenchant. Later works seemed undisciplined, derivative, conventional.

BY COMPASSION MADE WISE

February 21, 1983

HANS-JÜRGEN SYBERBERG'S film *Parsifal*, now playing at the Guild Theatre, is a rich and beautiful production of Wagner's opera. The musical performance is of high distinction. The visual imagery is arresting, resonant, and colorful. A return of color to the Wagnerian stage has long been due. Wieland Wagner's first *Ring* production at Bayreuth, in 1951, was colorful—set against expanses of shining blue sky or brilliant fire that spanned the stage. In the work of his emulators, all grew dark. Black backcloths and wings became the rule. Blacks, browns, and grays dominated the stage pictures. Light dwindled to spots on the principals, picked out amid the encircling gloom. Magic fires shrank to a flicker. Siegfried's exultant cry to the sea of flame—the joyful glare rolling down from the mountain peak, in which he is eager to bathe—rang hollow. The radiance of Brünnhilde's greeting to sun, light, and glorious day was mocked by dimness. (Wagner's remark "Having created the invisible orchestra, I now feel like inventing the invisible stage" seemed to be taken literally. But it was a little joke, made as he contemplated the *Parsifal* rehearsals: "And the inaudible orchestra," he continued.) Much was lost: on the simplest level, the ability to read the libretto off the singers' lips and to see in the singers' eyes what they are thinking and feeling. (After voice, eyes are the chief medium of communication between us. Wagner's librettos are filled with references to the expressiveness of glance or gaze.) And, on deeper levels, the sense of eternal nature which should run through the *Ring*, setting the deeds of gods and men against forest and flood, sky and storm, untamed and intractable.

Parsifal is also a nature cycle—a long winter of pain and waiting ended at last by the Good Friday spell. The great *Parsifal* production of our day has been Wieland Wagner's at Bayreuth, first seen in 1951, maintained there for nearly a quarter century, and renewed annually, until Wieland's death, in 1966, by further thoughts, by revisions sometimes small and sometimes large, and by the director's sensitivity to particular singers and what they might achieve. Its imagery was essentially that of Wagner's original Bayreuth production, in 1882, but purged of nineteenth-century pictorialism. The technical resources of the modern theatre, Wieland said, had at last made Adolphe Appia's scenic ideas realizable. The shapes were simplified. Painted canvas was replaced by plays of light. About the 1951 production Ernest Newman wrote, "This was not only the best *Parsifal* I have ever seen and heard but one of the three or four most moving spiritual experiences of my life.... On the stage we had, for the first time in my experience, the combination of beauty of singing tone and dramatic insight that the subtle work demands.... No one who heard this performance will ever forget it." And I, who went on seeing this *Parsifal* year after year, can echo his words. It was recorded in 1951, by London, and the discs still re-create some of the production's deep enchantment.

Nevertheless, it was not the whole of *Parsifal*. Wieland's colors were muted. The "shadowy, sombre, but not gloomy forest" of the first scene was achieved by slanting beams of light and a shadowy hint of tree trunks, all gray. The Hall of the Grail was monochrome. No more than an unhealthy purplish flush suffused Klingsor's flower garden; some sinuous scrawls on the backcloth recalled Appia's 1922 design for the scene. No more than a hint of soft-glowing vernal green softened the starkness of the Good Friday meadow. The inspiration for the Hall of the Grail built in Bayreuth in 1882 was Siena's black-and-white cathedral, but when it reached the stage, in Paul von Joukowsky's designs, the cathedral had been transformed and was clad in gleaming polychrome mosaics. In Joukowsky's sketches for Klingsor's garden, inspired by the park of the Palazzo Rufalo, in Ravello, bright red flowers blaze amid luxuriant greenery. Wieland's production was beautiful and moving, but it had been designed as if by the redeemed, redeeming Parsifal and the penitent Kundry. It was spiritual from the start, never voluptuous in its visual imagery. Although in later editions it became less severe—the columns of the Hall of the Grail, plain gray cylinders in 1951, were duskily gilded and acquired capitals; the flower garden burgeoned with a backcloth of opaline efflorescence—it remained an essential *Parsifal*, a distillation, a sharply focussed "minimalist" presentation of great intensity and purity. It held one intent on only the work itself. Syberberg's *Parsifal*, on the other hand, embraces and presents those abundant, varied elements from which Wagner's most profound and beautiful opera was distilled: his life, his reading, his thinking, his passions, his response to art and nature, his earlier compositions. Specific biographical references—a casement of the room in the Palazzo Vendramin where Wagner died; heads of Aeschylus, King Ludwig, Marx, Nietzsche, and Wagner himself lying at the foot of Klingsor's throne; glimpses of Mathilde Wesendonk and Judith Gautier among the flower maidens—mingle with an allusiveness more oblique: some puppet sequences suggest at once Wagner's theatrical mastery and his readiness to manipulate people to his own ends.

Moreover, Syberberg takes into his subject not just what went into the making of *Parsifal* but also what it has meant to people and how it has been considered and performed during its century of existence. The first approach to the Hall of the Grail—to take a simple example —is down a flag-lined corridor: a procession backward in time past swastika banners, imperial standards, medieval pennons into a world of myth. For a phrase or two, the Grail Knights appear as a band of hard, eager S.S. troopers. Later, they are olden-time Arthurian chevaliers. It is also a procession to the center of Wagner's thought. Hitherto the action has played on and around a large knoll that is a giant reproduction of Wagner's death mask; the path to the Hall of the Grail cuts through and into it. The density of allusion is great. Caspar David Friedrich, Ingres, Goya, Dürer, Titian, Caravaggio, Bramante figure in the imagery. The allegorical statues of the Synagogue and of Faith on Strasbourg Cathedral are invoked. Titurel lies royally in the crypt of Saint-Denis. Scenes from Wieland Wagner's Bayreuth productions, notably his *Tristan,* and from Patrice Chéreau's Bayreuth *Ring* put in appearances. So do the 1882 *Parsifal* scenes and other images of Bayreuth's early days; when encountered in puppet form, the characters are modelled after the first interpreters of their roles. There is a reminiscence of Fritz Lang's *Siegfried* film. And there are links with Syberberg's earlier films *Ludwig: Requiem for a Virgin King* (1972), *Karl May: In Search of Paradise Lost* (1974), and *Our Hitler: A Film from Germany* (1977). Kundry makes her first entrance as a doll riding a toy Valkyrie flying horse from the 1876 *Ring* across a toy theatre's starry sky. (I had always taken the young squire's "Does she ride through the air?" to be an exclamation occasioned by her wild horsemanship, not a question to which the answer is yes.) Then the living woman appears Ophelia-like in a forest pool, which is also a lake of tears collected on Wagner's death mask. The Palazzo Vendramin casement, rain streaming down it like tears, is beside her; projected in the background is the Palazzo Giustiniani, whence in 1858 Wagner wrote to Mathilde Wesendonk, "A strangely world-daemonic woman, the Grail's messenger, is dawning on me with ever greater life and fascination." In Syberberg's book about his film, *Parsifal: Ein Filmessay,* I discover that there is also an allusion here to the actress of Kundry, Edith Clever, of the Berlin Schaubühne, in one of her famous stage roles—Clytaemnestra. That anticipates Klingsor's later designation of Kundry as a she-devil who has known many incarnations.

Watching the film is in some ways like reading Cosima Wagner's wonderful diary and marvelling at the breadth and depth of Wagner's thought, observation, and reading, compounded with emotions and with vivid and revealing dreams—a ferment in which his great music was formed. The episode of the murdered swan is more moving in the film, and more closely linked to the main religious drama, than I have ever known it be on the stage. It chimes with the remarks Cosima reported on July 31, 1879 (a day on which Schopenhauer, thoughts of destiny, Calderón, the Catholic Renaissance, Daudet, the "Waldstein"

Sonata, Beethoven's first period, *A Winter's Tale,* and ˉ*Henry IV* also passed in review):

> He says religion should be linked with compassion for animals; human beings' treatment of one another is already bad enough, for they are so vindictive... the noble teachings of Christianity are scarcely applicable. One should begin with quiet and patient creatures, and people who felt compassion for animals would certainly not be harsh toward human beings. "We must preach a new religion."

Syberberg's most controversial stroke, the assigning of the title role to two actors, a young man and a young woman (the latter takes over after Kundry's kiss; they stand side by side in the finale), recalls Cosima's entry for June 27, 1880. That evening, they look at engravings after Italian masters. Richard condemns Raphael's "Pietà" on the ground that classical beauty is inapt to the subject. Leonardo's sketch for the head of Christ in "The Last Supper" he finds too effeminate, but, he says, the finished painting made quite a different impression on him.

> He then plays the first theme of *Parsifal* to himself and, returning, says that he gave the words to a chorus so that the effect would be neither masculine nor feminine, Christ must be entirely sexless, neither man nor woman; Leonardo, too, in "The Last Supper," attempted that, depicting an almost feminine face adorned with a beard.

In his book, Syberberg says, "Would not Richard Wagner have delighted in this feminine image of his androgynous Parsifal? Had he not, apropos of Wilhelmine Schröder-Devrient's female Romeo, hailed the idea and called tenors 'stage dummies'?" It is true that in *Mein Leben* Wagner praised the "daring, romantic figure of the youthful lover," the "wonderful, thrilling, and entrancing impersonation of Romeo by Schröder-Devrient." True, too, that he composed the role of young Adrian, in *Rienzi,* for a woman. (Schröder-Devrient first sang it.) But Parsifal is not Christ. Kundry makes that confusion; Wagner made the distinction clear in his writings and very clear in Gurnemanz's lines:

> *Creation cannot perceive the Redeemer Himself on the cross:*
> *So it looks up to the redeemed man,*
> *One who feels himself free of the burden of sin and dread,*
> *Made pure and whole by God's loving sacrifice.*

(If I remember rightly, the English subtitles, which for English-speakers enormously increase the impact of the film, skimped the full sense of the difficult, important lines.) And Wagner's Parsifal is not "androgynous" and not "entirely sexless" but wholly virile—a boy until he meets Kundry in Act II and thereafter a man. In this film, at Kundry's kiss he becomes a girl. The enchantress's kiss denatures him.

To play Parsifal, Syberberg cast a young Swiss photographer, Michael Kutter, and a young Swiss puppeteer, Karin Krick—neither of them a professional actor. Mr. Kutter has piquant, slightly gypsy looks and seems younger than his twenty-three years. He moves through the part with grave, wide-eyed wonder, attending carefully to everything that is said, answering directly and simply, and leaving "expression" to Parsifal's voice on the soundtrack, where the role is sung with great freshness, intelligence, and sensitivity by the Dresden tenor Reiner Goldberg. It is plain that this youth has not the resources to take into himself, at the climax of the action, Amfortas's searing passion and pain and Kundry's wild despair and yearning. The new maturity and understanding is not difficult to enact in the opera house, given a tenor with musical insight: Wagner's music does it for him. Syberberg's drastic image seems to deny the music. Miss Krick's features are pure, regular, and unsensual. Like Mr. Kutter, she maintains a single expression—one of calm, pitying tenderness (which in some shots takes on a slightly prim, even priggish, aspect). Wagner's Parsifal is not unmanned by Kundry's kiss. Eroticism at its fullest floods him; he understands all that Amfortas felt, all that Kundry feels. He learns what sin is, and does not commit it. In our day, unchaste sexual activity may seem to be an old-fashioned symbol of sin, but it is as basic to *Parsifal* as to *Tannhäuser* and cannot be evaded. Wagner felt close to Amfortas. Both he and Cosima understood Kundry. On August 30, 1878, Malwida Meysenbug congratulated Cosima on bringing to Wagner the happiness that had made Bayreuth possible. "I listen to her with a thankful heart and remind her of my life's transgression, which enabled me to live for him alone and in him to find my salvation." In Syberberg's film, Cosima is among the company that, from high in the dome of the Hall of the Grail, sings the promise of redemption.

The sensuality, the voluptuousness, that is important in *Parsifal* finds expression in the opulence of Syberberg's imagery and in a wonderfully potent and subtle joint portrayal of Kundry by the actress Miss Clever and the singer Yvonne Minton. Physical warmth also flows, less expectedly, from Gurnemanz. Robert Lloyd sings the role nobly and plays it as a man young and handsome. (The original Gurnemanz, Emil Scaria, seemed to be eighty in the first scene, Cosima said, and ninety in the last.) His embracing of Parsifal in Act I and of Kundry in Act III is unwontedly tender.

One must not leave the impression that this *Parsifal* is primarily a puzzle picture ("Identify the artist," "Spot the allusion") or an elaborate set of footnotes to the opera—a visual essay in origins and analogues. Syberberg's claims that Wagner's music dictated the rhythms of his film and that his intention was to make the music visible are justified. Bayreuth forbade the use of a Bayreuth recording. The film, shot in the Bavaria Studios, was built on the foundation of a new recording made in Monte Carlo in 1981 with the Monte Carlo Philharmonic, which plays with great breadth and beauty of tone and subtlety of solo inflection, and the Prague Philharmonic Choir, whose singing is firm and full. The Swiss conductor Armin Jordan is revealed as an outstanding Wagnerian; his performance is as lucid as that of Pierre Boulez, and far more poetic. I saw the film in Alice Tully Hall, where the sound was good; the Erato/RCA album of the recording reassures me that I was not swept away by the pictures to overrate the musical merits of the production. The synchronization of image and soundtrack is careful. The camera dwells, for the most part, on whoever is singing. Inevitably, the actors, even when acting to their own voices (Mr. Lloyd as Gurnemanz, Aage Haugland as Klingsor), do not breathe as deeply or prepare and "place" their notes as evidently as singers do. One gets used to this and also—with a little more difficulty—to the sound of a tenor voice pouring from a smooth female throat. (With men, the Adam's apple rises and falls like a pitch indicator.) Mr. Jordan himself enacts Amfortas and for much of the time is held in such closeup that the result is like a physiological demonstration of how lips, teeth, and tongue move to frame vowels and consonants. He also drifts briefly across the background, conducting, during the Good Friday music—reflecting the fact that here the drama has passed to the orchestra, that the solo oboe, as Syberberg puts it, is animating nature. Amfortas's wound, separate from Amfortas—a piece of flesh borne on a little litter of its own—is a disgusting image, as was no doubt intended.

In the third act, the director's control becomes looser. The Good Friday meadow is a section of the death mask neatly overlaid with sods and studded with tight clumps of gaudy polyanthus. Gurnemanz has evidently taken up horticulture; in his hut more polyanthus are set out in trays. It's a poor emblem of spring's return, of verdant nature, for polyanthus, as the Britannica remarks, is a "florists' flower," man-made, derived from a cross between primrose and cowslip. (In his *Filmessay*, the director notes frankly that it was difficult to obtain suitable flora in November, the month of the shooting.) At the approach to the final scene, the imagery starts straying and spraying rather than closing in to a climax. The camera stalks the characters round the set, revealing techniques and mechanics of the staging. It is quite interesting but irrelevant. It suggests a rather desperate attempt to find something new to hold the audience's attention. The final assembly in the Hall is diffusely presented. The costumes range centuries and nations, but at this point, I think, Syberberg loses Wagner's steady rhythm. All in all, there is plenty to criticize. The Grail rite of the second scene is evaded. The giant death mask when seen complete and the various smaller reproductions of it that appear become on repetition too crudely obvious a symbol. And yet—above all, on someone who already knows *Parsifal*—this thoughtful, inventive, and very ambitious film casts a powerful spell. One drinks it in with eyes and ears intent, marvelling.

GENEROUS YOUTH

February 28, 1983

RICHARD STRAUSS'S first opera, *Guntram,* appeared in 1894, in Weimar. It was one of the less successful new operas of the year. Before the century was out, several other 1894 pieces had been performed widely, internationally, in various languages: not only Massenet's *Thaïs, Le Portrait de Manon,* and *La Navarraise* but also August Enna's *Cleopatra,* Emile Jaques-Dalcroze's *Janie,* Nicola Spinelli's *A basso porto,* Rudolf Raimann's *Arden Énok,* Spiro Samara's *La Martire,* Leonhard Emil Bach's *The Lady of Longford,* Pietro Floridia's *Maruzza,* and Jenö Hubay's *A Cremonia Hegedüs.* By 1900, two of the Massenets, *A basso porto,* and *A Cremonia Hegedüs* had all been heard in New York; *A basso porto* was also done in St. Louis. *Guntram,* however, had to wait almost ninety years for its American première: it was done last month in a concert performance, in Carnegie Hall, by the Opera Orchestra of New York, conducted by Eve Queler. I've not heard a note by Enna, Spinelli, Samara, or the rest but am prepared (if only for that reason) to wager that Strauss's music is better than theirs. And in 1894 Strauss was no mere novice: *Don Juan, Macbeth, Tod und Verklärung,* and some of his most celebrated songs had already appeared. But *Guntram* was tepidly received in Weimar, and its second production, in Munich the following year, was withdrawn after a single performance. Revivals in Prague (1901) and in Frankfurt (1910) failed to establish the piece. Strauss dug a grave in his garden and erected a tombstone with the inscription "Here lies the honorable and virtuous youth GUNTRAM, Minnesinger, who was horribly slain by the symphony orchestra of his own father." After *Guntram,* Strauss returned to tone poems: *Till Eulenspiegel, Also sprach Zarathustra, Don Quixote,* and *Ein Heldenleben* (in which *Guntram* themes are prominent among the Hero's Works of Peace). It was seven years before his second opera appeared; this was *Feuersnot,* which tells of a romantic young magician's revenge on the men of Munich who had failed to appreciate either his art or that of his great master. References to a "waggoner" who was "daring" (a double pun on *Wagner*) and to the new "warfare" *(Strauss)* that the disciple has brought to Munich find appropriate musical vesture—the latter a citation of the war theme from *Guntram.*

In 1933, Berlin Radio celebrated Strauss's seventieth year with a performance of *Guntram,* conducted by Hans Rosbaud. According to the composer's *Reminiscences,* it "revealed that the work...contained so much beautiful music that *Guntram* well deserved revival, if only for its historical interest as the first essay of a dramatic composer who later became renowned." Strauss shortened his score here and there and thinned his formerly "fatal" orchestration. In the revised version, *Gun-*

tram has enjoyed a few modern revivals. A BBC performance with American principals—Carole Farley as the heroine, Freihild, and William Lewis in the title role—and John Pritchard as conductor has circulated on pirate discs. The American première had foreign principals—Ilona Tokody as Freihild and Reiner Goldberg as Guntram—and also used the revised edition.

Often, but not always, the early works of good composers are more interesting and more rewarding to hear than the mature works of less good composers. Wagner's *Die Feen, Das Liebesverbot,* and *Rienzi* are operas largely underrated because by *Der fliegende Holländer, Tannhäuser,* and all that followed they were eclipsed. Yet it can be claimed that an opera company that produces Meyerbeer's *Les Huguenots, Le Prophète,* or *L'Africaine* when it could be doing *Das Liebesverbot* and *Rienzi* has its musical and moral priorities wrong. Mozart's *Lucio Silla, La finta giardiniera,* and *Il rè pastore* are operas musically richer than Cimarosa's *Il matrimonio segreto* and Paisiello's *Il barbiere di Siviglia,* but they are less often staged. That, too, seems wrong. Against that claim it can, of course, be argued that a second-rate master's mastery comes off and pleases the public in a way that a great composer's early, ambitious, but perhaps ill-proportioned works do not, and that operatic fare should be as rich and varied as possible. (Do Raimann and L. E. Bach have their modern champions?) The *Guntram* performance raised questions easier to pose than to answer, about survival, revival, and what the repertory should be. Still, no one is compelled to attend the Met's presentation of Cilea's *Adriana Lecouvreur.* And thanks to concert performances, to the radio and the phonograph, and to the enterprise of such companies as the San Diego Opera, which this season has staged Chabrier's *Gwendoline* and Saint-Saëns' *Henry VIII,* the curious, questing operagoer—provided he has the time, and the means to travel—can slake whatever his particular thirsts may be. Public radio should and if properly funded could do more than it does, by broadcasting across the country as a matter of course whatever is not locally available in live performances. The Carnegie *Guntram* was not carried to California. Gluck's *Armide,* which Alan Curtis conducted in Berkeley last month, was not carried to New York. Nor were *Gwendoline* and *Henry VIII.* The widest public availability would help to justify the large expenditure of public money incurred by any opera performance.

In his 1908 book on Strauss, Ernest Newman, a clear-eared, clear-minded critic not given to rash enthusiasms, wrote about *Guntram*:

> The bulk of the score touches a high plane of beauty, and curiously enough, in spite of the occasional Wagnerism of the music, the style throughout gives one the impression of being personal to Strauss.... Altogether *Guntram* is a great work, the many merits of which will perhaps some day restore it to the stage from which it is now most unjustly banished.

The musical Wagnerisms in *Guntram*—almost literal citations from *Tristan,* a cadence in the hero's first monologue lifted from Siegmund's

"Winterstürme"—are evident and unimportant. The music relates more closely, on the one hand, to Strauss's tone poems and, on the other, to operas still in the future—*Die Frau ohne Schatten, Die ägyptische Helena*—in the rich, euphonious orchestral writing and the glowing stretches of slow-moving diatonic music animated by chromatic counterpoint. But "a great work," one "most unjustly banished" from the stage? I think not. *Guntram* is likable for its earnestness, for its generosity of invention, and for an absence of cold calculation. Strauss, carried away, made no compromises with practicability. He wrote an impossibly demanding title role: Guntram has three immense monologues, two of them as taxing as Tannhäuser's Rome narration. Willi Schuh's *Richard Strauss: A Chronicle of the Early Years, 1864–1898*, an amply documented study that has now been published in English translation by Cambridge, includes a long, intelligent review, by Oskar Merz, of the 1895 Munich performance. The protagonist, Max Mikorey, "confined himself to singing the notes as correctly as possible," Merz says. "This was all that could have been expected when he was cast in this gigantic part, which (according to a particularly conscientious statistician) amounts...to a hundred and sixty bars more than the role of Tristan." Much the same could be said about Mr. Goldberg in Carnegie Hall. I doubt whether any tenor could throw himself into the role with all the ardor, intensity, and powerful dramatic accents that Strauss requires and make it through. This was Mr. Goldberg's American début. As Parsifal in Hans-Jürgen Syberberg's film he sings with more variety, poetry, and passion.

The libretto, Strauss's own, is not without interest. Guntram, a pacific social reformer, a member of a medieval order that preaches peace through universal love and reinforces its preaching with the power of song, sets about the conversion of a tyrannous duke. He saves the duke's wife, Freihild, from suicide, falls in love with her, and kills the duke in a scuffle. Although the deed is not unjustified, Guntram feels himself morally compromised, because love for Freihild directed his hand. He renounces her, renounces his order, and sets forth "to expiate the guilt of my existence—forever lonely, my soul lost in contemplation of the Divine—to draw near to the Saviour's grace." Much of the diction reads like a parody of late Wagner; much of the stage action echoes *Tannhäuser* without sharing Wagner's theatrical flair. Strauss's idea is clumsily executed. The opera's future, I think, lies mainly in concert performances of the preludes to Acts I and II and in concert performances of Guntram's Spring narration and Peace narration. These are lofty, beautiful music. And a tenor uncumbered by the whole role could sing the long solos fully, fearlessly.

Miss Tokody, a soprano of the Budapest and the Vienna Operas, was also making her American début. She was confident, accurate, and efficient. Geraldine Decker sang an old woman's curse ("Fluch dem Herzog! Fluch seinem Geschlecht!"), musically close to Isolde's curse, with Isolde-like passion. Roger Roloff in the small role of the old duke,

Freihild's father, revealed a baritone voice of admirable firmness and focus and a strong command of the text. Miss Queler's conducting was at once spirited and disciplined.

Strauss's tenth opera, *Arabella* (1933), has achieved a foothold on the fringe of the international repertory. Both London companies have productions—Covent Garden's being international and sung in German, the English National's being in English, staged by Jonathan Miller, with the wonderful Josephine Barstow its heroine. The Met first staged *Arabella* in 1955, in English, with Eleanor Steber (and, later, Lisa Della Casa) in the title role; the production lasted for ten years and twenty-two performances. This month, it has been replaced by a new version, sung in German, designed by Günther Schneider-Siemssen, and directed by Otto Schenk, with Kiri Te Kanawa as its heroine.

About *Arabella* I have shuttlecock feelings. It is an operetta action written and composed as a full-scale opera. Arabella herself is the battledore. If—as Miss Della Casa's Arabella was—she is charming and interesting, warm and spontaneous, brave and intelligent, and potentially a tragic heroine, impelled by a decadent, selfish society toward unhappiness until the rich, handsome Mandryka turns up to end her and her family's troubles, all is well; the opera can seem worth doing. If not, then Arabella's two solos and her duets with her sister Zdenka and with Mandryka are all we need bother about; the rest is skillful confection. Strauss was aware of the dangers. When Hofmannsthal's first-draft libretto reached him, he called Arabella "insufficiently interesting and almost unattractive." By several canny suggestions he sought to make all the characters warmer, richer, more human, and to sharpen their emotional conflicts.

Dame Kiri, I thought, hardly brought the heroine or the opera to life. Her performance seemed studied, unspontaneous, self-contained to a point where her relationship with the others on the stage was small. Her tones were often beautiful, but her phrasing was not impulsive. Kathleen Battle was a delightful Zdenka. Her singing was sweet, and her playing was unmannered and nicely impetuous, although the voice was small for a lyric role in so large a house. She herself is so much smaller of frame than Dame Kiri that it seemed even less likely than usual that the young officer Matteo could go to bed in the dark with one sister thinking her to be the other. Realistic portrayals were not much in evidence. The most eligible of the Noble Ninnies—the composer's designation of Arabella's three aristocratic suitors—looked like a butcher, and the shy, touching one was played as a mincing fop. Matteo—a role that "should always be given to a decently proportioned, fairly handsome tenor," as William Mann observes in his book on Strauss's operas—was plump and unromantic. Bernd Weikl, once so promising a romantic baritone, sang Mandryka's music rawly, often out of tune, with little feeling for lyrical line. Gwendolyn Bradley, the Fiakermilli, was pure and deft, but soft-grained, not sparky enough, in timbre. Donald Gramm gave a polished performance as the girls' father.

The size of the house and the decision to sing the piece in German both told against its effectiveness. Mr. Schneider-Siemssen's sets are realistic, attractive, distinguished, perhaps a shade too constantly muted in color. They reduce the proscenium opening to a narrow slot, and this further distances the action—makes it seem like live opera aspiring to the condition of a television show. Mr. Schenk's staging is carefully pianned and nicely detailed. Erich Leinsdorf's conducting was dry and unemotional.

MAGICAL OPERA

March 14, 1983

IN THIS country, Handel has still to take his due high place in the operatic repertory. He begins to: next season the Metropolitan Opera stages *Rinaldo,* and the New York City Opera *Alcina.* The last decade has not been quite Handel-less: the City Opera put on a lamentable *Giulio Cesare;* in Houston and in Ottawa there were spectacular, if musically barbarous, productions of *Rinaldo;* San Francisco imported the English National's *Cesare.* And among small-theatre presentations there were two so remarkable as to be, I'd say, international landmarks in the Handel revival. One was the American Repertory Theatre's *Orlando,* conducted by Craig Smith and directed by Peter Sellars, which ran for forty performances in Cambridge in 1981–82 (see page 199), and the other, Washington University in St. Louis's *Orlando,* directed musically and dramatically by Nicholas McGegan, which was performed thrice last month as part of the university's Baroque Festival.

Scenically, these two shows were at poles of Handelian presentation. Cambridge's *Orlando* opened in Mission Control at Cape Canaveral and moved into the Everglades, where Dorinda, in cutoff jeans, lived in an Airstream camper; Orlando wore an orange space suit. St. Louis's *Orlando* was set in a loving reconstruction of a Baroque stage; Orlando wore that unhappy eighteenth-century stage garment the tonnelet, a wired skirt (but wore it with more grace than perhaps anyone since Nijinsky in *Le Pavillon d'Armide* has shown). In other ways, the two *Orlandos* had much in common. They were set on an axis of belief that Handel is a great composer and a great dramatist whose operas do not need to be cut and shuffled. (That creed seldom sounds in big-house produciions.) Both were complete; *Orlando* contains two and a half hours of music. (The Ottawa *Rinaldo* held only fourteen whole airs of the thirty-one in the original version; the City Opera *Cesare* only three of its thirty-one.) Both observed the elaborate stage directions in full—with the difference that Cambridge represented them in modern guise. In Act I, "the Magician comes forth and waves his Wand, at which a large Fountain rises out of the Earth and conceals *Medoro*." In Cambridge it was a square steel drinking fountain that rose from the stage, in St. Louis a Baroque affair with glistering tinsel water jets. At the close of Act II, the hero was borne skyward by, respectively, a space rocket and a swan-drawn chariot amid bursts of aerial fireworks. Both productions eschewed realistic acting and adopted a repertory of formalized movement carefully matched to the music. The St. Louis singers suggested eighteenth-century stage prints and drawings animated, while the Cambridge singers found contemporary analogues of the emblematic poses and gestures of heroic resolve, playfulness, etc.

I first came across and admired Mr. McGegan's work twelve years ago when he, an undergraduate at Cambridge University, conducted François-André Danican Philidor's *Tom Jones,* in his own edition. He later came to Philidor's defense in London, conducting productions of *Blaise le savetier, Le Jardinier et son seigneur, Tom Jones* again, and *Le Maréchal ferrant;* recorded Rameau's *La Princesse de Navarre* and *Naïs* (a production of which he also conducted at the theatre in Versailles and at the Old Vic), on Erato; and in castles near Vienna put on candlelit enactments of Handel's *Apollo e Dafne* and *La resurrezione.* His concern for Baroque music played on the proper instruments and sung in a true style spread to concern for all aspects of effectively presenting the Baroque repertory. The *Orlando* he directed for Washington University was the most thoroughgoing essay in Handelian operatic reconstruction I have encountered; it brought together all the research and experiment that have been conducted in the fields of musical execution, stage setting, lighting, acting style, and orchestra-to-stage relationship.

The stage of the university's Edison Theatre was lit by a warm, living glow of simulated candlelight—candle bulbs and gilt reflectors placed where eighteenth-century candles would have been, with just enough flicker introduced to animate the effect, and not so much as to be distracting. (The technique was developed from one used now in the eighteenth-century Drottningholm Theatre, outside Stockholm, where old sets and machinery survive.) Except by two chandeliers suspended above the orchestra the house itself was unlit—not willingly, I was told, but because the electric circuits offered no choice between darkness and a modern glare, intermediate settings being unstable. The facsimile of the 1732 bilingual libretto which was available had to be conned in advance. Because the theatre has small wing space, scene changes were effected not by the sliding wings and shutters of the eighteenth century but by flown wings and backcloths. Although the movement was vertical, not horizontal, the effect of one scene in painted perspective swiftly covering or revealing another was preserved. The décor was by Scott Blake, a junior from Tennessee. Behind a painted proscenium flanked by the traditional niched statues of Music and Painting he created groves, grottoes, and temples. A surging ocean rolled on two long, stage-spanning cylinders; a fabulous sea beast traversed its surface. At the close, the stage direction "At this Instant the Statue of *Mars* rises in the Middle of the Temple, with a Fire kindled on the Altar" was faithfully carried out. Mr. Blake's figure drawing is still weak—his God of Love and Heroes of Antiquity looked like caricatures, and his Mars appeared to be drunk—and the actual painting of the scenes was perhaps too impressionistic in application. But as a zestful, enthusiastic vision of a Baroque stage in motion this was a brilliant achievement, a modern evocation of the stages pictured in the enthralling exhibition, "Baroque Theatre and Stage Design," that was also part of the university's festival. Donna Keesee's costumes were admirable in cut and color. There was an orchestra of twenty-four—including three harpsichords and two theorbos—made up of the ten-strong Toronto ensemble Tafelmusik, members of the university's collegium, and two guests. It was disposed as in the old seating plans, not sunk into a modern pit. Mr. McGegan presided at the central harpsichord, with the continuo cello beside him, playing from the same score. Most of the instrumentalists—including the continuo and the obbligato players—could see and hear and take cues directly from the singers; balance and ensemble were sensitive and just. Pitch was A 415. Only the pair of horns that should second the hero as he compares himself to Alcides and Peleus' son was missing. The recorders, which have only twenty-nine bars all evening (assisting at a scene change in Act I, and breathing a sudden new enchantment over the landscape of Angelica's "Verdi piante," in Act II), were present. The beauty, the gentleness, the vigor and variety of Handel's scoring were revealed as by a modern orchestra they cannot be. The *violette marine* lines that accompany Orlando's arioso (when the maddened hero, believing he has slain Angelica, sinks into a stupefied slumber) were taken by a viola d'amore and a muted viola; the sad yet soothing dusky-gold sound ravished the senses.

The title role was written for an alto castrato, the great Senesino. Winton Dean, in his *Handel and the Opera Seria,* remarks that castrati "appear to be among the few facilities not available at an American university." When Handel himself lacked one for a revival, he usually reassigned the role to a woman, and big houses today usually follow suit, with Janet Baker (in London) or Tatiana Troyanos (in San Francisco) as Caesar, Marilyn Horne (in Houston and Ottawa, soon in New York) as Rinaldo. But there is an increasing tendency to use countertenors; good countertenors seem to be in abundant supply now, and as a rule they are steadier, less vibrato-prone, than most female singers. (Perhaps the time has come for an "authentic" revival of Bellini's first opera, *Adelson e Salvini,* in which Nelly, Fanny, and Mme. Rivers were first played by young men.) In St. Louis, Orlando was sung by Drew Minter, a New York countertenor most often heard here in consort work with Concert Royal and Pomerium Musices. He is a bewitching artist. Most of what the composer Johann Joachim Quantz said about Senesino can be applied without reserve to Mr. Minter as Orlando:

> He had a clear, equal and sweet contralto voice, with a perfect intonation and an excellent shake. His manner of singing was masterly. Though he never loaded Adagios with too many ornaments, yet he delivered the original and essential notes with the utmost refinement. He sang Allegros with fire, and marked rapid divisions in an articulate and pleasing manner. His countenance was well adapted to the stage, and his action was natural and noble.

From Quantz's description only "powerful," "great" before "fire," "from the chest" after "divisions," and references to Senesino's "elocution unrivalled" and "majestic figure" have been omitted. Mr. Minter's voice is not powerful, although in the little theatre, a 650-seater, his passages of parade and his bravura cadenzas rang out brilliantly. Some low notes that he touched in tenor tones were agréeable, but he shunned sudden, startling register shifts—baroque in every sense—such as the countertenor René Jacobs espouses for special effect. His Italian was clear and correct rather than forcefully uttered. "Natural" may be a surprising epithet for the vividly mannered action Mr. McGegan had taught his cast, but Mr. Minter executed it with confidence and conviction that made it seem the music's natural counterpart. His beauty of timbre and of phrasing was enhanced by beauty of person—a potent weapon in any opera singer's artistic armory. Christine Armistead (Angelica), Sally Bradshaw (Dorinda), Deborah Harrison (Medoro), and Nicholas Solomon (Zoroaster) were fluent Handelians with light, clear, accurate voices and stylishly eloquent manners. There were a few moments of impure timbre or less than perfect intonation, it is true, but generally the singers were alluring, beguiling, affecting.

Musically, *Orlando* is one of Handel's richest and most rewarding operas. Emotionally and dramatically, it treads the varied, intricate tracks of love's mazes with delicacy, urgency, and passion. And, as Mr. Dean remarks, "its situations are psychologically and universally true and can carry a profound symbolic content." In connection with it he cites *The Magic Flute*. Reviewing the Cambridge production, I cited *Figaro* and *Così fan tutte*. (The heroine of the last, like her heroic namesake in the *Orlando furioso*, resolves to follow her beloved to the wars; he likens himself to the infatuate Orlando and the love-smitten Medoro. In Handel's opera, as in the *Flute*, the hero is watched over by a wise, benign bass, Zoroaster.) It is easy to understand why the people of Boston and Cambridge, able to visit *Orlando* again and again, did so. I saw the St. Louis *Orlando* twice, entering and gladly reëntering a world of delight, enchantment, and adventure. I hope the people who put on the Met *Rinaldo* and the City Opera *Alcina* have seen and learned from both the Cambridge and the St. Louis productions. Large houses, with orchestras and, often, singers unversed in eighteenth-century music, have a harder time of it. They need all the help they can get.

• • •

The Juilliard American Opera Center's production of Bellini's *I Capuleti ed i Montecchi*, in the Juilliard Theater last month, conducted by Denis Vaughan and directed by Ian Strasfogel, was a rather tame affair. In earlier operas, Bellini laid the foundations of *canto d'azione*, that vigorous, even violent declamatory style. When *I Capuleti* appeared, in Venice in 1830, the audience was surprised to discern what one critic called "a completely new genre, not noisy, but pensive, harmonious, and very gentle." This manner Bellini then made his specialty, while Donizetti and then Verdi developed the *canto d'azione*. But *I Capuleti* is not all gentle. Much of it should be fiery. Wilhelmine Schröder-Devrient—Beethoven's great Leonore in 1822, then Wagner's first Adriano, Senta, and Venus—was a fiery, dashing, impetuous Romeo, as Wagner recalls in *Mein Leben*. Wagner's niece Johanna, his first Elisabeth, made her London début in 1856 as Romeo, and in the reminiscences of Benjamin Lumley, the impresario of Her Majesty's, we read:

> She appeared: tall, stately, self-possessed, clothed in glittering gilded mail, with her fine fair hair flung in masses upon her neck: a superb air that seemed to give full earnest of victory, and a step revealing innate majesty and grandeur in every movement....She sang! The sonorous voice, which heralded the mission of the young warrior to his enemies, rang through the house as penetrating and as awakening as the summons of a clarion.

The Juilliard Romeo, Lucille Beer, made her entrance meekly, diffidently. She seemed not to have studied how gallant young warriors bear themselves and move or to have reflected that Bellini's Romeo is not Shakespeare's but the dreaded, dauntless captain of the Ghibelline army. Her voice was backward, without flash or urgency. Her musical interpretation was sluggish and sentimental, if not without feeling. The Juliet, Katherine Terrell, was a dull actress until, upon awakening in the tomb, she became deplorably kittenish. Her voice is pretty, and there were some sweetly turned phrases; sometimes she pushed it instead of letting it flow. The Tybalt, Franco Farina, was beefy, not elegant or buoyant, and reluctant to spin refined phrases in head voice.

All the *Capuleti* performances I have heard—conducted by Lorin Maazel, Claudio Abbado, Giuseppe Patanè, Eve Queler, now Mr. Vaughan—have lacked brio, have been monotonous and below tempo. All but one: Sarah Caldwell's in Boston in 1975. There the "pensive, harmonious, and very gentle" episodes were thrown into relief by the reckless glitter of the spirited scenes. One doesn't go to a school performance expecting polished perfection; one does expect verve and enthusiasm. Mr. Strasfogel's direction was flat (in the quintet the principals stood like dummies), and sometimes silly (before the duel Tybalt poked at Romeo through bars). Ming Cho Lee's set was an arcaded chapter house panelled in green marble, with different arches opened to suggest the six different scenes. From Bellini's autograph (which is published in facsimile by Garland), Mr. Vaughan had restored Bellini's original, sometimes unorthodox, and delicately deliberate orchestration. He had also made several little cuts—among them, the final page.

The Met revived *Don Carlos* last week, still in Italian translation. The plain wooden towers of David Reppa's unit set have now been clad in gilt-framed metallic panels and topped with tracery. They look richer. The *site riant* outside the Yuste monastery is less bleak, but the immense trees and the carpet of myraid flowers that the chorus and Tybalt tell of are still left to the imagination. In the coronation scene there is no stinting on supers, but the necessary onstage band fails to put in an appearance.

Mirella Freni returns to the company after a fifteen-year absence, to sing Elizabeth. Like Renata Scotto, she is a lyric soprano who has deserted her natural repertory in order to tackle heavier roles. For Karajan in Salzburg she sang Elizabeth in 1975, Aida in 1980. That first Elizabeth was exquisitely voiced, dulcet and gentle, meltingly beautiful in the final duet; so was the Elizabeth she sang for Abbado at La Scala two years later. At the Met, she sought volume and penetration at the cost of purity and sweetness; the lines did not float. Her vocalism was controlled and accurate—she has not become strident, as Miss Scotto has—but lacked amplitude and did not have the compensatory charm of timbre that once informed it. She is not a tragic actress—a dignified little doll of a queen, rather.

Nicolai Ghiaurov's Philip was a late, fainter impression of what began over twenty years ago as a boldly etched, if never particularly subtle, portrayal. Grace Bumbry was a loud, commanding Eboli whose singing seldom suggested the "extreme elegance, frivolity, and capriciousness" required of the character. The Carlos, Ermanno Mauro, deputizing for an ill Placido Domingo, had ardent, ringing high notes, but in softer passages the voice lost quality. Louis Quilico was an off-the-rack Rodrigo. The director, John Dexter, did much to prevent close attention to the principals: Philip's air was dwarfed by a play of moving lights across the huge El Greco fresco behind him; Rodrigo's prison air accompanied the maneuvers of two armed men, marching and countermarching across the scene, now on the beat, now not. But the audience, which had come to hear the famous singers, not Verdi's noblest opera, was loud in its appreciation. After her final air, that sombre, passionate entreaty to the shade of Charles V, Queen Elizabeth acknowledged the thunderous applause that greeted her and blew a kiss to the conductor, James Levine. He at least finds more in the work than a vocal circus, but his lofty conception was executed with too insistently energetic and inflexible a beat.

ALL-AMERICAN

March 21, 1983

JOHN ROCKWELL'S *All American Music: Composition in the Late Twentieth Century,* just published by Knopf, is an intelligent, impressive, and important book. There are twenty chapters, each dealing with a composer or (in two cases: the Art Ensemble of Chicago and Talking Heads) a group, and also with "broader issues epitomized by those composers, their music and their place in American cultural life." Thus, the first chapter treats of Ernst Krenek and "The Rise of American Art Music and the Impact of the Immigrant Wave of the Late 1930s"; the second of Milton Babbitt and "The Northeastern Academic Establishment and the Romance of Science"; the third of Elliott Carter and "American Intellectual Composers and the 'Ideal Public'"; the eighteenth of Babbitt's celebrated pupil Stephen Sondheim and "Urban Popular Song, the Broadway Musical, the Cabaret Revival, and the Birth Pangs of American Opera"; and the last of Talking Heads and "Art-Rock, Black vs. White, and Vanguard Cross-Pollination." The selection of composers, Rockwell says, is "based not just on the inherent quality of each composer's music (indeed, in a few cases I don't find the music of paramount interest) but also on what they suggest about contemporary American composition in general." The others are John Cage, Ralph Shapey, David Del Tredici, Frederic Rzewski, Robert Ashley, Philip Glass, Laurie Anderson, David Behrman, Max Neuhaus, Walter Murch, Keith Jarrett, Ornette Coleman, Eddie Palmieri, and Neil Young. There is much to agree with, much to feel challenged by, much to think about, and—for anyone less open than Rockwell to the full range of American contemporary composition— much to learn. During a decade in America, I have tried to remain open and have heard at least some music by all his twenty composers, but with eight of them can claim no more than slight acquaintance. While there are still Haydn quartets, Bach cantatas, Monteverdi madrigals, and Josquin masses I have never heard, I have grudged giving much time to, say, Ashley's *Perfect Lives (Private Parts)* or Anderson's *United States.* Threescore years and ten is a short span in which to carry out Cage's prescription "If something is boring after two minutes, try it for four. If still boring, try it for eight, sixteen, thirty-two, and so on." And the Ashley and Anderson works go on for hours. In Rockwell's book there are no glib conclusions, but there does, as he hopes, emerge a tale, which he describes as "a tale of traditional, cultivated music opening itself up to the diversity of the true American musical experience."

•   •   •

The New York pianist Alan Feinberg, a prize-winner in the first John F. Kennedy Center/Rockefeller Foundation International Competition for Excellence in the Performance of American Music, in 1978, gave a Merkin Hall recital this month. (The title of the event is now slimmed to International American Music Competition, and since 1981 Carnegie Hall has replaced the Kennedy Center as co-sponsor.) Unable to attend the recital, I caught up with it on tape: Mr. Feinberg is someone not to miss. He is a virtuoso with a musical mind as quick and precise as his technique; a pianistic "presence"; a romantic in his ardent, elegant championship of whatever he plays. His program was assembled in the belief that the last half century has produced a body of piano music so rich and "pianistic" that performers can, as he put in a program note, have with it "the same relation that our current-day virtuosi have with the eighteenth, nineteenth, and perhaps the first decade or so of the twentieth centuries" (a still closer relation, one might suggest, insofar as Mozart, Beethoven, Schubert, and even Brahms and Debussy when played on a modern grand must be to some extent "transcriptions," while the music Mr. Feinberg plays is composed for the instrument on which he plays it) and can "tap with it the same excitement and desire for transport which make people attend piano recitals so avidly." In a program free of "the dulling effects of crusadership or academicism," he spanned more than the half century, including an exquisitely shaped, very beautiful account of Stravinsky's lyrical 1924 Sonata and ending with a captivatingly poetic Ravel *Ondine* (1908). The recital began with Charles Wuorinen's Capriccio, which was composed in 1981 for Robert Miller, inspirer and inspired advocate of much new piano music, but was first played as a memorial to Miller, by Mr. Feinberg in April last year. It is a rich, substantial piece, urgent and inventive. Stefan Wolpe's dark, strong Passacaglia was given a performance at once lucid and emotionally charged. Shulamit Ran's *Verticals* (1983) —a grand, passionate, Lisztian composition, rhapsodic and shapely, seventeen minutes long—had its première. Milton Babbitt's *My Complements to Roger* (1978), one of several pieces with which Babbitt has hailed Sessions birthdays, had its first public performance, as the centerpiece of three miniatures—the others being *Partitions* (1957) and *Playing for Time* (1977). Rockwell in his Babbitt chapter says stern things about Babbitt's complexity, his "polemics and proselytization," and the baleful influence of the "Columbia-Princeton school," but he also remarks, "Yet the surprising, rather wonderful thing is that... Babbitt's own music *sounds* so good." It certainly sounds good as Mr. Feinberg played it. The three pieces are fiendishly difficult in notes, in rhythms, and in dynamics, but when these are mastered they cohere. Miniatures in length only—*Partitions* lasts two minutes, *Complements* rather less, and *Playing for Time* about two and a half—they then become jewelled constructions intricately wrought; airy towers of delight seven octaves high; a world of fantasy, swift emotion, and orderly wit. In his program note, Mr. Feinberg said, "As with Chopin études, one can never play them too well: these Babbitt works have all the exhilaration of virtuoso études together with a kind of Dixieland freshness."

I enjoyed Aleck Karis's spirited account of Babbitt's *Reflections* (1974), for piano and tape, at a Robert Miller memorial concert put on by the Group for Contemporary Music, in Symphony Space in November. (Mr. Miller's own performance on New World Records—the piece was composed for him—is still more delicately and pungently thoughtful.) Several pianists joined in the memorial tribute. Matthias Kriesberg played his exuberant *a3520* (1980), dedicated to Mr. Miller. Ursula Oppens gave the New York première of Tobias Picker's *When Soft Voices Die*, a lush outpouring that might be described as neo-Brahmsian. (It is recorded by Miss Oppens on CRI.) Kriesberg and Picker have both been Wuorinen and Babbitt pupils but do not qualify for inclusion in Rockwell's "generation of dry-as-dust, unthinking clones." Gilbert Kalish, one of the four pianists for whom Elliott Carter wrote his *Night Fantasies* (1980)—the others are Miss Oppens, Paul Jacobs, and Charles Rosen—became the third of them to play it in New York. He gave, I thought, a contained, measured, accurately shaped, but less than impulsive performance. It came at the end of a long evening filled with many exacting notes, and I was probably flagging. There had also been ensemble pieces: Webern's String Trio and the world première of Harvey Sollberger's *Life Study*, an elaborate affair for mezzo, flute, and harp. Mr. Rosen plays *Night Fantasies* in Carnegie Hall next month, and his recording of it, on the Dutch label Etcetera (distributed here by Qualiton), is now published. Mr. Karis played the piece last month at a Guild of Composers concert in Christ and St. Stephen's.

Wolpe's Passacaglia has a complicated history. He composed it in Jerusalem in 1936 for piano, as one of *Four Studies on Basic Rows*, and orchestrated it the following year. In America in 1971, he revised both the orchestral and the piano versions. At an American Composers Orchestra concert in Alice Tully Hall last month, Garrick Ohlsson played the piano version—he gave a performance enthusiastic but less penetrating than Mr. Feinberg's—and then Mr. Wuorinen conducted the première of the orchestral score. Fascinating juxtaposition! The first statements of the theme and, above all, the coda are so pianistic that orchestral dress seems unneeded. But the tremendous climax gains in force, the linear play is clarified, and the instrumental tints are unexpected, individual. On the other hand, there seems to be something more heroic still in a single player's setting out to grapple with the exacting, exalted material. Either way, the Passacaglia is a landmark of German music by one of the most influential émigré masters who settled in this country. Wuorinen readily owes his debt to Wolpe. The ACO concert began with the first performance of Wuorinen's Short Suite for Orchestra. Its "basic fabric" is derived from his glittering sextet *Arabia Felix* (1973). In six short movements, it exhilarated ear and mind.

More Wolpe—late, American Wolpe—began Speculum Musicae's December concert in Alice Tully Hall: his *Street Music No. 1* (1962). It's a rough, sketchy piece, not fully worked out, and the Speculum performance was less than convincing. The group, both here and at an October concert up at Columbia, was playing somewhat below its best form. It did not seem to know Peter Maxwell Davies's *Shakespeare Music* (1964) very well. But David Schiff's Elegy for String Quartet (1978), an excellent composition, was movingly done, with John Graham as the viola soloist, whose long, lyrical song runs like a cantus firmus through a shapely and arresting discourse. Davies's Fantasia and Two Pavans (1968), Purcell transformations, fared no better at one of Gerard Schwarz's Music Today concerts, in Merkin Hall in November. This concert brought the New York première of Ellen Taaffe Zwilich's *Passages* (1981), for soprano, flute, clarinet, string trio, piano, and percussion. It's a setting of six A. R. Ammons lyrics, with interludes in which the voice becomes an eighth instrument. It's fresh, bright, charming, intimate—a small recital in itself. Hearing it was like making a new friend who is at once the poet, the composer, and the singer—even if Clamma Dale's performance was hardly more than a lively first sketch. She didn't yet have the songs by heart. I hope she keeps *Passages* in her repertory.

More Wuorinen—the première of his *New York Notes* (1982)—closed a good concert given by the New York New Music Ensemble in November in Carnegie Recital Hall. The Ensemble is a sextet—Schoenberg's *Pierrot* quintet (flute, clarinet, violin, cello, piano) plus percussion, like the Fires of London—with a director, Robert Black, who is also a fine pianist. In *New York Notes*, which Mr. Black conducted, Wuorinen wrote for the six players as soloists, as duos, and as an ensemble: twenty minutes; three movements, the first intense, the second pensive, the third brilliant. Before it, there had been a quartet (Mario Davidovsky's short, striking *Synchronisms No. 2*, of 1964, for flute, clarinet, violin, cello, plus tape; the balance was awry, the tape too soft), a trio (Ingolf Dahl's *Concerto a tre*, of 1947, for clarinet, violin, and cello, which wears well), and three duos. Mr. Black and Mr. Feinberg were trim in Stravinsky's Three Pieces (1914) for piano duet. Jayn Rosenfeld and Daniel Druckman were alluring in Barbara Kolb's succulent, skillful *Homage to Keith Jarrett and Gary Burton* (1976), for flute and vibes. Jean Kopperud and Eric Bartlett were lyrical in Ran's *Private Game* (1980), for clarinet and cello, which is brief, romantic, and attractive. That leaves unnamed only the outstanding violinist: he was Gregory Fulkerson, the 1980 winner of the American Music Competition.

Ran is one of two Chicago composers (the other being Shapey) who have been prominent in New York this season. Besides *Verticals* and *Private Game*, there were New York premières of her *Excursions*, at another of Merkin Hall's Music Today concerts, and *A Prayer* (1982), at a Composers' Showcase concert this month given by the Contemporary

Chamber Ensemble, conducted by Arthur Weisberg, in a cramped, acoustically bleak room in Sotheby's. The concert honored Paul Fromm and celebrated thirty years of activity by the Fromm Music Foundation, which commissions works from composers both new and established, and underwrites their performance at Tanglewood and across the country. Ran's piece, for horn, clarinet, bass clarinet, bassoon, and timpani, is beautiful: a stretch of affecting wordless song.

Mr. Fromm figures in Rockwell's Shapey chapter, which is subtitled "Romantic Defiance, Enlightened Patronage, and Misanthropy in the Midwest." Shapey's *Songs of Ecstasy* (1968), at the Showcase concert, a work the composer describes as "a paean to the joy of union between man and woman," seemed to me near-pornographic in its employment, on tape and from soprano soloist, of the glutted sighs and sexy murmurs of "ye-e-es" which accompany lovemaking. I missed his Concerto Grosso for Woodwind Quintette, given its première last month by the Boehm Quintet, at the Guggenheim. His Songs for Soprano and Piano, which had its première at Elsa Charlston's recital in Merkin Hall in November, is a more pleasing example of his passionate, visionary, defiantly individual music. The text is compiled from lines in the Oxford Dictionary of Quotations indexed under "dream," "hope," and "death" and is set as a kind of free-floating yet coherent poetic dream.

Miss Charlston—a vivid and precise interpreter of difficult new music—also gave the New York première of John Eaton's *A Greek Vision,* for soprano, flute, and live electronics. Eaton defies categorization. He has an unmatched command of vocal gesture, a sure ear for telling, eloquent sound, and an amazing command of the expressive possibilities of new sounds and new harmonies made available by advanced instrumental and electronic techniques. He was trained at Princeton, where he worked with Babbitt and Sessions; he began his career as a jazz pianist; he works now in Bloomington, Indiana, away from either East Coast or West Coast "coteries." Although unmentioned in Rockwell's book, he exemplifies what Rockwell calls the "spiritual independence that seems, better than anything else, to define what is characteristic about the best American music." Since Eaton has invited me to collaborate with him on an opera [The Tempest, *given its first performance by the Santa Fe Opera, in 1986*], I'll say no more, but what I've just said I said years ago, after hearing his operas *Danton and Robespierre* and *The Cry of Clytaemnestra.*

NEW WORLD SYMPHONY

March 28, 1983

HANS WERNER HENZE's Fifth Symphony was composed, twenty years ago, for the New York Philharmonic's first season at Lincoln Center and was first conducted by Leonard Bernstein, its dedicatee. The orchestra revived it this month under Christoph von Dohnányi. I had not heard it live before. (There is a fine Berlin Philharmonic recording, conducted by the composer, on Deutsche Grammophon.) It was exciting to hear the piece in New York, for it is a symphony about this city as it struck a romantic tone-poet who sings of his life freely, fluently, generously, passionately. In Henze's *Essays*, there is a page headed "1962, Fifth Symphony," which begins, "Let me be brief! The human spirit is in a glorious state when it reveres, when it worships, when it exalts and is exalted by some object; but it must not stay long in that condition—generalizing chills it, idealizing brings exaggeration." Some Goethean life-into-art reflections then break into a Whitmanesque paean:

> Manhattan mon amour...Doves of Gurre, gulls, crying round the outcrops of shiny, Abruzzi-colored metal on skyscraper walls, rain on the asphalt. Fairytales, all the nightmares of childhood, all avenues end in the ocean, ancient Europe drifts in like a myth. Salt breeze, tang, vice, raids, minorities, clavichords, Edwardian rooms...Electric-hued nylon, gangs, God, Neon, jeans, bangs, hot dogs, cops. W.H. and dear C. in the Village...Silks, gold, ebony, subway shafts, black velvet, *maraviglioso fior del vostro mare....*

Much of Henze's music is about being in love—with a place, a person, an idea, or all three at once. The romance of this city needs to be sung. The exhilaration of first impressions here fades easily into harassed routine. Dirt and noise soon dull it. When a longing for grass, healthy trees, bird-song grows unbearable (finches sing on my Broadway terrace but cannot sound the full-throated dawn chorus to which Londoners wake), it is time to rediscover New York's different allurements: to walk over Brooklyn Bridge again; read Whitman; hear Roberto Gerhard's Fourth Symphony, "New York" (another Philharmonic commission, but unplayed here since 1967), Elliott Carter's Symphony of Three Orchestras (which the Philharmonic is reviving next season), and Henze's Fifth Symphony. Henze *was* brief: his symphony lasts under twenty minutes. Like Gerhard's and Carter's symphonies, it is picturesque—packed with vivid, varied incident and scored in bright colors. Musical logic gives order to the phantasmagoria evoked by the composer's essay: the first movement is a sonata-form construction, the second a stretch of song in which alto flute, viola, and English horn are unaccompanied solo singers, and the finale a moto perpetuo that is also a set of variations on the second-movement song.

Mr. Dohnányi, the conductor-elect of the Cleveland Orchestra, did not exactly get the Philharmonic to play rapturously, but the performance was sharp, clean-cut, impressive. He is a Henze specialist—he gave the premières of Henze's operas *The Young Lord* and *The Bassarids* —who finds the pathway through the composer's generously luxuriant sound-thickets and is good at clarifying form. The concert began and ended in G major with Haydn's Symphony No. 88 and Dvořák's Eighth Symphony, Opus 88. I had not before heard Mr. Dohnányi conduct standard repertory—only Franz Schreker's *Der ferne Klang*, the Henze operas, and (on records) Schoenberg's *Erwartung* and Berg's *Wozzeck* and *Lulu*. Grove declares, rather unkindly, that "he is more successful in works requiring intricate conducting technique than in those calling for a purely musical approach," but the Haydn showed him a poised classicist, alert to the marvels and surprises of the score. The string force was reduced, but the woodwinds were doubled. The interpretation was linear, not bulky, and very different from Szell's six-cylinder recording with the Cleveland. I enjoyed the work so much that I regretted we were given the first movement only in half measure, without the repeats. The Dvořák was more controversial: an odd, neurotic reading—the transformation of a work commonly described as lyrical, flowing, and happy into something abrupt, violent, and Expressionist. Dvořák's biographer Otakar Šourek says, in a preface to the study score he edited, that the symphony shows "no traces of the tough, turbulent defiance and bitter anguished yearning that fill the preceding symphony, the D minor...as if here only a contented and joyful soul were singing, proud of the goal attained and the means of attaining it, as if it wished to communicate a feeling of happy satisfaction with its own achievement and the fresh impressions awakened by a loving communion with the countryside." The symphony also has its dark moments but, as another biographer, John Clapham, remarks, "despite its deep shadows, is one of the composer's happiest creations." Not in Mr. Dohnányi's performance, however, which was a thing of harsh, sudden contrasts, strain, and formal striving. The Philharmonic needs little encouragement to play with hard, forceful tone. The strings were steely, and the brass was aggressive. It was a charmless but not an uninteresting performance. It held one's attention on every turn the music took, and challenged one to hear the familiar work as something sterner, less smilingly serene, than ever before.

Bernd Alois Zimmermann's Violin Concerto, first played in 1950, had its American première this month at a Brooklyn Philharmonic concert conducted by Lukas Foss in the Opera House of the Brooklyn Academy of Music. This is a strenuous piece, not long (about eighteen minutes) and not particularly likable. But after some effort and some work at it (there's a rather stark recording on the Candide label, coupled with Henze's early Violin Concerto, of 1947) one can discern the features and the merits of the composer whose later works are so potent and whose history—he ended his life in 1970—and musical personality are so moving. Zimmermann was born in 1918, eight years before Henze. Both of them had swiftly to absorb after 1945 the Stravinsky, Schoenberg, and Hindemith that Hitler had denied them, and seem now to have packed two decades of excited discovery into the compositions of a quinquenniad. Zimmermann's gritty concerto, with its sudden spans of traditional sweetness amid earnest neoclassical scrubbing, its abrupt tempo switches, its rumba-rhythm episodes, points to the pluralistic style he later handled so surely.

The soloist was the German violinist Christiane Edinger, efficient, assured, insistent. The Brooklyn Philharmonic is a band of virtuosi, its roster studded with names familiar from Manhattan's new-music concerts; Benjamin Hudson is the concertmaster. A fleet Haffner Symphony began the concert: too fleet, for many of Mozart's miracles were sped through rather than sounded. The Academy's Opera House— New York's handsomest hall and one of the easiest to reach (thirteen subway lines and Long Island Rail Road trains all stop near its doors) —has this year acquired a new concert shell, designed by Christopher Jaffe. For the first part of the concert, I sat centrally in the "orchestra," or platea, and felt that, new shell notwithstanding, the sound lacked boldness and intimacy. For the second half, consisting of the Eroica, I moved up to the first of the two balconies. Everything came to life. The woodwinds lifted their voices above the strings. In the trio of the scherzo, one heard the horn calls move from player to player across the platform. It was an Eroica of clear, living lines, not of massed sonorities. (How telling the drum part when played as Richard Fitz played it!) Mr. Foss was not so much "conducting" as coördinating a group of committed, eager players, attentive to one another as chamber musicians are. It was a heroic and stirring performance.

Henry Herford, the Scottish baritone who won last year's International American Music Competition, gave a recital this month at the 92nd Street Y. Of American music, he sang three songs by Arthur Shepherd, six songs by Charles Ives, and Conrad Susa's slight, agreeable cycle *Hymns for the Amusement of Children*. He began with a Schubert group (done in German). English and French cycles formed the core of his recital: Britten's *Songs and Proverbs of William Blake* and Ravel's *Histoires naturelles*. Of both he gave polished, detailed, and very successful performances—and that despite far from unflawed vocalism. The upper fourth of his range was often loose and fluffy, the tone not secure, forward, or unfailingly steady. Lines that should have been smooth and even were not. And yet one listened, and listened with enjoyment, reflecting the while that presence, personality, lively musical instincts, rhythmic verve, clever timing, and a feeling for words and their sense are assets perhaps more important to a songster than a carefully cultivated voice. David Bispham, that great champion of American contemporary song at the beginning of our century, urged singers to avoid at all costs the reproach of *"Vox, et praeterea nihil."* (But he united verbal liveliness to a wonderfully clear, forward, true, firm voice.) Precepts set out in his autobiography, *A Quaker Singer's Recollections,* should be followed more often. Learn Italian, French, and German, he says, but above all learn English:

> To all American singers I say, sing your songs in well-chosen English if singing to an English-speaking audience, and sing them so that every one understands your words; enunciate so clearly that the audience can tell even how every word is spelled. Get away from this foreign-language fad, and you will find yourself nearer the heart of your public.

Mr. Herford could do with more *vox* of the kind Bispham displays on his records and with a shade less reliance on physical effects (winsome cocking or slow, soulful shaking of the head; enacting the strut of each fowl in Ravel's barnyard a trifle too fully). Nevertheless, in an age when levels of accepted vocal competence are lower than those of instrumental, when most young lieder singers are dull, when many of them (unlike Mr. Herford) remain score-bound, when Phyllis Curtin and Donald Gramm seem to be just about the last of the great American line (the wonderful Joan Morris being something different), he gave a recital that was constantly engaging.

MORALITIES

April 4, 1983

Anna Karenina recounts two histories. One is that of Constantin Dmitrich Levin, the central character of the novel. Through country and town scenes, through encounters, conversations, and reflections, and in relation to his wife, his brothers, his sister-in-law and brother-in-law, his friends, and his peasants, we follow Levin's progress toward temporary, workable answers to his questions "Why do I live?" and "How ought I to live?" The answers will not satisfy a modern quester unless he, too, decides that it is enough to try to do the best work he can in his field while harming others as little as possible; the book breaks off rather than coming to a close. (Tolstoy's later novel *Resurrection,* more troubling to the conscience, is even less conclusive.) But the characters are drawn from the life; they ring true. And Levin's concerns—encompassing the land and its ownership, labor, profit, privilege, social justice, and personal relationships—his joys, and his troubles become the reader's. They do not lend themselves easily to dramatic or operatic representation. The subplot, Anna Arkadyevna Karenina's adulterous affair with Count Alexei Kirilovich Vronsky, provides matter more conventionally musicable. There have been seven or more *Anna Karenina* operas. At least two of them—Igino Robbiani's, first performed in Rome in 1924, and Iain Hamilton's, commissioned and first performed in London by the English National Opera, in 1981, and performed last month by the Los Angeles Opera Theater—are Levinless.

Anna and Vronsky are creations of a novelist's artifice. References to their physical attributes—to Anna's black curls escaping from whatever she has on her head (a hat, a pansy wreath, white lace, a top hat), to Vronsky's strong white teeth—recur like Homeric epithets. Anna first appears at the Moscow railroad station; she plays a crucial scene with Vronsky amid whirling snow on the platform of a country station; and from another she ends her life. (Hamilton begins and ends his opera in the Moscow station.) Anna has a recurrent nightmare about a peasant with a bar of iron; Vronsky has the same dream the night before Anna decides to defy her husband and see her lover again; and in two of the railroad scenes it is linked with the man who taps the wheels of the train. (Through Robbiani's opera, whose libretto is based on a "treatment" of the Tolstoy book by Edmond Guiraud, there stalks Il Mugik, a mysterious bass figure personifying the dream, who at the end leads Anna beneath the wheels of the approaching train.) Robbiani's opera is in four acts: set at the racecourse and in Karenin's study (where his son Sergey is entertained by a Cossack song); in Venice (where a gondolier sings and a commedia-dell'arte troupe plays); back in the study, which is now Sergey's; and on the terrace of a villa outside Moscow, beside a railroad track. It is a coherent if rather arty construction. Hamilton's opera, in three acts, with fifteen scenes, to his own libretto, is closer to the book, but it leaves out so much—or, to put it another way, it includes so much without fully explaining anything—that it is probably hard to follow by anyone who does not know the novel.

Janáček is the composer who could have entered into and made sense of Anna. Tolstoy presents her, Vronsky, and their behavior as a series of données. (Anna's maternal love for Sergey, for example, which is important to the plot, is merely asserted, while her sister-in-law Dolly's love for her children is revealed in a hundred unstressed realistic details.) Janáček did embark on an *Anna Karenina,* in 1907, but soon abandoned it. (The most remarkable of the surviving sketches, his biographer Jaroslav Vogel says, are concerned with Levin and his wife, Kitty.) Hamilton had a clear idea of what he wanted to achieve. In an introductory article about his opera, he said:

> When choosing a subject for an opera I like to feel I can state in a few words the central theme of the work.... In *Anna Karenina* one thing matters above all else—love. It is born, rejoiced in, suffered through, betrayed, and finally lost.

Hamilton is a seasoned opera composer. *Anna Karenina* is his sixth opera. His first, *Agamemnon* (1958, revised in 1969), remains unperformed. His second, *The Royal Hunt of the Sun* (1968), was produced by the English National Opera in 1977. His third, the one-act *Pharsalia,* appeared at the Edinburgh Festival in 1969. *The Catiline Conspiracy*, commissioned by Scottish Opera, appeared in 1974. His fifth opera, *Tamburlaine*, a BBC commission, was broadcast in 1977, and has now been expanded into a full-length theatre work. The latest Hamilton catalogue includes, after *Anna Karenina*, a *Dick Whittington* (1981; another English National Opera commission) and a *Lancelot* (1983). Although for twenty years Hamilton—Scottish-born, London-trained—lived in this country, *Anna Karenina* is the first of his operas to be performed here. It is also the first of them I've heard. The reviews of its predecessors which I have read were, on the whole, appreciative but not exactly enthusiastic; they left me mildly eager, not very eager, to hear them. *The Catiline Conspiracy* is by all accounts the most exciting of them. Of *Anna Karenina*, Winton Dean wrote that, on first hearing, it

> seemed a thoroughly viable opera of the second rank—a rarer and more considerable achievement than the qualification may seem to imply. It held attention for a full three hours, and made a less stale impression than some of Strauss's late operas (a natural comparison); though it explores no new ground, it avoids the twin pitfalls of pretentiousness and triviality.

Anna Karenina is not pretentious in effect, despite its ambition in tackling, however partially, Tolstoy's great novel, and it is not trivial. But Dean's mention of Strauss suggests an essential weakness: the lyrical invention is limited. (I should add that I do not find Strauss's last operas—*Friedenstag, Daphne, Die Liebe der Danae*, and *Capriccio*—"stale." They seem to me wonderful late flowerings of an ever-fertile composer, and works more honest and attractive in tone than some of the Hofmannsthal-influenced confections.) A quarter century or so ago, Hamilton abandoned traditional tonality. *Anna Karenina* marks his fullest return to it. Characters and ideas have not only their leitmotifs but also their keys: D for Anna, E-flat for Vronsky, A for their mutual love. According to an article in *Opera*, "when Iain Hamilton found he would be using key-signatures again in his music for *Anna Karenina*, he was afraid he might have forgotten how." His fear was not unjustified. One sits through the piece as through many an earnest, high-minded, well-planned post-verismo opera, waiting for what Verdi called *il motivo*—a melodic phrase to open the listener's heart to the character— and waits largely in vain.

The Los Angeles production, given in the Wilshire Ebell Theatre, staged by Richard Pearlman, designed by Ronald Chase, and lit by Nananne Porcher, was one of high technical accomplishment. The English National used a revolving stage and rear projections to achieve swift, numerous scene changes. Los Angeles used projections on a front gauze, with the actors and some furniture in pools of light behind it. It was skillfully done, and any particular scene looked good, but it killed the piece, for all evening long one watched the drama— and seemed to hear it—through a fog. The effect was something like that of a three-dimensional movie—but one where the lions, instead of leaping out into your lap, remained behind the screen. In addition, the orchestral interludes, which should pack a dramatic charge, were reduced to being an accompaniment for movies or slide shows. (How few modern directors understand that stretches of instrumental music without action or "visuals" provide opera composers with a powerful dramatic resource! In the Covent Garden *Ring*, Siegfried is seen paddling his canoe during the Rhine Journey.) Emily Rawlins, the Anna, has a soprano whose tone became acid under pressure; she etched a strong performance and was impressive in the final mad scene. Judith Christin's Princess Dolly was warmly and attractively played. Evan Bortnick's Alexey looked right, but his tenor lacked character. There were three good baritones: Lawrence Cooper, the Stiva; Roger Roloff, the Karenin (odd, though, to hear a baritone Karenin, for Tolstoy makes repeated reference to his high voice); and James Rensink, the Yashvin. Chris Nance conducted with a sure but slightly heavy hand.

Die Walküre, last heard at the Metropolitan six seasons ago, was revived last month. It was a light-weight affair. Silvio Varviso, returning to the house after a fourteen-year absence, was booed. I didn't think he deserved it, quite. The Met is no longer a place where first-league conductors appear much (not Abbado, Kleiber, Muti, or Solti, not even Maazel or Mehta, has been here during the Levine régime), and Mr. Varviso was not exceptionally bad. He wasn't dreary. But he seemed to have no sure command of the longer rhythms, and there was some careless orchestral playing. The cast—all but Mignon Dunn's strong, strident Fricka—was new. Hildegard Behrens, the Sieglinde, was clear but not rapturous. Manfred Jung, the Siegmund, was clear but prosaic. Hans Tschammer, from the Dusseldorf Opera, made his Met (and American) début, as Hunding, producing firm, dark-brown tone of quality; his manner was less than formidable. Gwyneth Jones's first Met Brünnhilde found her in fairly steady and accurate form, but the radiance that can fill her did not shine. Franz Ferdinand Nentwig's Wotan was correct until in Act III it began to flag. All in all, it was hardly more than another repertory *Walküre*.

The production—Karajan's in 1967, and since then staged by Wolfgang Weber—seems to consist now of moves made after the book (the local prompt book, not Wagner's careful libretto) rather than in any natural, apparently spontaneous reaction to what happens. Siegmund and Sieglinde spend far too much time on their knees, and even Wotan falls to his knees after his worsting by Fricka. (Wagner wanted him to fling himself dejectedly into a rocky seat; but there's no rocky seat around in the Met décor.) There are vulgar touches: when Siegmund draws forth the sword, Sieglinde lies squirming on the floor; at curtain-fall the two have begun to copulate; and Wotan lies down full-length on his daughter to implant his farewell kiss. In Act II, Siegmund now dies in Wotan's arms—a "touch" borrowed, perhaps, from the Chéreau production. Lighting stronger than Karajan's was is welcome, but it turns the mandorla of mystic shine which used to surround Brünnhilde as Herald of Death into a hank of cheesecloth.

Hans Werner Henze's two-act ballet *Orpheus,* a rich and moving score, composed after a powerful libretto by Edward Bond, was first performed in Stuttgart, in 1979, with choreography by William Forsythe. That summer, the Stuttgart Ballet brought the piece to the Met and by performing it in that gilded hall threw into question much of what goes on there during the rest of the year.

> Poets have sung of Orpheus
> Who returned from hell
> In this century day after day
> Many have gone to hell
> In war or prison
> Or walked there through the streets
> And returned home in the evening
> Like Orpheus without their passion
> With barely a reason for living
> Of these should Orpheus sing

That's the first of Bond's *Canzoni to Orpheus.* The third of them begins:

> After the war a philosopher said
> In this hell Orpheus should be silent
> Let no poet speak
>
> But Orpheus has always sung in hell

And Bond has continued to write plays, and Henze to write music, in which—like the Orpheus of their ballet—they reject the narcotic power of Apollo's lyre but not its ability to stimulate and to celebrate. Lincoln Center, despite the words graven in bronze on a tablet by its pool—"The arts are not for the privileged few, but for the many. Their place is not on the periphery of daily life, but at its center. They should function not merely as another form of entertainment"—is seldom a scene of high moral endeavor or of political awareness. What *Fidelio, The Ring,* or *Don Carlos* actually says is veiled in a foreign language. What might accumulate on the conscience is discharged by applause for the stars and for the scenery. But there are exceptions: the Met's *Lulu* and the City Opera's *Street Scene* and *Lily* come to mind—and *Orpheus.*

In 1980, Henze extracted a concert suite from his ballet. *Dramatic Scenes, Part 1, from Orpheus* was given its first New York performance last week, in Carnegie Hall, by the Cincinnati Symphony, conducted by Michael Gielen. It lasts about twenty minutes. It is a noble stretch of intensely imagined, highly colored music, exciting in its fast episodes, glowing in its lyrical stretches, picturesque, packed with incident, and brilliantly scored for very large forces (including heckelphone, saxophone, and harpsichord). The Cincinnati players played as if revelling in all the chances Henze gave them.

Britten's first chamber opera, *The Rape of Lucretia*, appeared at Glyndebourne in 1946. It reached Chicago the following year, and Broadway the year after that, staged by Agnes de Mille, with Kitty Carlisle as its heroine. Since the New York City Opera production of 1958, there has been a fairly steady flow of American performances. The latest of them was put on last month in the "Showcase" season of the San Francisco Opera Center, one of the cluster of troupes and activities around the big San Francisco company. Five of the cast were Adler Fellows—young singers being nurtured at the start of their careers.

It was about twenty years before *Lucretia* received general acceptance as a masterpiece. The 1954 Grove calls Britten's "experiment" in composing for the twelve-player instrumental ensemble of the English Opera Group "not musically satisfactory." In a 1949 *Hudson Review*, Joseph Kerman declared that the librettist, Ronald Duncan, "has no idea of drama whatsoever," and found "his philosophy...neither sensible nor coherent." Even today, the libretto troubles people, and they ask how the final Christian moral can fitly be drawn from the classical tragedy. The music shows how. As the New Grove puts it, "musically the sublime resolution of this final section is the goal towards which the whole opera has been directed." The coherent tonal scheme, the formal balance of the chorale's return after the great passacaglia, and the satisfying motivic relations can be shown by analysis. And they are audible. The listener who stops fretting with the text (there's much of it I would be reluctant to defend) hears scene after scene of beautifully wrought music, some of it lyrically sensuous, some exciting and passionate. He hears magical orchestral writing with an almost Baroque purity of instrumental colors, and vocal lines that move freely and eloquently through the careful structures. He is stirred. And, beyond that, he has at least the feeling that it all holds together and amounts to an opera that matters.

The San Francisco performance was sensitively shaped by Richard Bradshaw—he was both poetic and intense—and it was well played. Edward Hastings's staging, on a simple, effective set by Noel Uzemack, was more successful in its general lines than in the details of the individual actors' performances; there was some gauche demeanor. Richard Stead's wigs and makeup were deplorable: the chaste Lucretia was painted like a barmaid; Collatinus sported a curly comedy beard. Jeffrey Thomas, the Male Chorus, is a pleasingly intelligent and musical artist, but the voice was small for the role. Nikki Li Hartliep was a very distinct Female Chorus, but one missed the warmth and gentleness that Joan Cross, the first singer of the part, used to bring to it. That 1946 cast (Peter Pears, Miss Cross, Kathleen Ferrier as Lucretia, Margaret Ritchie and Anna Pollak as her maids) can still be heard; Discocorp, of Berkeley, publishes a record of substantial excerpts from a 1946 performance conducted by the composer. Perhaps the cold, erratic acoustics of the Herbst Theater were partly to blame for the fact that the women of the San Francisco cast—Laura Brooks Rice was Lucretia, Carla Cook a telling Bianca, and Ruth Ann Swenson a limpid, delicate Lucia—sometimes pushed their voices beyond the bounds of sweetness and purity, as Britten's performers never did. Vocally, the other men were strong: John Matthews a gleaming Tarquin, Thomas Woodman a vigorous Junius, and James Patterson—a bass to watch—a Collatinus sonorous and beautiful in timbre.

DIVINE SPARK

April 11, 1983

THE PHILHARMONIC has given concert performances of two operas this season, within the subscription series. In February, there was Schoenberg's monodrama *Erwartung,* with Hildegard Behrens true, accurate, and expressive as its unhappy heroine. Zubin Mehta conducted. Last month, Janáček's last opera, *From the House of the Dead,* had its American full-length première. (There was an abridged television adaptation in 1969.) This is a powerfully affecting piece that in the theatre proves overwhelming, although it is an unconventional opera. There is no plot, and next to no action. One young prisoner is a soprano role, and otherwise (apart from three phrases from a harlot) the cast is all male. The main matter appears to be the three narratives, one in each act, in which convicts recount the crimes that brought them to the Siberian prison. Much of the music is violent and some of it is bleak, and yet it shines with a strange, noble beauty. Berg's *Wozzeck,* which Janáček admired, seems to have left a mark on some of it. As an epigraph to his opera Janáček placed the phrase "In every creature a spark of God." Dostoyevsky's *Memoirs from the House of the Dead,* from which the composer adapted his libretto, is a terrible but not a depressing book. (The Russian censor's main objection to it, it seems, was that it might present too "seductive" a picture of prison life.) The opera is brief, amazingly intense, and a masterpiece.

The best introduction to it is a superb recording (London) conducted by Charles Mackerras, sung by Czechoslovakian artists, and played by the Vienna Philharmonic. The New York Philharmonic's performance was not on this level. It was conducted with evident passion by Rafael Kubelik, but he allowed monotonously noisy playing from the orchestra, and there was little of the fine-grained, emotionally keen, lyrical phrasing one hears from the Vienna instrumentalists. The balance was wrong. The soloists and chorus were set on a raised platform well behind the orchestra, and the perspective was dramatically and acoustically awry. Most of the singers barked or bellowed;

perhaps their distance from the audience tempted them to do so. Few of them *sang*. Other things conspired, too, to make this *From the House of the Dead* less than wholly successful. The soprano role was taken, an octave down, by a tenor. The edition used, Mr. Kubelik's own, is based on the composer's autograph and is closer to Janáček's first intentions than the heavily edited version one used to hear before Mr. Kubelik's restoration appeared, some twenty years ago. But Sir Charles employs an edition closer to the composer's final intentions. Janáček's autographs (as John Tyrell explains in an essay that accompanies the London recording) were superseded by fair copies made under his supervision which include his revisions, refinements, and second thoughts; and these are heard in the recording.

The leading roles were taken by Richard Cassilly (Luka), Donald Grobe (Skuratov), and Norman Mittelmann (Shishkov). Some thought had been given to providing an appropriate atmosphere. (In *Erwartung*, the "staging" was limited to Miss Behrens's wearing an elegant, beautiful dress in period style: at some performances the white dress with red roses on it specified in the libretto, at others an elegant Klimtian creation.) Players, singers, and conductor were clad all in black, not in the customary formal black and white. The lighting was gloomy: desk lamps, not overhead light, for the orchestra; light on the singers only while they stood to sing; a glow in the hall enough to read the libretto by, just (but not enough to let one glance at the text, as one might glance at subtitles, and then pay attention to the performers). This was misconceived, I think. An essential symbolic element—as anyone who has seen the opera in the theatre knows—is the wide sky overhead. The first and last of the four scenes (Act III has two) are set in a courtyard—morning light in Act I, sunshine in Act III. An eagle, wounded in Act I, soars, healed, into the sky in Act III, amid cries of "Liberty!" from the convicts. Act II is set on the banks of a broad river, lit by the evening sun, with a steppe visible in the distance. The consistently somber, funereal Philharmonic presentation gloomed the piece and tended to extinguish the divine sparks that should shine in it.

The opera was sung, rightly, in English—in a sensitive, intelligent, and musical new translation by Yveta Synek Graff and Robert T. Jones. A printed libretto was distributed gratis (and the program book contained two good essays by Mr. Jones). I trust there will be a chance soon to hear it in the theatre. Janáček's *Jenůfa* and *Kát'a Kabanová* are now—the *Times* told us recently—"part of the repertories of major companies around the world." But New York is still waiting for a professional staging of *Kát'a*.

Last month, Maurizio Pollini brought to Avery Fisher Hall a program of pieces he has played with especial success in several musical cities: Beethoven's Diabelli Variations, Webern's Opus 27 Variations, and Karlheinz Stockhausen's Piano Piece No. 10. His performance of the Diabelli was unremarkable, however—immaculately polished but lacking in wit, humor, fantasy, and suddenness. (It also could serve as a demonstration that Beethoven's indicated dynamics are literally unobservable on a modern Steinway grand, with its mighty sustaining power.) The Webern variations were bewitching. The Stockhausen brought the audience to its feet, cheering. No. 10—a work that is played in cotton mittens and calls for now palms, now arms to be smashed down on the keyboard—is the most flamboyant of the Piano Pieces and needs a creative executant to give form to its ideas. Mr. Pollini's inventions, some ferocious, some almost reticent, were as exciting as his pianism. The encores were Schoenberg's Six Little Piano Pieces, Opus 19, and the third of Beethoven's Opus 126 Bagatelles. Both were most beautifully rendered, with exquisite sonorities and with a sense of high adventure within a tiny time span.

The Mother of Us All and *Porgy and Bess* are two great American operas. A new production of *Porgy* plays in the immense Radio City Music Hall. The latest production of *Mother*, put on by the Music-Theatre Group/Lenox Arts Center, is in the ninety-nine-seat theatre fitted into St. Clement's Church, on West 46th Street. It is a reduced version similar to that done in the Guggenheim Museum ten years ago: the orchestra is again a quartet—piano, organ, trumpet, and percussion—and the thirty-one roles of the original are distributed among a cast of ten. (The Guggenheim had only eight.) Except at Queens College in 1975, I have heard a full-scale *Mother* only in recordings: a tape of the 1947 première, at Columbia, and the New World Records album of Santa Fe's 1976 production. The première, conducted by Otto Luening, with Dorothy Dow as Susan B. Anthony, remains a performance in some respects unsurpassed. The Santa Fe show was unevenly cast; some of the singing, too broad and general, overrides the fine markings of Virgil Thomson's score. Although Thomson's orchestral ear is keen, the musical essence of his opera is not lost in a modest, continuo-accompanied realization; nor is the largeness of the issues it treats of or the diversity of its characters. The work lives, like Monteverdi's *Poppea*, in the vocal writing. The declamation of Gertrude Stein's fine-spun text is marvellously dexterous, subtle, and surprising—a model of American word-setting. The simple-seeming harmonies are cunningly disposed. The forms are varied and carefully proportioned. The tunes constitute what the composer has called "a memory-book of Victorian play-games and passions...with its gospel hymns and cocky marches, its sentimental ballads, waltzes, darned-fool ditties and intoned sermons...a souvenir of all those sounds and kinds of tunes that were once the music of rural America."

All this survives in—indeed, is enhanced by—an intimate production. The St. Clement's cast is well balanced. Carmen Pelton plays Susan B. with gentle, unrufflable confidence—sometimes a shade close to blandness—and has the steady, floating high notes for the part. Kate Hurney (Constance Fletcher), Linn Maxwell (Anne and Indiana Elliot), John Vining (Jo the Loiterer), and James Javore (Chris the Citizen and Ulysses S. Grant) are outstanding. The neat, simple staging, directed by Stanley Silverman, has settings by Power Boothe and admirable costumes by Lawrence Casey. Richard Cordova's musical direction is deft.

SONGS OF EXPERIENCE

April 25, 1983

ON THE whole, London enjoys better opera than New York. The reason is not that the Royal Opera and the English National Opera singers are superior to those of the Metropolitan and the City Opera: vocally, the levels of the two international and of the two national houses are pretty well comparable. But for at least two reasons singers in London have a better chance to perform at the height of their abilities: the theatres are smaller; and productions are carefully prepared, and run their course with stable casts. From February 12 to February 21, the Royal Opera, at Covent Garden, played only *Tosca;* from February 25 to March 12, only *Carmen.* Eight *Magic Flutes* followed while the company prepared a *Don Carlos* revival, which opened on March 31. The Royal Opera shares its theatre with the Royal Ballet; the English National Opera, at the Coliseum, plays more often but does only two or three different operas in any week, also in coherent, overlapping runs. The New York companies, on the other hand, heavily dependent on subscription sales, must shovel on one opera after another as best they can. The 1983–84 season opens at the City Opera with five different works in four days, and at the Metropolitan with four in five. (*La Bohème* figures on both bills.) Furthermore, the British conditions—coupled, of course, with the possibility in London of combining an operatic stint with recording and concert dates—can attract better guest conductors than the Met and the City Opera seem able to engage. The Covent Garden bills may seem sparse (things look up in July, when consecutive days offer *Fidelio, Macbeth,* and a revival of Peter Maxwell Davies's *Taverner*), but in fact, as readers of *Opera* know, Londoners enjoy an operatic repertory of unmatched richness. In smaller theatres, the works of such men as Lully, Philidor, Handel, Cherubini, Moniuszko, Pacini, and Dvořák reach the stage. And outside the metropolis—instead of our wasteful East Coast system of many local enterprises whose costly productions may be played only two, three, or four times—several year-round companies tour the country, from their home bases, doing each show many times, in different towns. I went over to London for six April days, primarily to see *Don Carlos* and the English National *La forza del destino.* Within easy reach, the Welsh National Opera, Scottish Opera, Kent Opera, Opera

North, and Opera 80 were also playing—with, among other things, carefully prepared and much-discussed productions of *Kát'a Kabanová, The Cunning Little Vixen, Wozzeck, Parsifal, Don Giovanni, Così fan tutte, Fidelio,* and *Madama Butterfly* in its less sentimental, original version. In London itself, John Harbison's *Full Moon in March* had its European première, from the New Opera Company, on a bill with a new Australian piece, Brian Howard's *Inner Voices.*

In fact, neither *Carlos* nor *Forza* was staged with distinction. Both were unimaginative revivals, by staff directors, of once exciting, now worn productions—Luchino Visconti's famous 1958 *Carlos,* Colin Graham's 1968 *Forza.* The merits—and they were considerable—lay elsewhere: in superb conducting, by Bernard Haitink and by John Mauceri; in some individual performances; and, above all, in the sense that each work was being performed by everyone concerned in it not as just another assignment but in the passionate conviction that it was one of the greatest operas in the world. They were two long, grand evenings, totally engrossing. Verdi's belief that in these works he had written operas of a new, elevated, and integrated kind, operas in whose execution every detail should tell, was amply justified. I've never admired them with fewer reservations. *Don Carlos* had the added interest of being performed—for the first time since 1867 by one of the world's major companies—in the original language. The Met continues to use the bad old Italian translation. French-Italian score in hand, I listened to the Met broadcast of *Carlos* shortly before going to London, and noted again how grievously the translation blunts fine points of Verdi's declamation, and, also, how negligent the famous singers have become about fine points of Verdi's dynamics, accents, and phrasing. Haitink worked for faithful observance of these. The Carlos-Posa friendship vow was sung *piano* and *pianissimo,* with the correct articulations, which the Italian words destroy. The whole score seemed nobler, more eloquent, than ever. The cello solo at the start of Act IV (played by Robert Truman) was heartrending. There was no pushing, no rude forcing of the pace or crude recourse to mere loudness. The energy surged from a broad, unhurried command of the long movements, allowing plenty of breathing space for the rubato and the "stretching" of lines which are implicit, if unwritten, in the score. Haitink had decided to use the first, 1867 version of the opera, pared of the Paris ballet but amplified by the passages that the composer cut during rehearsals and never brought to performance or publication: among them the introductory chorus, a Posa solo, and the Elizabeth-Eboli and the Carlos-Philip duets. This 1867 score also has ampler versions of the Carlos-Posa duet, the quartet, and the finale, and is consistent in a way that the familiar revised score of 1883, with its more concise numbers amid the old material, is not. It includes the scene where Elizabeth and Eboli change masks and Eboli has a brief, voluptuous solo incorporating a memory of her veil song. (The Covent Garden performance ran for nearly five hours, with two intermissions.) In just two places Haitink preferred 1883: for the Posa-Philip duet and for the insurrection scene. The newly worked duet is more powerful than what it replaced, but the new insurrection proved too brief to bring the original, large-scale Act IV to an effective conclusion.

The production was an important but only partial demonstration that *Don Carlos* sounds best in the original. The Bulgarian Elizabeth, Stefka Evstatieva, the Hungarian Eboli, Livia Budai, and the Basque Carlos, Peyo Garazzi, showed no very sensitive command of French. Miss Evstatieva was tolerable, and at least she has a voice of the right caliber for the role—something I'd not heard since Montserrat Caballé's Elizabeth. Miss Budai made heavy weather of the veil song's flamenco cadenzas; she should perhaps have chosen one of the composer's alternatives to the piqué F–A sequences. Mr. Garazzi had difficulty with his upper notes. But Thomas Allen, the Posa, was magnificent—phrasing like another De Luca, charging the part with ardor and alert, youthful nobility, never forcing his virile, beautiful voice beyond the bounds of true, pure tone. Robert Lloyd, the Philip, was grand and moving, and will be even more moving if, taking Pol Plançon or Vanni-Marcoux, not Boris Christoff, as his model, he aims at a finer, less "resonated" timbre—at line firmly drawn with the smoothest of pencils, not a powerful brush. These two, John Tomlinson's sonorous, focussed Charles V, and Joseph Rouleau's trenchant Inquisitor all made much of the French. The director, Christopher Renshaw, was stuck with the Visconti scenery, which often contradicts the text (pine trees, myriad flowers, laurels, a window wan with the gray light of dawn all missing; a feeble auto-da-fé setting), but he should not have allowed ladies-in-waiting to invade the monastery that —as Eboli tells us—no woman but the Queen may enter, or deprived Charles V, at the close, of his imperial crown and robe. Covent Garden, like the Met, failed to supply an onstage band.

The English National *Forza* is done in Verdi's 1869 revised version. Back in 1968, this production—perhaps the first in our day to present the opera uncut—was almost as influential as Covent Garden's 1958 *Carlos* in persuading people that the two works, once deemed "problem" operas, are not sprawly, inchoate assemblages of tableaux. Mr. Graham imposed geographical unity on *Forza* by setting it all in Spain, during Napoleon's Peninsular War: this removed the coincidence of having five separate Spaniards turn up on the same Italian battlefield, but it weakened the forceful role played by Destiny in bringing about a series of just such improbable encounters. His larger achievement was to balance the individual and the genre scenes so skillfully that the driving inner theme of the opera—roughly, the tragic impossibility, in this busy world, of evading responsibility or finding rest—became apparent. Increased familiarity with Verdi's original, 1862 score has led me now to prefer that bolder handling of a drama he described as "powerful, singular, and truly vast...something quite out of the ordinary." He revised it in response to repeated criticisms and draped its savage close in a mantle of Manzonian piety. But the new finale he wrote is inspired. Both versions of *Forza*, like all versions of *Carlos*, merit performance.

Josephine Barstow was an incandescent heroine. Della Jones's spunky Preziosilla was the best I have heard. Kenneth Collins's Alvaro was ringing and clear, but unromantic in timbre and in manner. Neil Howlett's Carlo was powerful and richly voiced. Mr. Mauceri, making his London début, won a triumph. He has conducted *Carlos* for the Welsh National and *Otello* for Scottish Opera, but in this country no Verdi except a Yale *Falstaff*. Why don't the American companies have the wit to engage him? By comparison with this *Forza*, most of the Verdi conducting heard at the Met or at the City Opera seems crude, unidiomatic, unphrased, and anachronistic. Like Mr. Haitink, Mr. Mauceri gave his singers time to express themselves. His rhythms were supple, but within a framework of tempi firmly felt. There survives in Paris the score of *Forza* from which Verdi conducted a Madrid production of 1863 (and there is a film of it in the archive of the American Institute for Verdi Studies, at New York University). It is abundantly marked up with passing tempo modifications, fermatas, slurs, and accents of the kind we hear in recorded performances by singers Verdi admired—and could hear in Mr. Mauceri's performance. Good singers feel them naturally; insensitive modern conductors, beating to the letter of the printed text, destroy the singers' individual expression of the words. Miss Barstow's account of "Me pellegrina ed orfana" was well-nigh as free and as personal as Eugenia Burzio's, recorded early this century, and, like it, was both passionate and shapely. A conductor's task is incomplete, Wagner said, until the audience is quite unaware of his presence. Most of his work must be done in rehearsal; at the performance the singers take over. Mr. Mauceri was never obtrusive. While no mere accompanist, he threw the focus of attention on the stage—on the singers and on what they were saying—and seconded the drama with marvellously eloquent orchestral playing.

Dvořák's *Rusalka* (1901), the ninth of his ten operas, is a lovely work —melodious, emotional, picturesque, and richly scored—but one that outside Czechoslovakia has gained no firm place in the repertory. Neither the Metropolitan nor the City Opera has essayed it. (The Juilliard did it in 1975, and two weeks later San Diego gave the American professional première, in a cruelly abridged version.) In England, it reached the professional stage only in 1959, at Sadler's Wells, with Joan Hammond its heroine, and the production did not last. But *Rusalka* has now returned to London in a production, at the English National, that is a hit of the season and draws full houses.

Presenting a dramatic narrative as a dream of one of the characters has become modish. (Tchaikovsky's *Queen of Spades* as Hermann's hallucination and *The Magic Flute* as Tamino's dream are two recent British examples.) Today, the device is a cliché, but for a while it provided jaded directors with an easy way to add a pinch of novelty. Other easy ways were a recourse to flashback—as often in *La traviata*—and the use of exotic or anachronistic settings. (Outside London, Opera 80 is playing *Così fan tutte* in Japanese dress; the young men return to their beloveds disguised as Pinkertons. In Bonn, Norma has been singing "Casta Diva" standing on the hood of an army truck.) Converting *The Flying Dutchman* into Senta's dream does little harm so long as Senta dreams the opera that Wagner composed (Wagner's own dream at one remove, as it were); distorting it into the Steersman's dream that Jean-Pierre Ponnelle mounted in San Francisco and at the Met made non-sense of the drama. Much depends on the work. *Don Carlos* would gain nothing—and lose much—if it were staged as Rodrigo's reverie, Philip II's fantod, or Carlos's chimera; and I've no wish to see Florestan's fantasy or Norma's nightmare. But the English National's "dream" presentation of *Rusalka* does no violence to Dvořák's score and lends interest to a libretto that has stood in the way of the work's general acceptance.

The "lyrical fairy tale," its text by the dramatist Jaroslav Kvapil, combines La Motte Fouqué's *Undine* and Andersen's *The Little Mermaid*. Essentially, it is a version of the incompatibility, or Cupid-and-Psyche, myth. A mortal and a supernatural being fall in love. Sometimes, after tests successfully passed, the tale has a happy ending (Wagner's *Die Feen*, Strauss's *Die Frau ohne Schatten*). Sometimes one partner fails a test, or seems to, and then the lovers can be united only in death *(Swan Lake, The Flying Dutchman)* or must part forever (the Mélusine stories, *La Sylphide, Lohengrin, Rusalka* and its sources). By extension, the pursuit of the elusive or unattainable can become an allegory of the artist and his muse *(The Fairy's Kiss)*. The Helen act of Goethe's *Faust* is the strangest and grandest statement. Kvapil's version takes the form of a series of dreamlike emotional scenes—the water nymph sings to the silver moon of her love for a mortal, the water goblin pours out his grief at her defection, the wood nymphs' hymning of enchanted nature turns to lament when they learn of Rusalka's fate—varied, almost too conscientiously, by episodes of Bohemian rustic comedy (for the gamekeeper and the kitchen boy) and witchcraft, and by a stately court scene. Dvořák set it all as a long, beautiful tone poem with contrasting movements. Václav Kašlík and Josef Svoboda, in a memorable 1960 Prague production, directed and designed it as such, seeking not to interpret or explain the action but simply to deck it appropriately. David Pountney, the director of the English National staging, treats it as an adventure of adolescent sexuality.

Rusalka lies sleepless in her late-Victorian nursery. The wood nymphs are her carefree prepubescent sisters. The witch is her formidable governess, and the kindly, understanding old goblin is her grandfather, in a wheelchair. Since this is an Oedipal interpretation, Rusalka dreams of being embraced by her handsome father; he is ready to pet her, but sadly she sees him return to the gleaming, adult charms of the princess, a glamorous young mother figure. Mr. Pountney's working is not rigid or schematic but something more sensitive and more exciting—part dream, part allegory of experience, and part playful transposition. The wood nymphs sport on rocking horse and scooter. Gamekeeper and kitchen boy are two rag dolls that tumble from the toy closet. The magic in the music finds its reflection. The nursery floor opens to disclose a forest pool, above which Rusalka hovers on the nursery swing. Stefanos Lazaridis's elegant white settings and Nick Chelton's lighting are beautiful. Maybe there is just a hint of chic, tony advertising—of the Magritte-like adventures awaiting heroines who sip Smirnoff or bathe in Badedas—but the precision and poignancy of the images dispel any color-supplement taint. In Act II, a huge glass tank fills most of the stage, dividing Rusalka from the adult world she longs to join. The aqueous metaphors of the original are echoed as people peer in mockingly at her—at the queer fish their prince has brought home. Father dances voluptuously with Mother, while Rusalka's partners are courteous little boys. In Act III, the security of the nursery walls is shattered; menacing forms from the world without have broken through them.

The production, delicate and rich in imaginative detail, is executed with a finesse that would be difficult to achieve in New York's less intimate houses. Although the Coliseum, seating twenty-four hundred, is London's largest theatre, it is hardly large by American opera-house standards. Built as a music hall, it was designed to make people feel close to the stage. (The Coliseum has eighteen rows of seats in the orchestra; the Met has thirty-one.) Grand opera there has the impact and directness of chamber opera, and chamber opera is not lost. There have been Met productions (*Lulu*, for one) and individual performances (Catherine Malfitano's Violetta) no less delicate and detailed, but less tellingly housed. The English National company also has the advantage of performing regularly in the language of its audience, and therefore presents not an exotic and irrational entertainment but drama that means something. Actresses are likely to act better when they know that their listeners are following what they say. Eilene Hannan, the Rusalka, onstage throughout the long opera, gave an exquisite performance, limpidly sung. All it lacked was a greater feeling for legato—an insistence on sustaining notes for their full value, so that they press against their neighbors and join into a line, instead of separating them in the modern manner. John Treleaven, the prince, was forthright, insufficiently romantic. Sarah Walker, the witch, and Lois McDonall, the princess, looked wonderful and acted splendidly, but sounded worn of voice in the upper reaches. Fiona Kimm's kitchen boy was bright and winning, and virtuoso in rag-doll movements. (As the heroine of Harbison's opera, which I saw in rehearsal, Miss Kimm both sang and danced with accomplishment.) A company débutante, Joan Rodgers, was a sweetly radiant first wood nymph. Richard Van Allan's goblin grandfather—like his Father Guardian in *Forza*—was gravely moving. Lionel Friend conducted a tender, richly played, very satisfying performance.

FEAST OF REASON, FLOW OF SOUL

May 2, 1983

CHARLES WUORINEN has been in fluent, fertile vein, composing copiously and composing well. In six April days, works of his appeared on the bills of at least five New York concerts; two of them were world premières, one was new to America, and one new to New York. I heard three of the premières; they were exhilarating pieces that left one regretful they were done only once. The most captivating of all was the Horn Trio (1981), given its first performance, last week, at a Group for Contemporary Music concert at the 92nd Street Y. It lasts ten and a half minutes. It is for horn, violin, and piano, and was played by Julie Landsman (to whom it is dedicated), Benjamin Hudson, and the composer. Their performance was cultivated, witty, and brilliant. The work's demands, especially on the lips and breath of the hornist, are virtuoso. Wuorinen has lately forsworn writing program notes, believing (so a program note for the Horn Trio said) "that the listener should simply listen." I simply listened. The first epithet that occurs to me is "Haydnish," by which I would indicate a play of musical ideas so dexterous, inventive, and happy that a listener to them smiles with pleasure. The music dances on its way, changing gait sometimes at a proposal from one of the three instruments, sometimes as if on a new impulse commonly shared. There is a seductive waltz episode. The work, in one movement, is "classical" in being a discourse on pregnant motifs, even on melodious themes. Excellently Haydnish is the surprise when an apparent close in (more or less) C proves to be not final: it dissolves, and there are two more turns in the path and a delightful stretch through which the players tripple merrily before the true, satisfying end is reached.

The other pieces employed consorts more exotic. *Archaeopteryx* (1978), for bass trombone and ten players, was given its New York première by the St. Luke's Chamber Ensemble in Merkin Hall three days before the Horn Trio. It is one of two works composed some years ago for the trombonist David Taylor; the companion is *Archangel*, for bass trombone and string quartet, which the Group introduced in December, 1978. Where *Archangel* is severe, dark, declamatory, *Archaeopteryx* is more jerkily animated. Wuorinen's renunciation of program notes leaves the listener guessing why the piece is named for a prehistoric bird, but the title inevitably sets up images in the mind. Rightly or wrongly, they seemed to be reflected in the music. The work lasts fifteen minutes. It begins with scrappy, punchy sounds, and then the soloist embarks on short flights, some of which inspire cadenza exchanges with members of the ensemble (three flutes, two clarinets, two horns, tuba, piano, and marimba). Sustained melodies alternate with skittering and dithering. Eventually, the music "fossilizes" (as the archaeopteryx did). Hard, bright stratified chords made a strange new sound that has continued to haunt me.

Two days earlier, the New Music Consort, in Carnegie Recital Hall, gave the world première of the Trio for Bass Instruments (double-bass, bass trombone, and tuba, played by Joseph Tamosaitis, Mr. Taylor, and David Braynard). It was composed in 1981. It is eight minutes of lively, diverting Stravinskian play—not an important piece but an attractive one, and lighter in touch than the forces involved would suggest. Wuorinen's debts to Stravinsky are unconcealed, joyfully acknowledged: in this Trio, in the Two-Part Symphony (a twelve-note symphony in C), in the layered wind sonorities of *The Winds* and *Archaeopteryx*. He is moving on paths toward which Stravinsky pointed. His music has been always exuberant, often glittering, never dull. In the latest works, there seems to be a new refinement and precision.

The Chicago Symphony's concert presentation of *Das Rheingold* in Carnegie Hall last week looked good. Platformed stage right, above a phalanx of harps, the three Rhinemaidens wore vivid shades of marine blue and green, and Wellgunde was spangled. The giants were platformed stage left, and Erda was there, too. Gods and dwarfs stood centrally, at the foot of the conductor's high podium. Fricka—no friend to animals, as we learn later in the cycle from the way she lashes her rams—had a white fox fur. The men wore conventional evening dress. The hall was held to a European level of brightness, which lent a festive air to the performance and also made it easy to follow a handsome bilingual libretto that was distributed free. The stage was brighter still, with spotlights playing upon the singers. It was a "production." The spatial distinctions added aural and visual interest to the progress of the score. Without this Chicago *Rheingold*, Wagner's centenary year would be passing in New York all but *Ring*-less: the Met's *Walküre* revival was unhappy, and the Bayreuth *Ring* on television proves unlistenable to and unwatchable by any serious Wagnerian.

The star of the evening was the Loge, Siegfried Jerusalem. When he made his Met début, in 1980, as Lohengrin, I admired his full, easy lyrical tenor and regretted his lack of dramatic presence; in the long white coat of the Met production, which René Kollo had worn as an earnest young doctor might, he resembled a diffident junior nurse. All that has changed. Loge was one of the two characters in this *Rheingold* fully realized. Without ever breaking histrionically out of the concert frame, Mr. Jerusalem listened to what the others were saying; he stood as Loge would stand; he used small but elegant gestures that told strongly. Nowadays, it has become common to assign the role to a

Spieltenor, a character tenor. In the first six *Ring* cycles of my youth, the part was played by the heroic tenor—Set Svanholm—who went on to sing Siegmund and Siegfried. And Wagner's own first Bayreuth Loge —Heinrich Vogl—was a Tristan, a Siegmund, and a Siegfried; he was an Otello, a Dalibor, an Aeneas in *The Trojans.* Loge is the only *Rheingold* personage who appears in all three subsequent *Ring* operas, blazing out in the last act of each. His later manifestations are not impersonated but left to the stage technicians and the orchestral players to represent; in *Das Rheingold* he has the longest solos. He needs big vocal resources that he can use lightly. Mr. Jerusalem, a Bayreuth Parsifal, filled the bill. Whereas in the television *Ring* Loge is distorted into a Uriah Heep, Mr. Jerusalem played him with the appropriate charm, wit, and airy grace.

The other fully live character was Alberich, in the person of Hermann Becht. He enacted the role in both his physical and, so to speak, his vocal bearing. I have been listening to a very fine HMV seven-disc album, "Wagner on Record, 1926—1942." Not only its three stars— Frida Leider, Lauritz Melchior, and Friedrich Schorr—but, by and large, all the singers represented show a psychological command of their roles, made manifest in individual rhythmic, tonal, and verbal inflections, superior to most of what we hear in today's elaborately directed Wagner performances. Mr. Becht had their way of bringing phrases—and the character and his significance—to life.

The Wotan, Siegmund Nimsgern, was plain. His voice is a fine, forthright bass-baritone, clear, steady, and incisive; the interpretation lacked grandeur, nobility, godlike authority. Gwynne Howell was a lyrical Fasolt, and Malcolm Smith a hollow-toned Fafner. Robert Tear was a spry Mime. Fricka is a soprano role accessible to and often sung by mezzos. Bernard Shaw praised the first Bayreuth Fricka, Friederike Sadler-Grün (she was also the soprano Norn), for her singing of Brangäne's, Senta's, and the Woodbird's music at Wagner's 1877 London concerts. The Chicago Fricka, Gabriele Schnaut, was a rather lugubrious and uneven young mezzo. Mary Jane Johnson's Freia was untidy. Donner and Froh, John Cheek and Dennis Bailey, were undercast (Wagner's first Bayreuth Froh also sang Siegfried), but there were some sweet notes in Mr. Bailey's account of his two ariettas. The Rhinemaidens, Michelle Harman-Gulick, Elizabeth Hynes, and Emily Golden, were conscientious and carefully tuned, not playful or lilting. Jan DeGaetani was miscast as Erda, lacking both weight and words.

Georg Solti conducted. Breadth of vision, spiritual force, profundity of emotion play small part in his Wagner performances. Admirers of Furtwängler, Knappertsbusch, and Reginald Goodall are readier to concede than to acclaim Sir Georg's virtues. He obtains immaculate and powerful orchestral playing. He has an excited, enthusiastic concern for the passing details of the music. He has keen and committed feelings—for the obvious. He is less hectic than once he was: some touches of vulgarity remained in this *Rheingold*—overboisterous banging of the drums for the giants' arrival, earsplitting anvils—but not many. From Solti's Wagner one hopes in vain for the sense of great events starting to move toward far-off conclusions, for long epic planning (needed especially in *Das Rheingold,* so largely built on pedal points). He stirs the pulse but not the soul of his listeners. Moreover, by his own standards this *Rheingold* was in some ways flawed. Oddities of orchestral balance were perhaps due to insufficient experiment with Carnegie seating plans. At the very start, the bassoons' B-flat was much louder than the double-basses' fundamental E-flat; the cycle began out of kilter. (There was no central bass foundation on which to build; all the double-basses were relegated to stage far left.) The solo harp accompanying the Rhinemaidens' lament—a backstage harp in theatre performances—was so far frontstage that the Rhinemaidens became the accompaniment. In general, the orchestral sound was not deep, rich, warm, enveloping. It suggested a sharp, clear modern recording. Real Wagner orchestral sound is what we hear from Furtwängler, Knappertsbusch, and Goodall—and from Carl Muck's *Siegfried* funeral march recorded in Berlin in 1927, which is very well transferred in the HMV album. Muck's famous Berlin recordings of orchestral Wagner are now available again on two In Sync cassettes.

THOUGHT-EXECUTING FIRES

May 9, 1983

THE CHIEF musical event of the festival Britain Salutes New York 1983 —in this bicentennial of the treaty by which Britain acknowledged the independence of her Thirteen Colonies—has been a set of three thronged concerts given in Symphony Space by Britain's leading chamber ensemble, the Fires of London. At the second of them, on St. George's Day, a mutual transatlantic salute was exchanged, between a great New York composer and the British group: Elliott Carter's latest composition, Triple Duo, had its first performance. It was commissioned by the BBC for the Fires and is "affectionately dedicated to that ensemble and its prime mover, Peter Maxwell Davies." It is the latest in a series of such exchanges: Carter's previous piece, *In Sleep, in Thunder,* was written for the London Sinfonietta, while among recent Davies compositions his Second Symphony was written for the Boston Symphony and his Brass Quintet for the Empire Brass Quintet.

Since Carter's Brass Quintet (1974), which was first played in London, by the American Brass Quintet, his chamber music has been for voice, or voices, and instruments: the Elizabeth Bishop cycle *A Mirror on Which to Dwell* (1975), for soprano and nine players; the cantata *Syringa* (1978), Greek and John Ashbery poems set for mezzo-soprano, bass, and eleven players; and *In Sleep, in Thunder,* six Robert Lowell poems set for tenor and fourteen players. Triple Duo marks his return

435

to a pure instrumental ensemble. The Fires of London were formerly called the Pierrot Players; their instrumental forces are those of Schoenberg's *Pierrot Lunaire* (a quintet of violin/viola and cello, flute and clarinet, and piano), plus percussion. Many works have now been composed for the group, by many composers. (Eight works were played at the Symphony Space concerts, all but Triple Duo being by Davies.) Much of the Fires' repertory is dramatic and includes a singer, dancer, or mime; in fact, they call themselves a music-theatre ensemble. Triple Duo is dramatic, too, in that it is a "play" for enactment by six instruments, its score a "scenario" in which three couples—violin and cello, flute and clarinet, piano and percussion—are the characters. They leap on-stage abruptly, jauntily—as sounds, I mean, not physically, but the musical gestures are graphic. Each strikes an attitude, and then they all start chattering at once. Babble swiftly clarifies into dialogue: into some twenty-two minutes of riveting discourse—a fantasy of discussions, arguments, agreements, seasoned by jests—which is high-spirited, boundlessly inventive, and beautiful in its shapeliness and its sonorities. Each "character" has many facets: flute and clarinet, for example, become almost adversaries when the flutist takes up a shrill piccolo while the clarinet drops its voice an octave, into the wise, lyrical tones of the bass instrument. In another episode, the aggressive little E-flat clarinet, shriller still, dominates the gentle flute. There is a magical, icy passage of tingling chords struck softly on crotales and high piano strings, inspiring the bowed strings to touch in high harmonics and the piccolo to essay a faint, drifting descant.

The Fires are virtuosos: Philippa Davies (flutes), David Campbell (clarinets), Rosemary Furniss (violin/viola), Jonathan Williams (cello), Stephen Pruslin (piano), Gregory Knowles (percussion). They have played Carter's earlier music and were trained to tackle the lively hexalogue of the new piece. They are quick, keen, subtle artists—six distinct personalities, and a peerless ensemble. I hope they record Triple Duo soon. [*They have, on Nonesuch.*]

At the same concert, Davies's *Image, Reflection, Shadow* (1982) had its American première. The title comes from a poem by Charles Senior. Across a scene of stillness, a gull flies; its clear white reflection speeds on the surface of the water; along the green seafloor, passing over weed and rock, its shadow traces a dark, distorted course. At the moment of change of tide,

> *mutations of light and movement*
> *on plant, stone and bird*
> *initiate their mysterious rhythms.*

It is an idea apt for music. There are passages in *Image, Reflection, Shadow* where it finds almost literal representation—where the movement of three differing but related lines generated by one impulse can be perceived. Back in 1961, when Davies's String Quartet appeared, I fumbled with metaphors about the play of changing light on some-

436

thing simple, satisfying, and beautiful in order to suggest the effects of chromatic and rhythmic play around a cantus firmus. Light and landscape and the movements, the sounds—and the silence—of nature are newly important in much of what Davies has composed since he went to live in the Orkneys, a decade or so ago. "Fancifully perhaps, I often see the great cliff-bound bay before my window where the Atlantic and the North Sea meet as a huge alchemical crucible, rich in speculative connotations, and at all times a miracle of ever-changing reflected light," he wrote in a note on the chamber piece *A Mirror of Whitening Light* (1977). And in a note on his Second Symphony (1980) that it was, among other things, "a direct response to the sounds of the ocean's extreme proximity, subtly permeating all of one's existence—from the gentlest of Aeolian harp vibrations as the waves strike the cliffs on the other side of the bay in calm weather, to explosive shudders through the very fabric of the house as huge boulders grind over each other directly below the garden during the most violent westerly gales." Much dwelling on natural analogues may begin to suggest, quite wrongly, a latter-day Mendelssohn plotting a new *Fingal's Cave*. It is the musical alchemy at work in *A Mirror* that makes it a beautiful and satisfying piece. In the symphony, the interaction of different wave forms which Davies observed has been transmuted into specifically musical procedures. On the other hand, much dwelling on technical matters—permutations of plainchants, the magic squares that can determine pitches and durations, the unconventional harmonic foundations on which Davies's recent works rest firmly—would begin to suggest composition by formula and system, and obscure the fact that he is one of the most expressive, communicative, and immediately inspired of contemporary composers. His music, like Carter's, offers a rich field to the analyst. It is scrupulously, thoroughly, and intricately made. Davies is readier than Carter to let the listener take into account any extramusical stimuli. But Carter has told how the birds, animals, insects, and plants of the Arizona desert influenced the evolution of his First String Quartet, and how Hart Crane's *The Bridge* suggested musical ideas in his Symphony of Three Orchestras. Davies is readier than Carter to let musics of the past—whether in the guise of a citation, an allusion, a parody, or a large-scale formal procedure—play an audible creative part in one of his compositions. But Carter, in a public discussion before the concert at which Triple Duo was played, revealed that a close study of Schubert's Octet went into its making. Davies is prolific and is actively concerned with performance. He is a chronicler and critic of, a participant in, and, indeed, a shaper of life in his society. He is prominent in Britain in a way that Carter—working in a land where music-making is in large part a branch of the entertainment industry, in some part a mere academic discipline, and in but small part a keeper of the public's social, political, and moral conscience—probably could not be without compromise of his adamantine integrity.

Enough of likenesses and differences. In short, both composers—

though one could hardly mistake a Davies score for a Carter score, so different are they in sound and facture—are among the creators who make a listener glad to be living when they are, eager to discover each new work as it appears, excited to explore the new imaginative realms that each one offers. In that note to *A Mirror of Whitening Light,* Davies said, "Over the last few years I have tried to evolve a musical language simple and strong enough to make the complex forms with which I became involved meaningful and audible—particularly with regard to functional harmony operating over and relating large spans of time." Carter might say something similar, but at the discussion he preferred to suggest that increasing familiarity with his earlier music has made his later works seem—as a colleague wrote of *In Sleep, in Thunder*—"so openly expressive, so directly approachable." A glance at either man's score will quickly dispel any notion that "accessibility" implies any of the Simple Simon banalities, staleness, or old-clothes parade sometimes hailed as a return to romanticism. In a note that accompanies Paul Jacobs's brilliant new recording of Carter's Piano Sonata and *Night Fantasies* (Nonesuch), the composer scorns the "musical journeyman, who employs easily worn-out routines developed by others or even himself," and writes of "the wish not to repeat oneself but to constantly explore more vivid ways of presenting the musical vision in all its freshness, to be always setting out on a new adventure."

Image, Reflection, Shadow is in three movements—the first a long, quiet unfolding, the second an extended scherzo, the third a slow passacaglia that accelerates into a brilliant dance. There are images of stillness—and of small, delicate movement within stillness—so beautiful that listeners catch their breath. There is exuberant, joyful energy that sets their pulses racing. The forty-minute piece is in some ways a serene-hearted companion and sequel to the poignant *Ave Maris Stella* (1975). In *Ave Maris Stella,* the percussionist plays a marimba, with its pure, mellow, "enchanted" sound. In *Image,* he plays a cimbalom, whose dusky twangle gives the new work its special color. (Mr. Knowles became fascinated by the instrument during a Fires tour of Hungary, acquired one, and mastered it.) It stamps out slow mid-range melodies as if in notes of ancient, dirty gold, a fuzz around their shine. With a buzz and a flurry, it can work itself up into a fine frenzy. There is a short cimbalom cadenza in the second movement and a long, expressive one in the third.

The Carter and Davies premières were framed by two of the arrangements of old music—clear, clean, and exquisite—that Davies has made for the Fires: *Kinloche His Fantassie* (from a seventeenth-century Scottish keyboard piece) and a set of Renaissance Scottish Dances. The two other concerts, conducted by John Carewe, were devoted to music theatre. At the first, *Le Jongleur de Notre Dame* (1978) had its American première. In Davies's setting of the old story, the abbot sings; a juggler juggles and mimes; the seated instrumentalists (cello and piano/celesta), on one side, provide a continuo; clarinettist, flutist, and percussionist play monks but "speak" their lines—questioning, scolding, clucking away like so many Melitones—on their instruments (Mr. Knowles taps and jingles an eloquent tambourine); and the Virgin signifies her approval of the juggler's act in a violin solo. A children's band (coming on this occasion from J.H.S. 143) plays a buoyant intrada and recessional, in 7/8. The monks' gifts to Our Lady take the form of virtuoso solos. (There is a marimba handy for Brother Gregory; devising an extended tambourine solo might overtax even Davies's and Mr. Knowles's powers of invention.) *Le Jongleur* is a fine-grained, intimate piece, containing episodes in old dance movements and permeated by a plainchant for the Nativity of the Virgin. I would like to hear it in a small, resonant church; both in Edinburgh Cathedral (where I first heard it) and in Symphony Space it sounded exquisite but slight.

The other music-theatre pieces—*Eight Songs for a Mad King* (1969), *Miss Donnithorne's Maggot* (1974), and *Vesalii Icones* (1969)—date from Davies's Expressionist years, when much of his music was violent, frequently painful, extravagantly adventurous in its means (the mad king is asked to span more than four octaves), promiscuous in its allusions, searing, shocking, and boundlessly exciting. The pieces have not lost their power to sear, shock, and excite—not in such performances as the Fires gave. Michael Rippon, a rather grossly jocular abbot in *Le Jongleur*, was memorable as George III, and through all his screaming, wheezing, mumbling—and singing—in all registers managed to make just about every word clear. Mary Thomas was a spectacular Miss Donnithorne (the possible model for Dickens's Miss Havisham), but I prefer the earlier production of the *Maggot*, in which the unfortunate lady burst from the moldy wreck of her giant wedding cake and had the players around her, to the current one, in which she keeps to one side of the stage and they keep to the other. These are ensemble pieces, chamber music, not solos with accompaniment: every player participates as an individual in the dramas. Other things being equal, I prefer sanity to madness, but the subject matter and Davies's fierce parody and distortion techniques are matched. Ideas are challenged; assumptions are tested.

In the final performance, of *Vesalii Icones*, for dancer and six players, the Fires' execution attained an intensity that—how can one put it?—somehow could make a listener feel that all he had ever heard, felt, suffered had been leading to this moment. Davies has likened the "levels" in the piece to the effect of disparate imagery on three parallel panes of glass: while the eye focusses on one, images from the others modify and distract its perceptions. The musical levels are plainchant (the Good Friday proper), cheap popular music (a blowsy Victorian hymn tune, a foxtrot), and "my 'own' music derived from the other two." Visually, there are also three levels: the Vesalius anatomical engravings; the Stations of the Cross, with their traditional iconography; and the dancer's own body. But musical and visual elements are fused,

439

too—more closely in this performance, with choreography by Ian Spink, and Tom Yang its dedicated and electric dancer, than in any other I have seen. The cellist, seated apart, becomes in the dancer's eyes now Pilate, now a scourger, now Veronica. Musical gestures and physical actions are barely distinguished as with every nerve alert one lives through the Passion.

PASTORAL-TRAGICAL

May 16, 1983

THE FIRST opera, if one reckons Jacopo Peri's *Dafne* a private experiment—a dramatic scene pointing the way—was his *Euridice,* produced in Florence in 1600. Some scenes from it were done in New York in 1894, at the Berkeley Lyceum, on a bill with Royall Tyler's *The Contrast* —the first opera paired with the first American comedy (1787). *Euridice* had its full New York première last month in Christ Church, on Park Avenue, given by the Camerata of the Mannes College of Music. Once opera had been invented, there was no stopping it. It changed musical history. It changed the appearance of our cities, in some of which the opera house is a more prominent monument than the cathedral. For nearly four centuries, it has claimed the chief attention of most composers and has swallowed up huge sums of private and public money. It was curious to sit in the church, enjoying a modest—but accomplished—production, and reflect that this was how opera began. Peri's *Euridice* was overshadowed by Monteverdi's greater treatment of the same subject, seven years later, in his *Orfeo.* Monteverdi and his librettist, Alessandro Striggio, built upon the work of Peri and his librettist, Ottavio Rinuccini, developing their ideas. Dr. Burney, who owned scores of the Peri, of Giulio Caccini's setting of the same text (performed in Florence in 1602), and of the Monteverdi, declared in his *History* that he was "unable to discover Monteverdi's superiority." It can be discovered. Nevertheless, Peri's *Euridice* provokes astonishment that the inventor of opera got most things right first time off, defining and turning to dramatic effect the tensions—between speech and song, recitative and aria, progressive narrative and formal repetition, solo and chorus, voices and instruments, singing and scenery, acting and dancing—in which opera, the most inclusive of the arts, has lived ever since. Monteverdi, Handel, Gluck, Mozart, Wagner, Roger Sessions, and Peter Maxwell Davies had strong foundations on which to build.

Four years ago, I urged Peri's *Euridice* on the Juilliard School as an opera dramatic, melodious, and well worth staging. Mannes College, quicker to scan the opened horizons of music-making in our day, has taken the lead. Last year, its production of Marco da Gagliano's *Dafne* (1608) was praised (see page 259). Next year, it moves onto unfamiliar ground, with Loreto Vittori's *Galatea,* published in Rome in 1639, and a reform opera at a time when decadence—in the shape of drama subordinated to spectacle—had already set in. The Mannes Camerata, directed by Paul Echols, has come far, fast. *Euridice* has a cast of seventeen. (In the Mannes production, three singers doubled roles, and—as in Howard Mayer Brown's performing edition—the roles of Charon and Rhadamanthus were merged.) Mr. Echols's artists were fresh and confident in their approach to a goal defined in his program note as "a full-bodied but extremely flexible voice capable of singing long, sinuous phrases, of negotiating intricate coloratura ornaments, and of employing vibrato as a coloristic device." The Orpheus, Toshiaki Kunii, achieved a fine crescendo of intensity in the strophes of "Funeste piagge," with its poignant refrain. Seven stanzas of prologue, from Tragedy, were not too many when Evelyn Simon decorated each of them differently. Marlene Hernandez, as Daphne, the nymph whose announcement of Eurydice's death suddenly clouds the pastoral rejoicing, held the listeners intent on her long narrative. Gregory Lorenz, as the shepherd Arcetrus, held them intent on his long narrative of Orpheus' despair and his meeting with Venus.

Euridice was sung in Italian. Authenticity would require a performance in the language of the audience. The expressiveness of comprehended words heightened by music was Peri's first aim; opera would not have caught on so surely had those first Florentine performances been given in, say, German. But Mannes is a teaching institution. Students need to master Italian (and other languages). On the other hand, students must also learn how to communicate directly and intimately with an audience—and that can be done fully only in the audience's language. Student productions should be sometimes in the original, sometimes in translation. Each way teaches different lessons. The Mannes singers evidently knew what they were saying. They uttered the words expressively even when they mispronounced them. There was a bigger band—seventeen players, plus a quartet of cornetts and dulcians in a gallery—than, on my reading of the scant surviving evidence, I believe Peri had in 1600. But opera orchestras soon grew larger, and in any case Mr. Echols's aim was not "to re-create the original performance" but "to recapture the over-all vocal style and instrumental sound of early Italian music drama." He is an adept at using available forces, spaces, and individual abilities stylishly. If his instrumentalists sat between the singers and the audience, not in the wings, if they often took the beat from their conductor, instead of watching and taking their cues directly from the singers they accompanied, and if their obbligatos were composed in an improvisatory style, instead of being improvised, there were practical reasons therefor. (For one, the church setting provided no wing space.) There was simple, effective scenery: tall pavilions rose up as if by magic in the sanctuary; moving panels suggested prospects of Arcady or Avernus. The 1600 production used lighting effects—a contemporary report tells of simulated daylight in the pastoral scenes and a coppery glow, with tongues of flame glimpsed through rifts, in the Underworld—and so did this one. Above all, the music drama moved affectingly and well. The familiar, wonderful tale—unfaded allegory of music's power to influence and alter our lives—was told in accents and with a scenic shapeliness that caught one up afresh in its emotional situations.

Critic after critic, year after year, has been returning from Finland— from visits to the Savonlinna Festival and to Helsinki—proclaiming that there, at least, opera is still taken seriously, that there "noble attempts, like those of Tippett and Berg, to revive its ancient function," of reëxpressing social myth, are not (as Christopher Small puts it in his *Music–Society–Education*) "doomed to triviality by the essential frivolity of its audience." In the last decade alone, fourteen new Finnish operas have been produced. (In fifteen years, the Met has not put on a single American opera—the last was Marvin David Levy's *Mourning Becomes Electra*, in 1967.) One of them, Joonas Kokkonen's *The Last Temptations*, first staged in 1975, is approaching its two-hundredth performance. Aulis Sallinen's *The Red Line*, first staged in 1978, is approaching its hundredth. Both were created in Helsinki by the Finnish National Opera, whose house holds five hundred, and have been played at Savonlinna, in a castle courtyard holding about two thousand. The company has taken the two works to Germany, Switzerland, and Sweden, and *The Red Line* to Russia. In 1979, it brought them to London, to Sadler's Wells. Both have been recorded. Last month, the Finnish National Opera visited the Met and gave two performances each of *The Last Temptations* and *The Red Line*.

They are certainly serious operas. A résumé of *The Last Temptations* begins:

> Paavo Ruotsalainen, a revivalist preacher, lies restless on his deathbed.... He relives in his imagination the trials of his life and his struggles with his own sinfulness and with his enemies. Again and again he dreams that he is prevented from going through the barrier of Heaven.

And a résumé of *The Red Line* begins:

> Topi, a poor crofter, lives with his wife Riika and their children in the bleak north Finnish backwoods, eking out a miserable livelihood near starvation level. A marauding bear... has just killed one of their precious sheep.

In *The Last Temptations*, Paavo and his wife, Riitta, "accidentally trample their baby underfoot" while struggling to prevent frost from destroying their meager crop. In *The Red Line*, Topi and Riika's undernourished children sicken, and "one after another they die." Kokkonen's opera ends happily in that Paavo gets to Heaven. (So the libretto suggests, although at the Met the wicket representing Heaven's bar remained closed.) Sallinen's opera ends with mingled hope and tragedy. The winning of a people's election—its ballot papers marked with a red line—brings "the promise of a new life," but not for Topi, who has gone off to fight the bear and, offstage, is lying dead: "Blood is pouring from his throat, in a red line."

The libretto of *The Last Temptations*, condensed from a play by Lauri Kokkonen, the composer's cousin, is close in matter to Ibsen's *Brand* but lacks its high dramatic images and vivid characterizations. Kokkonen's music has roots in Mussorgsky and Sibelius; some passages suggest Hindemith. In the Met, the piece seemed earnest but rather drab. It is more enjoyable in the recording; listening to the voices and the instruments in closeup and following the words in a bilingual libretto, one kindles to the sober intensity of Kokkonen's score and to glowing performances from artists who knew that what they said was being understood. (The recording, on Deutsche Grammophon, is of the 1977 Savonlinna performance.) The Met, too large a house to allow any opera to make its full effect, was particularly hard on *The Last Temptations*. The piece was played against black curtains on a bare stage, with a few pieces of furniture and hints of homestead—a kind of décor more effective in small theatres than in large, where it becomes funereal. Martti Talvela, for whom the main role was tailored, was ill; Jaakko Ryhänen, who played Paavo, has a big bass but was a stodgy actor. Ritva Auvinen, as Riitta, shines out on the records but in the Met sometimes pushed her soprano into impurity and unsteadiness. The other principal roles, Paavo's grown son Juhana, a tenor, and a village smith and revivalist, a baritone, were well taken by Matti Heinikari and Tapani Valtasaari. A semichorus of three women and three men playing various roles in the narrative offered keen, brilliant cameo performances. The choral writing is important; rugged old hymn tunes are prominent. In a smaller theatre, the Finnish chorus's sheer weight of fervent tone is probably tremendous, a dramatic presence in itself.

There is more professional skillfulness, less homespun, in the composition of *The Red Line*. Sallinen came to prominence with *The Horseman*, produced in Savonlinna in 1975. *The Red Line* is his second opera. (A third, *The King Goes Forth to France*, has been jointly commissioned by Covent Garden, the BBC, and Savonlinna.) Mussorgsky seems again to be an influence, traces of Prokofiev are evident, and throwing in the names of Janáček and Berg may begin to suggest something of the musical world. The libretto, Sallinen's own, is based on Ilmari Kianto's 1911 novel of the same title. Its allegories are somewhat ambivalent and obscure, perhaps deliberately so. The marauding bear, according to the synopsis, is "a symbol of hostile Nature," but its proximity to the Russian border is more than once stressed. The Socialist election victory may bring that "promise of a new life" to the people of Finland, but coincident with its announcement "the bear has awakened and has come to attack once again." A Socialist agitator and his glib clichés are treated satirically, and Act I ends with something close to a parody of a Prokofiev uplifting patriotic assertion. In an Act

II double-chorus of opposed ideologies, the group led by a young priest, questioning the benevolence of "the new reckless spirit" that flies over Finland on red wings, has the more eloquent music. In an *Opera News* interview, Sallinen observes that a Moscow critic of *The Red Line* complained that the working class had not been "positively" presented. He continues, "Well, I see problems in life, contradictions in the struggle toward belief, and I have to portray things as I see them." His young priest represents the voice of gentleness and seems to be the composer's spokesman. The village vicar—at least, in Topi's dream of him—is an inhumane monster. A cobbler and his wife, Kunilla, ardent Socialists, and a kindly, pious old peasant woman, Kaisa, who tells Riika that the children's deaths are God's punishment of her and Topi for voting the red line, represent other extremes. In the final scene, there is this dialogue:

> KUNILLA *(brandishing a newssheet):* News from Helsinki! Our party is winning. Now the power of gentry and priests will vanish from this land. "New land distribution! Pensions for the old!....Children to be clothed and educated!....The whole way of life will improve!"
>
> KAISA: How can people be so blind? Do you not see how the Lord has already chastised this house? . . .
>
> KUNILLA: It's you who are blind. Don't you see it's the gentry's fault that there is death in this house? If there had been money and medicine, the children would not have died like puppies.

And at that point the dogs start barking. It is spring: the bear has attacked again, and Topi goes out to do battle with it. Sallinen does not try to answer the questions he raises. But most movingly he presents Topi and Riika as people of simple, lovable, heroic goodness in their struggle for existence against the forces of both cruel nature and an unjust society. There is something of Janáček, and something of Kurt Weill, in his clear, unaffected, unpatronizing portraits of the brave couple. *The Red Line* is an opera one warms to. One would need to know the novel and the Finnish political situation before deciding that it is also, as it seems to be, a passionate if veiled denunciation of Russian Communism as something whose dangers outweigh its benefits, even to the oppressed—a remedy worse than the disease. The first act proved dramaturgically a shade scrappy; a peddler's song, reminiscent of Varlaam's song in *Boris,* seemed too deliberate an injection of variety. Act II moved more surely. Sallinen has a flair for evocative, theatrically telling orchestral timbres. There is a chilling midwinter moment when a naïve political discussion is suddenly cut short by mysterious, menacing sounds, with offstage horns. The dogs on both sides of the border start barking, for they "sense what the people cannot: the bear is turning in his sleep."

Jorma Hynninen and Taru Valjakka, Topi and Riika, were fine performers. He is a baritone with a quick, live, emotional quality in his utterance and a beautiful, unforced tone. She is a lustrous soprano.

Both are honest, unmannered, eloquent actors, good to look at, and portrayers of real people. There were first-rate performances from Matti Salminen (the peddler); Erkki Aalto (the young priest); Iris-Lilja Lassila (Kunilla, a speaking role), Anita Välkki, whom I last heard in 1961 at Covent Garden as a bright Brünnhilde (Kaisa); and Eero Erkkilä, the company's chorusmaster (the agitator). The setting—another almost bare stage, with black wings but, this time, a white backcloth— was far too large. But, to a woman and a man, the Finnish company, both here and in *The Last Temptations*, showed a fine command of stage space. I've seldom seen a chorus move so well, so surely. In the Met, the effect of these productions was impressive. In a house of more suitable scale—say, the Brooklyn Academy—it would have been overwhelming.

DESERT SONG

May 23, 1983

BRITAIN, HAVING sent over its best contemporary-music group, Peter Maxwell Davies's Fires of London, to salute New York, followed with some of its best Baroque-music singers and players: John Eliot Gardiner's Monteverdi Choir and English Baroque Soloists. They gave three concerts, in interestingly different venues: Alice Tully Hall, Town Hall, and the Cathedral Church of St. John the Divine. (In addition, the Soloists gave an instrumental concert in the Brooklyn Academy of Music.) The first concert, in Tully, brought a thrilling performance of Handel's *Israel in Egypt*. *Israel* (1739), a choral oratorio, and *Messiah* (1742), that unique amalgam of oratorio, Passion, and extended anthem, are odd ones out in the long series of Handel oratorios. They appeared between *Saul* and *Samson,* breaking for a while the sequence of dramatic oratorios with individual characters. *Israel* has fewer airs than any other Handel oratorio, and *Messiah* fewer than any but *Israel.* Neither work found much favor at its London première. *Messiah* became popular later, in the 1750s, but when Handel at last revived *Israel,* somewhat revamped, in 1756, his friend Mrs. Delany reported that it "did not take, it is too solemn for common ears." It pleased Victorian ears, however, and became a favorite second only to *Messiah*—in massive performances, with large choirs, large orchestras, and, despite Handel's heavy scoring, added instrumental lines. Mendelssohn composed an organ part. Tovey, in his lively essay on the oratorio, talks of performances with four thousand singers and players, and of a bill proudly announcing that the duet "The Lord is a man of war" would be sung by four hundred tenors and basses. In our day, *Israel in Egypt* fell back into critical disfavor. Winton Dean, in his great book on the oratorios, calls it "unsatisfactory as a whole and musically very unequal...rather a jumble of epic and anthem with a few scenes of great dramatic power." I summarize this history because with their performance of *Israel* the Monteverdi Choir and the Baroque Soloists have opened a new chapter in its critical appraisal—both in New York and, to judge from the London reviews, in England, where they performed it a few days before coming here.

Israel in Egypt is a triptych. The first panel, "The Lamentation of the Israelites Over the Death of Joseph," is Handel's immense Funeral Anthem on the Death of Queen Caroline ("The ways of Zion do mourn") with altered words. The second, "Exodus," tells of the plagues that smote Egypt and of the crossing of the Red Sea. The third is "Moses' Song"—the jubilant sequence of Exodus 15: 1–21, beginning and ending "I will sing unto [in verse 21, "Sing ye to"] the Lord, for he hath triumphed gloriously: the horse and his rider hath he thrown into the sea." Elegy, epic narrative, and epinicion: in each, Handel works with great blocks of choral and instrumental sound, building balanced structures in which there are light, air, and spaciousness as well as grandeur. No one has ever been deaf to the incidental, picturesque delights of the work: the hopping of the frogs "even in the King's chambers," the buzzing and the itchy, scratching string figures that accompany "all manner of flies and lice." Or to the dramatic power of the grim fugue on "They loathed to drink of the river," the mystery of the opaque, groping tonality in "He sent a thick darkness over all the land" ("Handel makes Egyptians of us all," Dean remarks), and the majesty of the chorus "The people shall hear and be afraid" ("in which all the noblest aspects of Handel's genius are concentrated and contrasted with a power unsurpassed and, I believe, unequalled, even in *The Messiah*," Tovey said). But few before Mr. Gardiner and his singers and players have been wholehearted and utterly convincing champions—I can't quite say of the work as a whole, for the "Lamentation" was represented only by its overture, but of "Exodus" and "Moses' Song" uncut. Even Tovey conducted only a selection from them. In this performance, they became a coherent masterpiece.

The Monteverdi Choir is a thirty-strong chorus (twelve clear, steady sopranos, six each of male altos, tenors, and basses), founded nearly twenty years ago, when Mr. Gardiner was a Cambridge undergraduate and conducted a notable performance of the Monteverdi Vespers. The English Baroque Soloists are an orchestra some forty strong, founded seven years ago to satisfy our age's demand to hear music performed on appropriate instruments and in appropriate styles. Together they have explored the seventeenth- and eighteenth-century repertories (Purcell's *Fairy Queen,* on Deutsche Grammophon, and Handel's *Semele,* on RCA/Erato, are two excellent recordings), and their performances now reach levels of achievement unattainable by more occasional bodies. (There are good Baroque singers, instrumentalists, and conductors in New York, but none who rehearse and perform large-scale music regularly and often.) *Israel in Egypt* was brought to life by, on the one hand, the clarity, freshness, and firmness of the sound, the alert articulation, the true intonation of both singers and players, and the excellent balance between voices, strings, woodwinds, and brasses. And by, on the other hand, Mr. Gardiner's zestful response to the glories of Handel's melody, counterpoint, and dramatic command of timbre. There was no whiff of pedantry in the performance. Once upon a time, "old music" in "authentic" performances seemed to mean— sometimes it still does—faltering string tone; errant oboes; bleached, expressionless singing; and direction now mannered and arty, now plodding. Not here. This *Israel in Egypt* moved swiftly, naturally, adventurously. When the last fanfare had been sounded, the audience rose to its feet and cheered.

The Town Hall concert began with a sensitive account of Purcell's anthem "My Beloved Spake," continued with a powerfully architectural account of Bach's Cantata No. 4, "Christ lag in Todes Banden," and closed with a very bold account of Handel's exuberant, extravagantly brilliant *Dixit Dominus*. The Cathedral program roamed the centuries as it roamed the spaces of Ralph Cram's enormous building, six hundred feet long, making imaginative and varied use of its wonderful resonances. Gesualdo on unaccompanied voices and Giovanni Gabrieli on voices and brasses stole out from the far-distant high altar. Choir and players then advanced to the crossing to sing Schütz and Monteverdi. Purcell's Funeral Music for Queen Mary was sounded antiphonally, spanning the full length of the building with its solemn responses: sackbuts and drum by the high altar, singers at the West end. Back in the crossing, four of Bruckner's glowing motets—unaccompanied, with organ, or with trombones and organ—were richly sung. The choir's words, whether English, German, or Latin, were always intelligibly and eloquently uttered. The soloists stepped, anonymously, from the choral ranks, and one after another of them produced fluent, well-formed, stylish phrases.

Political opera was played on the sidewalk outside the Boston Opera House last month, in protest at the Opera Company of Boston's association with the Marcos regime. (Last year, the Boston company signed an agreement with the Cultural Center of the Philippines to organize operatic activity in Manila, in return for a reported hundred thousand dollars a year.) The street opera, backed by the Boston Committee on Human Rights and the Arts and other concerned organizations, was called *The Legend of the Invisible City of Manila and the Princess Sarah,* and it told how a much loved princess who delighted her people with beautiful music had been seduced by the wicked King Ferdinand and Queen Imelda from beyond the sea; they came to her bearing as gifts magnificent golden treasures they had stolen from their subjects who lived, hungry and oppressed, in hovels invisible beyond Queen Imelda's castle wall. The piece was not efficiently executed; it needed the attention of someone like Sarah Caldwell, an adept at staging opera in a way to prick listeners' consciences. Inside the Opera House,

Miss Caldwell staged *The Legend of the Invisible City of Kitezh and the Maiden Fevronia*—Rimsky-Korsakov's penultimate opera and one of his most beautiful works—as the Opera Company of Boston's latest production. Rimsky is sometimes charged with heartlessness, with merely applying automatic glitter to Russian legends. Performances (they are all too rare) of his operas reveal his poetic, emotional response to the marvels of nature and of myth, and his joyful surrender to, above all, the pantheistic nature myths—Jungian truths within us—that can transfigure the world. A chapter in his autobiography describes the composition of his *Snow Maiden* in a summer village where everything around him—the scenery, the flowers, the singing birds—"was somehow in peculiar harmony with my pantheistic frame of mind," so that "a stump overgrown with moss appeared to me the wood demon or his abode, the forest Volchinyets a forbidden forest...the triple echo heard from our balcony the voices of wood sprites." Bird song, folk song, and new songs composed in their spirit welled up within him, to be set down in bright, clear colors. In *Kitezh,* composed some twenty years—and several operas—after *Snow Maiden,* his inventive vein runs as fresh as ever, and there is a new feeling for human character. (Gerald Abraham calls "the spiritually tormented drunken scoundrel Grishka" Rimsky's "psychological masterpiece.") In the Finnish operas I wrote about last week, nature is harsh and implacable: the hero of Aulis Sallinen's *The Red Line* is killed by a marauding bear. In *Kitezh,* nature smiles: a bear that runs on from the Russian forest in the first scene, to be fed by Fevronia, is young, playful, and affectionate. But *Kitezh* is an opera not less serious than *The Red Line.* Both works are tragedies—in *Kitezh* harmonious nature and the civilized life of cities are alike destroyed by brutal invaders—that end with visions of hope.

The production was not one of Miss Caldwell's most spirited, inspired, or revelatory. It was plain; sometimes it seemed even perfunctory. Robert O'Hearn's simple décor was drab and inapposite (far too much black, too little enchantment). Timothy Miles's costumes were bright and pleasing. Sarah Reese's lustrous soprano proved rather ripe in timbre for the virginal Fevronia, but her singing was clear and beautiful, and her manner pleasantly natural. Noel Velasco was a graceful, chivalrous Prince Vsevolod. John Moulson, Felsenstein-trained, but no longer as disciplined as when I used to see him at the Berlin Comic Opera, gave one of his fiercely charged performances as Grishka. There were good performances from James Rensink (Fyodor and the Bard), Harry Dworchak (Bedyai), and Steven Schnurman (a bear tamer). There was a wise, noble performance from Donald Gramm, as Prince Yury, the ruler of Kitezh; all who sing in English should study Mr. Gramm's way of bringing every phrase to life by his timing and his inflection of the words. Neville Dove conducted with a fine flair for Rimsky's bewitching orchestral colors. Sometimes he pushed the music on a little too intently, instead of letting it flow out spaciously into the theatre. And there were some unwelcome cuts.

In a well-ordered world, Miss Caldwell would be treated as a national treasure, freed from financial and administrative cares, and enabled to concentrate all her spiritual, dramatic, and musical fire on the performance of operas. In the papers, we have read of her Boston company's financial plight and of her new commitments to opera in the Philippines, and now in Israel, too. Her exuberance and energy seem limitless, and perhaps nothing will prove too much for the woman who gave us, in Boston, the American premières of *Moses and Aaron, The Trojans, War and Peace, Montezuma, The Ice Break, The Soldiers.* (And to critics of her Philippine connection she might reply that in Manila this year she began operations with *The Magic Flute,* an opera directed against injustice, oppression, and absolutism on the part of rulers.) This *Kitezh* was enjoyable, but it was impossible to feel that it had received her undivided attention. It lacked the true Caldwell stamp.

TOO-LOORAL-LAY!

May 30, 1983

FEW MUSICIANS would rate *The Mikado* the best of Sullivan's operas. True, in 1933 Bernard Shaw wrote that "we compare the score of *The Mikado* today not with the score of *Les Brigands* and *La Grande Duchesse* but with that of *Die Meistersinger;* and can now appreciate its delicacy and the tenderness which redeems its witty levity and preserves the more ephemeral topicalities of Gilbert from perishing." There are one or two dullish numbers in it, and the dramaturgy is sometimes dicey. Yet, for reasons not hard to find, it remains the public's favorite, and this summer it is newly prominent. Next month, the New York Gilbert and Sullivan Players revive their traditional presentation in Symphony Space. In August, there are at least two new productions: by the Glimmerglass Opera Theater, in Cooperstown, and by the New York City Opera. And the Lyric Opera of Chicago has just put on an important new production. In the light of what one reads about doings at Chicago's City Hall, the piece is timely. "When Mayor Washington and his supporters abruptly adjourned an organizational meeting of the council and walked out," said a *Times* report, Alderman Edward R. Vrdolyak "took up the gavel and promptly rammed through his own program," whose new rules would "install allies of Mr. Vrdolyak as chairmen of all but three of the council's twenty-nine committees, wellsprings of power and patronage." Not *quite* Pooh-Bah behavior—that Lord High Everything would have assumed all twenty-six offices himself—but close enough. From the start, in 1885, *The Mikado* has been politically barbed: Prime Ministers from Mr. Gladstone to Mr. Heath have been indicated, by successive generations of Ko-Kos, as being on the little list of statemen who would none of 'em be missed.

Gilbert's shafts don't draw much blood, however. He allowed himself, Shaw (in 1891) noted with regret, "as a satirist, to depend for the piquancy of his ridicule on the general assumption of the validity of the very things he ridiculed." *The Pirates of Penzance* and *The Wild Duck* have essentially the same theme, but only the latter is "a grimly serious attack on our notion that we need stick at nothing in the cause of duty." All the same, Shaw discerned and admired "a substratum of earnest in Mr. Gilbert's joking," and so does Peter Sellars, the director of the Chicago *Mikado*. His production is not *grimly* serious. It is ebullient, high-spirited, and packed with good jokes—most of them sharp-edged, some of them unabashedly broad. It is serious in the way the best comedy productions are: nothing is unconsidered, nothing represents easy recourse to stock comic routines, and amid the fizz of ideas nothing is irrelevant or pointless. It's a show that keeps the audience's mind, as it were, on its toes.

The curtain rises during the overture, to reveal a drop curtain that bears the Northwest Orient logo. We're setting out for Japan: air hostesses onstage and in the aisles mime the familiar spiel about observing the nearest exits, donning oxygen masks in case of cabin pressure loss, inflating life jackets, and fastening seat belts. (On the first night, it went on too long; no doubt by now it has been tightened.) Act I plays in a large, shapely chamber, now airport lounge, now boardroom. Through the plate-glass picture window, commercial towers and signs for Seiko, Datsun, Minolta, Sony, Toshiba, and Coca-Cola are seen. The gentlemen of Japan are clone businessmen around the boardroom table. Indifferent to Nanki-Poo's sentimental song, they perk up at his patriotic ballad and endorse its refrain: "We shouldn't be surprised if nations trembled before the mighty troops of Titipu!" (As ever, Mr. Sellars, most musical of opera directors, finds his motivations and actions in the score.) The train of little ladies is a crocodile of uniformed, satcheled Japanese schoolgirls. The three little maids from school, Yum-Yum, Pitti-Sing, and Peep-Bo, are demure enough at their first appearance, but for an encore of their trio they make a lightning change, from scholastic trammels free, into punk gear. ("Three little maids" has been encored ever since the first night of *The Mikado*, and Mr. Sellars respects tradition—when it can be used for dramatic effect.) Nanki-Poo—need one say?—is a sequinned rock star, his "native guitar" an electrified instrument.

That Chicago's new *Mikado* is set in modern times is the least remarkable aspect of the show. Berlin had a jazz *Mikado* in 1927, with a blazered Nanki-Poo doing the Charleston, and Yum-Yum naked in a bathtub for "The sun whose rays." Chicago saw the W.P.A. *Swing Mikado* in 1938; New York saw both it and Mike Todd's *Hot Mikado* (with a bowler-hatted Mr. Bojangles in the title role) the following year. Changing the period of an opera—a Risorgimento *Nabucco*, an industrial-revolution *Ring*, a 1940s *Norma*, a space-age *Orlando*—is the simplest way to gain "freshness" and "new impact." In timeless tragedy, the relevances to modern life can be made apparent to the dullest watcher; in temporal comedy, the new jokes achieved by anachronism or by unexpected topicality are ready-made. As Peter Hall, apropos of the Bayreuth *Ring* he is directing this summer, remarked in an interview, that approach ("Wouldn't it be wonderful if we dressed all the Valkyries like the Household Cavalry") is "terribly easy—it doesn't take either much intelligence or much expertise." The larger challenge is "to do what the man asked you to do in the first place." Mr. Sellars, who is practical as well as visionary, declined the challenge of presenting a Victorian *Mikado* still fresh and sharp a century later, and adopted the easier formula. Having done so, he devised a *Mikado* sensitive to each turn of Sullivan's score; invested Gilbert's dialogue with new piquancy; and made sharp, subtle use of the frequent emotional tensions between the music and the words.

In a famous 1885 review, William Beatty-Kingston, the critic of *The Theatre*, praised the score of the new opera ("musical jewels of great price all aglow with the lustre of pure and luminous genius") but, in sentences that angered Gilbert, declared that its characters

> are carefully shown to be unsusceptible of a single kindly feeling or wholesome impulse; were they not manifestly maniacal they would be demoniacal. This view of them is rendered imperative by the circumstance that their dearest personal interests are, throughout the plot, made dependent on the infliction of a violent death upon one or other of them. Decapitation, disembowelment, immersion in boiling oil or molten lead are the eventualities upon which their attention (and that of the audience) is kept fixed with gruesome persistence.

Beatty-Kingston's account of "the grimmest subject ever yet selected for treatment from the comic point of view by any dramatic author" is partial but not untrue. It's disconcerting to learn that Queen Victoria "shook with laughter" at the Mikado's line "something humorous, but lingering, with either boiling oil or melted lead." It's not funny when kindly little Ko-Ko, who's never killed even a bluebottle, determines to acquire the skills a Lord High Executioner needs by beginning with a guinea pig and working his way through the animal kingdom. We are reminded of the millions of animals we torture in cruel experiments, of dogs force-fed with lethal doses of our household detergent in order that it may be licensed for sale. Mr. Sellars hasn't understated or prettified the ruthlessness of the piece. The brutality and inhumane values of hard businessmen and of self-serving politicians are on display. But so is much else. Sullivan did not share his collaborator's glee in ridiculing large mature women: "A dignified, stately, well made-up and well-dressed elderly lady is a charming feature in a piece... the elderly spinster, unattractive and grotesque, either bemoaning her faded charms or calling attention to what is still left of them, and unable to conceal her passionate longing for love, is a character which appeals to me vainly." He insisted on Gilbert's softening the portrait of

451

Katisha, and then he composed for her tragic music that makes her a sister of Donna Elvira. Like Elvira, Katisha is touching. Like Amneris, she is formidable and passionate. Like Fricka, she is formidable even when somewhat absurd. All this was very well handled by Mr. Sellars and by his Katisha, Diane Curry, herself an Amneris and a Fricka. Nor did Mr. Sellars neglect the picturesque japonaiserie that is one of the calculated charms of the opera, as it is of *Madama Butterfly*. The Act II curtain rose on a traditional *Butterfly* set pulled from stock—Chicago's venerable 1920 décor (in which Maria Callas sang in 1955). It had been slightly modernized: a fluorescent insect trap hung amid the cherry blossoms; the heroine had tacked rock-star posters to her pink bedroom wall and had left her Snoopy doll lying around. The effect was pretty, entertaining, and apt. It made its comment at once on the craze for things Japanese which was sweeping London when Gilbert wrote and on the visual taste of the opera-going public, and did so delightfully. Japonaiserie of another kind surrounds us today: we tell the time by it, listen to music through it, hear it beeping on the hour in our concert halls, ride in it. The Chicago Mikado made his entrance—in full Meiji uniform—charioted in a gleaming Datsun.

Ardis Krainik, the dynamic general manager of the Lyric Opera, drew the eyes and ears of the nation to Chicago when hers became the first big company to enlist the operatic flair, seriousness, and passion of Peter Sellars. (Broadway could have had his Gershwin musical *My One and Only* but lost its nerve, dismissed him during the tryout tour, and settled for a lowest-common-denominator reworking.) His earlier shows—among them Handel's *Saul* and *Orlando* in Cambridge, *Don Giovanni* for the Monadnock Festival—were on a smaller scale, and he would be the first to admit and regret the compromises that big-house opera entails. *The Mikado* was composed for a large theatre—D'Oyly Carte's Savoy seated thirteen hundred—but not a giant one like the Lyric, which seats over thirty-five hundred and must use amplification if spoken dialogue is to be audible. (The horseshoe-shaped Savoy packs all the audience as close to the stage as possible; the rectangular Lyric stretches like a football field, without side balconies or boxes.) The director had not quite succeeded in persuading all his opera singers not to behave like opera singers. Despite the amplification, some of them pushed their voices at times on the first night, and there were episodes in Act I when the dialogue dropped into City Opera slowness and the action hung fire. But more often there was imagery, choreography, musical emotion made visible that—as in the Cambridge *Orlando*—could move listeners to unmodified rapture. The staging of "The sun whose rays," of the madrigal "Brightly dawns," and of the trio "Here's a how-de-do!" was particularly exciting. Neil Rosenshein was a bonny Nanki-Poo. Michelle Harman-Gulick was a Yum-Yum both attractive and very wide awake. Sharon Graham (Pitti-Sing) and Dan Sullivan (Pish-Tush) were good, and William Wildermann (Pooh-Bah) was outstanding. Donald Adams, who made his

American début as the Mikado nearly thirty years ago, and has sung the role over two thousand times, was as impressive, alarming, sharply focussed, and precise as ever. I've never met a convincing Ko-Ko, and on record even the great Sir Henry Lytton proves disappointing. John Reed, the D'Oyly Carte buffo of the sixties, good in many other parts, was a Ko-Ko frisky in ways unrelated to the drama and the music. So, in Chicago, was James Billings. The first Ko-Ko, George Grossmith, introduced extraneous business, was rebuked for it by Gilbert, and protested that by it he got a big laugh. Mr. Billings and his director might say the same about the routine capers their Ko-Ko cuts. They should remember Gilbert's chilly retort to Grossmith: "So you would if you sat on a pork pie." The chorus was bright and accurate.

Adrianne Lobel's décor and Dunya Ramicova's costumes were exquisite, and exquisitely right for the production. Duane Schuler's lighting was hardly up to Sellars standards. Craig Smith conducted. On the first night, some of his earlier tempi seemed uncertain; but soon everything began to move surely and eloquently. I wish I could have stayed on to see the alternative cast and watch how the show developed. (Mr. Sellars, like Felstenstein, continues to work with his artists through the run of a production.) But in New York Alfred Brendel had begun his cycle of Beethoven piano sonatas (see page 482).

THALIA

June 6, 1983

COMEDY, THE great comedian Carlo Goldoni said, "was created to correct vice and to ridicule bad customs": it is a moral art, and when it aims merely to entertain people it loses its power of moving their hearts. Marc Blitzstein's sharp, moving, unfaded comic opera *The Cradle Will Rock*, first produced in 1937, when Roosevelt was trying to shape a juster American society, fulfills Goldoni's prescription. Paradoxically, musicians' and actors' unions sought to stop the première of the pro-union opera, but despite them it was given. Blitzstein had composed the piece with small-orchestra accompaniment, and the City Opera did it that way in 1960. Most productions have been piano-accompanied: the première; Leonard Bernstein's Cambridge presentation in 1939; a 1964 revival recorded on CRI; the Lyric Theater of New York production five years ago; and, most recently, John Houseman's revival at the American Place Theater, with alumni of his Acting Company. The last was a fervent, spirited performance. I hope that a revival of Blitzstein's *No for an Answer* is on the way.

Goethe's much-set singspiel *Jery und Bätely*, first seen in Weimar in 1780, is a warmhearted but rather heavy-handed little comedy. Scribe's reworking of it for Adolphe Adam, as *Le Chalet*, first seen at the Opéra-Comique in 1834, is elegant, sparkling, and a trifle slick. Donizetti's reworking of *Le Chalet* as *Betly,* first seen in Naples in 1836, is the most lovable version of all. Donizetti wrote both the words and the music. His comedies—although one might not guess it from the farcical, sitting-on-a-pork-pie productions we often suffer—are based on wise, loving observation of human behavior. He treats his characters tenderly. When the plot inflicts touches of unkindness on them—as that of *Don Pasquale* does—his music seems to regret it, and he is eager to soothe the hurt as swiftly as possible. Verdi, in D'Annunzio's famous phrase, "wept and loved for all of us." So did Donizetti, and in his comedies he smiled for us as well.

Betly is a delightful Swiss miss perhaps just a little too proud of her neat, pretty cottage and a little too fond of her independence. By a stratagem, she is induced to share her life with young Daniele, who loves her dearly: her brother Max, unseen by her since childhood, returns and pretends to be a rough, menacing soldier; Daniele risks his life in defense of Betly and her cottage, and wins her heart. Donizetti was at the height of his powers when he composed the piece—just after *Lucia* and that noble tragedy *Belisario.* The music bubbles out— tender, touching, irresistibly attractive, exquisitely fashioned. *Betly,* which had not been staged in New York since 1861, was revived in April by the Opera Shop of the Vineyard Theatre, at full length but on a tiny scale: the three principals (musical cousins to Adina, Nemorino, and Belcore in *L'elisir*), a chorus of four, and the orchestra a quintet of piano and four winds. There were alternating casts. Mine had a deft Betly, Iris Hiskey; an ardent Daniele, David Kellett; and a spirited, confident Max, Gary Giardina, to be faulted only for singing louder than he needed to. In the Vineyard, a sixty-five-seater, there is no call to force the volume. Apt scenery, by Sally Locke; neat stage direction, by Joseph LoSchiavo; lively musical direction, by Scott Thompson, maestro al cembalo. It was perverse to perform the piece in Italian. Would a Vineyard drama company do *The Cherry Orchard* in Russian, *Ghosts* in Norwegian?

Much New York opera is played in theaters too large (the Met, the State Theater) or too small. *Cradle* in the American Place and the scaled-down *Betly* in the Vineyard were good fits, but Boito's extremely grand grand opera *Nerone* had to be shoehorned into the Amato Opera's hundred-seat house on the Bowery. *Nerone,* left incomplete at Boito's death, in 1918, and first performed (without the final act) at La Scala in 1924, had its American première last year, when Eve Queler and the Opera Orchestra of New York gave a concert performance in Carnegie Hall, (see page 264), and its American stage première last month, in the Amato production. Anthony Amato is an adept at suggesting grandeur in intimate surroundings, and his *Nerone,* richly and skillfully designed by Richard Cerullo, was impressive. Spectacle is partly a matter of proportion. This show had a cast of seventy, pouring on to pack every inch of the theater in the first-act finale. To achieve a comparable cast-to-audience ratio, a Met *Nerone* would need a cast of well over two thousand.

Boito's libretto is more interesting than his music. The piece was sung in a well-fashioned English translation by Lucy Weed. The grandiose score, which calls for six lutes, and antique Roman trumpets, was sketched in by piano and a few wind instruments ("ensemble" would be an inappropriate word). Mr. Amato conducted, and sang any dropped cues. Different casts assemble for each of the ten performances. (One takes pot luck at Amato. Distinguished singers—among them Mignon Dunn and Neil Shicoff—made early appearances there.) In my *Nerone* cast, Rene De La Garza, a baritone I expect to hear again, was a gleaming, potent Simon Magus. Lynn Dolce was a passionate Asteria, and Katherine Enders a pure-toned Rubria. Alan Fischer, in the title role, was appropriately wild-eyed of aspect and ringing of voice.

The Carnegie and the Amato performances were complementary. The former did justice to the music. The latter suggested how Boito's ambitious vision—his attempt at a larger *Troyens*, a *Götterdämmerung* of imperial splendor—might work in the theatre. Amato included a presentation of the uncomposed final act, one of the strangest scenes in opera: while Rome blazes to destruction all around, Nero—pursued by his own Furies, confusing the specter of Clytemnestra with that of his murdered mother, Agrippina—in his private theater plays Orestes in a version of the *Eumenides* invaded by his victims and by the Kundry-like Asteria. It ends not with acquittal but with condemnation. The scene was partly spoken, partly set to music found in Boito's sketches or repeated from earlier in the opera. And it is needed to bring Boito's astounding drama of history and myth, actuality and illusion, eroticism and religious passions, philosophy and psychology to its resolution.

Carnegie Hall's series of Rossini operas with Marilyn Horne as hero came to a close last week with a glittering *Tancredi*. Six years ago in Houston and five years ago in Carnegie, Miss Horne was a vocally brilliant Tancred, singing the music with matchless energy, accuracy, and bravura. To that brilliance she has added a new command of the words and the moods. She began, it is true, in slightly brazen voice; it was well suited to the fanfares ("Ecco le trombe") of her martial duet with the tenor. In the later scenes, her timbre became warmer, more beautiful, and more varied in its emotional colors: it was exciting to hear someone complete mistress of a difficult role, able to do whatever she wanted with the notes and the phrases. Lella Cuberli, an American prima donna admired in Europe and admired in San Francisco (Donna Elvira) and Philadelphia (Anaï in Rossini's *Moïse*), made her New York début as the heroine, Amenaide. Her true, precise singing, the even, unforced flow of her voice through all its range, its agility, its pure focus, and its agreeable tone were acclaimed. Her manner is attractively modest, and during ovations she remained "in character." She is a sensitive artist.

Opera has its inescapably absurd side. There is something ridiculous in the spectacle of a hall of grownup people enraptured by a portly gentleman who throws wide his arms and cries a high C at them. That may be an unkind way to write of Chris Merritt, the Argirio. He has a tenor at once burly and fluent. He's like a Siegmund who can take in his stride the intricacies of Count Almaviva's music in the *Barber*. Effortlessly and in full voice he sailed up to high D's and E-flats. But he had no dramatic presence, no fantasy, no charm of musical manner. The subaltern roles were taken by Rose Taylor and Patricia Schuman (Isaura and Roggiero, who have an uninteresting aria apiece), and Justino Díaz (Orbazzano, who has no aria). *Arie di sorbetto* give the principals a break, but in Carnegie Hall one can hardly slip out for a sherbet during them. Ralf Weikert was a trim little conductor, responsive to the finely pointed instrumental writing (which was well played by members of the American Symphony), and a careful accompanist. But, I felt, he lacked true Rossinian verve—the sense of revelling, along with his cast, in the composer's exuberant inventions.

The Carnegie series had opened with *La donna del lago,* one of Rossini's most romantic operas, and continued with *Semiramide,* the towering crown of his Italian compositions. *Tancredi,* the early opera that established his fame, is hardly their equal. The *candeur virginale* that Stendhal praised wears thin after repeated exposure. Perhaps I've just heard the piece too often. The dramaturgy is static. A simple sentence from the heroine ("That compromising letter was written to you, dear Tancred, not to our enemy Solamir") could clear up the misunderstanding that gives rise to these floods of decorative music. Miss Horne sang the "tragic" finale that Rossini devised for a Ferrara production but then discarded. It's a surprising, audacious piece: a string-accompanied recitative, and a "cavatina" of broken parlando utterances, punctuated by string chords, as Tancred dies. (At this performance, the light in the hall faded to a glow on Miss Horne while she sang it.) Philip Gossett—who uncovered the music a few years ago (it had remained with the heirs of Luigi Lechi, author of its text and lover of Adelaide Malanotte, the first Tancred) and recomposed the forty-seven measures of lost recitative needed to introduce it—feels that "the tragic conclusion elevates the drama and banishes the insipid happy ending." The progressions, as David Hamilton has observed, recall the melodrama of Beethoven's *Egmont*. (Both that and the *Fidelio* melodrama could have been known to Rossini in vocal score.) Gossett declares that "one feels in the presence of the Gluckian ideal." Nevertheless, the artificially sustained tensions of the florid opera are perhaps more fittingly released by the brilliant, if rather trivial, trio of Rossini's original finale.

Berlioz's *Benvenuto Cellini,* an opera not yet staged in New York (Sarah Caldwell gave the American stage première in Boston eight

years ago, with Jon Vickers in the title role), had a concert performance in Carnegie last month, done by Miss Queler and the Opera
Orchestra. Berlioz began the work as a grand opera, recast it as an
opéra comique, then completed it as a grand opera again, with
comic elements, for its first production, at the Opéra in 1838. There
were further reworkings, by Liszt, by Bülow, and by Berlioz himself,
for subsequent productions. (These occasioned Wagner's famous
remarks "Is this artificial remodelling of old ideas real artistic
creativeness?...Children! Make something new, new, and once again
new!") Miss Queler returned to Berlioz's 1838 version, which is more
exuberant and shapely than the reworkings. Nicolai Gedda, whom I
first heard sing Cellini twenty-two years ago, sang it again, with vigor
unabated, with a clarion high C and a sweet high D. (There is nothing
absurd about the ardent high notes of a Berlioz hero.) Mariella Devia
was an accurate and stylish Teresa. Two Frenchmen, Marc Vento as
Balducci and Jean-Philippe Lafont as Fieramosca, were lively and entertaining. Donald Gramm was a wonderfully suave and polished
Clement VII. Miss Queler's conducting was a shade tighter, a shade
less exciting, than it usually is. But it was a good evening.

The Montreal Symphony, on a visit to Carnegie, performed Act II of
Saint-Saëns' *Samson et Dalila,* with Jessye Norman a majestic and commanding heroine and James McCracken in ardent voice as Samson.
Miss Norman would be better still if she cultivated a fuller legato and
emulated the voluptuous portamento of the famous French Delilahs.
The program began with Berlioz's *Corsaire* overture and ended with
The Rite of Spring. Conductors who not only conduct but actually dance
out the *Rite* on the podium usually inspire mistrust, but Charles Dutoit's interpretation, if choreographically somewhat flamboyant, was
musically exciting. The Montreal woodwinds have tangy, individual
timbres. The brasses are narrow, focussed, and fiery—pungent without being blatant. The kettledrummer was crisp but overenthusiastic.
The strings are full-toned, athletic, and exact. Montreal has a fine orchestra.

Some years ago, Daniel Barenboim recorded Berlioz's Te Deum (on
Columbia) in the Church of Saint-Eustache, where Berlioz first performed it. The long echoes as the initial chords, alternating from orchestra and organ, roll through the building are impressive. Berlioz
himself was delighted with the sound of his music in Saint-Eustache
but remarked that the "Tibi omnes" and the "Judex crederis" would
have benefitted from acoustics less resonant. The recording confirms
his observation. St. John the Divine, where a choir of seventy and an
orchestra of seventy performed the Te Deum last week, under Richard
Westenburg, is a building even more resonant. Last year, Berlioz's Requiem sounded splendid there. This year, once that first solemn dialogue was done, there was more mush than majesty. And the balance
seemed awry. Were the forces differently placed? The orchestra
drowned the chorus, and the organ dwarfed the orchestra. Carroll

Freeman, the tenor soloist, sang down into his score instead of letting his voice soar into the loftiness. The Te Deum was preceded by Richard Strauss's *Deutsche Motette,* a sustained stretch of choral virtuosity, converted by the cathedral acoustics into vague washes of glowing sound.

BEGUN, THE ETERNAL WORK

June 13, 1983

LAST MONTH, the San Francisco Opera opened its summer season with the first two installments—*Das Rheingold* and *Die Walküre*—of a new *Ring* production. *Siegfried* is to follow next year, and the complete cycle in 1985. Ever since Bayreuth reopened, in 1951, and presented what became known as the Wieland Wagner—not the Karajan or the Knappertsbusch—*Ring,* it has been customary to devote critical attention first to the staging and the scenery, not to the musical aspect, of *Ring* presentations. I follow the custom, not without regret that the limelight now settles so regularly on a director and his designer rather than on the singers and their conductor. The San Francisco *Rheingold* and *Walküre* took their color and character from the contributions of Nikolaus Lehnhoff, the director, and John Conklin, the designer. "Colorless" and "characterless" are hard but not unfair words to apply to Edo de Waart's conducting.

Six months ago—in words that cheered all Wagnerians who had had enough of black-and-gray *Rings,* of *Rings* staged throughout on a ring, of *Rings* where romance and picturesqueness are sacrificed to didactic point-making—Terence McEwen, the general director of the San Francisco company, announced what he had in mind: "Our *Ring* has been planned as a return to romanticism, color, and the kind of majestic beauty that most of the music suggests. That is not to say that it will be an old-fashioned *Ring* or look like something produced in the nineteenth century. There will be a couple of surprises. The important thing is that we believe we have worked in the spirit of the words and music, and produced something we consider very beautiful." It *is* beautiful to look at. In brief, the landscapes are after Caspar David Friedrich, and the architecture is after Karl Friedrich Schinkel. They provide good models for giving scenic form to Wagner's visions: the great German Romantic painter who observed nature so lovingly and set her down on canvas with a Feuerbach-like moral fervor; the great German Neoclassic architect who began his career in the theatre. On each side, two dull-gold neoclassical portals frame Mr. Conklin's stage pictures.

Das Rheingold begins, it seems, not in the depths of the Rhine but where a tall, gold-tipped Lorelei rock breaks through the river's surface—bad symbolism but a pretty picture. Six ballet girls impersonate the three Rhinemaidens. No more than three are visible at a time, but they pop up in ways to make the mechanics of the blocking all too plain, and although they open and shut their mouths more or less in time to the music it is evident they are not singing; the voices come from elsewhere. Singing and "swimming" Rhinemaidens, wire-suspended, darted about in my first *Ring,* at Covent Garden in 1949, which I remember as a Flagstad-Hotter *Ring,* not for its stage director; and also for Gabriel Volkoff's sets, dating from 1934—the only *Ring* décor I've ever seen in which all Wagner's stage directions could be enacted. Modern opera houses, for all their technical resources, seem to have lost the old theatre-magic skills.

In San Francisco's second scene, the gods hold court in a temple ruin that recalls elements of Friedrich's painting, now in Dortmund, of the Temple of Juno at Agrigentum. Behind, the giants have erected for them a splendid new nineteenth-century palace to plans by Schinkel. It's a beautiful stage picture, and the symbolism is apt—provided one views Wotan's enterprise not as a first attempt to impose order on primeval political chaos but as an attempt at reordering after an earlier great civilization has fallen into decay. The proviso is important. It underlies much of the production. In a program note, Mr. Lehnhoff dwells on crimes Wotan committed before curtain rise, before the *Ring* begins: his rending of the World Ash, his "enslaving" of Loge, and his offer of Freia, the goddess of love, as payment for the palace-fortress. Wotan—before Alberich did so, and deliberately, not provoked, as Alberich was—destroyed the world's natural harmony and renounced love in order to gain power. And now "Wotan's power politics have brought chaos to the world.... You see the gods, especially Wotan, as helpless, arrogant, vain, entangled by guilt.... What you as director have to show is this arrogant 'swimming-pool society,' these gods sitting around at the pool, saying that they can live on forever." The San Francisco gods are clad in colorful, high-fashion classical dress—the men in short skirts, the women in Botticelli draperies—with light billowing cloaks, not useful but decorative, to swish and swirl. Froh, complete with lyre, is a costume-ball Apollo. They look like the gods in a grand, elegant production of *Orphée aux enfers.* (Loge is the exception: he comes on in a frock coat as a Victorian lawyer, reading the *Wall Street Journal*—a callow idea that should have been dismissed before it reached the stage.) This is not rugged Nordic mythology; nor is it an attempt to picture the Aeschylean basis of Wagner's tragedy; rather, it suggests a neoclassical romp to the very serious music. Should someone not found a Society for the Defense of Wagner's Wotan? I'd join. Fricka's charges against Wotan ("Oh, carefree, frivolous lightness;" "Heartless, most disagreeable man"), Fasolt's ("Son of Light, lightly swayed"), and Alberich's ("You live up in the clouds, laughing and making love") are not without substance, but they are not the whole truth about the god. From the start, Wagner's music tells us that he has—but directors increasingly deny him—majesty, grandeur, benevolence. His plans for world peace are founded on a poisoned premise. In the long run, they cannot succeed. He grasps at expedients, and he sinks low before finally renouncing his power. But to portray him as merely a frivolous, power-seeking aristocrat is to diminish Wagner's careful, reasoned demolition—weighing the good with the wrong—of benevolent oligarchy. It may be that the San Francisco *Ring* is planned in part as a parable against the wickedness of nuclear deterrence; the close of *Das Rheingold* suggests that.

In Nibelheim, the stage is filled with a towering mass of gold, in a smoky cavern. Alberich's transformations into menacing dragon—a splendid sixty-foot pantomime monster with snapping jaws—and hopping toad are entertaining, as they should be. A giant industrial cogwheel overhead strikes a false note and seems a bit of debris left over from Patrice Chéreau's Bayreuth *Ring*. Back on the heights, there is a fine coup de théâtre when Donner's clouds, having gathered to hide the distant Valhalla from view, part to reveal the palace now close at hand. There is no rainbow bridge; one of Friedrich's monochrome bows appears on the backcloth. The giants are clubless. While the music depicts Fafner clubbing Fasolt to death, this Fafner takes a sword from the Nibelung horde and stabs his brother. When Wotan's "grand resolve" motif rings out, the god draws the sword, now bloodstained, from Fasolt's corpse, brandishes it, and then hands it to Donner, who holds it aloft as he leads the procession into Valhalla. The "grand resolve" motif (which in *Die Walküre* becomes associated with Nothung the sword) has caused much discussion. In the first *Ring*, Wagner instructed his Wotan to pick up a sword that the giants had improbably but conveniently overlooked when packing up their treasure. Bad idea: it suggests, first, that Wotan has in a flash conceived not just the general notion but the details of his "Excalibur" scheme to save the world through his son, and, second, that Nothung is a mere chance-found, dwarf-forged weapon (whereas in *Siegfried* we learn that it resists working by even the cunningest of dwarf smiths). Mr. Lehnhoff compounds the confusion. I see the attraction of laying the ring's curse upon Nothung, upon Wotan's grand design: in this reading, the power symbols of the cycle—ring, spear, and sword—are all three accursed. But Wagner's score gives no warrant for it. His three symbols are distinct, and the clear, bright C-major sword motif is surely pure, untainted by evil.

It seems to me that Mr. Lehnhoff has produced an intelligent, subtle, and very interesting version of the *Ring* libretto. It is theatrical, arresting, and—thanks to Mr. Conklin—beautiful to behold. When it departs from Wagner's carefully written play, which it does often, it does so in ways that illumine or elaborate on ideas implicit elsewhere in the text. But, I feel, Mr. Lehnhoff has perhaps concentrated on the text at the expense of the music—not listened to, studied, and given due weight to what the score says. He has aimed to clarify and make sense of what the words say. Wagner was emphatic that his words alone did not make sense. "How much there is that, because of the whole nature of my poetic aim, becomes clear only through the music." "The gods' downfall does not arise out of the dramatic turns of events; these could be interpreted in any way." Mr. Lehnhoff takes his stand on the text even when Wagner's music contradicts it or, in ambiguous situations, imposes a different interpretation. The prehistory of the *Ring* belongs only to the text; the music tells of a primeval start. In a straightforward unfolding of the cycle as Wagner wrote it, a listener is untroubled by the double time scale, but Mr. Lehnhoff's temple ruins suggest a nagging need for explication.

Die Walküre opens in the courtyard of the Villa Hunding, where Sieglinde later serves drinks on the terrace—but in plastic goblets rather at odds with the rich, gilded furniture. The first person we see is Wotan. Mr. Lehnhoff has been insufficiently attentive to the sense not only of Wagner's music but also of his stage directions—his dramatic imagery. The director plainly remembers that in all three prose drafts of the scene Wotan appeared, to witness the meeting of his twin children. But Wagner changed his mind and composed his music accordingly: Sieglinde's inspired "Der Männer Sippe" resulted. If Wotan is to appear at the start, then the music must be recomposed—the Valhalla-Wotan motif must be added as a counterpoint to the storm music (it could easily be done)—to account for it. Why do directors not realize that in works as carefully constructed as Wagner's (or Verdi's) recomposing the action is as jarring as recomposing the music would be? There is more doing-down of Wotan when his motif steals through Siegmund's narrative, after "den Vater fand ich nicht": Siegmund fills the solemn measures by taking a gulp of mead. Hunding is dressed, not inaptly, as a Hun chieftain. He comes home inappropriately accompanied by henchmen (as in Chéreau). The open-air scene looks good but destroys the essential dramatic symbolism: a closed room, refuge for Siegmund as he flees the storm, stifling prison for Sieglinde. There *is* a great door in the outer walls which could fly open to signify release; instead, the whole walls slide away into the wings, and by overelaboration Wagner's image is weakened.

Act II begins in an airy atrium of Valhalla. It might be Potsdam. At the back, Wotan is sporting with the junior Valkyries. Brünnhilde lounges on a throne, her feet up; in a short, saucy skirt and silver boots, she resembles Mercure in *Orphée aux enfers*. Fricka, an impeccably dignified Prussian empress, exquisitely dressed and coiffed, enters the throne room saying to her husband, "In the mountains where you hide...I have sought you." While she lectures Wotan, he lolls back on a throne with his legs crossed; he's not actually puffing a cigar but might as well be. Wotan's great narrative is seriously handled—and is sung with insight and passion by Thomas Stewart—but, because the Offenbach atmosphere has been so strongly established, it loses some of its power. For Sieglinde and Siegmund's entrance, the scene changes to the craggy place where the act should have started, and three evocative Friedrich landscapes appear in turn as its background. The crucial encounter of spear and sword—opposition of symbols made visible—doesn't happen; the sword doesn't shatter on the spear. Siegmund (as in Chéreau, but not in Wagner) dies sentimentally in his father's arms.

Act III is set, it seems, on a treeless version of Arnold Böcklin's "Isle of the Dead"—a cliff-girt semicircle. No pine forest, no mossy bank beneath a wide-branching tree for Brünnhilde's enchanted sleep. As in other recent *Ring*s, slain warriors litter the stage; here the Valkyries are mopping them, making them presentable for resurrection as Valhalla guards. Then things return to course, more or less, until the magic fire is due. There's no sudden flash of flame at Wotan's summons. There's no magic fire—no tongues of flame, no flicker—but merely a dense steam cloud, much like the mists that rose from the Rhine. A press release informed us that each performance requires a ton of dry ice.

Everything is played behind a silvered scrim, which softens the pictures. Its only practical purpose can be to contain dry-ice clouds that would otherwise spill into the house: nothing is projected on it, and scene changes are effected behind a drop curtain. It is less obtrusive than most scrims are (but sometimes weapons and armor throw glinting reflections on it). I wonder whether the *malerisch* tone it lends is worth an apparent loss in dramatic immediacy. It doesn't seem to dull the acoustics, however; the words, especially in *Die Walküre*, were excellently clear. Thomas Munn's lighting—apart from an errant follow spot on Loge—was exquisite.

The casts included both veterans and Wagnerian newcomers. Gods first: Michael Devlin's first Wotan was assured, although his bass-baritone lacks the nobility of timbre which the music—if not this production—calls for. He sang cleanly and distinctly but gave too even an emphasis to his sentences—rather as if he had learned to pronounce German but not to speak it. Mr. Stewart, in *Die Walküre*, was more eloquent and more moving; a Bayreuth and a Salzburg Wotan, he remains a master of the great role. Hanna Schwarz, the *Rheingold* Fricka, was vocally clumsy; Helga Dernesch, the *Walküre* Fricka, was splendidly incisive, intelligent, dignified, and sure. William Lewis's Loge was nimbly sung and played, but his tone was horribly dry, and Loge's lyrical narration gave no pleasure. Froh, Walter MacNeil, and Donner, John Del Carlo, were strong. Mary Jane Johnson's bright, impulsive Freia was less untidy than when she sang it for Solti in Carnegie Hall this spring. Erda, Reinhild Runkel, was heavily amplified.

Walter Berry's first Alberich was resourcefully tackled, but his voice sounded worn. David Gordon's Mime was a discovery: it combined character with charm of timbre; it was admirably *sung*. Hans Tschammer was a dull, blunt Fasolt, making nothing of his love music, but a sonorous and formidable Hunding. Erich Knodt was a keen Fafner. Peter Hofmann plays a handsome Siegmund but seems to have become a dull, insensitive singer. Leonie Rysanek's Sieglinde—admired at Bayreuth in 1951, in San Francisco in 1956, and often since—remains a wonderfully fresh, warm, delicate portrayal, and it was easy to forgive some lapses of pitch, some husbanding of tone. Jeannine Altmeyer's Brünnhilde was clear, accurate, and direct. Her soprano is not yet a large-house Brünnhilde voice: it lacks amplitude—large, effortless radiance. But it may grow. Hers was a performance both pleasing and promising. The Rhinemaidens' singing was not light, lilting, or pretty. The Valkyries, led by the Gerhilde and Helmwige of Luana DeVol and Nancy Gustafson, were a vivid, exciting team. By high Wagnerian standards, only Miss Dernesch and Mr. Gordon should be deemed outstanding. By current *Ring* standards—those set by Bayreuth, Covent Garden, the English National, Munich, the Met—these were, by and large, uncommonly well-sung performances. The orchestral playing was accomplished—neat, well prepared, well tuned, and agreeable in tone. But Mr. de Waart's conducting lacked feeling for phrase and shape, on the large scale as on the small. One example: the transformation music between the first and second scenes of *Das Rheingold*, when the ambivalent ring motif dissolves and the Valhalla motif gradually takes its place, was simply beaten through, unbreathed, unmolded.

"Tradition" in operatic performance is good when it means, in a master-to-disciple succession, drawing on fine interpretative insights and practices of the past, testing and trying them, and adopting or adapting those that can ring true within a new, individual interpretation. It represents wisdom accumulated; only foolish, insecure artists are reluctant to study what their great predecessors did. But tradition brings with it the danger of mere accretion: layer upon layer of interpretative ideas obscuring the fresh original. Then a new Mahler (who denounced such thoughtless tradition as *Schlamperei*) or a new Toscanini is needed, to cut through the embellishments and reveal aright what the composer—or dramatist, or composer-dramatist—actually wrote. Traditions grow up swiftly. Consider "Sieglinde's scream." In the *Walküre* program book, Miss Rysanek recalls its origin, during a Bayreuth rehearsal at which "I was so emotionally high...that, when Siegmund tore out the sword [from the tree], I just let out a scream." She expected to be chided; instead, there was an enthusiastic "Keep it in." A generation of Sieglindes has grown up adopting Miss Rysanek's spontaneous scream of excitement, uncalled for by Wagner, and has embroidered upon it—falling to the ground during it, making it one of Sieglinde's "big moments." A generation of *Ring*-goers has grown up expecting it. (Miss Rysanek was not the first Sieglinde to scream, however. Göta Ljungberg, in a 1927 recording of the scene, with Walter Widdop, also emitted that scream.)

Mr. Lehnhoff's production is within the "new tradition." I have indicated some of the standard modern embellishments he has taken over; having been less than assiduous recently in international *Ring* attendance, I cannot report whether other aberrations are of his own invention—potential new "traditions"—or not. Fafner and Fasolt appear in quadruplicate—a posse of eight giants, although only two of them sing. Erda fails to materialize; her disembodied voice is piped in, ineffectively, by loudspeaker, and another of Wagner's great theatrical images is lost. A synopsis in the *Walküre* program declared that at Wotan's contemptuous "Geh!" Hunding simply goes: he "slinks off into the forest." He didn't. Perhaps Mr. McEwen put his foot down at a silly contradiction of Wagner's direction "Hunding falls dead to the ground." Hunding fell dead. But elsewhere we seemed often to be viewing a production based on a corrupt text—something like Nahum Tate's version of *King Lear*—in which many of the author's essential passages (in the form of dramatic imagery) have been lost, and additions not by the author have been given prominence. Tate's *Lear* was not without merit; it held the stage, to the exclusion of Shakespeare's, from 1681 until 1838, when Macready did Shakespeare's *Lear* at Covent Garden. It is a long time since we have seen Wagner's *Ring;* perhaps Peter Hall will produce it at Bayreuth this summer. The San Francisco *Rheingold* and *Walküre* are very far from being without merit, and long stretches of them are close to Wagner. Careful, conscientious editing could bring them closer still.

The *Ring* represents the summit of grand opera. It is the largest task a company can undertake. It remains ceaselessly interesting. It continues to rouse strong feelings. (The San Francisco theatre was picketed by people whose leaflets perpetuated Hitler's distortion of Wagner's artistic aims.) And this San Francisco half cycle is a high, serious, and beautiful achievement—adventurous, unponderous, technically brilliant, spectacular in its staging. Although one may disagree with much of what Mr. Lehnhoff did, one is challenged, stimulated, stirred, and, I should add, entertained (for this is one of the few *Ring*s where the jolly episodes are not dulled). One looks forward eagerly to *Siegfried* and *Götterdämmerung*.

TUMULT OF MIGHTY HARMONIES

June 20, 1983

UNDER THE general title Horizons '83 and the subtitle "Since 1968, a New Romanticism?," the Philharmonic is presenting six summer concerts devoted to music composed in the last fifteen years. In addition, there are meet-the-composer sessions before the concerts, symposia on the "new romanticism?" (billed always with the question mark) in music, dance, and the visual arts, and an open rehearsal of two new scores by young composers. So far—as I write, there are still three concerts to come—the events have been well attended, and by an enthusiastic and discriminating audience, prepared to cheer what delights it and to boo what displeases it. This is a celebration, a festival—and more deserving of that title (which it does not claim) than are many events that do call themselves festivals.

What is being celebrated? At the initial symposium, a panel of three composers (Jacob Druckman, George Rochberg, and John Adams) and a former critic (Elliot Galkin) discussed what "a new romanticism?" might mean. They reached no firm conclusion. How could they? How can one draw the line that barred Roger Sessions, Elliott Carter, Pierre Boulez, and Milton Babbitt from the festival programs and admitted Donald Martino, Fred Lerdahl, John Harbison, Charles Wuorinen, and Peter Maxwell Davies? And in what sense can Davies and David Del Tredici (the *Alice* composer), Wuorinen and Adams (a "minima-list"), Lerdahl and Rochberg (a convinced, unabashed pasticheur) be considered bedfellows? Mr. Druckman, the Philharmonic's current composer-in-residence and the artistic director of its Horizons '83, tried to explain. In a program essay, he wrote:

> Just as the surface of the seas can be agitated by storms and smoothed by doldrums while there is a cosmic tide that moves from one pole to another, undisturbed by momentary tempests, so there is a rhythm in the progress of the arts that moves from one pole to another. This great and steady shift seems to happen repeatedly between two distinctly different artistic climates. On the one hand there is the Apollonian, the Classical—logical, rational, chaste and explainable; and on the other hand, the Dionysian, the Romantic —sensual, mysterious, ecstatic, transcending the explainable.

Boulez, Babbitt, and Carter "present the quintessential statement of those Apollonian ideals." But

> during the mid-1960s the tide began to change.... We can sense a gradual change of focus, of spirituality and of goals.... One can discern a steady re-emergence of those Dionysian qualities: sensuality, mystery, nostalgia, ecstasy, transcendency.... Once again the scent of Byron's "Western Wind" is in the air.

Byron's western wind is new to me; I suppose it resembles Shelley's west wind, that wild spirit moving everywhere, destroyer and pre-server, rather than the longed-for western wind ("When will thou blow?") familiar to musicians, which inspired sixteenth-century Masses by Taverner, Tye, and Sheppard. But I see what Mr. Druckman means. His formulation, no less than the choice of compositions for the festival, has, however, caused some dissension. A young woman rose at the symposium to ask, "Can I be the only person here tonight who has an emotional reaction to Carter's music and to Babbitt's, who finds in them sensual, mysterious, and ecstatic qualities?" A burst of congratulatory applause told her she was not. In a list of "romantic" compositions I have heard in the last decade, Sessions's *When Lilacs Last in the Dooryard Bloom'd,* Carter's Symphony of Three Orchestras and his *Syringa,* Babbitt's *My Ends Are My Beginnings,* and Boulez's *Rituel* would figure. "Romantic," one of the panelists remarked, is little more than an approbatory epithet individuals apply to music that has moved them. A committed modernist might deduce that among attributes qualifying a work for inclusion in the Horizons programs were triadic harmony and other minimalist devices conveniently summarized in the title of Adams's *Common Tones in Simple Time,* pastiche of what Mahler, Richard Strauss, and Alban Berg have already composed (evidenced in pieces by, respectively, Rochberg, Del Tredici, and Toru Takemitsu); construction in washes of sound, evocative timbres à la Ligeti, in which the precise musical communication afforded by discernible pitches and thematic discourse is abandoned; instant attractiveness masking an absence of any intellectual challenge to the listener. A "swing to the right" can be as pernicious in music as in politics if it leads to the repudiation of newly enlightened ways, the reinforcement of old prejudices, the championship of easy mediocrity, and self-indulgent nostalgia. (This is tricky ground: some of our most deeply reactionary music is composed by dedicated Marxists.) There were aspects of the festival which made one uneasy. Yet in an age when Davies can take Sibelius as a symphonic model and Carter can make increasing use of consonance, something certainly is stirring. Perhaps it is a new acknowledgment, surely more Apollonian than Dionysian, of the natural laws—the 1:3:5 relationship that yields a common triad—on which our music is based. In an age when the only American opera done at the Met (although not by the Met) in fifteen years is Philip Glass's *Einstein on the Beach,* and when Del Tredici's *Alice* extravaganzas fill concert halls, other, possibly related forces are stirring.

Let me try another approach. At a party given by the Da Capo Press to mark its publication of David Schiff's *The Music of Elliott Carter,* I remarked to a young composer—Ellen Taaffe Zwilich, a "romantic" and successful young composer—that in New York this spring I'd heard more whole programs of enjoyable, interesting new music, pouring out at concert after concert in Merkin Hall, Symphony Space, the Y, Carnegie Recital Hall, than during any comparable period of a long critical career. Eyes sparkling, she agreed with me: "We've entered a Golden Age for composition, and not enough people seem to realize it." A reason for it, she suggested, was that the father figures Schoenberg and Stravinsky no longer seemed formidable and exigent: young composers, freed from dogmas and orthodoxies, were more relaxed, adventurous, and individual. The compositions I had been enjoying were solo or chamber works. The orchestral composer must take into account both the conservative tastes of symphony audiences and the fact that he writes for what is essentially a turn-of-the-century "instrument," whose players are versed in turn-of-the-century music. Whether he disdains or embraces such considerations, they affect the public outcome of his work.

The open rehearsal made some of Mr. Druckman's points rather well. Not long ago, new compositions tended to bear bleak titles like *Hyperprism, Structures, Synchronisms.* The compositions rehearsed at the

466

Horizons event had more evocative names: *Dream of the Morning Sky,* by Aaron Jay Kernis (born in 1960), and *Symphony from Silence,* by Nicholas Thorne (born in 1953). Between them, there was a brief rehearsal and play-through of a fragment from George Crumb's work-in-progress *A Haunted Landscape.* The Crumb (a Philharmonic commission), which was rehearsed by Arthur Weisberg, begins with Bartókian "night music"—taps, rustles, chirrups suddenly shot through with bright calls and cries. The fragment was picturesque. To discover how it comes out, Mr. Weisberg said, we must come back next year. The works by the young composers, which were rehearsed by Zubin Mehta at his most decisive and impressive, were both of them large pieces for large orchestra, and both of them contained episodes so noisy as to cross a listener's threshold of physical pain. That's another sign of the times. Sometimes I wonder—when walls shake to the thud of a neighbor's hi-fi or when, passing by some headphoned walker, I hear clearly what music is being shrilled at earsplitting volume into his ears—whether a generation has grown up partly deafened since youth by electric amplification. People who attend concerts wearing wristwatches that beep on the hour can hardly be delicate listeners. There's no silence in New York—not even in concert halls. Most of them are sonically polluted by the hum of machinery. Alfred Brendel played his Beethoven recitals in Carnegie against a mechanical bourdon. Merkin Hall is a happy exception; Carnegie Recital Hall is maddening. In Avery Fisher Hall, fine-tuned by Cyril Harris into silence, the audience's shuffling on the resonant sounding board of the new wooden floor undoes his good work. (Music would gain if visitors were required to take their shoes off or don felt overshoes, as when entering Japanese temples.) The old composers wrote their music against a background of silence. So does Crumb. But young composers who write for the partly deafened seem to feel they must make very loud noises indeed if they are to be impressive. Richard Strauss was a heavy scorer, and so was Mahler, but in their day the human voice had its limits. Strauss pushed his sopranos to those limits in *Salome* and *Elektra,* Mahler his tenor in *Das Lied von der Erde.* But the soprano in the finale of Kernis's *Dream of the Morning Sky* was armed with a microphone and electric amplification—with inhuman, limitless volume, able at the turn of a knob to cut through a large orchestra in full cry. The soprano in Del Tredici's *Alice* pieces is similarly magnified. "Gargantuan" is an apter epithet than "Dionysian" for some of the phenomena that appear on our new horizons. (Apollo should sentence the grosser offenders to months in a silent cell with only a clavichord for company.) Mr. Mehta, who has a good ear, made some good suggestions during the rehearsal: that a tune clashed out in octaves by heavy metal percussion sounded needlessly strident; that a line blared by three trumpets might more effectively be played by one. But Mr. Kernis stoutly maintained that what he had written was what he wanted. Although some of the sound is laid on too thick, *Dream of the*

467

Morning Sky is—so far as one can judge from the rehearsal—a rich and imaginative piece, a little spoiled at the last by the rhetorical insistence of the pantheistic text (a poem by N. Scott Momaday): some twenty-five lines, each beginning "I am." The amplification turned Gwendolyn Bradley's light, pretty voice into a supersoprano but at the same time endowed it with supertremolo.

Thorne's *Symphony from Silence*, subtitled *A Piano Symphony*, is uninhibitedly, inordinately "romantic." Its five movements are called Communion, The Silence, Canticle, Offering, and Benediction. The sound world at times recalls Messiaen at his least restrained. There are static passages dense with busy minimalist figuration, and passages where the solo pianist noodles away furiously against full orchestra as if in parody of a note-filled neo-Romantic concerto. I enjoyed the first ten minutes or so and then began to feel glutted. Christopher Oldfather played brilliantly.

The fare at the first three concerts was lightened by a chamber work in each program. At the first, it was Davies's lovely *Ave Maris Stella*, sensitively played by the New York New Music Ensemble. The piece needs a smaller setting than Fisher Hall. The concert began with the world première of Marc-Antonio Consoli's *Afterimages*. The composer's program note spoke of "dreams, fulfilled, unfulfilled"; of "a new intensity of emotion"; of music that is "moody—now sad, now bursting with anger, but always reflective." The music itself seemed drab. Takemitsu's *Far calls. Coming far!* (the title from the close of *Finnegans Wake*), a lush, wandering, Bergian movement for violin and orchestra, had its New York première and drifted by as agreeably and unmemorably as when I heard it in San Francisco. Then Del Tredici's *All in the Golden Afternoon* was done. When *Final Alice*, the eighth of Del Tredici's Lewis Carroll compositions to appear, was first played here, in 1977, I ended a long review by wondering whether the piece, and the whole huge Alicead it apparently crowned, was impressive, touching, profound, absurd, or all four at once. *Final Alice* proved far from final. Four large pieces have followed: *In Memory of a Summer Day, Quaint Events, Happy Voices,* and *All in the Golden Afternoon*. Together they make up an evening-long entertainment, *Child Alice,* for large orchestra and amplified soprano. The welcome accorded the earlier pieces has, I fear, led Del Tredici into undisciplined excess—long bouts of sentimental, elephantine wallowing in the enchanted golden world of childhood. The heroines of the Dormouse's tale, Elsie, Lacie, and Tillie, who lived at the bottom of a treacle well, became ill—*very* ill—on their diet of treacle. There's too much thick syrup in Del Tredici's *Child Alice* recipe for my taste. And far too much racket in the works that result. Alice seldom raised her voice; Carroll is never vociferous or vehement. After the shrieking and screeching of the *Alice* pieces, the assaults by forces Mahler reserved for proclaiming such things as "Resurrection!," the relentlessly thick scoring, one returns with relief to Alice's own clear, reasonable voice and Carroll's gentler expression of profound emotions. The popular success of the *Alice* pieces is a sign, a symptom, of something happening in symphonic music today, and it was right to include one of them in the festival. Del Tredici's exuberance, generosity, gusto remain attractive. Phyllis Bryn-Julson was the soprano, and the concert was conducted by Raymond Leppard.

The second program, conducted by Mr. Weisberg, began with Fred Lerdahl's *Chords*, composed in 1974 and here receiving its première in a revised version. It seemed a product more of the old schematicism than of the new romanticism. "The concept was to construct a piece entirely from a succession of 'chord-color-rhythms,'" the composer wrote. The triadic base—"the vision was of an infinitely peaceful yet powerful B-flat major triad cutting through a welter of orchestral sound"—presumably won it a place at the festival. Harbison's Violin Concerto (1980), which followed, is, like all his music, hard to categorize and easy to enjoy. It pleases the mind but is composed with a freedom properly called "romantic." Harbison is a poetic, civilized, courteous composer. His fancy ranges, but he doesn't shout and stamp. Charles Rex, the Philharmonic's associate concertmaster, was the honeyed soloist at this New York première. Leonard Rosenman's *Foci I* (1981), which ended the program, had a large number of notes amounting, it seemed, to rather little. Being, the composer said, "the first of a projected series of pieces dealing with magnification, micrification, and the transitions between these processes," it lay oddly in the festival frame; it was a "processes" piece. Before it, the Group for Contemporary Music, conducted by Harvey Sollberger, played Donald Martino's Triple Concerto (1977), for soprano, bass, and contrabass clarinets and a chamber orchestra of winds and percussion. Slowly, slowly, I'm learning to love this severe piece, with its charming triple cadenza. There is a fine Group recording on Nonesuch, with the same soloists: Anand Devendra, Dennis Smylie, and Les Thimmig.

Three of the four works making up the third program seemed to provide token representation of strands in contemporary music. More persuasive examples of each could have been chosen. And those who distinguish composers by sex had not failed to point out, at the first symposium, that the fourth work, Barbara Kolb's *Chromatic Fantasy*, was the only piece of the twenty-five on the festival bills composed by a woman. It's a neat, epigrammatic work for narrator and six instruments. Electronic music was represented by Morton Subotnick's *Ascent into Air* (1981), for ten players and computer-generated sound, conducted by Larry Newland. It's a gruff piece, not one of Subotnick's pretty ones. Sándor Balassa's *Lupercalia* (1972), a New York première, represented Central Europe by a carefully fashioned, modest composition. Something by Robin Holloway or George Benjamin would have afforded stronger evidence of transatlantic new romanticism. (But already two of the five foreign composers included were British; three might have been too many.) Adams's *Grand Pianola Music* (1982), for two pianos, two sopranos and mezzo-soprano (amplified), and string-less orchestra, another New York première, conducted by Mr. Druckman, represented minimalism. The categorization is inevitable, although in a program note Adams pointed out that his "essentially triadic" harmony "modulates far more rapidly than most 'minimal' music." Not rapidly enough. The last of the three movements, entitled "On the Dominant Divide," oscillates "almost exclusively between dominant and tonic, thereby giving birth to The Tune"—a tune of stupefying banality. After Adams's *Harmonium* and *Common Tones,* both captivating pieces, *Pianola* was a disappointment. Alan Feinberg and Ursula Oppens were indefatigable soloists. The orchestra, I thought, was somewhat heavy, coarse-toned, and ill tuned.

BRANCH LINE

June 27, 1983

JEAN-PHILIPPE RAMEAU's three-hundredth birthday falls in September. He is a musician who inspires passionate advocacy. Ten years ago, his *Naissance d'Osiris* was played in the Smithsonian's natural-history museum, a setting that blended Encyclopédiste science with marbled splendor. (One passed a tiger poised to spring and a trumpeting elephant—each the largest of its kind—to reach the theatre, and sipped wine afterward beneath a blue whale lit by aqueous blue flickers.) After it, I declared that of great opera composers Rameau was the most cruelly neglected. Since then, many of his dramatic works have been revived in London. *La Princesse de Navarre, Hippolyte et Aricie* (twice), and *Castor et Pollux* were staged at Covent Garden and *Naïs* was staged at the Old Vic—not by the resident troupes but as part of the English Bach Festival. (Bach and Rameau are near-contemporaries.) In Inigo Jones's Banqueting House, the Festival presented *Pygmalion,* and in the Queen Elizabeth Hall a costumed performance of *Zoroastre.* In that hall, John Eliot Gardiner's Monteverdi Choir and Orchestra gave concert performances of *Dardanus, Les Fêtes d'Hébé,* and—a world première—*Les Boréades,* Rameau's last tragédie, and a masterpiece. *Les Boréades* was then repeated at the Proms. Rameau began to seem a composer British by adoption, like Berlioz. France recognized the merits of a largely neglected son when the English Bach Festival took its *Princesse de Navarre* and *Hippolyte* to Versailles and Mr. Gardiner mounted his *Boréades* at the Aix-en-Provence festival and in Lyons. (This summer, he conducts *Hippolyte* at Aix, with Jessye Norman as Phaedra.) American annals for the decade are slimmer. An abridged *Dardanus* at the Juilliard, a *Pygmalion* in St. Louis, a *Pygmalion* done by Concert Royal at Pace University, and a single entrée from *Les Fêtes* given in Tully Hall by the Concert have come my way. Nothing at the Met; nothing at the City Opera. But last month *Zoroastre* had its American première, presented in Cambridge at the start of Boston's Early Music Festival; and in September *Pygmalion* and the unfinished *Io*—possibly a world première—are due in Fayetteville, Arkansas.

Zoroastre, the fourth of Rameau's five surviving tragédies, has hitherto enjoyed less esteem than its predecessors, and modern performances of it have been few. One reason is that the Rameau Oeuvres Complètes, begun in 1895, petered out, uncompleted, in 1924, before reaching *Zoroastre.* The eighteenth-century printed scores lacked inner parts; a 1964 French edition appeared with downward transpositions and with written-out ornaments, making it unsuitable for modern Baroque performers. But for the English Bach Festival performance, four years ago, Graham Sadler prepared a new score, and this was used again in Cambridge. *Zoroastre* is a work of extraordinary beauty and radiance. In thumbnail characterizations of the tragédies, one might call *Hippolyte* the most directly and potently dramatic (it is where the Met or the City Opera should start), *Castor* the most moving, and *Dardanus* the most fanciful, while *Les Boréades,* which crowns the achievement, seems to be Rameau's *Otello* and *Falstaff* in one. It is tempting to be especially enthusiastic about the latest Rameau opera—as about the latest Mozart—one has heard. This didn't quite happen with *Zoroastre;* the Cambridge performance was less than ideally persuasive. But it was good enough to reveal the particular qualities of the piece. *Zoroastre* has something in common with *The Magic Flute* and something with *Lohengrin.* Its concern is the conflict of bright forces with the powers of darkness; enlightenment triumphs at last over moral and political tyranny. (The term "tragédie" did not preclude a happy ending.) Some commentators have been distressed that the eponymous hero is not a grave, low-voiced mage, like Handel's Zoroastro or Mozart's Sarastro, but a high tenor, and one, moreover, in love with the heroine. "Sacrilegious absurdity," Cuthbert Girdlestone declares in his Rameau monograph, and "It seems almost blasphemous to depict a figure like Zarathustra in love." *Also sprach* Girdlestone. But the near-divine, miraculous Zarathustra, as Rameau and his librettist, Louis de Cahusac, surely knew, was a creation of later legend. (Strauss, it is said, composed his tone poem in the belief that Zarathustra was an invention of Nietzsche's, and was rather cross when he learned otherwise.) The prophet Zoroaster of the earlier accounts, apostle of a sun-based religion well suited to the Persian clime, was a man—one who married and had children. And the character described by those who have read the Avesta (I've only heard it chanted, in Persepolis and from a fire temple beneath the tomb of Darius, as part of Peter Brook's *Orghast)* is that of Rameau's hero: a human being credible and sympathetic, now hopeful, now despondent, beset not only by his enemies but also by wavering on his adherents' part and by his own misgivings.

Zoroastre survives in two versions: the orginal, of 1749, and the revision, of 1756. When Rameau revived his tragédies, he reworked them, sometimes drastically. Generally, he tightened the drama but removed lovely music that one loses only with a pang. (Verdi did much the same when he revised *Don Carlos.*) The happy result is that listeners' voyages of delighted discovery grow longer. (I've heard *La traviata* a hundred times or more and *Nabucco* often, but there is music Verdi composed for *La traviata* and for *Nabucco* which—like music Mozart composed for *Figaro* and for *Don Giovanni*—I've yet to hear in the theatre.) Cambridge did the 1756 *Zoroastre;* the 1749 *Zoroastre*, with its glorious second act, a cresendo of light, remains a treat in store. In both versions, *Zoroastre* seems to me a strong drama, raised on a firm allegorical foundation but enacted by characters who are brought to life by their utterances. The chorus plays many parts—Bactrians, Indians, mages, priests, "elementary" forces (spirits of air and of earth), shepherdesses and shepherds—and is always part of the action. In the revised version, the characterization of Érinice—a cousin to Amneris and to Ortrud: a proud woman rent by political ambition, fierce love for Zoroastre, and jealousy of Amélite, whom Zoroastre loves—is so vivid as almost to unbalance the plot. The Cambridge production was given in Sanders Theater, without scenery apart from a rococo portico added to the back wall of the platform. (Sanders, part of Harvard's Memorial Hall—Henry James' "great bristling brick Valhalla"—is a décor in itself, but not exactly what Rameau had in mind.) The execution was not for the unconverted. Anyone whose idea of early music in an authentic performance is thin, out-of-tune orchestral playing, singers in fancy dress who strike odd poses and emit mannered noises, primping dancers, and plodding musical direction was likely to have his prejudices confirmed. (That early music, properly performed, means nothing of the sort has been amply proved elsewhere—recently, by that Handel *Orlando* in St. Louis.) Banchetto Musicale, which provided the band and the chorus, is a Boston Baroque ensemble of some renown, but it hadn't got the hang of Rameau. Georg Muffat, a seventeenth-century analyst of national styles, declared that one should "hear" French dance music through one's feet as well as one's ears. There was no springiness in Martin Pearlman's direction. The dance music didn't dance. The infernal music was not formidable. The continuo cellist, instead of sharing the harpsichordist's score and, as it were, living along the singers' phrasing and breaths and gestures, seemed individually intent on her part. The bassoons, which have important contributions to make, scarcely came through. The chorus, in modern dress, sang in its share of the drama from seats at one side of the stage. The dancers were three couples from the Boston Ballet, doing unstylish choreography by Violette Verdy. The lighting, by N. B. Goldstein, was insensitive to the progress of the drama and the score. Jean Claude Orliac, in the title role, sang truly but didn't begin to act. Sophie Boulin, the Amélite, was sometimes painfully out of tune.

Doing Rameau is not easy. The critic Pierre Lalo, one of Rameau's first modern champions, wrote that the music needs

an extremely precise and at the same time extremely sensitive interpretation, intelligent, penetrating, and felt.... Each fiddle, each flute, each oboe needs an execution that follows and adapts itself to every movement of the musical line, one that can mold and so to speak sculpt itself on its clear, precise, supple, and tight outline, without overlooking any inflection, accent, or intention, on pain of losing touch with the thought and with the feeling.

Each singer and each dancer needs that kind of execution, too. And, since Lalo wrote (he died in 1943), new work has been done on every aspect of Rameau performance; instrumental and vocal style, staging, costuming, acting, dancing, lighting. Mr. Pearlman and Philippe Lenaël, the stage director of *Zoroastre*, aimed to take the new researches into account. They can be forgiven for failing in the letter where difficulties practical (Sanders does not have an equipped stage) or economic (the band was woefully undersized) held them back. Failing in the spirit is more serious. This *Zoroastre* seemed more a polite antiquarian charade than a life-and-death struggle between right and wrong. My passion for Rameau was kindled by a Birmingham University production of *Hippolyte*, nearly twenty years ago (Janet Baker was the Phaedra, Anthony Lewis the conductor), at which the instruments were modern and the acting was untouched by Baroque rhetorical gesture. By modern scholarly standards, it was a primitive show; it would not be done that way now. But the thought and the feeling in it proved overwhelming. And I know other Ramellians who date their enthusiasm for the composer from hearing the Oiseau-Lyre *Hippolyte* recording derived from that production. The Birmingham show was sung in English. A general public will not respond to Rameau fully until it can follow the words: paradoxically, perhaps, the dramatic music most closely linked to the texts it expresses—Monteverdi's, Rameau's, Janáček's—stands most in need of theatre performance in the audience's tongue. The Oiseau-Lyre recording was made in French—rightly, since a bilingual libretto could be provided. The Cambridge *Zoroastre* was sung in French—rightly at an international scholarly festival. A bilingual libretto was on sale. Two translators, the Scientific and Cultural Service of the French Consulate in Boston, and a Libretto Translation Coördinator were credited in the program. Too many cooks? They rendered the line "Il faut briser ses fers"—an injunction to Zoroastre to rescue the imprisoned Amélite—as "You have to give her up."

Some of Debussy's music criticism is tiresome and flip, but when he heard Vincent d'Indy conduct an act of *Castor*, in 1903, he took trouble with his review and wrote with unwonted enthusiasm. His tone is chauvinist: Rameau, in whom he discerns "a purely French tradition," comes in handy for whacking Gluck, who, along with later Germans, is blamed for diverting French composers from the paths of Ramellian clarity of expression and conciseness and precision of forms. Rameau's works, Debussy says, "combine a charming and delicate tenderness with precise tones and strict declamation in the recitatives." One of Pollux's airs he finds so eloquent and original that "Rameau seems like one of our contemporaries whom we could congratulate as we left the theatre." The beauty and shapeliness of Rameau's melodies, the expressiveness of his orchestral colors—newly fresh in our age of Baroque instruments—and his sense of proportion are evident; praise must not overlook the sheer dramatic force of his tragédies when they are performed with feeling. Debussy ended with an apology for dwelling on the music of the past, but, he said, "moments of real joy in life are rare." Rameau can still provide them.

HARMONY AND GRACE

July 11, 1983

LEONARD BERNSTEIN'S new opera, *A Quiet Place,* had its first performance last month, in Houston. It is a two-hour piece—a score as long as *Rigoletto,* longer than *La Bohème* or *Elektra*—in four scenes divided by interludes and played without intermission. Written to be done on a double bill with Bernstein's 1952 opera *Trouble in Tahiti* (as it was in Houston), it is a sequel to and resolution of the earlier piece. The title is the refrain of a dream aria sung, on a psychiatrist's couch, by the heroine of *Trouble in Tahiti:*

> *There is a garden:*
> . *Come with me . . .*
> *There love will teach us*
> *Harmony and grace,*
> *Then love will lead us*
> *To a quiet place.*

Trouble in Tahiti, a domestic tragedy set in American suburbia, is a forty-five-minute chamber opera for five voices—mezzo-soprano and bass-baritone principals (Dinah and Sam) and a crooning trio as "a Greek Chorus born of the radio commercial"—and small orchestra. The music is wry, neoclassical, and deft—skillful and eloquent in its deployment of catchy commercial-vernacular idioms to gloss over, without concealing, deep emotion. Dinah and Sam, unable to find a way to their "quiet place," bicker, neglect their son, and seek escape from despair in meaningless macho achievement at office or gym, in suburbia's material consolations ("up-to-date kitchen: washing machine: colorful bathrooms, and Life Magazine"), and, when those fail, in "the bought-and-paid-for magic, waiting on a Super Silver Screen." (The opera is named for the South Sea movie the couple is setting out for at curtain fall; Dinah has already seen it that afternoon and has told us its plot in a vivid aria.) The libretto, Bernstein's own, is (as the quotations suggest) somewhat facile in its satire and banal in its poetic flights, but the situation is serious, and it is seriously handled in music that unites verve with Mahlerian irony. The rhythms dance, the scoring is spare and brilliant, and at each hearing new Rossinian felicities emerge. (There have been two recordings; both are out of print.) *Trouble in Tahiti* is a small but important landmark in the course of American opera.

A Quiet Place, which has a libretto by Stephen Wadsworth, opens some thirty years later. Characters that Dinah and Sam refer to in *Trouble in Tahiti* now appear: their son, Junior, nine years old at the time of *Tahiti;* Dinah's brother Bill, her friend Susie, and her analyst. And there are new characters: a daughter, Dede, ten years younger than Junior; François, Junior's Canadian lover, now married to Dede; the family doctor and his free-mouthed wife; a funeral director. Dinah has been killed in a drunken, probably suicidal car smash. Her funeral brings the family together: Sam has not seen Junior for twenty years and has never met his twice-over, as it were, son-in-law. There ensue a series of reminiscences, recriminations, and revelations and, at the same time, a series of moves, fumbling at first, toward forgiveness, understanding, and love. Dinah has left an enigmatic letter:

> Dear loved ones, I've never felt closer to you than now. Forgive this all, so messy. . . . The bottom line is, Accept or die. . . . But who will accept and live, you whom it may concern? We're only who we are.

It is hard to relate the plot without making it sound mawkish. Scene 2 is a double duet: in the master bedroom, Dede, who has put on one of her mother's dresses, and her father embrace; in Junior's bedroom, Junior's psychotic outbursts—he tells François of incest with Dede and of his father's shooting him—end with a cry of "I love you, Daddy" as he falls into François' arms. Then, in the hallway between the rooms, François embraces Dede passionately for the first time, and when they retire Sam comes into Junior's room to kiss his sleeping son. In an interlude, we see Dinah's healing influence extend to the subsidiary characters: Bill, who loved his sister and is now "free," finds comfort in Susie's arms, while Mrs. Doc confesses to her bathroom mirror that she was in love with Dinah. The last two scenes give stage form to the "garden gone to seed, choked with ev'ry kind of weed," where Dinah's dream in *Tahiti* began. Dede has been weeding her mother's garden, and there the outstanding family junctions are effected. In Scene 3, Dede and Junior play and kiss, and Sam hugs François. In the final scene, the new edifice of family love all round threatens to collapse in a spat over who will sleep where, but François recalls Dinah's letter ("It's your Ten Commandments, it's your Constitution, your bill of fucking rights!"), and the opera ends with Sam hugging Junior, François tenderly kissing Junior's hand, and Dede reaching out toward François.

The opera closest to *A Quiet Place* in content is perhaps Michael Tippett's *The Knot Garden,* but while that piece alternates scenic realism with scenic metaphor—the rose garden re-forms as an alarming labyrinth—*A Quiet Place* takes all its imagery from realistic suburbia. And Bernstein's cast includes no Prospero character to direct the figures of the dance. The maze of violent emotions may also recall that of an Ivy Compton-Burnett novel but is not plotted with Miss Compton-Burnett's clarity. The characters in *A Quiet Place* are uneducated. Their feelings, thinking, and utterances are inchoate. They do not talk with wit and precision: sentences remain unfinished, trains of thought leave the rails, and some of the language is coarse. All that is deliberate. The opera is an ambitious, arresting attempt to fashion an orderly work of art from material lifelike in its vagueness and unruliness. The music gives shape to the piece. The underlying form is that of a four-movement symphony, with the linked nocturnal duets as a slow movement and games in the garden as a scherzo, and the score is one of the richest Bernstein has composed. His use of the four principals, the comprimari, and a chorus in a variety of flexible textures is masterly. The scoring, in which the composer had two collaborators, is for full orchestra. (In Houston, the string section was small, and some episodes sounded needlessly brassy.) The melodic lines are as sharp-eared as Janáček's in their transformation of speech rhythms and speech inflections into music. Musical and verbal links with *Trouble in Tahiti* abound —not so much direct quotations as derivations and developments of a Wagnerian kind. And there is indeed a sense in which the double bill of *Trouble in Tahiti* and *A Quiet Place* can be likened to an American *Ring*—if one can imagine the *Ring* as a family drama played out not with Aristotelian magnitude but in a Great Neck home (Patrice Chéreau's Bayreuth production makes such imagining easier), in suburban speech. Wotan-Fricka, Wotan-Brünnhilde, and Wotan-Siegfried encounters find clear vernacular reflections here. And the "moral" is essentially that proclaimed by Brünnhilde at the close of Wagner's cycle (in lines that the composer left in the published libretto, although he decided not to set them to music): "Not goods, not gold, or godly magnificence; not house, not hall, or lordly splendor; not [I make free with some hard German] astutely drawn-up legal contracts, or hypocritical observance of the conventions; but only *Love* can bring happiness in weal or woe."

A Quiet Place was commissioned jointly by the Houston Grand Opera, the Kennedy Center, and La Scala. It will be played in Washington in early October, and in Milan next June. It opened in the largest of the three début theatres—Jones Hall, which is a handsome building but has a cavernous auditorium. (Construction begins soon on a new, twenty-three-hundred-seat, more compact home for the Houston company.) A monitory note in the *Tahiti* vocal score says, "If the words are not heard, there is no opera." In Jones Hall, an amplification system of the kind called "enhancement" helped to pipe the words—and the orchestral sound, too— throughout the theatre; in

Kennedy Center's Opera House and in La Scala, more direct performances will be possible. The Houston execution of both works was first-rate. David Gropman's designs and William Ivey Long's costumes were fresh, pretty, and entertaining; Mr. Gropman was perhaps more acute at devising fifties "nostalgic" touches in *Tahiti* than at presenting an unmistakably 1983 suburban home in *A Quiet Place*. Peter Mark Schifter's stage direction was crisp and observant, and if he slightly overelaborated the scenic action of *Tahiti* the vastness of the theatre can be his excuse. The disparity of scale between the two operas does bring problems, which arise not only from the increased size of cast, of orchestra, and of musical numbers in the later work but also from its wider harmonic range and its emotional and musical complexity. The difference is greater than that between *Das Rheingold* and *Götterdämmerung: Trouble in Tahiti* was conceived on a small scale; it had its first popular success on television; and "Simplicity of execution should be the keynote throughout" is the opening injunction of the production note in the vocal score. *A Quiet Place* is not at all simple. (I'm glad I was able to hear it twice.) Nevertheless, *Tahiti* is far from being a mere curtain-raiser; it serves as the necessary exposition to the grand opera that follows. A critic's task is to describe, not to tell composers and executants what they should have done. All the same, it may be that a revised scoring of *A Quiet Place*—perhaps for an orchestra, like that of *Tahiti*, with double, not triple, winds—and productions in which the two pieces are scenically more closely linked than they were in Houston would help audiences to discern more clearly the extent of Bernstein's and Wadsworth's achievement. And also help to give the bill wide currency. Campus and conservatory productions will surely be frequent. [*At the Washington and Milan productions,* Trouble in Tahiti *was played as a flashback, after the first scene of* A Quiet Place, *and some cuts were made. The campus and conservatory performances I hoped for have not taken place, but there has been a production at the Vienna State Opera.*]

Houston had assembled a cast of alert, able young singers with strong personalities, good voices, and the right looks. And they provided what Bernstein needs: fearless emotional exposure coupled with expert technical control. (It is in halfhearted performances that Bernstein's music sounds most sentimental.) For *Trouble in Tahiti*, Diane Kesling and Edward Crafts were an expert pair, and in the final scene Miss Kesling eloquently suggested the Dinah whose presence shines on in *A Quiet Place*. In the second opera, Sheri Greenawald, Timothy Nolen, and Peter Kazaras gave exact, vivid performances as Dede, Junior, and François. An older singer, Chester Ludgin, was a powerful and moving Sam. Carolyne James (Mrs. Doc), Dana Krueger (Susie), Douglas Perry (the analyst), Theodor Uppman (Bill), Charles Walker (the funeral director), and Peter Harrower (Doc) were all excellent. John DeMain's musical direction was clear and confident, if a shade cool in espressivo passages.

American opera is seldom created in New York, where the Met has long shunned it, where the City Opera has done little that is new since Leon Kirchner's *Lily* (1977), Dominick Argento's *Miss Havisham's Fire* (1979), and Gian Carlo Menotti's *La Loca* (1979). Across the country — in Houston, St. Louis, Minneapolis, Bloomington, Santa Fe — new operas continue to appear. When *A Quiet Place* goes to La Scala, it can show Europe that good American operas on contemporary subjects are still being composed.

A TORCH, A FLAME, A WILL-O'-THE-WISP

July 18, 1983

DELIUS'S SIX operas are strange, beautiful works in which an aristocratic disdain for the operatic conventions yields, at times, to disconcertingly clumsy attempts to observe them. All but the earliest opera, *Irmelin,* have been recorded (*A Village Romeo and Juliet* twice), but only *The Magic Fountain* and *Margot la Rouge* remain in print (both on Arabesque). Two at least of the six can hold the stage. *A Village Romeo* (1901), Delius's fourth opera, is a masterpiece: tender, poignant, ecstatic, breathtakingly beautiful, and like no other work in the repertory. A 1972 Washington production came to New York, and for three seasons the City Opera played it. I hope it returns to the State Theater soon. And *Fennimore and Gerda* (1901), the last of the six, contains several episodes that Eric Fenby, the composer's companion and amanuensis in his last, blind years, rightly describes as "miracles of loveliness." The Opera Theatre of St. Louis gave the American première of *Fennimore* two years ago, and this summer takes it to the Edinburgh Festival. There are "miracles of loveliness" in the four other Delius operas, too, but also theatrical infelicities that make them caviare to the general. I am one of the few people who can have seen *Irmelin* (1892): it has been done only once, by Beecham in Oxford in 1953. Delius's second opera, *The Magic Fountain* (1895), set in Florida, has never been staged, but in 1977 the BBC gave the studio performance that was later issued on record. The third, *Koanga* (1897), set in Louisiana, was highly acclaimed at its American première, in Washington in 1970.

Delius's fifth opera, *Margot la Rouge,* was composed in 1901 and was entered for the publisher Sonzogno's competition for one-act operas — a competition instituted in 1883 (when Puccini's *Le villi* remained unplaced) and repeated in 1889 (when Mascagni's *Cavalleria rusticana* won), in 1892, and in 1903. *Margot la Rouge* did not win, and it remained unstaged until last month, when it was done by the St. Louis company. A piano-vocal score, prepared by Ravel, had appeared in about 1905. In 1930–32, Delius and Fenby adapted some of the lyrical music of *Margot* to lines from *Leaves of Grass* (starting with "Once I pass'd through a populous city"), as *Idyll,* for soprano, baritone, and

478

orchestra. Later, the full score of *Margot* was mislaid. A few years ago, Fenby—with *Idyll*, the Ravel piano score, and his own intimate knowledge of Delius's practice to guide him—produced a new orchestration of the opera, which was performed by the BBC and then issued on disc. Fenby's score is convincingly Delian but in places a shade fuller than Delius's original, which turned up again in time to be used for the St. Louis production. Fenby conducted.

Margot, like *Cavalleria*, has a verismo plot. (The libretto, by Berthe Gaston-Danville, is in French doggerel.) In a Paris dive frequented by pimps and prostitutes, a soldier, Sergeant Thibault, dropping in to shelter from the rain, perceives among the girls his former village sweetheart Marguerite, known now as Margot the Redhead. The two recall the past and plan to leave the wicked city, but Margot's pimp turns up and bars their way. In a quarrel, he kills Thibault. Margot kills him. The police enter, asking for Margot la Rouge, and she lifts high her bloodstained hands. As verismo plots go, it's not a bad one, but the dramaturgy is ineffective: more than half the forty-minute opera is taken up with desultory conversation among the clientele, and nothing much of interest happens until Margot and Thibault start reminiscing. The opera consists, roughly, of a ravishing "idyllic" prelude, with a winding English-horn solo; a good deal of musically dull dialogue; and a lyrical duet. The best music reappears in *Idyll*.

Frank Corsaro and Ronald Chase, the director and the designer of the Washington *Koanga* and *Village Romeo* and of the St. Louis *Fennimore*, collaborated again on *Margot*. The opera was performed behind a gauze semicylinder, played upon by slide projections of Paris façades, streets, and bridges, with the singers in pools of light behind. This cinematic mode of presentation can be effective, but often it seems to me more decorative than theatrical: it dissipates dramatic tensions by pulling the eye away from the living actors. (The gauze also puts up a dramatic—and probably, to some extent, an acoustic—barrier between the stage and the house.) Employed by Mr. Corsaro and Mr. Chase for the City Opera's production of Erich Korngold's *Die tote Stadt*, it made much of that score seem like a soundtrack to a Bruges travelogue. In *Margot*, the action strayed out from the bar into the streets and onto the quais. The slender work might well seem stronger if concentrated in the single, realistic set of the composer's prescription—one whose seaminess would throw into contrast the lovers' dreams. ("On Sundays, we'll go and gather white violets in the woods and watch our reflections in the streams, silver mirrors, far from evil desires and evil people.") On the whole—if not always—operas are most successfully produced in the way their creators intended, and the dreamy, "drifting" aspects of Delius's music need no visual underlining. It might be better to emphasize the clarity and precision of his forms. Nevertheless, on its own terms the production was adept, sensitive, and good to look at, and the young cast, led by Melanie Sonnenberg, as Margot, and James Anderson, as Thibault, was admirable. The St. Louis Symphony produced some beautiful playing for Mr. Fenby, who was conducting his first opera.

Margot was paired with a production of Poulenc's first opera, *Les Mamelles de Tirésias*, directed and designed by the same team. It was a smart, entertaining, and stylish presentation—far more successful and poetic than the Met's. Susan Peterson, as the wife who becomes a man for a while, and Allan Glassman, as the husband who turns to child-bearing, were both charmingly deft. In small roles, St. Louis young regulars (Judith Farris, David Parsons, John Davies, Joseph McKee) and young débutants (Katherine Henjum, Edmund Alex Robb) were excellent. So was the dapper young chorus. (There is a new chorus master this season, Donald Palumbo.) William Harwood, conducting, showed that Poulenc's exquisitely fashioned score is indeed, as Grove remarks, "both funny and beautiful."

St. Louis continues to assemble some of the most attractive and ac-complished of young American singers and to present them in well-re-hearsed productions where they can shine. All the operas are sung in English, and so the shows are dramatically alive. The usual pattern is a Mozart, a standard Italian piece, a new or unusual opera, and an ad-venturous double bill. This year, the Mozart was *Don Giovanni* (done in my translation). The standard piece was *La traviata*. Kerry McCarthy (Violetta), Tonio di Paolo (Alfredo), and John Brandstetter (Germont) could all with advantage have sung more softly at times, and more variously—paying greater attention to words and to phrasing. In the St. Louis theatre, which seats about nine hundred, any forcing beyond the limits of pure, flowing tone is even less forgivable than elsewhere. Subtlety, however, had probably been discouraged by the styleless, er-ratic conducting of Henry Lewis, on which the show foundered. Colin Graham's stage direction was somewhat overpointed. John Conklin's décor was dowdy. The standard piece often turns out to be the least rewarding of the season's offerings. For next year, *Madama Butterfly* is billed. It could be unstandard if the company revived Puccini's stronger, unconventional, less sentimental first version. [*In fact, it did his third version, which is also a more arresting drama than the familiar, fourth version.*] The hit of the season was Berlioz's last opera, *Béatrice et Béné-dict*. Berlioz described it as "a caprice written with the point of a nee-dle" and as "one of the liveliest and most original things I have done." The St. Louis performance was bewitching. Just about everything was right. The minor reservations that arise at an imperfectly balanced production were dispelled by this one. One left the theatre elated, en-tranced. In the warm, soft air, fireflies were darting over the sur-rounding lawns; if nightingales existed in America, they would doubtless have been singing. St. Louis, like Glyndebourne, has eve-nings when all things seem to conspire for delight. (At Glyndebourne, bats sometimes flitter through the *Figaro* garden; at the last St. Louis *Béatrice*, fireflies flickered in the theatre.) Berlioz's opera, as David

Cairns puts it, "evokes a special, recognizable world...the noonday Italian brilliance of *Benvenuto Cellini* softened to the translucent light of late afternoon"; romantic love that lasts forever may be—as Beatrice and Benedick remind us—an illusion, but "it is a beautiful illusion, with eternal power over the minds of men."

Hero, Berlioz's embodiment of that love, was embodied by Sylvia McNair, a radiant young soprano, limpid and pure and true of voice: a singer so instinctively musical and so joy-giving that I reach back to memories of Sena Jurinac at Miss McNair's age—just twenty-seven—for comparisons. She is less experienced onstage than Miss Jurinac—who had sung her first professional Mimì at twenty-one and three years later became a star of the Vienna State Opera—was at that age, but her free, unaffected singing holds a similar warmth and candor. The darker, more complicated timbres of Susanne Mentzer, a Beatrice with a not displeasing touch of resin in her tone, made a fine contrast; she was spirited, witty, and moving. The warm, carefully graded contralto of Janice Taylor, as Ursula, joined beautifully in the nocturnal duet with Hero and in the women's trio. All three singers were St. Louis débutantes, but I'd admired all three before—Miss Taylor as Pauline in an Ottawa *Queen of Spades,* Miss McNair in her student days at Bloomington, Miss Mentzer in her student days at the Juilliard. Michael Myers, the Benedick, was less elegant of tone than a Benedick should be, but he was energetic, passionate, and manly. Mr. Parsons was a frank, winning Claudio. Mr. Davies (Somarone) and Mr. McKee (Don Pedro) were admirable. Mr. Conklin had designed a pretty set—an eighteenth-century architectural capriccio peopled by characters in nineteenth-century dress. It was delicately lit by Peter Kaczorowski—if a trifle fussily during Beatrice's aria, with that tiresome "mood" lighting which underlines each turn of the music. Sometimes *Béatrice* can seem a *Much Ado* diminished—the play divested of its dark side (Berlioz omitted Don John, his machinations, and all the hurt they cause) and then padded out in an almost masquelike way with musical numbers. Berlioz's claim that the "dialogue is almost word for word from Shakespeare" is misleading. About half is. The dialogue is important, since the musical numbers themselves are theatrically static. In what might be called a pre-Mozart, an almost Handelian, manner, they sustain and make vivid a particular emotion or conflict of emotions. Colin Graham, the director of *Béatrice,* had prepared dialogue so skillfully drawn from Shakespeare that the numbers fell naturally into place. The result was not a *Much Ado* manqué but a complete, self-sufficient drama based, as the composer said, on "a part of Shakespeare's play." It was beautifully paced and proportioned. It was well spoken and well acted besides being well sung. John Nelson's conducting caught both the quicksilver brilliance and the soft-pulsing enchantment.

PIANISTS

THE MOST stirring concerts of the season were probably the seven of Alfred Brendel's Beethoven sonata cycle in Carnegie Hall, given in three weeks of May. They dominated New York's music, even though the city's busy, varied musical life makes hard a single-minded, Bayreuth-like attention to one composer. I missed two of them. The cycle is still being discussed and will be remembered.

Brendel, who is fifty-two, has been long associated with the sonatas. In the early 1960s, he recorded them for Vox, taking two years to do so. He played them in the Wigmore Hall, in London, in 1962. Between 1971 and 1978, he recorded them again, for Philips. (Both sets remain in print.) In the winter of 1976-77, he played them in the Queen Elizabeth Hall, and in the spring he brought a three-concert sampler of that cycle to Carnegie—a program apiece of early, middle, and late sonatas. This season, Brendel played the cycle extensively—in ten European cities before New York. In Europe, he took out just one program at a time on the ten-city circuit and made the round seven times. Then in Carnegie he brought all the programs together. He began with Opus 2, No. 1, and ended with Opus 111, but otherwise disposed the sonatas, not chronologically, to form seven balanced programs. The fame of his latest cycle preceded him. The day after the London concerts (again given in the Elizabeth Hall) ended, the London *Times* had an editorial, entitled "A Whole World in His Hands," which told of "famous poets, writers, administrators, historians, as well as musicians, critics, and musical analysts at these concerts, in the midst of rapt capacity audiences," and of "hundreds of music lovers turned away." Hundreds of music lovers did not have to be turned away from Carnegie, but thousands came. The hall, which holds almost three thousand —the Elizabeth Hall holds a little over a thousand—was well filled for the first concert and was packed for the last.

Why an *intégrale,* as the French call it? On the simplest level, it's a feat and a challenge—to bring thirty-two intellectually and technically demanding works up to performance point. In his collection of essays *Musical Thoughts and Afterthoughts* (Princeton), Brendel tells us not to underestimate "the extent to which the circus is reflected in concert-giving," where "the interpreter puts himself on display: a juggler, tightrope-walker and trapeze-artist of piano-playing." This aspect, he suggests, "rather than the communication of musical essentials ... even today draws many deeply serious listeners to the concert hall, unaware of their motivation." Saint-Saëns at his Paris début, in 1846, an eleven-year-old prodigy, offered as an encore to play any of the thirty-two sonatas from memory. Gary Goldschneider, I read, recently played all thirty-two in a single, twelve-hour recital. The first public *intégrale*, it seems, was Charles Hallé's, at eight London concerts in 1861. Carl Wolfsohn played all the sonatas in Philadelphia in 1863, and later in New York and Chicago. Artur Schnabel, the supreme Beethoven pianist of our century, played the first of his *intégrales* at seven Berlin concerts in 1927, the centenary of Beethoven's death, and he made his famous recordings of the sonatas across four years, 1932–35, in London. The last important cycle in New York before Brendel's was probably Claudio Arrau's, in Town Hall in 1953–54; Arrau's recorded *intégrale*, made from 1962 to 1966, is also on Philips.

There is, of course, a nobler reason than the circus one for attending a Beethoven sonata cycle. It can be stated briefly: the sonatas are the greatest music written for the piano. David Hamilton's program notes for the Brendel concerts carried as epigraph some sentences from *Musical Thoughts and Afterthoughts* defining the sonatas' uniqueness:

> First, they represent the whole development of a genius, from his beginnings to the threshold of the late quartets.... Secondly, there is not an inferior work among them.... Thirdly, Beethoven does not repeat himself in his sonatas; each work, each movement is a new creation.

Elsewhere, after citing Busoni's aphorism on Mozart "Along with the mystery he provides the solution," Brendel observes that Beethoven's sonatas, on the other hand, remain forever elusive. We go with confidence to hear his latest accounts of them because for twenty years he has been their committed and illuminating interpreter, making new discoveries and finding new insights he is eager to share—to put to the test, one might say, of public performance.

I chose the epithet "stirring" to characterize the concerts partly because of Beethoven, partly because of Brendel. In a 1920 essay, Busoni—about whose performances of the late sonatas Edward Dent wrote so eloquently—remarked:

> You might speak of "the divine Rossini." You can also speak of "the divine Mozart." But you cannot say "the divine Beethoven." That does not sound right. You must say "the human Beethoven."... Beethoven's heart was great and pure, and it felt for humanity.... His proverbial struggles may be nothing else but the difficult endeavor to put human strivings...into musical forms.

To call Brendel stirring is more provocative. He has said, "Although I find it necessary and refreshing to *think* about music, I am always conscious of the fact that *feeling* must remain the Alpha and Omega of a musician," but many people find him unemotional. My colleague at *New York*, after paying tribute to his "keen musical intelligence as well as his physical stamina and mental concentration," called his playing "so correct, so immaculate, so dry-eyed, so infuriatingly objective" that he decided not to stay the course.

I never heard Schnabel play (he was born in 1882 and died in 1951) but was brought up on his records. In live performance, I learned Beethoven's piano music from Wilhelm Backhaus, who embodied an earlier, more romantic, less "intellectual" approach to Beethoven than Schnabel's; from Edwin Fischer (Brendel's teacher), who was poetic, unselfconscious, and entirely lovable; from Walter Gieseking, who realized everything in terms of beautiful tone, and Wilhelm Kempff, who magisterially blended charm, caprice, and profundity; from Arrau, Rudolf Serkin, Solomon, and, among my near-contemporaries, Julius Katchen. None of them sounded as Brendel sounds. I believe that musical sound-ideals in the 1980s are different from those of the 1950s, and very different from those of the 1930s; that ears (corrupted, perhaps, by the prevalence of amplification, and slightly deafened by everyday din) are tuned to different expectations; and that conductors, players, and instrument-makers, perhaps unconsciously, strive for a clearer, harder, stronger, less warmly beautiful timbre than their fathers did. In another essay, Brendel says, "When listening to the records of Cortot, Fischer or Schnabel, I feel as if I were sitting in a good seat in a good hall; the timbre of the great pianist is there, the piano sounds homogeneous in all registers, dynamic climaxes and hushed tones come over with equal conviction." Whereas modern recording techniques, he implies, are less closely related to what one hears in the concert hall from modern pianists. I agree with the first part of his proposition. When listening to Cortot or to Fischer records, I do hear the pianist that I used to listen to so eagerly in concert halls. But if Brendel were able to sit in the body of a concert hall today and listen to himself play I think he might hear, perhaps to his consternation, the pianist that is heard in his recordings. Records reflect, capture, and then reinforce the sound-ideals of their day. Beecham on records and Furtwängler on records sound much as Beecham and Furtwängler did in concert. Solti and Muti on records sound much as Solti and Muti do now in concert. Many factors, not only instruments and the way they are played, are at work. Modern concert halls with hard, clinical acoustics are accused of aspiring to the sonic condition of modern high-fidelity recordings. This is all an impression, not something easily proved. Records are factual "documents" about such matters as tempo, phrasing in time, and the degree of portamento the strings employ; in matters of timbre and balance they can be misleading. But it is a fair presumption that engineers aim at producing the kind of sound most admired at the time, and so in this respect records can be evidence, too—evidence that needs careful interpretation and some knowledge of recording techniques.

Every musician, I imagine, carries "memory tapes" in his mind of particular performances. I can rerun mine for a Michelangeli *Gaspard* that provided the most bewitching piano sound I have ever heard, or my first hearing of Horowitz as he stroked the opening theme of Rachmaninoff's Third Concerto from the keyboard. They are "audio-visual" memories; I'm back in, respectively, the Florence Comunale and London's Festival Hall. How accurate they are from a sound point of view I can't tell. There are other unforgotten performances—among them a Fischer Pathétique, a Kempff Hammerklavier, a Gieseking Waldstein, a Katchen Diabelli, Brendel's playing of the last three sonatas at York University in 1969—the vivid memories of which seem to be confirmed, but have possibly now been colored, by the artists' recordings of those works.

I'm going a long way about to find reasons for things that puzzle me—the divergence of reactions to Brendel, the defensive note in even the most laudatory accounts of him, my own mixed feelings—while weighing the fact that recordings now play as large a part in musical life as live concerts do. Are Beethoven pianists always controversial? When Hans von Bülow played twenty-two of the sonatas in New York, in 1889, Henry Krehbiel wrote, "Those who wish to add intellectual enjoyment to the pleasures of the imagination derive a happiness from Bülow's playing which no other pianist can give to the same degree." But James Huneker was unimpressed: "All intellect... cerebral, not emotional... the temperament of a pedant." Schnabel, the great Schnabel, was and still is chided for rushing and for imperfect technical command. Memory can't be dismissed. Appraisal is made against knowledge of both the works and how others have played them. A young enthusiast tells me he was tempted to cry to two elderly members of Brendel's audience who went rambling on about the Cortot and the Schnabel recitals they had attended, "You can keep your memories. Enough for me that I have heard Brendel!" I envy him that freshness. Will he decades hence—how will Beethoven's sonatas be played then?—become in turn a *laudator temporis acti*? To my ears, Brendel's playing lacks charm of timbre—lacks warmth in cantabile melodies, lightness and ripple in quick figurations, and ethereal beauty of sound in the hushed trilling of the late sonatas. From where I sat in Carnegie (about midway back, on the left aisle), rapid notes often tended to become smudges or blurs—abrupt single gestures rather than detailed, delightful filigrees. (Examples: the sixteenth-note bubbles that burst into the scherzo theme of Opus 2, No. 2; the sixteenth-note arpeggio sweep into its rondo theme.) Charm of timbre, I'm told, is not Brendel's concern. But I miss it. The other Beethoven players I've mentioned had it. Brendel does have charm of thought. It would be oversimplifying to suggest that, where earlier pianists rendered Beethoven's sonatas in color, Brendel gives us renderings in black and white. Some such analogy is tempting: one perceives relations, proportions, and form more readily in a line drawing than when the eye is allured by richness and seductiveness of color. One perceives them in Brendel's playing. Should we call it "post-Schenkerian"? Although Heinrich Schenker's analytical editions of the late sonatas began to appear in 1913 and were known to earlier generations, it is in our day

that people have begun to listen to Beethoven in a more formally analytical way.

There is another factor that affects contemporary Beethoven performance: the increased awareness on both pianists' and listeners'
parts that the pianos Beethoven composed for were unlike the pianos
of today. As Brendel has written, "we have to resign ourselves to the
fact that whenever we hear Beethoven on a present-day instrument,
we are listening to a sort of transcription." He goes on to argue in
favor of using the modern grand all the same, as being a richer and
more versatile instrument, even though some effects Beethoven requires can only be approximated on it. Charles Rosen has argued similarly. Both pianists, I think, now play Beethoven on modern grands
with a keener knowledge of their specific limitations than earlier pianists possessed. Thoughts about sound and thoughts about structure are
hardly separable. Rosen's observations on the Waldstein pedal indications, in a chapter of Dominic Gill's *The Book of the Piano* (Cornell), are
lucidly and convincingly supported by Rosen's performance of the
Waldstein in a Nonesuch album of middle-period sonatas. My ideal
Waldstein finale now combines Gieseking's poetic, captivating tone
quality with Rosen's firm structural definition.

Brendel, it is perhaps too seldom remarked, is an uneven pianist. I
was disappointed by his second recital. The third, which closed with a
thrilling, wayward Appassionata, held me spellbound. He often starts a
concert apparently tense, ill-at-ease; then after the intermission he settles, fingers and mind begin to flow together, and he seems to be in
rapport with his listeners. (In a hall as big as Carnegie, the number of
coughers, fidgeters, premature applauders, and wearers of beeping
wristwatches is large.) Because of his unevenness, it is hard to generalize; from jottings and memories of what he did here, what there—and
what now, what then—let me try. The early Vox recording shows
Brendel at his most unaffectedly strong and poetic. This is a young
man's Beethoven—buoyant, fiery, and generous. By contrast, the Philips cycle is thoughtful, point-making, and exploratory even to a fault.
There are many rare insights, but it is Beethoven in tight closeup. The
Carnegie cycle was freer, fresher, bolder. There were things I didn't
like at all (a lack of impetus in the first and the last movements of the
Pastoral, for example, and a mannered delay accent on the third note
of its theme) and others that were daring, even reckless. There was a
welcome sense that Brendel, far from endeavoring to set out his current "definitive" interpretations, was venturing—was ready to take
chances that might (as in the Hammerklavier finale) or might not (as in
the first movement of Opus 109) come off. At times, he seemed almost
to be improvising—on the secure basis of his ten recent performances
of the same sonata. It wasn't divine Beethoven, and Opus 111 was not
sublime. But it was human Beethoven. That London editorial put it
well:

It is not that his touch is finer, the sounds he produces more beautiful, or his pedaling more subtle than that of other pianists: indeed on all these counts he could be surpassed. But his grasp of the issues at stake in the music is incomparable.

In May, Vladimir Horowitz played a recital in the Metropolitan Opera House that began with a grotesque Opus 101 (which Brendel had played the week before), distorted as if to validate the contentious conclusion of the New Grove entry on him: "Horowitz illustrates that an astounding instrumental gift carries no guarantee about musical understanding." Then came Schumann's *Carnaval*—clattery and pointlessly eccentric. A Chopin group after the intermission brought some traces of the old wizard. The thumbnail characterizations in *The Book of the Piano* say of Horowitz that "even at his most provocative and controversial, he compels his critics to suspend judgment, listen, and marvel." Not this time.

In April, Charles Rosen ended his Carnegie Hall recital with an inspired performance of *Carnaval*—one with a line that ran firmly from piece to piece, that made it a coherent, colorful progress. It's years since I've listened to *Carnaval* so avidly or followed it with such delight in Schumann's inventions. Before it, Rosen played Schumann's bold, beautiful, rarely heard Impromptus on a Theme of Clara Wieck, Opus 5. The recital began with Chopin—two nocturnes and the B-minor Sonata—and continued with the most brilliantly shaped account we've had yet of Elliott Carter's *Night Fantasies*. I don't *always* enjoy what Rosen has to say, but when he hits the mark he is dazzling.

Later that week, there was more rare Schumann in Carnegie, from Emil Gilels: the Piano Pieces, Opus 32. It was followed by the Symphonic Studies. The recital began with the first book of Brahms's Paganini Variations and his Opus 116 Fantasias. Ever since Gilels's London début, in the fifties, I've thought him a solid, strong, sure, totally reliable, but rather uninteresting pianist. This is not received opinion. Mr. Gill, in Grove, mentions him in a breath with Sviatoslav Richter. I still can't hear why, though I keep trying.

Let me, while writing about pianists, praise Joseph Horowitz's *Conversations with Arrau* (Knopf) as one of the best books about a performing artist ever written. Mr. Horowitz, a former *Times* critic, asks the right, intelligent questions. Arrau answers fluently and frankly. It's an enthralling, free-flowing, but shapely compound of reminiscences and of observations on music, on particular pieces (and particular measures in those pieces), on piano playing, and on individual pianists. And let me deplore Glenn Plaskin's *Horowitz* (Morrow) as a coarse, gossipy chronicle that makes no musicianly attempt to examine why Horowitz is the most famous pianist of our day.

INDEX

Compositions reviewed are indexed under their composers. Boldface figures indicate extended discussion or, in long entries, distinguish reviews of the work or the performer in question from passing references. Musical organizations outside New York based in a particular city are generally listed under that city (e.g., Boston, Opera Company of).

Aalto, Erkki, 445
Abanes, Richie, 360
Abbado, Claudio, 52–53, 60–63, 130, 152, 337, 352, 407, 408
Abert, Hermann, 200
Abingdon: Unicorn Theatre, 278
Abraham, Gerald: *Hundred Years of Music*, 135
Accademia Monteverdiana, 305
Adam, Adolphe: *Chalet*, 453–54
Adams, Donald, 452–53
Adams, John, **107–8**, 465
  Common Tones in Simple Time, 106, 108, 466, 470
  Grand Pianola Music, **470**
  Harmonium, 106, 108, 113, 470
  Phrygian Gates, 108
Addison, Joseph, 278–79, 282
Adler, Kurt Herbert, **35–36**, 102–3, 317–318
Aeschylus, 265, 394, 459
  Oresteia, 368
Agate, James, 23
Agler, David, 101–2
Ahlstedt, Douglas, 375
Ahrend, Jürgen, 108
AIA Guide, 39, 261
Akhmatova, Anna: *Requiem*, 131
Albert, Donnie Ray, 64, 163–64, 370
Alboni, Marietta, 62
Albrecht, Gerd, 100
Alcantara, Theo, 140
Alden, David, 283
Aler, John, 140, 163–64

Alexander, Carlos, 176
Alexander, John, 282, 334
Allen, Ross, 121, 243, 245
Allen, Thomas, 24, 428
Allío, René, 194
Alma-Tadema, Lawrence, 37
Almeida, Antonio de, 242, 262-63
Altman, Robert, 347
Altmeyer, Jeannine, 463
Amadé Trio, 230
Amato, Anthony, 454–55
Amato Opera, 454–55
American Brass Quintet, 435
American Composers Orchestra, 258, 351–53, 383–84, 411
American Institute for Verdi Studies, 38, 190
American Lyric Theater, 117
American Musicological Society, 346
American Opera Project, 36
American Philharmonic, 312
American Repertory Theatre, 196–99, 271, 403–4, 406
American Society for Music Theory, 346
American Symphony Orchestra, 235–36, 376
Ammons, A. R., 412
Amsterdam, 111, 115
  Concertgebouw Orchestra, 340, 352
Anania, Michael, 117
Andersen, Hans Christian: *Little Mermaid*, 430
Anderson, Alfred, 348

Anderson, James 479–80
Anderson, June, 63, 150, 275–76, 372, **374,** 376
Anderson, Laurie: *United States,* 409
Anderson, T. J.: *Soldier Boy, Soldier,* **361**
Andrade, Rosario, 265–66
Ann Arbor *News,* 347
Appia, Adolphe, 112, 394
Archbold, Larry, 108–9
Argento, Dominick: *Miss Havisham's Fire,* 477–78
Arico, Fortunato, 229
Ariosto, Lodovico, 79–80, 230
 Orlando Furioso, 199, 205
Aristotle, 476
Armistead, Christine, 406
Armstrong, Rebecca, 222
Arne, Thomas, 304
Arnold, David, 43
Arrau, Claudio, 324, 483–84, 487
Artpark, 111, 114, 115–16, 346
Arts Council of Great Britain, 165
Ashbery, John, 435
Ashley, Robert, 391
 Perfect Lives (Private Parts), **104,** 409
Ashton, Frederick, 178
Asia, Daniel, 345
Assad, James, 149
Aston Magna Foundation for Music, 309–11
Asturias, Rodrigo: Piano Sonata No. 4, 257
Atherton, James, 316
Atlanta, Choral Guild of, 217
Auden, W. H., 33, 354
Audubon Quartet, 106
Auer, Edward, 19, 292
Auerbach, Cynthia, 42, 44, 236
Aulos Wind Quintet, 255
Austen, Jane, 200
Austin, Frederic, 304–5
Austin, Michael, 185
Autant-Lara, Claude, 367
Auvinen, Ritva, 443
Avshalomov, Jacob: *Tom O'Bedlam,* 222
Azito, Tony, 20
Azouri, Maroun, 223

Babbitt, Milton, 12, 121, 210, 291, 381, 409, **410–11,** 413
 Arie da Capo, 211
 Ars Combinatoria, **392**
 Correspondences, **137–38**
 Dual, 212
 Elizabethan Sextette, 212

Fabulous Voyage, 212
Minute Waltz, 249
My Complements to Roger, 410
My Ends Are My Beginnings, 465
Paraphrases, 212
Partitions, 410
Playing for Time, 249, 410
Reflections, 411
Tableaux, 257
Bach, C. P. E., 66
Bach, Jan: *Student from Salamanca,* **50**
Bach, Johann Sebastian, 21, 108–9, 141, 143, 211, 216, 270–71, 353
 Cantatas: No. 4, 447; No. 26, 294
 Mass in B-minor, 130, **195**
 Orchestral Suites, 163
 Partita No. 2, 365
 Preludes, 114
 St. John Passion, **245–46**
Bach, John Christian, 110
Bach, Leonard Emil: *The Lady of Langford,* 399
Bach Ensemble, 195
Backhaus, Wilhelm, 484
Bacquier, Gabriel, 315
Badea, Christian, 185, 348
Baglioni, Bruna, 317
Bailey, Dennis, 296, 434
Baker, Janet, 64, **192–93,** 405
Baker, Julius, 235
Baker, Sharon, 198
Balanchine, George, 242
Balassa, Sándor: *Lupercalia,* 469
Baldani, Ruža, 317
Baldner, Thomas, 121
Balfe, Michael William, 241
Balk, H. Wesley, 118–19
Balkwill, Bryan, 72, 176
Ballard, Louis: *Xactcé 'óyan,* **352–53**
Ballet Rambert, 48
Baltimore: Lyric Theater, 319, 322
 Meyerhoff Symphony Hall, 320, 322
Baltimore Opera, 174
Baltimore Symphony, 318–19, 322
Banchetto Musicale, 472
Barbaux, Christine, 24
Barber, Samuel: Adagio for Strings, 379, 381
 Canzonetta, **190–91**
 String Quartet, 191
Barbieri-Nini, Marianna, 189, 275–76
Barbireau, Jacques, 220
Bardot, Brigitte, 367
Barenboim, Daniel, 88, 457
Barnes, Edward: Concerto for Piano,

Percussion, and Strings, 137
Barnum, P. T., 57
Barraqué, Jean: Piano Sonata, **246–48**
Barstow, Josephine, 277, 402, 429
Barth, Karl, 238
Bartlett, Eric, 412
Bartók, Béla, 153
 Concerto for Orchestra, 151
 String Quartet No. 1, 191
Bartoli, Cosimo, 76
Barzun, Jacques, 273
Bassett, Ralph, 29, 63, 65, 158
Bassi, Luigi: *Rigoletto* fantasia, 343
Bath Festival, 153, 165
Battle, Kathleen, 201, 233, 317, 402
Bauer-Ecsy, Leni, 70
Bayreuth, 112, 116, 127–28, 208,
 238–39, 325, 393–95, 397,
 433–34, 451, 458, 460, 462–64
BBC, 53, 165, 168, 194–95, 215, 217,
 255, 267, 287, 400, 419, 435, 478–
 479
 Young Conductors Contest, 209
BBC Symphony Orchestra, 131, 377
Beach, Amy, 292
Beaman, Don, 354
Beaser, Robert, 344–45
 Seven Deadly Sins, 344
Beattie, Herbert, 65, 308
Beatty-Kingston, William, 451
Beaumont, Cyril, 178
Becht, Hermann, 434
Beckett, Lucy: *Parsifal*, 238
Beecham, Thomas, 109, 172, 201, 305,
 478, 484
Beer, Lucille, 407
Beethoven, Ludwig van, 65, 95, 109,
 132, 141, 142–43, 153, 165, 213,
 234, 247, 318, 407, 467
 Bagatelles, 153: Op. 126, 425
 Christus am Ölberge, 68
 Diabelli Variations, 424–25, 485
 Egmont, 456
 Fidelio, 21, 22, 51, 91, 112, 192, 216,
  239–40, 241, 280, 421
 Leonore, **239–40**
 Leonore No. 3 overture, 91
 Piano Sonatas, 9–10, 453, **482–87**;
  Op. 2, No. 1, 482; Op. 10, 67; Op.
  13, 66, 67, 485; Op. 53, 485, 486;
  Op. 101, 487; Op. 106, 485; Op.
  111, 482, 486
 String Quartets, 248, 254; *Grosse
  Fuge*, 153; Op. 59, No. 2, 153; Op.
  131, 191; Op. 132, 250

 Symphonies, 338; No. 3, 372, 416;
  No. 5, **33,** 34, 186, 325, 337, **364–
  365;** No. 9, 365
 Violin Concerto, 345
Beethoven Quartet, 253
Beethoven Reader, 239
Behr, Randall, 102
Behrens, Hildegard, 334, 420, 423
Bell, Donald, 283
Bellincioni, Gemma, 10
Bellini, Vicenzo, 56, 161, 277, 372
 Capuleti e i Montecchi, 216, **407–8**
 Norma, 25, 29, 62, **132–34, 318,** 450
 Puritani, **139–40,** 146–47, **150,** 236–
  237
 Sonnambula, 132
Belluschi, Pietro, 30
Belt, Philip, 66, 67
Benedetto, Rose, 41
Benedyktowicz, Milosz, 350
Benelli, Sem, 218
Beni, Gimi, 63
Benjamin, George, 469
Bennett, Richard Rodney, 106, 266
Benois, Nicola, 135, 178
Bent, Ian, 335
Berg, Alban, 202, 211, 254, 288, 387,
 442
 Chamber Concerto, 160, 309
 Lulu, 87, 88, **90–94,** 286, 415, 421
 Wozzeck, 90, 91, 119, 286, 415, 423
Bergeson, Scott, 304
Bergman, Ingmar, 179, 347
Bergonzi, Carlo, 158, 190
Berg Society, 90–91, 92
Berio, Luciano, 10, 88, 106, 385
 Calmo, 385
 Concerto, 83
 Coro, **82–85**
 Opera, 83
 Sinfonia, 83
Beriozoff, Nicolas, 72
Berkeley, 106–9
 St. Joseph of Arimathea Chapel,
  108–9
Berkeley Contemporary Chamber
 Players, 106
Berkeley Symphony, 104–5, 106
Berlin: Comic Opera, 194, 448
 Singakademie, 270
 Überbrettl cabaret, 256
Berlin, Isaiah, 89
Berlin Festival, 210
Berlin Philharmonic, 324, **337–39,** 340
Berlin Radio, 399

Berlioz, Hector, 34, 42, 145, **185–90,** 277, 355, 470
  Béatrice et Bénédict, 24, **480–81**
  Benvenuto Cellini, **456–57,** 480–81
  Cinq mai cantata, 188
  Corsaire, 189; overture, 457
  Funeral and Triumphal Symphony, 186, 187
  Funeral March for the Last Scene of "Hamlet," 188
  Impériale, **186–88,** 272
  Lélio, 24, **273–74**
  Memoirs, 272–73
  Mort d'Ophélie, 188
  Nuits d'été, 24
  Requiem, 185–86, **272–73**
  Rob Roy, 146–47
  Roman Carnival, 33
  Roméo et Juliette, 274
  Sardanapale, 274
  Symphonie Fantastique, 24, **273–74,** 338
  Te Deum, 185–86, **457–58**
  Troyens, 206, 434, 455
  Waverley, 146–47
Bernardi, Mario, 158, 278–79, 283
Bernstein, Leonard, 10, 21, 110, 151, 213, 240, 381, 414, 453
  Candide, 327, **329–33,** 336
  Halil, **234–35**
  Jeremiah Symphony, 381
  Quiet Place, **474–78**
  Trouble in Tahiti, **474–77**
Berry, Walter, 462
Bertolli, Francesca, 280
Betterton, Thomas, 95
Billings, James, 63, 303, 453
Billington, Elizabeth, 162
Billington, Ken, 332
Bilson, Malcolm, **66–67,** 142, 228–29
Binghamton, SUNY: Chorus, 222
Binkley, Thomas, 243, 245, 336
Binns, Malcolm, 142
Birmingham Repertory Theatre, 332
Birmingham University, 473
Birtwistle, Harrison, 173
Bishop, Elizabeth: "Insomnia," 166, 256, 435
Bishop, Henry: *Knight of Snowdoun,* 146, 148
Bispham, David, 416–17
  Quaker Singer's Recollections, 416
Bizet, Georges: *Carmen,* 36, 56–57, 72, 117, 296, 426

Djamileh, 44
Fair Maid of Perth, 44
Ivan IV, 44
Pêcheurs de perles, **42–44,** 296
Björling, Jussi, 180
Blachly, Alexander, 76–77, 262, 326
Black, Leo, 53
Black, Robert, 160, 247–48, 412
Blake, David: *Toussaint,* 112
Blake, Rockwell, 29, 63, 149
Blake, Scott, 404–5
Blatt, Josef, 59
Blaustein, Susan: *Ricercate,* 258
Bleeke, Mark, 271
Blegen, Judith, 88, 154, 157, 313
Bliss, Anthony, 313
Bliss, Arthur, 304
  Clarinet Quintet, 47
  Oboe Quintet, 47
  Pastoral: "Lie strewn the white flocks," 47
Blitzstein, Marc, 224
  Cradle Will Rock, **453,** 454
  No for an Answer, 453
Blom, Eric, 20–21
Bloomington: *see* Indiana University
Böcklin, Arnold: "Isle of the Dead," 462
Bode, Hannelore, 103
Böhm, Karl, 35, 90, 337
Boito, Arrigo, 316
  Mefistofele, 265
  Nerone, **264–66, 454–55**
Bolcom, William, 18–19, 213
Bolt Beranek & Newman (BBN), 31–32, 34
Bonazzi, Elaine, 308
Bonci, Alessandro, 158
Bond, Edward: *Canzoni to Orpheus,* 421
Bonnefous, Jean-Pierre, 177
Bonynge, Richard, 133, 305, 318
Boone, Charles, 107
Boothe, Power, 426
Borgese, G. Antonio, 206–8
Borgioli, Dino, 25
Borodin, Alexander: *Prince Igor,* **70–72,** 73
Borodin Quartet, 252–53
Bortnick, Evan, 420
Boston: Camerata, 353–54
  Early Music Festival, 471, 473
  Orpheum, 207
  Symphony Hall, 319–20
Boston, Opera Company of, 72, 202-7,
  Kitezh, **447-49**

Boston Ballet, 472
Boston Committee on Human Rights and the Arts, 447
Boston Opera House, 447–48
Boston Symphony, 34, 52, 53, 85, 89, 106, 150–53, 170, 250, 319, 340, 352, 378, 435; *see also* Tanglewood
Botticelli, Sandro, 459
Bouleyn, Kathryn, 23, 287
Boulez, Pierre, 52, 54, 90, 106, 160, 173, 213, 291, 382, 388, 392, 397–398
  Notations, **88–89,** 130
  Piano Sonata No. 2, 168–69, 247
  Pli selon pli, 82, 178
  Rituel, 385, 465
  Structures, 266; *I*, 381–82, 386
Boulin, Sophie, 472
Boult, Adrian, 52, 142, 236, 377
Bowman, James, 81
Boyagian, Garbis, 102
Braccioli, Grazio, 78–81
Brackenridge, Rosanne, 195
Bradley, A. C., 95
Bradley, Gwendolyn, 178, 402–3, 468
Bradshaw, Richard, 64, 104, 109, 422
Bradshaw, Sally, 406
Brahms, Johannes, 142, 145, 206, 215, 236, 295
  Fantasias, Op. 116, 487
  German Requiem, 365
  Horn trio, 19
  Intermezzi Op. 118, 365
  Nänie, 188
  Piano Quartets, 17
  Schicksalslied, 188
  Symphonies: No. 1, **339;** No. 2, 40, **339;** No. 3, **339;** No. 4, 339
  Variations on a Theme by Paganini, 487
Brandstetter, John, 480
Braun, Victor, 296
Bream, Julian, 329
Brecht, Bertolt, 71, 202, 306
Brendel, Alfred, 9–10, 168, 277, 467, **482–87**
  Musical Thoughts and Afterthoughts, 482, 483
Brendel, Wolfgang, 37, 101
Brenneis, Gerd, 139, 150
Brenner, Peter, 103
Bretón, Tomàs: *Verbena de la paloma*, 287
Breuer, Marcel, 39

Brewbaker, Daniel: Piano Sonata No. 2, 392
Brewer, Daniel, 72
Brey, Carter, 292
Briggs, Robert, 68
Bristol University, 351
British Festival, 169, 173
Britten, Benjamin, 18–19, 68, 171–72, 173, 224, 304–5
  Curlew River, 383
  Fantasy Quartet, 46, 47
  Illuminations, 172
  King Lear, 95, 98
  Midsummer Night's Dream, 86
  Peter Grimes, 169, 225–26, 286
  Rape of Lucretia, **422–23**
  Six Metamorphoses after Ovid, 46–47
  Songs and Proverbs of William Blake, 416
  Spring Symphony, 109
  String Quartet No. 3, 383
  Temporal Variations, 46, **47**
  Two Insect Pieces, 46
  Young Person's Guide to the Orchestra, 86
Broch, Hermann: *Death of Virgil*, 246–247
Brockes, Barthold Heinrich, 370
Brody, Alan, 361
Broecheler, John, 134–35
Bronx Opera, 263
Brook, Peter, 125, 126–27, 198
  Empty Space, 234
  Orghast, 113–14
Brooklyn Academy of Music, 114, 330–31, 445
  Leperc Space, 222–23
  Opera House, 415–16
Brooklyn College: Chorus and Orchestra, 186, 188
  Preparatory Center Chorus, 187–88
  Whitman Hall, 186, 187
Brooklyn Philharmonia Chorus, 246
Brooklyn Philharmonic, 222, 415–16
Brown, Earle, 266, 382
  Centering, 385
Brown, Janet, 198
Brown, Zack, 157
Brown Bag Opera, 36, 102
Brown University, 191
Bruckner, Anton, 351, 447
Brusilow, Anshel, 294
Bruson, Renato, 38–39, 158–59
Bryden, Jane, 198, 222, **271**
Brymer, Jack, 61

493

Bryn-Julson, Phyllis, 131, 163–64, 469
Bryson, Roger, 391
Büchner, Georg: *Lenz,* 119–21
  Woyzeck, 119, 202
Buckley, Emerson, 269
Budai, Livia, 428
Budapest Opera, 401
Budden, Julian, 158, 190, 275
  Operas of Verdi, 232
Buffalo Philharmonic, 114
Buller, John: *Theatre of Memory,* 130
Bülow, Hans von, 337, 457, 485
Bumbry, Grace, 132, 134, 135, 241–42,
  408
Bunyan, John, 288
Buontalenti, Bernardo, 259
Burchinal, Frederick, 39
Burge, David, 46–47
Burgess, Anthony, 314
Burnett, Carol, 54–55
Burney, Charles, 76, 161, 278–79,
  304–5, 440
Burrows, Stuart, 232–33
Bury, John, 358
Burzio, Eugenia, 429
Busching, Marianna, 371
Busenello, Francesco, 360
Businger, Toni, 101
Busnois, Antoine, **219–20**
  "O crux lignum" Mass, 220
  "Regina coeli," 220
  "Victimae paschali," 220
Busoni, Ferruccio, 483
Bussotti, Sylvano, 391
  Catalogo è questo I, 385
  Pearson Piece, 386, 387
  Per tre, 386
Buswell, James, 19
Butlin, Roger, 193, 348–49
Buttolph, David, 222
Buxton Festival, **23–24**
Bynner, Witter, 17
Byron, George, 188–89, 274, 465

Caballé, Montserrat, 19, 133, 136, 213,
  277, 317, 372, 374, 428
Caccini, Giulio, 440
  Rapimento di Cefalo, 260
Caecilian Chamber Ensemble, 47, 49
Cage, John, 266, 268, **381–83,** 392, 409
  Atlas Eclipticalis, 267
  Imaginary Landscape No. 4, 381–82,
    386
  Music of Changes, 381–82, 386

Piano Concerto, 382–83
Cagnoni, Antonio: *Re Lear,* 95
Cahusac, Louis de, 471
Cain, James M., **284–86**
  Postman Always Rings Twice, 284–85
Cairns, David, 338, 480–81
Caldara, Antonio, 78
Calder, Alexander, 382
Caldwell, Sarah, 45–46, 202, 204, 205,
  206, 407, 447–49
California, University of: Berkeley, 104,
  106–7, 109
  Davis, 104
  Marching Band, 187
Callas, Maria, 11, 26–27, 43, 56, 132,
  136, 158, 192–93, 240, 318, 363
Calleo, Riccardo, 237
Calvé, Emma, 42, 296
Cambreling, Sylvain, 194
Cambridge: Sanders Theater, 472
Cambridge University, 404
Cammarano, Salvatore, 96, 139
Campbell, David, 436
Campbell, Patton, 157
Caniglia, Maria, 159
Canova, Antonio, 185
Canterbury Choral Society, 68, 340
Capell, Richard, 313
Capobianco, Tito, 27, 64, 135, 276,
  278, 355
Cappella Nova, 219–20, 362–63
Cappuccilli, Piero, 19
Cardew, Cornelius, 266–68, 386
Carewe, John 438
Carlisle, Kitty, 54, 422
Carlson, Lenus, 94
"Carmina Burana," **243–45, 354**
Carner, Mosco, 182
Carr, John, 23–24
Carreras, José, 19, 183
Carroli, Silvano, 317
Carroll, Lewis, 468–69
  Alice's Adventures in Wonderland, 32, 33
  Through the Looking Glass, 32, 33
Carroll Musical Instrument Service
  Corporation, 32
Carter, Elliott, 12, 151, 171, 291, 292,
  378–79, 381, 409, **435–38,** 466
  Brass Quintet, 167, 435
  Concerto for Orchestra, 167
  Double Concerto, 167
  Duo for violin and piano, 166, 167
  In Sleep, in Thunder, 435, 438
  Mirror on Which to Dwell, 166, 172,
    256, 435

Night Fantasies, **165–69,** 256, 411, 438, 487
Piano Concerto, 167
Piano Sonata, 167, 168, 438
Pieces for Four Timpani, 160
String Quartets, 166; No. 1, 295, 437
Symphony of Three Orchestras, 166, 167, 414, 465
Syringa, 166, 435, 465
Triple Duo, **435–36,** 437
Variations for Orchestra, 381, 385
Caruso, Enrico, 36–37, 42, 56, 158
Carver, Alison, 239
Casals, Pablo, 10, 172
Casey, Lawrence, 426
Cassilly, Richard, 179, 424
Castel, Nico, 94
Castiglione, Baldassare, 76
Castro-Alberty, Margarita, 159
Catania, Claudia, 178
Cathcart, Allen, 70
Caudwell, Christopher, 267
Cavalli, Francesco, 345
Cavallo, Enrica, 18
Cembala, J. M., 351
Cernay, Germaine, 36, 296
Cerullo, Richard, 454
Cervantes, Miguel de: *Cave of Salamanca, 50*
Jealous Old Man, 50
Chabrier, Emmanuel: *Gwendoline,* **355–56,** 400
Roi malgré lui, 355
"Villanelle des petits canards," 344
Chadman, Christopher, 242
Chailly, Riccardo, 219
Chalia, Rosalia, 343
Chalker, Margaret, 138
Chandler, Dorothy, 363
Chard, Geoffrey, 391
Charkey, Stanley, 271
Charles V, Holy Roman Emperor, 205
Charlston, Elsa, 413
Charpentier, Gustave, 345
Louise, 191, **194,** 195
Chase, Ronald, 419, 479
Chausson, Carlos, 278
Chausson, Ernest: *Poème de l'amour et de la mer,* 345
Cheek, John, 434
Chekhov, Anton: *Cherry Orchard,* 454
Chelton, Nick, 431
Chéreau, Patrice, 93, 395, 420–21, 460
Cherubini, Luigi, 21
Lodoiska, 372

Médée, 213, **240–42,** 327–28, 345
Chicago: Orchestra Hall, 52
Chicago, Lyric Opera of, 449–53
Chicago Symphony, 19, **52–54,** 60, 169–70, 318–19, 323–24, 351, 385, 433
Chicago Symphony Chorus, 53
Childs, Lucinda, 113
Chopin, Frédéric, 66, 143, 168, 258, 384
Ballades: No. 1, 159; No. 4, 159
Barcarolle, 142, 144
Études, 410–11
Mazurkas, 144
Nocturnes, 144, 167, 487
Piano Sonata No. 3, 487
Prelude in A, 144
Waltzes, 159
Chorley, Henry F., 25–26, 27, 241, 375
Christin, Judith, 214, 420
Christoff, Boris, 428
Christos, Marianna, 42–43
Ciannella, Giuliano, 157
Ciesinski, Kristine, 344
Cigna, Gina, 132
Cigoj, Krunoslav, 150, 265
Cilea, Francesco: *Adriana Lecouvreur,* 355, 400
Cimarosa, Domenico: Matrimona segreto, 400
Cincinnati Opera, 225, 226–27
Cincinnati Symphony, 421–22
Clapham, John, 415
Clarion Concerts, 68, 159–60
Clark, James, 29, 158
Clark, Lincoln, 105
Clark, Richard, 105
Clarksville Apple Shed, 304, 308
Classical String Quartet, 229–30
Clayton, Desmond, 99–100
Clayton, Jay, 222
Clément, Edmond, 296
Clement IX, Pope, 104
Cleveland Orchestra, 60, 82–83, 415
Clevenger, Dale, 19
Clever, Edith, 395, 397
Coates, Edith, 330
Cocteau, Jean: *Voix humaine,* 50
Cohen, Joel, 353
Colavecchia, Franco, 149
Colbran, Isabella, 148, 372–73, 374
Cole, Vinson, 59, 154
Collegiate Chorale, 209
Collet, Robert, 144
Collins, Kenneth, 429

Cologne Radio Chorus, 83–84
Comissiona, Sergiu, 158, 322
Commanday, Robert, 35, 98
Compton-Burnett, Ivy, 476
Concert Royal, 405–6, 470–71
Concord String Quartet, 292
Congreve, William: *Way of the World*, 366, 367
Conklin, John, 58, 242, 287, 318, 458, 460, 480–81
Conlon, James, **59–60**, 315
Connors, Carla, 348
Consoli, Marc-Antonio: *Afterimages*, 468
Contemporary Chamber Ensemble, 412–13
Contemporary Music Network, 165
Conwell, Julia, 225
Cook, Carla, 423
Cook, Deborah, 292
Cook, Rebecca, 37–38, 109, 317
Cooke, Deryck, 52, 61, 339
Cooper, James Fenimore, 117
    Last of the Mohicans, 116
    Red Rover, 189
Copper, Kenneth, 159–60
Cooper, Lawrence, 420
Coopersmith, J. M., 160
Copenhagen Wind Quintet, 255
Copland, Aaron, 10, 137, 353
    Appalachian Spring, 379, 380–81
    Lincoln Portrait, 380
    Our New Music, 377, 378–79
Copley, John, 193, 214, 368
Corbeil, Claude, 296
Cordero-Saldivia, Alvaro, 210
    Ausencias, 212
Cordova, Richard, 426
Corigliano, John: Clarinet Concerto, 40
Coronado, Francisco Vasquez de, 294
Corot, Jean-Baptiste, 112
Corsaro, Frank, 40–41, 50, 149, 150, **154–56,** 157, 217, 278–80, 282, 479
    Maverick, 156
Cortés, Hernán, 205
Cortot, Alfred, 484
Cossa, Dominic, 43, 64
Cossotto, Fiorenza, 19
Costa, Mary, 330
Costa-Greenspon, Muriel, 65, 332
Cotrubas, Ileana, 334
Couperin, François, 142
Courbet, Jean, 183
Covent Garden, (Royal Opera, Royal Ballet) 25, 35, 36, 41, 44, 48, 55, 81,

101, 138, 146, 180–81, 196, 214, 218, 304–5, 359, 363, 369, 390, 402, 426, 445, 459, 464, 470
    Alceste, **192–94,** 333, 349
    Don Carlos, **426–28**
    Semele, **366–69**
Cox, Ainslee, 110
Cox, John, 44, 204
Cox, Kenneth, 278
Craft, Robert, 212, 254, 347, 379–80
Crafts, Edward, 477
Craig, Patricia, 227
Cram, Ralph Adams, 261, 447
Crane, Hart: *Bridge*, 437
Craven, Dorothy, 223
Craven Singers, 223
Creech, Philip, 178, 233
Crespin, Régine, 102
Crist, Richard, 68, 118
Crocker, Richard, 108
Crosby, John, 263, 296
Cross, Joan, 422
Cross, Richard, 269
Crozier, Catharine, 164
Crumb, George, 381
    Haunted Landscape, **467**
Cuberli, Lella, 101, 149, 374, **455–56**
Cuccaro, Costanza, 283
Cummings, Claudia, 115–16, 269
Cummings, Conrad: *Summer Air,* 256
Curran, Alvin, 266
Curry, Diane, 64, 242, 452
Curtin, Phyllis, 58, 344, 417
Curtis, Alan, 104, 283, 400
Curtis, Jan, 225

Dahlhaus, Carl, 238
Dalcroze Society of America, 222
Dale, Clamma, 412
Dallapiccola, Luigi: *Four Machado Songs,* 271
Dallas Ballet, 293–94
Dallas Civic Opera, 72–73, 78, 80–82
Dal Monte, Toti, 25
Daltrey, Roger, 127
Damiani, Luciano, 201
Damsel, Charles, 209
Daniele, Graciela, 20
D'Annunzio, Gabriele, 217–18, 454
Dante Alighieri, 237, 346, 387
    Divine Comedy, 95, 184
Da Ponte, Lorenzo, 45, 199, 359
Darmstadt, 382
Darrenkamp, John, 315
Dashnaw, Alexander, 246

Davies, Dennis Russell, 351–52
Davies, John, 481
Davies, Peter Maxwell, 173, 291,
   435–40, 465–66
 Ave Maris Stella, **248–49,** 438, 468
 Brass Quintet, **249–50,** 435
 Cinderella, 24
 Eight Songs for a Mad King, 439
 Fantasia and Two Pavans, 412
 Image, Reflection, Shadow, **436–38**
 Jongleur de Notre Dame, **438–39**
 Kinloche His Fantassie, 438
 Mirror of Whitening Light, **437–38**
 Miss Donnithorne's Maggot, **439**
 Renaissance Scottish Dances, 438
 Salome, **293–94**
 Shakespeare Music, 412
 String Quartet, 436–37
 Symphonies, 82, 292; No. 2, 106,
   130, 150, 250, 435, 437
 Vesalii Icones, **439–40**
Davies, Philippa, 436
Davis, Andrew, 86, 205, 321
Davis, Colin, 86–87, 152, 187, 352
Davis, Leonard, 234–35
Davy, Gloria, 360
Dean, Robert, 195
Dean, Winton, 42–43, 63, 160–62,
   239–40, 419
 Handel and the Opera Seria, 81,
   278–79, 281, 405, 406, 445-46
Debussy, Claude, 48, 68, 155, 178, 355,
   473–74
 Mer, 151, 338
 Ondine, 365–66
 Pelléas et Mélisande, 37, 191, **194–95,**
   217–18, 286, 296
 Promenoir des deux amants, 18–19
 Sonata for violin and piano No. 3, 18
 Trois Ballades de François Villon, 18–19
Decker, Geraldine, 401
DeGaetani, Jan, 434
de Gaulle, Charles, 242
DeJong, Constance, 111, 113
De La Garza, Rene, 455
Delany, Mary, 445
Del Carlo, John, 462
Del George, Roseann, 185
Del Monaco, Mario, 37
Delibes, Léo: *Lakmé,* **72–73**
Delius, Frederick, 172
 Fennimore and Gerda, 478, 479
 Idyll, 478–79
 Irmelin, 478
 Koanga, 478, 479

Magic Fountain, 478
Margot la Rouge, **478–80**
Village Romeo, 478, 479
Della Casa, Lisa, 402
Del Mar, Norman, 304–5, 339
Del Tredici, David, 171, 213, 465
 Adventures Underground, 32
 Alice pieces, **32–33,** 466, 467,
   468–69
 Alice Symphony, 32
 All in the Golden Afternoon, 32, 468
 Child Alice, **32–33,** 468
 Final Alice, 32, 468
 Happy Voices, 30, **32–33,** 34, 468
 In Memory of a Summer Day, 32, 468
 Pop-Pourri, 32
 Quaint Events, 32, 468
 Vintage Alice, 32
De Luca, Giuseppe, 42, 56
De Lucia, Fernando, 43, 180, 296, 316
DeMain, John, 224–25, 477
de Mille, Agnes, 422
Demuth, Leopold, 58
Denda, Gigi, 64, 355
Denisov, Edison: *Signs in White,* 257
Dennis, Carolyn, 360
Dent, Edward J., 25, 26, 196, 198, 199,
   304, 366, 483
DeRenzi, Victor, 41–42
Dernesch, Helga, 100, 462–63
Desprez, Josquin: *Homme armé* Mass, 77
 Malheur me bat Mass, **76–77**
Des Roches, Raymond, 160
Detroit Concert Band, 110
Deutekom, Cristina, 105, 133
Devendra, Anand, 469
Devia, Mariella, 457
Devlin, Michael, 218, 462
Devol, Luana, 463
Devriès, David, 296
de Waart, Edo, 33–34, 52, 54, 60, 109,
   152, 236, 458, 463
Dexter, John, 87, 93, 156, 176–77, 231,
   233, 314, 408
Diaghilev, Sergei, 178
Diamond, David: Symphony No. 4, 258
Díaz, Bernal, 205–6, 208
Díaz, Justino, 45–46, 135, 150, 158,
   237, 456
Dickinson, Emily: "Because I could not
   stop for death," 108
 "Wild Nights," 108
Dickson, Stephen, 58–59, 65
Dicterow, Glenn, 345
Dietsch, James, 190, 209

Diez, Werner, 238
DiGiuseppe, Enrico, 158
d'Indy, Vincent, 473
    Fervaal, 355–56
di Paolo, Tonia, 400
Doebler, Lawrence, 222
Dohnányi, Christoph, 414–15
Dolce, Lynn, 455
Dolmetsch, Arnold, 140
Domb, Daniel, 86
Domingo, Placido, 19, 37, 54–55,
    133–34, 218, 317, 408
Donatello, 76
Donatoni, Franco, 385
Donaueschingen Festivals, 83, 382, 385,
    387
Donington, Robert, 163, 335
Donizetti, Gaetano, 57, 65, **135–36,**
    184, 216, 372, 407
    Adelia, 342–43
    Ange de Nisida, 342
    Anna Bolena, **25–29,** 136
    Belisario, 454
    Betly, **453–54**
    Caterina Cornaro, 342–43
    Chiara e Serafina, 28
    Dom Sébastien, 342
    Don Pasquale, 26–27, 342–43, 454
    Duc d'Albe, **341–43**
    Elisir d'amore, 26–27, 102, 287
    Favorite, 26–27, 342
    Fille du régiment, 342–43
    Linda di Chamounix, 342–43
    Lucia di Lammermoor, 20, 24, 25, 135,
        139, 146–47, 283, 454
    Maria di Rohan, 342–43
    Maria Padilla, 342–43
    Maria Stuarda, **135,** 192
    Martyrs, 342
    Poliuto, 136, 342
    Rita, 342–43
    Roberto Devereux, 55, 56
Donne, John: "Negative Love," 108
Donnelly, Dorothy, 23
Dooley, Jeffrey, 371
Dorati, Antal, 230
Dostoyevsky, Fyodor: *House of the Dead*,
    423
Dove, Neville, 448
Dow, Dorothy, 425
Dowell, Anthony, 178, 179
Dowland, John, 271
Downes, Edward, 287
D'Oyly Carte Opera, 452–53
Drew, David, 51, 211

Drucker, Stanley, 40
Druckman, Daniel, 412
Druckman, Jacob, 388, **465–66,** 470
    Animus IV, **344**
    Prism, **345**
Drummond, Dean: *Columbus,* 258
Dubos, René, 272
Duchamp, Marcel: *Mariée mise à nu,* 107
Dudley, Raymond, 143, 144–45
Dufay, Guillaume, 326–27
    Ave regina celorum Mass, 326
    Ecce ancilla domini Mass, 327
Dugger, Edwin, 107
Dukas, Paul: *Ariane et Barbe-Bleue,* 355–
    356
Dulcken, J. L., 67
Dumas, Alexandre: *Dame aux camélias,*
    184
Duncan, Ronald, 422
Dunham, Clarke, 332
Dunn, Mignon, 150, 239, 315, 420
Du Pré, Jacqueline, 172
Duprez, Gilbert, 343
Durand, Diane, 271
Dusseldorf Opera, 420
Dutoit, Charles, 457
Dvořák, Antonín, 295
    Rusalka, **429–32**
    String Quartet in F, 292
    Symphony No. 8, 415
Dvorksý, Peter, 102
Dworchak, Harry, 327–28, 448

Eames, Emma, 55, 56
Early Music, 66
Eastman Philharmonia, 378–81
Eaton, John: *Cry of Clytaemnestra,* 100,
    103–4, 106, 413
    Danton and Robespierre, 112, 413
    Greek Vision, **413**
Eberle, Katherine, 348
Echols, Paul, 261, 441
Eda-Pierre, Christiane, 72, 218–19
Eddleman, Jack, 140
Eddy, Timothy, 18
Edinburgh Festival, 332, 418–19, 478
Edinger, Christiane, 416
Effron, David, 378–81
Eimert, Herbert: *Selektion I,* 387
Einstein, Alfred, 199
Eisler, David, 102, 327, 332
Eisler, Hanns, 268
Elder, Mark, 195
Elgar, Edward, 10, 169, 171–72, 271,
    351

Cello Concerto, 172
Enigma Variations, 235
Symphonies, 172
Violin Concerto, 173
Eliot, George, 200
Elliott, William, 20
Ellis, Brent, 103, 157, 291–92
Ellis, David: *Sequentia IV,* 106
Ellsaesser, Charlotte, 118, 119
Elvira, Pablo, 140, 232, 265–66, 317
Emerson, Ralph Waldo, 289
Emmanuel Wind Quintet, 255
Emmons, Beverly, 209
Empire Brass Quintet, 249–50, 435
Encompass, 51
Encyclopaedia Britannica, 398
Enders, Katherine, 455
English Bach Festival, 48, 470–71
English Baroque Soloists, 445–47
English Concert, 163
English National Opera, 125, 130, 184,
    191–95, 196, 205, 281–82, 286,
    359, 388, 402, 403, 417–19
  Forza del destino, **426–29**
  Orfeo, **125–28**
  Pelleas et Mélisande, 191, **194–95**
  Rusalka, **429–32**
English Opera Group, 422
Engstrom, Robert, 75
Enna, August: Cleopatra, 399
Entremont, Philippe, 319
Erickson, Arthur, 321
Erkkilä, Eero, 445
Eschenbach, Christoph, 340
Eschenburg, Johann Joachim, 97
Escudier, Léon, 357
Esham, Faith, 227
Eugene: Hult Center, 324–26
Eugene Symphony, 318–19, 325
European Broadcasting Union, 53
Evans, April, 217
Evans, Beverly, 50
Evans, Joseph, 43, 303
Evans, Lloyd, 50, 156
Evans, Peter, 379
Everding, August, 101
Evstatieva, Stefka, 428
Ewing, Maria, 103, 201

Fairbanks, Douglas, 20
Fall, Leo, 20–21
Falla, Manuel de: Harpsichord
    Concerto, 295
Farina, Franco, 407
Farley, Carole, 400

Farrell, Eileen, 54–55
Farrell, Ranger, 39
Fassini, Alberto, 73
Fauré, Gabriel, 19
Favour, Mollie, 326
Feinberg, Alan, 249, **410–11,** 412, 470
Feliciano, Richard: *Crystal,* 191
  from and to, with, 107
Feldhoff, Gerd, 37
Feldman, Morton, 382
Felsenstein, Walter, 448
Fenby, Eric, 478–80
Ferden, Bruce, 225, 227, 288, 328
Ferretti, Jacopo, 62
Feuillère, Edwige, 367
Fiacco, Michael, 292
Finnish National Opera, 442
Fiorella, Bernadette, 261, 371
Fires of London, **435–39**
Fischer, Ádám, 101
Fischer, Alan, 455
Fischer, Edwin, 484, 485
Fischer-Dieskau, Dietrich, 95, 98, 264
Fisk, Charles, 143–44
Fitch, Bernard, 283
Fitch, Kenneth, 354
Fitzgerald, Edward, 370
Fitzwilliam String Quartet, 250,
    253–54
Flagello, Ezio, 318
Flagstad, Kirsten, 132, 138, 192, 277,
    348, 459
Flanigan, Clifford, 243
Fletcher, John: *Two Noble Kinsmen,* 24
Flindt, Flemming, 293
Flint, Mark, 102, 118
Florence: Teatro Comunale, 484–85
Floridia, Pietro: *Maruzza,* 399
Florilegium Chamber Choir, 261–62
Floyd, Carlisle, **223–28,** 287
  Bilby's Doll, 224
  Markheim, 224
  Of Mice and Men, 224, 226
  Susannah, 213, 223, 224, **225–28,** 346
  Willie Stark, 224–25
  Wuthering Heights, 224
Foldi, Andrew, 94
Fonda, Henry, 380
Foreman, Richard, 49
Forrest, Leon, 361
Forsythe, William, 421
Foss, Harlan, 65
Foss, Lukas, 121, 415–16
  Thirteen Ways of Looking at a Blackbird,
    258

Foster, Elizabeth, 289
Fouqué, Friedrich de la Motte: *Undine*, 430
Fowles, Glenys, 65
France Littéraire, 273
Franck, César: Symphonic Variations, 322
   Symphony, 59, **60, 209**
Frank, Joseph, 292
Frankenstein, Alfred, 107
Fraser, Malcolm, 24
Frazzi, Vito, 240–41
   Re Lear, 96
Frederick, Edmund Michael, 142–43, 145
Fredricks, Richard, 54, 150, 154–55, 158
Frederick II, King of Prussia, 206
Freeman, Carroll, 287, 457–58
Freeman, David, 125–27
Freni, Mirella, 180, 183, 277, 408
Freni, RoseMarie, 59
Freud, Sigmund, 265
Frey, Gaby, 218
Friede, Stephanie, 308, 375
Friedrich, Caspar David, 458–60
Friedrich, Götz, 69
Friend, Lionel, 195, 432
Frisell, Sonja, 38, 317–18
Frobenius, Leo, 223
Fröhling, Michael, 120–21
Fromm, Paul, 413
Fromm Music Foundation, 413
Frost, James Daniel, 308
Fry, Joseph Reese, 29
Fulkerson, Gregory, 412
Fuller, Albert, 309–10
Fulton, Albert, 309–10
Fulton, Lauran, 118
Furlanetto, Ferruccio, 317
Furniss, Rosemary, 436
Furtwängler, Wilhelm, 109, 209, 319, 337–39, 434, 435, 484

Gabin, Jean, 367
Gabrieli, Giovanni, 447
Gagliano, Marco da: *Dafne*, 259, **260–61**, 440
Gall, Jeffrey, 198
Galli, Filippo, 28
Galterio, Lou, 58–59, 62, 157, 225, 263, 288
Galvany, Marisa, 240, 327
Galway, James, 54–55, 337–38

Gamley, Douglas, 305
Gandhi, Mahatma, 111–12
Garazzi, Peyo, 428
Garcia, Manuel, 317
Gardelli, Lamberto, 39
Garden, Mary, 217
Gardiner, John Eliot, 125, 445–47, 470
Garner, Erroll, 235
Garrick David, 95
Garrison, Jon, 227, 328, 348
Gast, Peter, 237
Gatt, Martin, 61
Gautier, Judith, 394
Gay, John: *Beggar's Opera*, **304–8**, 354
Gayarré, Giuliano, 316
Gedda, Nicolai, 266, 457
Gentele, Göran, 388
George, Alan, 253
George, Hal, 158
George, Stefan, 138
Gerhard, Roberto, 386
   Symphony No. 4, 414
Gershwin, George, 21
   Porgy and Bess, 227, 361, 425
Gerstenberger, Emil, 23
Gesualdo, Carlo, 447
Ghelderode, Michel de: *Balade du Grand Macabre*, 389
Ghiaurov, Nicolai, 408
Ghislanzoni, Alberto: *Lear*, 95–96
Ghislanzoni, Antonio, 95, 314
Giacomini, Giuseppe, 315, 358
Giacosa, Giuseppe, 182
Giaiotti, Bonaldo, 134, 315
Giannini, Dusolina, 132
Giardina, Gary, 454
Gibbon, Edward, 68
Gideon, Miriam: Piano Sonata, 248
Gielen, Michael, 152, 204
Gielgud, John, 97
Gieseking, Walter, 484, 485
Gigli, Beniamino, 158, 220
Gilbert, W. S., 19–20, 450–53
Gile, Bill, 304
Gilels, Emil, **484**
Gill, Dominic: *Book of the Piano*, 142, 486–87
Ginastera, Alberto: *Barabbas*, 389
   Piano Sonata No. 2, **365**
Giovaninetti, Reynald, 323–24
Girdlestone, Cuthbert, 471
Giulini, Carlo Maria, 130, **363–65**
Gladstone, Herbert, 449
Glass, Philip, 211
   Dance, 113

Einstein on the Beach, 82, 112, 113, 114, 466
Music with Changing Parts, 115
Satyagraha, **111–16**
Glassman, Allan, 50, 264, 480
Glazunov, Alexander, 70
Glimmerglass Opera Theater, 449
Glinka, Mikhail: *Russian and Lyudmila*, 72
Glock, William, 173
Gluck, Christoph Willibald, 68, 260, 277, 456, 473–74
Alceste, **191–94**, 327, 333, **348–50**
Armide, 400
Iphigénie en Tauride, 147, 372
Orfeo, 112
Glyndebourne, 70, 130–31, 201, 292, 311, 328, 334, 349, 358–59, 360, 368, 422
Gniewek, Raymond, 90
Godard, Benjamin, 44
Goehr, Alexander, 173
Goeke, Leo, 349
Goethe, Johann Wolfgang von, 33, 45, 120, 121, 273, 342, 414
Faust, 265, 430
Jery und Bätely, 453
Goetz, Hermann: *Widerspenstigen Zähmung*, 214–15
Golani-Erdesz, Rivka, 86
Goldberg, Reiner, 397, 400
Golden, Emily, 434
Golden, Ruth, 288
Goldoni, Carlo, 453
Goldschmidt, Hugo, 162
Goldschneider, Gary, 482–83
Goldstein, N. B., 472
Golub, David, 309
Gomberg, Harold, 190–91
Gonzalez, Dalmacio, 343
Goodall, Reginald, 103, 125, 434, 435
Goode, Richard, 258
Goossens, Leon, 47
Gordon, David, 462–63
Gore, Pamela, 198
Gorgensen, Bill, 276, 355
Gorr, Rita, 36
Gossett, Philip, 149, 239, 456
Gould, Morton: *Housewarming*, 322
Gounod, Charles, 36
Faust, 24
Mireille, 296
Romeo and Juliet, 100, **102**
Gozzi, Carlo: *Donna serpente*, 216
Graf, Herbert, 368

Graff, Yveta Synek, 424
Graham, Colin, 157, 178, 200, 284–87, 296, 305–8, 427, 428–29, 480–81
Graham, John, 412
Graham, Martha, 125–26
Graham, Sharon, 452
Grainger, Percy: "Power of Love," 309
"Spoon River," 309
Gramm, Donald, 54–55, 201, 315–16, 403, 417, 448, 457
Granados, Enrique, 137
Spanish Dances, 365–66
Grant, Cameron, 343–44
Graun, Karl: *Montezuma*, 206
Gray, Linda Esther, 125
Grayson, Robert, 209
Greco, El, 408
Greenawald, Sheri, 477
Greenberg, Noah, 354
Greene, Harry Plunket: *Interpretation in Song*, 208
Greenwood, Jane, 148
Greer, Gordon, 350
Gregor, Josef, 297
Greitzer, Sol, 137, 235
Grice, Garry, 237
Griffes, Charles T., 381
Poem, 236
Griffin, Hayden, 201
Griffiths, Paul, 248–49, 293, 346
Grillparzer, Franz: *Ahnfrau*, 274, 356
Grisi, Carlotta, 62
Grisi, Giulia, 132
Grobe, Donald, 424
Gropman, David, 477
Grossi, Pasquale, 73
Grossmith, George, 453
Grotowski, Jerzy, 125, 126–27
Group for Contemporary Music, 89, 160, 212, 258, 392–93, 411, 432, 469
Grout, Donald: *Short History of Opera*, 217
Grove, Sir George, 74
Groves, Charles, 52
Grove's Dictionary of Music and Musicians, 20–21, 79, 135, 142, 159, 173, 220, 229, 243–44, 251, 257, 262–63, 348, 353, 379, 385, 415, 422, 480, 487
New Grove, 70, **74**, 76, 79, 81, 87, 101, 130, 136, 159, 180, 212, 223, 236, 262, 296, 335, 338, 362, 422, 487
Gruber, HK, 213
Concerto for Orchestra, 210

Gruber, HK (cont.)
  Frankenstein!!, **210—11**, 212
  ... of shadow fragrance woven, 211
Guarducci, Tommaso, 161
Guarino, Robert, 190
Guarneri Quartet, 253
Guggenheim Concert Band, 110
Giubbory, Shem, 266
Guidry, Roland, 354
Guilbert, Yvette, 75
Guild of Composers, 256—57
Gulli, Franco, 18—19
Gurlitt, Manfred, 202
Gustafson, Nancy, 463
Guthrie, Tyrone, 305, 330
Gutknecht, Carol, 65, 350
Gutter, Robert, 273—74

Haber, John, 360
Hadley, Henry, 33
Hadley, Jerry, 288
Haffner, Elisabeth, 310—11
Hager, Ghita, 135
Hahn, Reynaldo, 242—43
Haik, Wojciech, 350
Haitink, Bernard, 130, 152, 239, 340,
  352, **427—28**, 429
Hale, Robert, 64, 228
Halfvarson, Eric, 375
Hall, Janice, 59, 278
Hall, Peter, 198, **356—59**, 360, 451, 464
Hallé, Charles, 482—83
Halle: Handel Festival, 160
Hallé Orchestra, 171
Hamari, Julia, 150, 217
Hambraeus, Bengt:
  Introduzione-Sequenze-Coda, 387
Hamburg Opera, 120, 121, 127—28
Hamilton, David, 152, 335, 456, 483
Hamilton, Iain, 205
  Agamemnon, 418
  Anna Karenina, **417—20**
  Catiline Conspiracy, 419
  Pharsalia, 418—19
  Royal Hunt of the Sun, 418
  Tamburlaine, 419
Hammond, Arthur, 43—44
Hammond, Joan, 429
Hampson, Thomas, 288
Handel, George Frideric, 10, 12,
  270—71, 304, 471
  Admeto, 281, 283
  Agrippina, 281—82
  Alcina, 196, 403, 406
  Belshazzar, **367—68**

Coronation Anthems, 164
  Deborah, 369
  Deidamia, 196
  Dixit Dominus, 447
  Esther, 160, 164, 367, **369—71**
  Giulio Cesare, 56, **63—65**, 103, 162,
    196, 281—82, 283, 311, 403
  Grand Concerti, Op. 6, 164; in
    D-major, No. 5, 311
  Hercules, 196, 368, 369
  Israel in Egypt, **445—47**
  Jephtha, 368, 369
  Lotario, 280
  Messiah, **161—64**, 366—67, 370
  Oboe Sonata, Opus 1, No. 6, 47
  operas, **196—99, 278—83**
  Organ Concerto, Op. 4, 164
  Orlando, **196—99**, 271, 278, 283,
    403—6, 450, 452
  Partenope, 281, 283
  Rinaldo, **278—83**, 403, 406
  Rodelinda, 281—82
  Samson, 368, 445
  Saul, 368, 445, 452
  Semele, 22, 196, **366—67, 368—69**
  Serse, 283
  Te Deums, 270
  Theodora, 368, 369, **371**
Handel Opera Society, 196, 368, 369
Hannan, Eilene, 195, 431
Hanover Opera House, 128
Hanson, Nina, 107
Harbison, John, 171, 295, 465
  Full Moon in March, 427
  Violin Concerto, 469
  Wind Quintet, **255—56**
Hardy, Hugh, 31
Harewood, Earl of 204
Harman-Gulick, Michelle, 434, 452
Harper, Heather, **348**
Harris, Cyril, 31—32, 301—2, 320, 467
Harris, Hilda, 94
Harris, Katherine, 360
Harris, Roy, 377
Harrison, Deborah, 406
Harrison, Lou: Concerto for Violin and
  Percussion, 106
  Symphony No. 3, 353
Harrold, Jack, 303
Harrower, Peter, 477
Hartliep, Nikki Li, 422
Hartman, Karen, 90
Hartman, Vernon, 41
Hartmann, Karl Amadeus, 387
Hartmann, Rudolf, 314

Hartwick College Choral Theater
Ensemble, 223
Harwood, William, 287, 291, 480
Haskell, Judith, 117
Hastings, Edward, 422
Haugland, Aage, 139
Haweis, H. R., 144–45
Hawkins, John, 307
Hawthorne, Nathaniel: "Celestial
Railroad," 288
Scarlet Letter, 224, 225
Haydn, Joseph, 10, 21, 66, 67, 141,
164, 166, **228–31**, 295, 362, 378,
432
Andante and Variations in F-minor,
229
Armida, 230
Baryton Trios, 229
Fantasy in C, 229
Orlando paladino, **230–31**
Piano Sonatas, 229
Songs, 229
String Quartets, 254; Op. 54, No. 1,
229; Op. 71, No. 2, 191; Op. 74,
No. 3, 153; Op. 77, No. 2, 229
Symphony No. 88, 415
Haydn Studies, 230
Heartz, Daniel, 81, 333, 335
Heath, Edward, 449
Hecht, Anthony, 344
Heeley, Desmond, 134
Heifetz, Jascha, 11
Hei-Kyung Hong, 209
Heinikari, Matti, 443
Heinrich, Reinhard, 194
Helgeson, Alice, 239
Hellman, Lillian, 330–32
Helper, Ross, 105
Hempel, Frieda, 42, 313
Hemsley, Gilbert V., Jr., 27, 236, 242
Henderson, Alva: *Last of the Mohicans*,
228
Henneberg, Claus, H., 97–98
Henze, Hans Werner, 68, 277, 416
Barcarola, **136–37**
Bassarids, 415
Doppio Concerto, 130
Dramatic Scenes from Orpheus, **421–22**
Essays, 414
Monteverdi's *Ritorno d'Ulisse*, new
version, 136–37
Moralities, 223
Music and Politics, 308
Ode to the Westwind, 137
Orpheus, 136–37, **421**

Royal Winter Music, 329
Symphonies: No. 1, 130; No. 5,
414–15
Tristan, 136–37
We Come to the River, 136
Young Lord, 415
Hepokoski, James, 359
Herbert, Bliss, 295
Herbert, Victor, 21, 110
Babes in Toyland, **89–90**
Herford, Henry, **416–17**
Herşcovici, Philipp, 90–91
Hervig, Richard: *Entertainment*, 258
Hesch, Wilhelm, 58
Hess, Willy: "Beethovens Oper Fidelio
und ihre drei Fassungen," 239–40
Hesse, Ruth, 37
Heuberger, Richard, 20–21, 22
High Fidelity, 48
Hildegard of Bingen: *Ordo virtutum*,
335–36
Hill, Aaron, 279
Hill, John Walter, 80
Hill Smith, Marilyn, 391
Hillman, David, 193
Hindemith, Paul, 353, 416, 443
Neues vom Tage, 50
Hines, Jerome, 150, 238
Hiskey, Iris, 454
Hitler, Adolf, 51, 252, 416
Hoback, James, 37–38, 227
Hockney, David, 176–78
Hodeir, André, 246–48
Hoffmann, E. T. A., 364–65
Hofmann, Peter, 239, 462
Hofmannsthal, Hugo von, 216, 296–97,
313, 402
Hofsiss, Jack, 23, 242
Holland Festival, 51, 83
Holliger, Heinz, 107, 130
Holliger, Ursula, 130
Holloway, David, 73
Holloway, Robin, 469
Holt, Henry, 105
Hope, Julian, 348–49
Hopkins, G. W., 246
Hoppin, Richard: *Medieval Music*, 243
Horace, 241
Horenstein, Jascha, 52
Horne, Marilyn, 19, 81, 88, 148, 204–5,
280, 282, 318, 325, 372, **374–75**,
376, 405, **455**, 456
Hornik, Gottfried, 103
Horowitz, Joseph: *Conversations with
Arrau*, **487**

Horowitz, Vladimir, 159, 228–29, 277,
  365–66, 392, 484, **487**
Horton, Priscilla, 95
Hose, Anthony, 24
Hot Mikado, 450
Hotter, Hans, 103, 138, 192, 296, 459
Houseman, John, 453
Houston Grand Opera, 146–49,
  155–56, 174, 224–25, 280, 282,
  474, 476–77
Howard, Brian: *Inner Voices*, 427
Howarth, Elgar, 390, 391
Howell, Gwynne, 125, 434
Howlett, Neil, 195, 429
Hsu, John, 229
Hubay, Jenö: *A Cremonia Hegedüs*, 399
Hudson, Benjamin, 160, 416, 432
Hudson Review, 422
Hughes, Ted, 113
Hugo, Victor, 188
Huneker, James, 485
Hunter College, 260
Hurney, Kate, 426
Hynes, Elizabeth, 23, 214, 303, 434
Hynninen, Jorma, 444–45

Ibsen, Henrik: *Brand*, 443
  Ghosts, 454
  Wild Duck, 20, 450
Igesz, Bodo, 72
Illica, Luigi, 182
Imai, Nobuko, 86
Imbrie, Andrew: *Roethke Songs*, 107,
  271
Indiana University, Bloomington, 392
  Early Music Institute, 243–45
  Office of Afro-American Affairs, 361
  Opera Theater, 70, 72, 103–4, 119,
  121, 174, 176, 354, 361
Indian Opinion, 112
Infantino, Luigi, 41
Ingalls, James F., 198
International String Quartet, 191
IRCAM (Institut de Recherche et de
  Coordination Acoustique-Musique),
  89, 211, 344, 392
Irwin, Virginia Davis, 101
Isaac, Heinrich, 219
  Argentum et Aurum Mass, **262**
ISCM (International Society for
  Contemporary Music), 47
ISCM Festivals, 377, 386
Iseler, Elmer, 321
Isham, Royce, 29
Israel, Robert, 112–13

Italian Radio, 341
Ithaca College Choir, 222
Ives, Charles, 187, 378, 381, 382, 416
  Decoration Day, **311–12**
  Holidays Symphony, 311–12
  Thanksgiving, 312
  Violin Sonata No. 4, 343–44

Jabloński, Roman, 383–384
Jacobs, Arthur, 63, 360
Jacobs, Paul, 165, 167–68, 256, 411,
  438
Jacobs, René, 163–64, 370, 406
Jacques-Dalcroze, Emile: *Janie*, 399
Jaffe, Christopher, 416
Jagger, Mick, 127
Jahn, Otto, 166
James, Carolyne, 73, 292, 477
James, William, 166
Janáček, Leoš, 155, **173–76**, 194, 220,
  418, 443, 444, 476
  Cunning Little Vixen, **150**, 157–58,
  174
  From the House of the Dead, **423–24**
  Jenůfa, **68–70**, 174, 424
  Kát'a Kabanová, 68, 174, 424
  Makropulos Affair, 68, 174
  Mr. Brouček's Excursions, **104–5,
  174–76**, 210
Janovický, Karel, 173–74
Javore, James, 426
Jeffery, Charles, 29
Jenkins, Newell, 68, 159–60
Jennens, Charles, 366–67
Jerusalem, Siegfried, 433–34
Joël, Nicolas, 37
John, Nicholas, 195
Johns, William, 103, 217
Johnson, Mary Jane, 434, 462
Johnson, Samuel, 307
Jones, Della, 429
Jones, Gwyneth, 420
Jones, Isola, 315
Jones, Neil, 72
Jones, Robert T., 424
Jordan, Armin, 397–98
Joseph, Rohan, 312
Josquin Choir, 77
Joukowsky, Paul von, 394
Journal of Musicology, 362
*Journal of the American Musicological
  Society*, 335
Joyce, James, 203
Juilliard School, 152, 386, 440, 470

American Opera Center, 126,
184–85, 205–9, 407–8
Conductors Orchestra, 209
Orchestra, 207, 340, 377, 392
Symphony, 59–60
Theatre, 207, 407
Jung, Carl, 52, 161, 448
Jung, Manfred, 139, 420
Jurinac, Sena, 69–70, 481

Kaczorowski, Peter, 481
Kafka, Franz, 120, 174
Kagel, Mauricio: *Anagrama*, **387**
Stattstheater, 388
Kaiser, Georg: *Silbersee*, **50–51**
Kalisch, Alfred, 314
Kalish, Gilbert, 165, 168, 411
Kallman, Chester, 29
Kálmán, E., 20–21
Kane, John, 391
Kaplan, Mark, 309
Karajan, Herbert von, 138, 184, 238,
324, **337–39**, 340, 352, 408,
420–21, 458
Karis, Aleck, 411
Karousatos, Nicholas, 209
Käslík, Václav, 430
Kasprzyk, Jacek, 350
Kastorsky, Vladimir, 72
Katchen, Julius, 484, 485
Katz, Martin, 280
Kavafian, Ani, 18–19, 292
Kay, Hershy, 23, 331
Kay, Ulysses: *Markings*, 40
Kays, Alan, 45, 118, 119, 225
Kazaras, Peter, 317, 477
Kean, Edmund, 95
Keating, Roderic, 391
Keats, John, 166
Keefe, Robert, 208
Keene, Christopher, 116, 225, 227, 236
Keesee, Donna, 405
Keiser, Reinhard, 78
St. Mark Passion, 246
Keller, Hans, 386
Kellett, David, 454
Kelly, Randolph, 170
Kemble, Fanny, 289
Kemble, John Philip, 95
Kempe, Rudolf, 363
Kempff, Wilhelm, 484, 485
Kennedy Center for the Performing
Arts, 41, 301, 320, 369, 476–77
Kentish Opera Group, 225
Kent Opera, 126, 281–82

Kentucky Opera, 327, **348–50**
Kenyon, Nicholas, 48
Kenyon College, 142–46
Kerman, Joseph, 422
Kern, Jerome, 21
Kernis, Aaron Jay: *Dream of the Morning
Sky*, **466–68**
Kesling, Diane, 477
Keynote, 152
Khrennikov, Tikhon, 257
Kianto, Ilmari, 443
Kidson, Frank, 307
Killebrew, Gwendolyn, 81
Kimbrough, Steven, 51–52
Kimm, Fiona, 431
King, James, 37
King, Martin Luther, Jr., 112, 379
Kirchner, Leon, 381
Lily, 235, 421, 477–78
Music for Flute and Orchestra,
235–36
Kirshbaum, Ralph, 19, 86
Kitching, Alan: *Handel at the Unicorn*,
278
Kleiber, Erich, 90
Klein, Allen Charles, 295
Klemperer, Werner, 233
Kline, Kevin, 20
Klobučar, Berislav, 37
Klotzman, Dorothy, 187
Knapp, J. Merrill, 160–61
Knappertsbusch, Hans, 340, 434, 435,
458
Knodt, Erich, 462
Knowles, Gregory, 436
Knussen, Oliver, 173
Ophelia Dances, No. 1, 170–71
Symphonies: No. 1, 171; No. 2, 171;
No. 3, 169–70, 171
Knutson, David, 100
Kohn, Karl, 106
Kohn, Margaret, 106
Kokkonen, Joonas: *Last Temptations*,
442–43, 445
Kokkonen, Lauri, 443
Kolb, Barbara: *Chromatic Fantasy*, 469
*Homage to Keith Jarrett and Gary
Burton*, 412
Kollo, René, 433
Kontarsky, Aloys, 386
Kopperud, Jean, 343–44, 412
Korf, Anthony, 212
Farewell, 89
Korngold, Erich: *Tote Stadt*, 479
Violanta, 264

Koshetz, Nina, 72
Koven, Reginald De, 21
Kowalke, Kim: *Kurt Weill in Europe*,
 50–51
Krainik, Ardis, 452
Kraus, Alfredo, 73
Krehbiel, Henry E., 59, 485
Krenek, Ernst, 48, 409
 Kitharaulos, 130
 "Marginal Remarks re *Lulu*," 92, 94
 String Quartets, 250–51
Krick, Karin, 396–97
Kriesberg, Matthias, **256–58**
 a3520, 257–58, 411
Krilovici, Marina, 341–42, 343
Krueger, Dana, 63, 477
Kubelik, Rafael, 337, 423–24
Kubrick, Stanley, 388
Kugel, Dale, 23
Kuhlmann, Kathleen, 369
Kuijken, Sigiswald, 283
Kunii, Toshiaki, 261, 441
Kupfer, Harry, 194–95
Kutter, Michael, 396–97
Kvapil, Jaroslav, 430
Kyung-Wha Chung, 172

Lachner, Franz, 240–41, 242
Laderman, Ezra: Symphony No. 4, 363
 Symphony for Brass and Orchestra,
 363–64
Lafont, Captain, 186
Lafont, Jean-Philippe, 457
La Jolla: Center for Music Experiment,
 391
Lake George Opera Festival, 116–19
Lalo, Pierre, 473
Lamb, Charles, 94–95
Lambert, Constant, 47–48
Lamberti, Giorgio, 39
Lanari, Alessandro, 356
Lancaster, Osbert, 330
Landi, Stefano: *Sant'Alessio*, **104**
Landowska, Wanda, 295
Landsman, Julie, 432
Lang, Daniel, 269
Lang, Fritz, 395
Lang, Paul Henry, 160–61
Langan, Kevin, 37–38, 39, 317
Langton, Sunny Joy, 292
Lankston, John, 50, 51, 332
Lanza, Mario, 23
Large, Norman, 65
Larocca, Frank, 107
Larsen, Jens Peter, 160–62, 229

LaSalle Quartet, 11, 263
Lassila, Iris-Lilja, 445
Lassus, Orlando de, 362–63
Latouche, John, 330
Lawrence, D. H., 223, 267
Lawrence, Marjorie, 192
Lawton, David, 190
Lay of Igor's Campaign, 71
Lazaridis, Stefanos, 431
Leach, Wilford, 20
Lear, Evelyn, 94, 269
Lee, Eugene, 225
Lee, Ming Cho, 27, 64, 147–48, 158,
 209, 225, 226, 315, 348, 407
*Legend of the Invisible City of Manila and
 the Princess Sarah*, 447
Lehár, Franz, 20–21
 Giuditta, 303
 Gold and Silver waltz, 262
 Merry Widow, 22, 125, 301–4
Lehmann, Lilli, 132, 318
Lehmann, Lotte, 58, 313
Lehnhoff, Nikolaus, 37, 458–59,
 460–61, 463–64
Leider, Frida, 434
Leinsdorf, Erich, 52, 138, 150, 403
 Composer's Advocate, 185
Leipzig: Neues Gewandhaus, 319
Lenaël, Philippe, 473
Leningrad Philharmonic, 345
Lenz, Jakob M. R., 119–21
 Soldaten, 119, 202, 203
Leonard, Peter, 352
Leonardo da Vinci, 396
Leoncavallo, Ruggiero, 48
 Pagliacci, 183
Leppard, Raymond, 101, 125, 348,
 361, 469
 Beggar's Opera (arr.), **305–8**
Lerdahl, Fred, 465
 Chords, **469**
 Episodes and Refrains, 255, 256
Lerner, Mimi, 29
Lesenger, Jay, 27, 44, 156
Levine, James, 35, 52, 61, 87, 91, 94,
 134, 152, 176–79, 184, 190, 201,
 232–33, 238, 314–15, 335, 359,
 408
Levine, Rhoda, 241
Levitt, Joseph, 176
Levy, Gerardo, 49
Lewis, Henry, 156, 372, 376, 480
Lewis, Robert, 225
Lewis, William, 70, 100, 400, 462
Liddell, Alice, 33

Liebling, Estelle, 55
Liège: Opéra Royal, 194
Ligeti, György, 392–93
  Apparitions, 387
  Atmosphères, **387–88**
  Aventures, 388
  Grand Macabre, **388–91**
  Kyrie, 388
  Lontano, 387–88
  Lux aeterna, 388
  Melodien, 388
  Nouvelles Aventures, 388
  Poème Symphonique, 388
  San Francisco Polyphony, 388
  Self-Portrait with Reich and Riley, 388
Light Opera of Manhattan (LOOM), 89
Lincoln Center for the Performing
    Arts, 39, 190, 421
  Alice Tully Hall, 18, 46, 59–60, 68,
    159, 210, 245–46, 250, 253, 255,
    258, 309–10, 340, 365, 397–98,
    411–12, 445
  Avery Fisher Hall, 31–32, 40, 169,
    217, 234, 301, 311–12, 320, 330,
    346, 363, 377–78, 383–84,
    467–68
  Damrosch Park, 110
  Library, 110
  New York State Theater, 21, 29, 41,
    44, 49, 50–51, 54, 55–56, 58–59,
    139, 301–2, 325, 478
  see also Juilliard School; Metropolitan
    Opera; New York City Opera; New
    York Philharmonic
Lind, Jenny, 57, 95
Lindsay String Quartet, 153, 191
Linfield, Nicholas, 354
Linley, Thomas, 304
Liotta, Vincent, 230
Liszt, Franz, 11, 142–43, 168, 457
  Ballade in B-minor, 159
  Berlioz's Symphonie Fantastique, piano
    transcription, 24
  "Drei Zigeuner," 344
  Funérailles, 144–45
  Hungarian Rhapsody No. 6, 365–66
  Mephisto Waltz, 144
  Symphony to Dante's Divine Comedy,
    59–60
Little, Frank, 94
Little, Gwenlynn, 45
Litton, Andrew, 209–10
Litvinne, Félia, 191–92
Livingston, William, 41
Lloveras, Juan, 154

Lloyd, Robert, 100, 397, 428
Lloyd Webber, Andrew: Joseph and the
    Amazing Technicolor Dreamcoat, 303
Lobel, Adrianne, 453
Locke, Sally, 454
Lockwood, Lewis, 239
Loewe, Carl: Sieben Schläfer von Ephesus,
    68
  "Tom der Reimer," 68
London: Albert Hall, 83, 85
  Coliseum, 125, 426, 431
  Drury Lane, 144, 304
  Festival Hall, 484–85
  Goldsmiths' Hall, 253
  Handel Opera Society, 196, 368, 369
  New Opera Company, 427
  Philharmonia Orchestra, 46
  Promenade Concerts, 83, 85–86,
    130–31, 170, 268, 470
  Queen Elizabeth Hall, 470, 482
  Regent's Park, 187
  Royal Academy of Music, 266, 267
  Royal Festival Hall, 324, 378
  Wigmore Hall, 253, 482
  see also Covent Garden; English
    National Opera; Fires of London
London Philharmonic, 352
London Sinfonietta, 435
London Symphony Orchestra, 60,
    61–62, 86, 169, 171, 352
London Times, 482
Long, William Ivey, 477
Longacre, James, 118
Long Island Opera Society, 190
Long Island University: C. W. Post
    Center, 346, 377–78
Longwith, Deborah, 102
López-Cobos, Jesús, 372
Lorenz, Gregory, 441
Loriod, Yvonne, 106, 247
Los Angeles: Wilshire Ebell Theatre,
    419
Los Angeles, Victoria de, 180, 277
Los Angeles Opera Theater, 417–20
Los Angeles Philharmonic, 363–65
LoSchiavo, Joseph, 454
Louisville: Macauley Theatre, 349
  see also Kentucky Opera
Louisville Orchestra, 352, 385
Lowell, Robert, 435
Lowinsky, Edward, 76–77
Lubin, Germaine, 191–92
Lucier, Alvin, 391
Ludgin, Chester, 100, 266, 477
Luedeke, Raymond: Fanfare, 321

Luening, Otto, 425
Lumley, Benjamin, 407
Lundberg, Mark, 72
Luther, Martin, 76
Lutoslawski, Witold, 382
  Cello Concerto, 381, **383–84**
  Concerto for Orchestra, 381, **384**
  Double Concerto, 130
  Jeux Vénitiens, 383
  Novelette, 381, **384**
  Variations on a Theme of Pagannini,
    106
Lutyens, Elisabeth, 173
Lytton, Henry, 453

Ma, Yo-Yo, 172
Maazel, Loren, 60, 84, 385, 407
Mabs, Linda, 164
McCabe, John: Variations on a Theme
  of Karl Amadeus Hartmann, 169,
  171
McCaffrey, Patricia, 288
McCarthy, Kerry, 480
McCauley, Barry, 43, 158, 296
McCracken, James, 457
Macdonald, Brian, 348
Macdonald, Hugh, 194–95
McDonall, Lois, 431
McEwen, Terence, 103, 458, 464
McGegan, Nicholas, 403–6
Machaut, Guillaume de, 337
Machlis, Joseph, 355
McIntyre, Donald, 139
McKee, Joseph, 481
Mackerras, Charles, 162, 193, 369,
  423–24
McLaughlin, Marie, 369
MacMillan, Ernest: *Blanche comme la
  neige*, 321
McNabb, Michael: *Dreamsong*, 107
McNair, Sylvia, 481
McNalley, Maureen, 75–76
MacNeil, Cornell, 317
MacNeil, Walter, 375, 462
McPhee, Colin: *Tabu-Tabuhan*, **352**
Macready, William Charles, 95, 464
Macurdy, John, 139, 179
Maddalena, James, 198
Maderna, Bruno, 382
  Aura, 385
  Biogramma, 381, 383, 384–85
  Oboe Concerto No. 2, 106, 107
  Quadrivium, 385
Maffei, Andrea, 127
Mahler, Gustav, 44–45, 51, 236, 254,

339, 351, 378, 468–69
Lied von der Erde, 467
Symphonies, 250; No. 1, 340; No. 2,
  54, **87–88**, 340; No. 3, 52, 54, 130,
  340; No. 4, 52–53; No. 5, 52–55,
  60–62, 130; No. 6, 60, **340**; No. 7,
  52, 340; No. 8, 30, **34, 52–54**, 340;
  No. 9, 52, **339**, 340
Wunderhorn cycle, 60–61
Mainwaring, John, 197
Makarova, Natalia, 178
Malfitano, Catherine, 157
Malgoire, Jean-Claude, 283
Malibran, Maria, 11
Mallarmé, Stéphane, 167, 382
Manahan, George, 222
Manhattan School of Music, 215, 258,
  263–64
Mann, Alfred, 160–61
Mann, Thomas: *Death in Venice*, 289
Mann, William, 402
Mannes College of Music, 266
  Camerata, 260–61, 440–41
Manning, Jane, 106
Mansouri, Lotfi, 158
Manuguerra, Matteo, 154, 353
Manzoni, Giacomo: *Masse: Omaggio a
  Edgard Varèse*, 340
Mao Tse-tung, 268
Marcello, Benedetto, 80
  Teatro alla moda, 79
Marchesi, Mathilde, 55
Marcos, Ferdinand and Imelda, 447
Marcoux, Vanni, 428
Marenzio, Luca, 259
Marlowe, Christopher, 263
Marschner, Heinrich: *Vampyr*, **51,** 216
Marsee, Susanne, 29, 63, 303, 327
Martin, Mary, 54–55
Martinelli, Giovanni, 36–37
Martino, Donald, 465
  Triple Concerto, **469**
Martinon, Jean, 351
Martinovich, Boris, 242
Marton, Eva, 150, 316–17
Maryland, University of, 160–61, 360
  Chorus, 160, 370
Maryland Handel Festival, 160–64,
  369, 370–71
Masaryk, Tomáš, 175
Mascagni, Pietro: *Cavalleria rusticana*,
  48, 183, 286, 316, 479
Mase, Ray, 262
Massenet, Jules, 345
  Manon, 56, 72, 296, 399

Navarraise, 399
Portrait de Manon, 399
Thaïs, 225, 399
Werther, 37, 72, 296
Masterson, Valerie, 194, 369
Matcham, Frank, 24
Mathias, Alice Hammerstein, 89
Matson, Margaret, 326
Matthews, John, 423
Mauceri, John, 46, 217, 331, 427, **429**
Mauro, Ermanno, 318, 408
Maurois, André, 330
Maxwell, Linn, 426
Maynor, Kevin, 72
Mazura, Franz, 94, 179
Mazzoleni, Ester, 133, 240
Mehta, Zubin, 40, 54, 88, 130, 137,
    190, 311–12, 345, 384, 467
Meier, Gustav, 348
Meier, Johanna, 105, 239
Mekler, Mani, 349
Melano, Fabrizio, 134, 135
Melba, Nellie, 55
Melchior, Lauritz, 434
Meltzer, Andrew, 23
Melville, Herman: *Billy Budd,* 289
    Confidence-Man, 288–90
Mendelssohn, Felix, 36, 57, 65, 214,
    340, 445
    Elijah, 68
    Fingal's Cave, 437
    Hebrides, 146–47
    Midsummer Night's Dream Overture,
       270
    Piano Concerto in G-minor, 33, 34
    Symphony No. 3, 146–47
    Te Deum in D, **270–71**
Mendès, Catulle, 355
Mengelberg, Willem, 61, 109
Menotti, Giancarlo, 29, 45–46, 50, 287
    Loca, 56, 228, 477–78
Mentzer, Susanne, 481
Merfeld, Robert, 271
Merman, Ethel, 54–55
Merola Opera Program, 36
Merrill, Nathaniel, 150, 269, 314
Merritt, Chris, 150, 456
Merz, Oskar, 401
Meschke, Michael, 389
Mesguich, Daniel, 389
Messiaen, Olivier, 88, 247, 468
    Transfiguration, 106
Mester, George, 340
Metastasio, Pietro, 373, 375
Metropolitan Opera, 12, 36, 42, 55, 68,
    72, 159, 192, 203, 205, 211, 213,
    264, 280, 301, 325, 346, 349, 354,
    400, 403, 406, 426, 430, 433, 442,
    454–55, 477–78, 487
    Arabella, 402–3
    Barbiere di Siviglia, 204–5
    Bohème, 180–84, 225
    Boris Godunov, 315–16
    Contes d'Hoffmann, 218–19
    Così fan tutte, 199–201
    Don Carlos, 408, 427, 428
    Entführung aus dem Serail, 232–34,
       283–84
    Forza del destino, 56, 314–15
    Gioconda, 316–17
    Idomeneo, 329, 333–35
    Lulu, 87, 88, 90–94
    Macbeth, 356–59
    Nightingale, 176–78, 179
    Norma, 132–34
    Oedipus Rex, 176–77, 178–79
    Parsifal, 238–39, 243
    Rheingold, 138–39
    Rigoletto, 154–57
    Rite of Spring, 176–77, 179
    Rosenkavalier, 313–14
    Siegfried, 138–39
    Traviata, 157–58, 286
    Vêpres siciliennes, 231–32
    Walküre, 420–41
Meyerbeer, Giacomo, 22, 42–43, 96,
    231, 342, 347, 372–74
    Africaine, 400
    Crociato in Egitto, 110, 373, 376
    Huguenots, 400
    Prophète, 217, 400
    Robert le diable, 356
Meysenbug, Malwida, 397
Miami: New World Festival of the Arts,
    268–70
Michelangeli, Arturo Benedetti, 484
Michelangelo, 76, 94–95, 185, 186
Michigan, University of (Ann Arbor),
    346–48, 351
Michigan Opera Theatre, 350–51
Migenes-Johnson, Julia, 94
Mikorey, Max, 401
Milanov, Zinka, 132
Miles, Timothy, 448
Milhaud, Darius, 107, 387
Miller, David, 229
Miller, David Alan, 209
Miller, Jonathan, 126, 288, 402
Miller, Robert, 89, 106, 410–11
Mills College, 104, 106–7

Mills, Erie, 283, 332
Milnes, Sherrill, 19, 54–55, 154, 228, 264, 315, 357–58
Milstein, Nathan, 345
Milton, John, 94–95
Minneapolis: Orchestra Hall, 30, 31, 301, 320, 325
Minnesota Orchestra, 30
Minter, Drew, 405–6
Minton, Yvonne, 397
Mitchell, Donald, 92
Mitchell, Leona, 315
Mitropoulos, Dimitri, 352, 377–78
Mittelmann, Norman, 424
MOB art & tone ART, 210–11
Moiseiwitsch, Tanya, 156, 157
Moldoveanu, Vasile, 317
Moliterno, Mark, 360
Moll, Kurt, 313
Mollicone, Henry: *Emperor Norton*, 102
Monadnock Festival, 165, 452
Moniuszko, Stanislaw, 384
  Halka, 350, 355, 361
  Straszny Dwór, **350–51,** 355
Monk, Allan, 183
Monte Carlo Opera, 237
Monte Carlo Philharmonic, 397
Montemezzi, Italo: *Amore dei tre re*, **217–18,** 264, 327, 355
Monteux, Pierre, 377
Monteverdi, Claudio, 68, 115, 155, 194, 271, 277, 447
  Arianna, 260
  Ballo delle ingrate, **100–101**
  Incoronazione di Poppea, **100–101, 360–61,** 425
  Orfeo, **125–28,** 260, 349, 440
  Ritorno d'Ulisse, 136–37, 360
  Vespers, 446
Monteverdi Choir, 445–**47,** 470
Montezuma II, Emperor of Mexico, 205
Montgomery, Kenneth, 296
Montreal Symphony, 457
Montresor, Beni, 217, 355
Moore, Douglas: *Ballad of Baby Doe*, 56
Moore, Eileen, 245
Moore, Frank Ledlie, 222
  Wagadougou, 223
Morel, Jean, 377
Morgan, Robert, 295
Morris, James, 183, 201, 227, 265–66
Morrison, Richard, 245
Morscheck, Stephen, 348
Morton, Thomas, 148

Moser, Edda, 232
Moshinsky, Elijah, 389–90
Mostly Mozart Festival, 110
Moszkowski, Moritz: *Caprice Espagnol*, 365–66
Motley, John, 342
Moulson, John, 448
Mount-Burke, William, 89
Mozart, Leopold, 333
Mozart, Wolfgang Amadeus, 20, 57, 65, 66, 68, 109, 127, 141, 165–66, 183, 211, 214–15, 231–32, 240, 255, 262, 278, 359, 483
  Così fan tutte, 197, **199–201,** 219, 280, 287, **288,** 308, 406
  Don Giovanni, **44–46,** 100, **101,** 118, 200, 307, 347, 356, 452, 480
  Entführung aus dem Serail, **117–19,** 160, 177, 201, **232–34, 283–84**
  Finta giardiniera, 400
  Idomeneo, 325, 329, **333–35**
  Larghetto and Allegro, K. 439b, 329
  Lucio Silla, 130–31, 213, 400
  Nozze di Figaro, 42, 80, 100, **101–2,** 197, 200, **213–14,** 305, 406
  Piano Sonatas: K. 332, 66, 67; K. 333, 66, 67; K. 488, 160
  Re Pastore, 213, 400
  Symphonies: K. 19a, 110; K. 201, 62; K. 250, **310–11;** K. 385, 416
  Zauberflöte, 21, 51, 166, 216, 327, 330, 372, 406, 426, 471
Mravinsky, Eugene, 345
Muck, Carl, 352, 435
Muffat, Georg, 472
Müller, Edoardo, 276
Munich Festival, 98–99
Munn, Thomas, 462
Munro, Leigh, 23
Mürger, Henry: *Scènes de la vie de Bohème*, 182, 184
Muse of Eloquence, Inc., 245–45
Musgrave, Thea: *Last Twilight*, 223
Musical Elements, 344
Musical Times, 163, 229, 266, 322–23
Music & Letters, 166
Music Review, 92
Music-Theatre Group/Lenox Arts Center, 425–26
Mussorgsky, Modest, 178, 194, 443
  Boris Godunov, 71, 100, **315–16,** 444
Muti, Riccardo, 359, 484
Muzio, Emanuele, 342
Myers, Michael, 283, 287, 481
Myers, Rollo, 355

Nagano, Kent, 105
Nagy, Robert, 315–16
Nancarrow, Conlon: String Quartet, 392–93
  Study No. 41, 392–93
Nance, Chris, 420
Napoleon III, Emperor of France, 186–88, 242
National Chorale, 110
National Public Radio, 228
National Symphony Orchestra, 266
Navarrete, Alfonso, 276
Negin, Mark, 280
Neighbour, O. W., 74–75
Nelson, John, 345, 481
Nelson, Judith, 104
Nelson, Nelda, 104
Nentwig, Franz Ferdinand, 139, 150, 420
Neruda, Pablo, 83–84
Ness, Joseph: *When Orpheus Last Sang,* 256
Neukomm, Sigismund, 68
Neumann, Frederick, 335
New Calliope Singers, 245–46
Newland, Larry, 385, 469
Newman, Ernest, 193–94, 265, 303, 394, 400; *Fanfare for Ernest Newman,* 25
New Mexico Symphony, 294
New Music Concert, 256, 433
New Orleans: Orpheum, 319
New Orleans Philharmonic, 301, 319
Newsweek, 57
New York: American Place Theater, 453, 454
  Berkeley Lyceum, 440
  Broadway Theater, 330–31
  Carnegie Hall, 9, 40, 46, 52–53, 60, 82, 84–85, 132, 169, 235, 264, 266, 320, 337–38, 341, 343, 363, 369, 372, 374–76, 378, 400, 411, 421, 433, 454–57, 462, 467, 482, 485–87
  Carnegie Recital Hall, 153, 191, 211, 248, 253, 256, 412, 433, 467
  Cathedral of St. John the Divine, 272–73, 445, 447, 457–58
  Chapel of St. Martin, 243
  Christ and St. Stephen's Church, 411
  Christ Church, 260–61, 440
  City Center, 301
  Columbia University, McMillin Theatre, 256–57
  Cooper Union, Great Hall, 344

  Corpus Christi Church, 76–77, 219, 245–46, 335–36
  Delacorte Theatre, 19
  Eastside Playhouse, 90
  Frick Collection, 252–53
  Good Shepherd-Faith Church, 51
  Guggenheim Museum, 74–75, 425
  Guild Theatre, 393
  Jolson Theatre, 22
  Kitchen, 268
  Lehman College Center for the Performing Arts, **39–40,** 41
  Martin Beck Theater, 330
  Marymount Manhattan Theater, 386, 392
  Merkin Concert Hall, 51, 66, 137, **138,** 228–29, 246–47, 261–62, 270, 271, 309, 326, 329, 343, 369, 371, 393, 410, 412–13, 432, 467
  Metropolitan Museum, 66, 67, 165, 220, 222, 256, 310, 312, 353
  92nd Street Y, 160, 165, 168, 195, 392–93, 416, 432
  Radio City Music Hall, 425
  St. Clement's Church, 425
  St. Joseph's Church, 219–20, 262, 362
  St. Thomas Church, 245–46
  Sotheby's, 412–13
  Symphony Space, 47, 89, 210, 212, 266, 268, 301, 411, 435, 439, 449
  Town Hall, 189, 249, 329, 445, 447, 483
  Xenon, 360
  see also Lincoln Center for the Performing Arts: Manhattan School of Music
New York, 483
New York, Lyric Theater of, 453
New York, Opera Orchestra of, 158–59, 217, 264, 341–43, 376, 399, 454, 456–57
New York City Ballet, 301
New York City Opera, 12, 23, 41, 57, 105, 119, 174, 179, 183, 203, 218, 227, 264, 288, 327–332, 346, 360–61, 374, 389, 403, 406, 421, 422, 426, 449, 452, 453, 477–78, 479
  Alceste, 327, 333, 348–49
  Amore dei tre re, 217–18, 327
  Anna Bolena, 25, 26–29
  Attila, 158, 237
  Candide, **327–33,** 336
  Cenerentola, 62–63, 65

New York City Opera *(cont.)*
  Cunning Little Vixen, 150, 157–58
  Don Giovanni, 44–46
  Fledermaus, 54–55
  Giulio Cesare, 63–65, 282, 283
  Grande-Duchesse de Gérolstein, 242, 263
  Lombardi, 236–37
  Maria Stuarda, 135–36
  Médée, 240–42, 327–28
  Merry Widow, 301–4
  Merry Wives of Windsor, 58–59, 65
  Nabucco, 105, 110–11, 134–35, 158, 237
  National Touring Company, 39, 40–42
  Nozze di Figaro, 213–14
  Pêcheurs de perles, 42–44
  Puritani, 139–40, 150
  Rigoletto, 154–57
  Silverlake, 50–51
  Student Prince, 21–23, 26
  Susannah, 225, 226–27
  Traviata, 40–42, **157–58,** 311, 328
New York Gilbert and Sullivan Players, 449
New York Lyric Opera, 360–61
New York New Music Ensemble, 248, 412, 468
New York Philharmonic, 12, 39, 40, 52, 54, 61, 82, 88, 128–30, 136–37, 151–52, 169–70, 190–91, 213, 221, 234–35, 250, 311–12, 340, 345–46, 351–52, 377, 381–85, 387–88, 391, 414–15, 423–24
  Horizons '83, 464–67, 470
New York Pro Musica Antiqua, 260, 354
New York Shakespeare Festival, 19
New York *Times,* 36, 169–70, 222, 285, 356, 424, 449, 487
Nicolai, Otto: *Merry Wives of Windsor,* **57–59, 65**
Nicolini, Giuseppe, 282
Nielsen, Carl: Wind Quintet, 255–56
Nierenberg, Roger, 270
Nietzsche, Friedrich, 237, 394
Nieuwenhuis, Hans, 115
Nijinsky, Vaslav, 177
Nikisch, Arthur, 236, 337
Nilsson, Birgit, 37–38, 130, 150, 312
Nimsgern, Siegmund, 434
Niska, Maralin, 135, 240, 301
Nixon, Richard, 380
Noble, Jeremy, 76–77
Noble, Timothy, 72, 104, 109

Nolen, Timothy, 225, 477
Nono, Luigi, 85, 385
Nordica, Lillian, 56
Norman, Jessye, 152, 457
North German Radio Symphony, 383
Nottingham University, 215
Nurmela, Kari, 105

Oakland: Paramount, 109, 319
Oakland Symphony, 106, 108, 109, 142, 236, 319
Oberlin, Johann Friedrich, 119–20
Oberlin College, 119
Oberlin Opera Theater, 359–60
O'Brien, Timothy, 389–90
Ochman, Wieslaw, 231–32, 315
Ockeghem, Johannes, 76, 219–20
Oeser, Fritz, 263
Oesterreichische Musik-Zeitschrift, 212
Offenbach, Jacques, **20–22, 262–63**
  Ba-Ta-Clan, 263
  Bluebeard, 22
  Brigands, 21, 449
  Contes d'Hoffmann, 21, **218–19,** 263, 296
  Geneviève de Brabant, 22
  Grande-Duchesse de Gerolstein, 100, **102, 242–43,** 263, 449
  Mariage aux lanternes, 263
  Orphée aux enfers, 459, 461
Ohanian, David, 250
O'Hearn, Robert, 42, 150, 314, 448
Ohyama, Heiichiro, 18
Oistrakh, David, 345
Oldfather, Christopher, 309, 468
Oliveros, Pauline, 391
Olivier, Laurence, 304
Olsen, Keith, 209
O'Neill, Claudia, 90
O'Neill, Eugene, 50
Opera, 139, 162, 419, 426
Opera News, 133, 149, 444
Oppens, Ursula, 165, 167–68, 256, 266, 411, 470
Opthof, Cornelis, 278
Orff, Carl: *Carmina Burana,* 243
Orliac, Jean Claude, 472
Ornstein, Leo, 392
  Three Moods, 393
Orpheon Chorale, 376
Oswald, Roberto, 103
Ottawa Festival, 278–84
Ottaway, Hugh, 252
Ovid: *Metamorphoses,* 259

Oxford University Opera Club, 192
Ozawa, Seiji, 52, 54, 89, 152, 378

Pace University, 470–71
Pachelbel, Johann, 291
Paganini, Niccolò, 11
Paik, Nam June: *Hommage à John Cage*, 386–87
Paisiello, Giovanni: *Barbiere di Siviglia*, 400
Pallo, Imre, 135, 214
Panerai, Rolando, 183
Panizza, Giacomo, 342
Papini, Giovanni, 96
Paris: Gaîté, 42
    IRCAM, 89, 211, 344
    Opera, 87, 91–93, 144, 231, 242, 274, 341, 457
    Opéra-Comique, 42, 72, 296, 453
    Pompidou Center, 104
    Théâtre-Lyrique, 42
    Variétés, 242
Paris, Orchestre de, 88
Parker, Dorothy, 330, 336
Parker, Hershel, 289
Parker, William, 18–19
Parloff, Michael, 156
Parnassus, 89, 212
Parsons, David, 287, 308, 481
Pasatieri, Thomas: *Before Breakfast*, **50**
Pasta, Giuditta, 11, **25–26,** 28, 213, 318, 376
Patané, Giuseppe, 156, 317, 407
Patinkin, Sheldon, 330
Patterson, James, 423
Patterson, Marjorie, 261
Pauk, György, 86
Paul, St., 238
Paulus, Stephen: *Postman Always Rings Twice*, **284–86**
    Village Singer, 284, 286-87
Pavarotti, Luciano, 57, 180, 212–13, 317, 334
Paxton, Larry, 72
Payer, Elisabeth, 139, 217
Payne, Anthony, 106
Payne, Patricia, 317
Pearlman, Martin, 472–73
Pearlman, Richard, 291, 419
Pears, Peter, 95
Pearson, William, 387
Peerce, Jan, 23
Pell, William, 102
Pelle, Nadia, 214
Pelton, Carmen, 425–26

Penderecki, Krzysztof, 388
Pennsylvania Opera Theater, 230–31
Penrod, Joseph, 261
Peoria: Civic Center, 323–24
Pepusch, Johann Christoph, 304–5
Peri, Jacopo: *Dafne*, 259–60, 440
    Euridice, 259–60, 261, **440–42**
Perle, George, 91–92
    Ballade, 258–59
    Concertino, 89
    Short Symphony, 89, 258
    Six Études, 258–59
Perlman, Itzhak, 152
Perry, Douglas, 115, 477
Persichetti, Vincent: *Lincoln Address*, 380
Perti, Giacomo Antonio, 271
Peters, Roberta, 23
Peterson, Susan, 480
Petina, Irra, 330
Petkov, Dimiter, 266
Petrella, Errico, 314
Petrie, Mollie, 351
Pharo, Carol, 354
Phelan, Kate, 360
Philadelphia, Opera Company of, 149
Philadelphia Orchestra, 52–53, 169–70, 340
Philidor, André: *Tom Jones*, 404
Phillips, Daniel, 292
Piaf, Edith, 337
Piave, Francesco Maria, 127, 189, 356
Picker, Tobias: *Blue Hula*, 249
    When Soft Voices Die, 411
Pini, Anthony, 172
Pinnock, Trevor, 163
Pinza, Ezio, 217
Pisaroni, Rosmunda, 148
Piston, Walter: String Quartet No. 2, 377
    Symphonies: No. 2, 381; No. 3, 381; No. 4, 377, **378–79**
Pittsburgh Pirates, 380
Pittsburgh Symphony, 110, **169–70,** 172–73, 351, 352, 377–78
Pizarro, Francisco, 205
Pizzi, Pier Luigi, 38, 81, 82
Plançon, Pol, 428
Plaskin, Glenn: *Horowitz*, 487
Plath, Sylvia, 171, 344
Play of Daniel, 244, **353–54**
Plishka, Paul, 73, 140, 315–16
Plowright, Rosalind, 275, 355
Poe, Edgar Allan, 289
Pokorny, Jan, 39

Polish National Radio Symphony, 383
Pollini, Maurizio, 168, 213, **424–25**
Pollock, Jackson, 382
Pomerium Musices, 76–77, 262,
    326–27, 405–6
Ponchielli, Amilcare: *Gioconda,* 316–17
Pond, Helen, 304
Ponnelle, Jean-Pierre, 98–100, 102,
    334, 358, 360–61, 430
Pons, Lily, 72
Ponselle, Rosa, 11, 56, 132, 217, 318
Porcher, Nananne, 419
Porco, Robert, 361
Porter, Cole, 21
Posnak, Paul, 143
Poulenc, Francis, 18–19, 176
    Mamelles de Tirésias, **480**
    Organ Concerto, 321
    Voix humaine, 50
Pound, Ezra, 203
Pountney, David, 115, 430–31
Poussin, Nicolas, 126
Prague Philharmonic Choir, 397
Pratt, Michael, 239
Prausnitz, Frederik, 206–7, 209
Preetorius, Emil, 37
Prescott, William H., 342
    History of the Conquest of Mexico, 205,
    208
Previn, André, 169, 172, 351, 377–78
Prévost, Robert, 284
Price, Henry, 23, 135, 269
Price, Leontyne, 54–55
Price, Margaret, 38–39
Prince, Harold, 51, 224–25, 331
Princeton University, 211, 239–40
Prior, Allan, 23
Pritchard, John, 378, 400
Pro Arte Chorale, 270–71
Proctor-Gregg, Humphrey, 360
Program Publishing Company, 65
Prokofiev, Sergei, 109, 277, 295, 353,
    443
    Love of the Three Oranges, 218
    Maddalena, 264, **287–88**
    Symphony No. 4, 150
    War and Peace, 286
Pruett, Elizabeth, 41, 311
Pruslin, Stephen, 248–49, 436
Puccini, Giacomo, 217–18, 263–64,
    269, 301, 340, 346
    Bohème, **180–84,** 225
    Madama Butterfly, 285, 290, 452, 480
    Rondine, 21
    Suor Angelica, 204

Tosca, 28–29, 274, 426
Purcell, Henry, 19, 277, 412
    Dido and Aeneas, **261–62**
    Funeral Music for Queen Mary, 447
    "My Beloved Spake," 447
Purnhagen, Gregory, 261
Putnam, Ashley, 135, 229, 236–37,
    288, 296, 328

Quantz, Johann Joachim, 406
Queens College, 425
Queler, Eve, 158–59, 217, 264–65,
    341–43, 399, 402, 407, 454,
    456–57
Quilico, Louis, 408
Quilley, Denis, 330

Rabelais, François, 77
Rachmaninoff, Sergei: Piano Concerto
    No. 3, 484
    Polkas, 159
    Preludes, 159, 365–66
Racine, Jean: *Athalie,* 369
    Esther, 369
Raffanti, Dano, 81, 149
Raffensperger, Fred, 354
Raftery, J. Patrick, 276, 355
Raimann, Rudolf: *Arden Enok,* 399
Raimondi, Gianni, 183
Raimondi, Ruggero, 232, 358
Rainier, Priaulx: *Aequora lunae,* 130
    Cello Concerto, 130
    Concertante for Two Winds, 130
Raintree Arts Council, 308
Rameau, Jean-Philippe, 271
    Boréades, 470, 471
    Castor et Pollux, 470, 471, **473–74**
    Dardanus, 470–71
    Fêtes d' Hébé, 470–71
    Hippolyte et Aricie, 470, 471, **473**
    Io, 471
    Naïs, 470
    Naissance d'Orisis, 470
    Princesse de Navarre, 470
    Pygmalion, 470–71
    Zoroastre, **470–73**
Ramey, Phillip, 235
Ramey, Samuel, 29, 44, 45, 213–14,
    227, 280, 282, 327, 372, 375
Ramicova, Dunya, 453
Ramm, Andrea von, **335–37,** 354
Ran, Shulamit: *Excursions,* 412–13
    Prayer, 412–13
    Private Game, 412–13
    Verticals, 410, 412–13

Raphael, 185, 396
Ratti, Eugenia, 183
Rattle, Simon, 131, 210
Ratz, Erwin, 340
Ravel, Maurice, 48, 142–43, 145, 176, 478–79
  Daphnis and Chloe suite No. 2, 321
  Gaspard de la nuit, 168, 484
  Histoires naturelles, 416
  Ondine, 410
  Trio for violin, cello, and piano, 19
Rawlins, Emily, 100, 420
Rawsthorne, Alan, 379
Record Guide, 36
Reed, Bruce, 65
Reed, John, 453
Reese, Gustave: *Music in the Renaissance*, 219
Reese, Sarah, 190, 448
Reich, Steve, 108, 211, 352
  Drumming, 222
  Music for Mallet Instruments, Voices, and Organ, 222
  Tehillim, **220–22**, 311, **312**
Reihe, Die, 210
Reimann, Aribert: *Fünf Gedichte von Paul Celan*, 98
  Lear, 95, **97–100**, 103–4, 106
  Melusine, 97
  Totentanz, 98
  Wolkenloses Christfest, 98
  Zyklus, 98
Reinhardt, Max, 202
Remedios, Alberto, 125
Rendall, David, 201
Rennert, Günther, 127–28, 368
Rennison, Michael, 70, 276
Renshaw, Christopher, 428
Rensink, James, 420, 448
Reppa, David, 408
Rescigno, Nicola, 73, 80–82, 157
Resnik, Regina, 193
Rex, Charles, 469
Reyer, Ernest: *Sigurd*, 355–56
Reynolds, Barbara, 80
Reynolds, Roger: *Archipelago*, 392
  Voicespace, **391–92**
Rhodes, Nancy, 117
Ricciarelli, Katia, 374
Rice, JoAnn, 261
Rice, Laura Brooks, 72, 423
Richter, Hans, 236
Richter, Sviatoslav, 308, 487
Ricordi, Giulio, 359
Ricordi, Tito, 218

Riddell, Richard, 112
Ridderbusch, Karl, 103
Ridler, Anne, 127
Riegel, Kenneth, 94
Riegger, Wallingford, 381
  Study in Sonority, 137
Rifkin, Joshua, 195
Rihm, Wolfgang: *Jakob Lenz*, **119–21**
Riley, Terry, 267
Rimsky-Korsakov, Nikolai, 70, 236
  Christmas Eve, 72
  Legend of the Invisible City of Kitezh, **447–49**
  Sadko, 100
  Show Maiden, 448
Rinuccini, Ottavio, 259–60, 440
Rippon, Michael, 439
Ristori, Giovanni Alberto, 79
Ritchie, Stanley, 311
Rizzuto, Charles, 341
Roar, Leif, 239
Robbiani, Igino: *Anna Karenina*, 417–18
Robbins, Carrie, 37
Robbins, Julien, 101
Robinson, Susan, 66, 229
Robison, Paula, 235–36
Rochberg, Gene, 289–90
Rochberg, George, 295, 381
  Confidence Man, 211, **288–92**
  String Quartets, 291–93
  String Quintet, **292**
Rochester, University of: Eastman School of Music, 378, 385
Rochlitz, J. F., 165–66
Rockstro, W. S., 366
Rockwell, John: *All American Music*, **409**, 410–11, 413
Rodgers, Joan, 431
Rodriguez, Santiago, **365–66**
Roerich, Nicholas, 177
Rogers, Noelle, 282
Rolandi, Gianna, 54, 64, 139–40, 150, 296
Rolfe Johnson, Anthony, 127
Roloff, Roger, 401–2, 420
Romani, Felice, 28–29
Romberg, Sigmund, 291
  Student Prince, **21–23**, 26
Rome Opera, 372
Ronstadt, Linda, 20
Roosevelt, Franklin D., 453
Rorem, Ned, **17–19**, 295
  Ariel, **344**
  Book of Hours, 17
  Day Music, 18

Rorem, Ned *(cont.)*
  Miss Julie, 228
  Night Music, 18
  Quaker Reader, 17
  Romeo and Juliet, 17
  Santa Fe Songs, **17–18**
  War Scenes, 18
Rosbaud, Hans, 399
Rose, George, 20
Rosen, Albert, 70
Rosen, Charles, 77, 108, 142, 165,
  167–68, 230, 411, 486, **487**
Rosen, David, 109
Rosen, Nathaniel, 292
Rosenfeld, Jayn, 412
Rosenman, Leonard: Chamber Music
  V, 309
  Foci I, **469**
Rosenshein, Neil, 291, 452
Ross, Adrian, 303
Rossi, Gaetano, 372–73, 374–75
Rossini, Gioachino, 28, 65, 161, 262,
  483
  Barbiere di Siviglia, **204–5,** 256
  Cenerentola, **62–63,** 65
  Donna del lago, **146–49,** 155–56, 456
  Ermione, 148
  Guillaume Tell, 48, 149
  Maometto II, 149
  Moïse et Pharaon, **149–50,** 186, 336
  Mosè in Egitto, 149, 336, 376
  Otello, 216, 217
  Ricciardo e Zoraide, 148
  Semiramide, **371–76,** 456
  Siège de Corinthe, **55**
  Stabat Mater, 130
  Tancredi, 147, **455–56**
  Turco in Italia, 56
Rostropovich, Mstislav, 266, 384
Röthlisberger, Max, 72, 121, 176, 243,
  361
Rouleau, Joseph, 428
Roussakis, Nicolas: *Night Speech,* 258
Routledge, Patricia, 20
Royal Ballet, 48, 426
Royal Shakespeare Company, 305
Royse, Robert, 33
Rozhdestvensky, Gennadi, 131
Rubin, Dorothy, 261
Rubini, Giovanni Battista, 28
Rudel, Julius, 37, 51, 54, 58, 63, 65
Rudhyar, Dane: *Epic Poem,* 248
Ruggles, Carl, 381
Runkel, Reinhild, 462
Rusconi, Carlo, 96, 356–57

Ryack, Rita, 198
Ryhänen, Jaakko, 443
Rysanek, Leonie, 37, 296, 462–63
Rzewski, Frederic, 211, 266, 267

Sacred Music Society, 110, 376
Sadie, Stanley, 74
Sadler, Graham, 471
Sadler-Grün, Friederike, 434
Sadler's Wells Opera, 368–69, 429, 442
Sadovnikoff, Mary, **66–67**
St. Louis, Opera Theatre of, 284–85,
  287–88, 304–8, 354, 478–81
St. Louis Symphony, 480
St Louis: Washington University
  Baroque Festival, 403–6
St. Luke's Chamber Ensemble, 432
Saint-Saëns, Camille, 482
  Clarinet Sonata, Op. 167, 343–44
  Henry VIII, 355, 400
  Samson et Dalila, 30, **36–37,** 457
St. Thomas Choir, 217
Salesky, Brian, 62
Salieri, Antonio: *Europa riconosciuta*
  overture, 159
  Piano Concerto in C, 159–60
  Symphony, 159
Sallinen, Aulis: *Horseman,* 443
  Red Line, **442–45,** 448
Salminen, Matti, 445
Saltzman, Harry, 188, 371
Salvi, Matteo, 341, 343
Samara, Spiro: *La Martire,* 399
San Diego Opera, 355, 400
  Verdi Festival, 274-78
San Francisco: Curran Theater, 100
  Davies Symphony Hall, **30–32,** 34,
  35, 52, 100, 109, 319, 320–21
  Herbst Theater, 423
  War Memorial Opera House, 30, 35,
  36
San Francisco: Arch Ensemble, 106
San Francisco Chronicle, 35, 98, 107
San Francisco Conservatory, 107–8
San Francisco Contemporary Music
  Players, 106
San Francisco: New Music Ensemble,
  106–8
San Francisco Opera, 30, 36–39,
  68–70, 95, 98–104, 118, 317–18,
  403, 422–23, 430, 458–64
San Francisco Symphony, 30, 33–34,
  35, 52, 53, 60, 100, 103, 106–8,
  109, 236, 377

San Jose, 106–7
Sanjust, Filippo, 368
Santa Fe: Paolo Soleri Theatre, 223
Santa Fe Chamber Music Festival,
    17–19, 292–95
Santa Fe Opera, 91–92, 286, 288,
    291–92, 295–96
Sargeant, Winthrop, 227–28
Sargent, Malcolm, 172, 307
Satie, Erik, 176
Savastano, Antonio, 150
Savonlinna Festival, 442–43
La Scala, 26–27, 36, 38, 55, 105, 133,
    158, 159, 180, 183–84, 240,
    264–65, 320, 357, 359, 363,
    371–72, 373, 375, 408, 454,
    476–77, 478
Scarlatti, Alessandro, 78, 271
Scarlatti, Domenico, 142
    Sonatas, 159
Schafer, Murray: *Sun*, 321
Scheffler, John, 291
Schenk, Otto, 218, 239, 402–3
Schenker, Heinrich, 485–86
Schiff, David, 385
    Elegy for String Quartet, 412
    Music of Elliott Carter, 466
Schifter, Peter Mark, 477
Schiller, Friedrich, 342
    Räuber, 274
Schillings, Max von: *Mona Lisa*, 264
Schinkel, Karl Friedrich, 458–59
Schiøtz, Aksel, 162
Schipa, Tito, 296
Schippers, Thomas, 341
Schlegel, A. W., 97
    Lectures on Dramatic Art and Literature,
        96, 356–57
Schlösser, Louis: "Memories of
    Beethoven," 165–66
Schmidt, Douglas, 37
Schnabel, Arthur, 11, 483–84
Schnaut, Gabriele, 434
Schneider, Hortense, 102, 242
Schneider-Siemssen, Günther, 138,
    218, 269, 402–3
Schnurman, Steven, 448
Schober, Franz von, 116
Schoenberg, Arnold, 21, 108, 236, 247,
    291, 387, 416
    Buch der hängenden Gärten, 74
    Chamber Symphony, 90–91, 340
    Erwartung, 50, 74, 415, 423
    Friede auf Erden, 222
    Glückliche Hand, 74

Gurrelieder, 130
"Nachtwandler," 256
Pelleas und Melisande, 345
Pierrot Lunaire, 48, 49, **74–76, 77**,
    412, 436
Six Little Piano Pieces, Op. 19, 425
String Quartets: No. 1, 90–91, 258;
    No. 2, 138
Wind Quintet, **255–56**
Schöffler, Paul, 103, 296
Schola Cantorum, 223
Schöne, Lotte, 58
Schorr, Friedrich, 434
Schreker, Franz: *Ferne Klang*, 51–52,
    415
    Gezeichneten, 264
    Songs, 51–52
Schröder, Jaap, 310–11
Schröder-Devrient, Wilhelmine, 11,
    396, 407
Schubert, Franz, 19, 66, 109, 116, 141,
    214, 416
    Octet, 437
Schubert, Peter, 245–46
Schuh, Willi, 401
Schuler, Duane, 453
Schuller, Gunther, 171, 210
    Contrabassoon Concerto, 258
    Spectra, 387
Schultz, Theodore, 34, 320–23
Schuman, Patricia, 456
Schuman, William, 295
Schumann, Robert, 142–43, 168, 214
    Arabesque, 144
    Carnival, 487
    Davidsbündlertänze, 144
    Fantasy, 144–45
    Faschingsschwank aus Wien, 144
    Impromptus on a Theme of Clara
        Wieck, 487
    Kreisleriana, 167
    Piano Pieces, Op. 32, 487
    Sonata in F-sharp-minor, 143–44
    Symphonic Studies, 487
Schütz, Heinrich, 447
Schwantner, Joseph: *New Morning for
    the World*, **379–80**
Schwarz, Boris, 251–52
Schwarz, Gerard, 137–38, 309, 412
Schwarz, Hanna, 462
Schwarzkopf, Elisabeth, 296, 303, 313
Schwertsik, Kurt, 210, 212
    Twilight Music, **345**
Schwisow, James, 288
Scimone, Claudio, 80–81, 149

Scott, Walter, 24
   Lady of the Lake, 146, 147–49
Scottish Opera, 349, 419, 429
Scotto, Renata, 54–55, **132–34**, 135,
   180, 183, 213, 232, **357–58**, 408
Scovotti, Jeanette, 281
Scratch Orchestra, 267
Scratch Orchestra, 267
Scriabin, Alexander: Piano Sonata in
   F-sharp, 365–66
   Studies, 159
Scribe, Eugène, 341, 453
   Gustave III, 276
Seabury, John, 278
Seattle Opera, 105
Segar, Kathleen, 350
Sego, Mary Kendrick, 198
Seiber, Mátyás, 386
Sellars, Peter, 198, 271, 278, 403,
   450–52, 453
Sendak, Maurice, 150
Sénéchal, Michel, 218
Senesino, 405–6
Senior, Charles, 436
Senn, Herbert, 304
Serafin, Tullio, 240–41
Serban, Andrei, 184
Serkin, Rudolf, 33, 484
Sessions, Roger, 107, 291, 293, 387,
   410, 413
   Concerto for Orchestra, **153–53, 378**
   Divertimento, 351, **352**
   Idyll of Theocritus, 152
   Montezuma, 152, **205–9**
   Questions About Music, **351–52**
   String Quartet No. 1, 377
   Symphonies: No. 1, 152; No. 2, 152,
      351, **352, 377–78**; No. 3, 152; No.
      7, **351–52**; No. 8, 152; No. 9,
      151–52
   Violin Concerto, 151, 152
   When Lilacs Last in Dooryard Bloom'd,
      152, 465
Severson, Jeff, 90
Shade, Ellen, 81
Shaffer, Peter: *Royal Hunt of the Sun*,
   205
Shakespeare, William, 57, 59, 63, 215,
   273, 278, 329, 407
   Hamlet, 80–81
   King Lear, 94–99, 368, 464
   Macbeth, 356–57
   Measure for Measure, 216
   Midsummer Night's Dream, 127, 198
   Much Ado About Nothing, 481

Two Noble Kinsmen, 24
Shane, Rita, 100, 242, 327
Shapey, Ralph: Songs for Soprano and
   Piano, 413
   Songs of Ecstasy, 413
Shaw, George Bernard, 20, 44, 140–41,
   214–16, 238, 365, 370, 370, 434,
   449–50
   Shaw's Music, 214
Shaw, Watkins, 161, 163
Shawe-Taylor, Desmond, 101
Shelley, Percy Bysshe, 339, 465
Shelton, Lucy, 256
Shepard, Sam: *Curse of the Starving
   Class*, 137
Shepherd, Arthur, 416
Sheppard, John, 465
Shere, Charles, 107
Sherry, Fred, 160
Shifrin, Seymour: Three Pieces for
   Orchestra, 106
Shirley-Quirk, John, 131, 266
Shore, Dinah, 54–55
Shostakovich, Dimitri, 295
   Lady Macbeth of Mtsensk, 251–52
   Piano Quartet, 292
   String Quartets, 250–54; No. 1, 251;
      No. 2, 251, 254; No. 4, 252–53;
      No. 7, 251; No. 8, 252–53; No. 12,
      253–54; No. 13, 253; No. 14, 253;
      No. 15, 252–54
   Symphonies, 338; No. 5, 251; No. 7,
      251–52; No. 8, 345–46; No. 11,
      251; No. 12, 251; No. 13, 251–52;
      No. 14, 251
   Viola Sonata, 252
   Violin Concerto No. 1, 345–46
Shostakovich, Maxim, 345
Sibelius, Jean, 293, 443, 466
Sibiriakov, Lev, 72
Siciliani, Alessandro, 149
Siddons, Sarah, 24
Siegal, Fritz, 170
Siegmund-Schultze, Walther, 160–61
Siems, Margarethe, 58
Siepi, Cesare, 39, 101
Sills, Beverly, 22, 26, **27**, 50, **54–57**, 64,
   65, 110–11, 136, 190
   Bubbles, 133
Silverman, Stanley, 21, 426
   Dr. Selavy, 50
   Hotel for Criminals, 50
   Madame Adare, **49–50**
Silverstein, Barbara, 230
Silvestrov, Valentin: *Elegy*, 257

Simionato, Giulietta, 371
Simmons, Calvin, 43, 109, 142, 236, 288
Simon, Evelyn, 441
Simon-Girard, Juliette, **242–43**
Sinclair, John, 375
Sinclair, Monica, 369
Sine Nomine Singers, 188, 369, 371
Sinopoli, Giuseppe, **340**, 383
   Lou Salomé, 384–85
Sitwell, Edith, 47–49
Skalicky, Jan, 231
Skidmore, Owings & Merrill, 30
Skinner, Philip, 176
Skrowaczewski, Stanislaw, 384
Slatkin, Leonard, 152
Slim, Colin, 147
Smartt, Michael, 121
Smedvig, Rolf, 250
Smetana, Bedřich, 224
   Bartered Bride, 21, 350
   Secret, 192
   Two Widows, 21
Smillie, Thomson, 349
Smith, Craig, 198–99, 403, 453
Smith, Jennifer, 127
Smith, Kevin, 391
Smith, Leonard B., 110
Smith, Malcolm, 434
Smith, Oliver, 330
Smith, Rex, 20
Smith, Sheila, 102
Smithson, Harriet, 24, 273
Smithsonian Chamber Players, 160, 370
Smoldon, W. L., 353–54
Smylie, Dennis, 469
Sobinov, Leonid, 72
Söderström, Elisabeth, **68–70**
   In My Own Key, 69
Sollberger, Harvey, 160, 256, 469
   Life Study, 411
   Riding the Wind, 258
Solomon, 484
Solomon, Maynard, 166
Solomon, Nicholas, 406
Solti, Georg, **52–54**, 61, 385, **434–35**, 462, 484
Somma, Antonio, 96–97
Sondheim, Stephen, 331, 409
Sondheimer, Hans, 214
Sonnenberg, Melanie, 308, 479–80
Sooter, Edward, 105, 239
Šourek, Otakar, 415
Sousa, John Philip, 110
South, Pamela, 101

Southern Methodist University:
   Meadows School of the Arts, 78, 82
Souzay, Gérard, 18
Soviero, Diana, 42, 158
Spacagna, Maria, 287
Spatz-Rabinowitz, Elaine, 198
Speculum Musicae, 210–12, 327, 412
Spenser, Edmund: *Faerie Queene*, 205
Sperry, Paul, 344
Spink, Ian, 439–40
Spinelli, Nicola: *A basso porta*, 399
Spivakovsky, Tossy, 151
Spohr, Louis, 68
Spoleto Festival, 158
Spontini, Gaspare: *Fernand Cortez*, 206, 372
Springfield Symphony, 273–74
Squire, W. H., 172
Stagno, Roberto, 316
Stalin, Joseph, 251–52, 384
Stanford University Center for Computer Research in Music and Acoustics, 107
Stanley, Edward, 116
Stapp, Olivia, 29
Starer, Robert: *Pantagleize*, 389
Stargell, Willie, 380
Staryk, Steven, 86
Stassov, V. V., 71
Stead, Richard, 422
Steane, John: *Grand Tradition*, 55–56
Steber, Eleanor, 402
Steele, Richard, 278–79, 282
Steigerwalt, Gary, 392
Stein, Gertrude, 425
Steinbach, Fritz, 236
Steinberg, Michael, 34, 159
Stendhal, 376, 456
Stephens, John, 288
Stevens, Denis, 101, 305
Stevens, John, 244
Stevens, Wallace, 258
Stevenson, John, 222
Stevenson, Robert Louis, 224
Stewart, John, 227
Stewart, Michael, 330
Steward, Thomas, 100, 238–39, 269, 461–62
Stiedry-Wagner, Erika, 75, 77
Stilwell, Richard, 183
Stine, Robert, 107
Stockhausen, Karlheinz, 85, 247, 383, 386–87, 388
   Aus den sieben Tagen, 267
   In Freundschaft, 129

Stockhausen, Karlheinz *(cont.)*
  Jubiläum, **128–30**
  Kontakte, 387
  Kreuzspiel, 381–82, 386
  Kurzwellen, 382
  Licht, 129
  Piano Piece No. 10, 424–25
  Sternklang, 82–83
Stokowski, Leopold, 179, 236
Stolz, Robert, 20–21
Stoltz, Rosine, 343
Stone, William, 158, 214, 328
Stony Brook, SUNY, 189–90
Stoppard, Tom: *Rosencrantz and*
  Guildenstern Are Dead, 24
Strasberg, Lee, 156
Strasfogel, Ian, 206–9, 407
Stratas, Teresa, 87, **93–94**, 180, 183
Straus, Oscar, 20–21, 256
Strauss, Johann, 20–22, 54, 262
Strauss, Richard, 68, 88, 109, 118, 236,
  258, 259, 288, 303, 419
  Ägyptische Helena, 296–97, 401
  Alpine Symphony, **339**
  Arabella, **402–3**
  Ariadne auf Naxos, 130–31
  Capriccio, 69, 297
  Daphne, 296–97
  Deutsche Motette, 458
  Elektra, 467
  Feuersnot, 399
  Frau ohne Schatten, 30, 35, **37–38**,
    150, 217–18, 401
  Guntram, **399–402**
  Heldenleben, 322
  Liebe der Danae, **296–97**
  Reminiscences, 399
  Rosenkavalier, **313–14**, 325
  Salome, 263, 467
Stravinsky, Igor, 48, 75, 180, 211–12,
  256, 362, 379–80, 416, 433
  Apollo, 339
  Nightingale, **176–79**,
  Oedipus Rex, **176–79**
  Orpheus, 177
  Piano Sonata, 410
  Rake's Progress, 103, **346–48**, 390
  Rite of Spring, **176–79**, 457
  Soldier's Tale, 49
  Symphony of Psalms, 150
  Three Pieces, 412
Strehler, Giorgio, 198, 201
Striggio, Alessandro, 127, 440
Strindberg, August: *Gustav III*, 51
Studio der Frühen Musik, 243, 336

Stuttgart Ballet, 421
Stuttgart Opera, 114
Styrian Autumn Festival, 392
Subotnick, Morton: *Ascent into Air*, 469
Sullivan, Arthur, **20–21**, 262
  H.M.S. Pinafore, 20
  Mikado, **449–53**
  Pirates of Penzance, **19–20**, 21, 23, 450
  Ruddigore, 36
Sullivan, Cornelius, 209
Sullivan, Dan, 214, 452
Sullivan, Louis, 320, 326
Sundine, Stephanie, 288
Susa, Conrad: *Black River*, 228
  Hymns for the Amusement of Children,
    416
Sutherland, Joan, 19, 56, 72, 132–33,
  136, 150, 162, 196, 218, 318, 343,
  371–72, 373–74
Svanholm, Set, 434
Svoboda, Josef, 231, 430
Svoboda, Thomas: *Eugene Overture*, 325
Swedish Opera, 388
Swenson, Ruth Ann, 423
Swing Mikado, 450
Syberberg, Hans-Jürgen, 393–98, 401
  Parsifal: Ein Filmessay, 395–96, 398
Sydney Opera House, 177
Sykora, Peter, 194
Sylvan, Sanford, 198
Szell, George, 415
Szymanowski, Karol, 283, 384
  Concert Overture, 345

Taddei, Giuseppe, 101, 118
Tafelmusik, 405
Taglioni, Paul, 62
Tagore, Rabindranath, 112
Takács, Klára, 265–66
Takemitsu, Toru: *Far Calls. Coming,*
  Far!, 106, 468
Talking Heads, 409
Talma, Louise: *Studies in Spacing*, 343–
  44
Talvela, Martti, 233, 315, 443
Tanenbaum, David, 329
Tanglewood, 171, 210, 258
Tannenbaum, Yadin, 234
Tanner, Michael, 238
Tanner, Tony, 303
Tappy, Eric, 101
Taruskin, Richard, 219–20, 362
Tate, Nahum: *King Lear*, 95, 464
Taucher, Dean, 231

Tauriello, Antonio, 355
Tavener, John, 465
  Akhamatova: Requiem, **131**
  Thérèse, 131
  Ultimos Ritos, 131
Taylor, David, 433
Taylor, Janice, 481
Taylor, Rose, 81, 456
Tchaikovsky, Peter Ilyich, 338
  Eugene Onegin, 290
  Iolanta, 266
  Nutcracker, 266
  Queen of Spades, 290, 481
  Symphony No. 4, 319
  Violin Concerto, 319
Tear, Robert, 162, 193, 369, 434
Tebaldi, Renata, 11, 277
Te Kanawa, Kiri, 201, 313, 402
Tempo, 210–11
Tenniel, John, 33
Tennstedt, Klaus, 340, 352
Ter-Arutunian, Rouben, 62, 296
Terrell, Katherine, 407
Terry, Ellen, 24
Tetley, Glen, 75–76
Tetrazzini, Luisa, 56, 81
Thatcher, Margaret, 173
Thimmig, Les, 469
Thomas, Ambroise: *Hamlet*, 24, 228, 327, 355
  Mignon, **295–96**
Thomas, Andrew: *In Memoriam*, 345
Thomas, Jeffrey, 317, 422
Thomas, Mary, 439
Thomas, Michael Tilson, 150, 170, 235–36
Thomas, Nova, 72
Thome, Joel, 75
Thompson, Scott, 454
Thomson, Heather, 45
Thomson, Virgil, 235
  Mother of Us All, **425–26**
Thoreau, Henry David, 289
Thorne, Nicholas: *From the Dying Earth*, 309
  Symphony from Silence, 466–67, **468**
Thouvenel String Quartet, 250–51
Thurber, Alistair, 241
Tiepolo, Giovanni Battista, 82
Tilbury, John, 266, 267, 268
Time, 57
Tinctoris, Johannes, 220
Tinsley, Pauline, 189
Tippett, Michael, 48, 173, 277, 351, 442
  King Priam, 71

Knot Garden, 475–76
Mask of Time, 85, 150
Midsummer Marriage, 85–86, 153
Piano Concerto, 153
Piano Sonata No. 3, 153
String Quartets: No. 3, 153; No. 4, 85, **153**
Symphonies: No. 3, 153; No. 4, 85
Triple Concerto, **85–87**, 169–70
Titus, Alan, 54, 63, 135, 303
Todd, David, 39
Todd, Mike, 450
Tokody, Ilona, 400–401
Tolstoy, Leo, 112
  Anna Karenina, 417–19
Tomlinson, John, 127, 195, 428
Tommasini, Vincenzo, 264
Toms, Carl, 140
Toney, Martha, 214
Toronto: Massey Hall, 319–20, 321, 322
  Roy Thomson Hall, 320–22
Toronto Mendelssohn Choir, 321–22
Toronto Symphony, 86, 321–22
Tortelier, Paul, 172
Toscanini, Arturo, 264, 338, 359
Tottola, Leone, 146
Tovey, Donald Francis, 91, 445–46
Tower, Joan: *Sequoia*, 345
Trakl, Georg, 171
Trapes, Diana, 308
Traubner, Richard, 22
Traver, Paul, 160–61, 163–64, 370
Treigle, Norman, 103
Treleaven, John, 194, 431
Trowell, Brian, 64
Troyanos, Tatiana, 133, 179, 218, 313, 405
Trussel, Jacque, 22–23, 100
Tschammer, Hans, 420, 462
Tucker, Norman, 176
Tudor, David, 266, 382, 391
Turek, Siegwulf, 105
Turner, Charles, 190
2001, 388
Tye, Christopher, 465
Tyler, Royall: *Contrast*, 440
Tyson, Alan, 239

Updike, John, 288
Uppman, Theodor, 477
U. S. Coast Guard Academy Singing Idlers, 217
Uzemack, Noel, 422

Valente, Benita, 282, 370
Valjakka, Taru, 444–45
Välkki, Anita, 445
Vallin, Ninon, 296
Val-Schmidt, Carolyn, 190
Valtasaari, Tapani, 443
Van Allan, Richard, 431–32
Vanarelli, Mario, 236
Van Dyck, Ernest, 10–11
Vaness, Carol, 44, 45–46, 58–59, 64,
    101, 154, 157, 214, 328
van Limpt, Adriaan, 277–78
Van Tieghem, David, 391
Van Vechten, Carl, 289
Varèse, Edgard: *Density 21.5*, 160
    Intégrales, 89, 103
Varnay, Astrid, 138, 192–93
Varona, José, 27
Varviso, Silvio, 420
Vaughan, Denis, 322–23, 325, 407–8
Vaughan, Williams, Ralph, 109,
    171–72, 173, 353
    Symphonies, 169; No. 5, 170, 172
Veasey, Josephine, 24
Velasco, Noel, 448
Velis, Andrea, 218
Veltri, Michelangelo, 277
Venice Biennale, 82
Vento, Marc, 457
Verdi, Giuseppe, 12, 92, 146–47, 161,
    340, 407, 419, 454
    Aida, 43, 180, 349, 372
    Alzira, 189, 277
    Attila, **158**, 237
    Ballo in Maschera, 36, 214, 274,
        276–78, 317–18
    Corsaro, **189–90, 274–76**
    Don Carlos, 242, 332, 343, 363, **408**,
        421, **426–28**, 430
    Due Foscari, **158–59**
    Ernani, 225
    Falstaff, 57–58, 166, 183, 265,
        359–60, 390, 429, 471
    Forza del destino, 56, 130–31, 225,
        314–15, 363, **426–27, 428–29**
    Giorno di regno, **105**
    Jérusalem, 189, 274
    King Lear, 95–98
    Lombardi, 132, 213, **236–37**, 275
    Macbeth, 95–96, 100, 127, 189, 190,
        274, 275, 343, **356–59**
    Masnadieri, 95, 189, 274
    Nabucco, 105, 110–11, **134–35**, 158,
        216, 237, 450

Otello, 38, 93, 100, 217, 265, 316,
    359, 471
Requiem, 109, 363
Rigoletto, 56, 100, **102, 154–57**, 231,
    358, 363
Simon Boccanegra, 30, **38–39**
String Quartet, 19
Traviata, 10, 22, 39, **40–42, 157–58**,
    184–85, 231–32, 286, 311, **328**,
    363, 429–30, 480
Trovatore, 20, 231, 363
Vêpres siciliennes, 38, **231–32**, 341,
    342
Verdi, Giuseppina, 132, 275
Verdi, Margherita, 275
Verdy, Violette, 472
Vermeulen, Matthijs, 387
Verrett, Shirley, 36, 132, 239, 345
Viardot, Pauline, 192, 277
Vickers, Jon, 37, 192, 368
Victoria, Queen of England, 451
Vienna: Theater an der Wien, 22,
    20–23
Vienna Opera, 401
Vienna Philharmonic, 61, 337, 340, 423
Vienna State Opera, 481
Villa-Lobos, Heitor, 353
    Uirapurú, 235
Vineyard Theatre: Opera Shop, 454
Vining, John, 426
Visconti, Luchino, 26–27, 158, 427, 428
Vishnevskaya, Galina, 266
Vivaldi, Antonio, 147
    Farnace, 78, 79
    Fida ninfa, 78
    Griselda, 78
    Incoronazione di Dario, 78
    Olimpiade, 78, 79
    Orlando finto pazzo, 79
    Orlando furioso, **78–82**
    Tito Manlio, 78, 79
    Two-Violin Concerto in D, 311
Vogel, Jaroslav, 173–74
Vogl, Heinrich, 434
Volkoff, Gabriel, 459
Volkov, Solomon: *Testimony: The Memoirs
    of Dmitri Shostakovich*, 251–52
Voltaire, 373, 375–76
    Candide, 330, 332
von Reichenbach, Susan, 68
von Stade, Frederica, 103, 148, 296,
    334
Vrdolyak, Edward R., 449
Vrenios, Anastasios, 375

Waddell, Helen: *Mediaeval Latin Lyrics*, 243
Wadsworth, Stephen, 475, 477
Wagner, Cosima, 395–96, 397
Wagner, James, 242, 327
Wagner, Richard, 12, 25, 26, 51, 88, 90–91, 92, 143, 174, 176–77, 288, 296, 312, 325, 340, 429
  Feen, 213, **215–17**, 400
  Fliegende Holländer, 44, 136, 216, 358, 400, 430
  Götterdämmerung, 149, 260, 455, 464, 477
  Liebesverbot, 215–16, 400
  Lohengrin, 237, 355, 471
  Mein Leben, 396, 407
  Meistersinger, 100, **103**, 105, 112, 214–15, 216, 237, 265, 449
  Parsifal, 115, 216, **237–39**, 243, **393– 398**
  Rheingold, **138–39**, 149, **433–35**, **458–61**, **463–64**, 477
  Rienzi, 110, 213, 215–16, **217**, 376, 396, 400
  Ring cycle, 138, 166, 216, 226, 237, 363, 393, 395, 421, 433–34, 450–51, **458–64**, 476
  Siegfried, **138–39**, 256, 395, 458, 464
  Tannhäuser, 216, 397, 400–401
  Tristan und Isolde, 33, 91, **105**, 125, 130, 136, 166, 216, 217–18, 237, 265, 274, 355, 359, 364, 395, 400– 401
  Walküre, 139, **420–21**, 433, **458**, **461–64**
Wagner, Robin, 205
Wagner, Wieland, 112, 127–28, 238, 349, 393–95, 458
Walker, Alan, 143
Walker, Charles, 477
Walker, Charles Dodsley, 340
Walker, George: *Eastman Overture*, 379
Walker, Sarah, 195, 431
Wallis, Delia, 63
Walser, Lloyd, 242
Walter, Anton, 66, 228
Walter, Bruno, 61, 201, 340
Walther, Geraldine, 292
Walton, William, 171–72, 173, 192
  Belshazzar's Feast, 321
  Façade, **47–49**
  Symphony No. 2, **172–73**
  Viola Concerto, 169, 172, 235
  Violin Concerto, 172

Ward, Michael, 360
Ward, Robert, 287
  Minutes till Midnight, **268–70**
Warlock, Peter, 106
Warner, Joseph, 351
Washington, DC: *see* Kennedy Center; Smithsonian Chamber Players
Washington, Harold, 449
Washington: Library of Congress, 160– 161
Waters, Willie Anthony, 101
Watts, Helen, 369
Weatherspoon, David, 360
Weber, Carl Maria von, 57, 65
  Freischütz, 104, 115, 147, 186, 216, 356, 372
  Grand Duo Concertant, 343–44
Weber, Ludwig, 138
Weber, Wolfgang, 420
Webern, Anton von, 247, 257, 387
  Piano Variations, 424–25
  String Trio, 411
Webster, James, 229
Webster, John, 263
Wechsler, Gil, 176, 201, 218, 315, 358
Wedekind, Erika, 58
Wedekind, Franz, 91–93, 94, 202, 285
Weed, Lucy, 455
Weikert, Ralf, 64, 456
Weikl, Bernd, 402
Weill, Kurt, 21, 48, 50, 211, 269, 444
  Mahagonny, 177
  Silverlake, **50–51**
  Street Scene, 23, 119, 227, 332, 421
Weir, Judith, 106
Weisberg, Arthur, 412–13, 467, 469
Weise, Klaus, 242, 328
Welitch, Ljuba, 277
Wells, Jeffrey, 350
Welsh National Opera, 43–44, 125, 281–82, 429
Welting, Ruth, 73, 218
Wendelken-Wilson, Charles, 27
Wesendonk, Mathilde, 394, 395
West, Philip, **46–47**
Westenburg, Richard, 272, 457
Westergaard, Peter, 239
West-German Radio (WDR), 83
Westney, William, 393
Wexford Festival, 349
WFMT, 53
Wheeler, Hugh, 23, 51, 331
White, Allen, 243
Whitman, Walt, 414

Whitman, Walt *(cont.)*
  Leaves of Grass, 478–79
Whittall, Arnold, 255
Wiant, Benjamin, 143
Wich, Günther, 204
Wiener, Gruppe, 210–11
Wilbur, Richard, 330
Wilde, Oscar: *Florentine Tragedy*, 263
  Tragedy, 288
Wildermann, William, 58–59, 452
Williams, Anne Martindale, 170
Williams, Jonathan, 436
Williams-Haik, Sally, 351
Wilson, Olly, 107
  Trilogy, 106
Wilson, Robert, 113
  Deafman Glance, 112
Winbergh, Gösta, 101
Windsor Festival, 171
Winslow, Walter, 107
Winter, Quade, 105
Wise, Patricia, 102
Wishart, Peter, 162
WNCN, 53, 152
WNET, 212–13
WNYC, 18, 225, 228, 256, 381,
Wolf, Hugo, 210–12, 271
Wolff, Christian, 266, 267, 382
Wolfram von Eschenbach, 238
Wolfsohn, Carl, 483
Wolpe, Stefan, 381
  Four Studies on Basic Rows, 411
  Passacaglia, 410, **411**
  Piece for Trumpet and Seven
    Instruments, 212
  Songs from the Hebrew, 212
  Street Music No. 1, 412
  String Quartet, 212
Wood, Pamela, 222
Woodman, Thomas, 37–38, 317, 423
Woodward, Roger, 247
Workers' Weekly, 266
WQXR, 89
Wuorinen, Charles, 381, 411, 465
  Arabia Felix, 411
  Archaeopteryx, **432–33**

Archangel, 432
Capriccio, 410
Chamber Concerto, 160
Horn Trio, **432**
New York Notes, 412
Short Suite for Orchestra, 411
Trio for Bass Instruments, **433**
Trio No. 2, 256
Tuba Concerto, 89
Two-Part Symphony, 433
Winds, 433
Wyner, Susan Davenny, 172

Xenakis, Iannis: *Anaktoria*, 344–45

Yang, Tom, 439–40
York, University of, 253, 485
Young, Karen, 245
Young, La Monte, 267

Zaccaria, Nicola, 81
Zander, Benjamin, 340
Zandonai, Riccardo: *Francesca da Rimini*,
  217–18, 264
Zangarini, Carlo, 241
Zbruyeva, Eugenia, 72
Zednick, Heinz, 139
Zeffirelli, Franco, **180–83**
Zehme, Albertine, 75
Zemlinsky, Alexander (von), 51
  Florentinische Tragöddie, **263–64**
  Lyric Symphony, 263
  String Quartet No. 2, 11, 263
Zimmermann, Bernd Alois: *Soldaten*,
  119, **202–4**
  Violin Concerto, **415–16**
Zimmermann, Jörg, 37
Zschau, Marilyn, 50, 158
Zurich Opera, 283
Zurich Tonhalle Orchestra, 137
Zwilich, Ellen Taaffe, 466
  Passages, **412**
  Symphony (Three Movements for
    Orchestra), 258
Zykan, Otto M., 210